SOURCES OF INDIAN TRADITION

VOLUME I

INTRODUCTION TO
ORIENTAL CIVILIZATIONS
WM. THEODORE DE BARY, EDITOR

Sources of Indian Tradition

VOLUME I

GENERAL EDITOR

Wm. Theodore de Bary

COMPILERS

A. L. Basham   R. N. Dandekar   Peter Hardy

V. Raghavan   Royal Weiler

COLUMBIA UNIVERSITY PRESS *New York*

The addition to the "Records of Civilization: Sources and Studies" of a group of translations of Oriental historical materials in a clothbound edition, from which this volume is taken, was made possible by funds granted by Carnegie Corporation of New York. That Corporation is not, however, the author, owner, publisher, or proprietor of this publication, and is not to be understood as approving by virtue of its grant any of the statements made or views expressed therein.

ISBN 0-231-08600-8

Printed in the United States of America

15 14 13 12 11

PREFACE

This book is part of a new edition of Introduction to Oriental Civilizations, the three-volume work dealing with the civilizations of Japan, China, and India and Pakistan published by Columbia University Press in the series *Records of Civilization*. It contains source readings that tell us what the peoples of India have thought about the world they lived in and the problems they faced living together. It is meant to provide the general reader with an understanding of the intellectual and spiritual traditions which remain alive in India and Pakistan today. Thus, much attention is given to religious and philosophical developments in earlier times which still form part of the Indian heritage and have experienced a considerable revival in the nineteenth and twentieth centuries. On the other hand, attention is also given to political, economic, and social thought, which other surveys, concentrating on classical Indian philosophy, have generally omitted.

Although our aim has been to combine variety with balance in the selection and presentation of materials, a few words are perhaps necessary concerning special points of emphasis. A glance at the contents will show that religion has furnished the general categories under which traditional Indian civilization is treated. This implies no judgment that religion was always the dominant factor in Indian life, but only that in the body of literature which provides us our texts, religious identities and continuities are more clearly distinguishable than are those based upon historical chronology or dynastic associations. Next, in this volume somewhat more attention is given to Theravāda Buddhism than to Mahāyāna because the latter is given fuller treatment in the volumes in this series dealing with China and Japan. In the case of Hinduism the reader will find that relatively greater emphasis is placed upon the social and devotional aspects of the religion, which have affected great numbers of Hindus, than upon the philosophical speculations which have generally commanded the first attention of educated Indians and Westerners and have already been widely reproduced in translation. In this volume, dealing with traditional Indian and Muslim civilization, most of the translations are new and many of them are of texts previously untranslated into any Western language.

Because of the unfamiliarity and complexity of many subjects not previously presented in translation, we have found it necessary to include more historical and explanatory material than is usual in a set of source readings. Nevertheless, the reader who seeks a fuller knowledge of historical and institutional background will do well to supplement this text by referring to a general survey of Indian history and culture.

Given the limitations of an introductory text, we could not hope to deal with every thinker or movement of importance, but have had to select those examples which seem best to illustrate the major patterns of Indian thought in so far as they have been expressed and preserved in writing. In the modern period the necessity for such selectivity is most apparent. Here particular prominence has been given to persons actively engaged in leading organized religious and political movements.

Compilation of *Sources of Indian Tradition* was originally undertaken by Andrew Yarrow in connection with the general education program in Columbia College. These readings were then substantially revised by the general editor with the assistance of Dr. Royal Weiler of Columbia and supplemented by Dr. Stephen N. Hay of the University of Chicago. In making revisions for the present edition, the general editor was assisted by Ainslie T. Embree of Columbia University. It goes without saying that this volume could not have been compiled without the cooperation of our principal contributors: R. N. Dandekar of the Bhandarkar Oriental Research Institute, Poona, prepared the materials for Chapters I, II, III, X, XI, and the selection from the Bhagavad Gītā in Chapter XIII; A. L. Basham of the School of Oriental and African Studies, University of London, prepared Chapters IV, V, VI, VII, and VIII; V. Raghavan of the University of Madras prepared Chapters IX, XII, and XIII; Peter Hardy of the School of Oriental and African Studies, University of London, prepared Chapters XIV, XV, XVII, XVIII, and XIX. Their contribution is all the more appreciated because of the patience and forbearance they have shown in regard to adjustments which the general editor has had to make in order to achieve uniformity and balance in the volume as a whole. For this reason, it should be emphasized, the editor must bear primary responsibility for the selection and presentation of the materials contained here.

The final version of these readings owes much to the critical examination and comment of scholarly colleagues. Dr. Basham wishes to record his appreciation to Dr. A. K. Warder for his reading of the draft on Jainism and Buddhism. S. M. Ikram, then of the Center for Pakistan Studies, Columbia University, is also to be thanked for reading the chapters on Muslim India. Visudh Busyakul of the University of Pennsylvania gave Dr. Weiler invaluable advice and assistance, as did Marjorie A. Weiler. Hans Guggenheim performed the exacting task of preparing the chapter decorations for Chapters I-XIX.

This series of readings has been produced in connection with the Columbia College General Education Program in Oriental Studies, which has been encouraged and supported by the Carnegie Corporation of New York. For whatever value it may have to the general reader or college student seeking a liberal education that embraces both East and West, a great debt is owed to Dean Emeritus Harry J. Carman, Dr. Taraknath Das, and Dean Lawrence H. Chamberlain of Columbia College, who contributed much to the initiation and furtherance of this program.

WM. THEODORE DE BARY

EXPLANATORY NOTE

The sources of translations given at the beginning of each selection are rendered as concisely as possible. Full bibliographical data can be obtained from the list of sources in the clothbound edition. In the reference at the head of each selection, unless otherwise indicated, the author of the book is the writer whose name precedes the selection. Where excerpts have been taken from existing translations, they have sometimes been adapted or edited in the interests of uniformity with the book as a whole.

Indic words appearing in italics as technical terms or titles of works are rendered in accordance with the standard system of transliteration as found in Louis Renou's *Grammaire Sanskrite* (Paris, 1930), pp. xi–xiii, with the exception that here ś is regularly used for ç. To facilitate pronunciation, other Sanskrit terms and proper names appearing in roman letters are rendered according to the usage of Webster's New International Dictionary, 2d edition, Unabridged, except that here the macron is used to indicate long vowels and the Sanskrit symbols for ś (ç) and ṣ are uniformly transcribed as sh. Similarly, the standard Sanskrit transcription of c is given as ch. In connection with Theravāda Buddhism, the form of technical terms is that of Pali rather than Sanskrit; the latter, however, is retained in connection with Jainism. Thus, in Buddhism Pali *dhamma* for Sanskrit *dharma,* but in Jainism Sanskrit *poṣadha* for Prakrit *posaha.* Deviations from these principles may occur in passages directly quoted from Indian writers of the seventeenth through twentieth centuries. A word list giving standard Indic equivalents for roman transcriptions will be found at the end of this volume.

In the pronunciation of Indic words, the accent is usually on the next to final syllable if long; otherwise on the nearest long syllable before it. The long syllable is indicated by the macron (e.g., ā, ī, ū) or a diphthong (e, o, ai, au), or a vowel followed by more than one consonant (except h).

a	as *u* in but
ā	as *a* in father
i	as *i* in pin
ī	as *i* in machine
u	as *u* in pull
ū	as *u* in rule
ri (ṛ), a vowel	as *er* in river
e	as *ay* in say
ai	as *ai* in aisle
o	as *o* in go
au	as *ow* in how
ch (c)	as in church
sh (ś, ṣ)	as *sh* in shape
g	as *g* in get
kh	as *ḳh* in lakehouse
gh	as *gh* in doghouse
th	as *th* in anthill
dh	as *dh* in roundhouse
bh	as *bh* in clubhouse
ph	as *ph* in uphill
ṃ or ṅ	as *ng* in sing

Guide to the Pronunciation of Persian and Indo-Persian Words

Short Vowels

a	Intermediate between the vowels in the English words *bed* and *bad*
i	As the vowel sound in the English *fen*
u	As in the English word *put*

Long Vowels

ā	as *a* in father
ī	as *i* in police
ū	as *u* in prude

Diphthongs

ai	as *ey* in they
au	as *ou* in out

In Indo-Persian the majhūl vowel sound ō rhymes with *toe;* the short vowel a is closer to the *u* in *sun;* and the diphthong au tends more to the majhūl sound, as the *o* in *hose* or *toe.*

ʿ represents the Arabic and Persian letter *ʿayn.* In Arabic *ʿayn* is a strong guttural preceding a vowel. In Persian, however, *ʿayn* at the beginning of a word is not pronounced separately from the vowel which goes with it; in the middle of a word, it has a sound—*sa'd* (or *sa'd*) like the bleating of a sheep; at the end of a word, in Persian, it is either silent or, more usually given a slight pronunciation between short "a" and "e" on a rising intonation.

' represents the *hamza* or glottal stop in Arabic words. It is a jerked hiatus; the Cockney pronunciation of "butter," "better," or "bottle" gives the sound in the middle of Arabic words; at the beginning of Arabic words it is indistinguishable from the vowel that goes with it; at the end it is like the Persian pronunciation of *'ayn* at the end of words.

In Persian words, ' also represents *hamza* when used to indicate a hiatus between two long vowels, as in the English pronunciation (very distinct) of "India Office," i.e., "India" (pause) "Office." (Example: Badā'ūnī.)

R.W. AND P.H.

Without the assistance of many publishers, a book of source readings such as this is not possible, and we are grateful for the cooperation of the following: Advaita Ashrama, Almora, India; Allen & Unwin, Ltd., London; All-Pakistan Political Science Association, Lahore; Mohammad Ashraf, Lahore; Asiatic Society of Mangal, Calcutta; Sri Aurobindo Ashram, Pondichéry, India; The Bodley Head, Ltd., London; Clarendon Press, Oxford; Current Book House, Bombay; Ganesh and Co., Ltd., Madras, India; S. P. Gokhale, Poona, India; Harvard University Press, Cambridge, Mass.; Hero Publications, Lahore; Indian Printing Works, Lahore; The India Press, Allahabad, India; Kitabistan, Allahabad, India; S. K. Lahin and Co., Calcutta; Luzac and Co., London; Macmillan & Co., Ltd., London and New York; al-Manar Academy, Lahore; Modern Review, Calcutta; John Murray, London, and the "Wisdom of the East" series; The Muslim World; G. A. Natesan and Co., Madras, India; The Navajivan Trust, Ahmedabad, India; P. M. Neogi, Calcutta; Orient Longmans Ltd., Calcutta; Oxford University Press, London; Pakistan Herald Press, Karachi; Panjab University Press, Lahore; People's Publishing House, Ltd., Bombay; Renaissance Publishers, Ltd., Calcutta; Roy and Son, Calcutta; A. W. Sahasvabuddhe, Sevagram, India; Sadharan Brahmo Samaj, Calcutta; Sarvodaya, Bombay; Theosophical Publishing Society, Banaras, India; Thomas and Co., Calcutta; Thompson and Co. Ltd., Madras, India; R. B. Tilak, Poona, India; The Vedanta Society, New York; Vedic Yantralaya, Ajmer, India; The Viking Press, Inc., New York; Visvabharati, Calcutta.

CONTENTS

CHRONOLOGICAL TABLE

Brahmanism

PREHISTORIC PERIOD

B.C.	c.2700–1700	Indus Valley civilization and height of Harappa Culture.
	c.1500–1200	Aryan invasions of the Indian subcontinent; composition of the earliest hymns of the *Rig Veda*.

VEDIC PERIOD

c.1200–900	Composition of the *Rig Veda*.
c.900	The great war depicted in the *Mahābhārata* epic.
c.900–500	Period of later Vedas, Brāhmanas, and early Upanishads.
c.800	Aryans reach eastern Bihar and Bengal.
c.600	End of Brāhmana period.

Jainism and Buddhism

B.C.	817	Traditional date of the birth of the Jain savior Pārshvanātha.
	c.563–483 [or, 558–478]	Siddhārtha Gautama, the Buddha.
	c.542–490	Bimbisāra, king of Magadha.
	c.490–458	Ajātashatru, king of Magadha.
	c.480	First Buddhist Council at Rājagriha.
	c.468 [or, 487, 477]	Death of Vardhamāna Mahāvīra.
	327–325	Invasion by Alexander of Macedon.

MAURYA PERIOD

c.322–298 [or, 317–293]	Chandragupta
c.300	Megasthenes, Greek ambassador of Seleucus Nicator visits court of Chandragupta.
c.298–273	Bindusāra.
c.273–237 [or, 269–232; 268–233]	Ashoka.
c.247–207	King Devanampiya Tissa of Ceylon converted to Buddhism by Thera Mahinda.
c.200–200 A.D.	Period of greatest Buddhist and Jain influence in India.
c.190	Greek Kingdoms in North-West India.
c.185 [or, 183]	End of dynasty.

	c.185–173 [or, 183–171]	Shunga Dynasty.
	c.185–149	Pushyamitra Shunga.
	c.170–165	Yueh-chi (Iranians) invade India.
	c.150	Milinda (Gk. Menander), greatest of Indo-Greek kings.
	c.90	Shakas invade North-West India.
A.D.	c.early 1st century	Kushānas invade India.
	c.79 [or, 82]	Division of Jains into Shvetāmbara and Digambara sects.
	c.78–101	Kanishka.
	c.100–200	Rise of Mahāyāna Buddhism. Ashvaghosha's *Buddhacarita.* Prominence of Mādhyamika School of Nāgārjuna (until 5th century).
	c.200–400	Kundakunda, Jain teacher of Digambara sect.
	c.400–500	Mahāyāna philosophers Asanga and Vasubandhu. Founding of great Buddhist monastery at Nālandā.
	c.454	Writing of Jain oral tradition at Council at Valabhī in Saurashtra.
	c.500–1000	Prominence of Mahāyāna Buddhist School of Yogāchāra or Vijnānavāda.
	c.600–700	Appearance of Tantricism in organized Buddhism.
	c.700–800	Buddhism spreads to Nepal and Tibet.
	c.770–810	Buddhist King Dharmapāla rules in Bihar and Bengal.
	c.900–1000	Sahajayāna or Sahajīya Tantric School marks last phase of Buddhism in India.
	c.1192	Muslim defeat of Hindus under Prithivi Rāj. Buddhism disappears as an organized religious force in India.

Hinduism

B.C.	c.500–500 A.D.	Period of Hindu lawbooks, epics, and development of the six orthodox systems of philosophy.
	c.300	Earliest core of Kautilya's *Artha Śāstra.*
	c.100–100 A.D.	Composition of *Bhagavad Gītā.*
A.D.	c.100–200	Early law code of Yājnavalkya.
	c.200–400	Bharata's *Treatise on Dramaturgy.*

GUPTA PERIOD

c.300–500	Īshvarakrishna's *Sāṅkhya Kārikās.* Christian community of the Nestorian (Syrian) sect in existence at Cochin in South India.
c.300–888	Pallava rulers of Kānchī in South India.

c.319 [or 318, 320]–335	Chandragupta I.
c.335–376	Samudragupta.
c.376–415	Chandragupta II.
c.400–500	Vātsyāyana's Aphorisms on Love.
c.405	Fa-hsien, Chinese pilgrim arrives in Magadha.
c.454	First Hūna invasion.
c.495	Second Hūna invasion.
c.540	End of Gupta dynasty.
c.550–753 [or, 757]	Kingdom of Western Chālukyas in Deccan.
606–647	Rule of King Harsha of Kanauj in North India.
c.629–645	Chinese pilgrim Hsüan-tsang visits India.
c.630–970	Eastern Chālukyas in Deccan.

MEDIEVAL INDIA

c.700–800	Tamil saint Mānikkavāchakar in Mathurai. Dandin, Sanskrit author and rhetorician.
c.760–1142	Pālas of Bihar and Bengal.
c.788–820	Traditional dates of Shankara.
c.800–900	*Bhāgavata Purāṇa. Policy of Shukra.* Jinasena's *Great Legend* (*Mahāpurāṇa*). Sundaramūrti, Shaiva *Nāyanār* of South India. Vāmana and Ānandavardhana, Hindu rhetoricians and aesthetic philosophers.
c.907–1310 [or, c.850–1267]	Chola Empire at Tanjore.
c.973–1189	Second Chālukya dynasty in Western and Central Deccan.
c.1000–1100	Abhinavagupta. Yāmuna Āchārya's (Tamil Ālavandār) *Āgamaprāmāṇya.* Saraha's *Dohākośa.* Rise of Hindu Tantricism.
c.1018–1055	King Bhoja of Mālwā.
c.1100–1200	Mammata's *Kāvyaprakāśa.* Basavarāja founds Vīrashaiva movement in South India.
c.1137	Death of Rāmānuja.
c.1197–1276 [or, 1199–1278]	Madhva Āchārya.
c.1200–1300	Shārngadeva's treatise on music, *Saṅgītaratnākara.* Lokāchārya's *Triad of Categories.*
1216–1327	Pāndyas of Mathura.
c.1275–1296	Jnāneshvara's *Jñāneśvarī.*
c.1300–1400	Lallā, poetess of Kashmir.
1336–1565	Vijayanagara, last great Hindu kingdom in India.
c.1420 [or, 1550]	Mīrā Bāī, Rājput poetess.
1440–1518	Kabīr.

c.1449–1568 Shankaradeva, Vaishnava saint of Assam.
c.1475 [or, 1479]–1531 Vallabha, Vedānta philosopher.
c.1480–1564 Purandaradāsa, poet-saint of Karnataka.
c.1485–1533 Chaitanya of Bengal.
c.1500–1600 Sūrdās, blind poet of Agra. Vādirāja's *Kṛṣṇastuti* and *Haryaṣṭaka*.
c.1532–1623 Tulasī Dās.
c.1542 St. Francis Xavier arrives in India.
c.1609–1649 [or, 1598–1649] Tukārāma, Mahārāshtra poet-saint.
c.1700–1800 Baladeva, Vaishnava mystic in Bengal.
c.1718–1775 Rāmaprasād in Bengal.
c.1767 [or, 1759]–1847 Tyāgarāja, saint-musician of South India.

Islam in Medieval India

c.570–632 Life and mission of Muhammad the Prophet.
711–715 Conquest of Sind by the Arabs under Muhammad ibn Qāsim.
962 Foundation of Turkish principality of Ghaznīn.
988 Capture of Kabul by Sabuktigīn of Ghaznīn.
999–1026 Mahmūd of Ghaznīn raids India.
1021 Foundation of Ghaznavid principality at Lahore.
1040 Battle of Dandanqan. Ghaznavids lose bulk of empire to Saljūqs.
1151 Burning of Ghaznīn by Jahān-Sūz. Rise of principality of Ghōr.
1186 Ghōrids capture Lahore. End of Ghaznavid principality.
1192 Ghōrid defeat of Prithivi Rāj. Delhi becomes Ghōrid headquarters in India.

DELHI SULTANATE

1211–1236 Reign of Īltutmish, first founder-sultan of Delhi.
1266–1287 Reign of Bālban, consolidator of Delhi sultanate.
1296–1316 Reign of Ala al-din Khaljī. Imperial phase of Delhi sultanate.
1306–1310 Conquest of South India by Delhi. Foundation of independent Bahmanī sultanate in the Deccan.
1325–1351 Sultan Muhammad ibn Tughluq, patron of historian and political theorist Barnī.
1351–1388 Reign of Delhi sultan, Fīrūz Shah Tughluq. End of imperial phase of Delhi sultanate.
1398–1399 Tīmūr's invasion of India and sack of Delhi. Rise of independent "provincial" Muslim principalities. Probable birth of Kabīr.
1451–1526 Lodī sultanate of Delhi.
1469 Birth of Guru Nānak, founder of Sikhism.
1504 Bābur occupies Kabul.

1526	First battle of Panipat. Mughals displace Lodīs as rulers of Delhi and Agra.
1540	Mughal ruler, Humāyūn, expelled from India by Shēr Shah Sūr.
1555	Humāyūn recovers Delhi.
1556	Accession of Akbar.
1569–1586	Mughal conquest of Chitor, Gujarat. Bengal, Kashmir.
1582	Promulgation of Dīn-i-Ilāhī, Akbar's "Divine Faith."
1600	Charter of incorporation granted to the East India Company.
1605–1627	Reign of Jahāngīr.
1627–1658	Reign of Shah Jahān.
1651	Foundation of East India Company's factory at Hugli.
1657–1658	War of Succession between Dārā Shikōh and Aurangzīb.
1707	Birth of Shah Walī-Ullāh. Death of Aurangzīb.
1739	Sack of Delhi by Nādir Shah.
1757	Battle of Plassey.

BRAHMANISM

Brahmanism, while not necessarily representing the most ancient religion of the Indian subcontinent, is that system of belief and ritual practice to which Indians have, historically, looked back as the source of their religious traditions. Whether in later Hinduism, which tenaciously holds to much of the Brahmanical tradition, or in Buddhism, which rejects much of it, there is presupposed this highly conscious and articulate cult, the central feature of a way of life made known through the ages by the earliest body of formal literature, the Veda.

As seen today, the earliest religious thought in India is known or deduced from archaeological evidence, such as seals, figurines, tablets, and other artifacts, belonging to a pre-Aryan civilization which existed in the valley of the Indus River during the latter part of the third millennium B.C. The only conclusions which may be drawn with any certainty, however, from materials associated with the culture uncovered at the site of Harappa, are a preoccupation with fertility symbols (e.g., terra-cotta figurines of pregnant females, stone phallic symbols, and the like) and the worship of a divinity similar to the god Shiva, the ascetic par excellence of historic Hinduism, who is frequently associated with a bull and is also often represented by a phallic symbol. Besides representations of fertility symbols, which imply the existence of a Mother or Earth Goddess cult, and the divinity reminiscent of Shiva, the Indus civilization also seemed to attach religious significance to certain animals, such as the tiger, buffalo, crocodile, elephant, and even multiheaded monsters and hybrid creatures, as well as trees and auspicious symbols, such as the swastika. Some seals point to religious motifs found in Mesopotamia, such as the Gilgamesh legend, the ibex, trefoil designs, and others, and suggest a possible origin of religious ideas even earlier than the datable artifacts of the Indus Valley civilization. Though it is difficult to establish a definite continuity in the development of religious ideas in India dating from the Indus civilization to modern times, it is, however, possible to distinguish a clearly non-Aryan—which may or may not be pre-Aryan—source for many of the concepts which characterize that religion which is known as "Hinduism" in India today.

A second, and perhaps somewhat more significant, source of Indian religious ideas was introduced by the Aryans who invaded India from the northwest about 1500 B.C., or earlier, and who may themselves have been responsible for the destruction of the Indus civilization. These Aryan invaders brought with them religious concepts consisting mainly of a pantheon of naturalistic or functional gods, a ritualistic cult involving the sacrificial use of fire and an exhilarating drink called *soma,* as well as the rudiments of a social order. To a certain extent their religion derived from primitive Indo-European times; that is to say, some of the gods mentioned in the scriptures of these people are found to have mythological counterparts in other Indo-European traditions, particularly those of Iran, Greece, and Rome, and thus indicate a common origin of such gods in antiquity. In addition to such specifically Indo-European concepts, the religion of the Aryans involved other ideas which may have developed in the course of their eastward migrations or may have resulted from the assimilation of indigenous religious notions encountered in the Indian subcontinent itself. From a sociological standpoint, the religion introduced by the Aryan invaders was limited to persons of Aryan birth, though some non-Aryan beliefs seem to have been accepted in a modified form or at least tolerated by the priesthood of the conquering Aryans.

The religion thus developed by the Aryans from the time of their invasion of India until roughly 500 B.C. was embodied in a collection of hymns, ritual texts, and philosophical treatises, called the *Veda.* From Aryan times down to the present, Hindus have regarded the Veda as a body of eternal and revealed scripture. Its final authority is accepted to some extent by all Hindus as embodying the essential truths of Hinduism. The earliest portion of the Veda consists of four metrical hymnals, known as *Saṃhitās,* being the *Rig Veda, Yajur Veda, Sāma Veda,* and *Atharva Veda.* The earliest of these texts is that of the *Rig Veda,* and it is this collection of hymns (*ṛc*) which constitutes the earliest source of knowledge concerning the Aryan religion. The most recent of these canonical collections is the *Atharva Veda,* which is somewhat more representative of the popular religion of Vedic times than are the other Vedas, which are more sacerdotal in character. The metrical hymns and chants of these texts gave rise to elaborate ritualistic prose interpretations called *Brāhmanas* and *Āranyakas* ("forest books"). Toward the end of the Vedic period, the earlier emphasis on ritual was translated symbolically. Thus, Vedic ideas of sacrifice and mythology were reinterpreted in terms of the macrocosm and microcosm. Cosmological inquiries of some of the later hymns of the *Rig Veda* were extended and an investigation of the human soul was undertaken. The speculations and interpretations along these lines were formulated by various philosophical schools in treatises collectively called *Upanishads*. Thus, the whole of Vedic literature consists of four Vedas or Samhitās, several expository ritual texts attached to each of these Vedas called Brāhmanas, and speculative treatises, or Upanishads, concerned chiefly with a mystical interpretation of the Vedic ritual and its relation to man and the universe.

Although the relationship between the various deities of the *Rig Veda* is not always clear, and different deities—often personifications of natural forces—may each in turn be regarded as the supreme god, nevertheless Indra (often referred to as *eka deva* "One God") stands out as pre-eminent and the core myth of the *Rig Veda* recounts his deeds. In terms of this central myth, creation proceeded when Indra, the champion of the celestial gods, slew a serpent demon, Vritra, who enclosed the waters and the sun requisite for human life. When Indra split open the belly of this demon the essentials of creation—moisture, heat, light—were released and cosmic order (rita) was established under the administration of the god Varuna. Gods and men then had specific functions (*vrata*) to perform in accordance with this cosmic order. After death those individuals who had fulfilled their obligations under the cosmic order went to a heavenly realm presided over by Yama, the first mortal. Two mythical dogs guarded the righteous on the path to this region, but the sinful were fettered and, unprotected, fell prey to various demons.

Cult practices developed an elaborate ritual based on a fire sacrifice, personified as the god Agni, and included various oblations of clarified butter and the production of the soma juice, deified as the god Soma, from an unidentified plant known also from Iranian sources. This ritual naturally necessitated a highly specialized priesthood. Just as the crackling of the sacrificial fire was viewed as the voice of Agni, the priest par excellence, so, too, great significance was attached to the chanting of hymns and invocations by the human priesthood. Later the sacrifice itself was viewed cosmologically and the correct performance of the sacrifice possessed a magical potency which could coerce even the gods. This magical power inherent in the sacrificial prayers thus developed into spells, called *bráhman*. He who recited them was a "pray-er" (*brahmán*), or one related to prayer (*brāhmaṇa*). From this concept developed the brāhman, or priestly, caste.

The spiritualization of prayer (brahman) and its relation to the gods and the universe through ritual sacrifice constitute the central conception of this early phase of Indian religious thought. When the Upanishads coupled this notion with an investigation of the individual self (ātman)—an idea closely allied to the earlier personification and deification of "Wind" or "Air" (*Vāyu*) and referring to human "breath"—the brahman came to be viewed as a universal principle. Thus, an essential feature of Vedic ritual, the "prayer" itself, was given cosmological and cosmogonic implications and became the principal subject of later Indian philosophical inquiry. It is on the basis of these ritualistic Vedic concepts that the earliest definable religious thought of India is identified as Brahmanism.

R. Weiler

CHAPTER I

THE COSMIC ORDER IN THE VEDIC HYMNS

Long before they entered into India the Vedic Aryans must have started producing prayers and songs (mantras) relating to their religion. The character of this religion was determined by the kind of life they had been living. At that early stage of their cultural history, the Vedic Aryans lived close to nature—as a part of it, rather than apart from it. It was, therefore, the vastness and brilliance of nature, its blessings and maledictions, and, above all, the inexorable and subtly operating law which regulated all its manifestations, that dominated their religious ideology. The earliest hymns of the Vedic Aryans, accordingly, pertained to this cosmic religion, to which they gave expression through such mythological concepts as those of the divine parents, Heaven and Earth, the cosmic law (rita), and the sustainer of that law, Varuna. Side by side with this cosmic religion, the Vedic Aryans had also developed a kind of fire worship. The cosmic religion of the Vedic Aryans tended toward anthropomorphism, but it was not idolatrous. Fire was, therefore, regarded as the liaison between gods and men.

Sun worship, which also figures prominently in the Veda, is, in a sense, just an aspect of fire worship; but it has greatly influenced many mythological concepts in the Veda with the result that divinities like Vishnu, who had originally little to do with the solar phenomenon, came to be regarded as sun-gods at some stage in the evolution of their character.

In the course of time there occurred a change in the conditions of life of the Vedic Aryans and consequently in their religious ideology. They set out toward India on campaigns of conquest and colonization, fought on their way a series of battles with several antagonistic tribes, whom they collectively called *Dāsas,* and finally emerged as victorious colonizers of that part of India which was known as the land of seven rivers, the present Punjab. In this epoch-making warlike enterprise the Vedic Aryans were apparently led by their heroic leader, Indra, whom they soon made into a god. Gradually history came to be transformed into mythology. In this process several elements were derived from an ancient primitive myth of the Hero and the Dragon. And later the Vedic Aryan war-god came to be invested with a cosmic character. This hero-religion eventually dominated the hymns produced by the Vedic poets, priests, and warriors.

Perhaps with a view to counteracting the growing influence of a mythology glorifying military prowess, the Vedic poets and priests deified the magical potency of their prayers and priestcraft in the forms of Brahmanaspati (Lord of Prayer), who is in some respects modeled after Indra, and Vāch, the goddess of Speech or Holy Word. He embodies prayer (*brahman*) itself, as well as ritual activity in general. Moreover, in the person of Brahmanaspati ritual and cosmological aspects are blended. He is often associated with Agni, the sacrifice personified, on the one hand, and Indra, the later cosmogonic principal (*tad ekam*), on the other. Thus the hymns dedicated to this god represent the emergence of prayer (*brahman*) as an extremely significant concept in early Vedic thought. It is not at all surprising then that the importance of ritual in Vedic religion should give rise to the central conception of later Vedic philosophical speculation regarding the true nature of the cosmological concept *brahman* and its relation to the human self.

Like many other primitive communities, the Vedic Aryans believed that the creation of the universe and the procreation of the human race were the result of a primeval sacrifice, namely of the self-immolation of a cosmic being. This cosmic being is represented in the Veda as the male, Purusha. Apart from this concept of the primeval cosmic sacrifice as the starting point of creation, there are represented in the Veda other significant currents of cosmogonic thought. According to one of them the source of all powers and existences, divine as well as earthly, was conceived as the "golden germ" (*hiraṇyagarbha*)—a form assumed by an unnamed Ur-god. This "golden germ" is the precursor of the universal egg (*brahmāṇḍa*) of the later cosmogony. Another cosmogonic theory is far more profound. It seeks to controvert the view that the world has evolved out of "nonbeing" (asat). At the same time this theory asserts that the source of this world can not be, strictly speaking, characterized as "being" (sat). In the beginning there was neither "nonbeing" nor "being," nevertheless That One (*tad ekam*) breathed, though breathless, through its own inherent power. Besides it nothing existed. This idea may suggest the mythological creation of the world by Indra, the One God (*eka deva*), who destroyed the cosmic demon Vritra. Finally, in the *Atharva Veda* both "being" and "nonbeing" have *brahman* as their source.

Side by side with the ritual, eschatology, mythology, and cosmogony of the upper classes among the Vedic Aryans there had also existed a religion of the non-Aryan subject peoples. This religion comprised a variety of charms, imprecations, and exorcistic practices which were primarily intended "to appease, to bless, and to curse." The motif recurring throughout this religion was, of course, magic.

Agni

The discovery of fire constitutes a significant landmark in the history of human civilization and it is not unnatural that fire should have been held in great awe from early times. The Aryans, however, developed the worship of Agni or Fire to an extraordinary degree.

The god Agni is the personification and deification especially of the sacrificial fire. He is the priest of the gods and the god of the priests. In the *Rig Veda* he is second only to Indra in prominence. He has three forms: terrestrial as fire, atmospheric as lightning, and celestial as the sun. Thus, his function as the sacrificial fire of the priests serves as a kind of liaison between man and the heavenly gods—specifically he carries the oblations which the brāhman priests pour into the fire to the gods. The correct propitiation of Agni in the Vedic ritual was thus of considerable importance to Aryan man.

[From *Rig Veda,* 1.1]

I extol Agni, the household priest, the divine minister of the sacrifice, the chief priest, the bestower of blessings.

May that Agni, who is to be extoled by ancient and modern seers, conduct the gods here.

Through Agni may one gain day by day wealth and welfare which is glorious and replete with heroic sons.

O Agni, the sacrifice and ritual which you encompass on every side, that indeed goes to the gods.

May Agni, the chief priest, who possesses the insight of a sage, who is truthful, widely renowned, and divine, come here with the gods.

O Agni, O Angiras ["messenger"], whatever prosperity you bring to the pious is indeed in accordance with your true function.

O Agni, illuminator of darkness, day by day we approach you with holy thought bringing homage to you,

Presiding at ritual functions, the brightly shining custodian of the cosmic order (rita), thriving in your own realm.

O Agni, be easy of access to us as a father to his son. Join us for our wellbeing.

Heaven and Earth

As the divine parents, Heaven and Earth are symbolic of the vastness, brightness, and bounty of nature. The myth of their conjugal union dates from primitive Indo-European times and probably represents the earliest Vedic conception of creation based on an indissoluble connection of the two worlds, celestial and terrestrial.

Note the constant emphasis in these prayers on the hope of obtaining material rewards.

[From *Rig Veda,* 6.70]

Rich in ghee [i.e., clarified butter considered as fertilizing rain], exceedingly glorious among beings, wide, broad, honey-dispensing, with beautiful forms, Heaven and Earth are, in accordance with Varuna's cosmic law (dharma), held asunder, both ageless and rich in seed.

Nonexhausting, many-streamed, full of milk, and of pure ordinance the two dispense ghee for the pious one. You two, O Heaven and Earth, ruling over this creation, pour down for us the seed [rain] which is wholesome to mankind.

The mortal, who, for the sake of a straightforward course of life, has offered sacrifice unto you, O Heaven and Earth, O Sacrificial Bowls, he succeeds; he is reborn through his progeny in accordance with the cosmic law. Your poured semen becomes beings of manifold forms, each fulfilling his own function.

With ghee are covered Heaven and Earth, glorious in ghee, mingled with ghee, growing in ghee. Wide and broad, these two have precedence at the time of the selection of officiating priests. The wise ones invoke these two with a view to asking them for blessings.

May Heaven and Earth, honey-dropping, honey-dispensing, with hon eyed courses, shower down honey for us, bringing unto the gods sacrifice and wealth, and for us great glory, reward, and heroic strength.

May Heaven and Earth swell our nourishment, the two who are father and mother, all-knowing, doing wondrous work. Communicative and wholesome unto all, may Heaven and Earth bring unto us gain, reward, and riches.

Varuna

Varuna is the administrator of the cosmic law (rita, dharma), which regulates all activities in this world, big and small. It is he, for instance, who has spread out the earth and set the sun in motion, and who pours out the rain but sees to it that the one ocean is not filled to overflowing by many rivers. He is, therefore, rightly called the world-sovereign. Naturally enough, this upholder of cosmic order is also regarded as the lord of human morality. It is the function of Varuna to ensure that there occurs no transgression of the law, cosmic or human.

[From *Rig Veda,* 5.85]

Unto the sovereign lord sing a sublime and solemn prayer (*brahman*), one dear unto glorious Varuna, who has spread out the earth, as the butcher does the hide, by way of a carpet for the sun.

Varuna has extended the air above the trees; he has put strength in horses, milk in cows, will-power in hearts, fire in waters, the sun in the heaven, and soma upon the mountain.

Varuna poured out the leather-bag, opening downward, upon the heaven and the earth and the mid-region. Thereby does the lord of the whole creation moisten thoroughly the expanse of earth, as rain does the corn.

He moistens the broad earth and the heaven. When Varuna would have it milked [i.e., would shower rain] then, indeed, do the mountains clothe themselves with clouds and the heroes, showing off their might, loosen those clothes [i.e., disperse the clouds].

This great magic-work (māyā) of renowned spiritual Varuna will I proclaim loudly; of Varuna, who, standing in the mid-region, has measured the earth with the sun as with a measuring rod.

No one, indeed, dare impugn this great magic-work of the wisest god, namely, that the many glistening streams, pouring forth, do not fill up one ocean with water.

If we, O Varuna, have offended against a friend, befriended through Aryaman or through Mitra [i.e., gods of hospitality and friendship], or if we have offended against an all-time comrade or a brother or an inmate —whether belonging to us, O Varuna, or a stranger—do you remove that offense from us.

If we have deceived, like gamblers in a game of dice, and whether we really know it or not, all that do you unbind from us, like loosened fetters, O god. Thus may we be dear unto you, O Varuna.

Dawn

In hymns such as this we find most movingly expressed the profound awe and sensitivity to the beauties of nature which underlie much of Vedic mythology. Here, however, there is less of the tendency to personify and deify natural forces which is so prominent a feature of Vedic religious thought, than a majestic description of the actual dawn itself in metaphorical language, giving us an insight into the cosmic harmony of man and nature. While later Indian philosophies often viewed nature and the visible world as in some sense evil or unreal, this loving appreciation of nature is characteristic not only of the more optimistic, life-affirming attitude of the Vedas but also of an important strain in Indian literature from the early epics and plays of Kālidāsa down to the modern works of Rabindranath Tagore.

We have chosen the excellent metrical translation of Professor Macdonell which suggests the stately rhythm and cumulative power of the original.

[From A. A. Macdonell, *Hymns from the Rigveda,* p. 38, hymn 1.113]

This light has come, of all the lights the fairest:
The brilliant brightness has been born effulgent.
Urged onward for god Savitar's uprising,
Night now has yielded up her place to morning.

Bringing a radiant calf she comes resplendent:
To her the Black One has given up her mansions.
Akin, immortal, following each other,
Morning and Night fare on, exchanging colors.

The sisters' pathway is the same, unending:
Taught by the gods alternately they tread it.
Fair-shaped, of form diverse, yet single-minded,
Morning and Night clash not, nor do they tarry.

Bright leader of glad sounds she shines effulgent:
Widely she has unclosed for us her portals.
Pervading all the world she shows us riches:
Dawn has awakened every living creature.

Men lying on the ground she wakes to action:
Some rise to seek enjoyment of great riches,
Some, seeing little, to behold the distant:
Dawn has awakened every living creature.

One for dominion, and for fame another;
Another is aroused for winning greatness;
Another seeks the goal of varied nurture:
Dawn has awakened every living creature.

Daughter of Heaven, she has appeared before us,
A maiden shining in resplendent raiment.
Thou sovereign lady of all earthly treasure,
Auspicious Dawn, shine here today upon us. . . .

Indra

Indra is the most prominent divinity in the *Rig Veda.* He is an atmospheric god often identified with thunder and wielding a weapon, called *vajra* ("thunderbolt"). As such he destroys the demons of drought and darkness and heralds the approach of the rain so vital to life in India. In the Veda, the most significant myth which recounts his deeds centers about his slaying of the demon Vritra, who encloses the waters (i.e., the rains) and the sun, and who is the very embodiment of cosmic chaos. Historically considered, this myth may represent the conquest of India by the Aryans inspired by a warrior-champion, Indra. From a mythological standpoint, the destruction of Vritra and the subsequent release of the essentials of life—water, heat, light—may be allegorically regarded as an early cosmogonic theory.

[From *Rig Veda,* 1.32]

Indra's heroic deeds, indeed, will I proclaim, the first ones which the wielder of the vajra accomplished. He killed the dragon, released the waters, and split open the sides of the mountains.

He killed the dragon lying spread out on the mountain; for him Tvashtar fashioned the roaring vajra. Like bellowing cows, the waters, gliding, have gone down straightway to the ocean.

Showing off his virile power he chose soma;[1] from the three *kadrukas*[2] he drank of the extracted soma. The bounteous god took up the missile, the vajra; he killed the first-born among the dragons.

When you, O Indra, killed the first-born among the dragons and further overpowered the wily tricks (māyā) of the tricksters, bringing forth, at that very moment, the sun, the heaven, and the dawn—since then, indeed, have you not come across another enemy.

Indra killed Vritra, the greater enemy, the shoulderless one, with his mighty and fatal weapon, the vajra. Like branches of a tree lopped off with an axe, the dragon lies prostrate upon the earth.

For, like an incapable fighter, in an intoxicated state, he [Vritra] had challenged the great hero [Indra], the mighty overwhelmer, the drinker of soma to the dregs. He did not surmount the onslaught of his fatal weapon. Indra's enemy, broken [-nosed],[3] was completely crushed.

Footless and handless he gave battle to Indra. He [Indra] struck him with the vajra upon the back. The castrated bull, seeking to become a compeer of the virile bull, Vritra lay shattered in many places.

Over him, who lay in that manner like a shattered reed[4] flowed the waters for the sake of man.[5] At the feet of the very waters, which Vritra had [once] enclosed with his might, the dragon [now] lay [prostrate].

Vritra's mother had her vital energy ebbing out; Indra had hurled his fatal weapon at her. The mother lay above, the son below; Dānu[6] lay down like a cow with her calf.

In the midst of the water-streams, which never stood still nor had any resting place, the body lay. The waters flow in all directions over Vritra's secret place; Indra's enemy lay sunk in long darkness.

With the Dāsa as their lord[7] and with the dragon as their warder, the waters remained imprisoned, like cows held by the Pani.[8] Having killed

[1] Presumably the juice of soma was originally used for ritualistic purposes only. In view of the peculiar strength-giving, entrancing properties of the drink, however, the war-lord Indra later used it to inspirit himself for his heroic deeds.

[2] *Kadrukas* are traditionally explained as the three days in a six-day soma-sacrifice. Perhaps the word originally meant the three wooden bowls from which soma was drunk.

[3] Or, the breaker of chariots.

[4] Or, bull.

[5] Manu. The exact meaning is unclear.

[6] Vritra's mother.

[7] Literally "having the demon as their lord" (*dāsapatnīs*). After Indra's victory over the demon, the waters became *arya-patnīs* (*Rig Veda,* 10.43.8), that is, "having the Aryans as their lord." Apart from its mythological significance, this fact may have an historical basis in the conflict of the Aryan invaders with indigenous tribal people.

[8] That is, the leader of the Panis, a gypsy-like, nomadic, trading people, who stole the cows belonging to the Aryans.

Vritra, [Indra] threw open the cleft of waters which had been closed.

You became the hair of a horse's tail, O Indra, when he [Vritra] struck at your sharp-pointed vajra—the one god (*eka deva*) though you were. You won the cows, O brave one, you won soma; you released the seven rivers, so that they should flow.

Neither did lightning nor thunder, nor mist nor hailstorm, which he [Vritra] had spread out, prove efficacious when Indra and the dragon fought. And the bounteous god remained victorious for all time to come.

Whom did you see, O Indra, as the avenger of the dragon, that fear entered into your heart, after you had killed the dragon, and frightened, you crossed nine and ninety rivers and the aerial regions like the falcon? [9]

Indra, who wields the vajra in his hand, is the lord of what moves and what remains rested, of what is peaceful and what is horned.[10] He alone rules over the tribes as their king; he encloses them as does a rim the spokes.

The Primeval Sacrifice

The origin of the universe from a primeval sacrifice, in which a cosmic being offers himself as an oblation, is not unknown in primitive mythological traditions. However, the sacrifice of the male Purusha here is not so much the primordial sacrifice of a world-giant or the type *Ur-mensch* found in Norse or Germanic mythology, as it is a cosmogonic idea based on ritual sacrifice itself as the origin of the universe. Thus, the nature of the Purusha is a secondary blend of characteristics derived from the Vedic deities Agni, the sacrifice personified and the typical male principle; Sūrya, the sun; and Vishnu, another solar deity who embraces earth, atmosphere, and sky. Emphasized here is the universality of Purusha and his function as the cosmic sacrifice. In this way the ritual sacrifice performed on earth by a priestly class eventually was translated into terms of cosmological significance by a process identifying microcosmic, with macrocosmic, elements.

This hymn makes the earliest reference to the four social orders, later known as castes. The passage is important in that it emphasizes the magico-ritualistic origin of castes. The brāhmans formed the highest social order, the literate intelligentsia which gave India its priests, thinkers, law-givers, judges, and ministers of state. The rājanyas, later called kshatriyas or rulers, were the

[9] Does this refer to some temporary setback which Indra suffered in his battles with the Dāsas?

[10] And, therefore, aggressive.

second social order, the Indian counterpart of feudal nobility: from this class were recruited kings, vassals, and warriors. The vaishyas formed the class of landowners, merchants, and moneylenders, while the shūdras, originally those peoples conquered by the Aryans, were workers, artisans, or serfs.

[From *Rig Veda,* 10.90]

Thousand-headed Purusha, thousand-eyed, thousand-footed—he, having pervaded the earth on all sides, still extends ten fingers beyond it.

Purusha alone is all this—whatever has been and whatever is going to be. Further, he is the lord of immortality and also of what grows on account of food.

Such is his greatness; greater, indeed, than this is Purusha. All creatures constitute but one quarter of him, his three quarters are the immortal in the heaven.

With his three quarters did Purusha rise up; one quarter of him again remains here. With it did he variously spread out on all sides over what eats and what eats not.

From him was Virāj [11] born, from Virāj the evolved Purusha. He, being born, projected himself behind the earth as also before it.

When the gods performed the sacrifice with Purusha as the oblation, then the spring was its clarified butter, the summer the sacrificial fuel, and the autumn the oblation.

The sacrificial victim, namely, Purusha, born at the very beginning, they sprinkled with sacred water upon the sacrificial grass. With him as oblation the gods performed the sacrifice, and also the Sādhyas [a class of semidivine beings] and the rishis [ancient seers].

From that wholly offered sacrificial oblation were born the verses [*ṛc*] and the sacred chants; from it were born the meters (*chandas*); the sacrificial formula was born from it.[12]

From it horses were born and also those animals who have double rows [i.e., upper and lower] of teeth; cows were born from it, from it were born goats and sheep.

When they divided Purusha, in how many different portions did they arrange him? What became of his mouth, what of his two arms? What were his two thighs and his two feet called?

[11] The precise meaning of Virāj is uncertain. Here it seems to represent a kind of cosmic source—perhaps the waters themselves—from which creation proceeds.

[12] The verses (*ṛc*), the sacred chants (*sāma*), and the sacrificial formula (*yajus*) may refer to the three Vedas.

His mouth became the brāhman; his two arms were made into the rājanya; his two thighs the vaishyas; from his two feet the shūdra was born.

The moon was born from the mind, from the eye the sun was born; from the mouth Indra and Agni, from the breath (prāna) the wind (vāyu) was born.

From the navel was the atmosphere created, from the head the heaven issued forth; from the two feet was born the earth and the quarters (the cardinal directions) from the ear. Thus did they fashion the worlds.

Seven were the enclosing sticks in this sacrifice, thrice seven were the fire-sticks made, when the gods, performing the sacrifice, bound down Purusha, the sacrificial victim.

With this sacrificial oblation did the gods offer the sacrifice. These were the first norms (dharma) of sacrifice.[13] These greatnesses reached to the sky wherein live the ancient Sādhyas and gods.

The Origin of the World

In the early Indra creation myth, the demon Vritra had to be slain before creation could proceed. Indra as the personal demiurge brought order out of chaos (asat); that is to say, he brought about the existent (sat) from the nonexistent (asat). In later Vedic cosmogonic speculation, the personal creator, Indra as the One God (*eka deva*) is conceived of as an impersonal creative impulse called That One (*tad ekam*). When the question arises (vs. 1) as to "what enclosed all," the answer is no longer Vritra according to the old myth, but rather that creation proceeds from a principle motivated by desire outside, or over and beyond, "being" and "non-being." In terms of this new cosmological interpretation of creation, only the sages were able to fathom in their hearts the relation of "being" and "nonbeing." The hymn ends on a note of skepticism, which anticipates the questioning mood of the Upanishads—"he who is the highest overseer in heaven, he certainly knows, on the other hand, perhaps he does not."

[From *Rig Veda,* 10.129]

Neither not-being nor being was there at that time; there was no air-filled space nor was there the sky which is beyond it. What enveloped all? And where? Under whose protection? What was the unfathomable deep water?

[13] The later sacrifices are modeled after the primeval cosmic sacrifice and are believed to be actually furthering the purpose of that sacrifice by ensuring the proper organization and functioning of the world and human society.

Neither was death there, nor even immortality at that time; there was no distinguishing mark of day and night. That One breathed without wind in its own special manner. Other than It, indeed, and beyond, there did not exist anything whatsoever.

In the beginning there was darkness concealed in darkness; all this was an indistinguishable flood of water. That, which, possessing life-force, was enclosed by the vacuum, the One, was born through the power of heat from its austerity.

Upon It rose up, in the beginning, desire, which was the mind's first seed. Having sought in their hearts, the wise ones discovered, through deliberation, the bond of being and nonbeing.

Right across was their [i.e., the wise ones'] dividing line extended. Did the below exist then, was there the above? There were the seed-planters, there were the great forces of expansion. Below there was self-impulse, above active imparting.

Who knows it for certain; who can proclaim it here; namely, out of what it was born and wherefrom this creation issued? The gods appeared only later—after the creation of the world. Who knows, then, out of what it has evolved?

Wherefrom this creation has issued, whether he has made it or whether he has not—he who is the superintendent of this world in the highest heaven—he alone knows, or, perhaps, even he does not know.

The Brahmachārī

The term *brahmachārī* means "going to, or according to, *bráhman* (the holy word)." Since the prayer or sacred word (*brahman*) came to be identified with the Vedic hymns or invocations themselves, a brahmachārī was regarded as a student of the Veda as well as a disciple of Brahman. In later Hinduism this remnant of early Brahmanism was preserved as the first prescribed stage (āshrama) of Aryan life, characterized by studentship under a competent teacher (guru) or authority on the Vedic texts, and adherence to a vow of celibacy. This stage itself is called *brahmacharya.* In this particular hymn, from the *Atharva Veda,* the brahmachārī is glorified in a cosmological sense as the sun "clothed in heat" and "with a long beard" (that is, with many rays), who is the primeval principle of the universe. The heat of the sun and the fervor generated through austerities are both called *tapas,* often seen as a factor in creation. Thus when Mahatma Gandhi later glorified *brahmacharya,* it was as a creative force sublimated by sexual continence.

[From *Atharva Veda,* 11.5.1–8, 17–26]

The Brahmachārī travels animating the two hemispheres; the gods become like-minded in him. He sustains earth and heaven; he fills his teacher with fervor.

The fathers, the god-folk, and all the gods collectively follow the Brahmachārī; the six thousand three hundred and thirty-three Gandharvas went after him. He fills all the gods with fervor.

When the teacher accepts the Brahmachārī as a disciple, he treats him as an embryo within his own body. He carries him for three nights in his belly; when he is born, the gods assemble to see him. . . .

Born prior to Brahman, clothing himself in heat, the Brahmachārī arose with his fervor. From him were born Brahmahood, the highest Brahman, and all the gods together with immortality.

The Brahmachārī goes forth, kindled by sacred fire-sticks, clothing himself with black-antelope skin, consecrated, long-bearded. Within one single day does he go from the eastern to the northern ocean; having gathered together the worlds, he fashions them repeatedly.

The Brahmachārī, begetting Brahman, the waters, the world, Prajāpati [Lord of Creatures], the most exalted one, creative force, having become an embryo in the womb of immortality, indeed, having become Indra, has shattered the demons.

The preceptor fashioned both these hemispheres, the wide and the deep, namely, earth and heaven. These two the Brahmachārī protects with his fervor; in him the gods become like-minded. . . .

Through Brahmacharya, through fervor, a king protects his kingdom. A teacher through Brahmacharya seeks a Brahmachārī for his student.

Through Brahmacharya a maiden finds a young husband. Through Bramacharya a steer or horse strives to obtain food.

Through Brahmacharya, through fervor, the gods dispelled death. Through Brahmacharya Indra brought heaven to the gods.

Plants, past and future, trees, the year and its seasons were all born from the Brahmachārī.

Animals of the earth and those of heaven, wild and domestic, wingless and winged, were all born from the Brahmachārī. . . .

The Brahmachārī fashioned these things on the back of the waters. He stood in the sea performing austerities. When he has performed ritual ablution, he shines extensively over the earth, brown and ruddy.

A Charm Against Jaundice

The contents of the *Atharva Veda* relate mainly to what may be considered indigenous traditions of popular religion. This religion consists of charms and imprecations accompanied by certain exorcistic practices, for the proper knowledge of which one has to depend entirely on an ancillary text of the Veda, like the *Kauśika Sūtra*. It is needless to add that the principal basis of these practices is symbolic magic.

[From *Atharva Veda,* 1.22]

Unto the sun let them both go up—your heartburn and your yellowness; with the color of the red bull do we envelop you.

With red colors do we envelop you for the sake of long life; so that this person may be free from harm and may become non-yellow.

Those cows [1] that have Rohinī [the Red One] as presiding divinity, as also cows which are red—their every form and every power—with them do we envelop you.

Into the parrots do we put your yellowness and into the yellow-green *ropaṇākā*-birds. Similarly into the turmeric [or yellow wagtail?] do we deposit your yellowness.

Exorcism of Serpents

The tradition designates this charm specifically to keep serpents away from the premises.

[From *Atharva Veda,* 6.56]

Let not the serpent, O gods, slay us with our children and with our men. The closed jaw shall not snap open, the open one shall not close. Homage to the divine folk [i.e., the serpents, by way of exorcistic euphemism].

Homage be to the black serpent, homage to the one with stripes across its body, homage to the brown constrictor [?], homage to the divine folk.

I smite your teeth with tooth, I smite your two jaws with jaw; I smite your tongue with tongue; I smite your mouth, O Serpent, with mouth.[2]

[1] Or herbs.

[2] Presumably the exorcist strikes the tooth, jaw, etc. of the symbolic figure of a serpent with the tooth, jaw, etc. of, perhaps, a dead serpent.

CHAPTER II

THE RITUAL ORDER IN THE BRĀHMANAS

To each of the four Samhitās or collections of hymns are attached certain expository liturgical texts called *Brāhmanas.* These somewhat bulky prose treatises give, in tedious detail, explanations of the Vedic ritual and its performance. Thus their principal concern is with the nature and use of the holy word, utterance, prayer, invocation, or divine power in the sacrifice, that is, *brahman.* The Sanskrit term *brāhmaṇa* means "relating to Brahman" or simply "brahmanic." Since the Veda contains both terms *bráhman* "prayer" and *brahmán* "pray-er," the Brāhmanas can be considered as either referring to the knowledge of *bráhman* or as belonging to the priesthood (*brāhmaṇa*), though the former interpretation seems more likely.

The Brāhmanas are significant for several reasons. First of all, they represent the oldest known specimens of Indo-European prose narrative, though earlier prose formulae are found in some of the hymn collections. Secondly, they constitute a fountainhead of information dealing with sacrifice, ritual, and priesthood. Thirdly, much of this ritualistic material is inspirited and illustrated by numerous myths and legends of all types. Even though the personalities of the gods of the *Rig Veda* tend to lose their virility and become submerged in a maze of ritual formulae, still this mythological and legendary lore provides numerous themes for poets and other writers of later times. Thus the Vedic tradition is kept very much alive even in the minds of that vast majority of Indians belonging to social classes considered beneath the priesthood.

The Brāhmana texts deal mainly with the theory and practice of sacrifice. The institution of sacrifice, elaborated by the brahmanic priests, is an amazingly intricate and complex affair. There are three principal categories of sacrifice—the cooked-food sacrifice, to be offered on the domestic fire, the oblation sacrifice, and the *soma*-sacrifice, the last two to be offered on the sacred *śrauta* (Vedic) fires. It is chiefly with the last two categories that the Brāhmana texts concern themselves. Broadly speaking, the contents of a Brāhmana text may be classified under two main heads—the precepts and the explanation. The precepts are detailed injunctions relating to the place and time, priests and sacred fires, deities and ritualistic formula, oblations and sacrificial utensils, priests' fees and expiatory rites, and several sacerdotal details in respect of a particular sacrifice. The explanation, as it were, seeks to "rationalize" these injunctions—the method of such rationalization often being, paradoxical as it may seem, not logical but magical. One of the commonest ways of emphasizing the appropriateness of any particular ritualistic detail was by taking recourse to etymology. For instance, water (*āpaḥ*) was used in connection with the preparation of a fire-place because "by means of water (*āpaḥ*), indeed, is all this world obtained [*āpta* from a different root, *āp*]; having thus obtained all this, as it were, by means of water, he sets up the sacred fire." Obviously most of such etymological exercises will not stand the test of modern scientific philology. Another way of justifying and, to a certain extent, glorifying a sacerdotal detail was by presenting it as a significant item in some myth, which latter often took the form of a contest for superiority between the gods and the demons. Then, too, there was the usual tendency to establish a kind of mystic bond between an item of the sacrificial procedure and some aspect of cosmic phenomena.

The Collection of Materials for the Sacred Fires

All *śrauta* (Vedic, as opposed to domestic) sacrifices presuppose the formal setting up of the sacred fires, usually three in number. The following extract deals with the collection of the specific materials to be used in connection with the preparation of a fire-place. An attempt is made to make the translation as literal as possible in order to bring out the peculiarities of the style developed in the Brāhmanas.

[From *Śatapatha Brāhmaṇa,* 2.1.1. 1–14]

Since, indeed, he collects (*sam + bhṛ*) them from this place and from that—that is why the materials used in connection with the preparation of the fire-place are called "collection" (*sambhāra*). In whatever place the essence of Agni (Fire) is inherent, from that very place he collects the materials. Collecting in this way, he thereby here makes him [Agni] thrive partly with glory, as it were, partly with cattle, as it were, partly with a mate, as it were.[1] Then the officiating priest draws with the wooden sword three lines on the spot selected for the fire-place. Whatever part of this earth is trodden upon or is defiled by being spit upon, that part of hers, indeed, he thereby symbolically digs up and removes away, and thus he sets up the sacred fires upon the earth which is now rendered worthy of being sacrificed upon: that is, indeed, why he draws lines upon the spot selected for the fire-place. Then he sprinkles the lines with water. This, indeed, constitutes the collecting of water [as a material for the preparation of the fire-place], namely, that he sprinkles the lines with water. That he collects water as a material in this connection is due to the fact that water is food; for, water is, indeed, food: hence, when water comes to this world, there is produced plentiful food in this world. By sprinkling water he makes him [Agni] thrive with plentiful food itself. Moreover, water is, indeed, female and Agni is male. By sprinkling water he makes him thrive with a procreating mate. By means of water (*āpaḥ*), indeed, is all this world obtained [*āpta*]; having thus obtained all this, as it were, by means of water, he sets up the sacred fire. That is why he collects water. . . . [The officiating priest then collects a piece of gold, representing the divine *semen virile;* saline soil, representing cattle and the flavors of heaven and earth; earth dug out by a wild rat, representing the flavor of this earth, affluence; and gravel, representing firmness of the earth, as proved by an *ad hoc* mythological story. He thus makes fire thrive with the magic potency derived from these materials.]

These five materials (*saṃbhāra*), indeed, does he collect (*sam* + *bhṛ*); for, five-fold is the sacrifice, five-fold is the sacrificial victim, five are the seasons of the year. As for the statement that there are five seasons in a year, they say: "Six, surely, are the seasons in a year [according to the Indian system]. There is thus a kind of deficiency in the foregoing prescription." But, verily, this very deficiency (*nyūna*) is rendered a procreative mate. For, it is from the *nyūna* [that is, the lower part of the body—a pun on the two meanings of the word *nyūna*] that progeny is procreated. Further, this fact, namely, that there are only five materials instead of six actually ensures for the sacrificer some scope for progress toward prosperity in future. That is why there are only five materials collected in connection with the preparation of the fire-place, even though there are

[1] The essence of Agni which is scattered in various places is, as it were, collected together and is again symbolically bestowed upon him so as to make him full and complete.

six seasons in a year. And if they still persist in arguing that there are, surely, six seasons in a year, we may retort by saying that Agni himself is the sixth among those materials and that, therefore, this whole procedure, surely, becomes nondeficient.

The Fetching of Sacrificial Grass

The *Śrauta Sūtras* are the most exhaustive and comprehensive manuals of Vedic sacrifice. They are the outcome of vigorous efforts made to systematize and consolidate the brahmanic ritual. It will be seen from the following passage how ritualist teachers added—perhaps purposefully—to the already existing complexities of the sacrificial procedure by expressing a variety of opinions even about a minor detail, such as the thickness of the bunch of sacrificial grass for the new-moon and full-moon sacrifices.

The text of the *Baudhāyana Śrauta Sūtra* and its supplements, *Dvaidha* and *Karmānta,* has been here rearranged so as to make it yield a connected account about this particular item in the sacrificial procedure. Baudhāyana was the preceptor of an eminent school of ritualists belonging to the Taittirīya branch of the *Black Yajur Veda.* Shālīki was another ritualist-preceptor, whose views were presumably treated with great respect.

[From *Baudhāyana Śrauta Sūtra,* 1.2; 20.2; 24.24–25]

With the formula, *devānām pariṣūtam asi* [1] [the officiating priest] should trace [by means of the sickle] a line round as small a cluster of *darbha*-grass as he considers to be sufficient for being used as strewing grass. As for the tracing round: Baudhāyana, indeed, says that [the officiating priest] should recite the formula three times and repeat the action of tracing a line round the *darbha* cluster also three times. He should act similarly at the time of tracing a hole for the sacrificial post, similarly at the time of tracing the foot-print [of the cow] with which soma is to be purchased, similarly at the digging of the hole for the branch of the *udumbara* tree, and similarly at the preparation of the [four] resonant pits. Shālīki on the other hand says that he should recite the formula only once, but should repeat the action of tracing round a line three times.

Then he should brush [the blades in the *darbha* cluster from the bottom] to the top [by means of the sickle] with the formula, *varṣavṛddham asi.* He should seize it by means of the sickle with the formula, *devabarhir mā. . .* He should cut off [as much grass as can be cut off in one

[1] In most cases, the Sūtra texts give only the initial words of a formula to indicate the whole formula.

stroke with the formula] *ācchettā te mā riṣam*. He should touch the stumps of grass remaining after the cutting with the formula, *devabarhiḥ śatavalśaṃ vi roha*. As for cutting off of the grass: The view expressed above is that of Baudhāyana. Shālīki on the other hand says that this formula should, indeed, be regarded as bestowing an indirect blessing. There should, therefore, be only indirect touching [of the stumps] by means of the formula. With the formula, *sahasravalśā vi vayaṃ ruhema*, he should touch himself [that is, he should touch his own heart]. He should cut off the *darbha* cluster entirely. Having tied up the *darbha* blades into a bunch to serve as strewing grass, he should place it aside with the formula, *pṛthivyāḥ saṃpṛcaḥ pāhi*.

For being used as strewing grass there should be tied up a bunch of *darbha* blades having a circumference equal to the one produced by joining the tips of nails [of the thumb and forefinger]—such is the view of some teachers. A bunch should be tied up of as many *darbha* blades as could be cut off in one stroke—such is the view of some teachers. . . . It should be tied up so as to be as thick as the handle of the sacrificial spoon—such is the view of some teachers. It should be tied up so as to be as thick as the thigh-bone—such is the view of some teachers. It should be tied up so as to be as thick as the thumb-joint—such is the view of some teachers. It should be tied up without being measured—such is the view of some teachers.

CHAPTER III

THE ULTIMATE REALITY IN THE UPANISHADS

Toward the end of the Brāhmana period, that is, c.600 B.C., another class of religious texts appeared called *Āranyakas* ("forest books"). The exact implication of this term is uncertain, but it seems probable that these works were recited by hermits living in the forests. The retirement to the forest prior to attaining religious salvation is usually considered the third prescribed stage (āshrama) in the life of the orthodox Hindu even as studentship (brahmacharya) represented the first. The Āranyakas contain transitional material between the mythology and ritual of the Samhitās and Brāhmanas on the one hand and the philosophical speculations of the Upanishads on the other. The ritual is given a symbolic meaning, and knowledge of this becomes more important than the actual performance of the ritual itself. This principle then becomes the starting point of Upanishadic speculation.

Like the Brāhmanas, each Upanishad is attached to one of the four Vedic Samhitās. The Upanishads represent both the final stage in the development of Vedic religious thought and the last phase of Brahmanism. They are thus the end of the Veda (*vedānta*). Later philosophical schools of classical Hinduism which base their tenets on the authority of the Upanishads are therefore called *Vedānta.*

The Upanishads cannot be regarded as presenting a consistent, homogeneous, or unified philosophical system, though there are certain doctrines held in common. Divergences of method, opinion, and conclusion are everywhere apparent even within a single Upanishad. It is for this reason that the Upanishads are considered speculative treatises. Another significant feature of the Upanishads, particularly the older ones, is that practically every basic idea expounded has its antecedent in earlier Vedic texts. What distinguishes the Upanishads is not so much their originality as their probing for new interpretations of the earlier Vedic concepts to obtain a more coherent view of the universe and man. Here the link between man and the cosmos is, as we have said, no longer the ritual act, but a knowledge of the forces symbolically represented in the ritual. These allegorical and symbolic interpretations are characteristic of the Upanishads. They are developed by Upanishadic thinkers in two ways: 1) by setting up various levels of comprehension suited to different individual intellectual capacities, and 2) by identifying partially or by degrees two seemingly dissimilar elements and arriving at a type of equation which, though at first sight irrational, will on further analysis or introspection reveal a unity. This pursuit of a unifying principle suggests that the duality apparent in the world is to some extent or in some sense unreal. The macrocosm is viewed universally as an extension of Vedic mythological and ritualistic concepts, specifically *brahman*. As a parallel to this, the microcosmic nature of the human self or soul (ātman) is explained. From this results the most significant equation of the Upanishads: *brahman* = *ātman*. It is the transcendent knowledge of this essential identity that is the chief concern of Upanishadic sages.

The Sacrificial Horse

The most elaborate and stupendous sacrifice described in the Brāhmanas is the horse-sacrifice (*aśvamedha*). It is an ancient rite which a king might undertake to increase his realm. In the following selection from perhaps the oldest of the Upanishads, the *Bṛhad Āraṇyaka* (Great Forest Text), the horse-sacrifice is given cosmological significance by equating various parts of the sacrificial horse with corresponding elements of the cosmos. To Upanishadic thinkers the real meaning of the horse-sacrifice was gained through a realization of the identity of the parts of this sacrifice and the universe. This type of mystical or transcendent knowledge is based on equations stressed by the word "verily" (*vai*) and is characteristic of the early Upanishads in particular. It should be noted that dawn, the sun, the wind, etc., besides being elements of the cosmos, were also deified naturalistic forces in Vedic mythology and still retain their identity as such in the following passage.

[From *Bṛhad Āraṇyaka Upaniṣad*, 1.1.1]

Dawn verily is the head of the sacrificial horse. The sun is his eye; the wind, his breath; the universal sacrificial fire (*agni-vaiśvānara*), his open mouth; the year is the body (ātman) of the sacrificial horse. The sky is his back; the atmosphere, his belly; the earth, his underbelly [?]; the directions, his flanks; the intermediate directions, his ribs; the seasons, his limbs; the months and half-months, his joints; days and nights, his feet; the stars, his bones; the clouds, his flesh. Sand is the food in his stomach; rivers, his entrails; mountains, his liver and lungs; plants and trees, his hair; the rising sun, his forepart; the setting sun, his hindpart. When he yawns, then it lightnings; when he shakes himself, then it thunders; when he urinates, then it rains. Speech (*vāc*) is actually his neighing (*vāc*).

Sacrifices—Unsteady Boats on the Ocean of Life

Some later Upanishads represent a reaction to the glorification of the sacrifice in which the brahmanic ritualists indulged. The teacher of the *Muṇḍaka Upaniṣad* quoted below seems to concede a place for sacrifice in man's life—by way of religious discipline; but he concludes that sacrifice is ineffectual as a means to the knowledge of the highest reality and to spiritual emancipation. On the other hand, as is suggested by the passage cited above, some earlier Upanishadic teachers substituted a kind of "spiritual" or "inner" sacrifice for the "material" or "external" sacrifice.

[From *Muṇḍaka Upaniṣad,* 1.2. 1, 2, 7–13]

This is that truth. The sacrificial rites which the sages saw in the hymns are manifoldly spread forth in the three [Vedas]. Do you perform them constantly, O lovers of truth. This is your path to the world of good deeds.

When the flame flickers after the oblation fire has been kindled, then, between the offerings of the two portions of clarified butter one should proffer his principal oblations—an offering made with faith. . . .

Unsteady, indeed, are these boats in the form of sacrifices, eighteen in number, in which is prescribed only the inferior work. The fools who delight in this sacrificial ritual as the highest spiritual good go again and again through the cycle of old age and death.[1]

Abiding in the midst of ignorance, wise only according to their own estimate, thinking themselves to be learned, but really hard-struck, these fools go round in a circle like blind men led by one who is himself blind.

Abiding manifoldly in ignorance they, all the same, like immature children think to themselves: "We have accomplished our aim." Since

[1] That is, they are reborn again and again in the phenomenal world. The doctrine of transmigration or reincarnation was probably unknown to the brāhman ritualists, but in the Upanishads man's salvation from this cycle of rebirths became a matter of great concern. It is suggested that the Vedic sacrifices could bring only a temporary respite in the abode of a god, not permanent release from the cycle.

the performers of sacrificial ritual do not realize the truth because of passion, therefore, they, the wretched ones, sink down from heaven when the merit which qualified them for the higher world becomes exhausted.

Regarding sacrifice and merit as most important, the deluded ones do not know of any other higher spiritual good. Having enjoyed themselves only for a time on top of the heaven won by good deeds [sacrifice, etc.] they re-enter this world or a still lower one.

Those who practice penance (tapas) and faith in the forest, the tranquil ones, the knowers of truth, living the life of wandering mendicancy—they depart, freed from passion, through the door of the sun, to where dwells, verily, that immortal Purusha, the imperishable Soul (ātman).

Having scrutinized the worlds won by sacrificial rites, a Brāhman should arrive at nothing but disgust. The world that was not made is not won by what is done [i.e., by sacrifice]. For the sake of that knowledge he should go with sacrificial fuel in hand as a student, in all humility to a preceptor (guru) who is well-versed in the [Vedic] scriptures and also firm in the realization of Brahman.

Unto him who has approached him in proper form, whose mind is tranquil, who has attained peace, does the knowing teacher teach, in its very truth, that knowledge about Brahman by means of which one knows the imperishable Purusha, the only Reality.

The Five Sheaths

In this passage an attempt is made to analyze man on five levels—proceeding from the grosser forms to the subtler, and therefore more real, forms. The "real" man transcends the physical, vital, mental, and intellectual aspects and has to be identified with the innermost, beatific aspect. It is, in the end, suggested that the real self of man is identical with Brahman, the ultimate principle, the absolute, which is his *raison d'être.*

[From *Taittirīya Upaniṣad,* 2.1–6 *passim*]

From this Self (ātman), verily, space arose; from space, wind; from wind, fire; from fire, water; from water, the earth; from the earth, herbs; from herbs, food; from food, man (purusha). This man here, verily, consists of the essence of food. Of him possessing the physical body made up of food, this, indeed, is the head; this, the right side; this, the left side; this, the body (ātman); this, the lower part, the foundation. . . . From food, verily, are produced whatsoever creatures dwell on the earth. Moreover, by food alone do they live. And then also into it do they pass at the end. . . . Verily, different from and within this body which consists of the essence of food is the body which consists of breath. The former body is filled with the latter. The latter body also is of the shape of man. According to the former one's being of the shape of man this latter body is of the shape of man. Of him possessing the body consisting of breath, the out-breath is head; the diffused breath, the right side; the in-breath, the left side; space, the body; the earth, the lower part, the foundation. . . . Verily, different from and within this body which consists of vital breaths is the body which consists of mind. The former body is filled with the latter. The latter body is also of the shape of man. . . . Verily, different from and within this body which consists of mind is the body which consists of intellectuality [or consciousness]. The former body is filled with the latter. That one also is of the shape of man. . . . Verily, different from and within this body which consists of intellectuality [or consciousness] is the body which consists of bliss.[1] The former body is filled with the latter. The latter body also is of the shape of man. . . . As to that, there is also this verse: "Nonexistent (asat), verily, does one become if he knows (believes) that Brahman is nonexistent.[2] If one knows that Brahman exists, such a one people thereby know as existent."

The Real Self

In this famous parable, the real, essential Self is successively identified with the bodily self, the dream self, and the self in deep sleep, and it is suggested that all these three teachings are quite inadequate, for in none of the three conditions, namely, of wakefulness, of dream, and of deep sleep, can the nature of Self be said to conform to the description given in the very first sentence of this passage. The real Self is neither body nor mind nor a complete negation of consciousness. The Self is certainly conscious, but of nothing else but itself. It is pure self-consciousness as such and it is in this condition that it is identical with the highest reality.

[From *Chāndogya Upaniṣad,* 8.7–12 *passim*]

"The Self (ātman) who is free from evil, free from old age, free from death, free from grief, free from hunger, free from thirst, whose desire

[1] Each succeeding body is within the preceding one and is, therefore, subtler and more real than it. The body of bliss is the most internal body. Bliss, accordingly, is the true nature of man.

[2] Man has, indeed, no existence as apart from Brahman. For a man to say that Brahman is non-existent is a contradiction in terms.

is the Real [*satya,* or truth], whose intention is the Real—he should be sought after, he should be desired to be comprehended. He obtains all worlds and all desires, who, having found out that Self, knows him." Thus, indeed, did the god Prajāpati speak. Verily, the gods and the demons both heard this. They said among themselves: "Aha! Let us seek after that Self—the Self, having sought after whom one obtains all worlds and all desires." Then Indra from among the gods went forth unto Prajāpati, and Virochana from among the demons. Indeed, without communicating with each other, those two came into the presence of Prajāpati with sacrificial fuel in hand [i.e., as students willing to serve their preceptor]. For thirty-two years the two lived under Prajāpati the disciplined life of a student of sacred knowledge (brahmacharya). Then Prajāpati asked them: "Desiring what have you lived the disciplined life of a student of sacred knowledge under me?" They said: "'The Self, who is free from evil, free from old age, free from death, free from grief, free from hunger, free from thirst, whose desire is the Real, whose intention is the Real—he should be sought after, he should be desired to be comprehended. He obtains all worlds and all desires, who, having found out that Self, knows him.' These, people declare to be the venerable master's words. Desiring him [the Self] have we lived the student's life under you." Prajāpati said to them: "That Purusha who is seen in the eye—he is the Self (ātman)," said he. "That is the immortal, the fearless; that is Brahman." "But this one, Sir, who is perceived in water and in a mirror—who is he?" Prajāpati replied: "The same one, indeed, is perceived in all these." "Having looked at yourself in a pan of water, whatever you do not comprehend of the Self, tell that to me," said Prajāpati. They looked at themselves in the pan of water. Prajāpati asked them: "What do you see?" They replied: "We see here, Sir, our own selves in entirety, the very reproduction of our forms, as it were, correct to the hairs and the nails." Then Prajāpati said to them: "Having become well ornamented, well dressed, and refined, look at yourselves in a pan of water." Having become well ornamented, well dressed, and refined, they looked at themselves in a pan of water. Thereupon Prajāpati asked them: "What do you see?" They replied: "Just as we ourselves here are, Sir, well ornamented, well dressed, and refined. . . ." "That is the Self," said he. "That is the immortal, the fearless; that is Brahman." Then they went away with a tranquil heart. Having looked at them, Prajāpati said to himself:

"They are going away without having realized, without having found out the Self. Whosoever will accept this doctrine as final, be they gods or demons, they shall perish." Then Virochana, verily, with a tranquil heart, went to the demons and declared to them that doctrine, namely: One's self [one's bodily self] [1] alone is to be made happy here; one's self is to be served. Making oneself alone happy here, serving oneself, does one obtain both worlds, this world and the yonder. Therefore, here, even now, they say of one who is not a giver, who has no faith, who does not offer sacrifices, that he is, indeed, a demon; for this is the doctrine of the demons. They adorn the body of the deceased with perfumes, flowers, etc., which they have begged, with dress and with ornaments, for they think they will thereby win the yonder world.

But then Indra, even before reaching the gods, saw this danger: "Just as, indeed, the bodily self becomes well ornamented when this body is well ornamented, well dressed when this body is well dressed, and refined when this body is refined, even so that one becomes blind when this body is blind, lame when this body is lame, and maimed when this body is maimed. The bodily Self, verily, perishes immediately after the perishing of this body. I see no good in this." With sacrificial fuel in hand, he again came back to Prajāpati. [Indra states his objection to Prajāpati, who admits its truth and asks him to live as a student under him for another thirty-two years.] Indra lived a student's life under Prajāpati for another thirty-two years. Then, Prajāpati said to him: "He who moves about happy in a dream—he is the Self," said he. "That is the immortal, the fearless; that is Brahman." Thereupon, with a tranquil heart, Indra went away.

But then, even before reaching the gods, he saw this danger: "Now, even though this body is blind, the Self in the dream-condition does not become blind; even though this body is lame, he does not become lame; indeed, he does not suffer any defect through the defect of this body. He is not slain with the slaying of this body. He does not become lame with the lameness of this body. Nevertheless, they, as it were, kill him; they, as it were, unclothe him. He, as it were, becomes the experiencer of what is not agreeable; he, as it were, even weeps. I see no good in this." [Again Indra returns to Prajāpati with his objection. The latter admits its truth but asks Indra to be his student for another thirty-two years.] Then Prajāpati said to him: "Now, when one is sound asleep, composed, serene,

[1] Ātman can refer to one's bodily self as well as the Supreme Self.

and knows no dream—that is the Self," said he. "That is the immortal, the fearless; that is Brahman." Thereupon, with a tranquil heart, Indra went away.

But then, even before reaching the gods, he saw this danger: "Assuredly, this Self in the deep sleep condition does not, indeed, now know himself in the form: 'I am he'; nor indeed does he know these things here. He, as it were, becomes one who has gone to annihilation. I see no good in this." [Indra once more returns to Prajāpati, who promises to tell him the final truth after another five years of studentship.] Indra lived a student's life under Prajāpati for another five years. The total number of these years thus came to one hundred and one; thus it is that people say that, verily, for one hundred and one years Maghavan [Indra, the Rewarder] lived under Prajāpati the disciplined life of a student of sacred knowledge. Then Prajāpati said to him: "O Maghavan, mortal, indeed, is this body; it is taken over by death. But it is the basis of that deathless, bodiless Self. Verily, the Self, when embodied, is taken over by pleasure and pain. Verily, there is no freedom from pleasure and pain for one who is associated with the body. The wind is bodiless; cloud, lightning, thunder—these are bodiless. Now as these, having risen up from yonder space and having reached the highest light, appear each with its own form, even so this serene Self, having risen up from this body and having reached the highest light, appears with its own form. That Self is the Supreme Person (*uttama puruṣa*).

The Essential Reality Underlying the World

Looking "outwards," the Upanishadic thinker comes to the realization that this world is merely a bundle of fleeting names and forms, that there is only one permanent reality underlying this manifold phenomenal world, and that, in the ultimate analysis, that reality (elsewhere called Brahman, but here sat, i.e., being, essence) is identical with the essential reality in human personality, namely, the Self (ātman).

[From *Chāndogya Upaniṣad,* 6.1–3, 12–14, *passim*]

There, verily, was Shvetaketu, the son of Uddālaka Āruni. To him his father said: "O Shvetaketu, live the disciplined life of a student of sacred knowledge (brahmacharya). No one, indeed, my dear, belonging to our family, is unlearned in the Veda and remains a brāhman only by family connections as it were." He, then, having approached a teacher at the age of twelve and having studied all the Vedas, returned at the age of twenty-four, conceited, thinking himself to be learned, stiff. To him his father said: "O Shvetaketu, since, my dear, you are now conceited, think yourself to be learned, and have become stiff, did you also ask for that instruction whereby what has been unheard becomes heard, what has been unthought of becomes thought of, what has been uncomprehended becomes comprehended?" "How, indeed, Sir, is that instruction?" asked Shvetaketu. "Just as, my dear, through the comprehension of one lump of clay all that is made of clay would become comprehended—for the modification is occasioned only on account of a convention of speech,[2] it is only a name; while clay as such alone is the reality. Just as, my dear, through the comprehension of one ingot of iron all that is made of iron would become comprehended—for the modification is occasioned only on account of a convention of speech, it is only a name; while iron as such alone is the reality. . . . So, my dear, is that instruction." "Now, verily, those venerable teachers did not know this; for, if they had known it, why would they not have told me?" said Shvetaketu. "However, may the venerable sir tell it to me." "So be it, my dear," said he.

"In the beginning, my dear, this world was just being (sat), one only, without a second. Some people, no doubt, say: 'In the beginning, verily, this world was just nonbeing (asat), one only, without a second; from that nonbeing, being was produced.'[3] But how, indeed, my dear, could it be so?" said he. "How could being be produced from nonbeing? On the contrary, my dear, in the beginning this world was being alone,[4] one only, without a second. Being thought to itself: 'May I be many; may I procreate.' It produced fire. That fire thought to itself: 'May I be many, may I procreate.' It produced water. Therefore, whenever a person grieves or perspires, then it is from fire [heat] alone that water is produced. That water thought to itself: 'May I be many; may I procreate.' It produced food. Therefore, whenever it rains, then there is abundant food; it is from water alone that food for eating is produced.

[2] The various objects made of clay, such as plate and pitcher, are *essentially* nothing but clay. But for the sake of convenience different names are, by convention, assigned to the different shapes or modifications which that clay is made to assume. Within the world of the objects made of clay, clay alone is essential, while the different names and forms of those objects are only incidental. This is the doctrine of extreme nominalism.

[3] As in *Rig Veda,* 10.72.

[4] Compare *Rig Veda,* 10.129, above.

. . . That divinity[5] (Being) thought to itself: 'Well, having entered into these three divinities [fire, water, and food] by means of this living Self, let me develop names and forms.[6] Let me make each one of them tripartite.' That divinity, accordingly, having entered into those three divinities by means of this living Self, developed names and forms. . . . It made each one of them tripartite. . . ."

"Bring hither a fig from there." "Here it is, sir." "Break it." "It is broken, sir." "What do you see there?" "These extremely fine seeds, sir." "Of these, please break one." "It is broken, sir." "What do you see there?" "Nothing at all, sir." Then he said to Shvetaketu: "Verily, my dear, that subtle essence which you do not perceive—from that very essence, indeed, my dear, does this great fig tree thus arise. Believe me, my dear, that which is the subtle essence—this whole world has that essence for its Self; that is the Real [*satya,* truth]; that is the Self; that [subtle essence] art thou, Shvetaketu."[7] "Still further may the venerable sir instruct me." "So be it, my dear," said he.

"Having put this salt in the water, come to me in the morning." He did so. Then the father said to him: "That salt which you put in the water last evening—please bring it hither." Even having looked for it, he did not find it, for it was completely dissolved. "Please take a sip of water from this end," said the father. "How is it?" "Salt." "Take a sip from the middle," said he. "How is it?" "Salt." "Take a sip from that end," said he. "How is it?" "Salt." "Throw it away and come to me." Shvetaketu did so thinking to himself: "That salt, though unperceived, still persists in the water." Then Āruni said to him: "Verily, my dear, you do not perceive Being in this world; but it is, indeed, here only: That which is the subtle essence—this whole world has that essence for its Self. That is

[5] Being, which has been referred to in an impersonal manner so far, is now spoken of as a personalized divinity with a view to indicating that pure, essential "Being," as such, is in no way connected with the process of creation—this latter being only the result of nominalism.

[6] Being penetrates into fire, water, and food as their life-force and thereby invests them with the capacity further to function in the process of creation, thus helping the evolution of the phenomenal world which is in reality but a bundle of names and forms.

[7] In this statement, which is repeated a number of times in this chapter of the *Chāndogya Upaniṣad,* the following important points have been made: sat or Being, which is the cause of this gross world, is itself subtle and imperceptible. It is Being which constitutes the true Self (ātman) or life-force of this world. In other words, without Being the world cannot exist. The only absolute reality, therefore, is Being. This Being is identical with the Self (ātman), which is the essential reality in human personality. There is, thus, one single essential reality underlying man and the world.

the Real. That is the Self. That art thou, Shvetaketu." "Still further may the venerable sir instruct me." "So be it, my dear," said he.

"Just as, my dear, having led away a person from Gandhāra [8] with his eyes bandaged, one might then abandon him in a place where there are no human beings; and as that person would there drift about toward the east or the north or the south: 'I have been led away here with my eyes bandaged, I have been abandoned here with my eyes bandaged'; then as, having released his bandage, one might tell him: 'In that direction lies Gandhāra; go in that direction.' Thereupon he, becoming wise and sensible, would, by asking his way from village to village, certainly reach Gandhāra. Even so does one who has a teacher here know: 'I shall remain here [in this phenomenal world] only as long as I shall not be released from the bonds of nescience. Then I shall reach my home.' "

[8] The western limit of Indian civilization.

THE BACKGROUND OF JAINISM AND BUDDHISM

Between the seventh and the fifth centuries B.C. the intellectual life of India was in ferment. It has been pointed out many times that this period was a turning point in the intellectual and spiritual development of the whole world, for it saw the earlier philosophers of Greece, the great Hebrew prophets, Confucius in China, and probably Zarathustra in Persia. In India this crucial period in the world's history was marked on the one hand by the teaching of the Upanishadic sages, who admitted the inspiration of the Vedas and the relative value of Vedic sacrifices, and on the other hand by the appearance of teachers who were less orthodox than they, and who rejected the Vedas entirely. It was at this time that Jainism and Buddhism arose, the most successful of a large number of heterodox systems, each based on a distinctive set of doctrines and each laying down distinctive rules of conduct for winning salvation.

The social background of this great development of heterodoxy cannot be traced as clearly as we would wish from the traditions of Jainism and Buddhism, which have to some extent been worked over by editors of later centuries. But it would appear that heterodoxy flourished most strongly in what is now the state of Bihar and the eastern part of Uttar Pradesh. Here the arrival of Aryan civilization and brahmanical religion seems to have been comparatively recent at the time. The people were probably little affected by the Aryan class system, and the influence of the brāhman was by no means complete. Quite as much attention was devoted to local chthonic gods such as yakshas and nāgas, worshiped at sacred mounds and groves (chaityas), as to the deities of the Aryan pantheon. Cities had arisen, where a class of well-to-do merchants lived in comparative opulence, while the free peasants who made up the majority of the population enjoyed, as far as can be gathered, a somewhat higher standard of living than they do today, when pressure of population and exhaustion of the soil have so gravely impoverished them.

The old tribal structure was disintegrating, and a number of small regional kingdoms had appeared, together with political units of a somewhat different type, which preserved more of the tribal structure, and are generally referred to as "republics" for want of a better word. Most of these republics were of little importance politically, and were dependent on the largest of the kingdoms, Kosala, which controlled most of the eastern part of modern Uttar Pradesh; one such was that of the Shākyas, in the Himalayan foothills, which might well have been forgotten entirely were it not for the fact that the founder of Buddhism was the son of one of its chiefs. The most important of these republics was that generally referred to as the Vajjian Confederacy, of which the largest element was the tribe of the Licchavis; this controlled much of Bihar north of the Ganges, and was apparently governed by a chief who derived his power from a large assembly of tribesmen, and ruled with the aid of a smaller council of lesser chiefs. Much of Bihar south of the Ganges formed the kingdom of Magadha. King Bimbisāra, who ruled Magadha during most of the time in which the Buddha taught, seems to have had more initiative in political organization than his rivals, and managed his little state with more efficiency and closer centralized control than any other chief or king of his time. His son, Ajātasattu, who began to reign some seven years before the Buddha's death, embarked upon a policy of expansion. Magadha soon absorbed the Vajjis and Kosala, and her growth continued until, about two hundred years later, the great emperor Ashoka annexed Kalinga, and Pātaliputra (modern Patna) became the capital of the whole Indian subcontinent except the southern tip.

The development of organized states and the advance of material culture were accompanied by the rapid spread of new religious ideas which were soon to become fundamental to all Indian thought. It is remarkable that in the Vedas and the earlier Brāhmana literature the doctrine of transmigration [1] is nowhere clearly mentioned, and there is no good reason to believe that the Aryans of Vedic times accepted it. It first ap-

[1] We use this term, which is the most usual one, with reference to the general Indian doctrine of reincarnation and rebirth; but it must be remembered that it is misleading when applied to Buddhism, which maintains that no entity of any kind migrates from one body to another.

KAMBOJA
Indus
GANDHĀRA
Taxila
KASHMIR
HIMALAYA
Jhelum
Ravi
PUNJAB
Sutlej
Mt. Kailasa
MTS.
Chenar
Harappa
Indraprastha
Brahmaputra
Indus
NEPAL
Yamuna
Ganges
RĀJPUTĀNA
Brindavan
Mohenjodaro
Mathura
Savatthi
Kapilavastu
Kanauj
Lumbini
Ajmir
Vaishali
Chanhu-Daro
Ayodhyā
Kusinara
Mithilā
RĀJASTHĀN
Sarnath
Prayaga
Pātaliputra
Champa
KĀMARŪPA
MOUTHS OF THE INDUS
Bhārhut
Kāshi
Nalanda
MĀLWĀ
Khajuraho
Bodhgaya
Gaya
AVANTI
Rājagaya
Sanchi
GUJARAT
BIHAR
Ujjain
Narbadā
MAGADHA
SURĀSHTRA
VINDHYA MTS.
MAHĀKOSALA
Mahānadi
BENGAL
Valabhi
MOUTHS OF THE GANGES
Girnar
Surat
Tapti
MAHĀRĀSHTRA
Konarak
Puri
KALINGA
Godavari
Poona
Arabian Sea
ANDHRA
Bay of Bengal
Vengi
Kistna
Tālikota
Amarāvati
Bādāmi
DECCAN
Vijayanagar
Tungabhadrā
PALLAVA
KĀRNĀTAKA
Kānchipuram
Māmallapuram
Mysore
Kāvāri
CHOLA
Shrirangam
Tanjore
KERALA
India
BEFORE 1200
Madura
PĀNDYA
Anurādhapura
Polonnāruva
100 200 300 400 500
Scale in Miles
Kandy
LANKĀ-SIMHALA

pears, in a rather primitive form, in the early Upanishads as a rare and new doctrine, to be imparted as a great mystery by master-hermits to their more promising pupils. In the next stratum of India's religious literature, the Jain and Buddhist scriptures, the doctrine of transmigration is taken for granted, and has evidently become almost universal. With this belief in transmigration came a passionate desire for escape, for union with something which lay beyond the dreary cycle of birth and death and rebirth, for timeless being, in place of transitory and therefore unsatisfactory existence. The rapid spread of belief in transmigration throughout the whole of northern India is hard to account for; it may be that the humbler strata of society had believed in some form of transmigration from time immemorial, but only now did it begin to affect the upper classes. It is equally difficult to explain the growth of a sense of dissatisfaction with the world and of a desire to escape from it. Several reasons have been suggested to account for this great wave of pessimism, occurring as it did in an expanding society, and in a culture which was rapidly developing both intellectually and materially. It has been suggested that the change in outlook was due to the break-up of old tribes and their replacement by kingdoms wherein ethnic ties and the sense of security which they gave were lost or weakened, thus leading to a deep-seated psychological unease affecting all sections of the people. Another suggested cause of the change in outlook is the revolt of the most intelligent people of the times against the sterile sacrificial cults of the brāhmans. No explanation is wholly satisfactory, and we must admit our virtual ignorance of the factors which led to this great change in the direction of religious thought which was to have such an effect on the life of India and the world.

Both the sages of the Upanishads and the heresiarchs of the unorthodox schools taught the way of knowledge, as opposed to the way of works Their primary aim was to achieve salvation from the round of birth and death, and to lead others to achieve it. Most of them maintained that salvation could only be obtained after a long course of physical and mental discipline, often culminating in extreme asceticism, but this was chiefly of value as leading to the full realization of the fundamental truths of the universe, after which the seeker for salvation was emancipated from the cycle of transmigration and reached a state of timeles bliss in which his limited phenomenal personality disintegrated or wa absorbed in pure being. The basic truths of the various schools differed widely.

In many passages of the Buddhist scriptures we read of six unorthodox teachers (often rather inaccurately referred to as "heretics"), each of whom was the leader of an important body of ascetics and lay followers. In one passage (*Dīgha Nikāya* 1.47 ff.) short paragraphs are quoted which purport to give the basic tenets of their systems. A glance at these will give some impression of the bewildering variety of doctrines which were canvassed by the ascetic groups of the time.

The first of the teachers mentioned, Pūrana Kassapa, was an antinomian, who believed that virtuous conduct had no effect on a man's karma:

> He who performs an act or causes an act to be performed, . . . he who destroys life, the thief, the housebreaker, the plunderer, . . . the adulterer and the liar . . . commit no sin. Even if with a razor-sharp discus a man were to reduce all the life on earth to a single heap of flesh he would commit no sin, neither would sin approach him. . . . From liberality, self-control, abstinence, and honesty is derived neither merit nor the approach of merit.

The second "heretic," Makkhali Gosāla, was the leader of the sect of Ājīvikas, which survived for some two thousand years after the death of its founder. He agreed with Pūrana that good deeds did not affect transmigration, which proceeded according to a rigid pattern, controlled by an all powerful cosmic principle which he called *Niyati,* Fate.

> There is no deed performed either by oneself or by others [which can affect one's future births], no human action, no strength, no courage, no human endurance or human prowess [which can affect one's destiny in this life]. All beings, all that have breath, all that are born, all that have life, are without power, strength, or virtue, but are developed by destiny, chance, and nature. . . . There is no question of bringing unripe karma [2] to fruition, nor of exhausting karma already ripened, by virtuous conduct, by vows, by penance, or by chastity. That cannot be done. Samsāra [3] is measured as with a bushel,

[2] It is perhaps unnecessary to mention that karma is the effect of any action upon the agent, whether in this life or in a future one. Most Indian sects believed that karma operated as a sort of automatic moral sanction, ensuring that the evil-doer suffered and the righteous prospered; but Pūrana, Makkhali, and Pakudha appear to have disagreed with this view, while Ajita the materialist evidently denied the existence of karma altogether. The Jains, as we shall see, still look on karma as a sort of substance adhering to the soul, and it would appear that the "heretics" did likewise, although later Hinduism and Buddhism take a less materialistic view of it.

[3] The cycle of transmigration, the round of birth, death, and rebirth.

with its joy and sorrow and its appointed end. It can neither be lessened nor increased, nor is there any excess or deficiency of it. Just as a ball of thread will, when thrown, unwind to its full length, so fool and wise alike will take their course, and make an end of sorrow.

The third heterodox teacher, Ajita Kesakambala, was a materialist. The passage in which his views are given is one of the earliest expressions of complete unbelief in immaterial categories in the history of the world's thought:

There is no [merit in] almsgiving, sacrifice, or offering, no result or ripening of good or evil deeds. There is no passing from this world to the next. . . . There is no after-life. . . . Man is formed of the four elements; when he dies earth returns to the aggregate of earth, water to water, fire to fire, and air to air, while the senses vanish into space. Four men with the bier take up the corpse; they gossip [about the dead man] as far as the burning ground, where his bones turn the color of a dove's wing, and his sacrifices end in ashes. They are fools who preach almsgiving, and those who maintain the existence of immaterial categories speak vain and lying nonsense. When the body dies both fool and wise alike are cut off and perish. They do not survive after death.

Pakudha Kacchāyana, the fourth of the six, was an atomist, a predecessor of the Hindu Vaisheshika school, putting forward his theories probably a century or more before Democritus in Greece developed a similar doctrine of eternal atoms:

The seven elementary categories are neither made nor ordered, neither caused nor constructed; they are barren, as firm as mountains, as stable as pillars. They neither move nor develop; they do not injure one another, and one has no effect on the joy or the sorrow . . . of another. What are the seven? The bodies of earth, water, fire, air, joy and sorrow, with life as the seventh. . . No man slays or causes to slay, hears or causes to hear, knows or causes to know. Even if a man cleave another's head with a sharp sword, he does not take life, for the sword-cut passes between the seven elements.[4]

The fifth teacher, Nigantha Nātaputta,[5] was no other than Vardhamāna Mahāvīra, the leader of the sect of Jains, which survives to this day, and the teachings of which will be considered presently. The sixth and last, Sanjaya Belatthiputta, was, as far as can be gathered from the passage attributed to him, a sceptic, who denied the possibility of certain knowledge altogether:

[4] These doctrines were apparently taken up by the Ājīvikas, who in later times maintained a theory of seven elements, which was evidently derived from that of Pakudha.

[5] Pāli, *Niganṭha Nātaputta;* Skt. *Nirgrantha Jñātṛputra.*

If you asked me "Is there another world?", and if I believed that there was, I should tell you so. But that is not what I say. I do not say that it is so; I do not say that it is otherwise; I do not say that it is not so; nor do I say that it is not not so.

It must be emphasized that the salvation promised by these teachers, and by others like them, was not dependent on the mere acceptance of the doctrine on the word of the teacher, or on belief in it on a cool logical basis. To achieve release from transmigration it was necessary that the fundamental doctrine should be realized in the inmost being of the individual, and such a realization could only be achieved by the mystical and ascetic practices generally known in the West as yoga. Each group, even that of the materialists who followed Ajita, had its special system of meditation and mental or spiritual exercises, each its organized body of followers, usually ascetics, pledged to strive together for emancipation. Lay devotees and patrons were generally thought to be on the lowest rungs of the spiritual ladder, and there was little or no chance of full salvation outside the disciplined order.

CHAPTER IV

THE BASIC DOCTRINES OF JAINISM

Originating at the same time and in the same region of India as Buddhism, Jainism has experienced its moments of triumph, periods when mighty kings supported it and the finest craftsmen in India worked on the embellishment of its temples. But it has never spread, like Buddhism, beyond the land of its origin to become one of the world's great religions; on the other hand it has not disappeared from India as Buddhism has, but has survived to the present day, a small but significant element in the religious life of the subcontinent.

THE ORIGIN AND DEVELOPMENT OF JAINISM

The figure to whom Jains look back as their great teacher, Vardhamāna Mahāvīra ("The Great Hero"), was a contemporary of the Buddha, often mentioned in the Buddhist scriptures under the name Nigantha Nātaputta, "the naked ascetic of the clan of the Jnātrikas." Mahāvīra is believed by the Jains to have been the twenty-fourth and last Tīrthankara ("Fordmaker") of the present period of cosmic decline. Pārshva, the twenty-third Tīrthankara, is said to have lived only two hundred and fifty years before Mahāvīra, and it would seem that in fact the latter teacher based his new community on existing groups of asectics, some of whom looked back to the earlier preacher Pārshva. The legends told by the Jains about Mahāvīra are in many ways less attractive than those told by Buddhists about Buddha, and most of them are equally doubtful from the point of view of the historian, but the main outline of his life-story is probably true. Mahāvīra is said to have been the son of Siddhārtha, a chief of the warrior clan of the Jnātrikas, and his wife Trishalā, sister of Chetaka, chief of the larger kindred tribe of the Licchavis; both tribes dwelled around the important city of Vaishāli, in what is now North Bihar. Thus, like the Buddha, Mahāvīra was a scion of the tribal "republican" peoples of India. He is said to have left his home at the age of thirty in order to seek salvation and to have wandered for twelve years far and wide in the Ganges valley, until, at the age of forty-two, he found full enlightenment, and became a "completed soul" (kevalin) and a "conqueror" (jina). From a derivative form of the second title the Jains take their name. Mahāvīra taught his doctrines for some thirty years, founding a disciplined order of naked monks and gaining the support of many layfolk. He died at the age of seventy-two at Pāvā, a village not far from Patna, which is still visited by thousands of Jains annually and is one of their most sacred places of pilgrimage. Most authorities believe that the date of his death was 468 B.C., although the Jains themselves place it some sixty years earlier.

Probably for a century or so after Mahāvīra's death the Jains were comparatively unimportant, because both the Jain and the Buddhist scriptures, though not wholly ignoring the existence of the other sect, look on the sect of the Ājīvikas as the chief rival of their respective faiths. Jainism, like Buddhism, began to flourish in the days of the Mauryas. A very strong Jain tradition maintains that the first Maurya emperor, Chandragupta (*c.* 317–293 B.C.), was a patron of Jainism and ultimately became a Jain monk. It is to this period that the great schism in Jainism is attributed by tradition. Between the death of Mahāvīra and this time, the order had been led by a series of pontiffs called *Gaṇadharas* ("Supporters of the Communities"). Bhadrabāhu, the eleventh *Gaṇadhara,* foresaw that a great famine would soon occur in northern India, and so, with a great following of naked monks, among whom was the ex-emperor Chandragupta, he departed for the Deccan, leaving behind many monks who refused to follow him, under the leadership of another teacher, Sthūlabhadra. When the famine was over Bhadrabāhu and many of the exiles returned to find that those who had remained in the north had adopted many dubious practices as a result of the distress and confusion of the famine, the most censurable of which was the wearing of white robes.

This, however, was not the only misfortune resulting from the famine. Bhadrabāhu was the only person who knew perfectly the unwritten sacred texts of Jainism. In order to conserve them Sthūlabhadra called a council of monks at Pātaliputra, but Bhadrabāhu was not present—

horrified at the corruption of the Order he had departed for Nepal, to end his days in solitary fasting and penance. So the original canon of Jainism was reconstructed as well as possible from the defective memory of Sthūlabhadra and other leading monks in the form of the eleven *Limbs* (*Aṅga*). Thus, according to tradition, Jainism was divided into two great sections, though in fact the division may have existed in germ in the days of Mahāvīra himself and did not become final until about two centuries later. On the one hand were the *Digambaras,* the "Space-clad," who insisted on the total nudity of their monks and who did not admit the full authenticity of the eleven *Limbs,* and on the other the Shvetāmbaras, or "White-clad," whose monks wore white robes and who accepted the *Limbs*. Today the Digambaras are to be found chiefly in the Deccan, especially in Mysore, while the Shvetāmbaras, who are much in the majority, dwell chiefly in Gujarat and Rajasthan. Though the teachers of the one group would in the past often write and speak very acrimoniously about the practices of the other, there has never been any fundamental difference in doctrine. There was no development in Jainism at all comparable to that which produced Mahāyāna Buddhism from Theravāda. All Jains, whatever their sect, maintain the same fundamental teachings, which have probably been little altered since the time of Bhadrabāhu. Though there have been superficial compromises with Hinduism, Jainism remains what it was over two thousand years ago.

There is no doubt that Jain monks did much to spread northern culture in the Deccan and the Tamil land, and in the early medieval period, until the eleventh century, many important south Indian kings gave Jainism their support. But the great wave of devotional theism which arose in South India almost overwhelmed it, and it never again became a major force in the religious life of the peninsula. In the west, too, after a period of triumph in the twelfth century, when King Kumārapāla of Gujarat became an earnest Jain, the religion declined. But its layfolk, unlike those of Buddhism, were bound to their faith by carefully regulated observances and the pastoral care of the monks. Solidly knit communities of well-to-do merchants forming their own castes, the Jains resisted both the violent attacks of the Muslims and the constant peaceful pressure of the brāhmans; where Buddhism perished Jainism survived.

Indeed in recent centuries Jainism has shown signs of vitality and growth. At Surat, in the early eighteenth century, a further significant schism occurred in the Shvetāmbara sect, under the leadership of a Jain monk named Vīrajī who, basing his views on those of earlier less successful reformers, taught that true Jainism should not admit iconolatry or temple worship. This schism, which undoubtedly owes some of its inspiration to Islam, is comparable on a much smaller scale to the Protestant Reformation in Christianity; it has resulted in the emergence of a new sect of Jainism which has given up the complex ritual dear to the Indian heart, and holds its religious meetings in the austere and unconsecrated *sthānakas* ("buildings") from which the sect has acquired its usual name —*Sthānakavāsī*.

In some respects the debt of Indian culture to Jainism is as great as it is to Buddhism. Of all the religious groups of India Jainism has always been the most fervent supporter of the doctrine of nonviolence (ahimsā), and undoubtedly the influence of Jainism in the spread of that doctrine throughout India has been considerable. But even if Jainism had never existed, it is probable that the idea of ahimsā would still have been almost as widespread in India as it actually is. It is in other and unexpected ways that Jainism has so greatly affected Indian life. Despite their very stern asceticism Jain monks have always found time for study, and, more than the Buddhists, they have devoted much attention to secular learning. The Jain monk is allowed and indeed encouraged to compose and tell stories if these have a moral purpose, and thus much medieval literature in Sanskrit, Prākrit, and the early vernaculars is the work of Jain monks, who also helped to establish and develop the literature of certain vernacular languages, notably Canarese and Gujarātī. Mallināthа, the author of the standard commentary on the works of India's greatest poet, Kālidāsa, was a Jain. Jain monks also contributed much to the indigenous sciences of mathematics, astronomy, and linguistics, and their libraries preserved from destruction many important ancient texts, often of non-Jain origin. In modern times also Jainism has had some significant influence, for Mahātmā Gāndhi was born in a part of India where Jainism is widespread, and he has himself admitted the great impression made on him by the saintly Jain ascetics whom he met in his youth. Many factors contributed to mold the mind of the young lawyer who was to become one of the greatest men of the twentieth century, and of these Jainism was not the least important.

JAIN DOCTRINES AND PRACTICES

The basic teaching of Jainism may be expressed in a single sentence: The phenomenal individual consists of a soul closely enmeshed in matter, and his salvation is to be found by freeing the soul from matter, so that it may regain its pristine purity and enjoy omniscient self-sufficient bliss for all eternity. In essence the Jain teaching closely resembles that of the early Sānkhya school of Hindu philosophy, and it is possible that both Jainism and Sānkhya share a common source in primitive hylozoistic ideas which were widespread in the Ganges valley before the time of Mahāvīra.

The Jain view of life is essentially materialistic, using that word in its strict sense. Jainism, in fact, looks back to a stage in the evolution of Indian thought when it was almost impossible to conceive of any entity except on the analogy of solid matter. For the Jain the soul, called *jīva* ("life") in contrast to the Vedāntic *ātman* ("self"), is finite, and of definite though variable dimensions. The primitive roots of Jainism are also shown in its attribution of souls to objects not generally thought of as living. Buddhism does not allow that plants have life in the sense of gods, human beings, or animals. Jainism, on the other hand, finds souls not only in plants, but in the very elements themselves. Among the many classifications of Jainism is one which divides all living things into five categories, according to the number of senses they possess. The highest group, possessing five senses, includes men, gods, the higher animals, and beings in hell. Of these men, gods, and infernal beings together with certain animals (notably monkeys, cattle, horses, elephants, parrots, pigeons, and snakes) possess intelligence. The second class contains creatures thought to have four senses only—touch, taste, smell, and sight; this class includes most larger insects such as flies, wasps, and butterflies. The class of three-sensed beings, which are thought to be devoid of sight and hearing, contains small insects such as ants, fleas, and bugs, as well as moths, which are believed to be blind because of their unfortunate habit of flying into lighted lamps. Two-sensed creatures, with only the sense of taste and touch, include worms, leeches, shellfish, and various animalculae. It is in the final class of one-sensed beings, which have only the sense of touch, that the Jain classification shows its most original feature.

This great class is in turn divided into five sub-classes: vegetable bodies, which may be simple, as a tree, containing only one soul, or complex, as a turnip, which contains countless souls; earth-bodies, which include earth itself and all things derived from the earth, such as stones, clay, minerals, and jewels; water-bodies, found in all forms of water—in rivers, ponds, seas, and rain; fire-bodies, in all lights and flames, including lightning; and wind-bodies, in all sorts of gases and winds.

Thus the whole world is alive. In every stone on the highway a soul is locked, so tightly enchained by matter that it cannot escape the careless foot that kicks it or cry out in pain, but capable of suffering nevertheless. When a match is struck a fire-being, with a soul which may one day be reborn in a human body, is born, only to die a few moments afterwards. In every drop of rain, in every breath of wind, in every lump of clay, is a living soul.

Like the monad of Leibnitz the jīva of Jainism in its pure state is omniscient, and mirrors the whole universe; but the soul's natural brightness and wisdom is clouded over by layers of matter, and every thought, word, or action is believed to affect the material integument of the soul. Karma, the cause of the soul's bondage, is thought of in Jainism as a sort of subtle matter, flowing in chiefly through the organs of sense. Acts of selfishness and cruelty result in the influx of much very heavy and inauspicious karma, which results in unhappy rebirths; good deeds, on the other hand, have no such serious effects; while suffering willingly undertaken dissipates karma already accumulated. The soul can never gain liberation until it has rid itself of its whole accumulation of karma, and therefore Jain ascetics subject themselves to rigorous courses of penance and fasting in order to set their souls free of the karma already acquired, while all their actions are most carefully regulated to prevent the further influx of karma in serious quantities. Actions carried out with full consciousness which do no harm to other living things and are not undertaken for unworthy motives or for physical satisfaction attract only very slight karma, which is dispelled almost immediately; on the other hand the unintentional killing of an ant through carelessness may have very serious consequences for the soul. Though a deliberate act of cruelty is more culpable than an accidental one, even the latter must be paid for dearly. If the soul at last escapes from all the layers of its material envelope, being lighter than ordinary matter, it rises to the top of the universe, where it remains forever in omniscient inactive bliss.

Injury to one of the higher forms in the scale of being involves more serious consequences to the soul than injury to a lower form; but even the maltreatment of earth and water may be dangerous for the soul's welfare. For the layman it is impossible not to harm or destroy lives of the one-sensed type, but even wanton and unnecessary injury to these is reprehensible. The Jain monk vows that as far as possible he will not destroy even the bodies of earth, water, fire, or wind. In order to remain alive he must of course eat and drink, but he will not damage living plants in order to do so, preferring to leave this to the lay supporters who supply him with food. The monk will not eat potatoes or other root vegetables, since these contain large colonies of plant-lives; he strains his drinking water, in order to do as little harm as possible to the souls within it; he wears a face-cloth, rather like a surgeon's mask, to ensure that he does no serious injury to the wind-lives in the air he breathes; he will not run or stamp his feet, lest he harm the souls in earth and stones, or destroy small insects; he refrains from all quick and jerky movements for fear of injuring the souls in the air. His whole life must be circumspect and thoroughly regulated. Buddhism demands similar circumspection on the part of its monks, though not taken to such extreme lengths, but with the Buddhist the purpose of this is to develop the monk's spiritual powers. With the Jain its purpose is simply to avoid injury to the lower forms of life and thereby to prevent the influx of karma in dangerous quantities.

The number of lives or souls in the universe is infinite. The consequences of this proposition were worked out by the Jains with ruthless logic. Most souls have no hope of full salvation—they will go on transmigrating indefinitely. This is inevitable, for the number of souls is infinite, and however many pass to the state of ultimate bliss an infinite number will still remain bound in the toils of matter, for infinity remains infinity, however much is subtracted from it.

Thus the process of transmigration continues eternally, and the universe passes through an infinite number of phases of progress and decline. Unlike the similar cyclic doctrines of Hinduism and Buddhism, in the Jain system there is no sharp break at the end of the cycle, but rather an imperceptible process of systole and diastole. Each cosmic cycle is divided into two halves, the ascending (*utsarpiṇī*), and the descending (*avasarpiṇī*). We are now in the phase of descent, which is divided into six periods. In the first, the "very happy" (*susama-suṣamā*), men were of enormous stature and longevity, and had no cares; they were spontaneously virtuous, so had no need of morals or religion. In the second period, the "happy" (*suṣamā*), there was some diminution of their stature, longevity, and bliss. The third period, called "happy-wretched" (*suṣama-duḥṣamā*), witnessed the appearance of sorrow and evil in mild forms. At first mankind, conscious of the decline in their fortunes, looked to patriarchs (*kulakara*) for guidance and advice, until the last patriarch, Rishabhadeva, knowing the fate which was in store for the world, established the institutions of government and civilization. He then took to a life of ascetism, making his son Bharata the first Universal Emperor (*Cakravartin*). Rishabhadeva was the first of the twenty-four Tīrthankaras ("Fordmakers" through life) of Jainism, and, according to Jain tradition, was the true founder of Jainism in this age, for religion was now necessary in order to restrain the growing evil propensities of men. Moreover with the cosmic decline men's memories had become so bad that they needed to commit their thoughts to writing; so Brahmī, the daughter of Rishabhadeva, invented the numerous alphabets of India. The fourth period, "wretched-happy" (*duḥṣama-suṣamā*), was one of further decline, and saw the birth of the other twenty-three Tīrthankaras, the last of whom was Mahāvīra. The fifth period, the "wretched" (*duḥṣamā*), began some three years after Mahāvīra's death, and is at present current. Its duration is 21,000 years, during which Jainism will gradually disappear, and the stature, virtue, and longevity of men will gradually diminish. The sixth and last period, the "very wretched" (*duḥṣama-duḥṣamā*), will also last for 21,000 years, and at its end the nadir of decline will be reached. People will live for only twenty years, and will be only a cubit tall. Civilization will be forgotten, and men will live in caves, ignorant of even the use of fire. Morality will be nonexistent, and theft, incest, adultery, and murder will be looked upon as normal. At the end of this age there will be fierce storms which will destroy many of the remaining pygmy inhabitants of the earth; but some will survive, and from now on the state of the world will imperceptibly grow better, for the age of ascent will have commenced. The six periods will be repeated in reverse order until the peak of human happiness and virtue is reached once more, and the cycle begins again.

In a universe which continually repeats itself in this way there seems little scope for human effort, but though on a large scale the processes of nature are strictly determined by natural law and neither men nor gods can influence them, the individual is free to work out his own salvation. The Jains vigorously rejected the fatalism of the Ājīvikas. It was to a life of earnest striving for perfection that Mahāvīra called his followers, whether laymen or monks.

Jainism differs from Buddhism in that its layfolk are expected to submit themselves to a more rigid discipline and are given more definite and regular pastoral care by the Jain clergy. The layman should in theory spend full- and new-moon days in fasting and penance at a Jain monastery. Few modern Jains keep this sabbath, called *poṣadha,* in so rigorous a form, except at the end of the Jain ecclesiastical year, usually in July, when there takes place a sort of Jain Lent, called *paryuṣanā,* which lasts for eight days with the Shvetāmbaras and for fifteen with the Digambaras. The year ends with a general penance in which all good Jains, monk and layman alike, are expected to confess their sins, pay their debts, and ask forgiveness of their neighbors for any offenses, whether intentional or unintentional. This ceremony of general confession and pardon, extending beyond the Jain church to embrace members of other religions and even animals, is perhaps the finest ethical feature of Jainism.

Despite their insistence on kindliness and nonviolence, Jain ethical writings often have a rather chilly character, their altruism motivated by a higher selfishness. The Jain scriptures contain nothing comparable for instance to the *Mettā Sutta* of the Buddhists (see Chapter VI), and the intense sympathy and compassion of the Bodhisattva of Mahāyāna Buddhism is quite foreign to the ideals of Jainism; for an advanced ascetic such sentiments are further bonds to be broken, mere evidence of human weakness, destroying the impassivity acquired after many years of hardship and penance. The chief reason for doing good is the furtherance of one's own spiritual ends. Violence is chiefly to be avoided not so much because it harms other beings as because it harms the individual who commits it. Charity is good because it helps the soul to break free from the bonds of matter. To implicate one's own feelings with those of others is dangerous to the welfare of the soul. The virtuous layman is encouraged to do good works and to help his fellows not for love of others but for love of his own soul; the monk turns the other cheek when attacked for the same reason.

We must not overemphasize this feature of Jainism. Moralists of all religions and none have often appealed to enlightened self-interest as the chief spur to virtuous conduct; moreover many passages in the Jain scriptures do encourage a more positive and truly altruistic morality. But their attitude is often one of cold detachment which, to the unbeliever, is rather unattractive.

In everyday life the Jains have been much influenced by the Hindus. They often perform all the domestic rites of Hinduism, employing brāhmans for the purpose. They worship many of the Hindu gods, who are believed to bestow temporal blessings, and they have their own versions of the most famous Hindu legends. Nevertheless Hinduism has made little impression on the heart of Jainism, which remains much as it was over two thousand years ago—a primitive science, purporting to give an explanation of the whole universe and to show man his way through it to its topmost point, where the conquerors and completed souls dwell forever in omniscient bliss. There have been no great changes in Jainism over the centuries, and it remains what it always has been—an atheistic ascetic system of moral and spiritual discipline encouraging honesty and kindliness in personal relations, and a rigid and perhaps sometimes exaggerated nonviolence.

JAIN LITERATURE

The Jain canon, as preserved by the Shvetāmbara sect, consists of forty-five texts of moderate size, chiefly composed in the Ardha-māgadhī dialect of Prākrit, in both prose and verse. These consist of eleven *Limbs* (*Aṅga*), twelve *Secondary Limbs* (*Upāṅga*), ten *Miscellaneous Texts* (*Prakīrṇaka*), six *Separate Texts* (*Chedasūtra*), four *Basic Texts* (*Mūlasūtra*), and two separate texts which do not fall into any of the foregoing categories, the *Blessing* (*Nandīsūtra*), and the *Door of Enquiry* (*Anuyogadvāra*). The Jains themselves, as we have seen, do not claim that these texts are the authentic productions of the founder of Jainism, but maintain that the eleven *Limbs* were codified some two hundred years after Mahāvīra's death, while the whole canon did not receive its definitive form until the fifth century A.D., when it was finally established at a council held at Valabhī in Saurashtra. In fact the canon contains matter of very varying date; it has received far less study than the canon of Pāli Buddhism, and much further work must be done on it before it can be arranged in chronological order. It appears, however, that the *Secondary, Miscellaneous,* and *Basic Texts* contain some material which is quite as old as much of the contents of the eleven *Limbs,* while much of the latter is probably no earlier than the beginning of the Christian era. However, the canon also contains matter with a very archaic flavor, which may be more or less correctly transmitted from the days of the founder himself. The language, allusions, and general atmosphere of the Jain canon show, however, that it is broadly speaking later than that of Theravāda Buddhism.

The canon contains passages of grace and beauty, especially in its verse portions, but its style is generally dry; lengthy stereotyped passages of description are repeated over and over again throughout the series of texts, and the passion for tabulation and classification, which can be detected in much Indian religious literature, is perhaps given freer rein here than in the scriptures of any other sect. From the literary point of view the Jain canon is inferior to that of the Buddhists.

There is, however, much noncanonical Jain literature in various Prākrits, Apabhramsha, Sanskrit, several vernaculars of India, and in English, and some of the medieval narrative literature is of considerable literary merit. *Legends* (*Purāṇas*) were composed on the Hindu model, together with lengthy tales of the lives of the Tīrthankaras and other worthies of Jainism. Gnomic poetry is very plentiful. Commentarial literature was produced in very large quantities in Sanskrit, as well as manuals of doctrine, and refutations of the views of other systems. Moreover Jain scholars wrote treatises on politics, mathematics, and even poetics, giving their works a Jain slant. The total of medieval Jain literature is enormous, and is often more interesting and attractive than the canonical works.

The brief anthology which follows includes passages from both the canon and later Jain literature. Some liberty has been taken in places with the originals, and here and there passages have been drastically abridged in order to make them more easily understandable to the Western reader. According to the conventional usage works in Prākrit are generally referred to by their Sanskrit titles.

Of Human Bondage

The opening verses of *The Book of Sermons* (*Sūtrakṛtāṅga*)[1] epitomize the teaching of Jainism. The text from which they are taken, a series of separate passages of various origin in prose and verse, is one of the oldest sections of the canon. The insistence on nonviolence and the disparagement of human emotions are among the leading themes of Jainism from its origin to the present day.

[From *Sūtrakṛtāṅga,* 1.1.1.1–5]

One should know what binds the soul, and, knowing, break free from bondage.

What bondage did the Hero[2] declare, and what knowledge did he teach to remove it?

He who grasps at even a little, whether living or lifeless, or consents to another doing so, will never be freed from sorrow.

If a man kills living things, or slays by the hand of another, or consents to another slaying, his sin goes on increasing.

The man who cares for his kin and companions is a fool who suffers much, for their numbers are ever increasing.

All his wealth and relations cannot save him from sorrow.

Only if he knows the nature of life, will he get rid of karma.

The Man in the Well

This famous parable is to be found in more than one source, and is known to the Hindus. The version given below in an abridged form is taken from *The Story of Samarāditya,* a lengthy tale in mixed prose and verse[3] written in Prākrit by Haribhadra, who lived in the seventh century. The story tells of the adventures of its hero in nine rebirths, and is intended to show the effects of karma, but its author was a master of words, and his moral purpose is often lost in descriptive writing of a charming floridity. In the grim little story which follows, told by a Jain monk to a prince in order to persuade him of the evils of the world, he remembers his main purpose. The parable needs little comment, for Haribhadra has interpreted it himself.

[From *Samarādityakathā,* 2.55–80]

A certain man, much oppressed by the woes of poverty,
Left his own home, and set out for another country.

[1] Prākrit, *Sūyagaḍaṅga.* The correct interpretation of the Prākrit term is very doubtful. Our title is based on the conventional Sanskrit equivalent.

[2] That is, "The Great Hero," Mahāvīra.

[3] A genre known as *campū.*

He passed through the land, with its villages, cities, and harbors,
And after a few days he lost his way.

And he came to a forest, thick with trees . . . and full of wild beasts. There, while he was stumbling over the rugged paths, . . . a prey to thirst and hunger, he saw a mad elephant, fiercely trumpeting, charging him with upraised trunk. At the same time there appeared before him a most evil demoness, holding a sharp sword, dreadful in face and form, and laughing with loud and shrill laughter. Seeing them he trembled in all his limbs with deathly fear, and looked in all directions. There, to the east of him, he saw a great banyan tree. . . .

And he ran quickly, and reached the mighty tree.
But his spirits fell, for it was so high that even the birds could not fly over it,
And he could not climb its high unscalable trunk. . . .
All his limbs trembled with terrible fear,
Until, looking round, he saw nearby an old well covered with grass.
Afraid of death, craving to live if only a moment longer,
He flung himself into the well at the foot of the banyan tree.
A clump of reeds grew from its deep wall, and to this he clung,
While below him he saw terrible snakes, enraged at the sound of his falling;
And at the very bottom, known from the hiss of its breath, was a black and mighty python
With mouth agape, its body thick as the trunk of a heavenly elephant, with terrible red eyes.
He thought, "My life will only last as long as these reeds hold fast,"
And he raised his head; and there, on the clump of reeds, he saw two large mice,
One white, one black, their sharp teeth ever gnawing at the roots of the reed-clump.
Then up came the wild elephant, and, enraged the more at not catching him,
Charged time and again at the trunk of the banyan tree.
At the shock of his charge a honeycomb on a large branch
Which hung over the old well, shook loose and fell.

The man's whole body was stung by a swarm of angry bees,
But, just by chance, a drop of honey fell on his head,
Rolled down his brow, and somehow reached his lips,
And gave him a moment's sweetness. He longed for other drops,
And he thought nothing of the python, the snakes, the elephant, the mice, the well, or the bees,
In his excited craving for yet more drops of honey.
This parable is powerful to clear the minds of those on the way to freedom.
Now hear its sure interpretation.
The man is the soul, his wandering in the forest the four types of existence.[4]
The wild elephant is death, the demoness old age.
The banyan tree is salvation, where there is no fear of death, the elephant,
But which no sensual man can climb.
The well is human life, the snakes are passions,
Which so overcome a man that he does not know what he should do.
The tuft of reed is man's allotted span, during which the soul exists embodied;
The mice which steadily gnaw it are the dark and bright fortnights.[5]
The stinging bees are manifold diseases,
Which torment a man until he has not a moment's joy.
The awful python is hell, seizing the man bemused by sensual pleasure,
Fallen in which the soul suffers pains by the thousand.
The drops of honey are trivial pleasures, terrible at the last.
How can a wise man want them, in the midst of such peril and hardship?

Kinsfolk Are No Comfort in Old Age

If in this brief anthology we quote several passages which lay stress on the miseries of ordinary life, we do but preserve the proportion of such passages in the Jain scriptures themselves. The following extract is taken from *The Book of Good Conduct,* the first *Limb* of the canon, which contains some of the most ancient passages of Jain literature.

[From *Ācārāṅga Sūtra,* 1.2.1]

[4] Divine, human, animal, and infernal.

[5] Until the introduction of Western methods of recording time the week was not used in India except in astronomy. In its place was the *pakṣa,* the "wing" of the lunar month, the bright *pakṣa* covering the period from new moon to full and the dark from full moon to new.

He who desires the qualities of things is deluded and falls into the grip of great pain. For he thinks, "I have mother, father, sister, wife, sons and daughters, daughters-in-law, friends, kin near and remote, and acquaintances. I own various properties, I make profits. I need food and clothes." On account of these things people are deluded, they worry day and night, they work in season and out of season, they crave for fortune and wealth, they injure and do violence, and they turn their minds again and again to evil deeds. Thus the life of many men is shortened.

For when ear and eye and smell and taste and touch grow weak, a man knows that his life is failing, and after a while his senses sink into dotage. The kinsfolk with whom he lives first grumble at him, and then he grumbles at them. . . . An old man is fit for neither laughter, nor playing, nor pleasure, nor show. So a man should take to the life of piety, seize the present, be firm, and not let himself be deluded an hour longer, for youth and age and life itself all pass away. . . .

Understanding the nature of all kinds of pain and pleasure, before he sees his life decline, a wise man should know the right moment [for taking up a life of religion]. . . . Before his senses weaken he should pursue his own true welfare.

All Creation Groans Together in Torment

The following passage is taken from the *Book of Later Instructions,* one of the *Basic Texts,* and of later date than the *Limbs* of the canon, from which we have quoted. The eloquent verses translated below are part of a long speech delivered by a prince named Mrigaputra, in order to persuade his parents to allow him to take up a life of religion. Much of this passage consists of a very gory description of the pains of purgatory, which we omit. The reader should remember what we have said about the hylozoism of the Jains—the iron on the blacksmith's anvil is also in pain.

[From *Uttarādhyayana Sūtra,* 19.61–67, 71, 74]

From clubs and knives, stakes and maces, breaking my limbs,
An infinite number of times I have suffered without hope.
By keen-edged razors, by knives and shears,
Many times I have been drawn and quartered, torn apart and skinned.
Helpless in snares and traps, a deer,
I have been caught and bound and fastened, and often I have been killed.
A helpless fish, I have been caught with hooks and nets;

An infinite number of times I have been killed and scraped, split and gutted.
A bird, I have been caught by hawks or trapped in nets,
Or held fast by birdlime, and I have been killed an infinite number of times.
A tree, with axes and adzes by the carpenters
An infinite number of times I have been felled, stripped of my bark, cut up, and sawn into planks.
As iron, with hammer and tongs by blacksmiths
An infinite number of times I have been struck and beaten, split and filed. . . .
Ever afraid, trembling, in pain and suffering,
I have felt the utmost sorrow and agony. . . .
In every kind of existence I have suffered
Pains which have scarcely known reprieve for a moment.

Creatures Great and Small

The following verses from the *Book of Sermons* exemplify the cardinal Jaiṅ doctrine that life pervades the whole world and that the lives of even the humblest living things should be respected. The first verse lists the various categories of life; the first two lines giving the five sub-classes of one-sensed beings, and the second two a fourfold subdivision of beings with two or more senses.

[From *Sūtrakṛtāṅga,* 1.1–9]

Earth and water, fire and wind,
  Grass, trees, and plants, and all creatures that move,
Born of the egg, born of the womb,
  Born of dung, born of liquids [6]—

These are the classes of living beings.
  Know that they all seek happiness.
In hurting them men hurt themselves,
  And will be born again among them. . . .

Some men leave mother and father for the life of a monk,
  But still make use of fire;

[6] Creatures born of dung are lice, bugs, and similar insects; those born of liquids are minute water insects, etc.

But He[7] has said, "their principles are base
Who hurt for their own pleasure."

The man who lights a fire kills living things,
While he who puts it out kills the fire;
Thus a wise man who understands the Law
Should never light a fire.

There are lives in earth and lives in water,
Hopping insects leap into the fire,
And worms dwell in rotten wood.
All are burned when a fire is lighted.

Even plants are beings, capable of growth,
Their bodies need food, they are individuals.
The reckless cut them for their own pleasure
And slay many living things in doing so.

He who carelessly destroys plants, whether sprouted or full grown,
Provides a rod for his own back.
He has said, "Their principles are ignoble
Who harm plants for their own pleasure."

The Eternal Law

For the Jains the term *dharma* has two meanings. In one sense the term is used to imply a sort of secondary space, without which movement would be impossible. In most contexts, however, *dharma* for the Jain is the universal rule of nonviolence, the eternal Law. The following passage on this theme is from the *Book of Good Conduct*.

[From *Ācārāṅga Sūtra,* 1.4.1]

Thus say all the perfect souls and blessed ones, whether past, present, or to come—thus they speak, thus they declare, thus they proclaim: All things breathing, all things existing, all things living, all beings whatever, should not be slain or treated with violence, or insulted, or tortured, or driven away.

This is the pure unchanging eternal law, which the wise ones who

[7] Mahāvīra.

know the world have proclaimed, among the earnest and the not-earnest, among the loyal and the not-loyal, among those who have given up punishing others and those who have not done so, among those who are weak and those who are not, among those who delight in worldly ties and those who do not. This is the truth. So it is. Thus it is declared in this religion.

When he adopts this Law a man should never conceal or reject it. When he understands the Law he should grow indifferent to what he sees, and not act for worldly motives. . . .

What is here declared has been seen, heard, approved, and understood. Those who give way and indulge in pleasure will be born again and again. The heedless are outside [the hope of salvation]. But if you are mindful, day and night steadfastly striving, always with ready vision, in the end you will conquer.

Respect for Life

Though "enlightened self-interest" is very frequently stated in the Jain scriptures to be the most important reason for leading the good life, numerous passages show that even the unimpassioned Jain monks who composed the canon were not entirely devoid of human feeling. The following extract, a much abridged version of the first chapter of the first *Limb* of the Jain canon, the *Book of Good Conduct,* exemplifies this point.

[From *Ācārāṅga Sūtra,* 1.1]

Earth is afflicted and wretched, it is hard to teach, it has no discrimination. Unenlightened men, who suffer from the effects of past deeds, cause great pain in a world full of pain already, for in earth souls are individually embodied. If, thinking to gain praise, honor, or respect, . . . or to achieve a good rebirth, . . . or to win salvation, or to escape pain, a man sins against earth or causes or permits others to do so, . . . he will not gain joy or wisdom. . . . Injury to the earth is like striking, cutting, maiming, or killing a blind man. . . . Knowing this a man should not sin against earth or cause or permit others to do so. He who understands the nature of sin against earth is called a true sage who understands karma. . . .

And there are many souls embodied in water. Truly water . . . is alive. . . . He who injures the lives in water does not understand the nature of sin or renounce it. . . . Knowing this, a man should not sin against water, or cause or permit others to do so. He who understands the nature of sin against water is called a true sage who understands karma. . . .

By wicked or careless acts one may destroy fire-beings and, moreover, harm other beings by means of fire. . . . For there are creatures living in earth, grass, leaves, wood, cowdung, or dustheaps, and jumping creatures which . . . fall into a fire if they come near it. If touched by fire, they shrivel up, . . . lose their senses, and die. . . . He who understands the nature of sin in respect of fire is called a true sage who understands karma.

And just as it is the nature of a man to be born and grow old, so is it the nature of a plant to be born and grow old. . . . One is endowed with reason, and so is the other; [8] one is sick, if injured, and so is the other; one grows larger, and so does the other; one changes with time, and so does the other. . . . He who understands the nature of sin against plants is called a true sage who understands karma. . . .

All beings with two, three, four, or five senses, . . . in fact all creation, know individually pleasure and displeasure, pain, terror, and sorrow. All are full of fears which come from all directions. And yet there exist people who would cause greater pain to them. . . . Some kill animals for sacrifice, some for their skin, flesh, blood, . . . feathers, teeth, or tusks; . . . some kill them intentionally and some unintentionally; some kill because they have been previously injured by them, . . . and some because they expect to be injured. He who harms animals has not understood or renounced deeds of sin. . . . He who understands the nature of sin against animals is called a true sage who understands karma. . . .

A man who is averse from harming even the wind knows the sorrow of all things living. . . . He who knows what is bad for himself knows what is bad for others, and he who knows what is bad for others knows what is bad for himself. This reciprocity should always be borne in mind. Those whose minds are at peace and who are free from passions do not desire to live [at the expense of others]. . . . He who understands the nature of sin against wind is called a true sage who understands karma.

In short he who understands the nature of sin in respect of all the six types of living beings is called a true sage who understands karma.

[8] The commentary justifies this statement. Plants manifest a degree of reason in knowing the right season in which to bear flowers and fruit, and in growing upwards and not downwards.

The Hero of Penance and Self-Control

To gain salvation a man must be absolutely sinless, and to achieve such complete purity he must become a Jain monk. His goodness must be such that he will not even accidentally tread on the insect which crosses his path. In order to avoid such acts of violence Jain monks often carry feather dusters, with which they sweep the ground on which they sit or walk. The following passage, exemplifying these teachings, is taken from the canonical *Book of Sermons.*

[From *Sūtrakṛtāṅga,* 1.2.1.10–14]

Oh man, refrain from evil, for life must come to an end.
Only men foolish and uncontrolled are plunged in the habit of pleasure.

Live in striving and self-control, for hard to cross are paths full of insects.
Follow the rule that the Heroes[9] have surely proclaimed.

Heroes detached and strenuous, subduing anger and fear,
Will never kill living beings, but cease from sin and are happy.

"Not I alone am the sufferer—all things in the universe suffer!"
Thus should man think and be patient, not giving way to his passions.

As old plaster flakes from a wall, a monk should make thin his body by fasting,
And he should injure nothing. This is the Law taught by the Sage.[10]

Cheerfully Endure All Things

The ideal which the Jain monk, and indeed as far as may be the Jain layman, strives for is complete imperturbability. But behind this he should feel a calm, patient cheerfulness in the knowledge that, whatever his hardships, he is wearing away his karma and preparing for the bliss of full salvation.

[From *Uttarādhyayana Sūtra,* 2.24–37]

If another insult him, a monk should not lose his temper,
For that is mere childishness—a monk should never be angry.
If he hears words harsh and cruel, vulgar and painful,
He should silently disregard them, and not take them to heart.
Even if beaten he should not be angry, or even think sinfully,
But should know that patience is best, and follow the Law.
If someone should strike a monk, restrained and subdued,
He should think, "[It might be worse—] I haven't lost my life!" . . .

[9] The twenty-four Tīrthankaras.

[10] Mahāvīra.

If on his daily begging round he receives no alms he should not be grieved,
But think, "I have nothing today, but I may get something tomorrow!" . . .
When a restrained ascetic, though inured to hardship,
Lies naked on the rough grass, his body will be irritated,
And in full sunlight the pain will be immeasurable,
But still, though hurt by the grass, he should not wear clothes.
When his limbs are running with sweat, and grimed with dust and dirt
In the heat of summer, the wise monk will not lament his lost comfort.
He must bear it all to wear out his karma, and follow the noble, the supreme Law.
Until his body breaks up, he should bear the filth upon it.[11]

Wise Men and Fools

The following passage from the *Book of Good Conduct* repeats a theme very common in Jain literature, the contrast between the life of the world and the life of religion.

[From *Ācārāṅga Sūtra,* 1.2, 3]

Who will boast of family or glory, who will desire anything, when he thinks that he has often been born noble, often lowly, and that his soul, [his true self] is neither humble nor high-born, and wants nothing?

Thus a wise man is neither pleased nor annoyed. . . . A man should be circumspect and remember that through carelessness he experiences many unpleasantnesses and is born in many wombs, becoming blind, deaf, dumb, one-eyed, hunchbacked, or of dark or patchy [12] complexion. Unenlightened, he is afflicted, and is forever rolled on the wheel of birth and death.

To those who make fields and houses their own, life is dear; they want clothes dyed and colored, jewels, earrings, gold, and women, and they delight in them. The fool, whose only desire is for the fullness of life, thinks that penance, self-control, and restraint are pointless, and thus he comes to grief. . . .

There is nothing that time will not overtake. All beings love themselves,

[11] Normally a Jain monk should not wash, for by doing so he is liable to injure both water-lives and the vermin on his body.

[12] *Śabala,* probably a reference to the skin disease leucoderma, very widespread in India, which produces white blotches on the skin.

seek pleasure, and turn from pain; they shun destruction, love life, and desire to live. To all things life is dear. They crave for riches and gather them together, . . . using the labor of servants both two-footed and four-footed; and whatever a man's share may be, whether small or great, he wants to enjoy it. At one time he has a great treasure, . . . while at another his heirs divide it, or workless men steal it, or kings loot it, or it is spoiled or vanishes, or is burned up with his house. The fool in order to get riches does cruel deeds which in the end are only of benefit to others, and stupidly comes to grief on account of the pain which he causes.

This the Sage (Mahāvīra) has declared—such men cannot and do not cross the flood; they cannot, they do not reach the other shore; they cannot, they do not get to the other side.

Though he hears the doctrine such a man never stands in the right place,
But he who adopts it stands in the right place indeed.
There is no need to tell a man who sees for himself,
But the wretched fool, delighting in pleasure, has no end to his miseries, but spins in a whirlpool of pain.

Two Ways of Life

For all the severity of the discipline of the Jain ascetic, the Jain scriptures contain numerous passages which mention the quiet inner happiness of the homeless life. The great sense of relief, of freedom, which comes with the abandonment of family ties, is often described in Hindu, Buddhist, and Jain texts. Moreover the life of asceticism is not looked on as weakly giving way before the sorrows of the world, but as a great spiritual struggle to be entered upon with courage and resolution like that of the soldier. These ideas are well expressed in the following passage, taken from the *Book of Later Instructions,* wherein we read of a semi-legendary king of Mithilā (North Bihar), who became an ascetic, and evidently did not regret it.

[From *Uttarādhyayana Sūtra,* 9]

With the fair ladies of his harem King Nami enjoyed pleasures like those of heaven,
And then he saw the light and gave up pleasure. . . .
In Mithilā, when the royal sage Nami left the world
And took to the life of a monk, there was a great uproar.
To the royal sage came the god Indra, disguised as a brāhman,
And spoke these words:

"There is fire and storm, your palace is burning!
Good sir, why don't you take care of your harem?"
Nami replied:
"Happy we dwell, happy we live, who call nothing whatever our own.
Though Mithilā burn, nothing of mine is burned!
When a monk has left his children and wives, and has given up worldly actions,
Nothing is pleasant to him, nothing unpleasant.
There is much that is good for the sage, the houseless monk
Set free from all ties, who knows himself to be alone."
Indra said:
"Build a wall, with gates and turrets,
And a moat and siege-engines; then you will be a true warrior."
Nami replied:
"With faith as his city, hardship and self-control the bolt of the gate,
Patience its strong wall, impregnable in three ways.[13]
With effort as his bow, circumspection in walking its string,
And endurance as its tip, with truth he should bend his bow,
And pierce with the arrow of penance the mail of his enemy, karma.
Thus the sage will conquer in battle, and be free [from samsāra]!"
Indra said:
"By punishing thieves and burglars, pickpockets and robbers,
Keep the city in safety; then you will be a true warrior."
Nami replied:
"Often men punish unjustly,
And the guiltless are put in prison, the guilty set free."
Indra said:
"Bring under your yoke, O lord of men, those kings
Who do not bow before you; then you will be a true warrior."
Nami replied:
"Though a man conquer a thousand thousand brave foes in battle,
If he conquers only himself, this is his greatest conquest.
Battle with yourself! Of what use is fighting others?
He who conquers himself by himself will win happiness." . . .

Throwing off his disguise, and taking his real shape,
Indra bowed before him and praised him with sweet words:

[13] By means of the three "defenses"—self-control in thought, word, and deed.

"Well done! You have conquered anger!
Well done! You have vanquished pride!
Well done! You have banished delusion!
Well done! You have put down craving!
Hurrah for your firmness!
Hurrah for your gentleness!
Hurrah for your perfect forbearance!
Hurrah for your perfect freedom! . . ."
Thus act the enlightened, the learned, the discerning.
They turn their backs on pleasure, like Nami the royal sage.

The Refuge of All Creatures

Here and there in the Jain scriptures the virtue of compassion (*dayā*) is praised, though for the monk it should never be allowed to lead to emotional involvement with other beings. In the following passage, however, the monk is declared to have other duties than merely working out his own salvation; in practice Jain monks have always been ready to help others with preaching, consolation, and spiritual advice.

[From *Ācārāṅga Sūtra,* 1.6, 5]

In whatever house, village, city, or region he may be, if a monk is attacked by men of violence, or suffers any other hardship, he should bear it all like a hero. The saint, with true vision, conceives compassion for all the world, in east and west and south and north, and so, knowing the Sacred Lore, he will preach and spread and proclaim it, among those who strive and those who do not, in fact among all those who are willing to hear him. Without neglecting the virtues of tranquillity, indifference, patience, zeal for salvation, purity, uprightness, gentleness, and freedom from care, with due consideration he should declare the Law of the Monks to all that draw breath, all that exist, all that have life, all beings whatever. . . . He should do no injury to himself or anyone else. . . . The great sage becomes a refuge for injured creatures, like an island which the waters cannot overwhelm.

The Final Penance

Though strongly opposed by the Buddhists, religious suicide is known to both Hindu and Jain ascetics, and Mahāvīra himself is said to have voluntarily starved himself to death by the protracted fast known as *itvara* or *sallekhanā*. A Jain monk who wishes to end his life in this way, and thereby rid his soul of a great deal of karma and perhaps even obtain full salvation, must prepare for the final penance by a course of graduated fasting lasting for as long as twelve years. If, however, he is sick and unable to maintain the course of rigid self-discipline to which he is vowed, he may starve himself to death without the preliminary preparation. The following passage from the *Book of Good Conduct,* though it refers to the rite as a "terrible penance," looks on it as the triumphant end to a life of spiritual struggle, and finds it no cause for tears.

[From *Ācārāṅga Sūtra,* 1.7, 6]

If a monk feels sick, and is unable duly to mortify the flesh, he should regularly diminish his food. Mindful of his body, immovable as a beam, the monk should strive to waste his body away. He should enter a village or town . . . and beg for straw. Then he should take it and go to an out-of-the-way place. He should carefully inspect and sweep the ground, so that there are no eggs, living beings, sprouts, dew, water, ants, mildew, drops of water, mud, or cobwebs left on it. Thereupon he carries out the final fast. . . . Speaking the truth, the saint who has crossed the stream of transmigration, doing away with all hesitation, knowing all things but himself unknown, leaves his frail body. Overcoming manifold hardships and troubles, with trust in his religion he performs this terrible penance. Thus in due time he puts an end to his existence. This is done by those who have no delusions. This is good; this is joyful and proper; this leads to salvation; this should be followed.

Moral Verses

Among the great classics of Tamil is *The Four Hundred Quatrains* (*Nālaḍi-nānnūrru*), better known simply as *The Quatrains,* a collection of fine verses on morality, perhaps of the fifth or sixth century A.D. They are known and loved by all Tamils, whether Hindu, Jain, Muslim, or Christian, since they contain much which all religions would approve, and little to which any would object; but they are by tradition the work of a large company of Jain monks who in a time of famine were sheltered and fed by a Tamil king, and, when they departed from his court, left each a quatrain as a blessing for his benevolence. The traditional ascription is borne out by the contents of the collection. Unlike the kindred collection of Tamil gnomic verse, the *Couplets* (*Kuraḷ*), which is theistic in outlook, the *Quatrains* contain no references to the gods, and their earnest and rather pessimistic attitude to life is very similar to that of literature of known Jain origin. They differ, however, from much other Jain literature in their warmth and real humanity—for the authors of the *Quatrains* right conduct was not merely the avoidance of doing evil and the performance of cold acts of charity, but was rooted in fellowship, sympathy, and love. The verses below are a small representative sample of the whole.

[From *Nālaḍiyār*]

There is no passing the fixed day [of death]. No one
On earth has escaped death, and fled, and gone free.
You who hoard up wealth, give it away! Tomorrow
The funeral drum will beat. [6]

My mother gave me birth, left me, and went
To seek her mother, who had gone on the same quest.
And so goes on the search of each man for his mother.
This is the way of the world. [15]

Men come uninvited, join the family as kinsmen,
And silently depart. As silently the bird
Flies far from the tree where its old nest remains,
Men leave their empty bodies to their kin. [30]

The skulls of dead men, with deep caves for eyes,
Horrid to see, grinning, address the living—
"Take heed, and keep to the path of virtue.
That is the blessing that makes the body worth having." [49]

When men rise up in enmity and wish to fight,
It is not cowardice, say the wise, to refuse the challenge.
Even when your enemies do the utmost evil,
It is right to do no evil in return. [67]

If you send a little calf into a herd of cows
It will find its mother with unfailing skill.
So past deeds search out the man who did them,
And who must surely reap their fruit. [107]

Cows are of many different forms and colors;
Their milk is always white.

The path of virtue, like milk, is one;
  The sects that teach it are manifold. [118]

Those who snare and keep encaged the partridge or the quail,
  Which dwell in the wilds where beetles hum around the flowers,
Shall [in a later life] till black and hungry soil,
  Their legs in fetters, as slaves to alien lords. [122]

Learning is a treasure that needs no safeguard;
  Nowhere can fire destroy it or proud kings take it.
Learning's the best legacy a man can leave his children.
  Other things are not true wealth. [134]

In the city of the gods, in the after-life,
  We shall learn if there is any greater joy
Than that when wise men, with minds as keen as steel,
  Meet together in smiling fellowship. [137]

You may bite the sugar-cane, break its joints,
  Crush out its juice, and still it is sweet.
Well-born men, though others abuse or hurt them
  Never lose their self-respect in words of anger. [156]

The greatness of the great is humility.
  The gain of the gainer is self-control.
Only those rich men are truly wealthy
  Who relieve the need of their neighbors. [170]

People speak of high birth and low—
  Mere words, with no real meaning!
Not property or ancient glory makes a man noble,
  But self-denial, wisdom and energy. [195]

This is the duty of a true man—
  To shelter all, as a tree from the fierce sun,
And to labor that many may enjoy what he earns,
  As the fruit of a fertile tree. [202]

Better hatred than the friendship of fools.
  Better death than chronic illness.
Better to be killed than soul-destroying contempt.
  Better abuse than praise undeserved. [219]

If I do not stretch out my hand and risk my life
  For a friend in need,
May I reap the reward of one who seduces the wife of a friend,
  While the wide world mocks me in scorn. [238]

Best is a life passed in penance,
  Middling, that spent with those one loves,
Worst, the life of one never satisfied,
  Cringing to rich men who care nothing for him. [365]

As a scroll read by one who well understands it,
  As wealth to the man of generous spirit,
As a sharp sword in the warrior's hand,
  Is the beauty of a faithful wife. [386]

CHAPTER V

JAIN PHILOSOPHY AND POLITICAL THOUGHT

Two of the most interesting and individual features of Jainism are the kindred doctrines of "Viewpoints" (*nayavāda*) and "Maybe" (*syādvāda*), which are often called together "the Doctrine of Manysidedness" (*anekāntavāda*). These ideas certainly existed in embryo at the time of Mahāvīra and the Buddha, as is evident from the passages in the Buddhist scriptures attributed to the teacher Sanjaya which appear to be based on a garbled version of some such "manysided" doctrine; but there is no good evidence that they were propounded by Mahāvīra, and they may have been introduced into Jainism some time after his death.

Western thought, from the days of the Greeks onward, has been largely governed by the logical rule known as the law of the excluded middle—"either *a* or not-*a*." Socrates must be a mortal or not-mortal—there is no other possibility. In India, on the other hand, this law of thought has never been so strongly emphasized as in Europe, and the Jains allow not two possibilities of predication, but seven. These are known as "the Sevenfold Division" (*saptabhaṅgī*) or "the Doctrine of Maybe" (*syādvāda*):

1. We may truthfully affirm a given proposition (*syādasti*). Thus when in winter I come home after a walk in the open air, I may say that my room is warm.

2. But from another point of view it is possible to negate the same proposition (*syānnāsti*). Thus someone who has been sitting in the same room for some time may say with equal truth that it is not warm.

3. Hence it is possible to predicate the truth of a proposition and its negation at one and the same time (*syādastināsti*). The room is both warm and not-warm.

4. But the true character of the room, which we have seen is from different points of view warm, not-warm, and warm-and-not-warm, may

be said to be indescribable (*syādavaktavya*). Its true character, *sub specie aeternitatis,* eludes us.

The first four of the seven divisions are fairly clear and intelligible. The last three divisions, on the other hand, are a pendantic refinement of the theory, and some early Jain schools did not accept them:

5. A characteristic may be predicated about an entity which is otherwise recognized to be indescribable (*syādastyavaktavya*).

6. It may not possess that characteristic and be otherwise indescribable (*syānnāstyavaktavya*).

7. It may both have and not have the same characteristic, and be otherwise indescribable (*syādastināstyavaktavya*).

Closely related to the doctrine of "Maybe" is that of "Viewpoints," which shows the seven ways of approaching an object of knowledge or study:

1. We may consider an object of thought, say a certain man, concretely (*naigama-naya*), as at the same time an individual and a member of the human species.

2. Or we may consider him purely as a representative of mankind, not taking note of his individual character, but thinking only of the characteristics which he has in common with other men (*saṃgraha-naya*).

3. On the other hand we may think of him primarily as, for instance, our old friend John Smith, with all his personal traits and idiosyncrasies, hardly considering him in relation to the human species at all (*vyavahāra-naya*).

4. We may think of him as at the present moment, taking no note of his past or future, as a mere phenomenon in a limited area of space and time (*ṛjusūtra-naya*).[1]

As with the Sevenfold Division, the last three viewpoints seem somewhat pedantic, and are connected rather with the words used to define objects and concepts than with the objects and concepts themselves:

5. We may think of him from the point of view of his specific name "man," considering its synonyms and its implications (*śabda-naya*). This is supposed to prevent misuse of words and terms.

6. We may think of him from the point of view of the conventional meaning of the word only, without considering its etymological implications (*samabhirūḍha-naya*).

[1] One of the chief Jain criticisms of the Buddhists was that they tended to view the world exclusively from the viewpoint of *ṛjusūtra,* virtually ignoring the others.

7. Or finally we may consider an object with respect to the etymology of its name (*evambhūta-naya*). This viewpoint cannot be well illustrated with the word "man." A favorite Jain illustration is the consideration of the god Shakra (better known as Indra) as a manifestation of pure power, because his name is derived from the root *śak,* "to be able."

Though the Jain doctrine of manysidedness, in its finished form, shows pedantic refinements which are perhaps the work of an unfruitful scholasticism, it is, in its fundamentals, a remarkable achievement of Indian thought. Implicit in the epistemological relativity of *anekāntavāda* is a recognition that the world is more complex than it seems, that reality is more subtle than we are inclined to believe. Our knowledge is less certain than we think. A given proposition, though generally accepted as true, may only be relatively so, and the absolute and whole truth can only be seen by the perfected soul, the siddha, who surveys the whole universe in a single act of timeless knowledge. There is a famous Indian parable, occurring in many sources, which tells of a king who, in a fit of practical joking, assembled a number of blind men and told them each to touch an elephant and tell him what they felt. The man who touched the trunk declared that it was a snake, he who touched the tail, a rope, he who touched the leg, a tree-trunk, and so on. The story concludes with violent altercations, each blind man maintaining that he knew the whole truth. So man, incapable of seeing things whole and from all aspects at once, must be satisfied with partial truths. All too often he maintains that he knows the whole truth, and his one-sided approach results in anger, bigotry, and strife. The Jain, trained in the doctrine of manysidedness, realizes that all ordinary propositions are relative to the aspect from which they are made, and tries to know the objects of his attention as thoroughly as possible by considering them from all points of view. Jain philosophers have often been just as forthright in their criticism of other systems as the teachers of rival Indian schools of thought, but Jainism has a record of tolerance and friendliness toward other sects which is at least in part due to the doctrine of the manysidedness of truth.

Of Space and Time

Jain theories of space, time, and matter are of considerable subtlety, and suggest the non-Euclidean conceptions of modern relativity physics. There are in Jainism three types of space: *ākāśa,* sometimes translated "ether," but which we translate as "space," the function of which is to contain other substances, and a secondary and a tertiary space, which permit movement and rest respectively. These latter are strangely called *dharma* and *adharma* ("non-dharma"). This *dharma* must not be confused with the term as used in its religious and ethical sense, which we translate as "the Law" or "Righteousness." In our translation below *dharma* and *adharma* in the special sense of Jain physics are left untranslated. As will be seen, space is made up of an infinite number of points and of time, which, as in relativity physics, almost takes on the character of a fourth dimension, and consists of an infinite number of atomic instants. Substances are composed of atoms. There seems to have been some uncertainty as to whether or not a single atom had dimension. Kundakunda, the author whom we quote, apparently believed that the material atom was infinitesimal.

The *Essence of the Doctrine* is the work of a teacher of the Digambara sect, Kundakunda, who is believed to have lived in the third or fourth century A.D. It is a concise versified outline of the main doctrines of Jainism, written in Shauraseni Prakrit. It was commented on at considerable length in Sanskrit by Amritachandra, of the tenth century, and our notes are largely based on his work. The passage we quote outlines the nature of the six substances of Jain physics—souls, matter, space, *dharma, adharma,* and time—which constitute the whole universe. One of our chief reasons for including this passage is to show the great subtlety of which early Indian thought was capable. Our notes do not half exhaust the matter discussed by the commentator, and they might be prolonged indefinitely. It is largely on account of their extremely recondite nature that we have included so little from the purely philosophical texts of Jainism and Buddhism.

[From *Pravacanasāra,* 2.41–49, 53]

The quality of space is to give room, of *dharma* to cause motion, of *adharma* to cause rest.[1]
The quality of time is to roll on, of the self,[2] awareness.
You should know, in short, that all these qualities are formless.

[1] The existence of *dharma* as a secondary space is proved to the Jain's satisfaction from the fact of motion; this must be caused by something; it cannot be due to time or the atoms, since they have no spatial extension, and that which is spaceless cannot give rise to movement in space; it cannot be due to the soul, since souls do not fill the whole universe, but motion is possible everywhere; it cannot be due to space, for space extends even beyond the universe, and if space was the basis of motion the bounds of the universe would fluctuate, which they do not; therefore motion must be caused by some other substance which does not extend beyond the universe, but pervades the whole of it; this is what is called *dharma*. The existence of *adharma* is proved by similar arguments.

[2] Here Kundakunda employs the Prakrit term *appa* (Skt. *ātman*) in the sense of *jīva,* the usual Jain term for soul.

Souls, aggregates of matter, *dharma, adharma,* and space
Contain innumerable dimensional points,[3] but time has no dimensional points [i.e., no dimensions].

Space is both in the universe and in that which is beyond it. *Dharma* and *adharma* extend throughout the universe only;
Likewise time, because it depends on the other two substances, these other substances being souls and matter.[4]

As the dimensional points of space, so are the dimensional points of other substances [except time].
The atom has no dimensional point, but hence is explained the development of dimensional points.[5]

But a moment has no dimensional point. It occurs when a substance with a single dimensional point
Crosses a dimensional point of space.

[3] *Pradeśa,* elsewhere translated "infinitesimal spatial units," or "spatial minima." The *pradeśa,* though it roughly corresponds to the point in Euclidean geometry, is not quite the same concept. The Euclidean point has no dimensions; the *pradeśa* has dimensions but they are infinitesimally small. It is a sort of atom of space, perhaps comparable to the point in the Gaussian system of geometry used by Einstein. The paradoxical "dimensional point" is perhaps as good a translation of this difficult term as any other.

[4] Time does not exist beyond the confines of the universe, because it can only function in relation with souls and matter, which do not exist except in the universe. Note that the universe (*loḳa*) is unique, and poised in absolutely empty space (*aloḳa,* "non-universe"). Unlike the Buddhists, the Jains do not admit the existence of a plurality of universe.

[5] The obvious interpretation of this is that the ultimate atom has no dimension, but that upon the juxtaposition of nondimensional atoms in different relationships dimensionally measurable substances are produced. The commentator, however, notices that three verses later Kundakunda defines the dimensional point as the space occupied by an atom. As the dimensional point possesses dimension, albeit in an infinitesimally minute measure, we are faced with a crux. The best Amritachandra can do to solve it is as follows: "Though, as has been said, matter, considered as a substance, is without dimensional points, on account of its having one dimensional point only, yet it has the characteristic of being the originator of dimensional points, through its innate nature, which has the power of developing qualities of viscousness and roughness (implying attraction and repulsion) of such character as to be the cause of the production of two or more dimensional points." It seems that "dimensional point" is here used in two senses, the distinction between which is not thoroughly recognized by the writer. Matter in the form of the atom is quite without dimension; the dimensional point, however, in which the atom is contained, is infinitesimally small, but not wholly without dimension, not an absolute Euclidean point; the nondimensional atoms of matter, in their infinitesimally small areas of space, create a specious sense of extension or dimension in material substances by their mutual attractions and repulsions.

A moment is equal to the time taken for an atom to move [from one dimensional point to another].
What lies before and after that moment is time. The moment originates and perishes.[6]

The space occupied by an atom is called a dimensional point.
It can find room for all atoms.[7]

One, two, many, innumerable or infinite
Are the dimensional points contained by substances, as are the moments of their duration.[8] . . .

The world is full of objects with spatial extension, complete and eternal.
That which knows it is the soul,[9] bound to the four vital forces.[10]

There Is No Creator

Jainism, though not denying the existence of superhuman beings, is fundamentally atheistic. Moreover, it never compromised with theism, or devised a pantheon of substitute gods, as did Mahāyāna Buddhism. From the earliest times to the present day Jains have strenuously rejected the doctrine that the universe is created or guided by a divine will or a divine mind—for them natural law is a sufficient explanation. Their literature contains many criticisms of the theist's position.

The following example of Jain dialectic is taken from the *Great Legend*

[6] The commentator points out that time as substance has no beginning or end, but as modified by its relations with other substances it originates and is subject to annihilation.

[7] Thus all the atoms in the universe can be contained in a single dimensional point. This is only logically possible if the atoms are infinitely small or completely without dimension.

[8] On this verse Amritachandra makes a remarkable comment: "The complex of dimensional points is horizontal, while that of which the function is characterized by moments is vertical." This clearly implies the concept of time as a sort of fourth dimension.

[9] The belief in soul-substance is said to be one of the most primitive features of Jainism, but the verses quoted will show how far Jain thought on the subject transcended primitive concepts. The soul is certainly a substance, but it is not material substance, any more than are space and time. Its chief function is knowledge, of which the other five substances are the objects.

[10] *Prāṇa:* this term literally means "breath." In the later Vedic literature it often has the sense of "the breath of life," hence "spirit" or "soul." In Hindu literature the word is used for one of the five "winds" of the body, residing in the heart and responsible for respiration. The Jains, however, used the word in a completely different sense; with them there were four prānas, which were particularly potent forms of karma, binding the soul within the body, and conditioning its powers of sensation, strength, longevity, and respiratory capacity respectively.

(*Mahāpurāṇa*), a lengthy poem in excellent Sanskrit, composed by the Digambara teacher Jinasena in the ninth century. This work is modeled on the Hindu Purānas and consists mainly of cosmology and legends of the patriarchs, Tīrthankaras, and other great men of former days. Like the Hindu Purānas again, it contains numerous philosophical and polemic excursi of which the following passage is one.

[From *Mahāpurāṇa,* 4.16–31, 38–40]

Some foolish men declare that Creator made the world.
The doctrine that the world was created is ill-advised, and should be rejected.

If God created the world, where was he before creation?
If you say he was transcendent then, and needed no support, where is he now?

No single being had the skill to make this world—
For how can an immaterial god create that which is material? [1]

How could God have made the world without any raw material?
If you say he made this first, and then the world, you are faced with an endless regression.[2]

If you declare that this raw material arose naturally you fall into another fallacy,
For the whole universe might thus have been its own creator, and have arisen equally naturally.

If God created the world by an act of his own will, without any raw material,
Then it is just his will and nothing else—and who will believe this silly stuff? [3]
If he is ever perfect and complete, how could the will to create have arisen in him?

[1] A very common line of argument among the Jains. One type of substance cannot produce another with completely different characteristics.

[2] He had previously to make the raw-material of the raw-material, and so on. The endless regression is a type of fallacy as well known in Hindu logic as in Western.

[3] The appeal to practical experience, with which Jains, like Samuel Johnson at a later date, made short work of idealist philosophers!

If, on the other hand, he is not perfect, he could no more create the universe than a potter could.

If he is formless, actionless, and all-embracing, how could he have created the world?
Such a soul, devoid of all modality, would have no desire to create anything.

If he is perfect, he does not strive for the three aims of man,[4]
So what advantage would he gain by creating the universe?

If you say that he created to no purpose, because it was his nature to do so, then God is pointless.
If he created in some kind of sport,[5] it was the sport of a foolish child, leading to trouble.

If he created because of the karma of embodied beings [acquired in a previous creation]
He is not the Almighty Lord, but subordinate to something else. . . .

If out of love for living things and need of them he made the world,
Why did he not make creation wholly blissful, free from misfortune?

If he were transcendent he would not create, for he would be free;
Nor if involved in transmigration, for then he would not be almighty.

Thus the doctrine that the world was created by God
Makes no sense at all.

And God commits great sin in slaying the children whom he himself created.
If you say that he slays only to destroy evil beings, why did he create such beings in the first place? . . . .

Good men should combat the believer in divine creation, maddened by an evil doctrine.

[4] Righteousness (dharma), profit (artha), and pleasure (kāma), a traditional Indian classification.
[5] An attack on the Vedāntic doctrine of creation.

Know that the world is uncreated, as time itself is, without beginning and end,
And is based on the principles,[6] life and the rest.

Uncreated and indestructible, it endures under the compulsion of its own nature,
Divided into three sections—hell, earth, and heaven.

The Plurality of Souls

Jain theorists never tired of attacking the idealist monism of Vedāntic Hinduism and Mahāyāna Buddhism, usually basing their arguments on appeals to experience and sturdy common sense. For the Jain the material universe is an ineluctible datum, not to be explained away by specious arguments however subtle. The existence of innumerable living beings in the universe is an obvious fact of experience. The fact of their being alive can be explained by the hypothesis that they possess a certain substance, life (jīva). But as their bodies are separate, so their lives are separate. And the life, for the Jain, is the soul.

This criticism of Vedānta is taken from the *Debates with the Disciples* of Jinabhadra, a Jain writer who probably lived in the early seventh century. The text purports to contain a series of discussions between Mahāvīra and the eleven ascetics who were later to become his chief disciples; in it each of these puts forward a proposition, and, after some discussion, is convinced of its fallaciousness and becomes a follower of Mahāvīra. The work is part of a longer one, a lengthy appendix (*niryukti*) to the canonical *Book of Obligatory Practices* (*Avaśyaka Sūtra*), and is composed in Prākrit verse.

[From *Gaṇadharavāda*, 1.32–39]

You should know that the chief characteristic of the soul is awareness,
And that its existence can be proved by all valid means of proof.
Souls may be classified as transmigrant and liberated,
Or as embodied in immobile and mobile beings.

If the soul were only one,
Like space pervading all bodies,

[6] *Tattva*, more accurately "facts." These, according to Jain classification, are seven—souls (*jīva*, lit. "life"); the other five substances (see p. 76) which are classified as non-soul (*ajīva*); the influx of karmic matter into the soul (*āsrava*); the bondage of the soul, arising from this (*bandha*); the stopping of the influx of karma (*saṃvara*); the destruction and expulsion of karmic matter previously absorbed (*nirjarā*); and final emancipation from bondage to karma (*mokṣa*).

Then it would be of one and the same character in all bodies.
But the soul is not like this.
There are many souls, just as there are many pots and other things
In the world—this is evident from the difference of their characteristics.

If the soul were only one
There would be no joy or sorrow, no bondage or freedom.[1]
The awareness, which is the hallmark of the soul,
Differs in degree from body to body.
Awareness may be intense or dull—
Hence the number of souls is infinite.[2]

If we assume the monist hypothesis, since the soul is all-pervading,
There can be no liberation or bondage, [for the soul is uniform] like space.
Moreover thus the soul is neither agent nor enjoyer, nor does it think,
Nor is it subject to transmigration—again just like space.

Again assuming monism, there can be no soul enjoying final bliss,
For there are many maladies in the world, and thus the world-soul can only be partly happy;
Moreover, as many phenomenal souls are in bondage
The world-soul cannot be released from transmigration, but only partly so.[3]

The soul exists only within the body,[4] just as space in a jar,
Since its attributes are only to be detected therein,

[1] These words are, of course, intended in their special sense of bondage to and freedom from karma and matter.

[2] The logic of the argument is not clear. The twelfth-century commentator Maladhārī Hemachandra (not to be confused with the great Hemachandra) gives an interpretation which may be paraphrased as follows: The awareness of the different souls may vary in degree from the all-embracing knowledge of the perfected being (siddha) to the almost complete senselessness of the stone. Between the one and the other there are an infinite number of gradations. Therefore the number of souls is infinite. The logic is still evidently unsatisfactory.

[3] Maladhārī Hemachandra expands this by comparing the fortunate Brahman of Vedānta to a man whose whole body is diseased with the exception of one finger, or to one whose whole body is fettered, with the same exception. The Jains, perhaps justly accused of pessimism, would have no truck with the unrealistic optimists who declared that all evil and sin were in some sense illusory.

[4] This does not involve materialism of the Western positivist type. The Jains, in common with most other Indian sects, believe that the soul is wrapped in a series of inner sheaths of subtle matter, which form an invisible body surrounding it. The statement of the text is

And since they are not to be found elsewhere,
  As a pot is different from a piece of cloth.

Therefore action and enjoyment,
  Bondage and release, joy and sorrow,
And likewise transmigration itself,
  Are only possible on the hypothesis that souls are many and finite.

A Modern Jain Apologist

In the last hundred years the Jains of India, one of the wealthiest and best-educated communities of the subcontinent, have maintained their solidarity and have tried to adapt their doctrines to modern needs and conditions. A good deal of money and labor has been spent on propaganda, not only to prevent younger members of the community from succumbing to the temptations of twentieth-century materialism, but also to obtain sympathizers, and even converts, from other communities. Among the most active Jain propagandists was the late Mr. Champat Rai Jain, an able barrister with a good command of English, Hindi, and Urdu, and a wide knowledge of his own and other religions, who devoted many years with self-sacrificing wholeheartedness to writing and speaking in favor of Jainism. In keeping with the earlier teachers of his faith, who interpreted the Hindu scriptures figuratively in a Jain sense, Mr. Jain, who had read widely in Christian and Muslim theology, succeeded in proving to the satisfaction of himself and many of his co-religionists that both the Bible and the Qur'an taught the eternal truths of Jainism, that the only God of any significance was the eternal soul of man, who should liberate himself from matter and karma as quickly as possible by ahimsā and ascesis. We cannot, however, give an extract from Mr. Jain's brilliant if unscientific interpretations of the stories of the Old Testament and the teachings of the New. Perhaps his most interesting achievement was in his use of modern concepts taken from psychology and science in the service of his religion. The passage below, based largely on the arguments of earlier Jain philosophers, but well expressed in twentieth-century terms, aims at showing that the soul, which for the Jain includes consciousness and indeed has conscious awareness as its chief characteristic, is a simple substance, and therefore in its uncompounded state is eternal.

[From C. R. Jain, *Essays and Addresses,* pp. 89–92]

Knowledge is an affection or feeling—the sense of awareness of an object or thing. Outside me are things, not knowledge; inside me is knowledge, not things.

not quite correct, for the siddhas, the perfected beings completely emancipated from karma who dwell in eternal omniscient bliss at the summit of the universe, are souls in a state of complete nakedness, according to orthodox Jain teaching.

The current of vibrations (sensory stimulus) that comes from the external object is not loaded with knowledge. It is only matter in motion or motion of matter (that is, matter or energy in one form or another). Only in contact with a conscious substance does it occasion knowledge (perception); otherwise only a material or mechanical phenomenon will ensue.

The mere formation of the outline of an object on the retinae or elsewhere will not account for perception. No image is formed through the senses other than sight. Visual perception itself only gives us an inverted image, which is the reverse of how things are perceived. There is, again, a great difference between the microscopic retinal image and the mental percept, which may represent half the world. The main difficulty remains yet to be stated. How is the retinal image itself perceived? Is it its outline that is *felt?* And by whom? Does perception merely consist in a feeling of contact with the image formed in the eye, or further back, say in the perceptive centers of the brain? If so it will only give us a number of simultaneous touch-feelings—a coextensive series of sensations of touch along the outlines or over the area filled by the image. But how shall we account for the brightness and color that play such an important part in visual perception? The external stimulus, it would thus seem, merely calls out what is already there *inside;* it is not itself transformed into perception—color, smell, sounds, etc.

Again, perception will be impossible for a composite substance. A composite substance lacks in individualization. Different parts of a composite substance, e.g., a mirror, will reflect different limbs or parts only of an object; the object in its entirety will not be, cannot be, reflected in any of the parts of the reflecting surface. It will, therefore, be impossible for any part of a composite perceiver to perceive the whole of an object. A compound, of course, does not cease to be a compound merely because it is given a simple name.

Consciousness perceives the whole as well as the parts of an object simultaneously. It must therefore be a simple (uncompounded) thing, unlike the mirror, which is devoid of individuality. . . .

Knowledge radically differs from the object in the world outside. The rose on the bush in the garden took a long time in putting in its appearance; a small cutting was first stuck in the soil; it germinated after a time; then appeared leaves and shoots; then a tiny little bud slowly formed on one of the branches; and after a time it bloomed into a rose.

Nothing like this tedious process occurs in consciousness at the moment of perception. The knowing faculty there and then produces from its mysterious nursery an exact *facsimile* of the external rose, and that without trouble. It would as easily produce two, three, four, or a basketful of roses, or any and all other flowers, whole gardens. . . . Its producing capacity is really wonderful—it is infinite!

Are these epistemological facsimiles of outside objects manufactured in any way in the background of consciousness? But knowledge is not atomistic, nor made of parts. Suppose you try to break up an idea, e.g., the percept of a house, into bits and parts. The physical structure can be demolished. . . . But with what instruments shall we demolish the mental counterpart of the material edifice? . . .

What does it all signify then? Is it meant that loose ready-made ideas are stocked in an immense "stores" somewhere in the mind?

No; for our consciousness is unitary and not composite. Loose ideas will be like external objects and will have to be perceived as external objects are perceived. With loose ideas the mind will itself become idealess, and devoid of knowledge. But knowledge consists, really, only in the states of the perceiving consciousness, which are inseparable from it.

The unity of knowledge may be further illustrated by another example. A man enters the field of my vision, and is perceived as one. A little later another man joins him. In my consciousness also the first man is joined by the second. Now in the world outside the two men are separate; the first remained where he was; the second merely came and sat down beside him. But in the mind the two constitute but one percept. While the second man was approaching the first one, the mind was continually furnishing new and ready-made mental pictures corresponding to the scene and the movements going on in the world outside. When the two men came together finally there was no blending or pasting together of two different percepts in the mind. . . . The secret is only this, that with each act of perception a new mental image is evoked and appears in the limelight.[1] . . . Thus a new percept is presented every moment by our consciousness, and it is a noncomposite, partless, and unbreakable presentation.

Furthermore I can have an idea of an object that may be rough, smooth,

[1] Outside the limelight of consciousness knowledge is not destroyed, but exists in the "sub-conscious" condition, owing to the inimical influence of the matter which is in association with the soul. [Author's footnote.]

hot, cold, light, heavy, hard, or soft; but the idea itself, that is my knowledge of the object, is neither cold, nor hot, nor smooth, nor rough, nor hard, nor soft. In the like manner color is to be found in the objects outside in the world; but none in the mind. This will also hold good of taste, smell, and sound.

Knowledge then: 1) consists in the states of a noncomposite and partless . . . substance; 2) is natural to, that is inherent (unmanufactured) in, the perceiving faculty; 3) is infinite; and 4) is devoid of material qualities, color, taste and the like.

Now a thing that is not made up of parts is eternal, being unbreakable, indestructible and indissoluble. The faculty of knowledge, the partless substance whose function is conscious perception, is, then, immortal. As such it is, and may properly be, termed soul.

The Ideal King I

The Jain attitude to rulership and government varied considerably. The state is a necessary feature of society in the period of decline in which we now find ourselves. It maintains the social order and is conducive to the good life, leading to liberation. In this respect Jain thought differs very little from that of Hinduism. In fact Jain writers set much the same ideals before rulers as do those of Hinduism, and their thought on the subject has few original features. A sample of typical Jain advice to kings is given later. Exceptional ideas, however, are to be found in the writings of Hemachandra, who appears to have had real influence on politics, which may still be indirectly felt in India to the present day. This teacher, the greatest doctor of Jainism, was born in or about 1089 in Gujarat. Entering the Jain order as a boy, he rapidly acquired a great reputation for learning, and was much patronized by the powerful king of the Chaulukya dynasty, Jayasimha (1094–1143), despite the fact that the latter was an orthodox Hindu. Jayasimha died childless, and was succeeded by Kumārapāla (1143–72) a distant relation who seized the throne by force. Under Hemachandra's influence Kumārapāla became a Jain, and, if we are to believe later Jain sources, enforced ahimsā so rigorously that two merchants were mulcted of all their wealth for the crime of killing fleas. There is no doubt that Kumārapāla did attempt to enforce ahimsā quite stringently, under the guidance of his Jain mentor, who composed several works in his honor. Hemachandra died a little before his pupil at the age of eighty-four, by fasting to death; Kumārapāla is said to have died in the same manner. His successor, Ajayapāla, introduced something of an orthodox reaction, and is referred to by the Jains as a violent persecutor of their faith.

Hemachandra was evidently a man of great versatility; among his works are philosophical treatises, grammars of Sanskrit and Prākrit, lexica of both languages, a treatise on poetics, and much narrative poetry which, if judged according to the canons of the time, is often very beautiful and brilliantly clever. The longest of his poems is *The Deeds of the Sixty-three Eminent Men* (*Triṣaṣṭiśalākāpuruṣacarita*), an enormous work telling the stories of the twenty-four Tīrthankaras and of other eminent figures in Jain mythology, including the patriarchs and various legendary world emperors. The last section of this forms an independent whole, *The Deeds of Mahāvīra,* and records the life story of the historical founder of Jainism. In its course Mahāvīra is said to have prophesied in his omniscience the rise to power of Hemachandra's patron Kumārapāla, and to have forecast the reforms he would inaugurate. It will be seen that Hemachandra's ideal king is a rigorous puritan, and that he has a rather pathetic faith that man could be made good by legislation.

[From *Mahāvīracarita,* 12.59–77]

The vows, especially those concerning . . . food,
He will keep regularly, and he will be generally celibate.
The king will not only avoid prostitutes
But will encourage his queens to remain chaste. . . .

He will not take the wealth of men who die sonless [1]—
This is the fruit of insight, for men without insight are never satisfied.

Hunting, which even the Pāndus [2] and other pious kings did not give up,
He will abjure, and all men will do likewise at his command.

When he forbids all injury there will be no more hunting or other cruel sports.
Even an untouchable will not kill a bug or a louse.

When he puts down all sin the wild deer of the forest
Will ever chew the cud unharmed, like cows in a stall. . . .

Even creatures who eat meat by nature, at his command,
Will forget the very name of meat, as an evil dream.[3]

[1] According to earlier Hindu law books, if a man died sonless and without male relatives the king was entitled to appropriate his property, though he was responsible for the maintenance of the widow and the dowering of the dead man's daughters. In accordance with the precept of the *Yājñavalkya Smṛti* Kumārapāla allowed the widow to inherit in such cases.

[2] The heroes of the *Mahābhārata.*

[3] It was a commonplace of Indian thought that the king had jurisdiction not only over the human beings of his kingdom, but also over the animals. His virtue or lack of it, moreover, was supposed directly to affect the course of nature.

Drink, which even pious [Jain] laymen had not given up,
He, perfect of soul, will forbid everywhere. . . .
Drunkards, whose fortunes were ruined by calamitous drink
Will once more prosper, when they have given it up at his command.

Gambling, which even princes such as Nala [4] could not abandon,
He will utterly put an end to, like the name of his worst enemy.[5]

Under his glorious rule, throughout the earth
There will be no more pigeon races or cock fights.

Continually bestowing his wealth on all men, he will redeem the debts of the whole world,
And will establish his own era upon earth.[6]

The Ideal King II

Other Jain writers set somewhat less puritanical ideals before their kings, and their concept of good conduct in matters of government differed little from that of the Hindus. This is exemplified in the *Nectar of Aphorisms on Polity* of Somadeva, a Digambara teacher of the tenth century. This is a collection of gnomic sentences on politics and good conduct, written in Sanskrit prose. We quote some of those concerning the ideal king.

[From *Nītivākyāmṛta,* 17.180–84]

A true lord is he who is righteous, pure in lineage, conduct and associates, brave, and considerate in his behavior.

He is a true king who is self-controlled whether in anger or pleasure, and who increases his own excellence.

All subjects are dependent on the king. Those without a lord cannot fulfill their desires.

Though they be rich, subjects without a king cannot thrive. How can human effort be of any avail in cultivating a tree without roots?

If the king does not speak the truth all his merits are worthless. If he deceives, his courtiers leave him, and he does not live long.

[4] A famous king of the *Mahābhārata* legend, who was ruined by gambling.

[5] This line shows, as is quite clear from other sources, that Hemachandra's idea of ahimsā did not include the renunciation of war.

[6] Several great kings of Hindu India established new eras, but that of Kumārapāla did not survive his death.

He is dear to the people who gives of his treasure.

He is a great giver whose mind is not set on frustrating the hopes of suppliants.

Of what use is the barren cow, which gives no milk? Of what use is the king's grace, if he does not fulfill the hopes of suppliants?

For an ungrateful king there is no help in trouble. His frugal court is like a hole full of snakes, which no one will enter.

If the king does not recognize merit the cultured will not come to his court.

The king who thinks only of filling his belly is abandoned even by his queen.

Laziness is the door through which all misfortunes enter. . . .

A king's order is a wall which none can climb. He should not tolerate even a son who disobeys his commands. . . .

He should never speak hurtfully, untrustworthily, untruthfully, or unnecessarily.

He should never be improper in dress or manners.

When the king is deceitful, who will not be deceitful? When the king is unrighteous who will not be unrighteous? . . .

He should personally look into the affairs of his people. . . .

He should not make offering to the spirits of the night. . . .

Bribery is the door through which come all manner of sins. Those who live by bribery cut off their mother's breasts. . . .

The king is the maker of the times. When the king rightly protects his subjects all the quarters are wishing-cows,[1] Indra rains in due season, and all living things are at peace.

Practical Advice on War and Peace

Though charity and forgiveness are, of course, looked on as cardinal virtues, the highest virtue, for the Jain, is nonviolence, the importance of which is repeated over and over again in Jain literature, with many variations. It is noteworthy that, despite its nonviolence, Jainism never strongly opposed militarism; several great Jain kings were conquerors, and the ideal Jain king, Kumārapāla, who is said to have enforced vegetarianism throughout his realm, is nowhere said to have given up warfare. No Jain monarch had the enlightened sentiments of Ashoka in this respect, and nowhere in the whole body of Jain literature is a plea for peace between states to be found such as that in the

[1] Legendary divine cows, which granted all the wishes of those who milked them.

Buddhist *Excellent Golden Light Sūtra.* Yet, in normal personal relations, ahimsā is repeatedly stated to be the greatest virtue.

With very few exceptions, Indian thinkers looked on warfare as legitimate. There were, however, two schools of thought on the subject. One, typified by the *Mahābhārata* and the *Lawbook of Manu* (*Manusmṛti*), looked on war as good in its own right, a very exciting, if very grim sport, and sometimes even as a religious duty. There was no question of justified and unjustified warfare here; wars of aggression, if waged fairly and with humanity toward the wounded, prisoners, and noncombatants, were just as legitimate as wars of self-defense. The other school of thought, most clearly expressed in the famous treatise on polity (*Arthaśāstra*) ascribed to Kautilya, looked on war as a "continuation of policy by other means," a legitimate last resort in achieving the aims of statecraft, but not to be embarked on lightly, since it was expensive, troublesome, and uncertain in its outcome.

Jainism supported the second point of view; the Jain writer on polity, Somadeva, who on practical grounds advises war only as a last resort, like the Hindu political theorists, looks on it as a normal activity of the king.

[From *Nītivākyāmṛta,* 344–56 *cento*]

The force of arms cannot do what peace does. If you can gain your desired end with sugar, why use poison? . . .

What sensible man would abandon his bale [of merchandise] for fear of having to pay toll on it? [2]

For when the water is drained from the lake the crocodile grows as thin as a snake.[3]

A lion when he leaves the forest is no more than a jackal.

And a snake whose fangs are drawn is a mere rope.

In union is strength. Even a mad elephant will trip on a twisted clump of grass. And the elephants of the quarters [4] are held by ropes of twisted fibers.

But what is the use of other means when the enemy can only be put down by force? Such expedients are like a libation of ghee poured on the fire [which makes it burn more fiercely].

The Miseries and Dangers of Politics

The passages which we have quoted from the work of Hemachandra and Somadeva typify two Jain attitudes to political life. The first saw it as a

[2] Implying that it is better for a king to pay tribute to a more powerful enemy, rather than to fight to the last and lose his kingdom altogether, and probably his life also.

[3] Thus even if the enemy conquers, and seems immensely powerful, he may yet lose much of his power by one means or another, and it will then be possible to resist him.

[4] Mythical divine elephants presiding over the cardinal points.

means of enforcing morality as Jainism understood it upon those who would not accept the restraints of religion willingly; the second, as a necessary feature of everyday life, which was perfectly legitimate provided it was conducted justly. A third attitude is that shown by Somaprabha, an author of the late twelfth century, in the passage which we quote. The work from which it is taken is a didactic poem, the *Arousing of Kumārapāla,* which purports to tell of the conversion of King Kumārapāla by Hemachandra, and of his reforms. The work is written in mixed Sanskrit, Prakrit, and Apabhramsha; our quotation is taken from a section composed in Apabhramsha.

Though both his main characters were keen politicians, Somaprabha, in the course of one of the stories told by the monk to the king, declares that political activity is inevitably sinful, and advises Jains to have nothing to do with it.

[From *Kumārapālapratibodha,* Apabhramsha sections, 2.51–60 (Alsdorf, 105)]

The achievement of the three aims [1]
Is the essence of man's life,
But advancement in office
Is a hindrance thereto.

For when it pleases the king's mind
A minister must harm others, and that is the source of sin.
How then can perfect righteousness arise in him,
Through which he may gain eternal bliss?

And the fortune which an officer extorts by force from others,
Like a leech sucking blood,
His master may take from him,
For he [the king] extorts from everyone.

Subservient to another, full of fears and cares,
Responsible for manifold affairs of state,
How can officials know the joys of love,
In which great happiness reveals itself? . . .

After tossing on the ocean of being, of which birth and death are waves,
You have come to man's estate.
Avoid the things of sense and pluck the fruit of human birth.[2]
Why give up ten million for the sake of a mere penny? . . .

[1] Righteousness, profit, and pleasure.

[2] Only human beings are capable of achieving complete salvation. The gods cannot gain it unless they are reborn as men, for in heaven there is not enough sorrow and pain to work off the residual evil karma.

If you spend only five days in the service of a king
  You bring sin upon yourself,
And you must go, O soul, to the dark gulf of hell,
  With its inevitable, intolerable, innumerable woes.

So give up the king's service; though it seems sweet as honey,
  It brings scorn and disillusion, it is basically wretched.
Work, O soul, for righteousness, and put aside your lethargy,
  Lest in hell you find not a few unpleasantnesses.

The soul that in youth does not strive after righteousness
  And does not avoid all reprehensible actions,
Will wring its hands in the hour of death,
  And be left like an archer with a broken bowstring.

CHAPTER VI

THERAVĀDA BUDDHISM

As we have already seen, the centuries which saw the rise of Buddhism and Jainism in India were marked by continuing social change and profound intellectual ferment. What has been said above about the conditions in which the heterodox systems developed in the sixth and fifth centuries must be borne in mind in the study of Buddhism.

The founder of Buddhism was the son of a chief of the hill-tribe of the Shākyas, who gave up family life to become an ascetic when he was some twenty-nine years old, and, after some years, emerged as the leader of a band of followers who pursued the "Middle Way" between extreme asceticism and worldly life. The legends which were told about him in later times are mostly unreliable, though they may contain a grain of historical truth here and there. Moreover many of the sermons and other pronouncements attributed to the Buddha [1] are not his, but the work of teachers in later times, and there is considerable doubt as to the exact nature of his original message. However, the historicity of the Buddha is certain, and we may believe as a minimum that he was originally a member of the Shākya tribe, that he gained enlightenment under a sacred pīpal tree at Gayā, in the modern Bihar, that he spent many years in teaching and organizing his band of followers, and that he died at about the age of eighty in Kusinārā, a small town in the hills. The Sinhalese Buddhists have preserved a tradition that he died in 544 B.C., but most modern authorities believe that this date is some sixty years too early.

The band of yellow-robed *bhiḳḳhus* [2] which the Buddha left behind him to continue his work probably remained for some two hundred years one small group among the many heterodox sects of India, perhaps fewer in numbers and less influential than the rival sects of Jains and Ājīvikas.

[1] "The Enlightened" or "Awakened," a religious title with which we may compare the Christian "Christ" (i.e., "Anointed") and "Savior." The Buddha's real name was Siddhārtha Gautama (Pali, Siddhattha Gotama).

[2] Literally, "beggars." This is the Pali form, used by the Theravāda Buddhists. The Sanskrit form is *bhiḳsu*. Here the word is generally translated "monk."

Though by Western standards its rule was rigid, involving continuous movement from place to place for eight months of the year and the consumption of only one meal a day, which was to be obtained by begging, it was light in comparison with the discipline of most other orders, the members of which were often compelled to take vows of total nudity, were not permitted to wash, and had to undergo painful penances. It is evident that between the death of the Buddha and the advent of Ashoka, the first great Buddhist emperor, over two hundred years later, there was considerable development of doctrine. Some sort of canon of sacred texts appeared, though it was probably not at this time written down, and the Buddhists acquired numerous lay followers. For the latter, and for the less spiritually advanced monks, the sect adapted popular cults to Buddhist purposes—notably the cult of stūpas, or funeral mounds, and that of the sacred pīpal tree. We have seen that these had probably been worshiped in the Ganges valley from time immemorial, and with such cults both Hinduism and Buddhism had to come to terms. Buddhist monks began to overlook the rule that they should travel from place to place except in the rainy season and took to settling permanently in monasteries, which were erected on land given by kings and other wealthy patrons, and were equipped with pīpal trees and stūpas, theoretically commemorating the Buddha's enlightenment and death respectively.

Quite early in the history of Buddhism sectarian differences appeared. The tradition tells of two great councils of the Buddhist order, the first soon after the Buddha's death, the second a hundred years later. At the latter a schism occurred, and the sect of *Mahāsaṅghikas* ("members of the Great Order") is said to have broken away, ostensibly on account of differences on points of monastic discipline, but probably on doctrinal grounds also. The main body, which claimed to maintain the true tradition transmitted from the days of the founder, took to calling their system *Theravāda*[3] ("The Teaching of the Elders"). By little over a century after this schism the whole of India except the southern tip had been unified politically by Magadha, after a long and steady process of expansion, which culminated in the rise of the first great Indian imperial dynasty, that of the Mauryas. The third and greatest of the Mauryas, Ashoka, became a Buddhist. According to his own testimony he was so moved by

[3] In Sanskrit *Sthaviravāda,* but the Pali form is generally used, as Pali was the official language of the sect.

remorse at the carnage caused by an aggressive war which he had waged that he experienced a complete change of heart and embraced Buddhism. His inscriptions, the earliest intelligible written records to have survived in India, testify to his earnestness and benevolence.

Buddhism seems to have received a great impetus from Ashoka's patronage. He erected many stūpas, endowed new monasteries, and enlarged existing Buddhist establishments. In his reign the message of Budhism was first carried over the whole of India by a number of missionaries, sent out, according to tradition, after a third council which met at Pātaliputra (the modern Patna) in order to purify the doctrine of heresy. It was in Ashoka's reign that Ceylon first became a Buddhist country, after the preaching of the apostle Mahinda, said to have been Ashoka's son, who had become a monk. From that day onwards Ceylon has remained a stronghold of the Buddhism of the Theravāda school; Mahāyāna and other Buddhist sects, though they have at times been influential, have never seriously shaken the hold of the form of Buddhism which Ceylon looks on as particularly its own.

It is probable that, by the end of the third century B.C., the doctrines of Theravāda Buddhism were in essentials much as they are now. The monks taught a dynamic phenomenalism, maintaining that everything in the universe, including the gods and the souls of living beings, was in a constant state of flux. Resistance to the cosmic flux of phenomena, and craving for permanence where permanence could not be found, led to inevitable sorrow. Salvation was to be obtained by the progressive abandonment of the sense of individuality, until it was lost completely in the indescribable state known as Nirvāna (Pali, *Nibbāna,* "blowing out"). The Buddha himself had reached this state, and no longer existed as an individual; nevertheless he was still rather inconsistently revered by his followers, and the less-learned Buddhist layfolk tended to look on him as a sort of high god.

The fundamental truths on which Buddhism is founded are not metaphysical or theological, but rather psychological. Basic is the doctrine of the "Four Noble Truths": 1) that all life is inevitably sorrowful; 2) that sorrow is due to craving; 3) that it can only be stopped by the stopping of craving; and 4) that this can only be done by a course of carefully disciplined and moral conduct, culminating in the life of concentration and meditation led by the Buddhist monk. These four truths, which are the common property of all schools of Buddhist thought, are part of the true Doctrine (Pali, *dhamma;* Skt. *dharma*), which reflects the fundamental moral law of the universe.[4]

All things are composite. Buddhism would dispute the Hegelian theory that units may organize themselves into greater units which are more than the sum of their parts. As a corollary of the fact that all things are composite they are transient, for the composition of all aggregates is liable to change with time. Moreover, being essentially transient, they have no eternal Self or soul, no abiding individuality. And, as we have seen, they are inevitably liable to sorrow. This threefold characterization of the nature of the world and all that it contains—sorrowful, transient, and soulless—is frequently repeated in Buddhist literature, and without fully grasping its truth no being has any chance of salvation. For until he thoroughly understands the three characteristics of the world a man will inevitably crave for permanence in one form or another, and as this cannot, by the nature of things, be obtained, he will suffer, and probably make others suffer also.

All things in the universe may also be classified into five components, or are composed of a mixture of them: form and matter (*rūpa*), sensations (*vedanā*), perceptions (*saññā*), psychic dispositions or constructions (*saṃkhārā*), and consciousness or conscious thought (*viññāna*). The first consists of the objects of sense and various other elements of less importance. Sensations are the actual feelings arising as a result of the exercise of the six senses (mind being the sixth) upon sense-objects, and perceptions are the cognitions of such sensations. The psychic constructions include all the various psychological emotions, propensities, faculties, and conditions of the individual, while the fifth component, conscious thought, arises from the interplay of the other psychic constituents. The individual is made up of a combination of the five components, which are never the same from one moment to the next, and therefore his whole being is in a state of constant flux.

The process by which life continues and one thing leads to another is

[4] The word *dharma* is employed in Buddhism a little differently from its use in Hinduism, and is strictly untranslatable in English. One leading authority has translated it as "the Norm"; in our extracts it is translated "the Doctrine," "Righteousness," or "The Law of Righteousness" according to context. The term *dharma* in Buddhism has also other connotations. Phenomena in general are dharmas, as are the qualities and characteristics of phenomena. Thus the Buddha's last words might be translated: "Growing old is the dharma of all composite things."

explained by the Chain of Causation (*Paṭicca-samuppāda,* lit. Dependent Origination). The root cause of the process of birth and death and rebirth is ignorance, the fundamental illusion that individuality and permanence exist, when in fact they do not. Hence there arise in the organism various psychic phenomena, including desire, followed by an attempt to appropriate things to itself—this is typified especially by sexual craving and sexual intercourse, which are the actual causes of the next links in the chain, which concludes with age and death, only to be repeated again and again indefinitely. Rebirth takes place, therefore, according to laws of karma which do not essentially differ from those of Hinduism, though they are explained rather differently.

As we have seen, no permanent entity transmigrates from body to body, and all things, including the individual, are in a state of constant flux. But each act, word, or thought leaves its traces on the collection of the five constituents which make up the phenomenal individual, and their character alters correspondingly. This process goes on throughout life, and, when the material and immaterial parts of the being are separated in death, the immaterial constituents, which make up what in other systems would be called the soul, carry over the consequential effects of the deeds of the past life, and obtain another body accordingly. Thus there is no permanent soul, but nevertheless room is found for the doctrine of transmigration. Though Buddhism rejects the existence of the soul, this makes little difference in practice, and the more popular literature of Buddhism, such as the *Birth Stories* (*Jātaka*), takes for granted the existence of a quasi-soul at least, which endures indefinitely. One sect of Buddhism, the *Sammitīya,* which admittedly made no great impression on the religious life of India, actually went so far as to admit the existence of an indescribable substratum of personality (*pudgala*), which was carried over from life to life until ultimately it was dissipated in Nirvāna, thus fundamentally agreeing with the pneumatology of most other Indian religions.

The process of rebirth can only be stopped by achieving Nirvāna, first by adopting right views about the nature of existence, then by a carefully controlled system of moral conduct, and finally by concentration and meditation. The state of Nirvāna cannot be described, but it can be hinted at or suggested metaphorically. The word literally means "blowing out," as of a lamp. In Nirvāna all idea of an individual personality or ego ceases to exist and there is nothing to be reborn—as far as the individual is concerned Nirvāna is annihilation. But it was certainly not generally thought of by the early Buddhists in such negative terms. It was rather conceived of as a transcendent state, beyond the possibility of full comprehension by the ordinary being enmeshed in the illusion of selfhood, but not fundamentally different from the state of supreme bliss as described in other non-theistic Indian systems.

These are the doctrines of the Theravāda school, and, with few variations, they would be assented to by all other schools of Buddhism. But the Mahāyāna[5] and quasi-Mahāyāna sects developed other doctrines, in favor of which they often gave comparatively little attention to these fundamental teachings.

Of the Lesser Vehicle only one sect survives, the Theravāda, now prevalent in Ceylon, Burma, Thailand, Cambodia, and Laos. There were several others in earlier times, some of which had distinctive metaphysical and psychological systems which approached more closely to those of the Greater Vehicle than did that of the Theravāda. The most important of these sects was perhaps that of the Sarvāstivādins, which stressed the absence of any real entity passing through time in transmigration, but on the other hand maintained the ultimate reality of the chain of events which made up the phenomenal being or object. A sub-sect of the Sarvāstivādins, the Sautrāntikas, emphasized the atomic nature of the component elements of the chain—every instant a composite object disappeared, to be replaced by a new one which came into being as a result of the last. This view of the universe, which appears in the systems of other Buddhist sects in a less emphatic form, is akin to the quantum theory of modern physics.

Another very interesting sect of the Lesser Vehicle was the Mahāsanghika, said to have been the first to break away from the main body of Buddhism. Subdivided into numerous schools, its chief characteristic was the doctrine that the things of the phenomenal world were not wholly real; thus it paved the way for the idealist world-view of Mahāyāna philosophy. Buddhas, on the other hand, according to the fully developed

[5] With the rise of the Mahāyāna form of Buddhism, Buddhist sects became divided into two major groups. The newer sects referred to their doctrine as the "Mahāyāna," the Greater Vehicle (to salvation), and to their rivals' as the "Hīnayāna," the Lesser Vehicle. We have generally preferred to call the latter group Theravāda from the name of its major sect.

doctrine of the Mahāsanghikas, had full reality, as heavenly beings in a state of perpetual mystic trance, and earthly Buddhas such as the historical Gautama were mere docetic manifestations of the Buddhas in their true state. It is possible that gnostic doctrines from the Middle East influenced this form of Buddhism, which came very close to Mahāyānism, differing only in the doctrine of bodhisattvas.

Buddhism also taught an advanced and altruistic system of morality, which was a corollary to its metaphysics, since one of the first steps on the road to Nirvāna was to do good to others, and thereby weaken the illusion of egoity which was the main cause of human sorrow. Buddhism set itself strongly against animal sacrifice and encouraged vegetarianism, though it did not definitely impose it. It tended towards peace, even if Ashoka's successors did not heed his injunctions to avoid aggression. Its attitude to the system of class and caste is not always definite; while passages in the Buddhist scriptures can be found which attack all claims to superiority by right of birth, the four great classes seem to have been recognized as an almost inevitable aspect of Indian society; but the Buddhist classification of these classes varies significantly from that of the Hindus, for in Buddhist sources the warrior is usually mentioned before the brāhman.

The total literature of Buddhism is so large that it is quite impossible for a single individual to master it in his lifetime. Each of the numerous sects of Buddhism had its version of the sacred scriptures written either in a semi-vernacular Prakritic language or in a form of Sanskrit with peculiar syntax and vocabulary, generally known as "Buddhist Sanskrit." Besides these there was a great body of commentarial literature, and much philosophical and devotional writing of all kinds. Much of the literature of the sects other than the Theravāda has been lost, or only survives in Chinese or Tibetan translations, but the complete canon of Theravāda Buddhism has been fully preserved in Ceylon. It is therefore of fundamental importance in any study of Buddhism. It is written in Pali, a language related to Sanskrit, and based on an ancient vernacular, probably spoken in the western part of India.

The canon is generally known as *Tripiṭaka* (the *Three Baskets*) after the three sections into which it is divided, namely *Conduct* (*Vinaya*), *Discourses* (*Sutta*), and *Supplementary Doctrines* (*Abhidhamma*). The first *Piṭaka* contains the rules of conduct of the Buddhist order of monks and nuns, usually in connection with narratives which purport to tell the circumstances in which the Buddha laid down each rule. The second *Piṭaka* is the most important; it contains discourses, mostly attributed to the Buddha, divided into five sections: the *Long Group* (*Dīgha Nikāya*) containing long discourses; the *Medium Group* (*Majjhima Nikāya*) with discourses of shorter length; the *Connected Group* (*Saṃyutta Nikāya*), a collection of shorter pronouncements on connected topics; the *Progressive Group* (*Aṅguttara Nikāya*), short passages arranged in eleven sections according to the number of topics dealt with in each—thus the three types of sin, in act, word and thought, occur in section three, and so on; and finally the *Minor Group* (*Khuddaka Nikāya*), a number of works of varying type, including the beautiful and very ancient Buddhist poems of the *Way of Righteousness* (*Dhammapada*) and a collection of verses which are filled out by a lengthy prose commentary to form the *Birth Stories* (*Jātaka*) relating the previous births of the Buddha.

The third *Piṭaka,* the *Supplementary Doctrines,* is a collection of seven works on Buddhist psychology and metaphysics, which are little more than a systematization of ideas contained in the *Discourses,* and are definitely later than the main body of the canon.

There is considerable disagreement about the date of the canon. Some earlier students of Buddhism believed that the *Conduct* and *Discourse Baskets* existed in much the same form as they do now within a hundred years of the Buddha's death. Later authorities are inclined to believe that the growth of the canon was considerably slower. On the other hand many of the discourses may look back to the Buddha himself, though all have been more or less worked over, and none can be specified with certainty as being his own words. The orthodox tradition itself admits that the *Basket of Supplementary Doctrines* (*Abhidhamma Piṭaka*) is later than the other two, and was not completed until the time of Ashoka. Sinhalese tradition records that the canon was not committed to writing until the reign of King Vattagāmani (89–77 B.C.), and it may not have finished growing until about this time. Thus it is possible that it is the product of as many as four centuries.

There are numerous other works in Pali which are not generally considered canonical. Perhaps the most important of these works are the standard commentaries on the books of the canon, most of which, it is said, were compiled in Ceylon by the great doctor Buddhaghosa, of the fifth century A.D., from earlier commentaries. As well as passages of explanatory character, the commentaries contain much ancient Buddhist tradition not to be found elsewhere, and the elucidation of the *Jātaka* verses, in plain and vigorous prose, contains some of the finest narrative literature of the ancient world. Buddhaghosa is also the reputed author of a valuable compendium of Buddhist doctrine, *The Way of Purification* (*Visuddhimagga*). Another very important Pali work of early date is *The Questions of King Menander* (*Milindapañha*), from which several passages are translated here. The inscriptions of Emperor Ashoka (c. 273–232 B.C.) must also be included in any survey, since they are inspired by Buddhism and are at least in part intended to inculcate the morality of Buddhism.

BASIC DOCTRINES OF THERAVĀDA BUDDHISM

The Four Noble Truths

According to Buddhist tradition this was the first sermon preached by the Buddha. After gaining enlightenment under the Tree of Wisdom at Gayā he proceeded to Vārānasī[1], where, in a park outside the city, he found five ascetics who had formerly been his associates, and who had left him in disgust when he gave up self-mortification and self-starvation as useless in his quest for supreme wisdom. In the presence of these five the Buddha "set in motion the Wheel[2] of the Law" by preaching this sermon, which outlines the Four Noble Truths, the Noble Eightfold Path, and the Middle Way, three of the most important concepts of Buddhism.

[From *Saṃyutta Nikāya,* 5.421 ff.[3]]

Thus I have heard. Once the Lord was at Vārānasī, at the deer park called Isipatana. There he addressed the five monks:

There are two ends not to be served by a wanderer. What are these two? The pursuit of desires and of the pleasure which springs from de-

[1] The ancient name of Banaras, now officially revived by the Indian government.

[2] The chariot wheel in ancient India symbolized empire and hence this phrase may be paraphrased as: "embarked on his expedition of conquest on behalf of the Kingdom of Righteousness."

[3] In all quotations from the Pali scriptures, except where specified, reference is made to the Pali Text Society's edition of the text.

sire, which is base, common, leading to rebirth, ignoble, and unprofitable; and the pursuit of pain and hardship, which is grievous, ignoble, and unprofitable. The Middle Way of the Tathāgata [4] avoids both these ends. It is enlightened, it brings clear vision, it makes for wisdom, and leads to peace, insight, enlightenment, and Nirvāna. What is the Middle Way? . . . It is the Noble Eightfold Path—Right Views, Right Resolve, Right Speech, Right Conduct, Right Livelihood, Right Effort, Right Mindfulness,[5] and Right Concentration. This is the Middle Way. . . .

And this is the Noble Truth of Sorrow. Birth is sorrow, age is sorrow, disease is sorrow, death is sorrow; contact with the unpleasant is sorrow, separation from the pleasant is sorrow, every wish unfulfilled is sorrow—in short all the five components of individuality [6] are sorrow.

And this is the Noble Truth of the Arising of Sorrow. It arises from craving, which leads to rebirth, which brings delight and passion, and seeks pleasure now here, now there—the craving for sensual pleasure, the craving for continued life, the craving for power.

And this is the Noble Truth of the Stopping of Sorrow. It is the complete stopping of that craving, so that no passion remains, leaving it, being emancipated from it, being released from it, giving no place to it.

And this is the Noble Truth of the Way which Leads to the Stopping of Sorrow. It is the Noble Eightfold Path—Right Views, Right Resolve, Right Speech, Right Conduct, Right Livelihood, Right Effort, Right Mindfulness, and Right Concentration.

The Nature of Consciousness and the Chain of Causation

The following *Discourse,* though it purports to be a single utterance of the Buddha, is evidently a conflation of separate passages, bearing on the character of consciousness. It contains a short statement of the contingent nature of consciousness or conscious thought, an appeal for an objective and clear realization that everything whatever is dependent on causes outside itself, an enumeration of the elements of the Chain of Causation, given first in reverse order, an exhortation to the monks not to bother unduly about the question of the survival of the personality and to realize the facts of the Doctrine for themselves, not taking them from the lips of the Teacher, and finally an impressive passage

[4] "He who has thus attained," one of the titles of the Buddha.

[5] *Sati,* lit. "memory." At all times the monk should as far as possible be fully conscious of his actions, words, and thoughts, and be aware that the agent is not an enduring individual, but a composite and transitory collection of material and psychic factors.

[6] Forms, sensations, perceptions, psychic dispositions, and consciousness.

comparing the life of the ordinary man with that of the Buddha, which we have not space to give here.

[From *Majjhima Nikāya,* 1.256 ff.]

Once a certain monk named Sāti, the son of a fisherman,[1] conceived the pernicious heresy that, as he understood the Lord's teaching, consciousness continued throughout transmigration. When they heard this several monks went and reasoned with him . . . but he would not give in, but held firm to his heresy. . . . So they went to the Lord and put the matter to him, and he sent a monk to fetch Sāti. When Sāti had come the Lord asked him if it was true that he held this heresy . . . and Sāti replied that he did hold it.

"What, then," asked the Lord, "is the nature of consciousness?"

"Sir, it is that which speaks and feels, and experiences the consequences of good and evil deeds."

"Whom do you tell, you foolish fellow, that I have taught such a doctrine? Haven't I said, with many similes, that consciousness is not independent, but comes about through the Chain of Causation, and can never arise without a cause? You misunderstand and misrepresent me, and so you undermine your own position and produce much demerit. You bring upon yourself lasting harm and sorrow!" . . .

Then the Lord addressed the assembled monks:

"Whatever form of consciousness arises from a condition is known by the name of that condition; thus if it arises from the eye and from forms it is known as visual consciousness . . . and so with the senses of hearing, smell, taste, touch, and mind, and their objects. It's just like a fire, which you call by the name of the fuel—a wood fire, a fire of sticks, a grass fire, a cowdung fire, a fire of husks, a rubbish fire, and so on."[2]

"Do you agree, monks, that any given organism is a living being?" "Yes, sir."

"Do you agree that it is produced by food?" "Yes, sir."

"And that when the food is cut off the living being is cut off and dies?" "Yes, sir."

[1] In theory the origins of a monk, once he had become a full member of the Order, were irrelevant, but the authors of the Pali scriptures often mention the fact that a given monk was of humble birth. It would seem that they were not altogether free from class-consciousness.

[2] The implication is that just as fire is caused by fuel and varies according to the fuel used, so consciousness is caused by the senses and their objects, and varies accordingly.

"And that doubt on any of these points will lead to perplexity?" "Yes, sir."

"And that Right Recognition is knowledge of the true facts as they really are?" "Yes, sir."

"Now if you cling to this pure and unvitiated view, if you cherish it, treasure it, and make it your own, will you be able to develop a state of consciousness with which you can cross the stream of transmigration as on a raft, which you use but do not keep?" "No, sir."

"But only if you maintain this pure view, but don't cling to it or cherish it . . . only if you use it but are ready to give it up?"[3] "Yes, sir."

"There are four bases which support all organisms and beings, whether now existing or yet to be. They are: first, food coarse or fine, which builds up the body; second, contact; third, cogitation; and fourth, consciousness. All four derive and originate from craving. Craving arises from sensation, sensation from contact,[4] contact from the six senses, the six senses from physical form, physical form from consciousness, consciousness from the psychic constructions, and the psychic constructions from ignorance. . . . To repeat: Ignorance is the cause of the psychic constructions, hence is caused consciousness, hence physical form, hence the six senses, hence contact, hence sensations, hence craving, hence attachment, hence becoming, hence birth, hence old age and death with all the distraction of grief and lamentation, sorrow and despair. This is the arising of the whole body of ill. . . . So we are agreed that by the complete cessation of ignorance the whole body of ill ceases.

"Now would you, knowing and seeing this, go back to your past, wondering whether you existed or didn't exist long ago, or how you existed, or what you were, or from what life you passed to another?" "No, sir."

"Or would you look forward to the future with the same thoughts?" "No, sir."

"Or would you, knowing and seeing this, trouble yourselves at the

[3] Buddhism is a practical system, with one aim only, to free living beings from suffering. This passage apparently implies that even the most fundamental doctrines of Buddhism are only means to that end, and must not be maintained dogmatically for their own sake. It suggests also that there may be higher truths, which can only be realized as Nirvāna is approached.

[4] Here we are told that craving arises from contact, through sensation, while in the previous sentence contact arises from craving. There is no real paradox, because the chain is circular, and any one link is the cause of any other.

present time about whether or not you really exist, what and how you are, whence your being came, and whither it will go?" "No, sir."

"Or would you, possessing this knowledge, say, 'We declare it because we revere our teacher'?" "No, sir."

"Or would you say, 'We don't declare it as from ourselves—we were told it by a teacher or ascetic'?" "No, sir."

"Or would you look for another teacher?" "No, sir."

"Or would you support the rituals, shows, or festivals of other ascetics or brāhmans?" "No, sir."

"Do you only declare what you have known and seen?" "Yes, sir."

"Well done, brethren! I have taught you the doctrine which is immediately beneficial, eternal, open to all, leading them onwards, to be mastered for himself by every intelligent man."

False Doctrines About the Soul

The early Buddhists never ceased to impress upon their hearers the fact that the phenomenal personality was in a constant state of flux, and that there was no eternal soul in the individual in anything like the Hindu sense. On the other hand the perfected being had reached Nirvāna, and nothing could be meaningfully predicated about him. The following passage, attributed to the Buddha himself, criticizes the soul theories of other sects.

[From *Dīgha Nikāya,* 2.64 ff.]

It is possible to make four propositions concerning the nature of the soul—"My soul has form and is minute," "My soul has form and is boundless," "My soul is without form and is minute," and "My soul is without form and boundless." Such propositions may refer to this life or the next. . . .

There are as many ways of not making propositions concerning the soul, and those with insight do not make them.

Again the soul may be thought of as sentient or insentient, or as neither one nor the other but having sentience as a property. If someone affirms that his soul is sentient you should ask, "Sentience is of three kinds, happy, sorrowful, and neutral. Which of these is your soul?" For when you feel one sensation you don't feel the others. Moreover these sensations are impermanent, dependent on conditions, resulting from a cause or causes, perishable, transitory, vanishing, ceasing. If one experiences a happy sensation and thinks "This is my soul," when the happy sensation ceases he will think "My soul has departed." One who thinks thus looks on his soul as something impermanent in this life, a blend of happiness and sorrow with a beginning and end, and so this proposition is not acceptable.

If someone affirms that the soul is not sentient, you should ask, "If you have no sensation, can you say that you exist?" He cannot, and so this proposition is not acceptable.

And if someone affirms that the soul has sentience as a property you should ask, "If all sensations of every kind were to cease absolutely there would be no feelings whatever. Could you then say 'I exist'?" He could not, and so this proposition is not acceptable.

When a monk does not look on the soul as coming under any of these three categories . . . he refrains from such views and clings to nothing in the world; and not clinging he does not tremble, and not trembling he attains Nirvāna. He knows that rebirth is at an end, that his goal is reached, that he has accomplished what he set out to do, and that after this present world there is no other for him. It would be absurd to say of such a monk, with his heart set free, that he believes that the perfected being survives after death—or indeed that he does not survive, or that he does and yet does not, or that he neither does nor does not. Because the monk is free his state transcends all expression, predication, communication, and knowledge.

The Simile of the Chariot

This passage from the *Questions of King Menander* is among the best known arguments in favor of the composite nature of the individual. The Greek king Milinda, or Menander, ruled in northwestern India about the middle of the second century B.C. According to the text he was converted to Buddhism by Nāgasena, and the wheel which appears on some of his numerous coins would suggest that he was in fact influenced by the Indian religion. The style of the *Questions* is in some measure reminiscent of the Upanishads, but some authorities have thought to find traces of the influence of Plato and have suggested that the author or authors knew Greek. Though in its present form the work may be some centuries later, its kernel may go back to before the Christian era.

[From *Milindapañha* (Trenckner ed.) pp. 25 f.]

Then King Menander went up to the Venerable Nāgasena, greeted him respectfully, and sat down. Nāgasena replied to the greeting, and the

King was pleased at heart. Then King Menander asked: "How is your reverence known, and what is your name?"

"I'm known as Nāgasena, your Majesty, that's what my fellow monks call me. But though my parents may have given me such a name . . . it's only a generally understood term, a practical designation. There is no question of a permanent individual implied in the use of the word."

"Listen, you five hundred Greeks and eighty thousand monks!" said King Menander. "This Nāgasena has just declared that there's no permanent individuality implied in his name!" Then, turning to Nāgasena, "If, Reverend Nāgasena, there is no permanent individuality, who gives you monks your robes and food, lodging and medicines? And who makes use of them? Who lives a life of righteousness, meditates, and reaches Nirvāna? Who destroys living beings, steals, fornicates, tells lies, or drinks spirits? . . . If what you say is true there's neither merit nor demerit, and no fruit or result of good or evil deeds. If someone were to kill you there would be no question of murder. And there would be no masters or teachers in the [Buddhist] Order and no ordinations. If your fellow monks call you Nāgasena, what then is Nāgasena? Would you say that your hair is Nāgasena?" "No, your Majesty."

"Or your nails, teeth, skin, or other parts of your body, or the outward form, or sensation, or perception, or the psychic constructions, or consciousness? [1] Are any of these Nāgasena?" "No, your Majesty."

"Then are all these taken together Nāgasena?" "No, your Majesty."

"Or anything other than they?" "No, your Majesty."

"Then for all my asking I find no Nāgasena. Nāgasena is a mere sound! Surely what your Reverence has said is false!"

Then the Venerable Nāgasena addressed the King.

"Your Majesty, how did you come here—on foot, or in a vehicle?"

"In a chariot."

"Then tell me what is the chariot? Is the pole the chariot?" "No, your Reverence."

"Or the axle, wheels, frame, reins, yoke, spokes, or goad?" "None of these things is the chariot."

"Then all these separate parts taken together are the chariot?" "No, your Reverence."

"Then is the chariot something other than the separate parts?" "No, your Reverence."

[1] The five components of individuality.

"Then for all my asking, your Majesty, I can find no chariot. The chariot is a mere sound. What then is the chariot? Surely what your Majesty has said is false! There is no chariot! . . ."

When he had spoken the five hundred Greeks cried "Well done!" and said to the King, "Now, your Majesty, get out of that dilemma if you can!"

"What I said was not false," replied the King. "It's on account of all these various components, the pole, axle, wheels, and so on, that the vehicle is called a chariot. It's just a generally understood term, a practical designation."

"Well said, your Majesty! You know what the word 'chariot' means! And it's just the same with me. It's on account of the various components of my being that I'm known by the generally understood term, the practical designation Nāgasena."

Change and Identity

After convincing Menander of the composite nature of the personality by the simile of the chariot, Nāgasena shows him by another simile how it is continually changing with the passage of time, but possesses a specious unity through the continuity of the body.

[From *Milindapañha* (Trenckner ed.), p. 40]

"Reverend Nāgasena," said the King, "when a man is born does he remain the same [being] or become another?"

"He neither remains the same nor becomes another."

"Give me an example!"

"What do you think, your Majesty? You were once a baby lying on your back, tender and small and weak. Was that baby you, who are now grown up?"

"No, your Reverence, the baby was one being and I am another."

"If that's the case, your Majesty, you had no mother or father, and no teachers in learning, manners, or wisdom. . . . Is the boy who goes to school one [being] and the young man who has finished his education another? Does one person commit a crime and another suffer mutilation for it?"

"Of course not, your Reverence! But what do you say on the question?"

"I am the being I was when I was a baby," said the Elder . . . "for through the continuity of the body all stages of life are included in a pragmatic unity."

"Give me an illustration."

"Suppose a man were to light a lamp, would it burn all through the night?" "Yes, it might."

"Now is the flame which burns in the middle watch the same as that which burned in the first?" "No, your Reverence."

"Or is that which burns in the last watch the same as that which burned in the middle?" "No, your Reverence."

"So is there one lamp in the first watch, another in the middle, and yet another in the last?"

"No. The same lamp gives light all through the night."

"Similarly, your Majesty, the continuity of phenomena is kept up. One person comes into existence, another passes away, and the sequence runs continuously without self-conscious existence, neither the same nor yet another."

"Well said, Reverend Nāgasena!"

The Process of Rebirth

In this little passage Nāgasena presses the analogy of the lamp further, and shows Menander how rebirth is possible without any soul, substratum of personality, or other hypothetical entity which passes from the one body to the other.

[From *Milindapañha* (Trenckner ed.), p. 71]

"Reverend Nāgasena," said the King, "is it true that nothing transmigrates, and yet there is rebirth?"

"Yes, your Majesty."

"How can this be? . . . Give me an illustration."

"Suppose, your Majesty, a man lights one lamp from another—does the one lamp transmigrate to the other?"

"No, your Reverence."

"So there is rebirth without anything transmigrating!"

Karma

Buddhism accepted the prevailing doctrine of karma, though it had an original explanation of the process whereby karma operated. In this passage from the

Questions of King Menander karma is adduced as the reason for the manifest inequalities of human fate and fortune. Had Nāgasena been disputing with an Indian king instead of with a Greek one the question would not have been asked, for the answer would have been taken for granted.

[From *Milindapañha* (Trenckner ed.), p. 65]

"Venerable Nāgasena," asked the King, "why are men not all alike, but some short-lived and some long, some sickly and some healthy, some ugly and some handsome, some weak and some strong, some poor and some rich, some base and some noble, some stupid and some clever?"

"Why, your Majesty," replied the Elder, "are not all plants alike, but some astringent, some salty, some pungent, some sour, and some sweet?"

"I suppose, your Reverence, because they come from different seeds."

"And so it is with men! They are not alike because of different karmas. As the Lord said . . . 'Beings each have their own karma. They are . . . born through karma, they become members of tribes and families through karma, each is ruled by karma, it is karma that divides them into high and low.' "

"Very good, your Reverence!"

Right Mindfulness

The following passage is of interest as showing the means which the monk should take in order thoroughly to realize the transience and otherness of all things, and thus draw near to Nirvāna. The *bhāvanās,* or states of mind, are practiced by Buddhist monks to this day, and are part of "Right Mindfulness," the seventh stage of the Noble Eightfold Path. The translation is considerably abridged.

[From *Majjhima Nikāya,* 1.420 ff.]

The Lord was staying at Sāvatthī at the monastery of Anāthapindaka in the Grove of Jeta. One morning he dressed, took his robe and bowl, and went into Sāvatthī for alms, with the Reverend Rāhula [1] following close behind him. As they walked the Lord, . . . without looking round, spoke to him thus:

"All material forms, past, present, or future, within or without, gross or subtle, base or fine, far or near, all should be viewed with full understanding—with the thought 'This is not mine, this is not I, this is not my soul.' " [2]

[1] The Buddha's son, who, after his father's enlightenment, became a monk.

[2] Or "self" (*atta*).

"Only material forms, Lord?"

"No, not only material forms, Rāhula, but also sensation, perception, the psychic constructions, and consciousness." [3]

"Who would go to the village to collect alms today, when he has been exhorted by the Lord himself?" said Rāhula. And he turned back and sat cross-legged, with body erect, collected in thought.

Then the Venerable Sāriputta,[4] seeing him thus, said to him: "Develop concentration on inhalation and exhalation, for when this is developed and increased it is very productive and helpful."

Towards evening Rāhula rose and went to the Lord, and asked him how he could develop concentration on inhalation and exhalation. And the Lord said:

"Rāhula, whatever is hard and solid in an individual, such as hair, nails, teeth, skin, flesh, and so on, is called the personal element of earth. The personal element of water is composed of bile, phlegm, pus, blood, sweat, and so on. The personal element of fire is that which warms and consumes or burns up, and produces metabolism of food and drink in digestion. The personal element of air is the wind in the body which moves upwards or downwards, the winds in the abdomen and stomach, winds which move from member to member, and the inhalation and exhalation of the breath. And finally the personal element of space comprises the orifices of ears and nose, the door of the mouth, and the channels whereby food and drink enter, remain in, and pass out of the body.[5] These five personal elements, together with the five external elements, make up the total of the five universal elements. They should all be regarded objectively, with right understanding, thinking 'This is not mine, this is not me, this is not my soul.' With this understanding attitude a man turns from the five elements and his mind takes no delight in them.

"Develop a state of mind like the earth, Rāhula. For on the earth men throw clean and unclean things, dung and urine, spittle, pus and blood, and the earth is not troubled or repelled or disgusted. And as you grow like the earth no contacts with pleasant or unpleasant will lay hold of your mind or stick to it.

"Similarly you should develop a state of mind like water, for men

[3] The five components of individuality. [4] One of the Buddha's chief disciples.

[5] This interesting passage will give the reader some notion of ancient Indian ideas of anatomy and physics, as it would have been assented to by most schools of thought. In

throw all manner of clean and unclean things into water and it is not troubled or repelled or disgusted. And similarly with fire, which burns all things, clean and unclean, and with air, which blows upon them all, and with space, which is nowhere established.

"Develop the state of mind of friendliness, Rāhula, for, as you do so, ill-will will grow less; and of compassion, for thus vexation will grow less; and of joy, for thus aversion will grow less; and of equanimity,[6] for thus repugnance will grow less.

"Develop the state of mind of consciousness of the corruption of the body, for thus passion will grow less; and of the consciousness of the fleeting nature of all things, for thus the pride of selfhood will grow less.

"Develop the state of mind of ordering the breath, . . . in which the monk goes to the forest, or to the root of a tree or to an empty house, and sits cross-legged with body erect, collected in thought. Fully mindful he inhales and exhales. When he inhales or exhales a long breath he knows precisely that he is doing so, and similarly when inhaling or exhaling a short breath. While inhaling or exhaling he trains himself to be conscious of the whole of his body, . . . to be fully conscious of the components of his mind, . . . to realize the impermanence of all things, . . . or to dwell on passionlessness . . . or renunciation. Thus the state of ordered breathing, when developed and increased, is very productive and helpful. And when the mind is thus developed a man breathes his last breath in full consciousness, and not unconsciously."[7]

The Last Instructions of the Buddha

The following passage occurs in the *Discourse of the Great Passing-away* (*Mahāparinibbāna Sutta*) which describes the last days and death of the Buddha. The Master, an old and ailing man, is on the way to the hills where he was born, and where soon he is to die. These are among his last recorded instructions to his disciples. Unfortunately we cannot be sure of their authenticity; the fine phrases concerning "the closed fist of the teacher" are particularly suspect, for they are just the sort of interpolation which an earnest Theravāda monk would be likely to make, in order to discredit

many passages Buddhist texts admit only four elements, rejecting space, which is looked on as an element in orthodox Hindu theory.

[6] Friendliness, compassion, joy, and equanimity are the four cardinal virtues of Buddhism.

[7] The state of mind in the last moments before death was considered extremely important in its effect on the next birth. Some of the Chinese and Japanese Buddhist sects perform rites at the deathbed similar to the Roman Catholic extreme unction.

the doctrines of schismatics of a Mahāyānist type, who claimed to possess the esoteric teachings of the Master. But, whether authentically the Buddha's words or not, the following passage perhaps gives the quintessence of Theravāda Buddhism, with its call for self-reliant striving against all that seems base and evil.

[From *Dīgha Nikāya,* 2.99 f., 155–56]

Soon after this the Lord began to recover, and when he was quite free from sickness he came out of his lodging and sat in its shadow on a seat spread out for him. The Venerable Ānanda went up to him, paid his respects, sat down to one side, and spoke to the Lord thus:

"I have seen the Lord in health, and I have seen the Lord in sickness; and when I saw that the Lord was sick my body became as weak as a creeper, my sight dimmed, and all my faculties weakened. But yet I was a little comforted by the thought that the Lord would not pass away until he had left his instructions concerning the Order."

"What, Ānanda! Does the Order expect that of me? I have taught the truth without making any distinction between exoteric and esoteric doctrines; for . . . with the Tathāgata there is no such thing as the closed fist of the teacher who keeps some things back. If anyone thinks 'It is I who will lead the Order,' or 'The Order depends on me,' he is the one who should lay down instructions concerning the Order. But the Tathāgata has no such thought, so why should he leave instructions? I am old now, Ānanda, and full of years; my journey nears its end, and I have reached my sum of days, for I am nearly eighty years old. Just as a worn out cart can only be kept going if it is tied up with thongs, so the body of the Tathāgata can only be kept going by bandaging it. Only when the Tathāgata no longer attends to any outward object, when all separate sensation stops and he is deep in inner concentration, is his body at ease.

"So, Ānanda, you must be your own lamps, be your own refuges. Take refuge in nothing outside yourselves. Hold firm to the truth as a lamp and a refuge, and do not look for refuge to anything besides yourselves. A monk becomes his own lamp and refuge by continually looking on his body, feelings, perceptions, moods, and ideas in such a manner that he conquers the cravings and depressions of ordinary men and is always strenuous, self-possessed, and collected in mind. Whoever among my monks does this, either now or when I am dead, if he is anxious to learn, will reach the summit." [p. 99 f.]

"All composite things must pass away. Strive onward vigilantly." [pp. 155–56]

The Buddha in Nirvāna

This brief passage from the *Questions of King Menander* illustrates the Theravāda conception of Nirvāna. It is not total annihilation, but at the same time it involves the complete disintegration of the phenomenal personality—a paradox which cannot be explained in words.

[From *Milindapañha* (Trenckner, ed.), p. 73]

"Reverend Nāgasena," said the King, "does the Buddha still exist?"

"Yes, your Majesty, he does."

"Then is it possible to point out the Buddha as being here or there?"

"The Lord has passed completely away in Nirvāna, so that nothing is left which could lead to the formation of another being. And so he cannot be pointed out as being here or there."

"Give me an illustration."

"What would your Majesty say—if a great fire were blazing, would it be possible to point to a flame which had gone out and say that it was here or there?"

"No, your Reverence, the flame is extinguished, it can't be detected."

"In just the same way, your Majesty, the Lord has passed away in Nirvāna. . . . He can only be pointed out in the body of his doctrine, for it was he who taught it."

"Very good, Reverend Nāgasena!"

The City of Righteousness

This fine passage, from the latter part of the *Questions of King Menander,* is probably the work of a hand different from that which composed the dialogues which we have already quoted. In it the Buddha almost takes on the character of a savior god, who, like Amitābha in the developed Mahāyāna mythology, built a heaven for his followers. Nirvāna is not described in negative terms, but in very positive ones, and the metaphor of the busy, populous, and prosperous city hardly suggests the rarified Nirvāna of the previous passage, but a heaven in which personality is by no means lost. It suggests in fact to the Western reader the New Jerusalem of the Book of Revelation. Clearly this passage is the work of a writer whose attitude approached closely to that of

Mahāyāna, but it must be remembered that Theravāda Buddhists look on the text from which it is taken as semi-canonical.

[From *Milindapañha* (Trenckner ed.), pp. 330 ff.]

The builder of a city . . . first chooses a pleasant and suitable site; he makes it smooth, and then sets to work to build his city fair and well proportioned, divided into quarters, with ramparts round about it. . . . And when the city is built, and stands complete and perfect, he goes away to another land. And in time the city becomes rich and prosperous, peaceful and happy, free from plague and calamity, and filled with people of all classes and professions and of all lands . . . even with Scythians, Greeks, and Chinese. . . . All these folk coming to live in the new city and finding it so well planned, faultless, perfect, and beautiful exclaim: "Skilled indeed must be the builder who built this city!"

So the Lord . . . in his infinite goodness . . . when he had achieved the highest powers of Buddhahood and had conquered Māra [1] and his hosts, tearing the net of false doctrine, casting aside ignorance, and producing wisdom, . . . built the City of Righteousness.

The Lord's City of Righteousness has virtue for its ramparts, fear of sin for its moat, knowledge for its gates, zeal for its turrets, faith for its pillars, concentration for its watchman, wisdom for its palaces. The *Basket of Discourses* is its marketplace, the *Supplementary Doctrines* its roads, the *Conduct* its court of justice, and earnest self-control is its main street. . . .

The Lord laid down the following subjects for meditation: the ideas of impermanence, of the nonexistence of an enduring self, of the impurity and of the wretchedness of life, of ridding oneself of evil tendencies, of passionlessness, of stopping the influx of evil tendencies, of dissatisfaction with all things in the world, of the impermanence of all conditioned things, of mindful control of breath, of the corpse in disintegration, of the execution of criminals with all its horrors; the ideas of friendliness, of compassion, of joy, of equanimity,[2] the thought of death, and mindfulness of the body. . . . Whoever wishes to be free from age and death takes one of these as a subject for meditation, and thus he is set free from passion, hatred, and dullness,[3] from pride and from false views; he crosses

[1] The spirit of the world and the flesh, the Buddhist Satan.

[2] The four cardinal virtues of Buddhism.

[3] The three "influxes" (*āsava*), the cardinal sins of Buddhism.

the ocean of rebirth, dams the torrent of his cravings, is washed clean of the threefold stain [of passion, hatred, and dullness], and destroys all evil within him. So he enters the glorious city of Nirvāna, stainless and undefiled, pure and white, unaging, deathless, secure and calm and happy, and his mind is emancipated as a perfected being.

THE ETHICS OF THERAVĀDA BUDDHISM

In the sphere of personal relations Buddhism inculcated a morality gentler and more humanitarian than the stern early Hindu ethic, based chiefly on duty rather than fellowship. The four cardinal virtues of Buddhism—friendliness, compassion, joy, and equanimity—are extolled in many passages of the scriptures. The *Birth Stories* teach friendly relations between man and man and between man and animal, and encourage the warm virtues of family love, brotherhood, and honesty (not to speak of shrewdness) in one's dealings with others. Though the surviving Buddhist religious literature is chiefly intended for the monastic community Buddhism certainly had, and still has, a message going far beyond the monastery to the millions of ordinary believers who have no hope of Nirvāna until after many lives, but who may yet rise in the scale of being by faith in the teaching of the Buddha, by service to the Buddhist Order, and by fair dealing with their fellows.

In this connection we would draw attention to the most important passage on lay morality in the Pali scriptures—the *Discourse of Admonition to Singāla* (*Siṅgālovāda Sutta*). It is a solid bourgeois morality that this text encourages. Like many older writings of Protestant Christianity it stresses the virtue of thrift—expensive ceremonies and domestic rituals are wasteful as well as useless; fairs and festivals lead men to squander precious time and wealth; from the layman's point of view drink and gambling are evil chiefly for the same reasons; to increase the family estates is a meritorious act. But there is more in the *Discourse* than this. In modern terms the ideal it sets forth is of a society in which each individual respects the other's personality, an intricate network of warm and happy human relationships, where parents and children, teachers and pupils, husbands and wives, masters and servants, and friends and friends look on one another as ends in themselves, and dwell together in mutual respect and affection, each helping the other upward in the scale of being through a cosmos which, though theoretically a vale of tears, yet contains pleasant places and gives many opportunities for real if transient happiness in fellowship with friends and kin. And the inevitable sorrow of all who are born only to grow old and pass away, the lonely anguish of the individual being who finds himself at odds with an unfriendly universe, can only be lessened, at least for the ordinary layman, by brotherhood.

The Morals of the Monk

The following extract is part of a long panegyric of the Buddha, leading up to a description of his perfect wisdom. The moral virtues attributed to him in the earlier part of the passage, which is quoted here, are those after which every monk should strive; and, allowing for their different circumstances, the monk's example should be followed as far as possible by the layman.

[From *Dīgha Nikāya,* 1.4 ff.]

The monk Gautama has given up injury to life, he has lost all inclination to it; he has laid aside the cudgel and the sword, and he lives modestly, full of mercy, desiring in compassion the welfare of all things living.

He has given up taking what is not given, he has lost all inclination to it. He accepts what is given to him and waits for it to be given; and he lives in honesty and purity of heart. . . .

He has given up unchastity, he has lost all inclination to it. He is celibate and aloof, and has lost all desire for sexual intercourse, which is vulgar. . . .

He has given up false speech, he has lost all inclination to it. He speaks the truth, he keeps faith, he is faithful and trustworthy, he does not break his word to the world. . . .

He has given up slander, he has lost all inclination to it. When he hears something in one place he will not repeat it in another in order to cause strife, . . . but he unites those who are divided by strife, and encourages those who are friends. His pleasure is in peace, he loves peace and delights in it, and when he speaks he speaks words which make for peace. . . .

He has given up harsh speech, he has lost all inclination to it. He speaks only words that are blameless, pleasing to the ear, touching the heart, cultured, pleasing the people, loved by the people. . . .

He has given up frivolous talk, he has lost all inclination to it. He speaks at the right time, in accordance with the facts, with words full of meaning. His speech is memorable, timely, well illustrated, measured, and to the point.[1]

He does no harm to seeds or plants. He takes only one meal a day, not eating at night, or at the wrong time.[2] He will not watch shows, or attend fairs with song, dance, and music. He will not wear ornaments, or adorn himself with garlands, scents, or cosmetics. He will not use a high or large bed. He will not accept gold or silver, raw grain or raw meat. He will not accept women or girls, bondmen or bondwomen, sheep or goats, fowls or pigs, elephants or cattle, horses or mares, fields or houses. He will not act as go-between or messenger. He will not buy or sell, or falsify with scales, weights, or measures. He is never crooked, will never bribe, or cheat, or defraud. He will not injure, kill, or put in bonds, or steal, or do acts of violence.

Care of the Body

The Buddhist Order was very solicitous for the bodily health of its members, and the Buddha is reported to have said, on one occasion: "He who would care for me should care for the sick." [1] Buddhist monasteries often served as dispensaries, and it has been suggested that one of the reasons for the spread of Buddhism in Southeast Asia and elsewhere was the medical lore of the Buddhist monks, which, though of course primitive by modern standards, was superior to anything known to the local inhabitants, and thus added to the reputation of the new religion.

The *Questions of King Menander* explains the apparent anomaly that a system which stressed so strongly the evils of the things of the flesh should also value physical wellbeing so highly.

[From *Milindapañha* (Trenckner ed.), pp. 73–74]

The King said: "Reverend Nāgasena, is the body dear to you wanderers?"

"No, your Majesty."

"Then why do you feed it and care for it so well?"

"Have you ever gone to battle, and been wounded by an arrow?"

[1] The layman in Buddhism is expected to follow the example of Gautama in all the points of morality above, except, of course, that in place of complete celibacy legitimate sexual relations are allowed. Many of the points that follow would be regarded as subjects of supererogation for the layman, though he might adhere to some of them for specified periods. It should be remembered, incidentally, that the vows of the Buddhist monk are not taken in perpetuity, and a Buddhist layman will often take the monk's vows for a short period.

[2] That is, after midday.

[1] *Vinaya Piṭaka* 1. 302 (*Mahāvagga* 8. 26).

"Yes, your Reverence, I have."

"And in such a case isn't the wound smeared with ointment, anointed with oil, and bound with a bandage?"

"Yes, that's what is done."

"And is the wound dear to you, your Majesty, that you care for it so well?"

"Certainly not! All those things are done to make the flesh grow together again."

"So, you see, wanderers do not hold the body dear, your Majesty! Without clinging to it they bear the body in continence, for the Lord declared that the body was like a wound. . . .

'Covered with clammy skin, with nine openings, a great wound,
The body oozes from every pore, unclean and stinking.' "

"Well spoken, Reverend Nāgasena!"

"Lay Not Up for Yourselves Treasures upon Earth. . . ."

In theory "right views" about the nature of the world are the first step along the Eightfold Path. But the Buddhist literature meant chiefly for laymen tends to emphasize right actions rather than right views. Whatever the beliefs of a man may be, his good deeds and self-discipline are an unfailing source of merit, and lead to a happier rebirth, which may give him the opportunity for further spiritual progress. We quote the following little passage partly because it recalls a famous verse of the Sermon on the Mount. Notice that the treasure "cannot be given to others." This is the doctrine of the Theravāda sect. The Mahāyāna teaches that the merit accruing from good deeds can be transferred by a voluntary act of will, and men are encouraged, by the example of the compassionate bodhisattvas (See Chapter VII), to make such transfers of merit.

[From *Khuddaka Pāṭha,* 8]

A man buries a treasure in a deep pit, thinking: "It will be useful in time of need, or if the king is displeased with me, or if I am robbed or fall into debt, or if food is scarce, or bad luck befalls me."

But all this treasure may not profit the owner at all, for he may forget where he has hidden it, or goblins may steal it, or his enemies or even his kinsmen may take it when he is careless.

But by charity, goodness, restraint, and self-control man and woman alike can store up a well-hidden treasure—a treasure which cannot be given to others and which robbers cannot steal. A wise man should do good—that is the treasure which will not leave him.

The Virtue of Friendliness

The following poem is evidently a conflation from two sources, for in the middle of the third verse its whole tone changes, and in place of a rather pedestrian enumeration of the Buddhist virtues we have an impassioned rhapsody on the theme of friendliness (*mettā*), the first of the four cardinal virtues. "Mindfulness of friendliness" is among the daily exercises of the monk, and can also be practiced by the layman; he detaches himself in imagination from his own body, and, as though looking down on himself, pervades himself with friendliness directed towards himself, for it is impossible to feel true friendliness or love for others unless, in the best sense of the term, one feels it for oneself; then he proceeds in imagination to send waves of friendliness in every direction, to reach every being in every corner of the world. After pervading the world with love he may repeat the process with the three other cardinal virtues—compassion, joy, and equanimity. These forms of the practice of "right mindfulness" are known as *Brahma-vihāras,* freely translated "sublime moods." They are still practiced by Buddhists throughout the world, and it is believed, especially among the Mahāyānist sects, that the waves of friendliness constantly poured out by many thousands of meditating monks have a very positive effect on the welfare of the world.

[From *Sutta Nipāta,* p. 143 ff.]

This a man should do who knows what is good for him,
Who understands the meaning of the Place of Peace [i.e., Nirvāna]—
He should be able, upright, truly straight,
Kindly of speech, mild, and without conceit.

He should be well content, soon satisfied,
Having few wants and simple tastes,
With composed senses, discreet,
Not arrogant or grasping. . . .

In his deeds there should be no meanness
For which the wise might blame him.

May all be happy and safe!
May all beings gain inner joy—

All living beings whatever
Without exception, weak or strong,
Whether long or high
Middling or small, subtle or gross,
Seen or unseen,
Dwelling afar or near,
Born or yet unborn—
May all beings gain inner joy.

May no being deceive another,
Nor in any way scorn another,
Nor, in anger or ill-will,
Desire another's sorrow.

As a mother cares for her son,
Her only son, all her days,
So towards all things living
A man's mind should be all-embracing.
Friendliness for the whole world,
All-embracing, he should raise in his mind,
Above, below, and across,
Unhindered, free from hate and ill-will.

Standing, walking or sitting,
Or lying down, till he falls asleep,
He should remain firm in this mindfulness,
For this is the sublime mood.
Avoiding all false views,
Virtuous, filled with insight,
Let him conquer the lust of the passions,
And he shall never again be born of the womb.

Hatred and Love

The idea of "turning the other cheek" in one's personal relations is frequently to be found in Buddhist literature. Nevertheless there are few condemnations of warfare, as distinct from acts of violence on the part of individuals, and the Theravāda scriptures contain no passages on this latter topic as forthright as

Ashoka's Thirteenth Rock-Edict (quoted later). The following verses from the *Way of Righteousness* exemplify these points.

[From *Dhammapada,* 3–5, 201]

"He insulted me, he struck me,
He defeated me, he robbed me!"
Those who harbor such thoughts
Are never appeased in their hatred. . . .
But those who do not harbor them
Are quickly appeased.

Never in this world is hate
Appeased by hatred;
It is only appeased by love—
This is an eternal law (*sanantana-dhamma*).[1]

Victory breeds hatred
For the defeated lie down in sorrow.
Above victory or defeat
The calm man dwells in peace.

Buddhism and Everyday Life

The *Admonition to Singāla* is the longest single passage in the Pali scriptures devoted to lay morality. Though put in the mouth of the Buddha, it is probably not authentically his; parts of it, however, may be based on a few transmitted recollections of his teaching. Like many other *Discourses* it seems to emanate from more than one source, for the earlier part, enumerating the many sins and faults to which the layman is liable, and describing the true friend, is divided by a series of verses from the later and finer passage, defining the duties of the layman in his sixfold relationship with his fellows.

The reader should notice the solid, frugal, mercantile virtues which are inculcated, especially in the first part. This sermon is evidently not directed chiefly at the very poor or the very rich, but at the prosperous middle class. Also noteworthy are the paragraphs on the duties of husbands and wives and masters and servants in the second part of the sermon—if read in terms of rights rather than of duties they seem to imply the wife's right to full control of household affairs and to an adequate dress allowance, and the employee's right to fair wages and conditions, regular holidays, and free medical attention.

[From *Dīgha Nikāyu,* 3.180 ff.]

[1] Skt. *Sanātana dharma,* a conventional term designating "Hinduism," redefined here in terms of Buddhist ethics.

Once when the Lord was staying in the Bamboo Grove at Rajagaha, Singāla, a householder's son, got up early, went out from Rājagaha, and, with his clothes and hair still wet from his morning ablutions, joined his hands in reverence and worshiped the several quarters of earth and sky—east, south, west, north, above, and below. Now early that same morning the Lord dressed himself, and with bowl and robe went into Rājagaha to beg his food. He saw Singāla worshiping the quarters, and asked him why he did so.

"When my father lay dying," Singāla replied, "he told me to worship the quarters thus. I honor my father's words, and respect and revere them, and so I always get up early and worship the quarters in this way."

"But to worship the six quarters thus is not in accordance with noble conduct."

"How then, Sir, should they be worshiped in accordance with noble conduct? Will the Lord be so good as to tell me?"

"Listen then," said the Lord, "and I'll tell you. Mark well what I say!"

"I will, Sir," Singāla replied. And the Lord spoke as follows:

"If the noble lay-disciple has given up the four vices of action, if he does no evil deed from any of the four motives, if he doesn't follow the six ways of squandering his wealth, if he avoids all these fourteen evils—then he embraces the six quarters, he is ready for the conquest of both worlds, he is fortunate both in this world and the next, and when his body breaks up on his death he is reborn to bliss in heaven.

"What are the four vices of action that he gives up? They are injury to life, taking what is not given, base conduct in sexual matters, and false speech. . . .

"What are the four motives of evil deeds which he avoids? Evil deeds are committed from partiality, enmity, stupidity, and fear.

"And what are the six ways of squandering wealth? They are addiction to drink, the cause of carelessness; roaming the streets at improper times; frequenting fairs; gambling; keeping bad company; and idleness.

"There are six dangers in addiction to drink: actual loss of wealth; increased liability to quarrels; liability to illness; loss of reputation; indecent exposure; and weakened intelligence.

"There are six dangers in roaming the streets at improper times: the man who does so is unprotected and unguarded; so are his wife and children; and likewise his property; he incurs suspicion of having committed crime;

he is the subject of false rumors; in fact he goes out to meet all kinds of trouble.

"There are six dangers in frequenting fairs: the man who does so becomes an insatiable addict of dancing; singing; music; story-telling; jugglers; or acrobats.

"There are six dangers in gambling: the winner incurs hatred; the loser regrets his lost money; there is obvious loss of wealth; a gambler's word is not respected in the law courts; he is scorned by his friends and counselors; and he is not cultivated by people who want to marry their daughters, for the rogue who's always dicing isn't fit to keep a wife.

"There are six dangers in keeping bad company: a man who does so has as his friends and companions rogues; libertines; drunkards; confidence men; swindlers; and toughs.

"And there are six dangers in idleness; A man says, 'it's too cold' and doesn't work; or he says, 'it's too hot'; or 'it's too early'; or 'it's too late'; or 'I'm too hungry'; or 'I'm too full.' And so all the while he won't do what he ought to do, and he earns no new wealth, but fritters away what he has already earned.

"There are four types who should be looked on as enemies in the guise of friends: a grasping man; a smooth-spoken man; a man who only says what you want to hear; and a man who helps you waste your money.

"The grasping man is an enemy on four grounds: he is grasping; when he gives a little he expects a lot in return; what duty he performs he does out of fear; and he only serves his own interests.

"The smooth-spoken man is an enemy on four grounds: he speaks you fair about the past; he speaks you fair about the future; he tries to win you over by empty promises; but when there's something to be done he shows his shortcomings.[1]

"The man who only says what you want to hear is an enemy on four grounds: he consents to an evil deed; he doesn't consent to a good one; he praises you to your face; but he runs you down behind your back.

"The wastrel is an enemy on four grounds: he is your companion when you drink; when you roam the streets at improper times; when you go to fairs; and when you gamble.

[1] The commentator Buddhaghosa gives a quaint example of the conduct of such a false friend—you send a message asking him to lend you his cart, and he replies that the axle is broken.

"But there are four types who should be looked on as friends true of heart: a man who seeks to help you; a man who is the same in weal and woe; a man who gives good advice; and a man who is sympathetic. . . .

The friend who is a helper,
  The friend in weal and woe,
The friend who gives good counsel,
  The friend who sympathizes—
These the wise man should know
  As his four true friends,
And should devote himself to them
  As a mother to the child of her body.

The wise and moral man
  Shines like a fire on a hilltop,
Making money like the bee,
  Who does not hurt the flower.
Such a man makes his pile
  As an anthill, gradually.
The man grown wealthy thus
  Can help his family
And firmly bind his friends
  To himself. He should divide
His money in four parts;
  On one part he should live,
With two expand his trade,
  And the fourth he should save
Against a rainy day.[2]

"And how does the noble lay-disciple embrace the six quarters? He should recognize these as the six quarters: mother and father as the east;

[2] These verses are undoubtedly popular gnomic poetry, adapted with little or no alteration to Buddhist purposes. They effectively give the lie to the picture, still popular in some circles, of ancient India as a land of "plain living and high thinking." The last three verses are evidently the product of a society quite as acquisitive as that of present-day Europe or America. The commentator Buddhaghosa found them difficult, for the ideal layman is here said to plow half his income back into his trade, but to devote nothing to religious or charitable causes. The phenomenal rate of reinvestment advocated suggests a rapidly expanding economy.

teachers as the south; wife and children as the west; friends and counselors as the north; slaves and servants as below; and ascetics and brāhmans as above.

"A son should serve his mother and father as the eastern quarter in five ways: having been maintained by them in his childhood he should maintain them in their old age; he should perform the duties which formerly devolved on them; he should maintain the honor and the traditions of his family and lineage; he should make himself worthy of his heritage; and he should make offerings to the spirits of the departed. And thus served by their son as the eastern quarter his mother and father should care for him in five ways: they should restrain him from evil; encourage him to do good; have him taught a profession; arrange for his marriage to a suitable wife; and transfer his inheritance to him in due time. Thus he embraces the eastern quarter and makes it safe and propitious.

"A pupil should serve his teacher as the southern quarter in five ways: by rising [to greet him when he enters]; by waiting upon him; by willingness to learn; by attentive service; and by diligently learning his trade. And thus served by his pupil as the southern quarter a teacher should care for him in five ways: he should train him in good conduct; teach him in such a way that he remembers what he has been taught; thoroughly instruct him in the lore of every art [of his trade]; speak well of him to his friends and counselors; and protect him in every quarter. Thus he embraces the southern quarter and makes it safe and propitious.

"A husband should serve his wife as the western quarter in five ways: by honoring her; by respecting her; by remaining faithful to her; by giving her charge of the home; and by duly giving her adornments. And thus served by her husband as the western quarter a wife should care for him in five ways: she should be efficient in her household tasks; she should manage her servants well; she should be chaste; she should take care of the goods which he brings home; and she should be skillful and untiring in all her duties. Thus he embraces the western quarter and makes it safe and propitious.

"A gentleman should serve his friends and counselors as the northern quarter in five ways: by generosity; by courtesy; by helping them; by treating them as he would treat himself; and by keeping his word to them. And thus served by a gentleman as the northern quarter his friends and counselors should care for him in five ways: they should protect him when he is careless; they should guard his property on such occasions; they should be a refuge for him in trouble; in misfortune they should not leave him; and they should respect other members of his family. Thus he embraces the western quarter and makes it safe and propitious.

"A master should serve his slaves and servants as the lower quarter in five ways: he should assign them work in proportion to their strength; he should give them due food and wages; he should care for them in sickness; he should share especially tasty luxuries with them; and he should give them holidays at due intervals. Thus served by their master as the lower quarter they should care for him in five ways: they should get up before him; they should go to bed after him; they should be content with what he gives them; they should do their work well; and they should spread abroad his praise and good name. Thus he embraces the lower quarter and makes it safe and propitious.

"In five ways a gentleman should serve ascetics and brāhmans as the upper quarter: by affectionate acts; by affectionate words; by affectionate thoughts; by not closing his doors to them; and by duly supplying them with food. Thus served by a gentleman as the upper quarter they should care for him in six ways: they should restrain him from evil; they should encourage him to do good; they should feel for him with a friendly mind; they should teach him what he has not heard before; they should encourage him to follow what he has already learned; and they should show him the way to heaven. Thus he embraces the upper quarter and makes it safe and propitious."

SOCIETY AND THE STATE IN THERAVĀDA BUDDHISM

Few pages in the massive literature of Buddhism lay down definite instructions on social or political life, and the amount of speculation by Buddhist authors on the problems of state and society is not large. Indeed Buddhism has sometimes been stigmatized as not a true religion at all, but a mere system of self-discipline for monks, with no significant message for the ordinary man except that he should if possible leave the world and take the yellow robe. In fact Buddhists have always realized that not every layman was morally or intellectually capable of becoming a monk, and the scriptures, as we have seen above, do contain here and there instructions especially intended for layfolk, together with occasional passages with a social or political message. Nevertheless it may be that one of the reasons for the disappearance of Buddhism in the land of its birth was that it left the laymen too dependent on the ministrations of the brāhmans, and, instead of giving a lead in political and social matters, was too often willing to compromise with the existing ways of everyday life.

Though in practice Buddhism seems to have accepted the existence of a society with sharp class divisions and to have made no frontal attack on it, there are many passages in Buddhist literature in which the four classes of Hindu society are declared to be fundamentally equal, and in which men are said to be worthy of respect not through birth, but only through spiritual or moral merit. Though we cannot show that Buddhism had any definite effect on the Indian system of class and caste, its teachings obviously tended against the extremer manifestations of social inequality. In those lands where Buddhism was implanted upon societies little influenced by Hindu ideas the caste system in its Indian form is not to be found.

In politics Buddhism definitely discouraged the pretensions of kings to divine or semidivine status. While Hindu teachers often declared that kings were partial incarnations of the gods and encouraged an attitude of passive obedience to them, the Buddhist scriptures categorically state that the first king was merely the chosen leader of the people, appointed by them to restrain crime and protect property, and that his right to levy taxation depended not on birth or succession but on the efficient fulfillment of his duty. The *Birth Stories,* among the most influential of the Buddhist scriptures, contain several tales of wicked kings overthrown as a result of popular rebellion. Thus Buddhism had a rational attitude to the state. The constitution of the Buddhist order, in which each monastery was virtually a law unto itself, deciding major issues after free discussion among the assembled monks, tended toward democracy, and it has been suggested that it was based on the practices of the tribal republics of the Buddha's day. Though Buddhism never formulated a distinctive system of political ethics it generally tended to mitigate the autocracy of the Indian king.

On the question of war Buddhism said little, though a few passages in the Buddhist scriptures oppose it. Like the historical Ashoka, the ideal emperor of Buddhism gains his victories by moral suasion. This did not prevent many Buddhist kings of India and Ceylon from becoming great conquerors and pursuing their political aims with much the same ruthlessness as their Hindu neighbors. Two of pre-Muslim India's greatest conquerors, Harsha of Kanauj (606–647) and Dharmapāla of Bihar and Bengal (c.770–810), were Buddhists. In fact Buddhism had little direct effect on the political order, except in the case of Ashoka, and its leaders seem often to have been rather submissive to the temporal power. An Erastian relationship between church and state is indicated in the inscriptions of Ashoka, and in Buddhist Ceylon the same relationship usually existed.

Early travelers have left a number of valuable accounts of conditions in ancient India. Two of these, that of the Greek Megasthenes (c.300 B.C.) and that of the Chinese pilgrim Fa-hsien (A.D. c.400), are of special interest for our purposes, for the first was written before Buddhism had become an important factor in Indian life, and the second when it had already passed its most flourishing period and had entered on a state of slow decline. Megasthenes found a very severe judicial system, with many crimes punished by execution or mutilation. The existence of such a harsh system of punishment is confirmed by the famous Hindu text on polity, the *Arthaśāstra,* the kernel of which dates from about the same time. Under Chandragupta Maurya, the grandfather of Ashoka, the state was highly organized and all branches of human activity were hemmed in by many troublesome regulations enforced by a large corps of government officials. Fa-hsien, on the other hand, found a land where the death penalty was not imposed, and mutilation was inflicted only for very serious crime; and he was especially impressed by the fact that human freedom was respected and people were able to move freely from one part of the land to the other without passports or other forms of interference from the government. In Megasthenes' day all classes freely ate meat, while in the time of Fa-hsien only the outcastes did so.[1] It seems certain that Buddhism had something to do with the great change in the direction of mildness and nonviolence which had taken place in the seven hundred years between the two travelers. Certainly Buddhism was not the only factor in the change, for sentiments in favor of tolerance, mildness,

[1] If we are to believe the pilgrim, who may have exaggerated somewhat.

and nonviolence are to be found also in Hindu and Jain writings, but it is very probable that Buddhism was the greatest single factor, for it was the most active and vigorous religion in the period in question.

Though Ashoka was practically forgotten by India his message calling for good relations between rulers and ruled was not, and echoes of it may be heard in many non-Buddhist sources of later date. On the other hand his fond hope that aggressive wars would cease forever as a result of his propaganda was unfulfilled, and the successors of Ashoka seem to have been if anything more militant than his predecessors. It would seem that Buddhism had little effect in encouraging peace within the borders of India.

How the World Evolved

Buddhism, like all Indian religious systems, believed that the world goes through periods of evolution and decline. While it did not reject the existence of the gods, it denied that they had any significant effect upon the cosmic process. Brahmā, at the time of the Buddha a much more important figure than he became in later Hinduism, imagines that he is the creator, when in fact the world came into being through the operation of natural laws. In Brahmā's case the primal ignorance, which affects gods and men alike, has led to the wish fathering the thought. The following passage is attributed to the Buddha himself.

[From *Dīgha Nikāya,* 3.28 ff.]

There are some monks and brāhmans who declare as a doctrine received from their teachers that the beginning of all things was the work of the god Brahmā. I have gone and asked them whether it was true that they maintained such a doctrine, and they have replied that it was; but when I have asked them to explain just how the beginning of things was the work of the god Brahmā they have not been able to answer, and have returned the question to me. Then I have explained it to them thus:

There comes a time, my friends, sooner or later, . . . when the world is dissolved and beings are mostly reborn in the World of Radiance.[1] There they dwell, made of the stuff of mind, feeding on joy, shining in their own light, flying through middle space, firm in their bliss for a long, long time.

Now there comes a time when this world begins to evolve, and then

[1] *Ābhassara,* the third Buddhist heaven, above the World of Brahmā.

the World of Brahmā appears, but it is empty. And some being, whether because his allotted span is past or because his merit is exhausted, quits his body in the World of Radiance and is born in the empty World of Brahmā, where he dwells for a long, long time. Now because he has been so long alone he begins to feel dissatisfaction and longing, and wishes that other beings might come and live with him. And indeed soon other beings quit their bodies in the World of Radiance and come to keep him company in the World of Brahmā.

Then the being who was first born there thinks: "I am Brahmā, the mighty Brahmā, the Conqueror, the Unconquered, the All-seeing, the Lord, the Maker, the Creator, the Supreme Chief, the Disposer, the Controller, the Father of all that is or is to be. I have created all these beings, for I merely wished that they might be and they have come here!" And the other beings . . . think the same, because he was born first and they later. And the being who was born first lived longer and was more handsome and powerful than the others.

And it might well be that some being would quit his body there and be reborn in this world. He might then give up his home for the homeless life [of an ascetic]; and in his ardor, striving, intentness, earnestness, and keenness of thought, he might attain such a stage of meditation that with collected mind he might recall his former birth, but not what went before. Thus he might think: "We were created by Brahmā, eternal, firm, everlasting, and unchanging, who will remain so for ever and ever, while we who were created by the Lord Brahmā . . . are transient, unstable, shortlived, and destined to pass away."

That is how your traditional doctrine comes about that the beginning of things was the work of the god Brahmā.

The Origin of Society and the State

This most important and interesting legend should be read as a sequel to the former passage, since it describes a further stage in the process of cosmic evolution. It tells of the gradual progress of humanity, on account of its own greed, from the blissful golden age when there was no need of food or clothing to a fully evolved society with a king and class system. It should be noted especially that neither the state nor the class system has any ultimate sanction other than human expediency. The first king holds office by virtue of a contract with his subjects, and this is probably one of the world's oldest versions of the contractual theory of the state. The passage concludes by emphasizing the fundamental equality of all the four classes. Again the words are attributed to the Buddha.

[From *Dīgha Nikāya,* 3.80 ff.]

Sooner or later, after a long, long time . . . there comes a time when this world passes away. Then most living beings pass to the World of Radiance, and there they dwell, made of the stuff of mind, feeding on joy, shining in their own light, flying through middle space, firm in their bliss for a long, long time. Sooner or later there comes a time when this world begins to evolve once more. Then those being who pass away from the World of Radiance are usually born here on earth; but they are still made of the stuff of mind . . . and are firm in their bliss for a long, long time.

At that time the world is wholly covered in water, dark with a blinding darkness. No moon or sun, no constellations are to be seen, nor the forms of stars; there are no nights or days, no phases of the moon or months, no seasons or years. And there are no men or women then, for the beings living on earth are simply reckoned as beings. And for those beings, after a long, long time, a sweet earth is spread out on the waters, just as the skin forms on the surface of hot milk as it cools. And it had [2] color, fragrance and flavor, for it was the color of fine ghee or butter, and sweet as the choicest honey.

Then a certain being, greedy from a former birth, said, "What can this be?" and tasted the sweet earth with his finger. He was delighted with the flavor, and craving overcame him. Then others followed his example, and tasted the earth, . . . until they were all feasting on it, breaking off pieces with their hands. And as they did so their radiance faded; and as it faded the moon and sun appeared, with the constellations and the forms of stars, nights and days, phases of the moon and months, seasons and years. . . .

Beings continued thus, feeding on the sweet earth, for a long, long time. And the more they ate the more solid their bodies became, some beautiful and some ugly. And the beautiful scorned the ugly, boasting of their greater beauty. And as they became vain and conceited because of their beauty the sweet earth disappeared. . . .

Then growths appeared on the soil, coming up like mushrooms, with

[2] The change of tense occurs in the original.

color, scent and flavor like those of the sweet earth. The beings began to eat those growths, and so they continued for a long, long time . . . until the growths too disappeared.

Then creeping plants arose, growing like rattans; and the beings lived on them until the creepers too disappeared. . . .

Then, when the creepers had vanished, rice appeared, already ripe in the untilled soil, without dust or husk, fragrant and clean-grained. If they gathered it in the evening and took it away for supper it would grow and be ripe again by the next morning. If they gathered it in the morning for breakfast it would grow and be ripe again by the evening. It grew without a pause. And those beings continued to live on the rice . . . for a long, long time, and their bodies became more and more solid, and their differences in beauty, even more pronounced. In women female characteristics appeared, and in men male. The women looked at the men too intently, and the men at the women, and so passion arose, and a raging fire entered their bodies. In consequence they took to coupling together. When people saw them doing so some threw dust at them, others ashes, others cowdung, and shouted, "Perish, you foul one! Perish, you foul one!! How could one person treat another like that?" And even now people in certain districts, when a bride is led away after a wedding, throw dust or ashes or cowdung, and repeat the custom of long ago, but do not understand its significance.

What was considered immoral in those days is now considered moral. For in those days the people who took to coupling together were not allowed to enter a village or town for a month afterward or even for two. So, as they incurred so much blame for their immorality, they took to building huts in order to conceal it.

Then someone of a lazy disposition thought to himself, "Why do I go to the trouble of fetching rice night and morning? I'll fetch enough for supper and breakfast in one journey!" Then another man saw him and said, "Come on, my friend, let's go and fetch our rice!" "I've got enough," the first man replied, "I've fetched enough in one journey for both supper and breakfast." So the second man followed the first man's example, and fetched enough rice for two days at once. [Thus gradually people took to storing enough rice for as much as eight days at a time]. . . . And from the time that people took to feeding on stored rice the grain became covered with dust, and husks enveloped it; the reaped stems did not grow again, and there were pauses in its growth, when the stubble stood in clumps.

Then the people gathered together and lamented, saying: "Evil customs have appeared among men. Once we were made of the stuff of mind . . . and were firm in our bliss for a long, long time. . . . But now, through our evil and immoral ways, we have degenerated until our grain has become covered with dust . . . and the stubble stands in clumps. So let us divide the rice fields, and set up boundary marks."

Then someone of a greedy disposition, while watching his own plot, appropriated another plot that had not been given to him, and made use of it. The people seized him and said: "You've done an evil deed in taking and using a plot which was not given to you. Don't let it happen again!" "Very well," he replied. But he did the same thing again and yet a third time. Once more the people seized him and admonished him in the same terms, but this time some of them struck him with their hands, some with clods, and some with sticks. From such beginnings arose theft, censure, false speech, and punishment.

Then the people gathered together and lamented, saying: "Evil ways are rife among the people—theft, censure, false speech, and punishment have appeared among us. Let us choose one man from among us, to dispense wrath, censure, and banishment when they are right and proper, and give him a share of our rice in return. So they chose the most handsome, . . . attractive, and capable among them and invited him to dispense anger, censure, and banishment. He consented and did so, and they gave him a share of their rice.

Mahāsammata means approved (*sammata*) by the whole people (*mahājana*), and hence Mahāsammata was the first name to be given to a ruler. He was lord of the fields (*khettānam*) and hence *khattiya* [Skt. *kṣatriya*] was his second name. He pleases (*rañjeti*) others by his righteousness—hence his third name, *rājā*.[3] This was the origin of the class of kshatriyas, according to the tale of long ago.[4] They originated from those same folk and no others, people like themselves, in no way different; and their origin was quite natural and not otherwise.

Then it happened that some men thought, "Evil ways are rife among

[3] It is hardly necessary to say that these etymologies of *khattiya* and *rājā* are false, as are those which follow. They are significant nevertheless.

[4] It is noteworthy that in the Pali scriptures the kshatriya is regularly mentioned before the brāhman.

the people. . . . Now let us put away such evil and unwholesome ways." The word *brāhman* implies that they put away (*bāhenti*) such evil and unwholesome ways, and so brāhman became their earliest name. They built themselves huts of leaves in the woodland, and there they sat and meditated. They had no more use for charcoal or the smoke of cooking, or for the pestle and mortar, but they went out to villages, towns, or cities, seeking their food, in the evening their supper, in the morning their breakfast. When they had enough to eat they came back and meditated in their huts, and so they were given the second name of mystics (*jhāyaka*) because they meditated (*jhāyanti*).

Now some of them grew tired of meditating in their huts, and so they went away, settled on the outskirts of villages and towns, and made books.[5] When they saw this the people said, "These good folk can't meditate!", and so they were called teachers (*ajjhāyaka*),[6] and this became their third name. In those days these teachers were looked on as the lowest of brāhmans, but now they are thought the best. This was the origin of the class of brāhmans. . . . They originated quite naturally and not otherwise.

There were other people who married and took to all kinds of crafts and trades; and because they took to all kinds (*vissa*) of crafts and trades they were called *vessa* [Skt. *vaiśya*]. This was the origin of the class of vaishyas. . . . They originated quite naturally and not otherwise.

Those who remained were hunters. Those who live by hunting (*ludda*) have a mean (*khudda*) trade, and thus they were called *sudda* (Skt. *śūdra*). This was the origin of the class of shūdras. . . . They originated quite naturally and not otherwise.

Then there came a time when a kshatriya, scorning his own way of life, went out from his home and took up the homeless life, thinking to become an ascetic—[and then a brāhman, a vaishya, and a shūdra did the same]. From these four classes arose the class of ascetics. . . . And they too originated quite naturally and not otherwise.

A kshatriya who has led a bad life, whether in deed, word, or thought, and who has had wrong views about the world, because of his outlook and his deeds will be reborn after parting with his body in the waste and woe-

[5] According to the commentary, the three Vedas.

[6] An untranslatable play on words. *A-jhāyaka* means a non-meditator, and *ajjhāyaka* a reciter or teacher of the Vedas.

ful pit of purgatory. And a brāhman, a vaishya, and a shūdra will fare likewise. If on the other hand they lead good lives in thought, word, and deed, and have right views about the world, they will be reborn in the happy world of heaven. If their lives and their views are mixed they will be reborn in a state where they feel both happiness and sorrow. But if they are self-restrained in body, speech and mind . . . they may find Nirvāna, even in this present life.

For whoever from among the members of these four classes becomes a monk and later a perfected being, with all his stains destroyed, has done what he had to do; he has laid down his burden, gained salvation, destroyed the bonds of becoming; he is free in his perfect wisdom. And he is declared to be to the chief of them all, by the law of Righteousness and not otherwise; for the Law is the best thing men can have, both in this life and the next.

The Ideal of Government, and the Decay and Growth of Civilization

The following *Discourse,* again attributed to the Buddha, attempts, like the preceding one, to account for the origin of crime and evil, but it gives a different answer. According to a former passage crime began in the state of nature, and kingship was introduced to suppress it. Here government precedes crime. The golden age has its governments and indeed its conquests, but they are not conquests by the sword. It seems more than likely that this account of the Universal Emperor's peaceful victories over his neighbors is in some way linked with Ashoka's "Conquest by Righteousness," and we are inclined to believe that the present passage is post-Ashokan. Note that sin and crime, and the consequent lowering of the standards of civilization and of human conditions generally, are said to be due to the shortcomings of the ruler, and especially to his failure to continue the policy of his predecessors in caring for the poor. Hence crime appears, morality declines, and with it the standards of life deteriorate, until, after a brief period of complete anarchy, human love and fellowship again prevail, and gradually restore the golden age. Interesting is the reference to Metteya (Sanskrit, *Maitreya*), the future Buddha. This indicates that the *Discourse* is a comparatively late one. Our version is considerably abridged.

[From *Dīgha Nikāya,* 3.58 ff.]

In the past . . . there was a king called Dalhanemi. He was a Universal Emperor . . . a king of Righteousness, a conqueror of the four quarters, a protector of his people, a possessor of the Seven Jewels—the Wheel, the Elephant, and Horse, the Gem, the Woman, the Householder, and the General.[7] He had over a thousand sons, all heroes brave of body, crushers of enemy armies.[8] He conquered the earth from ocean to ocean and ruled it not by the rod or by the sword, but by the Law of Righteousness.

Now after many thousands of years King Dalhanemi ordered one of his men thus: "When you see that the Divine Wheel has sunk or slipped from its place, come and tell me." . . . And after many thousand years more the man saw that the Divine Wheel had sunk . . . and went and told the King. So King Dalhanemi sent for his eldest son, and said: "Dear boy, the Divine Wheel has sunk, and I've been told that when the Wheel of a Universal Emperor sinks he has not long to live. I have had my fill of human pleasure—now the time has come for me to look for divine joys. Come, dear boy, you must take charge of the earth. . . ." So King Dalhanemi duly established his eldest son on the throne, shaved his hair and beard, put on yellow robes, and left his home for the state of homelessness. And when the royal sage had left his home seven days the Divine Wheel completely vanished.

Then a certain man went to the King, the anointed warrior, and told him that it had vanished. He was beside himself with sorrow. So he went to the royal sage his father and told him about it. "Don't grieve that the Divine Wheel has disappeared," he said. "The Divine Wheel isn't an heirloom, my dear boy! You must follow the noble way of the Universal Emperors. If you do this and keep the fast of the full moon on the upper terrace of your palace the Divine Wheel will be seen again, complete with its thousand spokes, its tire, its nave, and all its other parts."

"But what, your Majesty, is the noble way of the Universal Emperors?"

"It is this, dear boy, that you should rely on the Law of Righteousness, honor, revere, respect, and worship it. You should be yourself the banner

[7] A Universal Emperor (Pali, *Cakkavatti;* Skt. *Cakravartin*) is a figure of cosmic significance, and corresponds on the material plane to a Buddha on the spiritual. Thus, according to the legend of the Buddha, it was prophesied at the birth of Siddhārtha Gautama that he would either become a Buddha or a Universal Emperor. Universal Emperors invariably have the Seven Jewels, which are perfect specimens of their kinds, and are the magical insignia of their owners. The Woman is of course the chief queen. In most lists the Crown Prince takes the place of the Householder.

[8] The Universal Emperor is not thoroughly adapted to the ethics of Buddhism, and though he conquers by force of character even the Buddhist author cannot disconnect him wholly from the usual militancy of the Indian king.

of Righteousness, the emblem of Righteousness, with Righteousness as your master. According to Righteousness you should guard, protect, and watch over your own family and people, your armed forces, your warriors, your officers, priests and householders, townsmen and country folk, ascetics and brāhmans, beasts and birds. There should be no evil-doing throughout your domains, and whoever is poor in your land should be given wealth. . . . Avoid evil and follow good. That is the noble way of the Universal Emperors."

"Very good, your Majesty," the King replied, and he followed the way of the Universal Emperors, until one day the Divine Wheel revealed itself . . . complete and whole. And he thought: "A king to whom the Divine Wheel reveals itself thus becomes a Universal Emperor—so may I now become such a Universal Emperor." He uncovered one shoulder, took a pitcher of water in his left hand, and sprinkled the Divine Wheel with his right, saying: "Roll on, precious Wheel! Go forth and conquer, lordly and precious Wheel!"

Then the precious Wheel rolled on toward the east, and the King followed it with his fourfold army. Wherever the Wheel stopped the Universal Emperor encamped with his army, and all the kings of the east came to him and said, "Come, your Majesty! Welcome, your Majesty! All this is yours, Your Majesty! Command, us, your Majesty!" And the Universal Emperor said, "Do not take life; do not take what is not yours; do not act basely in sexual matters; do not tell falsehoods; do not drink spirits.[9] Now enjoy your kingdoms as you have done in the past." And all the kings of the east submitted to him.

Then the Divine Wheel plunged into the eastern ocean, and rose again and rolled towards the south. And so the Wheel conquered the south, west, and north, until it had covered the whole earth from sea to sea. Then it returned to the capital, and stood at the door of the Universal Emperor's private apartments, facing the council hall, as though fixed to the place, adorning the inner palace.

With the passage of many thousands of years other kings did as this one had done, and became Universal Emperors—and it all happened as it had done before. But one day a Universal Emperor left his palace to become an ascetic, and his son, who succeeded him, heard that the Divine Wheel had vanished, but, though grieved at its disappearance, did not go

[9] These are the five precepts which all Buddhist laymen must do their best to follow.

to his father, the royal sage, to ask about the noble way of the Universal Emperors. He ruled the land according to his own ideas, and the people were not governed as they had been in the past; so they did not prosper as they had done under former kings who had followed the noble way of the Universal Emperors.

Then the ministers and counsellors, the officers of the treasury, the captains of the guard, the ushers, and the magicians, came to the King in a body and said: "The people do not prosper, your Majesty, because you govern them according to your own ideas. Now, we maintain the noble way of the Universal Emperors. Ask us about it and we will tell you." The King asked them about it and they explained it to him. When he had heard them he provided for the care and protection of the land, but he did not give wealth to the poor, and so poverty became widespread. Soon a certain man took what had not been given to him, and this was called stealing. They caught him and accused him before the King.

"Is it true that you have taken what was not given to you?" asked the King.

"It is, your Majesty," replied the man.

"But why did you do it?"

"Because I'd nothing to live on, your Majesty."

Then the King gave him wealth, saying, "With this keep yourself alive, care for your father and mother, children and wife, follow a trade, and give alms to ascetics and brāhmans, to help yourself along the way to heaven."

"I will, your Majesty," he replied.

And another man stole and was accused before the King, and the King rewarded him in just the same way. People heard of this and thought that they would do the same in order to receive wealth from the King. But when a third man was brought before the King and accused of theft the King thought: "If I give wealth to everyone who takes another man's property theft will increase. I'll put a stop to this! I'll sentence him to execution and have him beheaded!"

So he ordered his men to tie the culprit's arms tightly behind him with a strong rope, to shave his head with a razor, to lead him from street to street and from square to square to the strident sound of the drum, and to take him out of the southern gate of the city, and there to cut off his head. And they did as the King commanded.

But when people heard that thieves were to be put to death they thought: "We'll have sharp swords made, and when we steal we'll cut off the heads of those we rob." And they did so, and looted in village and town and city, besides committing highway robbery.

Thus, where formerly wealth had been given to the poor, poverty became widespread. Hence came theft, hence the sword, hence murder . . . and hence the span of life was shortened and men lost their comeliness, until where the fathers had lived for eighty thousand years the sons lived for only forty thousand.

Then it happened that a certain man stole and was accused, and when the King asked him whether it was true that he had stolen he replied, "No." Thus lying became widespread, and where the fathers had lived for forty thousand years the sons lived for only twenty thousand.

And again, when a certain man took what was not given him, another man came to the King and said: "So and so has taken what was not given him, he has committed . . . theft." Thus he spoke evil of the thief. So speaking evil of others became widespread, until where the fathers had lived for twenty thousand years the sons lived for only ten thousand.

Now some people were handsome and some ugly. And the ugly were jealous of the handsome, and took to committing adultery with other men's wives. So base conduct in sexual matters became widespread, and men's life-span and comeliness diminished until where the fathers had lived for ten thousand years the sons lived for only five thousand.

Next abusive speech and foolish gossip increased, and so where the fathers had lived for five thousand years the sons lived some for two thousand five hundred and some for two thousand years. Then cupidity and ill-will increased, and the life-span became only one thousand years. With the growth of false doctrines it fell to five hundred, and then incest, inordinate greed, and unnatural lust spread, and hence the span of life dropped to two hundred and fifty or two hundred years. Finally three further sins—disrespect for father and mother, disrespect for ascetics and brāhmans, and refusal to heed the head of the family—reduced man's life to one hundred years.

A time will come when the descendants of these people will live for only ten years, and when girls will reach puberty at the age of five. Then there will not be even the taste of ghee, butter, sesamum oil, sugar, or salt, and the finest food of the men of that time will be mere millet, where now it is rice and curry. Among those men . . . good deeds will entirely disappear, and evil deeds will flourish exceedingly—there will not even be a word for good, much less anyone who does good deeds. Those who do not honor mother and father, ascetic and brāhman, and those who do not heed the head of the family will be respected and praised, just as today those who do these things are respected and praised.

Among those people there will be no distinction of mother or aunt or aunt-by-marriage or teacher's wife—society will be just as promiscuous as goats and sheep, fowls and pigs, dogs and jackals. There will be bitter enmity one with another, bitter ill-will, bitter animosity, bitter thoughts of murder, and parents will feel toward their children, children toward their parents, brothers toward their brothers . . . as a hunter feels toward a deer.

Then there will be a transitional period of the Seven Days of the Sword, during which men will look upon one another as wild beasts, and with sharp swords in their hands will take one another's lives. . . . But a few will think: "We don't want anyone to kill us and we don't want to kill anyone. Let us hide in grassland, in jungle, in hollow trees, in river-marshes, or in the rough places of the mountains, and live on the roots and fruits of the forest."

And thus they will survive. And after the Seven Days of the Sword are passed they will come out and embrace one another, and with one accord comfort one another, saying, "How good it is, my friend, to see you still alive!" Then they will say: "We have lost so many of our kinsfolk because we took to evil ways—now we must do good! But what good deed can we do? We must stop taking life—that is a good custom to adopt and maintain!"

They will do this, and increase in both age and comeliness. And their virtues will increase until once more they live to the age of eighty thousand years and girls reach puberty at the age of five hundred. . . . India will be rich and prosperous, with villages and towns and cities so close together that a cock could fly from one to the next. India will be as crowded then as purgatory is now, as full of people as a thicket is of canes or reeds. Vārānasī . . . will be a rich and prosperous capital, full of people, crowded, and flourishing, and there will be born Sankha, a Universal Emperor, who will . . . like Dalhanemi . . . conquer the earth from ocean to ocean and rule it . . . by the Law of Righteousness

And among those people will be born the Lord Metteya, the perfected being, the fully enlightened, endowed with wisdom and virtue, the blessed, the knower of all the worlds, the supreme guide of willing men, the teacher of gods and men, a Lord Buddha, even as I am now. Like me, with his own insight, he will know the world and see it clearly, with its spirits, with Māra, with Brahmā, with its ascetics and brāhmans, with its gods and men. He will teach the Law of Righteousness in spirit and in letter, lovely in its beginning, lovely in its middle, lovely in its end, and he will live the pure life of celibacy in all its completeness, just as I do now. But he will have thousands of monks as his followers, where I have only hundreds.

Conditions of the Welfare of Societies

The following passage occurs in the *Discourse of the Great Passing-away,* which describes the last days and death of the Buddha. Though the words are put into his own mouth, it is quite likely that the passage is based on a series of popular aphorisms current among the Vajjian tribesmen themselves. It is followed by a longer passage in which the Buddha is purported to have adapted the list of the seven conditions of the welfare of republics to the circumstances of the Buddhist Order. According to a tradition preserved by the commentator Buddhaghosa, King Ajātasattu's wily minister Vassakāra, hearing the Buddha's words, set to work by "fifth column" methods to sow dissension among the leaders of the Vajjis, with the result that Magadha was able to annex their lands within a few years.

Notice especially the third condition. No early Indian sect took kindly to innovation, and according to orthodox Hindu thought the purpose of government was not to legislate, but only to administer the eternal law (*Sanātana-dharma*). Though the Buddhists had a somewhat different conception of dharma they shared the conservatism of the Hindus in this respect. Nevertheless new legislation was enacted from time to time, as will be seen later in the edicts of Ashoka.

[From *Dīgha Nikāya,* 2.72 ff.]

Once the Lord was staying at Rājagaha on the hill called Vulture's Peak . . . and the Venerable Ānanda was standing behind him and fanning him. And the Lord said: "Have you heard, Ānanda, that the Vajjis call frequent public assemblies of the tribe?" "Yes, Lord," he replied.

"As long as they do so," said the Lord, "they may be expected not to decline, but to flourish."

"As long as they meet in concord, conclude their meetings in concord, and carry out their policies in concord; . . . as long as they make no laws not already promulgated, and set aside nothing enacted in the past, acting in accordance with the ancient institutions of the Vajjis established in olden days; . . . as long as they respect, esteem, reverence, and support the elders of the Vajjis, and look on it as a duty to heed their words; . . . as long as no women or girls of their tribes are held by force or abducted; . . . as long as they respect, esteem, reverence, and support the shrines of the Vajjis, whether in town or country, and do not neglect the proper offerings and rites laid down and practiced in the past; [10] . . . as long as they give due protection, deference, and support to the perfected beings among them so that such perfected beings may come to the land from afar and live comfortably among them, so long may they be expected not to decline, but to flourish.

Birth Is No Criterion of Worth

Though in practice it would seem that Indian Buddhists maintained the system of class and caste, the theoretical attitude of Buddhism was equalitarian. We have seen that the division of the four classes was believed to be a functional one, with no divine sanction. The Buddhist view is summed up in the verse of the *Discourse Section* (*Sutta Nipāta,* verse 136):

> No brāhman is such by birth.
> No outcaste is such by birth.
> An outcaste is such by his deeds.
> A brāhman is such by his deeds.

In the following passage the Buddha puts forward numerous arguments in favor of this view, though many other passages show that lay Buddhists were encouraged to treat worthy brāhmans with respect.

[From *Majjhima Nikāya,* 2.147 ff.]

Once when the Lord was staying at Sāvatthī there were five hundred brāhmans from various countries in the city . . . and they thought: "This ascetic Gautama preaches that all four classes are pure. Who can refute him?"

At that time there was a young brāhman named Assalāyana in the city, . . . a youth of sixteen, thoroughly versed in the Vedas . . . and in all brāhmanic learning. "He can do it!", thought the brāhmans, and so they

[10] Note the respect paid to popular religion, which Buddhism adapted in the cults of the sacred tree and the stūpa, and later in that of the image.

asked him to try; but he answered, "The ascetic Gautama teaches a doctrine of his own,[1] and such teachers are hard to refute. I can't do it!" They asked him a second time . . . and again he refused; and they asked him a third time, pointing out that he ought not to admit defeat without giving battle. This time he agreed, and so, surrounded by a crowd of brāhmans, he went to the Lord, and, after greeting him, sat down and said:

"Brāhmans maintain that only they are the highest class, and the others are below them. They are white, the others black; only they are pure, and not the others. Only they are the true sons of Brahmā, born from his mouth,[2] born of Brahmā, creations of Brahmā, heirs of Brahmā. Now what does the worthy Gautama say to that?"

"Do the brāhmans really maintain this, Assalāyana, when they're born of women just like anyone else, of brāhman women who have their periods and conceive, give birth and nurse their children, just like any other women?"

"For all you say, this is what they think. . . ."

"Have you ever heard that in the lands of the Greeks and Kambojas and other peoples on the borders there are only two classes, masters and slaves, and a master can become a slave and vice versa?"

"Yes, I've heard so."

"And what strength or support does that fact give to the brāhmans' claim?"

"Nevertheless, that is what they think."

"Again if a man is a murderer, a thief, or an adulterer, or commits other grave sins, when his body breaks up on death does he pass on to purgatory if he's a kshatriya, vaishya, or shūdra, but not if he's a brāhman?"

"No, Gautama. In such a case the same fate is in store for all men, whatever their class."

"And if he avoids grave sin, will he go to heaven if he's a brāhman, but not if he's a man of the lower classes?"

[1] *Dhammavādi:* Our translation is on the basis of Buddhaghosa's commentary as generally interpreted. Dr. A. K. Warder suggests that the term may here mean "a teacher maintaining that the world is governed by natural law."

[2] According to the *Puruṣa Sūkta* (*Rig Veda,* 10.90) brāhmans are born from the head of the primeval man, while the other three classes are born from his arms, trunk, and feet, respectively.

"No, Gautama. In such a case the same reward awaits all men, whatever their class."

"And is a brāhman capable of developing a mind of love without hate or ill-will, but not a man of the other classes?"

"No, Gautama. All four classes are capable of doing so."

"Can only a brāhman go down to a river and wash away dust and dirt, and not men of the other classes?"

"No, Gautama, all four classes can."

"Now suppose a king were to gather together a hundred men of different classes and to order the brāhmans and kshatriyas to take kindling wood of sāl, pine, lotus or sandal, and light fires, while the low class folk did the same with common wood. What do you think would happen? Would the fires of the high-born men blaze up brightly . . . and those of the humble fail?"

"No, Gautama. It would be alike with high and lowly. . . . Every fire would blaze with the same bright flame." . . .

"Suppose there are two young brāhman brothers, one a scholar and the other uneducated. Which of them would be served first at memorial feasts, festivals, and sacrifices, or when entertained as guests?"

"The scholar, of course; for what great benefit would accrue from entertaining the uneducated one?"

"But suppose the scholar is ill-behaved and wicked, while the uneducated one is well-behaved and virtuous?"

"Then the uneducated one would be served first, for what great benefit would accrue from entertaining an ill-behaved and wicked man?"

"First, Assalāyana, you based your claim on birth, then you gave up birth for learning, and finally you have come round to my way of thinking, that all four classes are equally pure!"

At this Assalāyana sat silent . . . his shoulders hunched, his eyes cast down, thoughtful in mind, and with no answer at hand.

Ashoka: The Buddhist Emperor

The great emperor Ashoka (c.268–233 B.C.), third of the line of the Mauryas, became a Buddhist and attempted to govern India according to the precepts of Buddhism as he understood them. His new policy was promulgated in a series of edicts, which are still to be found, engraved on rocks and pillars in many parts of India. Written in a form of Prakrit, or ancient vernacular, with several local variations, they can claim little literary merit, for their style is crabbed and often ambiguous. In one of these edicts he describes his conversion, and its effects:

[From the Thirteenth Rock Edict]

When the king, Beloved of the Gods and of Gracious Mien, had been consecrated eight years Kalinga[1] was conquered, 150,000 people were deported, 100,000 were killed, and many times that number died. But after the conquest of Kalinga, the Beloved of the Gods began to follow Righteousness (Dharma), to love Righteousness, and to give instruction in Righteousness. Now the Beloved of the Gods regrets the conquest of Kalinga, for when an independent country is conquered people are killed, they die, or are deported, and that the Beloved of the Gods finds very painful and grievous. And this he finds even more grievous—that all the inhabitants—brāhmans, ascetics, and other sectarians, and householders who are obedient to superiors, parents, and elders, who treat friends, acquaintances, companions, relatives, slaves, and servants with respect, and are firm in their faith—all suffer violence, murder, and separation from their loved ones. Even those who are fortunate enough not to have lost those near and dear to them are afflicted at the misfortunes of friends, acquaintances, companions, and relatives. The participation of all men in common suffering is grievous to the Beloved of the Gods. Moreover there is no land, except that of the Greeks, where groups of brāhmans and ascetics are not found, or where men are not members of one sect or another. So now, even if the number of those killed and captured in the conquest of Kalinga had been a hundred or a thousand times less, it would be grievous to the Beloved of the Gods. The Beloved of the Gods will forgive as far as he can, and he even conciliates the forest tribes of his dominions; but he warns them that there is power even in the remorse of the Beloved of the Gods, and he tells them to reform, lest they be killed.[2]

For all beings the Beloved of the Gods desires security, self-control, calm of mind, and gentleness. The Beloved of the Gods considers that

[1] The coastal region comprising the modern Orissa and the northern part of Andhra State.

[2] Note that Ashoka has by no means completely abandoned the use of force. This passage probably refers to the wild uncivilized tribesmen of the hills and jungles, who still occasionally cause trouble in Assam and some other parts of India, and in ancient days were a much greater problem.

the greatest victory is the victory of Righteousness; and this he has won here (in India) and even five hundred leagues beyond his frontiers in the realm of the Greek king Antiochus, and beyond Antiochus among the four kings Ptolemy, Antigonus, Magas, and Alexander.[3] Even where the envoys of the Beloved of the Gods have not been sent men hear of the way in which he follows and teaches Righteousness, and they too follow it and will follow it. Thus he achieves a universal conquest, and conquest always gives a feeling of pleasure; yet it is but a slight pleasure, for the Beloved of the Gods only looks on that which concerns the next life as of great importance.

I have had this inscription of Righteousness engraved that all my sons and grandsons may not seek to gain new victories, that in whatever victories they may gain they may prefer forgiveness and light punishment, that they may consider the only [valid] victory the victory of Righteousness, which is of value both in this world and the next, and that all their pleasure may be in Righteousness. . . .

Ashoka's Buddhism, as his title shows, did not lessen his belief in the gods. Here he expresses his faith in Buddhism, and declares that the gods have appeared on earth as a result of his reforms: [4]

[From a minor Rock Edict (Maski Version)]

Thus speaks Ashoka, the Beloved of the Gods. For two and a half years I have been an open follower of the Buddha, though at first I did not make much progress. But for more than a year now I have drawn closer to the [Buddhist] Order, and have made much progress. In India the gods who formerly did not mix with men now do so. This is the result of effort, and may be obtained not only by the great, but even by the small, through effort—thus they may even easily win heaven.

Father and mother should be obeyed, teachers should be obeyed; pity . . . should be felt for all creatures. These virtues of Righteousness should be practiced. . . . This is an ancient rule, conducive to long life.

[3] Antiochus II Theos of Syria, Ptolemy II Philadelphus of Egypt, Antigonus Gonatas of Macedonia, Magas of Cyrene, and Alexander of Epirus. Classical sources tell us nothing about Ashoka's "victories of Righteousness" over these kings. Probably he sent envoys to them, urging them to accept his new policy and his moral leadership. Evidently he never gave up his imperial ambitions, but attempted to further them in a benevolent spirit and without recourse to arms.

[4] Some authorities have put different interpretations on the relevant phrases, but in our opinion there can be little doubt about their meaning.

[From the Ninth Rock Edict]

It is good to give, but there is no gift, no service, like the gift of Righteousness. So friends, relatives, and companions should preach it on all occasions. This is duty; this is right; by this heaven may be gained—and what is more important than to gain heaven?

The emphasis on morality is if anything intensified in the series of the seven Pillar Edicts, issued some thirteen years after the Rock Edicts, when the king had been consecrated twenty-six years:

[From the First Pillar Edict]

This world and the other are hard to gain without great love of Righteousness, great self-examination, great obedience, great circumspection, great effort. Through my instruction respect and love of Righteousness daily increase and will increase. . . . For this is my rule—to govern by Righteousness, to administer by Righteousness, to please my subjects by Righteousness, and to protect them by Righteousness.

Ashoka's solicitude extended to the animal life of his empire, which in ancient India was generally thought to be subject to the king, just as was human life. He banned animal sacrifices at least in his capital, introduced virtual vegetarianism in the royal household, and limited the slaughter of certain animals; his policy in this respect is made clear in his very first Rock Edict:

[From the First Rock Edict]

Here[5] no animal is to be killed for sacrifice, and no festivals are to be held, for the king finds much evil in festivals,[6] except for certain festivals which he considers good.

Formerly in the Beloved of the God's kitchen several hundred thousand animals were killed daily for food; but now at the time of writing only three are killed—two peacocks and a deer, though the deer not regularly. Even these three animals will not be killed in future.

[From the Second Pillar Edict]

I have in many ways given the gift of clear vision. On men and animals, birds and fish I have conferred many boons, even to saving their lives; and I have done many other good deeds.

[5] There is some reason to believe that the adverb implies the royal capital of Pātaliputra.

[6] *Samāja*, generally interpreted as a fair or festival, but perhaps a society or club. A tone of rather pompous puritanism is sometimes evident in the edicts, and suggests a less congenial side of Ashoka's character.

In accordance with the precepts of Buddhism Ashoka, for all his apparent other-worldliness, did not neglect the material welfare of his subjects, and was specially interested in giving them medical aid:

[From the Second Rock Edict]

Everywhere in the empire of the Beloved of the Gods, and even beyond his frontiers in the lands of the Cholas, Pāndyas, Satyaputras, Keralaputras,[7] and as far as Ceylon, and in the kingdoms of Antiochus the Greek king and the kings who are his neighbors, the Beloved of the Gods has provided medicines for man and beast. Wherever medicinal plants have not been found they have been sent there and planted. Roots and fruits have also been sent where they did not grow, and have been planted. Wells have been dug along the roads for the use of man and beast.

Ashoka felt a moral responsibility not only for his own subjects, but for all men, and he realized that they could not lead moral lives, and gain merit in order to find a place in heaven, unless they were happy and materially well cared for:

[From the Sixth Rock Edict]

I am not satisfied simply with hard work or carrying out the affairs of state, for I consider my work to be the welfare of the whole world, of which hard work and the carrying out of affairs are merely the basis. There is no better deed than to work for the welfare of the whole world, and all my efforts are made that I may clear my debt to all beings. I make them happy here and now that they may attain heaven in the life to come. . . . But it is difficult without great effort.

He speaks in peremptory tones to the officers of state who are slow in putting the new policy into effect:

[From the First Separate Kalinga Edict]

By order of the Beloved of the Gods. Addressed to the officers in charge of Tosali.[8] . . . Let us win the affection of all men. All men are my children, and as I wish all welfare and happiness in this world and the next for my own children, so do I wish it for all men. But you do not realize what this entails—here and there an officer may understand in part, but not entirely.

[7] Tamil kingdoms, in the southern tip of the Peninsula.

[8] The chief town of Kalinga, the region conquered by Ashoka in his last war of aggression.

Often a man is imprisoned and tortured unjustly, and then he is liberated for no [apparent] reason. Many other people suffer also [as a result of this injustice]. Therefore it is desirable that you should practice impartiality, but it cannot be attained if you are inclined to habits of jealousy, irritability, harshness, hastiness, obstinacy, laziness, or lassitude. I desire you not to have these habits. The basis of all this is the constant advoidance of irritability and hastiness in your business. . . .

This inscription has been engraved in order that the officials of the city should always see to it that no one is ever imprisoned or tortured without good cause. To ensure this I shall send out every five years on a tour of inspection officers who are not fierce or harsh. . . . The prince at Ujjain shall do the same not more than every three years, and likewise at Taxila.

Later, in his Pillar Edicts, Ashoka seems more satisfied that his officers are carrying out the new policy:

[From the Fourth Pillar Edict]

My governors are placed in charge of hundreds of thousands of people. Under my authority they have power to judge and to punish, that they calmly and fearlessly carry out their duties, and that they may bring welfare and happiness to the people of the provinces and be of help to them. They will know what brings joy and what brings sorrow, and, conformably to Righteousness, they will instruct the people of the provinces that they may be happy in this world and the next. . . . And as when one entrusts a child to a skilled nurse one is confident that . . . she will care for it well, so have I appointed my governors for the welfare and happiness of the people. That they may fearlessly carry out their duties I have given them power to judge and to inflict punishment on their own initiative. I wish that there should be uniformity of justice and punishment.

In numerous passages Ashoka stresses the hard work which the new policy demands of him. He has given up many of the pleasures of the traditional Indian king in order to further it, including, of course, hunting:

[From the Eighth Rock Edict]

In the past kings went out on pleasure trips and indulged in hunting and similar amusements. But the Beloved of the Gods . . . ten years after his consecration set out on the journey to Enlightenment.[9] Now when he goes on tour . . . he interviews and gives gifts to brāhmans and ascetics; he interviews and gives money to the aged; he interviews the people of the provinces, and instructs and questions them on Righteousness; and the pleasure which the Beloved of the Gods derives therefrom is as good as a second revenue.

As we have seen, Ashoka, though a Buddhist, respects brāhmans and the members of all sects, and he calls on his subjects to follow his example:

[From the Twelfth Rock Edict]
The Beloved of the Gods . . . honors members of all sects, whether ascetics or householders, by gifts and various honors. But he does not consider gifts and honors as important as the furtherance of the essential message of all sects. This essential message varies from sect to sect, but it has one common basis, that one should so control one's tongue as not to honor one's own sect or disparage another's on the wrong occasions; for on certain occasions one should do so only mildly, and indeed on other occasions one should honor other men's sects. By doing this one strengthens one's own sect and helps the others, while by doing otherwise one harms one's own sect and does a disservice to the others. Whoever honors his own sect and disparages another man's, whether from blind loyalty or with the intention of showing his own sect in a favorable light, does his own sect the greatest possible harm. Concord is best, with each hearing and respecting the other's teachings. It is the wish of the Beloved of the Gods that members of all sects should be learned and should teach virtue. . . . Many officials are busied in this matter . . . and the result is the progress of my own sect and the illumination of Righteousness.

Though he was by no means a rationalist, it appears that Ashoka thought little of the many rituals and ceremonies of Indian domestic life:

[From the Ninth Rock Edict]
People perform various ceremonies, at the marriage of sons and daughters, at the birth of children, when going on a journey . . . or on other occasions. . . . On such occasions women especially perform many cere-

[9] This phrase probably merely implies that Ashoka made a pilgrimage to the Bodhi Tree at Gayā.

monies which are various, futile, and useless. Even when they have to be done [to conform to custom and keep up appearances] such ceremonies are of little use. But the ceremonies of Righteousness are of great profit —these are the good treatment of slaves and servants, respect for elders, self-mastery in one's relations with living beings, gifts to brāhmans and ascetics, and so on.[10] But for their success everyone—fathers, mothers, brothers, masters, friends, acquaintances, and neighbors—must agree—"These are good! These are the ceremonies that we should perform for success in our undertakings . . . and when we have succeeded we will perform them again!" Other ceremonies are of doubtful utility—one may achieve one's end through them or one may not. Moreover they are only of value in this world, while the value of the ceremonies of Righteousness is eternal, for even if one does not achieve one's end in this world one stores up boundless merit in the other, while if one achieves one's end in this world the gain is double.

We conclude this selection of the edicts of Ashoka with his last important inscription, in which the emperor, eighteen years after his conversion, reviews his reign:

[From the Seventh Pillar Edict]

In the past kings sought to make the people progress in Righteousness, but they did not progress. . . . And I asked myself how I might uplift them through progress in Righteousness. . . . Thus I decided to have them instructed in Righteousness, and to issue ordinances of Righteousness, so that by hearing them the people might conform, advance in the progress of Righteousness, and themselves make great progress. . . . For that purpose many officials are employed among the people to instruct them in Righteousness and to explain it to them. . . .

Moreover I have had banyan trees planted on the roads to give shade to man and beast; I have planted mango groves, and I have had ponds dug and shelters erected along the roads at every eight kos.[11] Everywhere I have had wells dug for the benefit of man and beast. But this benefit is but small, for in many ways the kings of olden time have worked for the welfare of the world; but what I have done has been done that men may conform to Righteousness.

[10] With this compare the *Admonition to Singāla* (pp. 119 ff.).

[11] There is some uncertainty about the interpretation of this phrase. If that given above is correct, it implies intervals of about sixteen miles, or a day's journey.

All the good deeds that I have done have been accepted and followed by the people. And so obedience to mother and father, obedience to teachers, respect for the aged, kindliness to brāhmans and ascetics, to the poor and weak, and to slaves and servants, have increased and will continue to increase. . . . And this progress of Righteousness among men has taken place in two manners, by enforcing conformity to Righteousness, and by exhortation. I have enforced the law against killing certain animals and many others, but the greatest progress of Righteousness among men comes from exhortation in favor of noninjury to life and abstention from killing living beings.[12]

I have done this that it may endure . . . as long as the moon and sun, and that my sons and my great-grandsons may support it; for by supporting it they will gain both this world and the next.

[12] For all his humanitarianism, Ashoka did not abolish the death penalty, as was done by some later Indian kings.

CHAPTER VII

MAHĀYĀNA BUDDHISM: "THE GREATER VEHICLE"

From about the first or second century A.D. onwards, a new and very different kind of Buddhism arose in India. The new school, which claimed to offer salvation for all, styled itself *Mahāyāna,* the Greater Vehicle (to salvation), as opposed to the older Buddhism, which it contempuously referred to as *Hīnayāna,* or the Lesser Vehicle. The Mahāyāna scriptures also claimed to represent the final doctrines of the Buddha, revealed only to his most spiritually advanced followers, while the earlier doctrines were merely preliminary ones. Though Mahāyāna Buddhism, with its pantheon of heavenly buddhas and bodhisattvas and its idealistic metaphysics, was strikingly different in many respects from the Theravāda, it can be viewed as the development into finished systems of tendencies which had existed long before—a development favored and accelerated by the great historic changes taking place in northwestern India at that time. For over two hundred years, from the beginning of the second century B.C. onwards, this region was the prey of a succession of invaders—Bactrian Greeks, Scythians, Parthians, and a Central Asian people generally known to historians of India as Kushānas. As a result of these invasions Iranian and Western influences were felt much more strongly than before, and new peoples, with backgrounds very different from those of the folk among whom the religion arose, began to take interest in Buddhism.

A tendency to revere the Buddha as a god had probably existed in his own lifetime. In Indian religion, divinity is not something completely transcendent, or far exalted above all mortal things, as it is for the Jew, Christian, or Muslim, neither is it something concentrated in a single unique, omnipotent, and omniscient personality. In Indian religions godhead manifests itself in so many forms as to be almost if not quite ubiquitous, and every great sage or religious teacher is looked on as a special manifestation of divinity, in some sense a god in human form. How much more divine was the Buddha, to whom even the great god Brahmā himself did reverence, and who, in meditation, could far transcend the comparatively tawdry and transient heavens where the great gods dwelt, enter the world of formlessness, and pass thence to the ineffable Nirvāna itself? From the Buddhist point of view even the highest of the gods was liable to error, for Brahmā imagined himself to be the creator when in fact the world came into existence as a result of natural causes. The Buddha, on the other hand, was omniscient.

Yet, according to theory, the Buddha had passed completely away from the universe, had ceased in any sense to be a person, and no longer affected the world in any way. But the formula of the "Three Jewels"—"I take refuge in the Buddha, I take refuge in the Doctrine, I take refuge in the Order"—became the Buddhist profession of faith very early, and was used by monk and layman alike. Taken literally the first clause was virtually meaningless, for it was impossible to take refuge in a being who had ceased to exist as such. Nevertheless the Buddha was worshiped from very early times, and he is said to have himself declared that all who had faith in him and devotion to him would obtain rebirth in heaven. In some of the earliest Buddhist sculpture, such as that of the stūpa of Bharhut (second or first century B.C.), crowds of worshipers are depicted as ecstatically prostrating themselves before the emblems of the Buddha—the wheel, the footprints, the empty throne, or the trident-shaped symbol representing the Three Jewels. At this time it was evidently not thought proper to portray the Buddha or to represent him by an icon; but in the first century A.D., whether from the influence of Greco-Roman ideas and art forms or from that of indigenous popular cults, the Buddha was represented and worshiped as an image.

A further development which encouraged the tendency to theism was the growth of interest in the *bodhisattva*. This term, literally meaning "Being of Wisdom," was first used in the sense of a previous incarnation of the Buddha. For many lives before his final birth as Siddhārtha Gautama the Bodhisattva did mighty deeds of compassion and self-sacrifice, as he gradually perfected himself in wisdom and virtue. Stories of the Bodhisattva, known as *Birth Stories* (*Jātaka*) and often adapted from popular legends and fables, were very popular with lay Buddhists, and numerous illustrations of them occur in early Buddhist art.

It is probable that even in the lifetime of the Buddha it was thought that he was only the last of a series of earlier Buddhas. Later, perhaps through Zoroastrian influence, it came to be believed that other Buddhas were yet to come, and interest developed in *Maitreya,* the future Buddha, whose coming was said to have been prophesied by the historical Buddha, and who, in years to come, would purify the world with his teaching. But if Maitreya was yet to come the chain of being which would ultimately lead to his birth (or, in the terminology of other sects, his soul) must be already in existence. Somewhere in the universe the being later to become Maitreya Buddha was already active for good. And if this one, how many more? Logically the world must be full of bodhisattvas, all striving for the welfare of other beings.

The next step in the development of the new form of Buddhism was the changing of the goal at which the believer aimed. According to Buddhist teaching there are three types of perfected beings—*Buddhas,* who perceived the truth for themselves and taught it to others, *Pratyeka-buddhas,* "Private Buddhas," who perceived it, but kept it to themselves and did not teach it, and *Arhants,*[1] "Worthies," who learned it from others, but fully realized it for themselves. According to earlier schools the earnest believer should aspire to become an Arhant, a perfected being for whom there was no rebirth, who already enjoyed Nirvāna, and who would finally enter that state after death, all vestiges of his personality dissolved. The road to Nirvāna was a hard one, and could only be covered in many lives of virtue and self-sacrifice; but nevertheless the goal began to be looked on as selfish. Surely a bodhisattva, after achieving such exalted compassion and altruism, and after reaching such a degree of perfection that he could render inestimable help to other striving beings, would not pass as quickly as possible to Nirvāna, where he could be of no further use, but would deliberately choose to remain in the world, using his spiritual power to help others, until all had found salvation. Passages of Mahāyāna scriptures describing the self-sacrifice of the bodhisattva for the welfare of all things living are among the most passionately altruistic in the world's religious literature.

The replacement of the ideal of the Arhant by that of the bodhisattva is the basic distinction between the old sects and the new, which came to

[1] Pali, *arahant,* usually translated "perfect being" in our extracts.

be known as *Mahāyāna*. Faith in the bodhisattvas and the help they afforded was thought to carry many beings along the road to bliss, while the older schools, which did not accept the bodhisattva ideal, could save only a few patient and strenuous souls.

The next stage in the evolution of the theology of the new Buddhism was the doctrine of the "Three Bodies" (*Trikāya*). If the true ideal was that of the bodhisattva, why did not Siddhārtha Gautama remain one, instead of becoming a Buddha and selfishly passing to Nirvāna? This paradox was answered by a theory of docetic type, which again probably had its origin in popular ideas prevalent among lay Buddhists at a very early period. Gautama was not in fact an ordinary man, but the manifestation of a great spiritual being. The Buddha had three bodies—the Body of Essence (*Dharmakāya*), the Body of Bliss (*Sambhogakāya*) and the Body of Magic Transformation (*Nirmāṇakāya*). It was the latter only which lived on earth as Siddhārtha Gautama, an emanation of the Body of Bliss, which dwelled forever in the heavens as a sort of supreme god. But the Body of Bliss was in turn the emanation of the Body of Essence, the ultimate Buddha, who pervaded and underlay the whole universe. Subtle philosophies and metaphysical systems were developed parallel with these theological ideas, and the Body of Essence was identified with Nirvāna. It was in fact the World Soul, the *Brahman* of the Upanishads, in a new form. In the fully developed Mahāyānist cosmology there were many Bodies of Bliss, all of them emanations of the single Body of Essence, but the heavenly Buddha chiefly concerned with our world was *Amitābha* ("Immeasurable Radiance"), who dwelt in *Sukhāvatī*, "the Happy Land," the heaven of the West. With him was associated the earthly Gautama Buddha, and a very potent and compassionate Bodhisattva, Avalokiteshvara ("the Lord Who Looks Down").

The older Buddhism and the newer flourished side by side in India during the early centuries of the Christian era, and we read of Buddhist monasteries in which some of the monks were Mahāyānist and some Hīnayānist. But in general the Buddhists of northwestern India were either Mahāyānists or members of Hīnayāna sects much affected by Mahāyānist ideas. The austerer forms of Hīnayāna seem to have been strongest in parts of western and southern India, and in Ceylon. It was from northwestern India, under the rule of the great Kushāna empire (first to third centuries A.D.) that Buddhism spread throughout central Asia to China; since it emanated from the northwest, it was chiefly of the Mahāyāna or near-Mahāyāna type.

We have already outlined the typical Mahāyāna teaching about the heavenly Buddhas and bodhisattvas, which is a matter of theology rather than of metaphysics. But Mahāyāna also produced philosophical theories which were argued with great ability, and which were influential on the thought of Hinduism, as well as on that of the Far East. The two chief schools of Mahāyāna philosophy were the *Mādhyamika* (Doctrine of the Middle Position) and the *Vijñānavāda* (Doctrine of Consciousness) or *Yogācāra* (The Way of Yoga). The former school, the founder of which was Nāgārjuna (first to second centuries A.D.), taught that the phenomenal world had only a qualified reality, thus opposing the doctrine of the Sarvāstivādins. A monk with defective eyesight may imagine that he sees flies in his begging bowl, and they have full reality for the percipient. Though the flies are not real the illusion of flies is. The Mādhyamika philosophers tried to prove that all our experience of the phenomenal world is like that of the short-sighted monk, that all beings labor under the constant illusion of perceiving things where in fact there is only emptiness. This Emptiness or Void (*Śūnyatā*) is all that truly exists, and hence the Mādhyamikas were sometimes also called *Śūnyavādins* ("exponents of the doctrine of emptiness"). But the phenomenal world is true pragmatically, and therefore has qualified reality for practical purposes. Yet the whole chain of existence is only real in this qualified sense, for it is composed of a series of transitory events, and these, being impermanent, cannot have reality in themselves. Emptiness, on the other hand, never changes. It is absolute truth and absolute being—in fact it is the same as Nirvāna and the Body of Essence of the Buddha.

Nāgārjuna's system, however, went farther than this. Nothing in the phenomenal world has full being, and all is ultimately unreal. Therefore every rational theory about the world is a theory about something unreal evolved by an unreal thinker with unreal thoughts. Thus, by the same process of reasoning, even the arguments of the Mādhyamika school in favor of the ultimate reality of Emptiness are unreal, and this argument against the Mādhyamika position is itself unreal, and so on in an infinite regress. Every logical argument can be reduced to absurdity by a process such as this. The ontological nihilism of Mādhyamika dialectic led to the development of a special sub-school devoted to logic, the *Prāsaṅgika*[2] which produced works of great subtlety.

The effect of Mādhyamika nihilism was not what might be expected. Skeptical philosophies in the West, such as that of existentialism, are generally strongly flavored with pessimism. The Mādhyamikas, however, were not pessimists. If the phenomenal world was ultimately unreal, Emptiness was real, for, though every logical proof of its existence was vitiated by the flaw of unreality, it could be experienced in meditation with a directness and certainty which the phenomenal world did not possess. The ultimate Emptiness was here and now, everywhere and all-embracing, and there was in fact no difference between the great Void and the phenomenal world. Thus all beings were already participants of the Emptiness which was Nirvāna, they were already Buddha if only they would realize it. This aspect of Mādhyamika philosophy was specially congenial to Chinese Buddhists, nurtured in the doctrine of the *Tao,* and it had much influence in the development of the special forms of Chinese and Japanese Buddhism, which often show a frank acceptance of the beauty of the world, and especially of the beauty of nature, as a vision of Nirvāna here and now.

The Vijnānavāda school was one of pure idealism, and may be compared to the systems of Berkeley and Hume. The whole universe exists only in the mind of the perceiver. The fact of illusion, as in the case of the flies in the short-sighted monk's bowl, or the experience of dreams, was adduced as evidence to show that all normal human experience was of the same type. It is possible for the monk in meditation to raise before his eyes visions of every kind which have quite as much vividness and semblance of truth as have ordinary perceptions; yet he knows that they have no objective reality. Perception therefore is no proof of the independent existence of any entity, and all perceptions may be explained as projections of the percipient mind. Vijnānavāda, like some Western idealist systems, found its chief logical difficulty in explaining the continuity and apparent regularity of the majority of our sense impressions, and in accounting for the fact that the impressions of most people who are looking at the same time in the same direction seem to cohere in a remarkably consistent manner. Bishop Berkeley, to escape this dilemma,

[2] So called from its preoccupation with *prasaṅga* the term used in Sanskrit logic for the *reductio ad absurdum.*

postulated a transcendent mind in which all phenomena were thoughts. The Vijnānavādins explained the regularity and coherence of sense impressions as due to an underlying store of perceptions (*ālayavijñāna*) evolving from the accumulation of traces of earlier sense-impressions. These are active, and produce impressions similar to themselves, according to a regular pattern, as seeds produce plants. Each being possesses one of these stores of perception, and beings which are generically alike will produce similar perceptions from their stores at the same time. By this strange conception, which bristles with logical difficulties and is one of the most difficult of all Indian philosophy, the Vijnānavādins managed to avoid the logical conclusion of idealism in solipsism. Moreover they admitted the existence of at least one entity independent of human thought—a pure and integral being without characteristics, about which nothing could truly be predicated because it was without predicates. This was called "Suchness" (*Tathatā*) and corresponded to the Emptiness or Void of the Mādhyamikas, and to the Brahman of Vedānta. Though the terminology is different the metaphysics of Mahāyāna Buddhism has much in common with the doctrines of some of the Upanishads and of Shankara. The latter probably learned much from Buddhism, and indeed was called by his opponents a crypto-Buddhist.

For the Vijnānavāda school salvation was to be obtained by exhausting the store of consciousness until it became pure being itself, and identical with the Suchness which was the only truly existent entity in the universe. The chief means of doing this, for those who had already reached a certain stage of spiritual development, was yogic praxis. Adepts of this school were taught to conjure up visions, so that, by realizing that visions and pragmatically real perceptions had the same vividness and subjective reality, they might become completely convinced of the total subjectivity of all phenomena. Thus the meditating monk would imagine himself a mighty god, leading an army of lesser gods against Māra, the spirit of the world and the flesh. The chief philosophers of the school were Asanga (fourth century A.D.) and Vasubandhu,[3] of about the same period. According to tradition Dinnāga, the greatest of the Buddhist logicians, was a disciple of Vasubandhu.

The canons of the Mahāyāna sects contain much material which also

[3] There may have been two Vasubandhus, one the approximate contemporary of Asanga and the other about a century later.

occurs in Pali, often expanded or adapted, but the interest of the Mahāyānists was largely directed to other scriptures, of which no counterparts exist in the Pali canon, and which, it was claimed, were also the pronouncements of the Buddha. These are the *Vaipulya Sūtras,* or "Expanded Discourses," of greater length than those in the Pali *Basket of Discourses* (*Sutta Piṭaka*), and written in Buddhist Sanskrit; in them the Buddha is supposed to have taught the doctrine of the heavenly Buddhas and bodhisattvas. Of these Mahāyāna sūtras pride of place must be taken by *The Lotus of the Good Law* (*Saddharmapuṇḍarīka*), which propounds all the major doctrines of Mahāyāna Buddhism in a fairly simple and good literary style with parables and poetic illustrations. In translation it is the most popular Buddhist scripture in China and Japan, the Japanese Buddhists of the Nichiren sect making it their sole canonical text. An important group of Mahāyāna texts is the *Discourses on the Perfection of Wisdom* (*Prajñāpāramitā Sūtras*), of which several exist, generally known by the number of verses[4] they contain, ranging from 700 to 100,000. The primary purpose of these is to explain and glorify the ten perfections (*pāramitā*) of the Bodhisattva, and especially the perfection of wisdom (prajnā), but they contain much of importance on other aspects of Buddhism. Other Mahāyāna sūtras are too numerous to mention.

The Bodhisattva

The essential difference between Mahāyāna and Theravāda Buddhism is in the doctrine of the bodhisattva, who, in Mahāyāna, becomes a divine savior, and whose example the believer is urged to follow. It must be remembered that all good Buddhists, from the Mahāyāna point of view, are bodhisattvas in the making, and the many descriptions of bodhisattvas in Mahāyāna texts provide ideals for the guidance of monk and layman alike. One of the chief qualities of the bodhisattva is his immense compassion for the world of mortals.

[From *Aṣṭasāhasrikā Prajñāpāramitā,* 22.402–3]

The bodhisattva is endowed with wisdom of a kind whereby he looks on all beings as though victims going to the slaughter. And immense compassion grips him. His divine eye sees . . . innumerable beings, and he is filled with great distress at what he sees, for many bear the burden of past

[4] Or more correctly the number of verses of 32 syllables each which they would contain if they had been versified. They are actually in prose.

deeds which will be punished in purgatory, others will have unfortunate rebirths which will divide them from the Buddha and his teachings, others must soon be slain, others are caught in the net of false doctrine, others cannot find the path (of salvation), while others have gained a favorable rebirth only to lose it again.

So he pours out his love and compassion upon all those beings, and attends to them, thinking, "I shall become the savior of all beings, and set them free from their sufferings."

The Mahāyāna Ideal Is Higher Than That of the Theravāda

Mahāyāna teachers claimed that the ideal of the Theravādins—complete loss of personality as perfected beings in Nirvāna—was fundamentally selfish and trivial. The truly perfected being should devote all his powers to saving suffering mortals. The following passage elucidates this point. It purports to be a dialogue between the Buddha and one of his chief disciples, Shāriputra (Pali *Sāriputta*).

[From *Pañcaviṃśatisāhasrikā Prajñāpāramitā,* pp. 40–41]

"What do you think, Shāriputra? Do any of the disciples[1] and Private Buddhas[2] ever think, 'After we have gained full enlightenment we will bring innumerable beings . . . to complete Nirvāna'?"

"Certainly not, Lord!"

"But," said the Lord, "the bodhisattva (has this resolve). . . . A firefly . . . doesn't imagine that its glow will light up all India or shine all over it, and so the disciples and Private Buddhas don't think that they should lead all beings to Nirvāna . . . after they have gained full enlightenment. But the disc of the sun, when it has risen, lights up all India and shines all over it. Similarly the bodhisattva, . . . when he has gained full enlightenment, brings countless beings to Nirvāna.

The Suffering Savior

In many passages of the Mahāyāna scriptures is to be found what purports to be the solemn resolve made by a bodhisattva at the beginning of his career. The following fine passage will appear particularly striking to Western readers, for in it the bodhisattva not only resolves to pity and help all mortal beings,

[1] *Śrāvaka,* literally "hearer," a term often applied by Mahāyāna writers especially to adherents of Theravāda.

[2] *Pratyeka-buddha,* one who has achieved full enlightenment through his own insight, but does not communicate his saving knowledge to others.

but also to share their intensest sufferings. Christians and Jews cannot fail to note resemblances to the concept of the suffering Savior in Christianity and to the "Servant Passages" of Isaiah (53:3–12). It is by no means impossible that there was some Christian influence on Mahāyāna Buddhism, for Christian missionaries were active in Persia very early, and it became a center from which Nestorian Christianity was diffused throughout Asia. From the middle of the third century A.D. Persian influence in Afghanistan and Northwestern India, which had always been felt, was intensified with the rise of the Sāsānian Empire; and it was in these regions that Mahāyāna Buddhism developed and flourished. Thus Christian influence cannot be ruled out. But it is equally possible that the similarities between the concepts of the suffering savior in Buddhism and Christianity are due to the fact that compassionate minds everywhere tend to think alike.

The work from which the following passage is taken, Shāntideva's *Compendium of Doctrine,* dates from the seventh century. It is extremely valuable because it consists of lengthy quotations from earlier Buddhist literature with brief comments by the compiler, and many of the passages quoted are from works which no longer survive in their original form. The following passages are quoted from two such works, the *Instructions of Akshayamati* (*Akṣayamati Nirdeśa*) and the *Sūtra of Vajradhvaja* (*Vajradhvaja Sūtra*).

[From *Śikṣāsamuccaya,* pp. 278–83]

The bodhisattva is lonely, with no . . . companion, and he puts on the armor of supreme wisdom. He acts himself, and leaves nothing to others, working with a will steeled with courage and strength. He is strong in his own strength . . . and he resolves thus:

"Whatever all beings should obtain, I will help them to obtain. . . . The virtue of generosity is not my helper—I am the helper of generosity. Nor do the virtues of morality, patience, courage, meditation and wisdom help me—it is I who help them.[3] The perfections of the bodhisattva do not support me—it is I who support them. . . . I alone, standing in this round and adamantine world, must subdue Māra, with all his hosts and chariots, and develop supreme enlightenment with the wisdom of instantaneous insight!" . . .

[3] These six, generosity (*dāna*), moral conduct (*śīla*), patience (*kṣānti*), courage or energy (*vīrya*), meditation (dhyāna) and wisdom (prajñā) are the *Pāramitās,* or virtues of the bodhisattva, which he has developed to perfection. Many sources add four further perfections—"skill in knowing the right means" to take to lead individual beings to salvation according to their several characters and circumstances (*upāyakauśalya*), determination (*praṇidhāna*), strength (*bala*), and knowledge (jñāna). Much attention was concentrated on these perfections, especially on the Perfection of Wisdom (*Prajñāpāramitā*), which was personified as a goddess, and after which numerous Buddhist texts were named.

Just as the rising sun, the child of the gods, is not stopped . . . by all the dust rising from the four continents of the earth . . . or by wreaths of smoke . . . or by rugged mountains, so the bodhisattva, the Great Being, . . . is not deterred from bringing to fruition the root of good, whether by the malice of others, . . . or by their sin or heresy, or by their agitation of mind. . . . He will not lay down his arms of enlightenment because of the corrupt generations of men, nor does he waver in his resolution to save the world because of their wretched quarrels. . . . He does not lose heart on account of their faults. . . .

"All creatures are in pain," he resolves, "all suffer from bad and hindering karma . . . so that they cannot see the Buddhas or hear the Law of Righteousness or know the Order. . . . All that mass of pain and evil karma I take in my own body. . . . I take upon myself the burden of sorrow; I resolve to do so; I endure it all. I do not turn back or run away, I do not tremble . . . I am not afraid . . . nor do I despair. Assuredly I must bear the burdens of all beings . . . for I have resolved to save them all. I must set them all free, I must save the whole world from the forest of birth, old age, disease, and rebirth, from misfortune and sin, from the round of birth and death, from the toils of heresy. . . . For all beings are caught in the net of craving, encompassed by ignorance, held by the desire for existence; they are doomed to destruction, shut in a cage of pain . . . ; they are ignorant, untrustworthy, full of doubts, always at loggerheads one with another, always prone to see evil; they cannot find a refuge in the ocean of existence; they are all on the edge of the gulf of destruction.

"I work to establish the kingdom of perfect wisdom for all beings. I care not at all for my own deliverance. I must save all beings from the torrent of rebirth with the raft of my omniscient mind. I must pull them back from the great precipice. I must free them from all misfortune, ferry them over the stream of rebirth.

"For I have taken upon myself, by my own will, the whole of the pain of all things living. Thus I dare try every abode of pain, in . . . every part of the universe, for I must not defraud the world of the root of good. I resolve to dwell in each state of misfortune through countless ages . . . for the salvation of all beings . . . for it is better that I alone suffer than that all beings sink to the worlds of misfortune. There I shall give myself into bondage, to redeem all the world from the forest of purgatory, from rebirth as beasts, from the realm of death. I shall bear all grief and pain in my own body, for the good of all things living. I venture to stand surety for all beings, speaking the truth, trustworthy, not breaking my word. I shall not forsake them. . . . I must so bring to fruition the root of goodness that all beings find the utmost joy, unheard of joy, the joy of omniscience. I must be their charioteer, I must be their leader, I must be their torchbearer, I must be their guide to safety. . . . I must not wait for the help of another, nor must I lose my resolution and leave my tasks to another. I must not turn back in my efforts to save all beings nor cease to use my merit for the destruction of all pain. And I must not be satisfied with small successes."

The Lost Son

One of the reasons for including this passage is its remarkable resemblance to the famous parable of St. Luke's Gospel (15:11–32). As the *Lotus of the Good Law,* from which the Buddhist story is taken, was probably in existence well before Christian ideas could have found their way to India via Persia, it is unlikely that this parable owes anything to the Christian one. Similarly it is unlikely that the Christian parable is indebted to the Buddhist. Probably we have here a case of religious minds of two widely separated cultures thinking along similar lines, as a result of similar, though not identical, religious experience. For this reason the resemblances and differences of the two stories are most instructive.[4]

The Prodigal of the Christian story squanders his patrimony in riotous living. The son in the Buddhist story is a wretched creature who can only wander about begging. His fault is not so much in squandering his property as in failing to acquire wealth (i.e., spiritual merit). The Prodigal returns to his father by his own free choice, after repenting his evil ways. In the Buddhist story it is only by chance that the son meets his father again; moreover the son does not recognize the father, though the father recognizes his son—thus the heavenly Buddha knows his children and works for their salvation, though they do not recognize him in his true character, and, if they get a glimpse of him, are afraid and try to avoid him—they feel much more at ease among their own earthbound kind, in "the poor quarter of the town," where their divine father sends his messengers (perhaps representing the Bodhisattvas) to find

[4] The text itself purports to give an interpretation of the parable in which the son toiling as a menial in his father's house is compared to the Hīnayāna monk, who is unaware of the true glory of the enlightenment to which he is heir. There is little doubt, however, that the story here turned to purposes of sectarian propaganda was originally meant to have a wider significance, and we believe our interpretation to be that demanded by the spirit of the parable.

them, bringing them home by force if need be. Here there is no question of a positive act of repentance, as in the Christian parable.

Unlike the Prodigal's father in the Christian story, who kills the fatted calf for his long-lost son, the father in the Buddhist story makes his son undergo a very long period of humble probation before raising him to the position which he merits by his birth. The heavenly Buddha cannot raise beings immediately from the filth and poverty of the earthly gutter to the full glory of his own heavenly palace, for they are so earthbound that, if brought to it at once, they would suffer agonies of fear, embarrassment, and confusion, and might well insist on returning to the gutter again. So they must undergo many years of preparation for their high estate, toiling daily among the material dross of this world, earnestly and loyally striving to make the world a tidier place. Like the father in the story, the heavenly Buddha will cover his glory with earthly dust and appear to his children as a historical Buddha to encourage and instruct them. Thus the Buddha shows the perfection of "skill in means," that is to say, in knowing the best means to take to lead each individual to the light according to the circumstances in which he is placed.

Gradually the son grows more and more familiar with the father, and loses his former fear of him, but still he does not know that he is his father's child. So men, even though pious and virtuous, and earnestly carrying out the Buddha's will, do not know that they are already in Heaven; their lives are still to some extent earthbound, and though the Buddha offers them all his wealth of bliss long habit keeps them from enjoying it.

Only when the father is near death does he reveal himself to his son. This seems at first to weaken the analogy, for heavenly Buddhas do not die. But in fact the conclusion of the parable is quite appropriate, for when man has fulfilled his tasks and carried out his stewardship, that is to say when he has reached the highest stage of self-development, he finds that the heavenly Buddha has ceased to exist for him, that nothing is truly real but the great Emptiness which is peace and Nirvāna.

[From *Saddharmapuṇḍarīka,* 4.101 ff.]

A man parted from his father and went to another city; and he dwelt there many years. . . . The father grew rich and the son poor. While the son wandered in all directions [begging] in order to get food and clothes, the father moved to another land, where he lived in great luxury, . . . wealthy from business, money-lending, and trade. In course of time the son, wandering in search of his living through town and country, came to the city in which his father dwelled. Now the poor man's father . . . forever thought of the son whom he had lost . . . years ago, but he told no one of this, though he grieved inwardly, and thought: "I am old, and well advanced in years, and though I have great possessions I have no son.

Alas that time should do its work upon me, and that all this wealth should perish unused! . . . It would be bliss indeed if my son might enjoy all my wealth!"

Then the poor man, in search of food and clothing, came to the rich man's home. And the rich man was sitting in great pomp at the gate of his house, surrounded by a large throng of attendants, . . . on a splendid throne, with a footstool inlaid with gold and silver, under a wide awning decked with pearls and flowers and adorned with hanging garlands of jewels; and he transacted business to the value of millions of gold pieces, all the while fanned by a fly-whisk. . . . When he saw him the poor man was terrified . . . and the hair of his body stood on end, for he thought that he had happened on a king or on some high officer of state, and had no business there. "I must go," he thought, "to the poor quarter of the town, where I'll get food and clothing without trouble. If I stop here they'll seize me and set me to do forced labor, or some other disaster will befall me!" So he quickly ran away. . . .

But the rich man . . . recognized his son as soon as he saw him; and he was full of joy . . . and thought: "This is wonderful! I have found him who shall enjoy my riches. He of whom I thought constantly has come back, now that I am old and full of years!" Then, longing for his son, he sent swift messengers, telling them to go and fetch him quickly. They ran at full speed and overtook him; the poor man trembled with fear, the hair of his body stood on end . . . and he uttered a cry of distress and exclaimed, "I've done you no wrong!" But they dragged him along by force . . . until . . . fearful that he would be killed or beaten, he fainted and fell on the ground. His father in dismay said to the men, "Don't drag him along in that way!" and, without saying more, he sprinkled his face with cold water—for though he knew that the poor man was his son, he realized that his estate was very humble, while his own was very high.

So the householder told no one that the poor man was his son. He ordered one of his servants to tell the poor man that he was free to go where he chose. . . . And the poor man was amazed [that he was allowed to go free], and he went off to the poor quarter of the town in search of food and clothing. Now in order to attract him back the rich man made use of the virtue of "skill in means." He called two men of low caste and of no great dignity and told them: "Go to that poor man . . . and hire him in your own names to do work in my house at double the normal daily wage; and if he asks what work he has to do tell him that he has to help clear away the refuse-dump." So these two men and the poor man cleared the refuse every day . . . in the house of the rich man, and lived in a straw hut nearby. . . . And the rich man saw through a window his son clearing refuse, and was again filled with compassion. So he came down, took off his wreath and jewels and rich clothes, put on dirty garments, covered his body with dust, and, taking a basket in his hand, went up to his son. And he greeted him at a distance and said, "Take this basket and clear away the dust at once!" By this means he managed to speak to his son. [And as time went on he spoke more often to him, and thus he gradually encouraged him. First he urged him to] remain in his service and not take another job, offering him double wages, together with any small extras that he might require, such as the price of a cooking-pot . . . or food and clothes. Then he offered him his own cloak, if he should want it. . . . And at last he said: "You must be cheerful, my good fellow, and think of me as a father . . . for I'm older than you and you've done me good service in clearing away my refuse. As long as you've worked for me you've shown no roguery or guile. . . . I've not noticed one of the vices in you that I've noticed in my other servants! From now on you are like my own son to me!"

Thenceforward the householder called the poor man "son," and the latter felt towards the householder as a son feels towards his father. So the householder, full of longing and love for his son, employed him in clearing away refuse for twenty years. By the end of that time the poor man felt quite at home in the house, and came and went as he chose, though he still lived in the straw hut.

Then the householder fell ill, and felt that the hour of his death was near. So he said to the poor man: "Come, my dear man! I have great riches, . . . and am very sick. I need someone upon whom I can bestow my wealth as a deposit, and you must accept it. From now on you are just as much its owner as I am, but you must not squander it." And the poor man accepted the rich man's wealth, . . . but personally he cared nothing for it, and asked for no share of it, not even the price of a measure of flour. He still lived in the straw hut, and thought of himself as just as poor as before.

Thus the householder proved that his son was frugal, mature, and mentally developed, and that though he knew that he was now wealthy he still remembered his past poverty, and was still . . . humble and meek. . . . So he sent for the poor man again, presented him before a gathering of his relatives, and, in the presence of the king, his officers, and the people of town and country, he said: "Listen, gentlemen! This is my son, whom I begot. . . . To him I leave all my family revenues, and my private wealth he shall have as his own."

Against Self-Mortification

Buddhists of both "vehicles" strongly deprecated the exaggerated ascetic practices of other sects, as they did taboos connected with food and ritual purity. Suffering, for the Buddhist, has no intrinsic value or purificatory effect, unless it is undertaken voluntarily for the sake of others, in the manner of the bodhisattva, who elects to dwell in all the purgatories in order to relieve the beings in torment there. The man who mortifies the flesh in order to gain rebirth in heaven is completely selfish and misguided, and his last state will be worse than his first.

The following verses are from the *Deeds of the Buddha,* a metrical life of the Buddha by Ashvaghosha (first to second centuries A.D.), which is among the masterpieces of Sanskrit poetry and one of the earliest known poems in the courtly style. Though it is written in Sanskrit it contains no specifically Mahāyāna features; but it is included among Mahāyāna literature, since it was preserved by the Mahāyānist sects. The verses are spoken by the future Buddha during his period of spiritual apprenticeship, when he realizes that self-mortification is useless and wrong.

[From *Buddhacarita,* 7.20 ff.]

Penance in its various forms is essentially sorrowful;
  And, at best, the reward of penance is heaven.
Yet all the worlds are liable to change,
  So the efforts of the hermitages are of little use.

Those who forsake the kin they love and their pleasures
  To perform penance and win a place in heaven
Must leave it in the end
  And go to greater bondage.

The man who pains his body and calls it penance
  In the hope of continuing to satisfy desire

Does not perceive the evils of rebirth,
  And through much sorrow goes to further sorrow.

All living beings are afraid of death
  And yet they all strive to be born again;
As they act thus death is inevitable,
  And they are plunged in that which they most fear.

Some suffer hardship for mere worldly gain;
  Others will take to penance in hope of heaven.
All beings fail in their hopeful search for bliss,
  And fall, poor wretches, into dire calamity.

Not that the effort is to be blamed which leaves
  The base and seeks the higher aim,
But wise men should labor with an equal zeal
  To reach the goal where further toil is needless.

If it is Right to mortify the flesh
  The body's ease is contrary to Right;
Thus if, by doing Right, joy is obtained hereafter
  Righteousness must flower in Unrighteousness.

The body is commanded by the mind,
  Through mind it acts, through mind it ceases to act.
All that is needed is to subdue the mind,
  For the body is a log of wood without it.

If merit comes from purity of food [5]
  Then even the deer gain merit,
And those who do not win the reward of righteousness
  But by an unlucky fate have lost their wealth. . . .

And those who try to purify their deeds
  By ablutions at a place which they hold sacred—

[5] From the context it appears that this verse is specially directed at the Jains, whose monks were given to very severe fasting, sometimes even to death.

These merely give their hearts some satisfaction,
For water will not purify men's sin.

Joy in All Things

Joy is one of the cardinal virtues of Buddhism, and the bodhisattva, who is the example which all Mahāyāna Buddhists are expected to follow as far as their powers allow, has so trained his mind that even in the most painful and unhappy situations it is still full of calm inner joy. The following passage is from the *Compendium of Doctrine;* the first paragraph is the work of the author, Shāntideva, while the second is quoted from a lost sūtra, the *Meeting of Father and Son* (*Pitṛputrasamāgama*).

[From *Śikṣāsamuccaya,* 181 f.]

Indeed nothing is difficult after practice. Simple folk, such as porters, fishermen and plowmen, for instance, are not overcome by depression, for their minds are marked by the scars of the many pains with which they earn their humble livings, and which they have learned to bear. How much the more should one be cheerful in a task of which the purpose is to reach the incomparable state where all the joys of all beings, all the joys of the bodhisattvas are to be found. . . . Consciousness of sorrow and joy comes by habit; so, if whenever sorrow arises we make a habit of associating with it a feeling of joy, consciousness of joy will indeed arise. The fruit of this is a contemplative spirit full of joy in all things. . . .

So the bodhisattva . . . is happy even when subjected to the tortures of hell. . . . When he is being beaten with canes or whips, when he is thrown into prison, he still feels happy.[6] . . . For . . . this was the resolve of the Great Being, the bodhisattva: "May those who feed me win the joy of tranquillity and peace, with those who protect me, honor me, respect me, and revere me. And those who revile me, afflict me, beat me, cut me in pieces with their swords, or take my life—may they all obtain the joy of complete enlightenment, may they be awakened to perfect and sublime enlightenment." With such thoughts and actions and resolves he cultivates . . . and develops the consciousness of joy in his relations with all beings, and so he acquires a contemplative spirit filled with joy in all things . . . and becomes imperturbable—not to be shaken by all the deeds of Māra.

[6] Here a long list of the most gruesome tortures is omitted.

The Good Deeds of the Bodhisattva

We have seen that the bodhisattva has ten "Perfections." A further list of good qualities is sometimes attributed to him. Notice that the emphasis is on the positive virtues of altruism, benevolence, and compassion.

[From *Tathāgataguhya Sūtra, Śikṣāsamuccaya,* p. 274]

There are ten ways by which a bodhisattva gains . . . strength: . . . .
He will give up his body and his life . . . but he will not give up the Law of Righteousness.
He bows humbly to all beings, and does not increase in pride.
He has compassion on the weak and does not dislike them.
He gives the best food to those who are hungry.
He protects those who are afraid.
He strives for the healing of those who are sick.
He delights the poor with his riches.
He repairs the shrines of the Buddha with plaster.
He speaks to all beings pleasingly.
He shares his riches with those afflicted by poverty.
He bears the burdens of those who are tired and weary.

The Evils of Meat-Eating

According to the scriptures of the Theravāda school the Buddha allowed his followers to eat flesh if they were not responsible for killing the animal providing the meat, and if it was not specially killed to feed them. To this day most Buddhists in Ceylon and other lands where Theravāda prevails eat meat and fish, which are supplied by Muslim or Christian butchers or fishermen. Like the great Ashoka, however, many Buddhists have felt that meat-eating of any kind is out of harmony with the spirit of the Law of Righteousness, and have been vegetarians. The following passage criticizes the Theravāda teaching on meat-eating, and enjoins strict vegetarianism. The words are attributed to the Buddha.

[From *Laṅkāvatāra Sūtra,* pp. 245 ff.]

Here in this long journey of birth-and-death there is no living being who . . . has not at some time been your mother or father, brother or sister, son or daughter. . . . So how can the bodhisattva, who wishes to treat all beings as though they were himself, . . . eat the flesh of any living being. . . . Therefore, wherever living beings evolve, men should feel toward them as to their own kin, and, looking on all beings as their only child, should refrain from eating meat. . . .

The bodhisattva, . . . desirous of cultivating the virtue of love, should not eat meat, lest he cause terror to living beings. Dogs, when they see, even at a distance, an outcaste . . . who likes eating meat, are terrified with fear, and think, "They are the dealers of death, they will kill us!" Even the animalculae in earth and air and water, who have a very keen sense of smell, will detect at a distance the odor of the demons in meat-eaters, and will run away as fast as they can from the death which threatens them. . . .

Moreover the meat-eater sleeps in sorrow and wakes in sorrow. All his dreams are nightmares, and they make his hair stand on end. . . . Things other than human sap his vitality. Often he is struck with terror, and trembles without cause. . . . He knows no measure in his eating, and there is no flavor, digestibility, or nourishment in his food. His bowels are filled with worms and other creatures, which are the cause of leprosy; and he ceases to think of resisting diseases. . . .

It is not true . . . that meat is right and proper for the disciple when the animal was not killed by himself or by his orders, and when it was not killed specially for him. . . . Pressed by a desire for the taste of meat people may string together their sophistries in defense of meat-eating . . . and declare that the Lord permitted meat as legitimate food, that it occurs in the list of permitted foods, and that he himself ate it. But . . . it is nowhere allowed in the sūtras as a . . . legitimate food. . . . All meat-eating in any form or manner and in any circumstances is prohibited, unconditionally and once and for all.

The Gift of Food

From the Buddhist point of view, as Ashoka said, there is no greater gift than the gift of the Law of Righteousness; but Buddhism never disparaged the value or merit of practical acts of kindness and charity. The Buddhists, as we have seen, set much store on physical wellbeing. The passage which follows will show that poverty and hunger, unless voluntarily undertaken for a worthy cause, were looked on as unmitigated evils, liable to lead to sin and hence to an unhappy rebirth.

This passage is from the Tamil classic *Maṇimēgalai,* perhaps of the sixth century A.D., which is wholly Buddhist in inspiration, and concludes with an exposition of Mahāyāna logic and the doctrine of the Chain of Causation. The poem tells of Manimēgalai, a beautiful girl who, after many adventures, realized the uselessness and sorrow of the world and became a Buddhist nun. Here, led by a demi-goddess, she finds a magic bowl, which gives an inexhaustible supply of food.

[From *Maṇimēgalai,* 11.55–122]

The bowl rose in the water and . . . moved toward her hand. She was glad beyond measure, and sang a hymn in praise of the Buddha:

"Hail the feet of the hero, the victor over Māra!
Hail the feet of him who destroyed the path of evil!
Hail the feet of the Great One, setting men on the road of Righteousness!
Hail the feet of the All Wise One, who gives others the eye of wisdom!
Hail the feet of him whose ears are deaf to evil!
Hail the feet of him whose tongue never uttered untruth!
Hail the feet of him who went down to purgatory to put an end to suffering. . . .
My tongue cannot praise you duly—All I can do is to bend my body at your feet!"

While she was praying thus Tīvatilagai told her of the pains of hunger and of the virtue of those who help living beings to satisfy it. "Hunger," she said to Manimēgalai, "ruins good birth, and destroys all nobility; it destroys the love of learned men for their learning, even though they previously thought it the most valuable thing in life; hunger takes away all sense of shame, and ruins the beauty of the features; and it even forces men to stand with their wives at the doors of others. This is the nature of hunger, the source of evil craving, and those who relieve it the tongue cannot praise too highly! Food given to those who can afford it is charity wasted,[7] but food given to relieve the hunger of those who cannot satisfy it otherwise is charity indeed, and those who give it will prosper in this world, for those who give food give life. So go on and give food to allay the hunger of those who are hungry."

"In a past life," said Manimēgalai, "my husband died . . . and I mounted the pyre with him. As I burned I remembered that I had once given food to a Buddhist monk named Sādusakkāra; and I believe it is because of this virtuous thought at the moment of death that this bowl of

[7] This may be a criticism of the Hindu virtue of *dāna,* which is usually translated "charity," but includes feasts given to brāhmans who may be much richer than the donor.

plenty has come into my hands. Just as a mother's breast begins to give milk at the mere sight of her hungry baby, so may this bowl in my hand always give food . . . at the sight of those who suffer hunger and wander even in pouring rain or scorching sun in search of food to relieve it."

The Three Bodies of the Buddha

The following passage expounds the doctrine of the Three Bodies (*Trikāya*). It is taken from Asanga's *Ornament of Mahāyāna Sūtras,* a versified compendium of Mahāyāna doctrine, with a prose commentary. The latter is quoted where it throws light on the difficult and elliptical verses.

[From *Mahāyānasūtrālankāra,* 9.60–66]

The Body of Essence, the Body of Bliss,[8] the Created Body—these are the bodies of the Buddhas.
The first is the basis of the two others.
The Body of Bliss varies in all the planes of the Universe, according to region,
In name, in form, and in experience of phenomena.
But the Body of Essence, uniform and subtle, is inherent in the Body of Bliss,
And through the one the other controls its experience, when it manifests itself at will.

Commentary: The Body of Essence is uniform for all the Buddhas, Because there is no real difference between them. . . .

The Created Body displays with skill birth, enlightenment, and Nirvāna,
For it possesses much magic power to lead men to enlightenment.
The Body of the Buddhas is wholly comprised in these three bodies. . . .
In basis, tendency, and act they are uniform.
They are stable by nature, by persistence, and by connection.

Commentary: The Three Bodies are one and the same for all the Buddhas for three reasons: *basis,* for the basis of phenomena[9] is indivisible; *tendency,* because there is no tendency particular to one Buddha and not

[8] *Sambhoga,* more literally "enjoyment"; in some contexts it implies little more than "experience."

[9] *Dharmadhātu,* the Absolute.

to another; and *act,* because their actions are common to all. And the Three Bodies have a threefold stability: by *nature,* for the Body of Essence is essentially stable; by *persistence,* for the Body of Bliss experiences phenomena unceasingly; and by *connection,* for the Created Body, once it has passed away, shows its metamorphoses again and again.

Emptiness

The doctrine of *Śūnyatā,* "Emptiness" or "the Void," is aptly expressed in these fine verses from the *Multitude of Graceful Actions,* a life of the Buddha in mixed verse and prose, replete with marvels and miracles of all kinds, which formed the basis of Sir Edwin Arnold's famous poem, *The Light of Asia.*

[From *Lalitavistara,* 13.175–77]

All things conditioned are instable, impermanent,
  Fragile in essence, as an unbaked pot,
Like something borrowed, or a city founded on sand,
  They last a short while only.

They are inevitably destroyed,
  Like plaster washed off in the rains,
Like the sandy bank of a river—
  They are conditioned, and their true nature is frail.

They are like the flame of a lamp,
  Which rises suddenly and as soon goes out.
They have no power of endurance, like the wind
  Or like foam, unsubstantial, essentially feeble.

They have no inner power, being essentially empty,
  Like the stem of a plantain, if one thinks clearly,
Like conjuring tricks deluding the mind,
  Or a fist closed on nothing to tease a child. . . .

From wisps of grass the rope is spun
  By dint of exertion.
By turns of the wheel the buckets are raised from the well,
  Yet each turn of itself is futile.

So the turning of all the components of becoming
  Arises from the interaction of one with another.
In the unit the turning cannot be traced
  Either at the beginning or end.

Where the seed is, there is the young plant,
  But the seed has not the nature of the plant,
Nor is it something other than the plant, nor is it the plant—
  So is the nature of the Law of Righteousness, neither transient nor eternal.

All things conditioned are conditioned by ignorance,
  And on final analysis they do not exist,
For they and the conditioning ignorance alike are Emptiness
  In their essential nature, without power of action. . . .

The mystic knows the beginning and end
  Of consciousness, its production and passing away—
He knows that it came from nowhere and returns to nowhere,
  And is empty [of reality], like a conjuring trick.

Through the concomitance of three factors—
  Firesticks, fuel, and the work of the hand—
Fire is kindled. It serves its purpose
  And quickly goes out again.

A wise man may seek here, there, and everywhere
  Whence it has come, and whither it has gone,
Through every region in all directions,
  But he cannot find it in its essential nature. . . .

Thus all things in this world of contingence
  Are dependent on causes and conditions.
The mystic knows what is true reality,
  And sees all conditioned things as empty and powerless.

Faith in Emptiness

The following passage needs little comment. Belief in *Śūnyavāda,* the doctrine of Emptiness, encourages a stoical and noble equanimity.

[From *Dharmasaṅgīti Sūtra, Śikṣāsamuccaya,* p. 264]

He who maintains the doctrine of Emptiness is not allured by the things of the world, because they have no basis. He is not excited by gain or dejected by loss. Fame does not dazzle him and infamy does not shame him. Scorn does not repel him, praise does not attract him. Pleasure does not please him, pain does not trouble him. He who is not allured by the things of the world knows Emptiness, and one who maintains the doctrine of Emptiness has neither likes nor dislikes. What he likes he knows to be only Emptiness and sees it as such.

Karma and Rebirth

In an illusory world, rebirth is also illusory. The things a man craves for have no more reality than a dream, but he craves nevertheless, and hence his illusory ego is reborn in a new but equally illusory body. Notice the importance of the last conscious thought before death, which plays a very decisive part in the nature of the rebirth. The chief speaker in the following dialogue is said to be the Buddha.

[From *Pitṛputrasamāgama, Śikṣāsamuccaya,* pp. 251–52]

"The senses are as though illusions and their objects as dreams. For instance a sleeping man might dream that he had made love to a beautiful country girl, and he might remember her when he awoke. What do you think— . . . does the beautiful girl he dreamed of really exist?"

"No, Lord."

"And would the man be wise to remember the girl of his dreams, or to believe that he had really made love to her?"

"No, Lord, because she doesn't really exist at all, so how could he have made love to her—though of course he might think he did under the influence of weakness or fatigue."

"In just the same way a foolish and ignorant man of the world sees pleasant forms and believes in their existence. Hence he is pleased, and so he feels passion and acts accordingly. . . . But from the very beginning his actions are feeble, impeded, wasted, and changed in their course by circumstances. . . . And when he ends his days, as the time of death approaches, his vitality is obstructed with the exhaustion of his allotted span of years, the karma that fell to his lot dwindles, and hence his previous actions form the object of the last thought of his mind as it disappears. Then, just as the man on first waking from sleep thinks of the country girl about whom he dreamed, the first thought on rebirth arises from two causes—the last thought of the previous life as its governing principle, and the actions of the previous life as its basis. Thus a man is reborn in the purgatories, or as an animal, a spirit, a demon, a human being, or a god. . . . The stopping of the last thought is known as decease, the appearance of the first thought as rebirth. Nothing passes from life to life, but decease and rebirth take place nevertheless. . . . But the last thought, the actions (karma), and the first thought, when they arise come from nowhere and when they cease go nowhere, for all are essentially defective, of themselves empty. . . . In the whole process no one acts and no one experiences the results of action, except by verbal convention.

Suchness

The Vijnānavādin school called their conception of the Absolute *Tathatā* or "Suchness," in which all phenomenal appearances are lost in the one ultimate being.

The following passage is taken from a text which was translated into Chinese in the seventh century from a recension more interesting than the extant Sanskrit form. The whole passage considers the "Suchness" of the five components of being in turn. Here we give only the passage relating to the first of these.[10]

[From *Mahāprajñāpāramitā,* ch. 29, 1]

What is meant by . . . knowing in accordance with truth the marks of form? It means that a bodhisattva . . . knows that form is nothing but holes and cracks and is indeed a mass of bubbles, with a nature that has no hardness or solidity. . . .

What is meant by . . . knowing in accordance with truth the origin and extinction of form? It means that a bodhisattva . . . knows . . . that when form originates it comes from nowhere and when it is extin-

[10] Translated by Dr. Arthur Waley from the Chinese version of Hsüan Tsang. Reprinted by permission of Messrs. Bruno Cassirer, Oxford, from *Buddhist Texts through the Ages,* ed. by Edward Conze, Oxford, 1954, p. 154 f.

guished it goes nowhere, but that though it neither comes nor goes yet its origination and extinction do jointly exist. . . .

What is meant by knowing . . . in accordance with truth about the Suchness of form? It means that a bodhisattva . . . knows . . . that Suchness of form is not subject to origination or extinction, that it neither comes nor goes, is neither foul nor clean, neither increases nor diminishes, is constant in its own nature, is never empty, false or changeful, and is therefore called Suchness.

All Depends on the Mind

The following passage expresses the idealism of Mahāyāna thought.

[From *Ratnamegha Sūtra, Śikṣāsamuccaya,* p. 121–22]

All phenomena originate in the mind, and when the mind is fully known all phenomena are fully known. For by the mind the world is led . . . and through the mind karma is piled up, whether good or evil. The mind swings like a firebrand,[11] the mind rears up like a wave, the mind burns like a forest fire, like a great flood the mind bears all things away. The bodhisattva, thoroughly examining the nature of things, dwells in ever-present mindfulness of the activity of the mind, and so he does not fall into the mind's power, but the mind comes under his control. And with the mind under his control all phenomena are under his control.

Nirvāna Is Here and Now

The two following passages, the first Mādhyamika, and the second Vijnānavādin in tendency, illustrate the Mahāyāna doctrine that Nirvāna, the highest state, Pure Being, the Absolute, the Buddha's Body of Essence, is present at all times and everywhere, and needs only to be recognized. Thus the older pessimism of Buddhism is replaced by what is almost optimism. With this change of outlook comes an impatience with the learned philosophers and moralists who repeat their long and dreary sermons on the woes of samsāra, the round of birth-and-death. Though this attitude may have contributed to the antinomian tendencies of tantric Buddhism, it will probably stir an answering chord in many Western minds. Most people are like the man in the parable of the Lost Son, who year after year cleared away the refuse of his father's house without knowing that he was the son and heir.

[11] An allusion to a famous simile. The world is like a firebrand which, when swung round in the hand, resembles a solid wheel of flame.

[From *Śikṣāsamuccaya*, p. 257]

That which the Lord revealed in his perfect enlightenment was not form or sensation or perception or psychic constructions or thought; for none of these five components come into being, neither does supreme wisdom come into being . . . and how can that which does not come into being know that which also does not come into being? Since nothing can be grasped, what is the Buddha, what is wisdom, what is the bodhisattva, what is revelation? All the components are by nature empty—just convention, just names, agreed tokens, coverings. . . .

Thus all things are the perfection of being, infinite perfection, unobscured perfection, unconditioned perfection. All things are enlightenment, for they must be recognized as without essential nature—even the five greatest sins [12] are enlightenment, for enlightenment has no essential nature and neither have the five greatest sins. Thus those who seek for Nirvāna are to be laughed at, for the man in the midst of birth-and-death is also seeking Nirvāna.

[From *Laṅkāvatāra Sūtra*, pp. 61–62]

Those who are afraid of the sorrow which arises from . . . the round of birth-and-death seek for Nirvāna; they do not realize that between birth-and-death and Nirvāna there is really no difference at all. They see Nirvāna as the absence of all . . . becoming, and the cessation of all contact of sense-organ and sense-object, and they will not understand that it is really only the inner realization of the store of impressions.[13] . . . Hence they teach the three Vehicles,[14] but not the doctrine that nothing truly exists but the mind, in which are no images. Therefore . . . they do not know the extent of what has been perceived by the minds of past, present, and future Buddhas, and continue in the conviction that the world extends beyond the range of the mind's eye. . . . And so they keep on rolling . . . on the wheel of birth-and-death.

Praise of Dharma

Dharma, the cosmic Law of Righteousness proclaimed by the Buddha, was revered quite as highly by the Mahāyānists as by the Theravādins. The ulti-

[12] Murdering one's mother, murdering one's father, murdering a perfected being (*arhant*), trying to destroy the Buddhist Order, and maliciously injuring a Buddha.

[13] *Ālayavijñāna*.

[14] The two "Lesser Vehicles" (to salvation) of the older Buddhism—namely, those of the disciples and of Private Buddhas—and the vehicle of the bodhisattva.

mate body of the Buddha, which was roughly equivalent to the World-Soul of the Hindus, was called the Dharma-body, and the basic element of the universe was also often known as *Dharma-dhātu,* "the Raw-material of the Law," especially by the Vijnānavāda.[15] The following passage, perhaps originally intended for liturgical purposes, exemplifies the mystical attitude toward Dharma, which was widespread in later Buddhism. Here Dharma seems to have much in common with the *Tao* of Lao Tzu. Notice that it is prior to the heavenly Buddhas themselves.

[From *Dharmasaṅgīti Sūtra, Śikṣāsamuccaya,* pp. 322–23]

The blessed Buddhas, of virtues endless and limitless, are born of the Law of Righteousness; they dwell in the Law, are fashioned by the Law; they have the Law as their master, the Law as their light, the Law as their field of action, the Law as their refuge. They are produced by the Law . . . and all the joys in this world and the next are born of the Law and produced by the Law. . . .

The Law is equal, equal for all beings. For low or middle or high the Law cares nothing.
So must I make my thought like the Law.
The Law has no regard for the pleasant. Impartial is the Law.
So must I make my thought like the Law.
The Law is not dependent upon time. Timeless is the Law. . . .
So must I make my thought like the Law.
The Law is not in the lofty without being in the low. Neither up nor down will the Law bend.
So must I make my thought like the Law.
The Law is not in that which is whole without being in that which is broken. Devoid of all superiority or inferiority is the Law.
So must I make my thought like the Law.
The Law is not in the noble without being in the humble. No care for fields of activity has the Law.
So must I make my thought like the Law.
The Law is not in the day without being in the night. . . . Ever firm is the Law.
So must I make my thought like the Law.
The Law does not lose the occasion of conversion. There is never delay with the Law.

[15] Or, as many philosophers of this school would have interpreted it, "the Raw-material of Phenomena," since *dharma* in Buddhism had also a special philosophical connotation.

So must I make my thought like the Law.

The Law has neither shortage nor abundance. Immeasurable, innumerable is the Law. Like space it never lessens or grows.

So must I make my thought like the Law.

The Law is not guarded by beings. Beings are protected by the Law.

So must I make my thought like the Law.

The Law does not seek refuge. The refuge of all the world is the Law.

So must I make my thought like the Law.

The Law has none who can resist it. Irresistible is the Law.

So must I make my thought like the Law.

The Law has no preferences. Without preference is the Law.

So must I make my thought like the Law.

The Law has no fear of the terrors of birth-and-death, nor is it lured by Nirvāna. Ever without misgiving is the Law.

So must I make my thought like the Law.

Perfect Wisdom Personified

Prajñāpāramitā, the Perfection of Wisdom, is praised in many passages of Mahāyāna literature. As with the early Jews, the divine Wisdom was personified,[16] but the process went much further with the Buddhists than with the Jews, for in India *Prajñāpāramitā* became a goddess worshiped in the form of an icon. She was especially cultivated in the Vajrayāna, but by no means neglected in Mahāyānist sects.

[From *Aṣṭasāhasrikā Prajñāpāramitā,* 7.170–71]

Perfect Wisdom spreads her radiance, . . . and is worthy of worship. Spotless, the whole world cannot stain her. . . . In her we may find refuge; her works are most excellent; she brings us to safety under the sheltering wings of enlightenment. She brings light to the blind, that all fears and calamities may be dispelled, . . . and she scatters the gloom and darkness of delusion. She leads those who have gone astray to the right path. She is omniscience; without beginning or end is Perfect Wisdom, who has Emptiness as her characteristic mark; she is the mother of the Bodhisattvas. . . . She cannot be struck down, the protector of the unprotected, . . . the Perfect Wisdom of the Buddhas, she turns the Wheel of the Law.

[16] Compare especially Proverbs 8 and 9:1–6.

The Blessings of Peace[17]

The following passage is one of the few in the literature of early India which call upon the many kings of the land to forget their quarrels and live together in peace. It seems to contain an implicit criticism of the Hindu ideals of kingship, which encouraged kings to aim at territorial aggrandizement, and to attack their neighbors without good reason, in order to gain homage and tribute.

In the sixth section of the *Sūtra of the Excellent Golden Light,* the four great Kings Vaishravana, Dhritarāshtra, Virūdhaka, and Virūpāksha, who are the gods guarding the four quarters of the earth and correspond to the *Lokapālas* or world-protectors of Hindu mythology, approach the Buddha and declare that they will give their special protection to those earthly kings who patronize monks who recite the sūtra, and encourage its propagation in their domains. The Buddha replies with the words which follow. The sūtra probably belongs to the third or fourth century A.D., before the full expansion of the Gupta empire, when warfare was widespread. The reference to the title *devaputra,* "Son of the Gods," in the passage quoted after the following suggests that it emanated from northwestern India, where *devaputra* was a royal title of the Kushāna kings.

[From *Suvarṇaprabhāsottama Sūtra,* 6, pp. 73–75]

Protect all those royal families, cities, lands, and provinces, save them, cherish them, guard them, ward off invasion from them, give them peace and prosperity. Keep them free from all fear, calamity, and evil portent. Turn back the troops of their enemies and create in all the earthly kings of India a desire to avoid fighting, attacking, quarreling, or disputing with their neighbors. . . . When the eighty-four thousand kings of the eighty-four thousand cities of India are contented with their own territories and with their own kingly state and their own hoards of treasure they will not attack one another or raise mutual strife. They will gain their thrones by the due accumulation of the merit of former deeds; they will be satisfied with their own kingly state, and will not destroy one another, nor show their mettle by laying waste whole provinces. When all the eighty-four thousand kings of the eighty-four thousand capital cities of India think of their mutual welfare and feel mutual affection and joy, . . . contented in their own domains, . . . India will be prosperous, well-fed, pleasant, and populous. The earth will be fertile, and the months and

[17] We are indebted to Dr. Edward Conze for drawing our notice to this and the following passage, which have not hitherto received from historians the attention they deserve.

seasons and years will all occur at the proper time.[18] Planets and stars, moon and sun, will duly bring on the days and nights. Rain will fall upon earth at the proper time. And all living beings in India will be rich with all manner of riches and corn, very prosperous but not greedy.

The Divine Right (and Duty) of Kings

As we have seen, the early Buddhists evolved the story of the first king Mahāsammata, which implies a doctrine of social contract. In Hinduism, however, ideas of a different kind developed, and from early in the Christian era it was widely proclaimed in Hindu religious literature that the king was "a great god in human form," made of eternal particles of the chief gods of the Hindu pantheon. It became usual to address the king as *Deva* or "god," and the older ideas of Buddhism on kingship were, at least in Mahāyāna circles, modified in consequence.

The *Sūtra of the Excellent Golden Light,* as well as the striking call for peace previously quoted, contains one of the few passages in the Mahāyāna scriptures in which problems of government are discussed. It is not admitted that the king is a god in his own right, but he holds his high estate by the authority of the gods, and therefore is entitled to be addressed as *Deva,* and as "Son of the Gods." This doctrine of divine appointment may be compared with that widely proclaimed in England during the Stuart period, and it is also closely akin to the Chinese doctrine of the "mandate of Heaven." Like the Son of Heaven in imperial China, the Indian "Son of the Gods" held his title on condition of fulfilling his function properly, and might incur the anger of his divine parents. The verses quoted implicitly admit the moral right of revolt against a wicked or negligent king, for in conspiring against him his subjects are serving the heavenly purpose, and plotting the overthrow of one who no longer enjoys the divine blessing on which his right to govern depends. This too is a doctrine well known in China.

This poem on government, in Buddhist Sanskrit, purports to be a speech of the high god Brahmā, delivered to the four Great Kings, whom we have met in the previous extract.

[From *Suvarṇaprabhāsottama Sūtra,* 12 (*cento*)]

How does a king, who is born of men, come to be called divine?
Why is a king called the Son of the Gods?

[18] Note that, as we have seen elsewhere, the welfare of the whole land, and even the regularity of the calendar and of heavenly phenomena generally, were believed to be dependent on the morality of men, and more especially on the morality of ruling kings. This idea, which is also found in Hinduism, was well known in China, where it developed independently.

If a king is born in this world of mortals,
How can it be that a god rules over men?

I will tell you of the origin of kings, who are born in the world of mortals,
And for what reason kings exist, and rule over every province.
By the authority of the great gods a king enters his mother's womb.
First he is ordained by the gods—only then does he find an embryo.

What though he is born or dies in the world of mortals—
Arising from the gods he is called the Son of the Gods.

The thirty-three great gods assign the fortune of the king.
The ruler of men is created as son of all the gods,
To put a stop to unrighteousness, to prevent evil deeds,
To establish all beings in well-doing, and to show them the way to heaven.
Whether man, or god, or fairy, or demon,
Or outcaste, he is a true king who prevents evil deeds.
Such a king is mother and father to those who do good.
He was appointed by the gods to show the results of karma. . . .

But when a king disregards the evil done in his kingdom,
And does not inflict just punishment on the criminal,
From his neglect of evil, unrighteousness grows apace,
And fraud and strife increase in the land.

The thirty-three great gods grow angry in their palaces
When the king disregards the evil done in his kingdom.

Then the land is afflicted with fierce and terrible crime,
And it perishes and falls into the power of the enemy.
Then property, families, and hoarded wealth all vanish,
And with varied deeds of deceit men ruin one another.

Whatever his reasons, if a king does not do his duty
He ruins his kingdom, as a great elephant a bed of lotuses.

Harsh winds blow, and rain falls out of season,
Planets and stars are unpropitious, as are the moon and sun,

Corn, flowers, and fruit and seed do not ripen properly,
And there is famine, when the king is negligent. . . .

Then all the kings of the gods say one to another,
"This king is unrighteous, he has taken the side of unrighteousness!"
Such a king will not for long anger the gods;
From the wrath of the gods his kingdom will perish. . . .

He will be bereft of all that he values, whether by brother or son,
He will be parted from his beloved wife, his daughter will die.
Fire will fall from heaven, and mock-suns also.
Fear of the enemy and hunger will grow apace.
His beloved counselor will die, and his favorite elephant;
His favorite horses will die one by one, and his camels. . . .

There will be strife and violence and fraud in all the provinces;
Calamity will afflict the land, and terrible plague.

The brāhmans will then be unrighteous,
The ministers and the judges unrighteous.

The unrighteous will be revered,
And the righteous man will be chastised. . . .
Where the wicked are honored and the good are scorned
There will be famine, thunderbolts, and death . . .
All living beings will be ugly, having little vigor, very weak;
They will eat much, but they will not be filled.
They will have no strength, and no virility—
All beings in the land will be lacking in vigor. . . .

Many ills such as these befall the land
Whose king is partial [in justice] and disregards evil deeds. . . .

But he who distinguishes good deeds from evil,
Who shows the results of karma—he is called a king.
Ordained by the host of gods, the gods delight in him.
For the sake of himself or others, to preserve the righteousness of his land,

And to put down the rogues and criminals in his domains,
Such a king would give up [if need be] his life and his kingdom. . . .

Therefore a king should abandon his own precious life,
But not the jewel of Righteousness, whereby the world is gladdened.

Magical Utterances

It would be wrong to depict Mahāyāna Buddhism as simply a system of idealist philosophy, with a pantheon of benevolent and compassionate deities and an exalted and altruistic ethical system. It contained many elements from a lower stratum of belief, as will be made clear from the following extract from the *Laṅkāvatāra Sūtra,* one of the most important sacred texts of Mahāyāna Buddhism, from which we have already given two quotations.

Belief in the magical efficacy of certain syllables, phrases, and verses is as old as the *Rig Veda.* The Pali scriptures, however, pay little attention to this aspect of popular religion, and it would seem that the early Buddhists who were responsible for the compilation of these texts took a comparatively rationalistic view of the world. The criticism of vain and useless rituals contained in the Pāli texts and in Ashoka's edicts was probably intended to cover the vain repetition of mantras or magical utterances. But from early in the Christian era onwards, such things became more and more closely associated with Buddhism, especially with the Mahāyāna sects. Hinduism and Buddhism alike developed schools which taught that the constant repetition of mantras was a sure means of salvation. The following passage is not strictly tantric, for it does not attribute to the mantras it quotes any efficiency other than in the dispelling of evil spirits; but the importance given to the mantras, and the fact that they are attributed to the Buddha himself, show that Mahāyāna Buddhism was, by the fourth or fifth century A.D., permeated with the ideas which were to lead to fully developed tantricism.

[From *Laṅkāvatāra Sūtra,* pp. 260–61]

Then the Lord addressed the Great Being, the Bodhisattva Mahāmati thus:

Mahāmati, hold to these magic syllables of the *Laṅkāvatāra,* recited . . . by all the Buddhas, past, present, and future. Now I will repeat them, that those who proclaim the Law of Righteousness may keep them in mind:

Tuṭṭe tuṭṭe vuṭṭe vuṭṭe paṭṭe paṭṭe kaṭṭe kaṭṭe amale amale vimale vimale nime nime hime hime vame vame kale kale kale kale aṭṭe maṭṭe vaṭṭe tuṭṭe jñeṭṭe spuṭṭe kaṭṭe kaṭṭe laṭṭe paṭṭe dime dime cale cale pace pace bandhe bandhe añce mañce dutāre dutāre patāre patāre ark̤ke ark̤ke sark̤ke sark̤ke cak̤re cak̤re dime dime hime hime ṭu ṭu ṭu ṭu ḍu ḍu ḍu ḍu ru ru ru ru phu phu phu phu svāhā. . . .

If men and women of good birth hold, retain, recite, and realize these magical syllables, nothing harmful shall come upon them—whether a god, a goddess, a serpent-spirit, a fairy, or a demon.[19] . . . If anyone should be in the grip of misfortune, let him recite these one hundred and eight times, and the evil spirits, weeping and wailing, will go off in another direction.

[19] The names of many other supernatural beings follow.

CHAPTER VIII

THE VEHICLE OF THE THUNDERBOLT AND THE DECLINE OF BUDDHISM IN INDIA

The early centuries after Christ were very prosperous ones for Buddhism. In the Northwest it seems to have been the major religion, for hardly any specifically Hindu remains of this period are to be found there. Elsewhere the influence of Buddhism can be measured by the numerous remains of stūpas and monasteries to be found in many parts of India, which are among the finest and most beautiful relics of ancient Indian civilization. From India Buddhism spread not only to Central Asia and China but also to many parts of Southeast Asia. It is certain that it had some effect on the religious thought of the Middle East, and Buddhist influence has been traced in Neo-Platonism, Gnosticism, and Manichaeism. Many authorities believe that early Christianity was influenced, directly or indirectly, by Buddhist ideas. In the Eastern churches the story of Buddha's abandonment of his home for a life of asceticism, "the Great Going-forth," has been adapted as a Christian legend, the name of its protagonist, St. Josaphat, being evidently a corruption of the word *bodhisattva*.

But never in any part of India did Buddhism wholly supplant the other cults and systems. Theistic Hinduism continued to develop even during the period when Buddhism was strongest, as did the six orthodox philosophical systems. Layfolk, though they might support Buddhist monks and worship at Buddhist shrines, would usually patronize brāhmans also, and call on their services for the domestic rites such as birth ceremonies, initiations, marriages, and funerals, which played and still play so big a part in Indian life. Outside the monastic order those who looked on themselves as exclusively Buddhist were at all times probably comparatively few, and Ashoka, when he called on his subjects to respect the members of all sects and patronized Buddhists and Ājīvikas and probably other sects also, merely followed the practice of most religiously minded Indians down to the present day. It must be remembered that Indian religion is not exclusive. The most fanatical sectarian would probably agree that all the other sects had some qualified truth and validity. Hence Buddhism was never wholly cut off from the main stream of Indian religion.

The fourth century A.D. saw the rise of a second great empire, which at its zenith controlled the whole of northern India from Saurashtra to Bengal. This was the empire of the Guptas, whose greatest emperors were Hindus and gave their chief patronage to Vaishnavism.[1] From this period Buddhism began to lose ground in India. Its decline was at first almost imperceptible. The Chinese traveler Fa-hsien, who was in India at the very beginning of the fifth century, testified to the numerous well populated Buddhist monasteries in all parts of the land. He noted, however, that Buddhists and Hindus joined in the same religious processions as though Buddhism was looked on as a branch of Hinduism, rather than as an independent religion. In the seventh century the later Chinese travelers such as Hsüan Tsang and I Tsing reported a considerable decline in Buddhism. Numerous monasteries, even in the sacred Buddhist sites, were deserted and in ruins, and many monks were said to be corrupt, and given to superstitious and un-Buddhist practices. Some access of strength no doubt resulted from the support of Harsha (606–647), one of the last Hindu emperors to control the major part of northern India, who is said by Hsüan Tsang to have ended his life as a devotee of Buddhism. The chief stronghold of Buddhism from this time onward was Bihar and Bengal. In Bihar the great Buddhist monastery of Nālandā, probably founded in the fifth century A.D., was one of the chief centers of learning in the whole of India, to which students came from as far afield as China and Java. In eastern India Buddhism continued to flourish until the twelfth century, with the support of the Pāla dynasty, which ruled Bihar and Bengal, and the kings of which, though by no means exclusive in their religious allegiance, gave their chief support to Buddhism. It was from this region that Buddhism was carried in the eighth century to Nepal and Tibet, to be revived and strengthened by later missions in the eleventh century.

The Buddhism which prevailed in India at this time was of a type very

[1] The cult of Vishnu.

ifferent from that known to the pious emperor Ashoka. The Hīnayāna chools had almost disappeared in eastern India, and allegiance was divided between the Mahāyāna and a new branch of Buddhism, often reerred to as a separate vehicle, "the Vehicle of the Thunderbolt" (*Vajraāna*). From the middle of the fifth century onwards, with the decline of he Gupta empire, Indians began to take more and more interest in the ults of feminine divinities and in the practice of magico-religious rites, vhich were believed to lead to salvation or to superhuman power, and vhich often contained licentious or repulsive features. There is no reason o believe that such practices were new—they can be traced in one form r another right back to the Vedas. But until this time they are little in vidence either in literature or in art, and we must assume that they had ot much support among the educated, but were practiced chiefly by the ower social orders. As with many other features of Hinduism, they gradually influenced the upper classes, until in the Middle Ages groups of nitiates, both Hindu and Buddhist, were to be found all over India, who racticed strange secret ceremonies in order to gain the magic power vhich, it was believed, would lead to salvation.

Earlier Buddhism had never been so rationalistic as to reject the superatural. Thus it was taken for granted that the monk who was highly dvanced in his spiritual training was capable of supranormal cognition nd of marvelous feats such as levitation. The Buddha himself is said o have made a mango tree grow from a stone in a single night and to ave multiplied himself a thousandfold; but these miracles were only erformed on a single occasion to show the superiority of Buddhism over ther sects, and the Master gave explicit instructions to his followers that hey were not to make use of their magical powers, the exercise of which night lead them astray from the straight path to Nirvāna. There were, owever, at all times hermit monks, living apart from the monasteries n solitude or semi-solitude, and it was probably among such monks that he practice of magic grew.

The new magical Buddhism, like the magical Hinduism which arose at bout the same time, is often known as *Tantricism,* from the *Tantras,* or criptures of the sects, describing the spells, formulas, and rites which the ystems advocated. Probably Tantricism did not appear in organized Budlhism until the seventh century, when Hsüan Tsang reported that certain monastic communities were given to magical practices. Tantric Buddhism was of two main branches, known as Right and Left Hand, as in Tantric Hinduism. The Right Hand, though it became very influential in China and Japan, has left little surviving literature in Sanskrit; it was distinguished by devotion to masculine divinities. The Left Hand sects, to which the name *Vajrayāna* ("Vehicle of the Thunderbolt") was chiefly applied, postulated feminine counterparts or wives to the Buddhas, bodhisattvas, and other divinities of the mythology of later Buddhism, and devoted their chief attention to these *Tārās,* or "Savioresses." As in Hinduism they were thought of as the personified active aspects of the deities in question. The lore of this form of Buddhism was not generally given to the ordinary believer, but was imparted only to the initiate, who need not be a monk, but might be a layman. Adepts who had learned the secrets of Vajrayāna at the feet of a spiritual preceptor (guru) would meet together usually at night, in small groups to perform their secret ceremonies.

Among the chief features of the ritual of Vajrayāna was the repetition of mystical syllables and phrases (mantra), such as the famous *Oṃ maṇi padme hūṃ.*[2] Yoga postures and meditation were practiced. But the Tantric groups also followed more questionable methods of gaining salvation. It was believed that once the adept had reached a certain degree of spiritual attainment the normal rules of moral behavior were no longer valid for him, and that their deliberate breach, if committed in an odor of sanctity, would actually help him on the upward path. Thus drunkenness, meat-eating, and sexual promiscuity were often indulged in, as well as such repulsive psychopathic practices as eating ordure, and sometimes even ritual murder. Such antinomianism was perhaps the logical corollary of one of the doctrines which Tantric Buddhism took over from the Yogāchāra school of Mahāyāna, that all things in the universe were on ultimate analysis the illusory products of mind.

We must not believe that the whole of Tantric Buddhism is included in the practice of unpleasant secret rites. Many Tantric circles practiced such rites only symbolically, and their teachers often produced works of

[2] "Ah! The jewel is indeed in the lotus!" Though there are other interpretations this seems the most probable significance of the mysterious and elliptical phrase, which is specially connected with the Bodhisattva Avalokiteshvara, and is still believed in Tibet to have immense potency. Its significance may be sexual, implying that the Bodhisattva has united with his Tārā.

considerable philosophical subtlety, while the ethical tone of some passages in the Tantricist Saraha's *Treasury of Couplets* (*Dohākośa*), one of the last Buddhist works produced in India is of the highest.

The Vajrayāna developed its own system of philosophy by adapting the doctrines of the Vijnānavādins and Mādhyamikas to its own world view. It admitted the emptiness of all things, but maintained that, once the emptiness was fully recognized, the phenomenal world was not to be disparaged, for it was fundamentally identical with the universal Emptiness itself. Thus the adept was encouraged to utilize the phenomenal world for his psychic progress to supreme wisdom. The world was a Means (*upāya,* a masculine noun in Sanskrit), and full consciousness of the Emptiness of all things was the Supreme Wisdom (prajnā, a feminine noun), often personified both in Mahāyāna and Vajrayāna circles as a goddess. Final bliss was to be obtained by the union of the phenomenal Means with the noumenal Wisdom, and the most vivid symbol of such union was sexual intercourse. Thus a philosophical basis was found for the erotic practices of Tantric Buddhism. The Vajrayāna position was rather like that of certain deviationist Christian sects, the morals of which were completely antinomian, because their members were the Elect, and thus above the law.

The end of Buddhism in India is still not completely elucidated. Buddhist monasteries survived in many parts of the land until the time of the Muslim invasions at the very end of the twelfth century. Though there had been some loss of ground to Hinduism, it is clear that the great monasteries of Bihar and Bengal were inhabited down to this time. Fine illustrated manuscripts of Mahāyāna and Tantric scriptures were produced in Eastern India, some of which found their way to Nepal, where they have survived to this day. Inscriptions and archaeological evidence show that there were still fairly prosperous Buddhist monasteries at the sacred sites of Sarnath, near Vārānasī, where the Buddha preached his first sermon, and Shrāvastī, in northern Uttar Pradesh, where he spent much of his actual life. In the Deccan and the Dravidian South there are few evidences of Buddhism after the tenth century, though here and there it survived. It would seem that the life of the monasteries became gradually more and more estranged from that of the people, and that the activities of the monks, grown wealthy from long standing endowments, became increasingly confined to small circles of initiates. This, however, is not the whole story, for Buddhists were among the earliest writers of Bengali, and this would indicate an attempt to make contact with a popular audience. Thus the end of Buddhism was not wholly due to the divorce of Buddhism and everyday life, or to corruption and decay, as some have suggested.

By the time of the Guptas we find the Buddha worshiped in his shrines as a Hindu god, with all the ritual of pūjā,[3] and Buddhist monks and Hindu priests joined in the same processions. The Pāla kings, who claimed to be "supreme worshipers of the Buddha," were also proud of the fact that they maintained all the rules of Hindu dharma,[4] and many of their ministers were orthodox brāhmans. We can perhaps imagine the attitude of the layman to Buddhism from this analogy. For ordinary folk living near a Buddhist monastery, Buddha would be one god among many; they might pay him special homage and worship because their ancestors had done so and because his temple was nearby, but they would not look upon his worship as in any way excluding them from the Hindu fold. Medieval Hinduism knew many sects, each specially devoted to one or other of the gods, who was looked upon as supreme, the lesser gods being mere emanations or secondary forms of the great one. From the point of view of the layman this would be the position of Buddhism—a sect of Hinduism with its own special order of devotees, the monks, pledged to the service of their god. It cannot be too strongly emphasized that Hinduism has always tended to assimilate rather than to exclude.

At this time anti-Buddhist activity was not completely unknown. There are traditions, most of them preserved only in Buddhist sources and therefore suspect of exaggeration, of occasional fierce persecution by anti-Buddhist kings, chiefly Shaivites,[5] some of whom are said even to have gone as far as to place a price on the head of every Buddhist monk. Allowing for all exaggerations, it is clear that some kings were strongly anti-Buddhist and took active steps to discourage Buddhism. More serious opposition came from certain medieval Hindu philosophers and their disciples. Teachers such as Kumārila and Shankara are said to have traveled far and wide throughout India preaching their own doctrines and attacking those of their rivals, and Buddhism seems to have been singled

[3] Worship of an idol with offerings of lights, flowers, food, etc.
[4] The Sacred Law.
[5] Worshipers of Shiva.

out for special attention by those reformers. Anti-Buddhist propaganda of one kind or another may have had a significant influence in the decline of Buddhism.

By the time of the Muslim invasion (1192 A.D.) Buddhism was rapidly merging in the body of Hinduism. The process is exemplified in the doctrine of the incarnations of Vishnu, which does not appear in its final form until just before the Muslim invasion. Here the Buddha figures as an incarnation of the Supreme God, who took human form in order either to put a stop to the sacrifice of living animals, or, according to some formulations, to destroy the wicked by leading them to deny the Vedas and so accomplish their own perdition. Thus the Buddha was placed, in theory at least, on the same exalted level as the great popular divinities Krishna and Rāma, and his devotees might worship him as a full member of the orthodox pantheon. There is no reason to believe that the cult of Buddha as a Hindu god was ever widespread, but certainly in the great temple of Gayā, the scene of the Master's enlightenment, he was adored by simple Hindu pilgrims with all the rites of Hinduism as a Hindu god until very recent times, when the ancient temple was transferred back to Buddhist hands. Other traces of Buddhism survive in parts of eastern India. Thus it is said that the peasants of Bengal and Orissa still worship a divinity called Dharma, who seems to be a faint folk recollection of the ancient religion of the land.

When the Turkish horsemen occupied Bihar and Bengal, slew or expelled the "shaven-headed brāhmans," as they called the Buddhist monks, and destroyed their monasteries and libraries, Buddhism was dead in India. The *purohitas* (chaplains) of Hinduism, who performed the domestic rites for the layfolk, and the Hindu ascetics who wandered from place to place, were in need of no organization and could survive the disruption of the Muslim invasion and the aggressive propaganda of the alien faith. Buddhism, dependent on the monasteries for its survival and without the same lay support as Hinduism received, was destroyed by the invader. It is noteworthy that Islam had its greatest success in those parts of India where Buddhism had been strongest, in the Northwest, and in Bengal. Only in the Himalayan regions, especially Nepal, did Buddhism survive, kept alive largely by contact with Tibet. Though in many parts of Asia it has flourished, and indeed spread and developed in the last seven hundred years, in the land of its birth it has died. Only in the last few decades have intelligent Indians begun once more to take an interest in the religion founded by India's greatest son. Thanks largely to the work of the Mahābodhi Society the sacred sites of Buddhism are once more cared for, and Buddhist monasteries again exist in many parts of India. Though the number of professing Buddhists in India and Pakistan is still very small, there is no doubt that the doctrines of Buddhism are beginning to influence more and more Indians, and Buddhism may well become a force to be reckoned with in the India of the future.

To the Pure All Things Are Pure

The doctrine that the round of birth-and-death was really the same as Nirvāna, the cult of feminine divinities, and the growing interest in magic, especially magical utterances, led to the appearance of Vajrayāna, or Tantric Buddhism. The rather dangerous view that all things are legitimate to those who fully know the truth is already to be found in specifically Mahāyāna texts. In the texts of Vajrayāna it is developed further, for it is declared that, at a certain stage of self-development, to give way to the passions, especially the sexual passions, is a positive help along the upward path. This passage is taken from a Tantric poem, *Disquisition on the Purification of the Intellect,* composed by Āryadeva [1] toward the end of the seventh century.

[From *Cittaviśuddhiprakarana,* pp. 24–38]

They who do not see the truth
  Think of birth-and-death as distinct from Nirvāna,
But they who do see the truth
  Think of neither. . . .

This discrimination is the demon
  Who produces the ocean of transmigration.
Freed from it the great ones are released
  From the bonds of becoming.

Plain folk are afflicted
  With the poison of doubt. . . .
He who is all compassion . . .
  Should uproot it completely.

[1] Not the same as an earlier Āryadeva, disciple of Nāgārjuna and author of the *Four-hundred Stanzas* (*Catuḥśataka*).

As a clear crystal assumes
  The color of another object,
So the jewel of the mind is colored
  With the hue of what it imagines.

The jewel of the mind is naturally devoid
  Of the color of these ideas,
Originally pure, unoriginated,
  Impersonal, and immaculate.

So, with all one's might, one should do
  Whatever fools condemn,
And, since one's mind is pure,
  Dwell in union with one's divinity.[2]

The mystics, pure of mind,
  Dally with lovely girls,
Infatuated with the poisonous flame of passion,
  That they may be set free from desire.

By his meditations the sage is his own Garuda,[3]
  Who draws out the venom [of snakebite] and drinks it.
He makes his deity innocuous,
  And is not affected by the poison. . . .

When he has developed a mind of wisdom
  And has set his heart on enlightenment
There is nothing he may not do
  To uproot the world [from his mind].

He is not Buddha, he is not set free,
  If he does not see the world
As originally pure, unoriginated,
  Impersonal, and immaculate.

[2] That is, the woman with whom the Tantricist practices his rites.
[3] A mythical, divine bird, the enemy and slayer of snakes.

The mystic duly dwells
  On the manifold merits of his divinity,
He delights in thoughts of passion,
  And by the enjoyment of passion is set free.

What must we do? Where are to be found
  The manifold potencies of being?
A man who is poisoned may be cured
  By another poison, the antidote.

Water in the ear is removed by more water,
  A thorn [in the skin] by another thorn.
So wise men rid themselves of passion
  By yet more passion.

As a washerman uses dirt
  To wash clean a garment,
So, with impurity,
  The wise man makes himself pure.

Everything Is Buddha

The last phase of Buddhism in India was the school of Tantricism sometimes known as *Sahajayāna* or *Sahajīya,* "the Vehicle of the Innate," which stressed the doctrine that Ultimate Being was ever present in all things living, a view not strange to Buddhism, and very well known in Hinduism. The Sahajayāna teachers, like other Tantricists, strongly supported the view that sexual activity and other forms of worldly pleasure were positive helps to salvation for those who made use of them in the proper spirit, but their teaching was distinguished by its emphasis on simplicity—it was possible for the ordinary layman, living a normal life in every respect, to achieve salvation, simply by recognizing the Buddha within himself and all things.

The teachers of this school began to write in the vernaculars, and a number of their poems and series of verses, composed either in Apabhramsha [1] or Old Bengali, survive from among the many which must now be lost. All these works date from the tenth to the twelfth centuries. Unlike Sanskrit poetry their verses are rhymed and they employ meters which are still widely used in

[1] The early medieval vernaculars, which had moved much further from Sanskrit than had Pali or the Prakrits, and were much closer to the modern languages of India.

the vernaculars. For these reasons they give an impression very different from that of earlier Buddhist poetry. In their simplicity of style, and in the simplicity of their doctrines, they seem to look forward rather than back—towards the simple mystical verse of Kabīr, who also taught that the Ultimate Being was to be found in one's own home, as one went about one's daily work. Like Kabīr's verses again they sometimes have a strong ethical content; for all their emphasis on the value of sex as a means of salvation, the Sahajayāna teachers, like all Buddhists, taught the virtues of compassion, kindliness, and helpfulness.

The following verses are taken from the *Treasury of Couplets* ascribed to Saraha, and written in Apabhramsha in the eleventh or twelfth century.

[From Saraha, *Dohākośa,* v. 102-end; as translated by D. S. Snellgrove in Conze, *Buddhist Texts,* pp. 238–39]

As is Nirvāna so is Samsāra.[2]
  Do not think there is any distinction.
Yet it possesses no single nature,
  For I know it as quite pure.

Do not sit at home, do not go to the forest,
  But recognize mind wherever you are.
When one abides in complete and perfect enlightenment,
  Where is Samsāra and where is Nirvāna?

Oh know this truth,
  That neither at home nor in the forest does enlightenment dwell.
Be free from prevarication
  In the self-nature of immaculate thought!

"This is my self and this is another."
  Be free of this bond which encompasses you about,
And your own self is thereby released.

Do not err in this matter of self and other.
  Everything is Buddha without exception.
Here is that immaculate and final stage,
  Where thought is pure in its true nature.

[2] Transmigration, i.e., this world.

The fair tree of thought that knows no duality,
  Spreads through the triple world.
It bears the flower and fruit of compassion,
  And its name is service of others.

The fair tree of the Void abounds with flowers,
  Acts of compassion of many kinds,
And fruit for others appearing spontaneously,
  For this joy has no actual thought of another.

So the fair tree of the Void also lacks compassion,
  Without shoots or flowers or foliage,
And whoever imagines them there, falls down,
  For branches there are none.[3]

The two trees spring from one seed,
  And for that reason there is but one fruit.
He who thinks of them thus indistinguishable,
  Is released from Nirvāna and Samsāra.

If a man in need approaches and goes away hopes unfulfilled,
  It is better he should abandon that house
Than take the bowl that has been thrown from the door.

Not to be helpful to others,
  Not to give to those in need,
This is the fruit of Samsāra.
  Better than this is to renounce the idea of a self.

He who clings to the Void
  And neglects Compassion,
Does not reach the highest stage.

[3] All things are ultimately one in the eternal and infinite Emptiness which is the body o the Buddha; therefore there is no real distinction between self and others, and on analysi the "fair tree" is nonexistent. But, as we shall see in the following verse, on a still highe plane of thought it shares the reality of the Ultimate Being, and therefore, to the ma who sees the world with complete clarity, acts of mercy and kindness are still valid.

But he who practices only Compassion,
  Does not gain release from toils of existence.
He, however, who is strong in practice of both,
  Remains neither in Samsāra nor in Nirvāna.

HINDUISM

Buddhism and Jainism, which appear from archaeological evidence to have achieved considerable influence in India from c.200 B.C. to A.D. c.200, were gradually displaced by what came to be known as Hinduism, so-called because at the time of the Muslim conquest (A.D. c.1200) it was already the religion of the vast majority of Indians (Persian *Hindū,* "Indian"). Even today, despite the long period of Muslim rule (thirteenth to eighteenth centuries), with its numerous conversions to Islam, and the century or two (depending on the area) of British rule, Hindus account for three-fourths of the inhabitants of the subcontinent; the Buddhists have disappeared except in outlying areas (e.g., Tibet, Ceylon, Southeast Asia, etc.); and the Jains form a minority of little but commercial significance.

Hinduism is divided into innumerable sects and has no well-defined, large-scale ecclesiastic organization. Its two most general characteristics are the caste system and agreement about the sacredness of its most ancient scriptures, the Veda, which though considered essentially eternal, were revealed to the sages, the rishis. The caste system is itself supposed to rest on the authority of the Veda and in a sense the whole society forms an ecclesiastical organization, with its own canon law, the Sacred Law (dharma), also based on the Veda. The apex of the pyramidal caste system is the brāhman class, who because they are the authoritative interpreters and transmitters of the Veda, and sole ministrants of the religious sacraments, are likewise considered sacred. The hierarchy of caste is based upon how close a caste comes in its way of life to the pattern set by the brāhmans, who are themselves ranged into a hierarchy of castes on the basis of scriptural learning, adherence to the Sacred Law, and birth (that is, on the recognition won by their particular caste over a long period of time).

Hindus generally believe that the soul is eternal but is bound by the law of karma ("action") to the world of matter, which it can only escape after spiritual progress through an endless series of births. Different schools and sects have different views about metaphysics and the nature and method of release (moksha) from transmigration. The *Song of the Lord* (*Bhagavad Gītā*) sets forth three basic paths: those of knowledge, selfless action, and devotion to God. They are regarded as complementary rather than mutually exclusive. As understood today, the path of knowledge implies an awareness that reality is one and spiritual, the Brahman, with which each apparently individual soul is identical, and which is sat, chit, ānanda—pure being, intelligence, and bliss. All distinctions, including the entire phenomenal world, have only a relative reality but are ultimately false and the result of the creative illusion (māyā) of the Brahman. The path of devotion implies belief in a supreme personal god as the ultimate reality, the creator, preserver, and destroyer of the universe; salvation, viewed as various degrees of nearness to, and communion with, God, is dependent on God's grace in response to the devotee's intense and unswerving devotion and service. The major division in Hinduism is between the devotees of Vishnu and those of Shiva.

Neither the path of knowledge nor that of devotion need be, or ordinarily is, strictly monistic or monotheistic in practice. After all, man's desires, needs, and sufferings are many, and corresponding to these there are hosts of minor gods as well as various incarnations, manifestations, and aspects of the major gods. All these are generally united mythologically to one or the other major god. Thus Krishna and Rāma are the most important incarnations of Vishnu; Shiva's spouse is the Mother Goddess, known as Devī, Kālī, etc. As the Hindu generally does not follow any rigid dogma, there is a great deal of interpenetration between the various views of the divine, with the result that in India there are polytheistic monists, dualistic monotheists, etc. The various views are ordered by the monists, who follow the philosophy of the Upanishads as interpreted by Shankara (ninth century A.D.) into descending levels of apprehension of one and the same truth. The monistic view, whether pure monism or not, is often referred to as Higher Hinduism, the other views as Popular or Sectarian Hinduism. Included in the latter are more humble beliefs among the lowest strata of the population, such as the worship of various animals, trees, diseases, and even stones.

Devotion to the devotee's chosen deity (*iṣṭa-devatā*) may be purely spiritual, but it is usually manifested by pūjā, the ritual of worship and service of an idol of the deity (bathing the idol, offerings of food and water, flowers, lights, music and dancing). Just as sacrifice (yajna) was characteristic of early Brahmanism, renunciation (sannyāsa) of the Upanishads (and Theravāda Buddhism and Jainism), pūjā is characteristic of Hinduism (and Mahāyāna Buddhism). The idol or idols must be housed and cared for, and this requires temples and priests. Temples grew more and more elaborate with time, as did the ritual of worship. In fact, temples came to play a most important religious, cultural and artistic, and even economic role in medieval India.

The orthodox Hindu believes that the ultimate truth in matters of religion is to be found in the Veda, which is called *Shruti,* revelation. Later scriptures represent interpretations or codifications of that truth and are therefore called *Smriti* (human) tradition. The sectarian may also believe that his god revealed a more explicit doctrine in some still more recent scripture (āgama or tantra). Thus the Hindu sees religious development in Hinduism as the emphasis of now this, now that aspect of the Veda, or as a gradually deeper and more complete perception of the truth which was there in the Veda all the time. Thus the six orthodox systems of philosophy all claim Vedic authority, a claim which later Hindus have accepted in the belief that all were complementary visions (darshanas) of the one Truth. Even the Hindu's major gods, Vishnu or Shiva, had been worshiped in Vedic times too (though both were quite minor figures in the early Veda), so that later theistic movements were seen as a continuation and expansion of an earlier faith.

We have seen how the ideal of cosmic ethical interdependence of the earliest (the hymnal) portion of the Veda, the Samhitā, gave way to the principle of ritualistic—sacrificial and magical—cosmic interdependence in the Brāhmana period, and the latter, in turn, to the conclusion that ultimate reality was one, the Brahman, identical with man's Self, Ātman, as revealed in the concluding portion of the Veda, namely, the Upanishads. The doctrine of the Upanishads was really only the expression within the Vedic or Brahmanical tradition of a great quietistic movement characterized by a deep disillusionment with life, probably closely associated with the elaboration of the doctrines of karma and rebirth. The same movement was the basis of the heterodox faiths of Buddhism and Jainism. Thus if the earlier periods of the Brahmanical tradition had emphasized the positive values of life, symbolized by the ritual designed to help achieve those values, namely, the sacrifice (yajna), the last period was pessimistic and its ideal was renunciation (sannyāsa) of worldly life for the life of a religious mendicant.

The new outlook affected first and most profoundly those groups of brāhmans who had been given to theosophical speculations since late Rig-Vedic times, many of whom already lived in forest hermitages. But the ritualists, who formed the great majority of brāhmans, were also affected to some extent and adopted, in the Sacred Law, renunciation as the ultimate religious ideal of man, though to be followed only after a man had fulfilled all his social obligations during most of his adult life. (The elaboration of the Sacred Law is contemporary with the Upanishads in its beginnings but continued on for several centuries after Christ.)

Side by side with these developments in hieratic and intellectual circles, there are indications cropping up even in early texts of more popular religious movements centering around the worship of various supreme gods. This may well be a popular expression of the same search for cosmic unity in an Absolute which we found at the intellectual level in the Veda: e.g., the Brahmā (Sanskrit *Brahman,* a masculine noun) of the *Mahābhārata,* an early supreme creator god, is a personalized form of the Upanishadic Brahman (neuter in Sanskrit). These theistic movements must have grown in importance over a long period before they took on the trappings of philosophical thought, e.g., in a late Upanishad glorifying Shiva, the *Śvetāśvatara,* and from this time we can follow the development of theism through its own vast literature. The somewhat later and much more famous *Song of the Lord* (*Bhagavad Gītā*), dedicated to Krishna further advocates action according to dharma, ordained duty, and thus the Sacred Law comes to form a part of the new dispensation. Thus fortified by philosophy and the Brahmanical Sacred Law, Hinduism, as the new theistic movements are called, spread rapidly and to a great extent absorbed the rival faiths of Buddhism and Jainism.

Intellectually, the Upanishadic doctrine of an eternal, immutable essence of all things was easier to reconcile with theism than the Buddhist doctrine of universal impermanence. Socially, the Sacred Law, evolved chiefly on the basis of the older Brahmanism, became the property of Hinduism and was applied and propagated by both kings and brāhmans. Politically, the monistic, monotheistic, and socially hierarchical tendencies of Hinduism accorded better with the growing power and divinization of kings. Finally, by slight adjustments of the mythology the Hindu gods could be given an antiquity far beyond human traditions, as well as the scriptural authority of the Veda. Thus Krishna became an avatār (incarnation) of the Vedic Vishnu, Shiva another name for the Vedic Rudra, and the other gods of the new pantheon were somehow brought into derivative relationship to these two. The mantle of Vedic authority also covered the Sacred Law, the orthodox systems of philosophy, and, in fact, the whole of Hinduism. Hinduism is thus both a new religion and, in certain respects, a continuation of the older Brahmanism.

In contrast to the earlier Brahmanism which was restricted in principle to those of Aryan birth, and in contrast also to Theravāda Buddhism and Jainism, which offered the prospect of immediate salvation only to the monk, the new theistic movements offered an easy path to salvation for all, the path of devotion to God, without the need for forsaking life in society. The new ideal was also egalitarian as regards the hope of salvation—were not all devotees, from whatever class, equally dear to God? Hinduism thus offered a strong religious bond, transcending class or caste distinctions, to a society threatened with disintegration by the foreign invasions and rule of the second century B.C. to A.D. c.300 and later.

The periods in which these developments were brought to their fullest expression in Hindu culture were the dynasties of the Guptas in the North (fourth and fifth centuries A.D.) and the Pallavas (c. fourth to ninth centuries A.D.) and Cholas (c. ninth to c. twelfth centuries) in the South. The Gupta Age is the classical period of Hindu culture, which was to be imitated but not surpassed by later ages. It was brought to an end in the North c.500 by repeated invasions of the Huns which must have greatly impoverished northern India and which ushered in what we refer to as the Indian medieval period, distinguished from the earlier, classical age not by any break in cultural continuity but rather by lesser creativity and the spread of popular religious movements centered on devotionalism and magic. Politically there was a gradual disintegration and centralized empires gave way to looser, more feudalistic types of political organization, which were no match for the Turkish Muslim raiders and invaders from Ghazni and Ghur in present Afghanistan (c.1000–1200).

While the Dravidian South, which had never been Brahmanical, had early been converted to Buddhism or Jainism, in the North from the Shunga (second to first centuries B.C.) to the Gupta period Hinduism had made much headway against the heterodox religions. From the North, probably due in part to the prestige of the Guptas, the movement spread to the South, and the Pallava rulers were converted to Hinduism. It was with their help and that of their successors, the Cholas, that southern India became the stronghold of the Hindu tradition after the Muslim invasions in the north.

From the foregoing it will be clear that Hinduism was much more than an aggregation of devotional cults and philosophical schools—it was a way of life. To understand this way of life in its fullness and variety, we must first see how the major fields of human endeavor were ordered, according to the traditional Hindu conception, in relation to the ultimate ends of man.

A. Yarrow

CHAPTER IX

THE FOUR ENDS OF MAN

One of the main concepts which underlies the Hindu attitude to life and daily conduct is that of the four ends of man (purushārtha). The first of these is characterized by considerations of righteousness, duty, and virtue. This is called *dharma.* There are other activities, however, through which a man seeks to gain something for himself or pursue his own pleasure. When the object of this activity is some material gain, it is called *artha;* when it is love or pleasure, it is *kāma.* Finally, there is the renunciation of all these activities in order to devote oneself to religious or spiritual activities with the aim of liberating oneself from the worldly life; this is *mokṣa.* These four are referred to as "the tetrad" (*caturvarga*).

In early texts it is more usual to find the aspirations of man stated as three: dharma, material gain, and love or pleasure. Dharma then refers to the religio-ethical ideal, which we may translate as "virtue." The basic meaning of dharma, a word derived from the root *dhṛ,* "to sustain," is the moral law, which sustains the world, human society, and the individual. Dharma thus replaced the Vedic word rita, the principle of cosmic ethical interdependence. Though dharma generally refers to religiously ordained duty, in other passages it may just mean morality, right conduct, or the rules of conduct (mores, customs, codes, or laws) of a group. When Upanishadic mysticism and quietism came to be included in the religio-ethical ideal, dharma was classified into two aspects, the one relating to activity (*pravṛtti*) and the other to retirement from life (*nivṛtti*). Then *nivṛtti* itself later became a separate end of man under the name moksha, spiritual liberation. When moksha, now representing the higher religious ideal, is opposed to dharma, the latter no longer refers to the whole of religion but continues to include all ritual activities and ethical duties and ideals, such as right, righteousness, virtue, justice, propriety, morality, beneficence, and nonviolence. Dharma is in fact a key word of Hindu culture, and Hinduism itself is sometimes designated as Sanātana Dharma, the Eternal Dharma.

The great epic, the *Mahābhārata,* carries dharma as its burden, for it states at the end as the essence of its teachings: "With uplifted arms I cry, none heeds; from dharma [religious duty], material gain and pleasure flow;[1] then, why is not dharma pursued? Neither for the sake of pleasure, nor out of fear or avarice, no, not even for the sake of one's life should one give up dharma; dharma stands alone for all time; pleasure and pain are transitory." While this great epic makes its hero, Yudhishthira, the very son of the God of Dharma (*Dharma-putra*) and one who had no enemy (*Ajātaśatru*), the other epic, the *Rāmāyaṇa,* makes its hero, Rāma, dharma itself in flesh and blood.

The pursuits of material gain and pleasure are both necessary for life—for no one can live without either acquiring some goods or enjoying things to some extent—but they should be controlled by considerations of dharma. While material gain and pleasure refer to actuality, dharma refers to an ideal principle or rule or norm to which man should conform in his activities in the world, with reference to himself or in relation to his fellow-beings. Dharma is therefore assigned first place, because it is the regulating factor, except for which the pursuit of material gain and pleasure would lead man to ruin or into conflict with his fellow-beings. The Upanishads call upon man not to covet another's wealth (*Īśāvāsya,* 1.1). Even kings, whose role in life is so closely bound up with material activities and considerations, are asked to observe and enforce dharma;[2] they are considered merely regents and executors of dharma. A king who follows the injunctions of dharma is called a royal sage (*rāja-ṛṣi*); his victories, the victories of dharma (as the poet Kālidāsa says); and his rule, the rule of dharma. The *Lawbook of Yājnavalkya* (*Yājñavalkya Smṛti*) states that where there is a conflict between principle and policy, righteousness and material advantage, dharma and artha, the former should prevail. Similarly control by dharma is insisted upon for love or pleasure (kāma) also. In a well-known passage, the *Bhagavad Gītā* (7.11) makes the Lord identify Himself with such desire (kāma) as is consistent with dharma. The Hindu ideal does not preach abstinence from pleasure for all or at all stages; it rather preaches, universally, the

[1] Fulfilling one's religious duties, which included both ritual and ethical duties, was thought to lead to material rewards and pleasures both in this life and in heaven.

[2] Ordained duty, especially justice, the first and main religious duty of a king, and social duties (i.e., the class system).

ideal of chastened love, or pleasure regulated by considerations of both morality and material wellbeing.

The pursuit of moksha or liberation is placed last, as according to the Hindu scheme of values, it ought to be the final and supreme aspiration of man. The desire for liberation from the endless cycle of transmigration to which the spirit is subjected is so ingrained in the Hindu that however much he may wander about in life, he does not fail in his later years to pursue this yearning of the soul. Even in these days of Western education many who have led a modern life find a change coming over them and heed the nostalgic call of the Hindu spirit. Examples of this change are not wanting even among politicians; be they Moderates, Congressmen, or Praja-Socialists, they hear that inner voice to which the national poet Kālidāsa gave expression as he laid down his pen: "And as for me, may Shivạ, the almighty, end this cycle of rebirth."

From the Science of Dharma

Each of the first three ends of man was the subject-matter of a separate science: dharma, religion, of the *Dharma Śāstra,* the science of dharma, which we translate freely as the Sacred Law; artha, material gain, of the *Artha Śāstra,* the science of material gain; and kāma, love or pleasure, of the *Kāma Śāstra,* the science of love. Moksha, spiritual liberation, is not separately mentioned in the readings given below, but is included under dharma.

[From *Manu Smṛti,* 2.224]

Some say that dharma [virtue] and material gain are good, others that pleasure and material gain are good, and still others that dharma alone or pleasure alone is good, but the correct position is that the three should co-exist without harming each other.

[From *Yājñavalkya Smṛti,* 2.2.21]

The science of dharma is of greater authority than the science of material gain.

From the Science of Material Gain: The Conduct of the Ideal King

[From *Kauṭilīyā Artha Śāstra,* 1.7]

Therefore by abandoning the six internal enemies,[1] one should gain the control of his senses; he should gain knowledge by associating himself with elders, use his intelligence department as his eye, acquire and conserve things by exertion, establish righteous rule by commands and directives, and discipline among the people by the extension of education, endear himself to the people by gifts, and provide livelihood to them with what is beneficial to each.

Having brought his senses under discipline he must avoid betaking to others' women, appropriating others' wealth, and injuring others; he must avoid also long sleep, fickleness, falsehood, gaudy dress, associations which would bring him to grief, and activities that are unrighteous and unprofitable.

He should enjoy pleasure without detriment to virtue or material gain; he ought not to deprive himself of pleasure. Or he should take to pursuits virtuous, profitable, and pleasant in such a manner that they are mutually helpful. Of these, virtue, material gain and pleasure, if one is pursued by him to the exclusion of the others, it affects him adversely as well as others.

From the Science of Love

[From Vātsyāyana, *Kāma Sūtra,* 1.1.1; 1.2.1, 14, 49]

Obeisance to virtue, material gain, and pleasure. [1.1.1]

Man, who could normally live up to a hundred years, must apportion his time and take to virtue, material gain, and pleasure in such a way that these are mutually integrated and do not harm each other. As a boy he must attend to accomplishments like learning; in youth he should enjoy himself; in later life he should pursue the ideals of virtue and spiritual liberation. [1.2.1]

When there are all three, virtue, material gain, and pleasure, their mutual superiority is in the order of their precedence. [1.2.14]

Thus taking to material gain, pleasure, and virtue, man attains here as

[1] Lust, anger, avarice, delusion, pride, and envy.

well as in the hereafter happiness which is unimpaired and complete. [1.2.49]

From the Rāmāyaṇa

The *Rāmāyaṇa,* one of the two national epics of India, is ascribed to Sage Valmīki.

[From *Rāmāyaṇa,* 2.21.57–58; 3.9.30]

My dear one! In this world, virtue, material gain, and pleasure are all to be found in the fruit accruing from the pursuit of virtue; I am sure they will all be found there even as in the case of a chaste wife who is also beloved and blessed with offspring. If there is a case in which the three are not found together, one should do only that in which there is virtue, for one who is intent solely on material gain is to be hated and to be engrossed completely in pleasure is also not praiseworthy. [2.21.57–58]

From dharma issue profit and pleasure; one attains everything by dharma, it is dharma which is the essence and strength of the world. [3.9.30]

From Kālidāsa

Kālidāsa (c. 400 A.D.), the foremost Indian poet, has enunciated the fundamental concepts of Hindu thought and culture in his poems and plays.

[From *Raghuvaṃśa,* 1.25; 17.57]

In that wise King Dilīpa, who punished only to maintain order and married only for the sake of progeny, even material gain and love [1] were based on virtue [i.e., religious duty]. [1.25]

King Atithi did not put a strain on virtue by his pursuit of material gain and pleasure, nor did he allow these two to suffer by his pursuit of virtue; he did not betake to pleasure at the cost of material gain nor vice versa; he was devoted to the three in a harmonious manner. [17.57]

[1] The basic meaning of kāma is clearly required in this context. The meaning is that the king performed the sexual act not for its own sake but for the sake of the male progeny required to "pay the debt to the Fathers" by continuing the rites to his ancestors. Likewise material possession, in the form of kingly rule, was for the sake of maintaining law and order.

CHAPTER X

DHARMA, THE FIRST END OF MAN

The older Brahmanism of the Samhitās and Brāhmanas, when faced with the popularity of the non-Brahmanic religions and the appeal among intellectuals of Upanishadic mysticism, began to consolidate, reorganize, and revitalize the Brahmanic way of life and thought. In this process a synthesis was achieved between the older Brahmanical ideal of action—of life viewed as a ritual—and the newer, quietistic ideal of withdrawal and renunciation developed in the Upanishadic period. This revivalist movement within Brahmanism touched all spheres of human life—religious, academic, domestic, and social. Indeed, it was then for the first time that conscious efforts were made to evolve a definite pattern of Brahmanical society. The movement found expression in the texts of the Sacred Law (*Smṛti* or *Dharma Śāstra*) as well as in the Epics, the *Mahābhārata* and *Rāmāyaṇa,* and in literature generally, even that dedicated to such profane subjects as material gain or love.

For vast numbers of Hindus throughout the ages there has been no more inspiring symbol of dharma than the hero of the epic *Rāmāyaṇa,* a text which gives expression to the two main tendencies of the new revivalist movement—social and devotional. Rāma, eldest son and rightful heir to Dasharatha, King of Ayodhyā, is deprived of the throne by his stepmother's sudden demand that Dasharatha, in fulfillment of a boon granted long before, crown her own son king and banish Rāma. So that his father may keep his pledge to his wife, Rāma voluntarily withdraws to live in the wilderness for fourteen years with his faithful wife Sītā. In the forest the sages who have been leading a life of penance and austerity seek help from the great warrior Rāma against demons who are harassing them. This brings Rāma into conflict with the demons, whose king abducts Sītā and keeps her captive in his stronghold, hoping to win her love. After many struggles Rāma and his allies, the monkeys, overcome Rāvana and rescue

Sītā. Thereupon Rāma is restored to his throne in Ayodhyā and sets an example as king of the most righteous and benevolent rule.

Rāma's noble example of devotion to duty, to his father, and to his people, as well as Sītā's long-suffering fidelity to Rāma, have been looked to as religious and ethical ideals down through the ages. Rāma is seen as the embodiment of dharma, and his triumph over wicked Rāvana as the overcoming of vice (*adharma*) in order that virtue and the moral law might prevail in personal and public life. Rāma, the embodiment of dharma, is also adored as the incarnation of the Supreme Lord who has come into the world to restore the moral order. In this form he became the object of a great devotional movement which swept the country in the first centuries A.D. Generation after generation, poets have celebrated Rāma in poems and plays, in both Sanskrit and vernacular; temples have been built to him, where sculpture, song, and drama told of his glory and enthroned him in the hearts of the masses. Eventually the *Rāmāyaṇa* spread to the whole world of Southeast Asia where one can still see Rāmāyana sculptures and Rāmāyana plays. Even today, the epic, in its original Sanskrit or its vernacular versions, is read and expounded to large gatherings of devout listeners and in the national struggle for freedom which Mahātmā Gandhi waged, he held forth the establishment of *Rāma-rājya,* a reign of truth and nonviolence, as the ideal.

The Sacred Law and the epics are viewed by the Hindus as only slightly less sacred than the Vedas and together form the body of semi-canonical scriptures called *Smriti* "(human) Tradition"—as opposed to the Vedas, which are *Shruti* "(divine) Revelation." Smriti is supposed to be based on Shruti, as indeed it largely is, and its authority is therefore only derivative. It is best represented in the Lawbooks, namely, the earlier *Aphorisms on the Domestic Ritual* (*Gṛhya Sūtras*) and *Aphorisms on Dharma* (*Dharma Sūtras*), in prose, and the later expanded versified codes, called *Dharma Śāstras* or *Smṛtis,* and related texts. The most famous of these latter codes are the *Lawbook of Manu* (*Manu Smṛti,* Shunga period, second to first centuries B.C.) and that of Yājnavalkya (*Yājñavalkya Smṛti,* early Gupta period, c. fourth century A.D.).

In time the major period of Smriti (the Lawbooks and epics) covers roughly a thousand years (c.500 B.C. to A.D. c.500). Smriti gave India an integrated philosophy of life and social organization which stood the test, on the one hand, of foreign invasions and rule over several centuries (second century B.C. to A.D. c.300), and on the other, of the heterodox religions, furnishing a pattern for the integration and absorption of both. The same period of foreign invasions and rule saw the rapid spread of theistic devotional cults, which after early opposition came to accept the authority of the Sacred Law and the Vedic scriptures, and in return gained the support of orthodox Brahmanism. The alliance soon grew into the single, dynamic movement—though divided into several schools and sects—known as Hinduism. In contrast to Brahmanism, Hinduism was a mass movement, which brought together into a single culture and polity, presided over by the Sacred Law of the brāhmans, various peoples, classes, and religious traditions. This fusion of diverse forces produced one of the world's great classical periods, that of Hindu culture in the Gupta Age (fourth and fifth centuries A.D.).

The central concept which was elaborated and emphasized by Smriti was that of dharma. The word has been used in most of the Brahmanic texts from the *Rig Veda* downwards, and in different contexts, as we have seen, it has denoted different ideas, such as, Vedic ritual, ethical conduct, caste rules, and civil and criminal law. The Sacred Law is the codification of dharma. Actually, the concept of dharma is all-comprehensive and may be, broadly speaking, said to comprise precepts which aim at securing the material and spiritual sustenance and growth of the individual and society. Another significant characteristic of dharma which deserves to be specially noted is that it was regarded as not being static. The content of dharma often changed in the changing contexts of time, place, and social environment.

In spite of the comprehensive character of dharma, in its most common connotation it was limited to two principal ideals, namely the organization of social life through well-defined and well-regulated classes (varnas) and the organization of an individual's life within those classes into definite stages (āshramas). Thus, in popular parlance, dharma almost came to mean just varna-āshrama-dharma, that is the dharmas (ordained duties) of the four classes and the four stages of life.

The system of the four classes has come to be regarded as the most essential feature of Brahmanic society. Even later Hinduism, which differs from Brahmanism in many significant respects, has scrupulously preserved this peculiar social organization. Though the word *varṇa-vyavasthā* is generally translated as caste system, it should be remembered that, strictly speaking, varna does not denote caste as we understand it today. Caste system is *jāti-vyavasthā,* which, no doubt, represents a ramification of the original system of classes. From the early Brāhmanic texts we can derive but little historical information regarding the origin and development of classes and castes. The aim of those texts was avowedly to glorify and defend the social organization governed by the concepts of classes and castes. They either speak of the divine origin of those social phenomena or give some mythical accounts in respect to them. A complex social phenomenon such as the caste system must be the result of the interaction of a variety of factors. The word *varṇa* (color, complexion) itself would indicate that one of these basic factors was racial distinction. In the *Rig Veda* we actually come across references to the *ārya varṇa* (the "Aryan color," i.e., the Vedic Aryans) and the *dāsa varṇa* ("the Dāsa color," the name collectively given to all racial groups other than the Vedic Aryans). In territories where the Aryans were dominant, the color-line dividing the three upper Aryan social orders from the fourth, that of the despised shūdras, was very strict. Draconian penalties were prescribed for the shūdra who struck or insulted an Aryan, or even presumed to sit on the same seat with him. This social cleavage was given religious sanction and was thus preserved to this day in the distinction between caste Hindus and shūdras. The shūdras were denied all access to the Veda, the Vedic sacrifices, and the Aryan sacraments, especially the investiture with the sacred thread symbolic of the Aryan child's admittance to membership in his class.

Another important factor was magico-ritualistic in character. The four main classes were distinguished from one another on account of the specific roles which they played in connection with the communal sacrifice. These were determined by certain definite concepts of taboo, pollution, and purification. Corresponding to their roles in the ritual these classes were assigned distinct colors, which fact also seems to have confirmed the use of the word *varṇa* with reference to them. This magico-ritualistic origin of the four classes is indirectly indicated by their mention in the Purusha Sūkta (*Rig Veda,* 10.90), as the limbs of the cosmic sacrificial Purusha. Then there was the impact on the social organization of the Vedic Aryans of the pattern of social life already evolved by the indigenous Indian communities, which must have also been responsible for the consolidation of this social phenomenon. In the initial stages, these classes were more or less fluid and elastic. But in course of time they hardened into a definite social system characterized by a large number of endogamous and commensal castes, sub-castes, and mixed castes. Elaborate discussions occur in texts of the Sacred Law regarding their respective duties, and social and legal privileges and disabilities.

Within these classes and castes, an individual's life was organized into four distinct stages, called āshramas, in such a manner that the individual should be enabled to realize, through a properly graded scheme, the four ends of life. These four stages of life are those of the student, the householder, the hermit or recluse, and the ascetic. It will be seen that the system of the four stages of life seeks to resolve the conflict between two ideals, namely, consolidation and progress of society on the one hand and the spiritual emancipation of the individual on the other. In connection with the scheme of the four stages the texts of the Sacred Law have stated clearly and at some length the Brahmanic ideals regarding such topics as education, position of woman, and family life. Attempts have also been made to render the broad scheme of the four stages more viable and effective by prescribing various sacraments (samskāras), which are, as it were, the lampposts on the road leading to the full-fledged growth of man's personality. These sacraments cover man's whole life, beginning from the prenatal and ending with the post-mortem condition.

It will thus be seen that the Brahmanists had developed a most comprehensive system of social thought. This system continues to constitute—though in a more or less modified form—the basis of Hindu society even to this day.

What Is Dharma?

It is difficult to find any one single passage wherein the comprehensive character of dharma is adequately brought out. Some typical passages are, therefore, given below with the idea that they might cumulatively indicate some characteristic features of this highly significant concept in Brahmanism and Hinduism.

[From *Taittirīya Āraṇyaka,* 10.79]

Dharma is the foundation of the whole universe. In this world people go unto a person who is best versed in dharma for guidance. By means of dharma one drives away evil. Upon dharma everything is founded. Therefore, dharma is called the highest good.

[From *Mahābhārata,* 12.110.10–11]

For the sake of the promotion of strength and efficacy among beings the declaration of dharma is made. Whatever is attended with nonviolence (ahimsā),[1] that is dharma. Such is the fixed opinion.

Dharma [from a root *dhṛ,* "to sustain"] is so called on account of its capacity for the sustenance of the world. On account of dharma, people are sustained separately in their respective stations.[2]

[From *Vaiśeṣika Sūtra,* 1.1.2]

That from which result material gain and spiritual good is dharma.

[From *Manu Smṛti,* 8.15]

Dharma, when violated, verily, destroys; dharma, when preserved, preserves: therefore, dharma should not be violated, lest the violated dharma destroy us.

The Sources and Extent of Dharma

A discussion about the more tangible nature and extent of dharma, as it is generally understood, is given in the following passages.

[From *Yājñavalkya Smṛti,* 1.1.1–3, 6–9]

Having paid homage to Yājnavalkya, the lord of yogins, the sages said: Please expound to us fully the dharmas of the four classes, the four stages of life, and others.

The lord of yogins, living in Mithilā [capital of Videha], having meditated for a moment, said to the sages: The laws of that country in which the black antelope roams freely,[3] do you understand carefully.

The four Vedas, together with the Purānas,[4] logic, the science of Vedic interpretation, the Sacred Law [Dharma Shāstra], and the [six] limbs of

[1] In thought, word, and deed: violence of any kind disturbs the proper functioning of the individual and society, and, therefore, represents the negation of dharma.

[2] Confusion regarding the respective duties and functions (and privileges and disabilities) of different classes unbalances society. One of the king's chief duties is to prevent such confusion.

[3] That is, the open grazing lands of the north Indian plain. According to Manu (2.23), such a country alone is fit for sacrifice, that is, for Aryan habitation.

[4] Semihistorical and religious legends.

the Veda,[5] constitute the fourteen seats of sciences and of dharma. . . .

In a certain country, at a certain time, through certain means, when a thing is given over to a deserving person with faith—then, in that case, all these items, among others, indicate the concept of dharma.[6]

The Vedic scriptures [Shruti], the Sacred Law [Smriti], the practices of the good, whatever is agreeable to one's own self, and the desire which has arisen out of wholesome resolve—all these are traditionally known to be the sources of dharma.

Over and above such acts as sacrifice, traditional practices, self-control, nonviolence, charity, and study of the Veda, this, verily, is the highest dharma, namely, the realization of the Self by means of yoga.

Four persons versed in the Vedas and dharma, or a group of those who are adept only in the three Vedas, constitute a court. Whatever that court declares would be dharma; or that, which even one person who is the best among the knowers of the lore of the Self declares, would be dharma.

This passage, which is of the nature of a table of contents, indicates the scope and extent of the Sacred Law, as it was traditionally understood.

[From *Manu Smṛti,* 1.111–18]

The creation of the universe, the procedure in respect of the sacraments, the practices relating to the vow of studentship [the respectful behavior toward teachers, etc.], the highest rule regarding the ceremonial bath [to be taken at the termination of studentship],

The taking of a bride, the definitions of various kinds of marriages, the regulations concerning the great sacrifices, the eternal rule of the obsequies,

The definition of the modes of gaining subsistence, the vows of a graduate in Vedic studies [i.e., of a brāhman householder], the rules regarding what may be eaten and what may not be eaten, the purification of men and the purification of things,

The laws concerning women, the rules relating to a hermit's life, spiritual emancipation, renunciation of worldly life, the whole set of the duties of a king, the deciding of law-suits,

The rules regarding the examination of witnesses, the law governing the relation between husband and wife, the law of inheritance and parti-

[5] They are: science of correct pronunciation and accentuation, aphorisms concerning Vedic ritual, etc., grammar, Vedic etymology, Vedic metrics, and astronomy.

[6] The various constituents of the activity of giving away, which is, indeed, the main basis of all dharma, at least in the final age of a cycle, form, according to the commentator, the causative attributes of dharma.

tion of ancestral property, the law concerning gambling, the removal of men who prove to be thorns of society,

The behavior of vaishyas and shūdras, the origin of mixed castes, the law for all four classes in times of distress, similarly the expiatory rites,

The threefold course of transmigration resulting from a person's karma, the spiritual good, the examination of merits and demerits of actions,

The laws of specific countries, the laws of specific castes, the eternal laws of individual families, the laws of heretics and [tribal] communities —all these topics Manu has expounded in this treatise.

Dharma Is Not Static

The following passage brings out a very significant characteristic of dharma, namely, that the concept and content of dharma change in accordance with the changing circumstances. Ancient tradition speaks of four ages (yugas)—Krita, Tretā, Dvāpara, and Kali—their duration, respectively, 1,728,000; 1,296,000; 864,000; and 432,000 human years. It is believed that each of these four succeeding ages is characterized by an increasing physical and spiritual deterioration. No one uniform set of dharmas can, therefore, be made applicable to all the four ages. It is further believed that when one cycle of four ages is completed, there occurs the end of the universe, which is followed by a new creation and a new cycle.

[From *Manu Smṛti,* 1.81–86]

Four-footed and complete is dharma in the Krita age—it is, verily, identical with Truth. Through behavior contrary to dharma, no gain of any kind accrues to men.

In the other three ages, by reason of some kind of gain [accruing to men even through behavior contrary to dharma], dharma is deprived successively of one foot [i.e., one-fourth]. On account of the prevalence of theft, falsehood, and deceitfulness, dharma disappears successively quarter by quarter.

In the Krita age men are free from disease, accomplish all their aims, and live four hundred years; but in the ages beginning with the Tretā, their span of life decreases successively by one quarter.

The span of life of mortals mentioned in the Veda, the desired results of sacrificial rites, and the special spiritual powers of the embodied souls (that is, of mortals)—these result as fruits of men's actions in this world in accordance with the character of a particular age.

One set of dharmas is prescribed for men in the Krita age, other sets of dharmas in the Tretā and the Dvāpara ages and still another set of dharmas in the Kali age, in accordance with the increasing deterioration characterizing each successive age.

Austerities [tapas] constitute the highest dharma in the Krita age; in the Tretā, sacred knowledge is declared to be the highest dharma; in the Dvāpara they speak of the performance of sacrifice as the highest dharma; giving alone is the highest dharma in the Kali age.[7]

Varna-Dharma or Organization of the Four Classes

As far as the Brahmanic-Hindu way of life was concerned, the essence of all dharma consisted in the proper functioning of the organization of the four classes or of its later complex development, namely, the caste system. Each class had its own set of duties and obligations (*sva-dharma*) definitely prescribed and, for the sake of the solidarity and progress of society as a whole, each class or social unit was expected to act up to the following teaching of the *Bhagavad Gītā* (3.35): "Far more conducive to the ultimate good is one's own code of conduct (*sva-dharma*), even though deficient in quality, than an alien code of conduct, far easier to be practiced though it may be."

The four classes of those born from the mouth and limbs of Purusha—the brāhman (priest), kshatriya (noble), vaishya (the bourgeois), the shūdra (serf)—formed a well-knit, almost self-sufficient society.[8]

Below this society, yet economically tied to it, were a number of "excluded" castes, whose contact, shadow, or even sight polluted. They performed impure work such as scavenging, disposing of the dead, leather-work, etc., and had to live outside Aryan communities. They were made to bear distinctive marks and to strike a piece of wood to warn people of their approach. The concept of excluded castes is continued today in the untouchable castes, some of which may go back to ancient times, others probably being added from time to time from primitive tribes coming to live near more settled communities.

Large parts of India were not conquered by the Aryans but were held by various indigenous peoples, some tribes or classes of whom were observed to have a status and occupations similar to those of the corresponding twice-born

[7] Disparity (particularly in respect of material possessions), which is, indeed, the root cause of all evil and ill-will among men in the present Kali age, can be removed only by "giving away." It is interesting to view in this light such movements in modern India as *Bhū-dāna* (giving away of land), *Sampatti-dāna* (giving away of wealth), *Śrama-dāna* (making physical labor available to society), etc.

[8] The brāhmans, kshatriyas, and vaishyas are called *dvija* or twice-born, because they are entitled as Aryans to the sacrament of initiation to the study of the Veda, which is regarded as their second or spiritual birth. The study or even overhearing of the Vedic scriptures by the non-Aryan shūdras was forbidden under the most drastic penalties.

classes. These were called *Vrātyas* and were thought to be twice-born castes degraded by neglect of the Vedic rites. Though assimilated in principle to shūdras, they were eligible to admission into the caste system as brāhmans, kshatriyas, or vaishyas by having a special sacrifice performed by brāhman priests. This device may have been largely responsible for the integration among the twice-born both of the non-Aryan upper classes found in India by the Aryans and of later invaders such as the Huns. All other foreigners were despised "barbarians" (*Mlecchas*).

[From *Manu Smṛti,* 1.87–98, 102, 107, 108]

For the sake of the preservation of this entire creation, [Purusha], the exceedingly resplendent one, assigned separate duties to the classes which had sprung from his mouth, arms, thighs, and feet.[9]

Teaching, studying, performing sacrificial rites, so too making others perform sacrificial rites, and giving away and receiving gifts—these he assigned to the brāhmans.

Protection of the people, giving away of wealth, performance of sacrificial rites, study, and nonattachment to sensual pleasures—these are, in short, the duties of a kshatriya.

Tending of cattle, giving away of wealth, performance of sacrificial rites, study, trade and commerce, usury, and agriculture—these are the occupations of a vaishya.

The Lord has prescribed only one occupation [karma] for a shūdra, namely, service without malice of even these other three classes.

Man is stated to be purer above the navel than below it; hence his mouth has been declared to be the purest part by the Self-existent One.

On account of his origin from the best limb of the Cosmic Person, on account of his seniority, and on account of the preservation by him of the Veda [brahman]—the brāhman is in respect of dharma the lord of this entire creation.[10]

For the Self-Existent One, having performed penance, produced the

[9] Cf. *Rig Veda,* 10.90. The divine origin of the four classes is indicated here. It is, therefore, almost sacrilegious for a lower order to assume the duties of a higher one.

[10] Even from the point of view of civil law the brāhman enjoyed certain special privileges. In connection with the treasure-trove, for instance, the *Manu Smṛti* lays down (8.37) that if a brāhman finds it he may keep the whole of it "for he is master of everything," while persons belonging to other classes cannot do so. The punishments prescribed for a brāhman offender are more lenient than those prescribed for the same offense by persons belonging to other classes. For perjury, persons of the three lower classes shall be fined and banished, but a brāhman shall only be banished. Similarly, a brāhman is not liable to corporal punishment (*Manu Smṛti* 8.123–24).

brāhman first of all, from his own mouth, for the sake of the conveying of the offerings intended for the gods and those intended for the manes and for the sake of the preservation of this entire universe.

What created being can be superior to him through whose mouth the gods always consume the oblations intended for them and the manes those intended for them?

Of created beings, those which are animate are the best; of the animate, those who subsist by means of their intellect; of the intelligent, men are the best; and of men, the brāhmans are traditionally declared to be the best;

Of the brāhmans, the learned ones are the best; of the learned, those whose intellect is fixed upon ritual activity; of those whose intellect is fixed upon ritual activity, those who carry out ritual activity; of those who carry out ritual activity, those who realize the Brahman.

The very birth of a brāhman is the eternal incarnation of dharma. For he is born for the sake of dharma and tends toward becoming one with the Brahman. . . .

For the sake of the discussion of the brāhman's duties and of those of the other classes according to their precedence, wise Manu, the son of the Self-existent One, produced this treatise. . . .

In this treatise there are expounded in entirety dharma, the merits and demerits of [human] actions, and the eternal code of conduct of the four classes.

The code of conduct—prescribed by scriptures and ordained by sacred tradition [the Sacred Law]—constitutes the highest dharma; hence a twice-born person, conscious of his own Self [seeking spiritual salvation], should be always scrupulous in respect of it.

The Origin of Mixed Castes

This is a conventional description of the origin and nature of the various castes and mixed castes. It can by no means be regarded as reflecting the complex system of more than three thousand real castes, subcastes, mixed castes, and exterior (untouchable) castes, which prevails in India at present. Only one factor is considered in relation to the complex variety of the caste system, namely, mixed marriages; no reference is made to such other factors as occupations, specific religious functions, enforcement of deliberate economic and administrative policies, etc.

[From *Yājñavalkya Smṛti,* 1.90–96]

By husbands belonging to a particular class upon wives belonging to the same class—the husbands and wives having been united in unblemished marriages—are begotten sons who belong to the same caste as that of the father and the mother [11] and who are capable of continuing the line.

The son [12] begotten by a brāhman upon a kshatriya woman is called *Mūrdhāvasikta;* upon a vaishya woman, *Ambaṣṭha;* upon a shūdra woman, *Niṣāda* or even *Pāraśava.*[13]

The sons begotten upon vaishya and shūdra women by a kshatriya are known by tradition respectively as *Māhiṣya* and *Ugra.* The son begotten by a vaishya upon a shūdra woman is known as *Karaṇa.* This rule is laid down only in respect of married persons.

The son [14] begotten upon a brāhman woman by a kshatriya is called *Sūta;* by a vaishya, *Vaidehaka;* by a shūdra, *Cāṇḍāla,* who is excluded from all considerations of dharma.

A kshatriya woman procreates from a vaishya a son called *Māgadha,* and from a shūdra, *Kṣattṛ.* A vaishya woman procreates from a shūdra a son called *Āyogava.*

By a Māhishya is begotten upon a Karana woman a son called *Rathakāra.*[15] As bad and good are to be regarded respectively the sons born of hypogamous [pratiloma] and hypergamous [anuloma] marriages.

The progressive advance in the social status [16] [of the various mixed

[11] There is a threefold division of Hindu marriage: 1) that in which the husband and the wife belong to the same class; 2) hypergamy, in which the husband belongs to a higher class than the wife; 3) hypogamy, in which the wife belongs to a higher class than the husband. The offspring of hypogamous unions was especially despised, in direct proportion to the disparity between the ranks of the parents: the Chāndāla, said to be the offspring of a shūdra by a brāhman woman, is the lowest untouchable.

[12] This and the next stanza refer to the mixed castes resulting from hypergamous marriages. The sons of hypergamous unions between Aryan parents were also Aryan, though of mixed caste.

[13] Two very low castes.

[14] This and the next stanza refer to the mixed castes resulting from hypogamous unions.

[15] The *Sūta* (charioteer, bard), *Kṣattṛ* (doorkeeper), *Māhiṣya* (attendant on cattle), *Rathakāra* (chariot-maker) must have originally had occupational significance. The Nishādas were an aboriginal tribe in origin and lived by fishing and hunting. *Ambaṣṭha* (healer, doctor), *Vaidehaka,* and *Māgadha* (trader) are clearly regional names, implying that these castes came from Ambashtha, Videha, or Magadha. It may be seen how the castes named in this treatise had the most varied origins and were somehow integrated into a hierarchical system based on the theory of hypergamy. We must admire, however, the Brāhman author's ingenuity in choosing appropriate occupational castes for the offspring of different hybrid unions.

[16] This stanza is important in that it speaks of the possibility of a mixed caste being

castes] should be known as resulting in the seventh or even in the fifth union.[17] In cases of inversion of duties one is reduced to the status equal [to that of the caste whose way of life he adopts also at the end of the same period]. The higher and lower [status of sons born of unions between real castes and mixed castes] is to be determined on the same principle as before [the principle of hypergamy].

Initiation to Studentship

A brāhman, kshatriya, or vaishya boy is formally taken to a preceptor to be initiated to the disciplined life of a student of sacred knowledge. This initiation (upanayana) constitutes his second or spiritual birth—his birth from his parents being only a physical birth. Persons belonging to the first three classes are therefore called *dvijas* or twice-born. With the initiation commences the first stage of life (āshrama), namely, Vedic studentship or brahmacharya. The different initiation ages for the various classes suggest that their courses of study were different. The brāhman boy's was without doubt intellectually the hardest and he was probably the only one expected to master a whole Veda. The kshatriya's education was also in the hands of a brāhman preceptor, but much emphasis must have been given to training in military arts and government. As we can see from the selection given below from a work dating several centuries before Christ, a long period of education was compulsory in principle for all Aryans, who thus learned a common language (Sanskrit) and acquired a common culture. The superior linguistic, cultural, and social cohesion of the Aryans vis-à-vis the various non-Aryan tribes and peoples insured Aryan domination—political, social, and cultural—over the greater part of India even more than their military victories.

[From *Āśvalāyana Gṛhya Sūtra,* 1.19.1–13; 20.1–7; 21.5–7; 22.1–5]

In the eighth year one should initiate a brāhman; or in the eighth year from the conception in the embryo; in the eleventh year, a kshatriya; in the twelfth, a vaishya. Until the sixteenth year the proper time for initiation has not passed for a brāhman; until the twenty-second year, for a

---

elevated to the status of the next higher real caste. It also makes the significant point that a change in occupation (in normal circumstances) often implies a change in caste. In other words, birth is not the only factor which determines caste, for a Brāhman family which lives by the profession of a shūdra continuously through seven generations becomes shūdra. It is interesting that there is no mention of a person following the profession of a social order higher than his.

[17] For instance a brāhman begets upon a shūdra wife of Nishāda daughter. Another brāhman marries this Nishāda daughter and begets a daughter. Upon the daughter born in this way in the sixth generation a brāhman husband would beget a son who is himself a brāhman and not a member of any mixed caste.

kshatriya; until the twenty-fourth year, for a vaishya. After that they become banished from Sāvitrī.[18] One should not initiate them, nor teach them, nor officiate at their sacrifices; people should not have any dealings with them.

One should initiate a boy who has put on ornaments, the hair on whose head is properly taken care of, who is clothed in a new garment that has not yet been washed, or in an antelope skin if he is a brāhman, in the skin of a spotted deer if he is a kshatriya, in a goat's skin if he is a vaishya. If they put on garments, they should put on colored ones: a brāhman, a reddish-yellow one; a kshatriya, a light red one; a vaishya, a yellow one. As for their girdles: that of a brāhman should be made of *muñja* grass; that of a kshatriya, a bow-string; that of a vaishya, woolen. As for their staffs: that of a brāhman should be of *palāśa* wood; that of a kshatriya, of *uḍumbara* wood; that of a vaishya, of *bilva* wood; or all sorts of staffs are to be used by students belonging to all classes.

Having offered an oblation while the student touches him on the arm [implying participation in the offering], the teacher should station himself to the north of the sacred fire facing toward the east. To the east of the sacred fire facing toward the west should the student station himself. The teacher should then fill with water the two cavities of the hands of himself and of his student and with the formula *tat savitur vṛṇīmahe* . . . should make the water flow down upon the full cavity of the student's hands by means of the full cavity of his own hands. Having thus poured out the water upon the student's hands, he should with his own hand take the student's hand together with the thumb with the words: "By the impulse of the god Savitar [the Impeller, i.e., the sun god], with the arms of the two Ashvins [heavenly physicians], with Pūshan's hand [god of prosperity] I take thee by thy hand, O so-and-so!" The teacher should take the student's hand a second time with the words: "Savitar has taken your hand, O so-and-so." The teacher should take the student's hand a third time with the words: "Agni [Fire, the god of sacrificial rites] is thy teacher, O so-and-so!" The teacher should make the student look at the sun and should then say: "God Savitar, this is thy student of sacred knowledge [brahmachārī]; protect him; may he not die." . . .

Having seized the student's hands with the student's garment and his

[18] From initiation and hence from class and Aryan society, Sāvitrī being the Vedic verse used at initiations.

own hands, the teacher should recite the Sāvitrī verse firstly fourth by fourth, then verse-half by verse-half, and finally the whole of it. He should make the student recite the Sāvitrī after himself as far as he is able to do so. On the region of the student's heart the teacher should place his hand with the fingers stretched upwards and say: "Into my vow I put thy heart; after my mind may thy mind follow; with single-aimed vow do thou rejoice in my speech; may God Brihaspati [heavenly priest of the gods] join thee to me."

Having tied the girdle round the student and given him the staff, the teacher should instruct him in the disciplined life of a student of sacred knowledge (brahmacharya) with the words: "A student of sacred knowledge thou art; sip water [a purification rite]; do the ritual act (karma); do not sleep in the daytime; remaining under the direction of the teacher study the Veda." For twelve years lasts the studentship for the Veda; or until the student has properly learned it. The student should beg food in the evening and in the morning. He should put fuel on the sacred fires in the evening and in the morning.[19]

Marriage and Householder's Duties

The second stage of life, that of the householder, is often characterized as the basis and support of the other three. It is, indeed, the only stage which affords full scope for the realization of the first three ends of man, namely, pleasure (kāma), material gain (artha), and virtue (dharma).

[From *Āśvalāyana Gṛhya Sūtra,* 1.5.1–3; 6.1–8]

One should first examine the family [of the intended bride or bridegroom], those on the mother's side and on the father's side, as has been said above.[20] One should give his daughter in marriage to a young man endowed with intelligence. One should marry a girl who possesses the characteristics of intelligence, beauty, and good character, and who is free from disease. . . .

The father [21] may give away his daughter after decking her with orna-

[19] The student lived with the teacher at his residence and helped him in connection with, among other things, his religious observances. He begged food daily for himself and his teacher. Society bore the responsibility for the maintenance of teachers and students.

[20] That is, through ten generations, as has been prescribed in Āshvalāyana's *Aphorisms on the Vedic Ritual* (*Ā. Śrauta Sūtra,* 9.3.20).

[21] This passage describes the eight forms of marriage. The three main factors involved in these different forms are money, love, and physical force. Traditionally, the first four forms

ments and having first offered a libation of water: This is the *Brāhma* form of marriage. A son born to her after such a marriage purifies twelve descendants and twelve ancestors on both her husband's and her own sides. The father may give her away after decking her with ornaments to an officiating priest while a Vedic sacrifice is being performed: that is the *Daiva*[22] form of marriage. A son born of such a marriage purifies ten descendants and ten ancestors on both sides. "Practice dharma together," —a marriage performed with this imposition on the bride and the bridegroom is the *Prajāpatya* form of marriage. A son born of such marriage purifies eight descendants and eight ancestors on both sides. A person may marry a girl after having first given a cow and a bull to her father: that is the *Ārṣa*[23] form of marriage. A son born of such marriage purifies seven descendants and seven ancestors on both sides. A person may marry a girl after having made a mutual agreement with her. That is the *Gāndharva*[24] form of marriage. A person may marry a girl after having satisfied her father with money: that is the *Āsura* ["demonic"] form of marriage. A person may carry off a girl while her people are sleeping or are careless about her: that is the *Paiśāca* ["devilish"] form of marriage. Having killed her people and broken their heads, a person may carry off a girl, while she is weeping, from her relatives who are also weeping: that is the *Rākṣasa* ["fiendish"] form of marriage.

[From *Yājñavalkya Smṛti,* 1.97–105, 115–16]

A householder should perform every day a Smriti rite [i.e., a domestic rite prescribed by the Sacred Law, Smriti] on the nuptial fire or on the fire brought in at the time of the partition of ancestral property. He should perform a Vedic rite on the sacred fires.

Having attended to the bodily calls, having performed the purificatory rites, and after having first washed the teeth, a twice-born [Aryan] man should offer the morning prayer.

Having offered oblations to the sacred fires, becoming spiritually composed, he should murmur the sacred verses addressed to the sun god. He should also learn the meaning of the Veda and various sciences.

---

of marriage are accepted as proper, while the remaining four are condemned. This becomes clear not only from the names given to the various forms but also from the conventional mention in respect of the first four forms of marriage of the purifying capacity of sons born of those marriages.

[22] Lit. "pertaining to the [Vedic] gods."
[23] Lit. "pertaining to the [Vedic] sages."
[24] Lit. "pertaining to the heavenly musicians."

He should then go to his lord for securing the means of maintenance and progress. Thereafter having bathed he should worship the gods and also offer libations of water to the manes.

He should study according to his capacity the three Vedas, the *Atharva Veda,* the Purānas, together with the Itihāsas [legendary histories], as also the lore relating to the knowledge of the Self, with a view to accomplishing successfully the sacrifice of muttering prayers [*japa-yajña*].

Offering of the food oblation [bali], offering with the utterance *svadhā,* performance of Vedic sacrifices, study of the sacred texts, and honoring of guests—these constitute the five great daily sacrifices[25] dedicated respectively to the spirits, the manes, the gods, the Brahman, and men.

He should offer the food oblation to the spirits [by throwing it in the air] out of the remnant of the food offered to the gods. He should also cast food on the ground for dogs, untouchables, and crows.

Food, as also water, should be offered by the householder to the manes and men day after day. He should continuously carry on his study. He should never cook for himself only.

Children, married daughters living in the father's house, old relatives, pregnant women, sick persons, and girls, as also guests and servants—only after having fed these should the householder and his wife eat the food that has remained. . . .

Having risen before dawn the householder should ponder over what is good for the Self. He should not, as far as possible, neglect his duties in respect of the three ends of man, namely, virtue, material gain, and pleasure, at their proper times.

Learning, religious performances, age, family relations, and wealth—on account of these and in the order mentioned are men honored in society. By means of these, if possessed in profusion, even a shūdra deserves respect in old age.

The Position of Women

Contradictory views have been expressed concerning the social status of a Hindu woman. On the one hand it is enjoined that she should be shown the

[25] This is an expansion of the older and basic concept of Brahmanical thought, that of the three debts, to the ancestors or manes, to the gods, and to the rishis or sages. The debt to the manes was discharged by marrying and continuing the race and thus the ceremonies originally intended to feed the ancestors. The debt to the gods was discharged by sacrifices and worship and that to the sages through the study and preservation of the scriptures.

utmost respect, while, on the other, she is said to deserve no freedom. This contradiction is more apparent than real, for the emphasis in the latter case is not so much on the denial of any freedom to a woman as on the duty of her near ones to protect her at all costs.

[From *Manu Smṛti,* 3.55–57; 9.3–7, 11, 26]

Women must be honored and adorned by their fathers, brothers, husbands, and brothers-in-law who desire great good fortune.

Where women, verily, are honored, there the gods rejoice; where, however, they are not honored, there all sacred rites prove fruitless.

Where the female relations live in grief—that family soon perishes completely; where, however, they do not suffer from any grievance—that family always prospers. . . .

Her father protects her in childhood, her husband protects her in youth, her sons protect her in old age—a woman does not deserve independence.

The father who does not give away his daughter in marriage at the proper time is censurable; censurable is the husband who does not approach his wife in due season; and after the husband is dead, the son, verily, is censurable, who does not protect his mother.

Even against the slightest provocations should women be particularly guarded; for unguarded they would bring grief to both the families.

Regarding this as the highest dharma of all four classes, husbands, though weak, must strive to protect their wives.

His own offspring, character, family, self, and dharma does one protect when he protects his wife scrupulously. . . .

The husband should engage his wife in the collection and expenditure of his wealth, in cleanliness, in dharma,[26] in cooking food for the family, and in looking after the necessities of the household. . . .

Women destined to bear children, enjoying great good fortune, deserving of worship, the resplendent lights of homes on the one hand and divinities of good luck who reside in the houses on the other—between these there is no difference whatsoever.

The Hermit and the Ascetic

In the third stage of life man is expected to retire from active family and social life and seek seclusion. But he should be available for advice and guidance to the family and society whenever they need them. In the last stage, namely, that

[26] Ordained duty, especially here religious rites.

of the life of an ascetic (sannyāsin), man completely renounces this worldly life and devotes himself exclusively to spiritual self-realization.

[From *Manu Smṛti,* 6.1–3, 8, 25, 33, 42, 87–89]

Having thus lived a householder's life according to the prescribed rules, a twice-born householder should, making a firm resolve and keeping his sense-organs in subjection, live in a forest as recommended in the Sacred Law.

When a householder sees his skin wrinkled and his hair gray and when he sees the son of his son, then he should resort to the forest.

Having given up food produced in villages [by cultivation] and abandoning all his belongings, he should depart into the forest, either committing his wife to the care of his sons or departing together with her. . . .

He should be constantly engaged in study and should be self-controlled, friendly toward all, spiritually composed, ever a liberal giver and never a receiver, and compassionate toward all beings. . . .

Having consigned the sacred fires into himself [27] in accordance with the prescribed rules, he should live without a fire, without a house, a silent sage subsisting on roots and fruit. . . .

Having thus passed the third part of his life in the forest, he should renounce all attachments to worldly objects and become an ascetic during the fourth part of his life. . . .

He should always wander alone, without any companion, in order to achieve spiritual perfection—clearly seeing that such attainment is possible only in the case of the solitary man, who neither forsakes nor is forsaken. . . .

The student, the householder, the hermit, and the ascetic—these constitute the four separate stages of life, originating from and depending upon the householder's life.

All these stages of life, adopted successively and in accordance with the Shāstras, lead the brāhman [28] following the prescribed rules to the highest state.

Of all these, verily, according to the precepts of the Veda and the Smriti

[27] The three sacred fires are the symbol of a householder's life. During the latter part of his life as a forest hermit the Hindu gives up his sacred fires; these are not to be destroyed but are symbolically consigned into his own self.

[28] And also persons belonging to the next two social orders.

the householder is said to be the most excellent, for he supports the other three.

The Sacraments

The sacraments (samskāras) help to render the scheme of the four stages of an individual's life more tangible and definite. They represent, as it were, the various landmarks in man's progress through the course of life, which aim at building up a full-fledged physical and spiritual personality. The following passage represents the earliest enumeration of the sacraments. Note the author's subordination of external ritual to moral qualities at the end of the passage.

[From *Gautama Dharma Sūtra,* 8.14–26]

1) The ceremony relating to the conception of the embryo; 2) the ceremony relating to the desired birth of a male child; 3) the parting of the pregnant wife's hair by the husband [to ward off evil spirits]; 4) the ceremony relating to the birth of the child; 5) the naming of the child; 6) the first feeding; 7) the tonsure of the child's head; 8) the initiation; 9–12) the four vows taken in connection with the study of the Veda; 13) the ceremonial bath [graduation]; 14) the union with a mate who would practice dharma together with him [i.e., marriage]; 15–19) the daily performance of the five sacrifices to gods, manes, men, spirits, and the Brahman; 20–26) and the performance of the following sacrifices, that is, of the seven cooked-food sacrifices . . . ; 27–33) the seven kinds of oblation sacrifices . . . ; 34–40) the seven kinds of soma sacrifices . . . these are the forty sacraments.

Now follow the eight good qualities of the soul, namely, compassion to all beings, forbearance, absence of jealousy, purity, tranquillity, goodness, absence of meanness, and absence of covetousness. He who is sanctified by these forty sacraments but is not endowed with the eight good qualities of the soul does not become united with the Brahman, nor does he even reach the abode of the Brahman. On the other hand, he who is, verily, sanctified by a few only of the sacraments but is endowed with the eight good qualities of the soul becomes united with the Brahman, he dwells in the abode of the Brahman.

CHAPTER XI

ARTHA, *THE SECOND END OF MAN*

As we have seen, the ancient Indian concept of dharma as religiously ordained duty touched all aspects of man's relation with the society. One such aspect was political in character and often manifested itself in the form of the relation between the subject and the state. In view of the fact that the state in ancient India was mostly monarchical, this aspect of dharma was known as the *Rāja-dharma,* the dharma (duty) of kings. Naturally enough, the *Rāja-dharma,* which, by and large, corresponded with political science, formed but one of the many topics dealt with in the larger scheme of Dharma Shāstra. The latter was normally divided into three main sections, namely, rules of conduct (*ācāra*), civil and criminal law (*vyavahāra*), and expiation and punishment (*prāyascitta*). The *Rāja-dharma* was included in the section embodying the rules of conduct. In the course of time, however, polity came to be considered important enough to be recognized as an independent branch of knowledge, under the name of *Artha Shāstra,* the science of profit or material gain. As against Dharma Shāstra, Artha Shāstra may be said to have given quite a new orientation to political theory and practice. This new orientation reflected, at least to a certain extent, the increasing intensity of the struggle for power in ancient India and the growing complexity of the methods used to gain and keep control over the land and its peoples. Indeed, it is possible to find some indications of this new political ideology in the *Mahābhārata* itself. In order to overpower the Kaurava warriors like Bhīshma, Drona, and Karna, the Pāndavas often employed, under the active direction of Lord Krishna himself, ruses and stratagems which were not in strict accordance with the traditional rules of righteous war (*dharma-yuddha*). The ultimate victory of the Pāndavas over the Kauravas symbolizes, in a sense, the predominance of the new Artha Shāstra ideal over the older epic ideal of chivalry. As for the essential difference between the sacred law and the science of material gain, it may be stated in broad and rather oversimplified terms as follows: While Dharma Shāstra insisted on the righteousness of both the means and the ends, Artha Shāstra concerned itself primarily with the attainment of the ends irrespective of the nature of the means employed for that purpose. It is not unlikely that one of the reasons why Artha Shāstra is traditionally believed to be a science ancillary to the *Atharva Veda* is the similarity of their attitude toward the means and the ends. The Artha Shāstra ideology completely dominated the polity of ancient India. Attempts were made, however, from time to time to reassert the superiority of Dharma Shāstra over Artha Shāstra by prescribing that, in case of conflict between the two, Dharma Shāstra should prevail.

It is probable that besides the mostly theoretical *Dharma Sūtras* (Aphorisms on Dharma) which do not seem to have been specifically related to any particular set of social and political conditions, there had existed some kind of Artha Shāstra literature—presumably in the form of sūtras or aphorisms and more realistic in outlook—which served as a practical guide for the pursuit and exercise of power. That literature is now unfortunately not available—except perhaps in fragments—and is mainly known through references to it in later works. In 1905, however, a remarkable monument belonging to the second phase of the evolution of that literature—the phase of thorough amplification of the older aphorisms—first came to public attention. This is the well-known *Treatise on Material Gain* (*Artha Śāstra*) [1] attributed to Kautilya, the minister of Chandragupta Maurya, who was a contemporary of Alexander the Great. Though the kernel of the work may perhaps look back to the fourth century B.C., in its present form it is possibly as late as the fourth century A.D. This work is of exceptional interest and value, for it has almost revolutionized the traditional view regarding certain aspects of ancient Indian history and culture.

The *Treatise on Material Gain* of Kautilya reflects, in a striking manner, the social and political forces which were at work in India during the fourth century B.C. Alexander's incursions into India (326–325 B.C.) had helped to emphasize the need for establishing a central political and military power. The *Treatise on Material Gain* has, accordingly, laid down policies aimed at welding together, into a more or less unified pattern and under the control—direct or indirect—of a single authority, the multi-

[1] *Śāstra* means treatise, collectively "a discipline *or* science."

plicity of smaller states that had crowded the stage of Indian history at that time. Interstate relations thus constitute one of the main topics in Kautilya's *Treatise*. Kautilya defines Artha Shāstra as the science which treats of the means of acquiring and maintaining the earth, and indeed deals with practical government administration more fully than with theorizing about the fundamental principles of political science. In social matters, Kautilya has transcended the exclusiveness of ancient Brahmanism and has at the same time successfully counteracted the renunciatory tendencies of the Upanishads and early Buddhism. The exaltation of royal power in the legislative sphere and the elaboration of a complex bureaucracy in the executive sphere were certainly new to Indian polity. It is not unlikely that in these matters Kautilya has derived inspiration from foreign—more particularly, Hellenistic—sources.

To the intense political and military activity of the early Maurya period, which is reflected in the teachings of the science of material gain, there was a reaction in the reign of Ashoka (c.273–232 B.C.), the grandson of Chandragupta and the third Maurya emperor, who turned away from the Machiavellian ways of Artha Shāstra to the ways of righteousness or dharma, and in particular to the teachings of the Buddha. Under Ashoka's patronage Buddhism received great impetus and, consequently, threw out a strong challenge to the ancient Brahmanic traditions. The last Maurya monarch's commander-in-chief, Pushyamitra Shunga, who overthrew his master and thereby established his own dynasty in Magadha, was, on the other hand, a strong adherent of Brahmanism. Therefore, when he came to power he made a bold bid to resuscitate the Brahmanic way of life and thought. He performed the traditional horse sacrifice, helped the promotion of the Sanskrit language and literature, and tried to reestablish the Brahmanic ideals in the social sphere. It is out of this last activity that the *Lawbook of Manu* (*Manu Smṛti*) has presumably evolved, but in whatever little the author has said about polity one finds hardly anything original. The epic *Mahābhārata,* which is, in its final literary form, more or less contemporaneous with the *Lawbook of Manu,* is definitely richer in political speculations. The entire *Rāja-dharma* ("dharma of kings") section of the *Śāntiparvan* ("the Book of Peace," the twelfth book), for instance, constitutes a veritable compendium of political theories, rules of diplomacy, and details of administration. But the main achievement of the *Mahābhārata* consists in the synthesis of the older theories which it has attempted rather than in the enunciation of any new ones. And perhaps more significant than such theoretical discussions are the indications of political thought and practice which can be gleaned from the events actually described in the epic. At any rate, the total polity of Hindu India throughout its history from the Shunga period (second to first centuries B.C.) onward may be said to have been the result of a blending together of the political ideology of Kautilya's *Treatise on Material Gain* (in its present or an earlier form) and the social ideology of the *Lawbook of Manu.*

Among later works in Sanskrit dealing with the subject of political science may be mentioned the *Lawbook of Yājnavalkya,* the *Essence of Policy of the School of Kāmandaki* (*Kāmandakīya Nīti Sāra*), and the *Policy of Shukra* (*Śukra Nīti*). What the Lawbook of Manu was in relation to the Shunga period, the *Lawbook of Yājnavalkya* may be said to have been in relation to the Gupta period (fourth to fifth centuries A.D.). Though the latter, like its predecessor, makes no original contribution to ancient Indian polity, it reflects, to a large extent, the social changes which had been brought about by the beginning of the Gupta epoch. The Gupta lawgivers brought all persons, irrespective of caste, property, and position in society, under the purview of the king's supreme law. No person was regarded as being above the law. For instance, the *Lawbook of Yājnavalkya* denied to the brāhmans several legal concessions which they had previously enjoyed. It also did away with the many legal inequities from which the shūdra suffered. The law relating to women was also considerably revised and brought in line with their changed social status. The Gupta rulers were by no means bent on social revolution; indeed they retain much that has the sanction of orthodox tradition. Nevertheless, it is significant that whereas in earlier lawbooks there is no distinction between secular and religious law, in the *Lawbook of Yājñavalkya* these two aspects of law are clearly separated and *vyavahāra* or law proper is discussed far more systematically. It further lays greater stress on private law than on criminal law.

The *Essence of Policy* . . . which also is traditionally ascribed to the Gupta period (A.D. c.400), is but a metrical conspectus of Kautilya's *Treatise on Material Gain*. Its author shows no originality whatsoever nor are any traces to be found in it of any practical experience of governmental administration on his part. The *Essence of Policy* indicates on the one hand the unique sway which Kautilya's work held over ancient Indian polity, and on the other, the general decline of political thought in the succeeding periods. The same may be said of the *Kuraḷ,* a comprehensive work in Tamil by Tiruvalluvar, which deals with the three ends of man. This work probably dates from A.D. 450–500 and, like most of the Tamil literature produced in that period, shows unmistakable influence of earlier Sanskrit works. Even a casual perusal of the section on polity in the *Kuraḷ* would make it quite evident that Tiruvalluvar was closely acquainted with Kautilya's *Treatise* and has derived his inspiration and material from that work. Contrary to our expectations, therefore, the *Kuraḷ* does not contain any political thought which can be characterized as peculiar to South India. The last phase of the history of ancient Indian polity is represented by the *Policy of Shukra,* which is usually ascribed to about A.D. 800. This work also is in the nature of a conspectus of earlier works on polity, but it is remarkable for its detailed treatment of the administrative machinery, foreign relations, and military policy.

Dharma As the Supreme Authority

The normal form of the state in ancient India was monarchy. Temporal sovereignty, however, was usually considered to be based on religious authority. Thus, the dharma, the religious and moral law, elaborated and preserved by the brāhmans, was thought to be the source of kshatra, the sovereign power of the king, and therefore superior to it. The coronation ceremony, it is true, represented the application of this spiritual power in the temporal realm, and in that respect the custodians of spiritual power on earth were regarded as subordinate to the temporal authority vested in the king. Nevertheless, the king's chaplain (purohita), who was considered the embodiment of brahman, spiritual power, served as the king's mentor in temporal as well as spiritual matters. In this capacity he and other brāhman advisers attempted to guide and restrain the king's exercise of power, reminding him that it was not absolute. In so far as they actually succeeded in inspiring respect for dharma in the ruler, the brāhmans were thereby able to serve as a kind of check on the monarchy.

Social prosperity and the harmonious functioning of society were believed to depend upon a society composed of the four social orders, namely, brāhman, kshatriya, vaishya, and shūdra, representing respectively spiritual authority, temporal power, wealth, and labor. The society could not flourish in the absence of any of its four constituents. The regulation and prosperity of such an ordered society was not so much the function of the king as it was of dharma or law. Thus, in the *Rig Veda* each person in the ordered universe (sat) had a particular function (*vrata*) to perform. The regulation of this ordered universe was established by cosmic law or order, rita or dharma. Hence, the performance of duty in accordance with this law brought about a state of harmony with the ordered universe (sat) and was regarded as *satya* (truth). In this way, cosmic law was identified with truth and was regarded as the ultimate authority to which even the king was obliged to yield. This supremacy of dharma is the basic concept of ancient Indian social and political thought.

[From *Bṛhad Āraṇyaka Upaniṣad,* 1.4.11–14]

Verily, in the beginning this [world] was brahman, being only one. That brahman, being one, did not prosper. It therefore brought forth an excellent form, kshatra, such as those among the gods who are embodiments of kshatra, namely Indra, Varuna. . . . Therefore, there is nothing higher than kshatra. Therefore, the brāhman sits below the kshatriya at the coronation [*rājasūya*] sacrifice. Thereby, indeed, brahman confers honor on kshatra. The source of kshatra, however, is this very brahman. Therefore, even though the king attains supremacy, finally he has to resort to brahman, which is, indeed, his own source. So a king who injures a brāhman attacks his own source. He becomes more sinful as does one who injures his superiors.

Still he did not prosper. He created the community [*viś,* i.e., the vaishyas], such as those classes of gods, who are designated by groups, namely, the Vasus, the Rudras, the Ādityas. . . .

Still he did not prosper. He created the menial class [*śūdra-varṇa*], such as Pūshan among the gods. Verily, this earth is Pūshan for it nourishes all this, whatever there is.[1]

Still he did not prosper. That brahman brought forth an excellent form, dharma [law]. This dharma is the sovereign power ruling over kshatra itself. Therefore, there is nothing higher than dharma. Thereby, even the weak can overcome the strong with the help of dharma as with the help of a king. Verily, that which is dharma is truth [*satya*]. Therefore, they say of a man who speaks dharma, that he speaks the truth, for, verily, these two are one and the same.

The Origin of Kingship

In Vedic literature there are various speculations, mostly embodied in mythical legends, about such topics as the origin and nature of kingship, the functions

[1] Pūshan is a Vedic deity represented as a pastoral divinity and pathmaker *par excellence.* The principal functions indicate his service to gods and men. Similarly, the shūdras are the servants of the three higher classes. There is here, too, a pun on Pūshan and the earth which nourishes (*puṣyati*) the world.

of the king, and types of sovereignty. Though the most frequent theory expounded is that of the divine origin of kingship, in the Vedic literature itself references to any divinity attaching to the person of an historical king are rare. Occasionally in the *Rig Veda* or *Atharva Veda* a king is referred to as half-god or even a god above mortals. In ancient India, however, the king is not regarded as an incarnation on earth of any one particular deity, though he is often represented as the embodiment of a number of divinities. The idea of the personality of a king having been formed of essential particles derived from different gods was developed, perhaps for the first time, in the *Lawbook of Manu* (e.g. *Manu Smṛti,* 7.4–8).

In some older texts there are also suggestions that the king was selected or chosen, usually on account of some pressing need or special urgency, such as war, and was expected to fulfill certain obligations to the people. Public opinion expressed itself through popular assemblies or councils (*sabhā, samiti*) and something akin to a social contract between the king and his subjects was understood to exist. However this may be, it should be remembered that the normal form of state in ancient India was monarchy, usually with some form of religious sanction, and that the normal form of monarchy was hereditary.

One theory of the divine origin of kingship is found in the *Mahābhārata,* where, for instance, Brahmā or Prajāpati, the lord of creatures, is said to have rescued the human race from a state of nature by laying down a code of conduct for all people and by creating the institution of kingship. In the following passage three distinct stages in the evolution of kingship are indicated, namely, the golden age of stateless society under the regulation of dharma, in which individuals were conscious of their duties toward themselves and their fellow men, and external agencies, like state or government, were unnecessary; the period of decadence characterized by the prevalence of a state of nature; and finally the period which saw the divine establishment of law and the first king, Virajas, as administrator of law.

[From *Mahābhārata,* 12.59.5, 13–30, 93–94]

Yudhishthira said: "This word 'king' (*rājā*) is so very current in this world, O Bhārata; how has it originated? Tell me that, O grandfather."

Bhīshma said: "Certainly, O best among men, do you listen to everything in its entirety—how kingship originated first during the golden age (krita-yuga). Neither kingship nor king was there in the beginning, neither scepter (*daṇḍa*) nor the bearer of a scepter. All people protected one another, by means of righteous conduct (dharma). Thus, while protecting one another by means of righteous conduct, O Bhārata, men eventually fell into a state of spiritual lassitude. Then delusion overcame them. Men were thus overpowered by infatuation, O leader of men, on account of the delusion of understanding; their sense of righteous conduct was lost.

When understanding was lost, all men, O best of the Bhāratas, overpowered by infatuation, became victims of greed. Then they sought to acquire what should not be acquired. Thereby, indeed, O lord, another vice, namely desire, overcame them. Attachment then attacked them, who had become victims of desire. Attached to objects of sense, they did not discriminate between right and wrong action, O Yudhishthira. They did not avoid, O king of kings, pursuing what was not worth pursuing, nor, similarly, did they discriminate between what should be said and what should not be said, between the edible and inedible, and between right and wrong. When this world of men had been submerged in dissipation, all spiritual knowledge [brahman] perished; and when spiritual knowledge perished, O king, righteous conduct also perished.

"When spiritual knowledge and righteous conduct perished, the gods were overcome with fear, and fearfully sought refuge with Brahmā, the creator. Going to the great lord, the ancestor of the worlds, all the gods, afflicted with sorrow, misery, and fear, with folded hands said: 'O Lord, the eternal spiritual knowledge, which had existed in the world of men has perished because of greed, infatuation, and the like, therefore we have become fearful. Through the loss of spiritual knowledge, righteous conduct also has perished, O God. Therefore, O Lord of the three worlds, mortals have reached a state of indifference. Verily, we showered rain on earth, but mortals showered rain [i.e., oblations] up to heaven. As a result of the cessation of ritual activity on their part, we faced a serious peril. O grandfather, decide what is most beneficial to us under these circumstances.'

"Then, the self-born lord said to all those gods: 'I will consider what is most beneficial; let your fear depart, O leaders of the gods.'

"Thereupon he composed a work consisting of a hundred thousand chapters out of his own mind, wherein righteous conduct (dharma), as well as material gain (artha) and enjoyment of sensual pleasures (kāma) were described. This group, known as the threefold classification of human objectives, was expounded by the self-born lord; so, too, a fourth objective, spiritual emancipation (moksha), which aims at a different goal, and which constitutes a separate group by itself.

"Then the gods approached Vishnu, the lord of creatures, and said: 'Indicate to us that one person among mortals who alone is worthy of the highest eminence.' Then the blessed lord god Nārāyana reflected, and brought forth an illustrious mind-born son, called Virajas [who became the first king]."

The Science of Polity

The important place of political and economic thought, in relation to the other major fields of human inquiry and speculation, is set forth in the passages which follow.

[From *Kauṭilīya Artha Śāstra,* 1.2, 3, 4, 7]

Philosophy, the Veda, the science of economics, and the science of polity—these are the sciences. . . .

Sānkhya, Yoga, and materialism—these constitute philosophy. Distinguishing, with proper reasoning, between good and evil in the Vedic religion, between profit and nonprofit in the science of economics, and between right policy and wrong policy in the science of polity, and determining the comparative validity and invalidity of these sciences [under specific circumstances], philosophy becomes helpful to the people, keeps the mind steady in woe and weal, and produces adroitness of understanding, speech, and action. . . .

The *Sāma Veda,* the *Rig Veda,* and the *Yajur Veda* constitute the trilogy of the *Vedas.* These, the *Atharva Veda,* and the *Itihāsa Veda* (the Veda of history and legends) make up the Vedas. Phonetics, ritual, grammar, etymology, metrics, and astronomy—these are the limbs [ancillary sciences] of the Veda. The way of life taught in the trilogy of the Vedas [and other Vedic works] is helpful on account of its having laid down the duties of the four classes and the four stages of life. . . .

Agriculture, cattle-breeding, trade, and commerce constitute the main topics dealt with in the science of economics; it is helpful on account of its making available grains, cattle, gold, raw material, and free labor. Through the knowledge of economics, a king brings under his control his own party and the enemy's party with the help of treasury and army.

The scepter [1] (*daṇḍa*) is the means of the acquisition and the preservation of philosophy, the Veda, and economics. The science treating with the effective bearing of the scepter is the science of polity (*Daṇḍa Nīti*). It conduces to the acquisition of what is not acquired, the preservation of what has been acquired, the growth of what has been preserved, and the

[1] That is, government as opposed to anarchy.

distribution among worthy people of what has grown. It is on it [the science of polity] that the proper functioning of society [lit., the world] depends. . . .

"Of the three ends of human life, material gain is, verily, the most important." So says Kautilya. "On material gain depends the realization of dharma and pleasure." [2]

[From *Śukra Nīti,* 1.4–19]

Other sciences treat of one or another field of human activity, while the science of policy (Nīti Shāstra) [3] is helpful in all respects and conduces to the stability of human society.

As the science of policy is the source of dharma, material gain, and pleasure, and as it is traditionally said to lead to spiritual emancipation, a king should always study it diligently.

Through the knowledge of the science of policy, kings and others become conquerors of their foes and conciliators of their own people. Kings who are skillful in working out the right policy always prevail.

Can the knowledge of words and their meanings not be acquired without the study of grammar, and of material categories without the study of logic, and the science of reasoning and of ritual practices and procedures without the study of the *Pūrva Mīmāṃsā?* [4] Can the limitations and destructibility of bodily existence not be realized without the study of the Vedānta texts? [5]

Further, these sciences treat only of their own special subjects. They are, accordingly, studied only by such persons as follow their respective teachings. Their study implies mere adroitness of intellect. Of what avail are they to people interested and engaged in everyday affairs? On the other hand, the stability of any human affairs is not possible without the science of policy, in the same way as the functioning of the physical bodies of men is not possible without food.

The science of policy conduces to the fulfillment of all desires and is, therefore, respected by all people. It is quite indispensable even to a king, for he is the lord of all people.

Just as diseases are bound to make their appearance in the case of per-

[2] Consequently the Artha Shāstra, the science of material gain (i.e., polity), is the most important science.

[3] Lit., science of wise conduct (*nīti*), another name for the science of material gain or polity (Artha Shāstra).

[4] The philosophy of ritual.

[5] The Upanishads.

sons who eat unwholesome foods, so do enemies make their appearance—some immediately and some in course of time—in respect of kings who are devoid of the knowledge of the science of policy; but it never happens that they do not make their appearance at all.

The primary duty of a king consists of the protection of his subjects and the constant keeping under control of evil elements. These two cannot possibly be accomplished without the science of policy.

Absence of the knowledge of the science of policy is, verily, the weakest point of a king—it is ever dangerous. It is said to be a great help to the growth of the enemy and to the diminution of one's own power.

Whoever abandons the science of policy and behaves independently [that is, without any consideration for the teachings of the science] suffers from misery. Service of such an independent [i.e., self-willed, capricious] master is like licking the sharp edge of the sword.

A king who follows the science of policy is easily propitiated,[6] while one who does not follow it cannot be easily propitiated. Where both—right policy and might—exist, there prevails all-round glory.

In order that the entire kingdom should, of its own accord, become productive of good, right policy should be employed and maintained by a king. This should, indeed, be done by a king also for his own good.

A kingdom divided within itself, the army disintegrated, the civil service headed by ministers disorganized—these are always the result of the ineptitude of a king who is devoid of the knowledge of the science of policy.

Duties of a King

Ancient Indian polity does not treat specifically of the rights and the privileges of the subject but leaves them to be inferred from the duties and the responsibilities of the king, with which it deals at some length. The following passage, which deals with the duties of a king, prescribes that the king regulate his activities according to a definite timetable. A king was expected to keep himself in touch with every department of administration. Special emphasis was put on the inadvisability of his isolation from his subjects.

[From *Kauṭilīya Artha Śāstra,* 1.19]

Only if a king is himself energetically active, do his officers follow him energetically. If he is sluggish, they too remain sluggish. And, besides,

[6] Or: has his own desires easily fulfilled.

they eat up his works.[1] He is thereby easily overpowered by his enemies. Therefore, he should ever dedicate himself energetically to activity.

He should divide the day as well as the night into eight parts. . . . During the first one-eighth part of the day, he should listen to reports pertaining to the organization of law and order and to income and expenditure. During the second, he should attend to the affairs of the urban and the rural population. During the third, he should take his bath and meal and devote himself to study. During the fourth, he should receive gold and the departmental heads. During the fifth, he should hold consultations with the council of ministers through correspondence and also keep himself informed of the secret reports brought by spies. During the sixth, he should devote himself freely to amusement or listen to the counsel of the ministers. During the seventh, he should inspect the military formations of elephants, cavalry, chariots, and infantry. During the eighth, he, together with the commander-in-chief of the army, should make plans for campaigns of conquest. When the day has come to an end he should offer the evening prayers.

During the first one-eighth part of the night, he should meet the officers of the secret service. During the second, he should take his bath and meals and also devote himself to study. During the third, at the sounding of the trumpets, he should enter the bed chamber and should sleep through the fourth and fifth. Waking up at the sounding of the trumpets, he should, during the sixth part, ponder over the teachings of the sciences and his urgent duties for the day. During the seventh, he should hold consultations and send out the officers of the secret service for their operations. During the eighth, accompanied by sacrificial priests, preceptors, and the chaplain, he should receive benedictions; he should also have interviews with the physician, the kitchen-superintendent, and the astrologer. Thereafter, he should circumambulate by the right[2] a cow with a calf and an ox and then proceed to the reception hall. Or he should divide the day and the night into parts in accordance with his own capacities and thereby attend to his duties.

When he has gone to the reception hall, he should not allow such persons, as have come for business, to remain sticking to the doors of the hall [i.e., waiting in vain]. For, a king, with whom it is difficult for the people to have an audience, is made to confuse between right action and wrong

[1] That is, spoil or bring to naught his works.

[2] As a mark of respect or reverence.

action by his close entourage. Thereby he suffers from the disaffection of his own subjects or falls prey to the enemy. Therefore he should attend to the affairs relating to gods,[3] hermitages, heretics, learned brāhmans, cattle, and holy places as also those of minors, the aged, the sick, those in difficulty, the helpless, and women—in the order of their enumeration or in accordance with the importance or the urgency of the affairs.

A king should attend to all urgent business, he should not put it off. For what has been thus put off becomes either difficult or altogether impossible to accomplish.

Seated in the fire-chamber and accompanied by the chaplain and the preceptor he should look into the business of the knowers of the Veda and the ascetics—having first got up from his seat and having respectfully greeted them.

Only in the company of the adepts in the three Vedas, and not by himself, should he decide the affairs of the ascetics as also of the experts in magical practices—lest these become enraged.

The vow of the king is energetic activity, his sacrifice is constituted of the discharge of his own administrative duties; his sacrifical fee [to the officiating priests] is his impartiality of attitude toward all; his sacrificial consecration is his anointment as king.

In the happiness of the subjects lies the happiness of the king; in their welfare, his own welfare. The welfare of the king does not lie in the fulfillment of what is dear to him; whatever is dear to the subjects constitutes his welfare.

Therefore, ever energetic, a king should act up to the precepts of the science of material gain. Energetic activity is the source of material gain; its opposite, of downfall.

In the absence of energetic activity, the loss of what has already been obtained and of what still remains to be obtained is certain. The fruit of one's works is achieved through energetic activity—one obtains abundance of material prosperity.

The Seven Limbs of the State

Though monarchy was the normal form of state in ancient India, the sovereign power was never concentrated in the person or the office of the monarch alone.

[3] This refers to endowments, etc. in the name of the gods. Note the relatively high importance of the "heretics," mostly Buddhists and Jains, coming right after Hindu temples and brāhman hermitages.

The state or sovereignty was regarded as an organic whole made up of seven constituents, which are called the "limbs" of the body politic—the monarch being just one of those constituents. The state can function effectively only if these constituents remain properly integrated with one another. Modern political theorists mention territory, population, and central government as together constituting the state. It is interesting to note the additional constituents mentioned by Kautilya, who is first among ancient Indian writers to advance the theory of the seven constituents of the state.

[From *Kauṭilīya Artha Śāstra,* 6.1]

The king, the ministers, the country, the forts, the treasury, the army, and the allies are the constituents of the state.

Of these, the perfection of the king is this: Born of a high family; non-fatalistic; endowed with strong character; looking up to [experienced] old men [for guidance]; religious, truthful in speech; not inconsistent [in his behavior]; grateful; having liberal aims; full of abundant energy; not procrastinating; controller of his feudatories; of determined intellect; having an assembly of ministers of no mean quality; intent on discipline—these are the qualities by means of which people are attracted toward him. Inquiry; study; perception; retention; analytical knowledge; critical acumen; keenness for the realization of reality—these are the qualities of the intellect. Valor; impetuosity; agility; and dexterity—these are the qualities of energy. Of profound knowledge; endowed with strong memory, cogitative faculty, and physical strength; exalted; easily controlling himself; adept in arts; rid of difficulties;[4] capable bearer of the scepter; openly responding both to acts of help and harm; full of shame [to do anything evil]; capable of dealing adequately with visitations of nature and the constituents of state; seeing far and wide; utilizing for his work the opportunities afforded by the proper place, time, and personal vigor; skilled in discriminating between conditions which require conclusion of a treaty and manifestation of valor, letting off the enemies and curbing them, and waiting under the pretext of some mutual understanding and taking advantage of the enemies' weak points; laughing joyfully, but guardedly and without loss of dignity; looking straight and with uncrooked brow; free from passion, anger, greed, obstinacy, fickleness, heat, and calumny; capable of self-management; speaking with people smilingly but with dignity; observing customs as taught by elderly people—these are the qualities of the personality.

[4] Or: not addicted to vices.

The perfection of the ministers has been described earlier.[5]

Firm in the midland and at the boundaries; capable of affording subsistence to its own people and, in case of difficulties, also to outsiders; easy to defend; affording easy livelihood to the people; full of hatred for the enemy; capable of controlling [by its strategic position] the dominions of the feudatories; devoid of muddy, rocky, salty, uneven, and thorny tracts, and of forests infested with treacherous animals and wild animals; pleasing; rich in arable land, mines, and timber and elephant forests; wholesome to cows; wholesome to men; with well-preserved pastures; rich in cattle; not depending entirely on rain; possessing waterways and overland roads; having markets full of valuable, manifold, and abundant ware; capable of bearing the burden of army and taxation; having industrious agriculturists, stupid masters,[6] and a population largely consisting of the lower classes [i.e., the economically productive classes, vaishyas and shūdras]; inhabited by devoted and respectable men—this is the perfection of the country.

The perfection of the forts has been described earlier.[7]

Lawfully inherited from his ancestors or earned by the king himself; mainly consisting of gold and silver; full of manifold and big precious stones and bars of gold; and such as would endure a calamity even of a long duration and also a state of things which brought in no income—this is the perfection of the treasury.

Coming down from father and grandfather; constant in its loyalties; obedient; having the sons and wives of soldiers contented and well provided for; not becoming disintegrated in military campaigns in foreign lands; everywhere unassailable; capable of bearing pain; experienced in many battles; expert in the science of all the weapons of war; regarding the rise and the downfall of the king as equivalent to their own and consequently not double-dealing with him; mainly consisting of kshatriyas [nobles]—this is the perfection of the army.

Coming down from father and grandfather; constant in their loyalties;

[5] *Kauṭilīya Artha Śāstra* 1.9. It is mentioned there that a minister should be, among other things, native, born of high family, influential, trained in arts, endowed with foresight, bold, eloquent, possessed of enthusiasm, dignity, endurance, etc.

[6] According to the *Essence of Policy* . . . (4.54), the leading personalities in the country should be stupid. The commentator explains: Where the leaders of the community are foolish, the king can rule according to his own sweet will and without any obstruction.

[7] *Kauṭilīya Artha Śāstra* 2.3. On all the boundaries of the kingdom there should be defensive fortifications. Mention is made of water-forts, mountain-forts, desert-forts, and forest-forts. Details regarding their construction are also given.

obedient; not double-dealing; capable of preparing for war on a large scale and quickly—this is the perfection of the allies.

Not born of a royal family; greedy; having an assembly of ministers who are mean; with his subjects antagonistic toward him; inclined toward injustice; non-diligent; overcome by calamities; devoid of enthusiasm; fatalistic; indiscreet in his actions; helpless; supportless; impotent; and ever doing harm to others—this is the perfection of the enemy. For such an enemy is easy to uproot.

Excepting the enemy these seven constituents, characterized by the development of their respective qualities and serving as limbs of sovereignty, are said to be intended for promoting the perfection of the sovereignty.

A king endowed with a significant personality makes the imperfect constituents perfect. A king without personality, on the other hand, destroys the constituents even though they are well developed and effectively attached to one another.

Therefore, even the ruler of the four ends of the earth, the constituents of whose sovereignty are spoiled and who is not endowed with a significant personality, is either destroyed by the constituents themselves or is overpowered by his enemies.

On the other hand, a ruler who is endowed with a significant personality, is blessed with perfect constituents of sovereignty, and is a knower of statecraft, though possessing a small dominion, verily, conquers the entire earth—he does not suffer a setback.

The Circle of States and Interstate Policy

The theory of the circle of states and that of the sixfold interstate policy, as formulated by the political theorists of ancient India, may appear rather doctrinaire, but they clearly involve certain principles which must have been derived from practical political experience. The normal state of affairs is seen as a balance of power among the various states, but the ruler is impressed with the need for always remaining on his guard, for tactfully watching the situation, and, whenever an opportunity offers itself, for acting as a hammer unto others lest he himself be turned into an anvil.

[From *Kauṭilīya Artha Śāstra,* 6.2; 7.1]

Repose and activity constitute the source of acquisition and maintenance of wealth. Effort toward the acquisition of the fruits of works undertaken is activity. Effort toward the continuance of the enjoyment of the fruits of works is repose. The source of repose and activity is the sixfold policy. Its possible results are deterioration, stagnation, and progress. Its human aspect is constituted of right policy and wrong policy; its divine aspect of good luck and bad luck. For the divine working and the human working together keep the world going. That which is brought about by unseen forces is the divine. Thereby, the acquisition of the desired fruit denotes good luck; that of the undesired, bad luck. That which is brought about by the visible forces is the human. Thereby, the accomplishment of acquisition and maintenance denotes right policy; nonaccomplishment, wrong policy. The human aspect can be thought about [and taken care of]; the divine cannot be thought about [and taken care of].

The king who is endowed with personality and the material constituents of sovereignty and on whom all right policy rests is called the conqueror.[8] That which encircles him on all sides and prevails in the territory immediately adjacent to his is the constituent of the circle of states known as the enemy. Similarly, that which prevails in the territory which is separated from the conqueror's territory by one [namely, by the enemy's territory] is the constituent known as friend. A neighboring prince having the fullest measure of antagonism is an enemy. When he is in difficulty, he should be attacked; when he is without support or has weak support, he should be exterminated. In contrary circumstances [that is, when he is strong or has strong support], he should be harassed or weakened. These are the peculiar attitudes to be taken toward an enemy.

From the enemy onward and in front of the conqueror are the friend, the enemy's friend, the friend's friend, and the enemy's friend's friend, ruling over the consecutively adjacent territories. In the rear of the conqueror there are the rear-seizer,[9] the challenger,[10] the ally of the rear-seizer, and the ally of the challenger [ruling over the consecutively adjacent territories].

The prince ruling over the territory immediately adjacent to that of the conqueror is the conqueror's "natural" enemy. One who is born in the same family as the conqueror is his "born" enemy. One who is himself

[8] The conqueror is the king with reference to whom all the teachings of Kautilya's *Treatise* are taught. He may, indeed, be said to be the hero of this treatise. It is he who is the center of the circle of states and who is expected to employ the sixfold interstate policy. A king, according to Kautilya, must always aim at victories over others.

[9] An inimical prince who attacks the rear of the conqueror.

[10] *Ākranda,* lit. one who shouts, is a prince who "challenges" the rear-seizer on behalf of the conqueror or who warns the conqueror of the rear attack.

antagonistic to the conqueror or creates antagonism toward him among others is his "factitious" enemy. The prince ruling over the territory immediately beyond the one adjacent to that of the conqueror is his "natural" friend. One who is related to the conqueror through the father or the mother is his "born" friend. One with whom the conqueror has sought refuge for the sake of wealth or life is his "factitious" friend.

The prince who rules over the territory adjacent to those of the enemy and of the conqueror and who is capable of favoring both of them, whether they are united or not, or of keeping them under restraint when they are not united, is the middle king.

The prince who rules over a territory lying beyond those of the enemy, the conqueror, and the middle king, who is stronger than the other kings constituting the circles of states, and who is capable of favoring the enemy, the conqueror, and the middle king, whether they are united or not, or of keeping them under restraint when they are not united, is the neutral king.

These twelve [11] are the primary kings constituting the circles of states.

The conqueror, his friend, and friend's friend are the three primary constituents of his own circle of states. They are, each of them, possessed of the five constituents of sovereignty, namely, minister, country, fort, treasury, and army. Each circle of states, accordingly, consists of eighteen constituents.[12] Hereby are explained also the circles of states belonging to the enemy, the middle king, and the neutral king.

Thus there are in all four circles of states.[13] There are twelve primary kings; [14] and sixty constituents of sovereignty; [15] in all, there are seventy-two constituents.[16] [6.2]

The circle of states is the source of the sixfold policy. The teacher says: "Peace, war, marking time, attack, seeking refuge, and duplicity are the

[11] Namely: conqueror, enemy, friend, enemy's friend, friend's friend, enemy's friend's friend, rear-seizer, challenger, rear-seizer's ally, challenger's ally, the middle king, and the neutral king.

[12] That is, six constituents of sovereignty for each state, omitting the seventh, the ally, which is already implicit in the scheme.

[13] Namely, those of the conqueror, the enemy, the middle king, and the neutral king.

[14] Namely, the same four main kings and their respective friends and friends' friends. The rear-seizer, the challenger, and their respective allies do not seem to have been included in this number.

[15] Each of the twelve kings has five constituents of sovereignty (besides himself), omitting the ally as above.

[16] The above sixty plus the twelve kings.

six forms of interstate policy." "There are only two forms of policy," says Vātavyādhi, "for the sixfold policy is actually accomplished through peace and war." Kautilya says: "The forms of policy are, verily, six in number, for conditions are different in different cases."

Of these six forms: binding through pledges means peace; offensive operation means war; apparent indifference means marking time; strengthening one's position means attack; giving oneself to another [as a subordinate ally or vassal] means seeking refuge; keeping oneself engaged simultaneously in peace and war with the same state means duplicity. These are the six forms of policy.

When one king [the would-be conqueror] is weaker than the other [i.e., his immediate neighbor, the enemy], he should make peace with him. When he is stronger than the other, he should make war with him. When he thinks: "The other is not capable of putting me down nor am I capable of putting him down," he should mark time. When he possesses an excess of the necessary means, he should attack. When he is devoid of strength,[17] he should seek refuge with another. When his end can be achieved only through the help of an ally, he should practice duplicity.

So is the sixfold policy laid down. [7.1]

State Administration

This statement about the qualifications and functions of the principal ministers of the king clearly indicates a very complex and highly specialized governmental organization. It is also typical of the ancient Indian writings on polity, which concerned themselves more with the concrete administrative details than with abstract political theorizing.

[From *Śukra Nīti,* 2.69, 70, 77–108]

The chaplain, the deputy, the premier, the commandant, the counsellor, the judge, the scholar, the economic adviser, the minister, and the ambassador—these are the king's ten primary officers. . . .

Well-versed in ritual formulas and practices, learned in the three Vedas, diligent about religious duties, conqueror of his sense-organs, subduer of anger, devoid of greed and infatuation, possessed of the knowledge of the

[17] Strength, as Kautilya has said elsewhere, is of three kinds: strength of wise counsel (which is made up of knowledge and wisdom), strength of sovereignty (which is made up of treasury and army), and strength of personal enterprise (which is made up of the will to martial glory).

six limbs of the Veda and of the science of archery together with its various branches, one fearing whose anger even the king becomes devoted to righteous conduct and right policy, skilled in polity and the science of weapons, missiles, and military tactics—such should the chaplain be; such a chaplain is, verily, also the preceptor—capable of cursing and blessing alike. Those with reference to whom the king thinks: "Without the proper advice of these primary officers, my kingdom may be lost and there may be a general setback"—they should be regarded as good ministers. Is the growth of the kingdom possible without such ministers whom the king does not fear? Just as women are to be adorned with ornaments, dresses, etc., so too should these ministers be adorned and propitiated. What is the use of those ministers, whose counsels conduce neither to any aggrandizement of kingdom, population, army, treasury, and good kingship, nor to destruction of the enemy?

He who can discriminate between what is to be done and what is not to be done is traditionally known to be qualified for the office of the deputy. The premier is the supervisor of all things, and the commandant is well versed in military science and technique. The counsellor is skilled in polity and the scholar is the master of the essential tenets of righteous conduct. The judge possesses the knowledge of popular customs and principles of law. One who possesses an insight into the proper time and place for any action is called the minister, while one who knows the income and expenditure of the state is known as the economic adviser. One who can delve into the innermost thoughts and the secret actions, who has good memory, who has an insight into the proper time and place for any action, who is a master of the sixfold policy, who is an effective speaker, and who is fearless—such a one should be made the ambassador.

The deputy should always advise the king about a thing which, though unwholesome, has to be done, about the time when a thing is fit to be done instantly, and about a thing which, though wholesome, should not be done. He should make him act, or himself act, or should neither act nor advise.[1] The premier should, indeed, find out whether a thing is effective or ineffective, and watch over all the working in connection with the state functions entrusted to all officers. The commandant should be in charge of elephants, as also of horses, chariots, and foot-soldiers, so of

[1] When he feels that such action or advice is not necessary.

strong camels and, verily, of oxen; of those who are studied in military musical instruments, code-languages, ensigns, and battle-arrays, of vanguards and rearguards; of bearers of royal emblems, weapons, and missiles; of menial servants; and of servants of middle and high grades. He should find out the efficacy of missiles, missile-throwers, and cavalry; he should also find out how many among the troops are capable of action, how many are old, and how many new; he should further find out how many among the troops are incapable of action, how many are equipped with arms, ammunition, and gunpowder, and how much is the quantity of war material. Having carefully thought over all this the commandant should properly report to the king as to what is to be done. The counsellor should consider as to how, when, and in respect of whom the policies of conciliation, bribery, dissension, and punishment are to be employed and as to what their result would be—whether great, moderate, or small. He should then decide on some action and report it to the king. The judge should always advise the king after examining, while seated in the court with his assessors, the plaints brought forth by men, by means of witness, written documents, rights accruing from possession, artifices, and ordeals—first finding out as to which of these means is effective in which suits—and after getting the decisions agreed upon by the majority confirmed through the application of logic, direct observation, inference, and analogy as also of popular customs. The scholar should study the rules of conduct which are current, which have become archaic, and which are observed by the people, which are prescribed in scriptures, which are not applicable at a particular time, and which are opposed to scriptures and popular customs, and recommend to the king such rules as would be conducive to happiness in this life and hereafter. The economic adviser should report to the king on the following items: the quantity of commodities like grass, etc., stored during a particular year; the quantity spent; and the quantity in movables and immovables which has been left as balance. The minister should investigate and report to the king on how many cities, villages, and forests there are, how much land is under cultivation, who received rent from it and how much, how much remains after paying off the rent, how much land is uncultivated, how much revenue is realized in a particular year by way of taxes and fines, how much revenue accrues from uncultivated land and how much from forests, how much is realized from mines and how much from treasure-troves, how much is added to the state treasury as not belonging to anybody, as lost [and found], as recovered from thieves, and as stored up.

The characteristics and functions of the ten ministers are thus briefly mentioned. The king should judge their competence by looking into their written reports and oral instructions. He should appoint them to each post by rotation. He should never make these officers more powerful than himself; he should invest these ten primary officers with equal authority.

CHAPTER XII

KĀMA, THE THIRD END OF MAN

The place of kāma or the pursuit of love and pleasure in the balanced Hindu scheme of life derives from the importance attached to the life of the married householder (*gṛhastha*). In more than one authoritative text, the householder's life is considered to be the greatest of the four stages of life. Hinduism does not hold up monasticism or eremitism as a common ideal for all; it considers, rather, that the strains and trials of household management, family life, and social obligations are a useful discipline contributing to the preparation of man for the final life of retirement and spiritual endeavor. The place assigned to pleasure provides also for its regulated enjoyment, rather than its suppression, and thus for the development of a well-rounded personality. Constantly reminding the householder of his duties (i.e., dharma) as also of the higher nature of the Ultimate Reality which was the final goal to be attained, the Hindu code of conduct saw to it that the normal man did not degenerate into an epicure or profligate. Love chastened by suffering was held up even by poets and dramatists as capable of effecting a lasting spiritual union, and some of the best poetry in Sanskrit reflects this spirit and attitude toward love. The longing of hearts in love was taken as the most effective image to depict the yearning of the devotee to God or the seeking by the individual soul of the Supreme Soul, a symbolism which is at the base of a greater part of the erotic art of India. Hindu aesthetes explained the philosophy of beauty in terms of the enjoyment or perception of a state of sublime composure or blissful serenity which was a reflection, intimation, image, or glimpse of the enduring bliss of the spirit in its true realization through knowledge.

As in the case of the science of material gain (i.e., of polity), the science of love or pleasure (Kāma Shāstra) also was studied systematically and in exhaustive detail, the object being to comprehend all types of persons and situations, normal and otherwise. The separate disciplines and techniques elaborated upon, however, as well as the special cases and situations dealt with, should be considered in relation to the general view of life from which these branches of knowledge were evolved, and which continued to regulate and guide them. The history of the growth of these separate disciplines is set forth at the outset in texts like the *Aphorisms on Love* (*Kāma Sūtra*) of Vātsyāyana, where it is said that it was the gods and sages that promulgated these sciences of material gain and pleasure, along with the sacred law, and that at the beginning it was all one comprehensive code of conduct. As time went by, each section was separately elaborated by later sages and teachers, in conformity with the comprehensive scheme of values represented by duty (dharma), material gain, pleasure, and spiritual emancipation.

The cultured person and in particular the courtesan of Sanskrit literature (the Indian equivalent of the Japanese geisha) was expected to be educated in sixty-four *kalās* (arts and sciences), a term often equated with *śilpa* "art" or *vidyā* "science." Though this number may vary in older Jain and Buddhist texts, a standard list of sixty-four is given by Vātsyāyana in the *Kāma Sūtra* and a slightly different one in the *Policy of Shukra*. These arts include dancing, singing, acting, flower-arranging, gambling, legerdemain, distillation of spiritous liquors, sewing and embroidery work, first-aid, metallurgy, cooking, chemistry, posture, dueling, gymnastics, horology, dyeing, architecture and engineering, minerology, calligraphy, swimming, leatherwork, archery, driving horses and elephants, composition and solution of riddles and other puzzles, nursing and rearing of children, and the like.

The Man of Taste and Culture

In contrast to the characterization of the Hindu outlook as pessimistic and other-worldly, is the following description, taken from Vātsyāyana's *Aphorisms on Love* (c. A.D. 400), of the man-about-town who enjoys the good things of life, has a cultured taste, and moves in the most refined social and artistic circles.

The word for civilization in Sanskrit is, like its Western counterpart, associated with the town and city (nagara). The *nāgaraka* in Sanskrit means the civilized or cultured urban individual.

[From Vātsyāyana, *Kāma Sūtra,* 1.4]

After acquisition of learning, a person should with the help of the material resources obtained by him through gifts from others, personal gain, commerce or service,[1] marry and set up a home, and then follow the ways of the man of taste and culture (*nāgaraka*).

He may make his abode, in accordance with the calling chosen by him, in a city, in a commercial center, or a town; any of these that he chooses should be inhabited by good people.

There he should make for himself a house, with water nearby, having a garden, provided with separate apartments for different activities, and having two retiring rooms.

In the retiring room in the forepart of the house, there shall be a fine couch, with two pillows, pliant at the center, having a pure white sheet; there shall be by its side another couch of lesser height [for lying down]; at the head, there shall be a wicker-seat [for doing his prayers] and a platform for the sandal paste left over after the night's use, a garland, a box for wax and scents, peelings of pomegranate fruit [a mouth deodorant] and betel leaves; a spittoon on the ground; a lute hanging on a bracket on the wall, a painting-board and box of colors, some books and garlands of *kuraṇṭaka* flowers; not far away on the floor, different kinds of seats; a dice-board; outside the room, cages for the birds kept for playing with; and at a remote end [outside], things for private use.

In the garden a swing, well covered and under the shade of a tree, as also an earthen platform strewn with the falling flowers of the garden. Such is to be the layout of his residence.

He must get up early in the morning, answer the calls of nature, wash his teeth, smear his body with just a little[2] fragrant paste, inhale fragrant smoke, wear some flower, just give the lips a rub with wax and red juice, look at his face in the mirror, chew betel leaves along with some mouth deodorants, and then attend to his work.

Every day he must bathe; every second day, have a massage; every third day, apply *phenaka*[3] to the legs; every fourth day have a partial shave and clipping of the nails; every fifth [?] or tenth day a more complete

[1] These four means of acquiring wealth—acceptance as gift, personal gain, commerce, and service—apply respectively to the four classes, brāhman, kshatriya, vaishya, and shūdra. This suggests that the refined accomplishments, cultural preoccupations, and pursuit of art and pleasure were not restricted to any single segment of society.

[2] The commentary hastens to state that too much of these do not speak well of the person's refinement.

[3] To ward off stiffness of the legs.

shave; he must frequently wipe off the perspiration in the armpit; have his food in the forenoon and afternoon.[4]

After eating [in the forenoon] comes playing with parrots and myna birds and making them talk; and indulging in cock and ram fights and in other artistic activities; also attending to the work he has with his friends and companions. Then a little nap. In the forenoon still, he dresses and goes out for social calls and for enjoyment of the company of others. In the evening he enjoys music and dance. At the end of it, in his own apartments, decorated and fragrant with smoke, he awaits, along with his companions, his beloved who has given him an engagement, or else sends her a message and himself goes out to meet her. . . . Such is the daily routine.

He should arrange excursions in parties for attending festivals, salons for enjoying literature and art, drinking parties, excursions to parks, and group games. Once a fortnight or month, on the day sacred to particular deities, the actors and dancers attached to the temple of Sarasvatī [the Goddess of learning] gather and present shows [for the cultured citizens of the place]; or visiting actors and musicians from other places present their programs in the Sarasvatī temple.

AESTHETIC SPECULATIONS

Beauty has been a subject of Indian comment and speculation since the earliest times. The Rig Vedic poet reveled in the beauties of both nature and man; he attached the highest value to beauty of expression in the art of poetry, and had, besides several general terms, the specific names Lakshmī and Shrī for beauty. In the supplementary hymns of the *Rig Veda* he had already devoted a poem to the concept of a deity presiding over beauty and prosperity. In the Brāhmanas we come upon the word *śilpa,* the common term for art in the sense of a perfect or refined form or replica, and the whole world is described as a brilliant piece of divine art or handiwork. The Upanishads, which conceive of the ultimate reality as the one imperishable substratum of the form of existence, knowledge, and bliss, speak of it also as the fullness of perfection and the fountainhead of all enjoyment, *rasa* (*Taittirīya,* 2.7); from it proceed literature and other

[4] But in the forenoon and evening, according to the medical authority Chārāyana.

forms of artistic expression (*Bṛhad Āraṇyaka,* 2.4.10); and to it, as in praise of the Supreme Being, all song is sung (*Chāndogya* 1.7.6). The epics, the *Rāmāyaṇa* and the *Mahābhārata,* along with the Purānas, set forth the conception of a personal God, who is the embodiment of all beauty, and the object of man's devotion, service, and rapturous exaltation. Whatever is beautiful here in this world is so because of the spark of this divine beauty in it, says the *Bhagavad Gītā* (10.41).

Musicians later developed their philosophy along lines indicated by the Vedas and Upanishads, according to which music and spiritual endeavor were closely linked. All songs were to be composed and sung in praise of God; less lofty themes were not considered acceptable. Furthermore, the very act of singing was likened to the yogic discipline involving the control of breath and concentration. Indian music is, unlike the harmonic system of the modern West, a melodic or modal system in which the highest form of art is the continued singing of pure melody (rāga) unaided by any words. This pure melodic elaboration helps both the singer and listener to become absorbed in the depths of his own being or transported to a plane where all mundane memory ceases to intrude or disturb the blissfulness, restfulness, or poise which the spirit achieves. The high spiritual value set upon music is not only attested in the texts and the songs, but is also demonstrated by the fact that all the great musicians of India have been revered as saints.

The art of sculpture, iconography, and painting, as exemplified in the temples and rockcut caves, had a similar spiritual inspiration, content, and purpose.

It is in the fields of drama and poetry that a theory of art was systematically developed. Though the popular roots of the drama are shown in some of its social forms, the highest type of drama was conceived to be the heroic play in which the acts of gods, incarnations of the Supreme Divinity, or the sublime royal heroes of the epics were "imitated" or "represented"; similarly the highest form of the poetic art was also the epic or the grand poem which was a continuation of the *Rāmāyaṇa* and the *Mahābhārata,* following them in theme and treatment, though at less length. The holding forth before the people of elevated character and action was, nevertheless, a secondary purpose; critics agreed that the didactic aspect of a play or poem should always be subordinated to the primary aim of artistic enjoyment.

But if enjoyment of poetry and drama is the primary end, what then is the essence of this enjoyment? If poetry and drama depict a variety of characters and actions, with a consequent mixture of pleasant and unpleasant feelings, how is it all rendered equally or uniformly relishable? What is there in art that distinguishes it from the world and nature? If the poem, play, or picture presents a different reality, what is the nature of this reality? To questions such as these Indian critics have addressed themselves.

For them the essential thing in poetry or drama is not story and character as such, but the emotion which they embody and which the poet tries to communicate. The emotional interest of a work centers around certain primary sentiments felt by all human beings, around which other secondary emotions hover. Thus love, heroism, pathos, and a few others are seen as ultimate sentiments which constitute their own explanation; not so the subsidiary or transitory feelings such as doubt or despondency, anxiety, longing, or jealousy—all of which require further and multiple explanations as to their causes. Now these major enduring senti ments (*sthāyī-bhāvas*) are embedded as impressions in every heart, and the portrayal of situations in poems and plays touches the corresponding emotional instincts in the cultivated reader or spectator. Though any human being possesses a similar emotional endowment, only the cultivated person can respond fully to artistic presentations. In others the response may be hindered either by a lack of culture or by momentary preoccupations arising from irrelevant and distracting circumstances. In overcoming or eliminating the latter, the artistic atmosphere of the theater, the music, the poetic diction are all helpful. One who is thus responsive is called "a person of attuned heart" (*sa-hṛdaya*), one who identifies himself with the representation. Because the rapport is achieved through an emotional response and appreciation, such a person is also called a *rasiḳa,* one who has aesthetic taste (rasa, lit. "flavor," "relish"). These words *rasa* and *rasiḳa* are as much key words of Indian culture as *dharma* or *brahman,* and suggest how in Indian culture there is an imperceptible shading-off from the spiritual to the aesthetic, and vice versa.

How can the designated emotions, circumscribed by person, time, and place, be shared by spectators or readers? In life, one's emotions produce in onlookers quite varied reactions; what happens to them, then, in art? Bharata said in his *Treatise on Dramaturgy* (*Nāṭya Śāstra,* c. second century B.C. to second century A.D.), and this was further elucidated by the tenth-century critic Bhatta Nāyaka,[1] that in the emotions of the world a process of universalization occurs, thanks to their artistic expression, in music, acting, etc., and it is in their universal aspect, as love or heroism as such, and not as the love and the heroism of such and such characters, that a spectator finds them appealing to his own corresponding instincts. Along with this universalization, there is also a process of abstraction which detaches a painful situation from its painful setting. When the worldly emotion ceases to have its former personal reference, its painfulness, loathsomeness, etc., are all transcended. Thus, all the emotions presented in art are transferred to a supramundane plane, and the so-called enjoyment comes to represent a unique category of experience unlike anything that is known to result from ordinary worldly pleasures. This universalization and sublimation also disassociates the emotion from its particularized form, e.g., love, etc., so that it is relished simply as aesthetic emotion (rasa).

This aesthetic emotion is therefore of the nature of a serenity (*viśrānti*) of the heart or spirit, a condition in which the restlessness attendant upon mundane activity[2] is stilled by the play of artistic presentation. It is in this respect that aesthetic bliss is considered akin to the Supreme Beatitude. This is not, of course, the same as the Supreme Beatitude, from which, when once attained, there is no falling away. The realization of aesthetic bliss is a condition brought about and brought to an end by the presentation and withdrawal of the artistic stimulus. Yet it offers a momentary glimpse of the Supreme Bliss, and continuous efforts to partake of it are a means of preparing the soul for its supreme self-realization.

Now the artistic stimulus which brought forth this end is neither real nor unreal; it is indescribable; the cognition of this is again unique, being none of the known types of actual perception, inference, memory, etc. It is best described by analogy to the nature of the world as seen in idealistic metaphysics such as that of Kashmir Shaivism or Shankara's Advaita (monism). Like Shaivism and Advaita, Sānkhya also contributed its

[1] His work is called the *Mirror of the Heart* (*Hṛdayadarpaṇa*).

[2] The critic Abhinavagupta adopts here the Sānkhya psychology of the three qualities or dispositions of the mind: the sublime, "purity"; the restless, "passion"; and the stupid, "darkness" (see below under Sānkhya). Sorrow is the outcome of the restless disposition of "passion," but thanks to the artistic presentation, the sublime disposition of "purity" dominates over it and sublimates the tragic situation.

ideas to the theory set forth above; it is from the Sānkhya system that Abhinavagupta (A.D. c.1000),[3] the foremost exponent of this point of view, seeks assistance when explaining the phenomenon of our enjoyment of tragic plays and the sentiment of pathos.

This notable theory of aesthetic bliss is first adumbrated in both its broad outlines and technical details in Bharata's comprehensive *Treatise on Dramaturgy,* which is the earliest extant work in the field. Later, critics asserted that the emotional theory applied primarily to drama, where the actual impersonation of characters by different actors, and actual acting, made emotional communication direct, while in poetry this communication was indirect, since everything had to be put into words. Therefore, according to these early rhetoricians, Bhāmaha, Dandin, Vāmana[4] (seventh, eighth, and ninth centuries) who dealt with poetry primarily, emotion or rasa was subordinated to expression, which was embellished by various elements such as style, figure, and elegance. Subsequently the school of neo-critics headed by Ānandavardhana[5] (ninth century) unified criticism by treating the problems of poetry and drama as fundamentally identical, and restoring the supreme place to emotion.

Ānandavardhana's thesis was elucidated and developed further by the Kashmirian Shaiva philosopher Abhinavagupta, but even after the work of this writer, some younger critics like Kuntaka,[6] almost contemporary with Abhinavagupta, reargued the case for poetic art being one preeminently of expression, to which everything else was subordinated. Bhatta Nāyaka, whose contribution to the problem of aesthetic emotion in the theory of universalization has already been noted, and who wrote a little before Abhinavagupta, also upheld the expressionistic view of poetry. He clearly distinguished poetry from scriptural injunction on the one hand, and story or news on the other. In scripture, the words or the letter of the text was the chief thing; in story or narrative, the ideas alone mattered; but in poetry the *way,* the *manner* in which one used words or put his ideas, was what mattered.

Even those who took their stand on rasa or emotion as the essence of

[3] Author of a commentary on Bharata's *Treatise on Dramaturgy* and another on the *Light on Suggestion* (*Dhvanyāloka*) of Ānandavardhana.

[4] The works of these writers are called, respectively: the *Ornaments of Poetry* (*Kāvyālankara*), the *Mirror of Poetry* (*Kāvyādarśa*), and *Aphorisms on the Ornaments of Poetry* (*Kāvyālankāra Sūtra*), with commentary by the same author.

[5] His classic is called the *Light on Suggestion.*

[6] Author of the *Life of Striking Expression* (*Vakroktijīvita*).

poetry had to take into consideration the unique character of poetic expression; they were required to explain how this communication of emotion took place. While ideas actually can be conveyed by words, emotions cannot be evoked by mere mention of them. Poetry must represent the attendant emotional factors, the human participants, the background of nature, and the actions resulting from those feelings which come in the train of a major sentiment. It is through these that the sentiments of love, etc., are aroused in a responsive reader or spectator. Now this realm of emotion is something which lies beyond the reach of either the primary sense or its secondary metaphorical shifts; it is only through *suggestion* that emotion can be communicated. Therefore the leading neo-critic, Ānandavardhana, expounded the doctrine of suggestion (*dhvani, vyañjanā*) or revelation (*prakāśa*) as the chief means by which art achieves its highest communication. This *dhvani,* which has to do with the overtones of words, could render even the communication of ideas and figurative turns more charming by the power of suggestion than by straightforward statement. One paramount reason adduced by Ānandavardhana in support of his claim that suggestion is the sole means of communication was the emotional response produced by music through the inarticulated sounds of pure melody, where there obviously could be no question of verbal communication, primary or secondary. And this was as true of sight as of sound. The look in a lady's eye might have a profound emotional significance, unexplainable except in terms of suggestion.

There were, however, a few critics who still refused to acknowledge the need to ascribe to words such an intangible quality as suggestion when known processes of verbal import or cognition existed, such as the speaker's intention, presumption, and inference. King Bhoja[7] (eleventh century), who tried to take a rather dispassionate view of the Kashmirian contributions from his distant Malwa, found it more reasonable to take an eclectic approach, which would not reject the idea of suggestion, but would make it part of the poet's intention. He tried also to reconcile the ancients and the neo-critics in regard to the respective importance of expression and emotion. The most noteworthy contribution of Bhoja lies in his theory of aesthetic emotion, which, however, few after him understood properly. Bhoja tackled the problem of poetry and the world

[7] His two works in this field are the *Necklace of Sarasvatī* (*Sarasvatīkaṇṭhābharaṇa* [Sarasvatī is the Goddess of learning]) and the *Illumination of Love* (*Śṛṅgāraprakāśa*).

together and tried to find some common basis for explaining culture itself. Aesthetic emotion, according to him, is a refinement of the human ego (ahamkāra) or the development of one's self-consciousness (*abhimāna*) which takes one's personality to that peak of perfection at which one reflects upon one's Self and feels the joy of its fulfillment. Such was the interpretation given to the word *śṛṅgāra* which ordinarily means love, but which to Bhoja meant the Self's Love for Itself, and of which the love for various persons and things in the world is only an empirical manifestation. This inner Self, not so much at rest with itself as aglow with its own essential energy of love, is the one aesthetic emotion which is fed and nourished by the other feelings arising out of it and surrounding it, like the flames of a fire. The poetic emotions, such as love, heroism, etc., only enkindle this inner fire of the Self; and in the measure of their contribution to the burnishment of this inner Self—this sublimated ego—the poetry, art, or cultural activity of the world may be considered fruitful.

Among the lesser critics, there was about the same time (eleventh century) in Kashmir, the pupil of Abhinavagupta, Kshemendra,[8] who worked out the idea of proportion and propriety, *jīvita,* as the very life of poetic beauty. Lastly, we might mention Jagannātha Pandita,[9] who flourished in the seventeenth century. Following in the main school of thought handed down by Abhinavagupta, he defined poetry as words which convey an idea of beauty, and beauty as the delectation of a unique category of supramundane joy.

DRAMATURGY

Bharata's Treatise on Dramaturgy

[From *Nāṭya Śāstra,* 1.14–15, 17, 104–8, 113–14; 6.10, 15–21, 31, 32; 27.49–53, 55, 56, 59–62; 36.72, 74–76]

[God Brahmā said:] I will create the lore of drama which promotes dharma [virtue], material gain, and fame, which will show for posterity all activities, which is enriched with the ideas of all branches of knowledge and presents all the arts; I shall create it, along with the story required for its theme, with its teachings and the summary of its topics.

[8] Author of the tract *Examination of Propriety* (*Aucityavicāracarcā*).
[9] Author of *The Bearer of the Ganges of Emotion.*

. . Brahmā extracted the text from the *Rig Veda,* songs from the *Sāma Veda,* actions from the *Yajur Veda,* and the emotions from the *Atharva Veda.* [1.14–17]

[Brahmā said:] The drama is a representation of the nature or feelings of the whole universe. In some place it depicts dharma, play somewhere else, material gain at another place, quietude in yet another, fun at one place, fight at another place, love at one place, and killing at another. The drama that I have devised is a representation of the activities of the world; the virtuous ones have here virtue, and the amorous ones, love; the undisciplined ones are tamed here, and the disciplined ones exhibit their discipline; it emboldens the weak, energizes the heroic, enlightens the ignorant, and imparts erudition to the scholars; it depicts the gaiety of lords, teaches fortitude to those tormented by misery, shows gains to the materially minded, and firmness to the agitated; thus it is endowed with variegated feelings and embodies varied states. [1.104–8]

There is no knowledge, craft, learning, art, practical skill, or action which is not found in drama. [1.113–14]

Emotions, their subsidiary moods, actions, technique, style, mode, production and success, song and instrumentation, and theater—these form the resume of the topics of dramaturgy. [6.10]

The great Brahmā mentioned eight emotions: love, humor, pathos, violence, heroism, fear, loathsomeness, and wonder.[1] The enduring moods from which these aesthetic emotions develop are love, laughter, sorrow, anger, effort, fear, loathing, and surprise. The transitory feelings are thirty-three, despondency, langor, apprehension, envy, elation [etc.]. [6.15–21]

We shall speak first of the emotions [rasas]. Nothing goes on in a drama without emotion. This emotion is manifested by the interaction of cause, effect, and accessory moods. What is the illustration? Just as a dish or culinary taste is brought about by the mingling of various viands, even so is an emotional state engendered by the coming together of various feelings or emotional conditions; just as by molasses and other food-materials, the six culinary tastes are made, even so the eight perma-

[1] Some recensions of the text read a ninth emotion, quietude; later, from the eighth century onwards, the ninth was not only accepted, but also considered the greatest of all the emotions.

nent emotional moods are brought to a state of relishability by the interaction of manifold emotional conditions. The Sages asked: What is the meaning of the word *rasa* [emotion; lit. flavor, relish]? The reply given is: rasa is so called because it is relished. How is rasa relished? The reply is: Just as healthy men, eating food dressed with manifold accessories, enjoy the different tastes [the sweet, the sour, etc.], and derive exhilaration, etc., even so, the spectators with attuned minds relish the permanent emotional states [love, heroism, etc.], which are presented and nourished with manifold feelings and their actions through limbs, speech, and involuntary physical manifestations. [6.31, 32]

I shall now set forth the characteristics of spectators. They should be men of character and pedigree; endowed with composure, conduct, and learning; intent on good name and virtue; unbiased; of proper age; well versed in drama and its constituent elements; vigilant, pure, and impartial; experts in instruments and make-up; conversant with dialects; adepts in arts and crafts; knowledgeable in the dexterous art of gesticulation and in the intricacies of the major and minor emotional states; proficient in lexicon, prosody, and different branches of learning—such men are to be made spectators for witnessing a drama. He who is satisfied when the feeling of satisfaction is portrayed, himself becomes sorrow-stricken when sorrow is shown, and attains the state of helplessness when helplessness is enacted—he is the proper spectator in a drama. [27.49–53, 55]

It is not expected that all these qualities will be present in a single spectator. . . . Those in youth will be pleased with the love portrayed, the connoisseurs with the technical elements, those devoted to mundane things with the material activities presented, and the dispassionate ones with the efforts toward spiritual liberation depicted; of varied character are those figuring in a play and the play rests on such variety of character. The valorous ones will delight in themes of loathsomeness, violence, fights, and battles, and the elders will always revel in tales of virtue and mythological themes. The young, the common folk, the women would always like burlesque and striking make-up. Thus he who is, by virtue of the response of the corresponding feeling or situation, able to enter into a particular theme is considered a fit spectator for that kind of theme, being endowed with those qualities needed for being a proper spectator. [27.56, 59–62]

The science and production of drama helps the intellectual growth of people; it has in it the activity of the whole universe, and presents the knowledge contained in all its branches. . . .

He who listens to this branch of knowledge promulgated by God Brahmā, he who produces a drama, and he who attentively witnesses it —such a person attains to that meritorious state which those versed in the Vedas, the performers of sacrifices, and the donors of gifts attain. Among the duties of the king, provision for the enactment of plays is said to be highly useful; to present to the people a play is a gift esteemed highly among various kinds of gifts. [36.72, 74–76]

POETICS

Mammata's Illumination of Poetry

A standard textbook of neo-criticism written c. A.D. 1100.
[From Mammata, *Kāvyaprakāśa,* Chapters 1, 4]

The muse of the poet is all glorious, bringing into being as it does a creation beautified by the nine sentiments [lit. flavors], free from the limitations imposed by nature, uniformly blissful, and not dependent on anything else. . . .

Poetry is for fame, material gain, worldly knowledge, removal of adversity, immediate realization of supreme bliss, and for instruction administered sweetly in the manner of one's beloved wife. . . .

The bliss that arises immediately on the delectation of the emotions depicted in the poem and which makes one oblivious of every other cognition forms the highest of all the fruits of poetry.

Scriptural texts like the Veda command like masters and in them the very letter of the text is the chief thing. The stories of the mythological books and epics have their main emphasis on just conveying the meaning, and they instruct like friends. Poetry, on the other hand, is different from these two kinds of writings. Poetry is the activity of the poet who is gifted in depicting things on a supramundane plane; his writing is consequently such that in it word and meaning are together subservient and the emphasis is on the unique poetic activity which aims at evocation of emotional response; [1] therefore poetry like a beloved spouse, makes

[1] This explanation of the difference between poetic expression and other writing was given by the critic Bhatta Nāyaka. According to him, poetry is an emphasis on the *manner* of saying a thing.

one absorbed in one emotion, wins over both the poet and the reader alike with its message that one should be virtuous like Rāma and not vicious like Rāvana.[2] Hence, one should put forth effort in the direction of poetic composition.

This poetry is word and sense devoid of flaws, and from it occassionally the figures [of speech and sound] may be absent; that is, word and sense in poetry always have the figures, but if in some place, the figure is not clearly recognizable, the fact of the expression being poetry is not affected. . . .

This poetry, the wise say, is the highest and is called "poetry of suggestion" if its suggested element excels the expressed one. . . . The poetry is middling and called "poetry in which the suggested is subordinated to the expressed" if the suggested is not dominant over the expressed. . . . That category of poetry is inferior in which there is no suggested element and there is only some strikingness of sound or sense. Strikingness includes stylistic qualities and figures. [Ch. 1]

Among the suggested elements are those in which the sequence of the process is not noticeable and another in which it is noticeable.[3] As, however, the causes, effects, and accessory feelings of an emotion are not themselves the aesthetic emotion [rasa], but are the conditions which bring that aesthetic emotion into being, there does exist a sequence in the process of their suggestion also; but this sequence is not perceivable. The emotion, its basic and accessory feelings, their semblance, the gradual fall, rise, and admixture of these, which are all imperceivably suggested, form the very "soul" of poetic expression; as such they are to be distinguished from the state in which they are subordinated to the charm of expression and function as embellishments thereof. . . .

Sage Bharata has said: "Emotion is manifested by the interplay of the causes, effects, and the accessory moods." This is expounded thus:

The causes of emotions are (a) the human substratum, and (b) the exciting conditions of environment, etc.; e.g., in love the woman is the human substratum and the garden, etc., form the exciting conditions. The permanent emotional state called love is engendered by this twofold cause. The effects or ensuants which render the emotion cognizable comprise, for instance in love, the sidelong glances, the disporting of the

[2] The hero and villain respectively of the epic *Rāmāyaṇa*.

[3] The former is the case of the emotions, rasas.

arms, etc. The attendant accessory moods which nourish the permanent emotional state, in the case of love, are despondency, langor, etc. The emotion [so nourished] is primarily in the character presented, e.g., Rāma; it is also seen in the actor by virtue of our contemplating Rāma's character in him. Such is the nature of emotion as Bhatta Lollata and other ancient writers expounded it. . . .

Bhatta Nāyaka said: This aesthetic relish [rasa] is not apprehended as existing either independently or in oneself; also, it is neither originated nor revealed; but in poetry and drama, there is, beyond the primary significance of the expression, a function [called "that which makes for imaginative enjoyment"], which universalizes the particular causes, ensuants, and accessories [belonging to a given context]; by this universalizing power the permanent emotional mood [like love] is called forth; there is then a state of repose of the consciousness, a blissfulness, engendered by the upsurge of the sublime mental quality; in that state the emotional mood is relished.

The blessed teacher Abhinavagupta observed: In the world one makes out the permanent mood [like love] from causes like woman; in poetry and drama, the same give up their [prosaic] character of causes, etc., and by reason of their artistic evocative nature come to be called by non-worldly designations *vibhāvas*,[4] etc. They are not apprehended as one's own, the enemy's or the middle man's, nor as not being one's own, the enemy's, or the middle man's; they are apprehended in their universal aspect, there being no mental resolve either to take or to discard a particular relation to oneself as friend, foe, or neutral. The permanent emotional state such as love is embedded as impression in the hearts of spectators and is manifested by these causes [*vibhāvas*], etc., and apprehended in their universalized aspect. Through the strength of the same universalization, this permanent emotional state, though appearing only in a particular cognizer, is yet apprehended as if by a cognizer who has awakened into an unbounded state, because, for the time being, his limited cognizership drops and he becomes rid of the touch of any other object of cognition. In this unlimited state, on account of the universalization enabling one to be in unison with all hearts, the permanent emotional mood, though, like one's Self, not really different, is yet brought within the range of apprehension. This apprehension or realization is essentially of the form

[4] "Cause," in dramaturgy.

of a relish and strictly confined to the duration of the evoking artistic conditions, causes, etc.; its relish is unitary like that of a composite drink in which the ingredients do not taste separately; this unique relish is such that it seems to quiver in front of one, it seems to throw everything else into oblivion, it seems to make one experience the ineffable beatitude of the Supreme Being; it produces a supramundane delectation; such is the nature of the experience of aesthetic emotion, love and the like. . . . The means of its cognition are not indeterminate, because the knowledge of causes, etc., is essential to it; nor is it determinate, for it is relished as a supramundane bliss, certified by one's own Self-experience. Being of neither form or of both forms, it shows only, as already stated, its non-worldly character, and no contradiction whatsoever. [Ch. 4]

The Bearer of the Ganges of Emotion[1]

[From Jagannātha, *Rasagaṅgādhara,* Chapter 1]

THE DEFINITION OF POETRY

Words which convey an *idea* endowed with *beauty* constitute *poetry.* *Beauty* is that whose contemplation gives rise to a *non-worldly delight.* . . . The means of realizing this is repeated contemplation, an activity of imagination, directed toward the thing characterized by that non-worldly delectation. "A son has been born to you," and "I shall give you money" —these are also sentences whose meaning produces delight but that delight is not non-worldly; therefore there can be no question of poetry in those sentences. Thus poetry is words conveying an idea whose imaginative contemplation is productive of a supramundane delectation. [Ch. 1]

MUSIC

From a Brāhmana

[From *Taittirīya Brāhmaṇa,* 3.9.14]

Two brāhman lutists are singing to the lute; this thing, the lute, is verily the embodiment of beauty and prosperity; and these musicians of the lute do verily endow him [the patron] with prosperity.

[1] This refers to Shiva as the Bearer of the Ganges (*gaṅgādhara*).

From an Upanishad

[From *Chāndogya Upaniṣad* 1.7.6]

These that sing to the lute indeed sing of Him [the Supreme Brahman] only; hence it is that they attain riches.

From a Lawbook (c. fourth century A.D.)

[From *Yājñavalkya Smṛti,* 3.4.112–15]

One attains the Supreme Being by practicing continuously the chanting of the *sāmans* [the sacred Vedic mantras set to music] in the prescribed manner and with mental concentration. The singing of the songs *Aparānta, Ullopya,* [etc.] . . . the songs composed by Daksha and Brahman, constitutes indeed liberation. One who knows the correct playing of the lute, has mastered the subtle semitones, and understands the rhythms, attains the path of liberation without any strain.

From the Purānas (early medieval)

[From *Viṣṇu Purāṇa,* 1.22.84]

Whatever poetic utterances there are, and the songs in all their entirety, are aspects of Lord Vishnu in his sonant form.

[From *Skanda Purāṇa, Sūta Saṃhitā,* 4.2.3.114–16]

The knowledge of music becomes an effective means of attaining oneness with Lord Shiva; for by the knowledge of music, one attains to a state of absorption and it is by attaining such a state that oneness with Shiva could be obtained. . . . One ought not to indulge, out of delusion, in worldly songs. . . .

From a Tantra (medieval)

[From *Vijñānabhairava Tantra*]

To the yogin whose spirit attains a unified state in the uniform bliss engendered by the delectation of objects like music, there occurs an absorption and anchoring of the mind in that bliss. Where there is a continuous and long flow of sounds from stringed instruments, one becomes freed of other objects of cognition and becomes merged in that ultimate and verily of the form of that Supreme Ether [the Brahman].

From a Standard Music Treatise (thirteenth century A.D.)

[From Shārngadeva, *Saṅgītaratnākara,* 1.3.1–2]

We adore that Supreme Being of the form of sound [Nāda-Brahman] which is the one bliss without a second, and the light of consciousness in all beings that has manifested itself in the form of the universe. By the adoration of sound [*nāda*] are also adored Gods Brahmā [the Creator], Vishnu [the Preserver], and *Maheśvara* [Shiva, the Destroyer], for they are the embodiments of sound.

From the Songs of Tyāgarāja

Tyāgarāja (1767–1847) was the famous saint-musician of South India. The songs are translated from the Telugu.

SAṄGĪTAJÑĀNAMU [1] (MELODY: *Sālagabhairavi*)

O Mind! The knowledge of the science and art of music bestows on a person the bliss of oneness with the Supreme Being.

Music such as is accompanied by the blissful oceanlike stories of the Lord which are the essence of love and all the other sentiments blesses a person with oneness with the Lord.

Music such as that cultivated by the discerning Tyāgarāja bestows on a person affection [for fellow beings], devotion [to God], attachment to good men, the Lord's Grace, austere life, mental concentration, fame, and wealth.

RĀGASUDHĀRASA (MELODY: *Āndolikā*)

O Mind! drink and revel in the ambrosia of melody; it gives one the fruit of sacrifices and contemplation, renunciation as well as enjoyment; Tyāgarāja knows that they who are proficient in sound, the mystic syllable *Oṃ,* and the music notes [2]—which are all of the form of the Lord Himself—are liberated souls.[3]

[1] Indian songs are usually identified, as here, by their beginning words.

[2] From abstract sound, the mystic syllable *Oṃ* appears and from it the seven notes of music. *Oṃ* is uttered at the beginning, and sometimes also at the end, of a Vedic recitation, prayer, or chant. In the Upanishads (especially the *Chāndogya*) *Oṃ* came to be regarded as the essence of the Vedas, indeed of the whole world.

[3] That is *jīvanmuktas,* those who are released from bondage while yet in an embodied state.

CHAPTER XIII

MOKSHA, THE FOURTH END OF MAN

The fourth and final aim of man, moksha, is the culmination of the other three, but especially of the religious ideal originally associated with dharma. In the earliest phase of Indian thought the observance of the cosmic and moral law (rita) and the performance of dharma in the form of sacrifice were believed in as means of propitiating the gods and gaining heavenly enjoyment in the afterlife. From this idea—that an act of dharma achieved some merit or benefit which might be enjoyed on death—developed the karma theory and its corollary, the doctrine of rebirth. At this point, however, the thought that one thus passed from life to life and that there was no end to this series led to deeper reflection. An act being finite cannot produce a result different from it or more lasting; a thing that does not last is imperfect and cannot be the ultimate truth; what has been conditioned by acts, namely, this life, is therefore perishable and hence not capable of producing real happiness. To one perplexed with this problem, Death itself, as in the *Kaṭha Upaniṣad,* revealed the secret. As one passed from birth to birth and death to death, what was it that endured and continued as the substratum of conditioned experience, of the happy and unhappy results of acts? What was it in man that formed the basis of all this transmigratory drama? If there was something which endured such changes, it might yield the secret of restfulness, infinite peace, and lasting happiness. To attain it, one would naturally have to turn away from the so-called limited good or happiness and the equally circumscribed means to it. To one intent on the supreme good or everlasting bliss, even the pleasures of life were no different from its miseries, as both lead to an endless cycle of experience and have to be transcended. As anything done within the sphere of cause and effect was caught up in the same chain, action was no remedy; knowledge of the truth alone could help one to rise above the transmigratory cycle or the world of cause and effect.

This line of thought serves as the common background for later systems which expounded the goal or the reality or the path in different ways. All were agreed that experience in this life was on the whole to be considered miserable and that deliverance (moksha) from it or its cessation was to be sought. The Upanishads considered that knowledge of the truth would lead to realization of the Self as such, beyond the conditioned existence in which it was involved; and that behind this world of cause and effect, underlying the phenomenon of things that come into being, change, decay, and disappear, there was one permanent reality: existence (sat), changeless and consequently sorrowless, and of which knowledge was not a quality but its very form. The Upanishads, for the most part, held this monistic view of one transcendent absolute, but sometimes they spoke also of the truth as a transcendent personality. While the former view led to a monism such as Shankara's, the latter view led to theistic schools, which considered one supreme god as the creator, sustainer, and destroyer of the universe, and which developed the doctrine of devotion, love, and surrender. To them release from the world (moksha or mukti) brought absorption into or essential identity with the Lord.

Like the first mentioned pantheistic Upanishadic or Vedāntic school, there were others which also took their stand on knowledge as the means of attaining the everlasting good. They likewise turned away from sacrifices and similar ritual to inquire into the nature of reality. Sage Kanāda, the founder of the Vaisheshika system, examined creation and the universe whose creation he attributed to atoms as the material cause; God was for him an efficient cause and also a teacher and helper; knowledge of all physical, mental, and spiritual categories—which comprised matter, mind, spirit or soul, both human and divine—and their respective qualities and differences contributed to the attainment of the everlasting good, *niḥśreyasa*.

Sage Gotama, the founder of the Nyāya school, asserted that the misery experienced by man was due to birth (which involved death), the latter to activity, activity to desire and dislike, and these to erroneous knowledge —a causal chain akin to that which the Buddha preached. The followers of this school were theists, pluralists, and realists, and for them release or moksha was a state in which the soul of man was absolutely rid of all experience of sorrow (inclusive of so-called "pleasure") and was like unto a stone.

The Sānkhya of Sage Kapila, whose doctrines are found echoed in the Upanishads, considered release from the misery of all life here and in the heavens as attainable by the knowledge of the truth concerning Self or soul, on the one hand, and the material universe on the other. The truth about these two is that all experiences are due solely to the latter and not to the ever-pure soul. It is only imagined that they belong to the soul because of its proximity to matter and its erroneous identification with matter as agent and enjoyer. The Yoga of Sage Patanjali set forth the process of psychological discipline by which one could attain this release (moksha) or isolation (*kaivalya*) of the soul from involvement with matter and its doings.

Now all these five schools of Hindu philosophy aimed at release from the misery (*duḥkha*) of mundane experience and transmigration (samsāra), and all emphasized knowledge of one kind or another. Among these, the school which primarily based itself on the Upanishads, the Vedānta, took different forms, monistic and pantheistic or theistic. The Mīmāmsā alone, as a school, still stood for the performance of ordained duties (dharma) and sacrificial and meritorious acts (karma). Action, of course, could not be eliminated so long as a man lived; the most philosophy could do was to take the sting out of action. The monistic philosophers, recognizing the disciplinary value of acts and duties, as indeed of ethics, accordingly assigned them a place under *sādhanas* or preparatory disciplines. Acts could function in this way as ancillary to knowledge providing they were not done with the expectation of personal gain, or from the theistic view, as an expression of devotion, provided they were dedicated to the Lord. Either way, the doer abandoned not the act, but the desire for its fruit. Thus when action was adjusted to Vedānta and qualified by knowledge or devotion, it too became a means of liberation.

This reconciliation of action with knowledge and devotion, which also removed the contradiction between dharma and moksha, was the great contribution of the *Bhagavad Gītā*. In modern times, when increased activity has become a dominant feature of Indian life, it is to this text with its philosophy of selfless and dedicated action that the whole Indian nation has turned for inspiration.

THE BHAGAVAD GĪTĀ

The *Song of the Lord* (*Bhagavad Gītā*), which is by far the best known religio-philosophical text in Sanskrit, may be considered the most typical expression of Hinduism as a whole and an authoritative manual of the Krishnaite religion (i.e., the popular cult of Krishna) in particular.

Even in very early times there had existed, side by side with the hieratic Vedic religion, several popular, tribal religions. The gods and goddesses of these tribal people differed from the divinities of the official Vedic pantheon, and the religious practices associated with them also differed fundamentally from the religious practices of the Vedic Aryans. Nevertheless, these indigenous religions eventually found a place under the broad mantle of the Vedic religion. While Brahmanism remained in the ascendancy, their sphere of influence was restricted to the tribes among which they had originated. But the gradual decline of Brahmanism, in the face of competition from Buddhism and Jainism, afforded these popular religions an opportunity to assert themselves; and indeed, the Brahmanists themselves seem to have encouraged this development to some extent as a means of meeting the challenge of the more heterodox movements. At the same time, among the indigenous religions, with their variety of gods and religious practices, a common allegiance to the authority of the Veda provided a thin, but nonetheless significant, thread of unity. This is the genesis of Hinduism, which brought together under its banner large masses of people, and, at the same time, kept the Vedic tradition alive.

One significant constituent of this all-embracing Hinduism was Krishnaism, which seems to have originated and spread among the tribes of Western and Central India, like the Vrishnis, the Sātvatas, the Ābhīras, and the Yādavas. Its principal teacher was Krishna, who was associated with the above-mentioned tribes as either their temporal or their spiritual leader, and was in course of time, transformed into a tribal god. That this tribal god and the religious movement inspired by him were originally not countenanced by the Vedic religion is suggested by the episode at the Govardhana mountain (*Harivaṃśa,* 72–73), which describes the antagonism to and subsequent subjugation by Krishna of the chief Vedic god Indra. This is clearly symbolic of the growing predominance of the popular religion over the hieratic Brahmanic religion. But the religion of Krishna typifies the paradoxical characteristic of Hinduism mentioned above, namely, that it was a fundamental departure from Brahmanism which nonetheless remained within the bounds of loyalty to the Veda.

The *Gītā*[1] forms part of the great epic of India, the *Great Poem* (or *War*) *of the Descendants of Bharata* (*Mahābhārata*), which has gathered a veritable encyclopedia around the epic story of the rivalry between the Kauravas, led by Duryodhana, and their cousins the Pāndavas, led by Yudhishthira. Both houses were descended from Kuru and ultimately from the famous Vedic tribe of the Bharatas which gave India her name *Bhārat.* The struggle culminated in the great war won by the Pāndavas and their allies with the help of Krishna. Chiefly due to its numerous and elevated passages on the subjects of wisdom, duty, and liberation from mundane existence, the epic, which probably underwent its last major revision c. fourth century A.D. in the Gupta period, became sacred to later Hindus as part of the Smriti scriptures.

When in the course of the growth of the *Mahābhārata,* the bardic historical poem relating to the Kuru-Bharatas was being transformed into an early form of the epic, two principal processes had been in operation, namely, the bardic enlargement of the original ballad-cycle relating to the Kuru-Bharatas, and the Krishnaite redaction of the bardic material. The *Gītā* must indeed have served as the cornerstone of this Krishnaite superstructure. Though the *Gītā* mainly epitomizes the teachings of Krishna, after it had been included in the epic it also was subjected, like the rest of the epic, to the final process of Brahmanic revision.

The religion of Krishna differed from the Upanishads, as well as from Buddhism and Jainism, first and foremost in its teaching about the goal of human life. The Upanishads generally put forth the view that, since this phenomenal world and human existence are in some sense unreal, man should renounce this worldly life and aim at realizing the essential identity of his soul with the Universal Self, which is the one and only absolute reality. The Upanishadic attitude toward life and society is fundamentally individualistic. The *Gītā,* on the other hand, teaches that man has a duty to promote *lokasaṅgraha* or the stability, solidarity, and progress of society. Society can function properly only on the principle of the

[1] The abbreviated title of the *Bhagavad Gītā.*

ethical interdependence of its various constituents. As an essential constituent of society, therefore, man must have an active awareness of his social obligations. The *sva-dharma* (lit. one's own dharma, set of duties) or the specific social obligations of different types of men are, according to the *Gītā,* best embodied in the doctrine of the four classes. The *Gītā,* however, emphasizes the metaphysical significance of that scheme, according to which all classes are equal and essential, while it insists mainly on man's active recognition of *sva-dharma* or his own specific social obligations.

The second fundamental point on which the *Gītā* differs from Upanishadic thought follows logically from the first. The Upanishadic ideal of spiritual emancipation through knowledge involves the acceptance of the unreal character of the phenomenal world. Through his actions, consciously or unconsciously, man becomes involved in the tentacles of this fictitious world and is thus removed farther and farther from his goal. A complete abnegation of action, therefore, came to be regarded almost as a *sine qua non* of a true seeker's spiritual quest. The ideal of social integrity (*lokasaṅgraha*) through *sva-dharma* enjoined by the *Gītā,* on the other hand, implies an active way of life. The *Gītā,* indeed, most often speaks in terms of yoga (application to work or self-discipline) rather than of moksha (release or liberation). The teacher of the *Gītā* has discussed, at great length, the why and the how of the yoga of action (karma-yoga). The activism inculcated by the *Gītā* is, however, not of the common variety. It is tinged—perhaps under the influence of Upanishadic and Buddhist thought—with an element of renunciation. It argues that action, as such, is not detrimental to one's attainment of his spiritual goal. It is only one's attachment to the fruits of action that keeps one eternally involved in the cycle of birth and death. The *Gītā,* therefore, teaches the art of "acting and yet not acting," i.e., acting without becoming personally involved in the action.

Whereas Vedic ritual practices were exclusive in character, Krishna sponsors a way of spiritual life in which all can participate. It is the yoga of devotion (bhakti yoga). In contrast to ritual sacrifice the *Gītā* offers a concept of sacrifice embracing all actions done in fulfillment of one's *sva-dharma* and without attachment to their fruits. This way of devotion presupposes the recognition of a personal god—in the present context, of course, Krishna himself—who is regarded as being responsible for the creation, preservation, and destruction of the universe. The devotee serves that God like a loyal servant, always craving some kind of personal communion with Him. The criterion of true worship, according to the doctrine of devotion, is not the richness or profuseness of the materials used for worship nor the number and variety of religious observances involved in it. It is rather the earnestness, the faith, and the sense of complete surrender to the Divine on the part of the devotee (bhakta). Such a devotee—whatever his age, sex, learning, and social status—compels God to become his friend, guide, and philosopher. The way of devotion is thus more simple, more direct, and more effective than any other religious practice. To this teaching of devotion, however, Krishna makes one significant addition. He insists that a true practitioner of the yoga of action (karmayogin) also become a true devotee, for, by following his own duty (*sva-dharma*), the karmayogin is doing the will of God and participating in the divine project.

Krishnaism cannot boast of any independent philosophical system of its own. The great virtue of the *Gītā* is that, instead of dilating upon the points of difference among the various systems of thought and practice, it emphasizes the points of agreement among them and thereby brings about a philosophical and religious synthesis. We have already suggested that the *Gītā* underwent a kind of Brahmanic reorientation. One of the more significant results of this reorientation, as far as the personality of Krishna is concerned, was that this tribal god, who was essentially non-Vedic in origin and whose character had already become syncretic, came to be regarded as an avatār (incarnation) of the Vedic god Vishnu, and as identical with the Upanishadic Brahman.

Due no doubt to this synthetic character, study of the *Bhagavad Gītā* has given rise to a variety of problems pertaining both to its form and its content. It is, for instance, asked whether the text of the *Gītā,* as we have it today, actually represents its "original" text. Then there is the question concerning the relation between the *Gītā* and the *Mahābhārata.* Can the elaborate teaching embodied in the *Gītā* have been imparted by Krishna to Arjuna just when the great battle of Kurukshetra was on the point of commencing? Further, can the various teachings of Krishna be said to have been presented in the present text of the *Gītā* in a logical sequence? Would a rearrangement of the text not yield better results in this respect? Coming to the teachings of the *Gītā,* some scholars aver that its main metaphysical foundations have been derived from the Sānkhya system, the Vedāntic (monistic) tendencies being superimposed on them only in a superficial manner, while other scholars are of the opinion that it is just the other way around. Arguments are again adduced in support of the two opposing views that the *Gītā* in its original form was a philosophical treatise only later adopted by Krishnaism, and, on the other hand, that basically it embodied the kshatriya code of conduct as sponsored by Krishna, the philosophical speculations having found their way in it only incidentally. There is also the problem concerning the norm of ethical conduct. The views expressed on the subject by the *Gītā* itself do not appear to be quite consistent. At some places (5.14; 18.59) it is said that it is man's inherent nature (*svabhāva* or prakriti) which determines his actions, while elsewhere (11.33; 18.61) man is described as functioning only as an instrument of the Divine Will. It is further suggested (2.35) that one should act in such a manner that he is not thereby subjected to public disgrace. The teacher of the *Gītā* also points (16.24) to scripture as the authority for determining what should be done and what should not be done, and concludes by saying (18.63) that, reflecting fully on the doctrine declared by him, one should act as one chooses. These are only some typical problems of the many which are often discussed in connection with the work. The *Gītā* need not be approached as if it were a systematic treatise, in which the principal subject is treated with scientific or logical rigor. Being included in the popular epic, the *Gītā* also inherited epic characteristics of style and presentation. Nevertheless, this original compendium of Krishnaite religion, philosophy, and ethics has been presented in the epic on a very dramatic background and in such a manner that there should be no ambiguity so far as its principal teachings are concerned.

You Have To Fight

When the armies of the Kauravas and the Pāndavas were arrayed on the battlefield of Kurukshetra, waiting for the signal to commence the fight, the Pāndava hero, Arjuna, seeing that relatives and friends were ranged against each other, was suddenly overcome by deep spiritual despondency. It would be sinful, he felt, to kill his own kindred for the sake of kingdom. Therefore, not as a coward, but as a morally conscientious and sensitive person, he lay down his bow and declared to his friend and charioteer, Krishna, that he would not fight. Krishna then attempted to convince Arjuna that he would be committing a sin if he failed to perform his own duty (*sva-dharma*) as a warrior. As for his concern over taking the lives of others, this arose from a delusion which Krishna proceeds to dispel in the following passage:

[From *Bhagavad Gītā,* 2.11–37]

The Blessed Lord said:

You grieve for those who should not be mourned, and yet you speak words of wisdom! The learned do not grieve for the dead or for the living.

Never, indeed, was there a time when I was not, nor when you were not, nor these lords of men. Never, too, will there be a time, hereafter, when we shall not be.

As in this body, there are for the embodied one [i.e., the soul] childhood, youth, and old age, even so there is the taking on of another body. The wise sage is not perplexed thereby.

Contacts of the sense-organs, O son of Kuntī, give rise to cold and heat, and pleasure and pain. They come and go, and are not permanent. Bear with them, O Bhārata.

That man, whom these [sense-contacts] do not trouble, O chief of men, to whom pleasure and pain are alike, who is wise—he becomes eligible for immortality.

For the nonexistent (asat) there is no coming into existence; nor is there passing into nonexistence for the existent (sat). The ultimate nature of these two is perceived by the seers of truth.[1]

Know that to be indestructible by which all this is pervaded. Of this imperishable one, no one can bring about destruction.

These bodies of the eternal embodied one, who is indestructible and incomprehensible, are said to have an end. Therefore fight, O Bhārata.

He who regards him [i.e., the soul] as a slayer, and he who regards him as slain—both of them do not know the truth; for this one neither slays nor is slain.

He is not born, nor does he die at any time; nor, having once come to be will he again come not to be. He is unborn, eternal, permanent, and primeval; he is not slain when the body is slain.

Whoever knows him to be indestructible and eternal, unborn and immutable—how and whom can such a man, O son of Prithā, cause to be slain or slay?

[1] Cf. *Rig Veda,* 10.129.

Just as a man, having cast off old garments, puts on other, new ones, even so does the embodied one, having cast off old bodies, take on other, new ones.

Weapons do not cleave him, fire does not burn him; nor does water drench him, nor the wind dry him up.

He is uncleavable, he is unburnable, he is undrenchable, as also undryable. He is eternal, all-pervading, stable, immovable, existing from time immemorial.

He is said to be unmanifest, unthinkable, and unchangeable. Therefore, knowing him as such, you should not grieve [for him].

And even if you regard him as being perpetually born and as perpetually dying, even then, O long-armed one, you should not grieve for him.

For, to one who is born death is certain and certain is birth to one who has died. Therefore in connection with a thing that is inevitable you should not grieve.

Unmanifest in their beginnings are beings, manifest in the middle stage, O Bhārata, and unmanifest, again, in their ends. For what then should there be any lamentation?

Someone perceives him as a marvel; similarly, another speaks of him as a marvel; another, again, hears of him as a marvel; and, even after hearing of him, no one knows him.

The embodied one within the body of everyone, O Bhārata, is ever unslayable. Therefore, you should not grieve for any being.

Further, having regard to your own dharma [duty] you should not falter. For a kshatriya there does not exist another greater good than war enjoined by dharma.

Blessed are the kshatriyas, O son of Prithā, who get such a war, which being, as it were, the open gate to heaven, comes to them of its own accord.

But if you do not fight this battle which is enjoined by dharma, then you will have given up your own dharma as well as glory, and you will incur sin.

Moreover, all beings will recount your eternal infamy. And for one who has been honored, infamy is worse than death.

The great car warriors will think of you as one who has refrained from battle through fear; having been once greatly respected by them, you will then be reduced to pettiness.

Those who are not favorably inclined toward you will speak many unutterable words, slandering your might. What, indeed, can be more painful than that?

Either, being slain, you will attain heaven; or being victorious, you will enjoy [i.e., rule] the earth. Therefore arise, O son of Kuntī, intent on battle.

Why Karma-Yoga?

In the preceding passage, Krishna has addressed himself specifically to the case of Arjuna. Now he initiates a more or less general discussion of the theory and practice of the yoga of action, arguing against the view that renunciation entails only physical renunciation of all activity, or that such a renunciation, by itself, is conducive to the attainment of one's spiritual goal.

[From *Bhagavad Gītā,* 3.4–24]

Not by nonperformance of actions does a man attain freedom from action; nor by mere renunciation of actions does he attain his spiritual goal.

For no one, indeed, can remain, for even a single moment, unengaged in activity, since everyone, being powerless, is made to act by the dispositions (gunas) of matter (prakriti).[2]

Whoever having restrained his organs of action still continues to brood over the objects of senses—he, the deluded one, is called a hypocrite.

But he who, having controlled the sense-organs by means of the mind, O Arjuna, follows without attachment the path of action by means of the organs of action—he excels.

Do you do your allotted work, for action is superior to nonaction. Even the normal functioning of your body cannot be accomplished through actionlessness.

Except for the action done for sacrifice,[3] all men are under the bondage of action. Therefore, O son of Kuntī, do you undertake action for that purpose, becoming free from all attachment.

Having, in ancient times, created men along with sacrifice,[4] Prajāpati

[2] Cf. note 19.

[3] That is, action done in the spirit of sacrifice does not entangle the doer in its consequences.

[4] In this and the following six stanzas Krishna develops another argument in favor of the yoga of action, namely, that every man has to recognize his role in the scheme of cosmic ethics and has actively to promote its functioning. If he fails to do so, the cosmos will be turned into chaos. This is the basic theory of early Brahmanism.

said: "By means of this [sacrifice] do you bring forth. May this prove to be the yielder of milk in the form of your desired ends.

"Do you foster the gods by means of this and let those gods foster you; [thus] fostering each other, both of you will attain to the supreme good.

"For the gods, fostered by sacrifice, will grant you the enjoyments which you desire. Whoever enjoys the enjoyments granted by them without giving to them in return—he is, verily, a thief."

The good people who eat what is left after the sacrifice [5] are released from all sins. On the other hand, those sinful ones who cook only for themselves—they, verily, eat their own sin.

From food creatures come into being; from rain ensues the production of food; from sacrifice results rain; sacrifice has its origin from action (karma).[6]

Know action to originate from the Brahman and the Brahman to originate from the Imperishable. Therefore, the Brahman, which permeates all, is ever established in sacrifice.

Whoever, in this world, does not help in the rotating of the wheel thus set in motion—he is of sinful life, he indulges in mere pleasures of sense, and he, O son of Prithā, lives in vain.

But the man whose delight is in the Self alone, who is content with the Self, who is satisfied only within the Self—for him there exists nothing that needs to be done.

He, verily, has in this world no purpose to be served by action done nor any purpose whatsoever to be served by action abnegated. Similarly, he does not depend on any beings for having his purpose served.

Therefore, without attachment, always do the work that has to be done, for a man doing his work without attachment attains to the highest goal.

For, verily, by means of work have Janaka and others attained perfection. You should also do your work with a view to the solidarity of society [*lokasaṅgraha*].

Whatever a great man does, the very same the common man does. Whatever norm of conduct he sets up, that the people follow.

There is not for me, O son of Prithā, in the three worlds, anything that

[5] That is, those whose first and foremost concern is the promotion of cosmic order which sacrifice sustains, and not any selfish interest.

[6] Action is, indeed, the basic force which sets and keeps in motion the cosmic wheel: action—sacrifice—rain—food—creatures—action.

has to be done nor anything unobtained to be obtained; and yet I continue to be engaged in action.

For if ever I did not remain engaged in action unwearied, O son of Prithā, men would in every way follow in my track.

These worlds would fall into ruin if I did not do my work. I would then be the creator of chaos and would destroy these people.

The Technique of Karma-Yoga

The *Gītā* essentially embodies a code of conduct. After having theoretically established that, in order to fulfill one's social obligations, one has inevitably to do one's appointed work, the *Gītā* now lays down the practical course by following which one can, even while engaging oneself in work, remain uninvolved in its consequences. The *Gītā* thereby meets the most common objection to the way of work. It is, indeed, this practical aspect of the yoga of action (karma-yoga) which has been dilated upon in the major part of the poem.

[From *Bhagavad Gītā,* 3.25–35; 4.13–20; 2.39–50]

The Blessed Lord said:

Just as the unwise act being attached to their action, even so should the wise act, O Bhārata, but without attachment, and only with a view to promoting the solidarity of society.

One should not create any conflict in the minds of the ignorant who are attached to action. On the contrary the wise man, himself acting in accordance with the technique of the yoga of action, should induce them willingly to undertake all [prescribed] actions.

Actions of every kind are actually done by the dispositions of matter [prakriti];[7] and, still, a person whose mind is deluded by the ego thinks: "I am the doer [of those actions]."

But he, O Mighty-armed One, who knows the truth of the distinctness of the soul from the dispositions of matter and from the actions [resulting therefrom], does not become attached [to the results of actions], realizing that the dispositions operate upon the dispositions.

Those who are deluded by the dispositions of matter become attached to the disposition and the actions [resulting from them]. One who knows the whole truth should not make such dullards, who do not know the whole truth, falter [by himself renouncing all action].

[7] Cf. note 23.

Renouncing into Me all actions, with your mind fixed on the Self, and becoming free from desire and all sense of "my-ness," do you fight, freed from your spiritual fever.

Those men, who, full of faith and without malice, always follow this My teaching—they are, verily, freed from the bondage of actions.

Those, on the other hand, who, treating My teaching with superciliousness, do not follow it—know them, who are utterly confounded in wisdom and are senseless, to be completely lost.

Even the man of knowledge acts in accordance with his own innate nature. Beings have to follow the dictates of their innate nature. What can repression avail?

The attraction and aversion of a sense-organ in respect of the objects of that sense-organ are inherently determined. One should not come under their sway for they are his waylayers.

Better is one's own dharma [class duties] which one may be able to fulfill but imperfectly, than the dharma of others which is more easily accomplished. Better is death in the fulfillment of one's own dharma. To adopt the dharma of others is perilous. . . .

The fourfold class system was created by Me in accordance with the varying dispositions and the actions [resulting therefrom]. Though I am its creator, know Me, who am immutable, to be a non-doer.[8]

Actions do not cling to Me, for I have no yearning for their fruit. He who knows Me thus [and himself acts in that spirit] is not bound by actions.

So knowing was action done even by men of old who sought liberation. Therefore do the same action [i.e., your class duties] which was done by the ancients in ancient times.

What is action? What is inaction?—as to this even the wise sages are

[8] In this stanza, three propositions have been set forth: 1) The scheme of the four classes, which ensures the promotion of social solidarity (*lokasaṅgraha*) in the most efficient manner, is created by God. Therefore all men, surrendering themselves to the Divine will, should fulfill their respective duties (*sva-dharma*) in accordance with that scheme. 2) That scheme is designed by God in accordance with the varying propensities and capacities of different sets of people. It is not arbitrary. 3) God created the four-class system as a part of His *sva-dharma.* He had to act in the fulfillment of that *sva-dharma,* but He acted in a perfectly disinterested and unattached manner. Therefore, even in spite of action, He remained free from bondage to action. In other words, though He was a "doer," as far as the consequences of His action were concerned, He was a "non-doer." He has thus demonstrated the efficacy of the technique of karma-yoga. It would appear that, out of these three propositions, in the present context, it is the last one which Krishna wants particularly to emphasize.

confounded. I will expound action to you, knowing which you will be liberated from evil.

One has to realize what is action; similarly, one has to realize what is wrong action; and one has also to realize what is inaction. Inscrutable, indeed, is the way of action.

He who sees inaction in action and action in inaction, he is discerning among men, expert in the technique of karma-yoga, the doer of the entire action [enjoined by his dharma].

He whose undertakings are all devoid of motivating desires and purposes and whose actions are consumed by the fire of knowledge—him the wise call a man of learning.

Renouncing all attachment to the fruits of actions, ever content, independent [9]—such a person even if engaged in action, does not do anything whatever.[10]

This concept has been set forth for you according to Sānkhya.[11] Listen now to this one according to Yoga, being endowed with which mental attitude, O son of Prithā, you will cast away the bondage of actions.[12]

Herein there is no loss of any effort, nor does there exist any impediment. Even a little practice of this dharma saves one from great fear.

In this [technique], one's mind is fixed on action alone [not its fruits]; it is single-aimed, O Joy [i.e., scion] of the Kurus, while the thoughts of those whose minds are not fixed on action alone are many-branched and endless.

This flowery speech, which the undiscerning proclaim, who are fondly attached to the Vedic [ritualistic] doctrine and who, O son of Prithā, assert that there is nothing else, whose minds are full of desires and who are intent on heaven—a speech which yields nothing but birth after birth as the fruit of action and which lays down various specialized rites for the attainment of enjoyment and supremacy—by that speech of the ritualists the minds of those who are attached to enjoyment and supremacy are carried away, and their minds, which should be fixed exclusively on action, are not established in concentration.

The Vedas have the operation of the three constituent properties of matter

[9] That is, not depending on any attachment or aversion to action.

[10] As far as the bondage of action is concerned.

[11] Cf. earlier selection, "You Have To Fight."

[12] Sānkhya and Yoga here represent respectively the theoretical approach and the practical approach to Arjuna's problem.

[i.e., the phenomenal world] as their subject-matter; transcend, O Arjuna, the operation of the three constituent properties. Become free from dualities,[13] ever abiding in pure essence (*sattva*), indifferent to acquisition and preservation, possessed of the Self.

As much purpose there is in a pond in a place which is flooded with water everywhere, so much purpose there is in all the Vedas for a brāhman who possesses true knowledge.

Action alone is your concern, never at all its fruits. Let not the fruits of action be your motive, nor let yourself be attached to inaction.

Steadfast in Yoga, engage yourself in actions, Dhananjaya, abandoning attachment and becoming even-minded in success and failure. Such even-mindedness is called *yoga.*

Far inferior is mere action to action done according to the technique of karma-yoga, O Dhananjaya. Seek refuge in the [right] mental attitude. Wretched are those who are motivated by the fruits of action. One who acts according to the technique of karma-yoga casts off, in this world, the consequences of both his good acts and his bad acts. Therefore take to this yoga. Yoga is skill in actions.

The Doctrine of Devotion

The *Bhagavad Gītā,* like most of the texts relating to popular Hinduism, recommends devotion (bhakti) as the most efficacious form of religion. Devotion, as described in the *Gītā,* presupposes the recognition of a personal God, who is omnipresent, omniscient, and omnipotent, and who confers His grace on the devotee—however lowly he may be—when he surrenders himself unreservedly to Him.

[From *Bhagavad Gītā,* 9.4–14]

GOD AND THE CREATION

The Blessed Lord said:

By Me is all this world pervaded through My non-manifest form. All beings abide in Me, but I do not abide in them.[14]

And yet the beings do not abide in Me; behold My supreme yoga, Sustainer of beings, but not abiding in beings, is My Self, the bringer into being of all beings.

[13] The pairs of opposites, such as pleasure and pain, attachment and aversion, etc.

[14] The distinction between the incarnate God and the transcendental Godhead is emphasized in this and the next stanza.

Just as the mighty air, always moving everywhere, abides in the sky, even so do all beings abide in Me.[15] Understand this well!

All beings, O son of Kuntī, pass into My material nature [prakriti, primal matter] at the close of the world cycle; and at the beginning of the next world cycle I again bring them forth.

Having recourse to My own material nature, I bring forth, again and again, this entire multitude of beings, which is helpless under the control of matter.

These acts do not, however, bind Me, O Dhananjaya, for I remain as if unconcerned, unattached to these acts.

With Me as the overseer does primal matter give birth to this world—movable and immovable; and by reason of this, O son of Kuntī, does the world keep revolving in its course.

The deluded despise Me, the great lord of beings, who have assumed a human body, not realizing My higher existence.

They of vain hopes, of vain actions, of vain knowledge, and devoid of wisdom partake of the deluding nature of fiends and demons.

The great-souled ones, on the other hand, O son of Prithā, partaking of the divine nature, worship Me with undistracted mind, knowing Me as the immutable source of all beings.

Ever glorifying Me, always striving in My service, and steadfast in vows, bowing down to me with devotion, they worship Me with constant application.

Divine Manifestations

Though God is universally immanent, His presence is to be realized through his most striking manifestations, that is to say, through whatever is endowed, in a special way, with glory, majesty, and vigor.

[From *Bhagavad Gītā,* 10.20–24, 40–42; 11.3–4, 8, 14–17, 21, 26–27, 31–34; 9.22–34; 18.66–69]

I am, O Gudākesha [i.e., Arjuna], the Self abiding in the hearts of all beings; I am the beginning, the middle, and also the end of beings.

Of the Ādityas I am Vishnu; of the luminaries, the radiant sun; I am Marīchi of the Maruts; of the stars I am the moon.

[15] The beings abide in God in the same sense and to the same extent as air abides in the infinite, universal space. That is to say, they do not in any way affect the immutable character of God.

Of the Vedas I am the *Sāma Veda;* of the gods I am Indra; of the sense-organs I am the mind; of living beings I am the sentience.

Of the Rudras I am Shankara [Shiva]; Kubera I am of the Yakshas and Rakshasas; of the Vasus I am Agni; Meru I am of peaked mountains.

Of the officiating priests, know me, O son of Prithā, to be the chief—Brihaspati; of the army commanders I am Skanda; of water reservoirs I am the ocean. . . .

There is no end to My divine manifestations, O Tormentor of the Foe. Here, however, has been proclaimed by Me the extent of My divine glory only through a few illustrations.

Whichever entity is endowed with glory and with majesty, and is, verily, full of vigor—each such entity do you know to have originated from a fraction of My splendor.

Or rather, what need is there, O Arjuna, for this detailed knowledge on your part? This entire world do I support and abide in with only a single fraction of Myself.

GOD'S OMNIFORM

Arjuna said:

As You have declared Your Self to be, O Supreme Lord, even so it is. I desire to see Your supreme form, O Supreme Person.

If You think that it can be seen by me, O Lord, then reveal to me Your immutable Self, O master of yoga. . . .

The Blessed Lord said:

But you cannot see Me just with this your own human eye. Here I give you the divine eye. Behold My supreme yoga. . . .

Then he, Dhananjaya, overcome with amazement, his hair standing on end, bowed down his head and, with folded hands, said to the God.

Arjuna said:

I see all the gods in Your body, O God, as also the various hosts of beings, the Lord Brahmā enthroned on a lotus-seat and all the seers and divine serpents.

I see You possessing numberless arms, bellies, mouths, and eyes, infinite in form on all sides. Neither Your end, nor Your middle, nor yet Your beginning do I see, O Lord of the universe, O omniformed.

Wearing the crown and bearing the mace and the discus, a mass of splendor radiating on all sides, I see you—hard to gaze at—all around me, possessing the radiance of a blazing fire and sun, incomprehensible. . . .

These hosts of gods here enter into You and some, in fright, extol You with folded hands. And bands of the great seers and the perfected ones, crying "Hail," praise You with manifold hymns of praise. . . .

And here all these sons of Dhritarashtra [i.e., the Kauravas] together with the hosts of kings, and also Bhīshma, Drona, and Karna, along with the chief warriors on our side too, are rushing forward and entering into Your fearful mouths which have formidable tusks. Some, caught between the teeth, are seen with their heads pulverized. . . .

Tell me who You are—You of formidable form. Salutation unto You, O Foremost among the gods, confer Your grace on me. I desire to know you fully, the primal one, for I do not comprehend Your working.

The Blessed Lord said:

Time am I, bringing about the destruction of the world, grown mature, now engaged in drawing in the worlds within Myself.[16] Even without you will they all cease to be—these warriors who are arrayed in the opposing armies.

Therefore arise and win glory; conquering the foes enjoy a prosperous kingdom. By Me, verily, are they even already slain; become a mere instrument, O Savyasāchin, and slay Drona, Bhīshma, Jayadratha, Karna, and likewise other warriors, who have been already slain by Me. Feel not distressed. Fight, you shall conquer your enemies in battle.

GOD AND THE DEVOTEE

Those persons who, meditating on Me without any thought of another god, worship Me—to them, who constantly apply themselves [to that worship], I bring attainment [of what they do not have] and preservation [of what they have attained].

Even the devotees of other divinities, who worship them, being endowed with faith—they, too, O son of Kuntī, [actually] worship Me alone, though not according to the prescribed rites.

For I am the enjoyer, as also the lord of all sacrifices. But those people do not comprehend Me in My true nature and hence they fall.

Worshipers of the gods go to the gods; worshipers of the manes go to

[16] This passage may suggest that Time (*kāla*) is the ultimate principle underlying the world, but it has not been further developed metaphysically. More probably, however, the rerference to Time means simply Death. Cf. *Gītā* 10.30, 33, 34 *passim.*

the manes; those who sacrifice to the spirits go to the spirits; and those who worship Me, come to Me.

A leaf, a flower, a fruit, or water, whoever offers to Me with devotion—that same, proffered in devotion by one whose soul is pure, I accept.

Whatever you do, whatever you eat, whatever you offer in sacrifice, whatever you give away, whatever penance you practice—that, O son of Kuntī, do you dedicate to Me.

Thus will you be freed from the good or evil fruits which constitute the bondage of actions. With your mind firmly set on the way of renunciation [of fruits], you will, becoming free, come to Me.[17]

Even-minded am I to all beings; none is hateful nor dear to Me. Those, however, who worship Me with devotion, they abide in Me, and I also in them.

Even if a person of extremely vile conduct worships Me being devoted to none else, he is to be reckoned as righteous, for he has engaged himself in action in the right spirit.

Quickly does he become of righteous soul and obtain eternal peace. O son of Kuntī, know for certain that My devotee perishes not.

For those, O son of Prithā, who take refuge in Me, even though they be lowly born, women, vaishyas, as also shūdras—even they attain to the highest goal.

How much more, then, pious brāhmans, as also devout royal sages? Having come to this impermanent, blissless world, worship Me.

On Me fix your mind; become My devotee, My worshiper; render homage unto Me. Thus having attached yourself to Me, with Me as your goal, you shall come to Me. . . .

Abandoning all [other] religious practices (dharma), betake yourself unto Me alone as shelter. I shall deliver you from all sins whatsoever; be not grieved.

Never is this to be spoken by you to one who does not lead a life of austerity, who is not a devotee, and who is not anxious to hear, or to one who treats Me with superciliousness.

He, on the other hand, who proclaims this supreme secret among My devotees, showing the highest devotion to Me, shall without doubt come straight unto Me.

[17] In this and the preceding stanza, the *Gītā* coordinates its two principal teachings, namely, devotion (bhakti) and the yoga of action.

There is none among men who does dearer service to Me than he; nor shall there be another dearer to Me than he in the world.

Philosophical Synthesis

The *Bhagavad Gītā* does not endorse any one system of philosophy among those current in its time, but rather aims at achieving a synthesis of the most prominent among them, the Sānkhya, Yoga, and the Vedānta. Though one cannot speak of any consistent metaphysical viewpoint underlying the *Gītā's* teaching, the author tends toward a kind of theistic Sānkhya which embraces the spirit-matter dualism of the Sānkhya, the ultimate monism of the Vedānta, and the all-powerful God of devotional religion, realized through the disciplined activity and meditation of the yoga.

[From *Bhagavad Gītā,* 13.19–23; 14.3–8; 15.16–19; 5.4, 5]

Primal matter [prakriti] and spirit [purusha]—know them both to be beginningless.[18] The modifications and the constituent properties [19]—know them as originated from primal matter.

Primal matter is said to be the cause in respect to the creatorship of the cause and effect [relation in the phenomenal world]. The spirit is said to be the cause in respect of being the experiencer of pleasure and pain.

For the spirit abiding in primal matter experiences the constituent properties born of primal matter. Its attachment to the constituent properties is the cause of its births in good or evil wombs.

And the Supreme Spirit in this body is called the Witness, the Permitter, the Supporter, the Experiencer, the Great Lord, as also the Supreme Self.[20]

He who thus knows the spirit and primal matter together with the con-

[18] According to Sānkhya, there are two ultimately and independently existing principles, primal matter (prakriti) and spirit (purusha). The spirit is sentient (cetana) but incapable of modification while primal matter is nonsentient but capable of modification. In the unmodified form of primal matter, its three constituent properties (gunas), namely, purity (sattva), passion (rajas), and darkness (tamas) are in a state of equipoise. This state of equipoise is disturbed as the result of the "seeing" of primal matter by the spirit. Primal matter then begins to be modified, according to a fixed plan, into the manifold phenomenal world. The various aspects of the phenomenal world, accordingly, are made up of the three constituent properties combined in different proportions.

[19] That is, the different combinations of the three constituent properties which constitute the phenomenal world.

[20] The concept of the Supreme Spirit over and above matter and the individual spirit or soul is unknown to the original Sānkhya. It reflects the monistic Vedānta concept of the highest Brahman (cf. "the Supreme Self," *paramātman,* in this stanza) and thus facilitates a kind of synthesis between Vedānta monism and Sānkhya dualism. For another, the Supreme Spirit is identified with the all-god (Krishna; cf. "the great lord," *maheśvara*) of devotional religion.

stituent properties[21]—even though he engages himself in action in any way, he is not born again. . . .

My womb is the Great Brahman;[22] in it I deposit the seed. Therefrom occurs the origination of all beings, O Bhārata.

Whatever forms are produced in all wombs, O son of Kuntī—of them the Great Brahman is the primal womb and I am the father implanting the seed.

Purity, passion, and darkness—these constituent properties born of primal matter bind down the immutable embodied one [i.e., the soul] within the body, O mighty-armed.[23]

Of these, purity, on account of its taintlessness, produces light and health. Through attachment to happiness and through attachment to knowledge it binds one down, O sinless one.

Know passion to be of the nature of emotion, the source of longing and attachment. It binds down the embodied one, O son of Kuntī, through attachment to action.

But know darkness to be born of ignorance and as causing infatuation to all embodied ones, It binds one down, O Bhārata, through negligence, indolence, and sleep. . . .

There are two spirits in this world, the mutable and the immutable; the

[21] That is, one who knows the true nature of spirit and matter and preserves the true nature of the spirit, namely, of being essentially isolated from matter, by not allowing it to become attached to the various modifications of primal matter.

[22] This expression is made up of two technical terms, one of which—the Great One (*Mahat*)—is borrowed from Sānkhya while the other—the *Brahman*—is taken from the Vedānta. According to Sānkhya, the first evolute of primordial matter is "the Great One," which is the source of all further evolution; while in Vedānta the Brahman is the ultimate essence and cause of the world. This entity (the Great Brahman), which clearly refers here to primordial matter, is presided over by Krishna, who infuses it with life (his "seed")—an attempt at a synthesis between theism and both schools of philosophy.

[23] Matter includes not only the external world and the body, but also what we would call the mind. The latter is regarded as active, like all of matter, but unconscious, consciousness being the fundamental characteristic of the spirit. The spirit is deluded by the ego faculty of the mind into identifying itself with the body-mind complex. All of matter is made up of the three dispositions (gunas). The word *guṇa* literally means "strand," as the strands of a rope, but it also came to mean "quality." Though the gunas had both cosmic and psychological significance, the latter use predominates in the *Gītā*. The translation "disposition" is more suggestive of this connotation. The three dispositions manifest themselves in the highest or directing faculty of the mind, i.e., the intellect (*buddhi*), as three fundamental tendencies or drives, which are present in all of us in various proportions. Even when "purity," the drive toward knowledge and liberation, predominates, it binds the soul to the world of matter and therefore to karma and rebirth; but once the intellect reaches the saving knowledge, the drive for knowledge and liberation, and *a fortiori* the other dispositions, now without purpose, wither away, leaving the soul, freed from specious connections to the phenomenal world, to enjoy its own immutable bliss.

mutable [i.e., matter] comprises all beings; what remains unchanged is called the immutable [the spirit or soul].

But other than these two is the Highest Spirit (*uttama-puruṣa*), called the Supreme Self, who, the Eternal Lord (*īśvara*), permeating the three worlds, sustains them.[24]

Since I surpass the mutable and am higher even than the immutable, therefore, I am celebrated as the Highest Spirit (*puruṣa-uttama*) among people and in scripture [lit. in the Veda].

Whoever, undeluded, thus knows me to be the Highest Spirit, he is the knower of all and worships me with his whole being, O Bhārata. . . .

Fools, not the wise, declare that Sānkhya and Yoga are different; a person who resorts to one of these correctly, obtains the fruit of both.

The position obtained by followers of Sānkhya is also obtained by the followers of Yoga. He who sees that Sānkhya and Yoga are one, he truly sees.

The Ideal Man

The *Gītā* mentions in different contexts the characteristics of the man who can be regarded as perfect according to Krishnaism. He is referred to variously as of steadfast wisdom, yogin, devotee, etc. In the characterization of the Ideal Man the principal teachings of the *Gītā* are also reflected.

[From *Bhagavad Gītā,* 2.55–59; 6.16–23; 12.13–19]

When one renounces all the desires which have arisen in the mind, O son of Prithā, and when he himself is content within his own Self, then is he called a man of steadfast wisdom.

He whose mind is unperturbed in the midst of sorrows and who entertains no desires amid pleasures; he from whom passion, fear, and anger have fled away—he is called a sage of steadfast intellect.

He who feels no attachment toward anything; who, having encountered the various good or evil things, neither rejoices nor loathes—his wisdom is steadfast.

When one draws in, on every side, the sense-organs from the objects of sense as a tortoise draws in its limbs from every side—then his wisdom becomes steadfast.

The objects of sense turn away from the embodied one [the soul] who

[24] Cf. note 20.

ceases to feed on them, but the taste for them still persists. Even this taste, in his case, turns away after the Supreme is seen. . . .

Yoga, indeed, is not for one who eats in excess nor for one who altogether abstains from food. It is, O Arjuna, not for one who is accustomed to excessive sleep nor, indeed, for one who always keeps awake.[25]

For one who is disciplined in eating and recreation, who engages himself in actions in a disciplined manner,[26] who properly regulates his sleep and wakefulness—for him yoga proves to be the destroyer of sorrow.

When one's properly controlled mind becomes steadfast within the Self alone and when one becomes free from all desires, then he is said to have accomplished yoga.

"Just as a lamp in a windless place flickers not"—this is the simile traditionally used in respect of a yogin whose mind is properly controlled and who practices the yoga of the Self.

Wherein the mind, restrained by the practice of yoga, is at rest; and wherein he, seeing the Self through the Self, finds contentment within his own Self;

wherein he finds that supreme bliss, which is perceived by the intellect alone and which is beyond the ken of the sense-organs; wherein, being steadfast, he does not swerve from reality;

having obtained which, he does not consider any other gain to be greater than it; and being steadfast in which, he is not shaken by even a heavy sorrow;

that state, one should know as the one called yoga—the disconnection from union with sorrow. This yoga should be practiced with resoluteness and with undepressed mind. . . .

He who does not entertain hatred toward any being, who is friendly and ever compassionate, free from all sense of "my-ness," free from egoism, even-tempered in pain and pleasure, forbearing;

he who is ever content, the yogin, possessing self-control, of unshakable resolve; who has dedicated to Me his mind and intellect—he, My devotee, is dear to Me.

[25] The *Gītā* prescribes a way of life which can be practiced by the common man. It was generally believed that yoga presupposed some austere physical and mental discipline. This kind of yoga was obviously beyond the reach of the common man. The *Gītā,* therefore, here teaches a different kind of yoga or self-discipline, the most essential feature of which is temperateness.

[26] A reference to the yoga (discipline) of action.

He from whom the world shrinks not and who does not shrink from the world; and who is free from elation, impetuosity, fear, and perturbation—he too is dear to Me.
He who has no expectation; who is pure, dexterous, unconcerned, and untroubled; who renounces all acts[27]—he, My devotee, is dear to Me.
He who neither exults nor hates, neither grieves nor yearns; who renounces good and evil; who is full of devotion—he is dear to Me.
He who behaves alike to foe and friend; who, likewise is even-poised in honor or dishonor; who is even-tempered in cold and heat, happiness and sorrow; who is free from attachment;
who regards praise and censure with equanimity; who is silent, content with anything whatever; who has no fixed abode,[28] who is steadfast in mind, who is full of devotion—that man is dear to Me.

HINDU PHILOSOPHY

The Upanishadic doctrine concerning the identity of the individual self (ātman) with the Absolute Brahman, which represented the culmination of philosophic thought in the Vedas, also served as the point of departure for Hindu philosophical speculation in later times. The term Vedānta, as we have seen, means "end of the Veda" (that is, the Upanishads), and came to be applied to those later texts which, accepting the scriptural authority of the Upanishads, attempted to formulate more systematically its teaching concerning the nature of Brahman. The *Brahma* or *Vedānta Sūtras,* from which readings are given below, are ascribed to Vyāsa or Bādarāyana. Other thinkers who expounded the doctrines of the Vedānta and are referred to by Vyāsa in the course of these discussions include such names as Jaimini, Āshmarathya, Audulomi, and Kāshakritsna.

Closely related to the Vedānta was another school devoted to the hymns and formulae found in the Samhitā portion of the Veda, with which different deities were to be propitiated and merit thereby accumulated for the attaining of heavenly enjoyment. These meritorious acts enjoined by the former part of the Veda constitute dharma, and the nature of this

[27] Namely, acts springing from selfish desires and emotions; or: the fruits of such acts.
[28] A fixed abode is the symbol of one's attachment to the experiences of this phenomenal world.

dharma as taught by the Veda in its ritualistic portion (*Karma Kāṇḍa*) is expounded in a system of thought called *Mīmāṃsā* ("inquiry") by the sage Jaimini. It is also referred to as *Pūrva* (earlier) *Mīmāṃsā;* while the *Vedānta* is, in this respect, referred to as *Uttara* (later) *Mīmāṃsā.* According to the earlier interpreters of the Vedic teachings, these two schools were taken together and it was considered proper to study first the Pūrva Mīmāmsā and then the Uttara Mīmāmsā. But Shankara Āchārya (Shankara the Teacher, A.D. c.850) the greatest exponent of Advaita,[1] showed that the philosophy of the Brahman and its pursuit have nothing to do with acts; acts can, according to him, serve only as a disciplinary accessory, aiding mental purification.

Apart from this, the Pūrva Mīmāmsā gave a whole system of exegetical principles employed in the interpretation of the Vedic texts, which are of use in the sphere of civil and religious law also.

Also closely related to the *Vedānta* is the system of thought called *Sāṅkhya,* which figures so importantly in the *Gītā. Sāṅkhya* means reasoning. Traces of the development of Sānkhya thought are met with in the Samhitā and Upanishads, and in Buddhism. The sage who supposedly first propounded this school was Kapila, a name already met in one of the more important later Upanishads. According to Kapila, there are two entities, spirit and matter, purusha and prakriti; the phenomenal world that we see, the beings and their activities, are all the manifold manifestations of matter. Matter is nonsentient and is constituted of three dispositions called *guṇa*[2]—purity (*sattva*), passion (*rajas*), and darkness (*tamas*). *Sattva* is light, revealing, and happy; *rajas* is active, passionate, restless, and sorrowful; *tamas* is heavy, stupid, and obscuring. When these three constituents are in a state of equilibrium, matter is static; but when the equilibrium is disturbed and one or the other constituent gains the upper hand, matter starts evolving into cosmic intellect, egoity, the subtle elements, and so on. The cause of this disturbance of equilibrium is the proximity of the spirit. The spirit alone is intelligent, and its intelligence is reflected in the evolutes of matter, namely, intellect, ego, mind, and senses (intellect and ego have both a cosmic and an individual function). The spirit, whose association with matter is responsible for evolution, experience, and misery, being by nature a mere spectator not actually involved in the doings of matter, real knowledge consists of the realiza-

[1] Lit. "non-duality," the monistic school of Vedānta.

[2] Lit. "strands."

ion of the distinctness of the spirit from matter and recognition of all nundane activities as due to the interplay of the material dispositions. By uch isolation, one frees oneself from material bondage and the consequent ufferings. The *Vedānta Sūtras* refute the Sānkhya in many places by ointing out that insentient matter cannot explain creation and that a entient Supreme Being alone can be the source of this universe.

Closely related to the Sānkhya is the school of Yoga, the aphorisms of vhich are ascribed to Sage Patanjali. The Yoga is presupposed by the Jpanishads and Buddhism. This school accepts the philosophical docrines of the Sānkhya, with one important difference in that it accepts a God (Īshvara) as the Supreme Omniscient ever-existing Teacher. For he rest, the Yoga sets forth a system for controlling the mind and body hrough physical and ethical disciplines, and for helping that one-pointed oncentration by which the aspirant could see the spirit established in s intelligence and isolated completely from the modifications and conaminations of matter. The Yoga is thus of practical value.

Two other systems of thought also arose which used logic to a large xtent, the Vaisheshika and Nyāya, both realistic and pluralistic in their enets. The Vaisheshika developed a view of the physical universe through s atomic theory according to which objects were constituted of atoms *aṇu*), the ultimately analyzable units, and as each was distinct by virue of its own ultimate particular quality called *viśeṣa,* the school came to e known as *Vaiśeṣika*. The philosophy of the Vaisheshika is acceptable o the Nyāya, which specialized in the methodology of thought and reaoning. The Nyāya accepted God only as an efficient cause, the architect f the universe, and used the teleological argument to prove His existence. The followers of both these schools were theists and worshiped Shiva as he Supreme God.

The above were the six schools of philosophy developed by the orthoox, as against the heterodox thinkers. All of these orthodox schools ccepted the Vedas as authoritative. Opposed to them were the purely naterialist thinkers called *Cārvākas* or *Lokāyatas* for whom there was no elf or entity beyond the material body and its needs, as also the schools f Buddhism and Jainism which repudiated Vedic authority.

One of the chief characteristics of the Indian systems of thought is that hey postulate at the very outset the criteria or sources of valid knowldge (*pramāṇas*) which each of them proposes to use and rely upon. Of the sources of valid knowledge, it is only the materialistic school which accepts direct sense perception (*pratyakṣa*) as the sole source of knowledge. The rest accept a number of sources of knowledge, two, three, four, and so on. The chief of these sources of knowledge are the direct perception already mentioned, inference (*anumāna*), analogy (*upamāna*), and verbal testimony (*śabda*), the last of which includes the words of a reliable person and the scriptural utterances. Just as each school sets forth the sources of knowledge acceptable to it, it enumerates also the categories of knowable objects (*prameyas*) accepted by it.

Among these schools, use is made to a varying degree of logic and inference on the one hand and scriptural authority on the other. The two Mīmāmsās assign the primary place to scripture, and according to the Vedānta, reasoning occupies only the secondary place, being resorted to only to interpret and reinforce revelation. Mere inference is like groping in the dark, says the grammarian and poet Bhartrihari. In the logical school of Nyāya also, where even God is proved on logical grounds, the authority of the Veda as the word of God is accepted. To the Indian thinker, philosophy is no mere intellectual game but a darshana or vision of Truth revealed by a seer and an experience realized and relived by the aspirant. Consequently, each school sets forth its own conception of the goal aimed at by the inquiry. All are agreed that the goal of the philosophical quest is liberation from the misery of going from birth to death and death to birth, and the attainment of everlasting Bliss. In some cases, the everlasting bliss is simply release (mukti or moksha) from the transmigratory cycle (samsāra) or the suffering caused by the material enslavement of the spirit; the Sānkhya-Yoga schools envisage their liberation thus; in Nyāya also, it is of the same type, though here, as in Yoga God's grace is sought as a help. In the theistic schools, of which an example is given below, the *summum bonum* is conceived in terms of different relationships to a personal God. In monistic Advaita, the final state which the aspirant strives for is the realization of the unity of his Self with Brahman.

As Indian philosophy aims at experiencing the Truth, all the schools include disciplines (*sādhanas*), practical means for the attainment of the spiritual goal. The Yoga, mentioned already, is the chief *sādhana* accepted by the orthodox as well as heterodox schools. Devotion to God, fulfillment of obligatory and ordained duties, ethical behavior—all these ar likewise part of the means employed. As all the schools have such a practical side, all of them emphasize the need and importance of a spiritual preceptor or teacher—a guru.

In their inquiry into the nature of reality, the schools adopt different theories of causation, and in epistemology, they have similarly different theories of truth and error. There are three main theories of causation—origination (*ārambha*), transformation (*pariṇāma*), and apparent transfiguration (*vivarta*). The logical Nyāya school holds the first view, the effects being, according to them, created from out of several causes; here the effect was previously nonexistent in any one cause (*asatkārya-vāda*). The Sānkhya school adopts the second view where the effect exists already in the cause and is merely brought out in a different form (*sat-kārya-vāda*). On the third theory, which the idealistic school of Advaita adopts, the effect is only an apparent manifestation on the basis of the cause which is thereby transfigured. In accordance with the first view, illustrated by the example of the potter making a pot out of clay, God creates the universe as an agent. In the second case, which resembles milk curdling into a different form, the entire phenomenal world represents but manifold evolutions of the same matter. The third view is exemplified by a rope mistaken for a snake, or water seen in a mirage; in the same manner, the entire phenomenal universe is but an appearance projected by the basic reality called the *brahman*. It will be seen that from the first theory to the second and from the second to the third, there is a progressive reduction of difference and increase in identity between cause and effect.

In the same manner, when there arises a wrong cognition, different schools explain the nature of error in different ways. This consideration is essential to understanding the conception of the universe and experience in the different schools. Consider the example of a piece of nacre shining as silver to an onlooker who rushes to take it, but is disappointed on closer examination. Here, according to the Nyāya, what is one thing shines as something else; this is *anyathā-khyāti* or misapprehension. According to one sub-school of Pūrva Mīmāmsā, erroneous cognition is a case of nonapprehension of something (*akhyāti*); that is, one sees nacre, not as nacre, but as just "this object in front"; the strong memory of silver experienced by him previously forces itself now to the fore and without being able to distinguish between actual cognition and a recollection, he rushes to the knowledge that it is silver. Among the Vedāntic schools, that of Rāmānuja thinks that in all such experiences, there is nothing invalid; and in reality, certain silver-elements inhere in nacre as a consequence of which such a cognition arises. This is an eclectic view of *akhyāti-cum-satkhyāti.* In Shankara's theory of the appearance of one thing on the substratum of another and the superimposition of something unreal on a basic reality, the case of seeing silver in nacre, with which the whole phenomenal world and experience are compared, is simply an apparent reality whose nature cannot be determined one way or the other as either real or unreal. It has a *relative* reality for the duration of the erroneous perception, when one rushes to pick it up as silver, but is *ultimately* unreal, being sublated on the rise of the correct perception of its being only nacre.

Of these schools of philosophy, each played its notable part for a time and became superseded later, leaving only some distinctive subsidiary aspect of it as its contribution. The Sānkhya was once the most widely and influentially expounded school, against which even Buddhism had to contend. The very name Sānkhya became synonymous with knowledge. Moreover, despite some earlier tendencies toward atheism, after the addition of a God in a more substantial manner than in Yoga, the Sānkhya became absorbed by the Purānas. At the same time, the rise of Vedānta made it superfluous, its doctrine of primordial matter being paralleled by the Vedāntic nescience (*avidyā*) or illusion (māyā) and its conception of unaffected spirit or purusha by the Vedāntic ātman or Brahman (the only difference being that in Sānkhya, spirit (purusha) was not one but many). In its concept of the three dispositions (gunas), the Sānkhya bequeathed a vital idea which was useful in all schools of thought and fields of activity for evaluating things and grading them as good, middling, and bad. The cognate system of Yoga, however, was likewise adopted by all schools and today has spread even beyond the confines of India. The word *yoga* has come to mean spiritual or religious path in general.

For a long time the logical school of Nyāya performed a great service in defending, against the attacks of Buddhistic atheists and nihilists, the doctrines of the existence of God, the reality of the world, the continuity of experience, and the substantiality of wholes as distinct from parts. Later, when Vedānta took over the task of criticizing Buddhist metaphysics, the Nyāya with its realism and pluralism, directed its criticism against Advaitic idealism and monism. As a school of philosophy the Nyāya was unable to maintain a separate existence, but its methodology in logical analysis—in definition, inference, sentence, word and meaning, etc.—came to be utilized by all schools of philosophy in their own dialectic. The Mīmāmsā,[3] for its part, had served to restore the authority of the Veda when it was assailed by the Buddhists; and Kumārila, one of its outstanding exponents in the seventh century, was responsible for defending and strengthening Hindu teachings against Buddhism. With the rise of Vedānta and the progressive decline of the belief in sacrificial rites and the path of acts, Mīmāmsā became more and more a theoretical scholastic discipline, its writers being, in conviction, Vedāntins of one school or another.

It is the remaining school, the Vedānta, that became, from the time of Shankara, the prevailing philosophy of India. The readings which follow are representative of the monistic or nondualistic (*Advaita*) school of Vedānta as expounded by Shankara in his commentary on the *Vedānta Sūtras*. Later interpretations of the *Vedānta Sūtras* were those of the Rāmānuja school of qualified nondualism (*Viśiṣṭādvaita*) and of Madhva Āchārya (Madhva the Teacher, 1199–1278) which inculcated a more theistic and pluralistic (*Dvaita*) interpretation of Vedānta.

The exact nature of the relation between the Supreme Being and the individual soul is the central problem in these systems. Already in the *Vedānta Sūtras* (1.4.20–22), the sages, Āshmarathya, Audulomi and Kāshakritsna, are seen to have held different views on this question. The first held that the individual souls, even as sparks issuing forth from a fire, were neither different from the Brahman nor non-different from It. The second held that the individual souls are different from the Supreme, but with the dropping of their embodied limitation, they become one with the Supreme. According to the third, it is the Supreme Soul that exists also as the individual soul. The early interpreters of the *Vedānta Sūtras* before Shankara mostly adopted the first view of difference-*cum*-identity (*bheda-abheda*), holding the evolutionary theory of the origin of things from the Brahman, and in the period immediately following Shankara also, this view was maintained by writers like Bhāskara (A.D. c.850) and Yādavaprakāsha (A.D. c.1100). Shankara, as also his grand-preceptor Gaudapāda, followed the third view, of Kāshakritsna, and expounded

[3] The Pūrva Mīmāmsā.

the identity of the two, of the individual soul as a state of the Supreme.

In Rāmānuja's (d. A.D. 1137) interpretation, the sentient and the nonsentient universe constitute the body of the Supreme Being, which is thus a personality endowed with attributes and is identified with the God Vishnu. While the sentient and nonsentient (i.e., souls and matter) are thus characteristic of the one Brahman and cannot exist independently of Him, there is nonetheless an inherent distinction between them. It is in this sense that Rāmānuja's nondualism is "qualified." Rāmānuja's understanding of the *Vedānta Sūtras* differs from Shankara's nondualism in that Brahman is for Rāmānuja not intelligence itself, as Shankara maintains, but is a Supreme Being whose chief attribute is intelligence. This latter conception of the Supreme Being as the cause of the universe and as possessing various attributes gives the Rāmānuja school of Vedānta a theistic character. It has tended to stress devotion (bhakti) rather than knowledge as the chief means of salvation. In fact, however, this devotion to Vishnu—the theistic Brahman—is seen to derive from knowledge, and to represent only a more direct path to salvation. Unbelief rather than ignorance is regarded as the fundamental obstacle to this goal.

Madhva was a realist and pluralist to whom the world was real, the souls were many and different, the Supreme God was Vishnu and the individual souls, His servants. Besides Shankara, Rāmānuja, and Madhva, there were other South Indian exponents of the *Vedānta Sūtras* who explained this relationship between the Supreme and the individual self in slightly different terms and who established in North India sects which are still widely followed there. Nimbārka, for instance, adopted the old standpoint of difference-*cum*-identity; and Vallabha Āchārya (A.D. c.1500) adopted Shankara's view with greater stress on the personal God and His grace. In Bengal Vaishnavism, founded by Chaitanya (b. A.D. 1485), Baladeva (eighteenth century) interpreted the relation between God and the individual soul as an inscrutable difference-*cum*-identity. All these schools were markedly theistic and practiced fervent devotion to God in the form of Krishna, the Lover Supreme.

ĪSHVARAKRISHNA

The Sāṅkhya Kārikās

This exposition of the Sānkhya is taken from the best-known compendium of that school dating perhaps from the fourth century A.D. The original is in pithy verse (kārikās) and to give an easy flow to the English version, the text is rendered in some places in an expanded manner.

[From Īshvarakrishna, *Sāṅkhyā Kārikās,* 1–33, 38–42, 44–45, 55–69]

Owing to man being assailed by the three kinds of misery,[1] there arises the desire in him to know the means for the removal of such misery. Such an inquiry into the cause of the removal of misery is not rendered useless because there are known and ready remedies, for such remedies are neither invariably nor completely effective. Like those worldly remedies are those that one knows from the scriptures [namely, the performance of Vedic sacrifices to attain the joyous status of heaven]; for that scriptural remedy is impure as sacrifices involve injury [to animals], and its fruits are both perishable [2] and liable to be excelled by other kinds of pleasure.[3] Therefore a remedy which is the opposite of these [the seen one of the world and the heard one of the scriptures] is more beneficial; and that remedy is to be had by knowledge, the discrimination of the manifest material creation, its unmanifest cause [the object], and the presiding sentient spirit [the subject].

Primordial Matter is not an effect [modification]; the intellect, etc., seven in number, are both cause and effect; there are sixteen categories which are only effects; the spirit is neither cause nor effect.[4]

The categories of knowledge are known from means of correct knowledge and in Sānkhya, three sources of valid knowledge are accepted: perception, inference, and valid testimony; all other means of correct

[1] Mental and physical; that caused by fellow beings, animals and nature; and that caused by atmospheric conditions, spirits and heavenly beings.

[2] The heavenly status is strictly governed by the duration of the fruit of sacrifices and at its lapse, the performer of the sacrifice enjoying heavenly status reverts to earthly existence. A limited act, such as it is, cannot produce a result which is everlasting, a state from which there is no lapse.

[3] Such a fruit admits of degrees, one doing a bigger sacrifice gaining a higher heaven or a bliss of longer duration; varying degrees are part and parcel of artificial acts operating under the laws of specific cause-and-effect relationships.

[4] These are the twenty-five categories of Sānkhya.

knowledge are included in these three. Perception is the determination of objects by their contact with the respective senses perceiving them. Inference is of three kinds, and it results from the knowledge of a characteristic feature and of an object invariably accompanied by that feature.[5] Valid testimony is what one hears from a reliable authority. Perception provides knowledge of sensible objects. Of things beyond the senses, knowledge is had through inference based on analogy;[6] and those that are completely beyond the senses and cannot be established even through that process of inference are ascertained through valid testimony. A thing may not be perceived because of too great distance, of too much proximity, injury to the senses, inattention of mind, smallness or subtlety, an intervening object, suppression by another, or merging in a similar thing.

Primordial matter is not perceived because it is too subtle, not because it does not exist; for it is known from its products [the phenomenal world]. And those products are intellect, etc.; products born of primordial matter are, in their characteristics, partly like it and partly unlike it.[7]

The effect already exists in the cause for the following reasons: what is nonexistent cannot be produced; for producing a thing, a specific material cause is resorted to; everything is not produced by everything; a specific material cause capable of producing a specific product alone produces that effect; there is such a thing as a particular cause for a particular effect.

The evolved [i.e., the product] has the following characteristics: it has been caused, it is noneternal, nonpervasive, attended by movement, manifold, resting on another, an attribute of its source in which it finally merges, endowed with parts, and depending on another for its existence. The nonevolved [i.e., the cause, primordial matter] is the opposite of all this. But the evolved and the unevolved [primordial matter] have these common properties: they are composed of three dispositions [gunas];

[5] Such a characteristic feature is, for instance, smoke which accompanies fire invariably. Thus, from the appearance of smoke on a mountain, the existence of fire on the mountain is inferred. The stock example of a five-membered inference is: 1) *thesis to be proved:* the mountain is on fire; 2) *ground:* because it has smoke; 3) *illustration:* everything that has smoke, e.g., a kitchen, has fire; 4) *application:* the mountain is such a thing; 5) *conclusion:* therefore the mountain is on fire.

[6] For example, when we infer, from the different positions of the sun that it moves, on the analogy of a person seen at different places owing to his movement.

[7] That is, an effect takes a new form but at the same time carries the features of the cause; there is a difference-*cum*-identity between cause and effect.

they are nondiscriminating and nonsentient; they are object; they are common; and their nature is to evolve. The spirit is opposed in its qualities both to one and to the other.

The three dispositions: they are of the form of pleasure, pain, and dejection; their purposes are illumination, activation, and checking; they function by prevailing over one another, resorting to one another, engendering one another, and acting in cooperation with one another.[8] They are purity [sattva], passion [rajas], and darkness [tamas]. Purity is light, revealing and desirable; passion is stimulating and active; darkness is dense and obscuring; their harmonious functioning is directed by unity of purpose, as in the case of a lamp [in which the ingredients, fire, oil, and wick, conjointly function for the one purpose of producing light].[9]

The properties like absence of discriminatory knowledge can be proved to exist in the evolved by reason of the latter being composed of the three dispositions and by the absence of this threefold composition of its opposite, namely the spirit. The existence of an unevolved primary cause is proved by the fact that the effect has the same properties as the cause.

The unevolved exists as the primordial cause because the diverse evolutes are all attended by limitations, because common features subsist through all of them [arguing inheritance from a common cause], because the evolved has come into being as the result of the potentiality of a cause, because the distinction of cause and effect apply to the entire world without exception.

The unevolved acts [evolves] through its three dispositions [purity, etc.] and through them conjointly, changing like water according to the difference pertaining to each of those dispositions.

As all aggregates imply one different from themselves whom they subserve, as that for whom they are intended should differ from their own nature, namely, being composed of three dispositions, etc., as such objects should have one as their presiding authority, as objects imply an

[8] All nature is composed of these three dispositions. They are not to be understood as attributes of nature, but they are the three modes in which nature itself is constituted. They are nature. All modifications of nature are but the products of the different kinds of proportions of the interplay or intermingling of these three modes.

[9] Opposed in nature and individually possessed of mutually destructive properties, these cooperate for the sake of a common object; even so the three modes of nature, whose common object is to allow the spirit to attain through experience discriminative knowledge and ultimate emancipation.

enjoyer, and as there is seen through evolution a striving for liberation, there exists the spirit. The plurality of spirits is proven because of the specified nature of birth, death, and faculties in respect of each person, because of the absence of simultaneous activity on the part of all, and because of the diversity of the nature of the three dispositions in different beings. By the same reason of differences from the unevolved [primordial matter] which is composed of the three dispositions, the spirit is proved to be only a spectator, distinct and unaffected, endowed with cognition but free of agency.

Hence, as a result of union with the spirit, the evolved though non-sentient, yet appears to be sentient; and on its part, the spirit, too, though the dispositions of matter alone act, appears to act but is really indifferent. It is for the sake of enlightenment of the spirit and the eventual withdrawal from primordial matter [i.e., liberation of the spirit from matter] that the two come together, even as the lame and the blind [10] come together for mutual benefit; creation proceeds from this union.

From primordial matter proceeds intellect; from it ego; from that the group of sixteen [the five subtle elements governing sound, touch, form, taste, and smell, the five senses of knowledge, the five of action, and the mind which is the internal sense presiding over the other ten senses]; from the five [subtle elements] among those sixteen, the five gross elements [ether, air, fire, water, and earth].

The intellect is of the form of determination; its sublime [purity-dominated] forms are virtue, knowledge, dispassion, and mastery; the opposites of these [darkness-dominated vice, ignorance, passion, and powerlessness] represent its forms in delusion.

Ego is of the form of identification; from it proceed twofold creation, the group of eleven [senses] and the five subtle elements. From that state of ego called *vaikṛta* [i.e., dominated by purity] proceed the eleven purity-dominated evolutes [the faculties]; from the state called *bhūtādi* [dominated by darkness, lit. the origin of gross natural elements], the five subtle elements, which are dominated by darkness; and from the state called *taijasa* [dominated by passion] both of these [the faculties as well as the subtle elements] proceed.[11]

[10] The blind can carry the lame and the lame can direct the blind; sentient spirit is lame as it is devoid of activity and active matter is blind as it is devoid of cognition.

[11] The sublime purity-dominated state is inactive, even so the degraded darkness-dominated state; to make each of these active and productive of their respective evolutes, namely,

The senses of knowledge are eye, ear, nose, tongue, and skin; those of action are voice, hands, feet, and the organs of excretion and generation. The mind is of both forms [of knowledge and action]: it is of the form of reflection and it is called a sense because of its similarity to the senses. The variety of organs is due to the modifications of the constituents, and so is the variety of objects comprehended by the senses. The function of the five organs of knowledge in respect of form, etc. [their respective objects] is of the form of indeterminate perception; of the five organs of action, speech, taking, moving, discharge, and enjoyment form the function. What has been set forth above forms the characteristic and distinctive function of each of these three [the senses of knowledge, those of action, and of the mind]; the five vital breaths [12] constitute their conjoint function.

In respect of a perceptible object the functioning of the four [intellect, ego, mind, and one of the senses] is known to be sometimes simultaneous, sometimes gradual.[13] In respect of the unseen the operation of the three [internal instruments of knowledge: intellect, ego, and mind] is based on a prior sense perception. The external and internal instruments of knowledge function in their respective capacity in coordination; the motive of their activity is only to subserve the purpose of the spirit; [besides this] there is naught else that promulgates the activity of the instruments. These instruments [intellect, etc.] are of thirteen kinds: [five organs of knowledge; five of action; and intellect, ego, and mind]; they gather, hold together, and reveal [their objects]; their results are tenfold [the five sense-perceptions and five activities], gathered, assimilated, and revealed. The inner organ is threefold [intellect, ego, and mind]; the external organs are ten [the five of knowledge and the five of action] and they form the object of the former triad; the external ones are confined to the present time, the internal organs comprehend all the three phases of time [present, past, and future]. . . .

The subtle elements are not of any specific character; from these five, the five gross elements of matter proceed and these gross elements have specified characters, peaceful, violent, and dormant [according to the relative preponderance of any of the three gunas]. These three specified

the eleven faculties and the five subtle elements, the association of passion, the principle of activity, is needed; hence the middle state (*taijasa*) is for the benefit of both states.

[12] The five vital breaths are those that sustain life, discharge excreta, etc.

[13] Gradual in cases of doubt at the first instance and resolution after reflection.

forms have again a threefold manifestation [in living beings]; the subtle body,[14] the gross body born of parents, together with the gross elements; the subtle ones endure [through transmigration], the gross ones are perishable. The former called the *liṅga*[15] is of unknown antiquity, not subject to any obstruction, is enduring, and comprises intellect, ego, mind, and the five subtle elements; it is not yet capable of experience [being without a gross body], but overlaid with the impressions of acts, it migrates from birth to birth. Just as there cannot be a picture without a substratum or a shadow without objects like the post, even so, the instruments of experience cannot exist without the subtle body [composed of the subtle elements]. According to the exigencies of the causes—virtue, vice, etc.—and the resultant higher or lower births, the subtle body (*liṅga*) prompted by the purpose of the spirit (viz. its liberation) makes its appearance like an actor in different guises, thanks to the capacity of the primary matter (prakriti) to manifest diverse forms. . . .

By virtue one progresses toward higher forms of embodied existence; by vice, one goes down toward lower forms; by knowledge liberation is gained and by its opposite bondage; by nonattachment to mundane objects, one reaches the state of merging in primordial matter;[16] from desire impelled by passion further transmigration results; unimpeded movement is gained through the attainment of mastery and from its opposite, the opposite of free movement. . . .

In this transmigratory journey, the sentient spirit experiences the misery due to old age and death till such time as the subtle body also falls away; hence, in the very nature of existence, everything is misery.

Thus this activity caused by primordial matter starting with intellect and ending with gross elements is for the release of each individual spirit; it is really for the spirit, though it appears to be for itself. Just as insentient milk flows out for the purpose of the growth of the calf, even so is the activity of primordial matter intended for the release of the spirit. Just as

[14] This is the form in which one is said to transmigrate from one kind of birth to another.

[15] The subtle body is called *liṅga* because it is eventually "merged" (*līyate*) back into primordial matter.

[16] This is an intermediate state from which one proceeds to final release or to further transmigration. There are three kinds of bondage due to three kinds of mistaken notion: considering the performance of various acts of merit as being enough; identifying the spirit with one of the intruments of knowledge; and mistaking primordial matter to be the spirit. Those engaged in acts continue to be involved in bodies produced by the effects; the other two produce a state of merger in primordial matter.

to rid oneself of a longing, one indulges in activities in the world, even so does primordial matter act for freeing the spirit [from its own experience]. Just as a danseuse displays her art to the public and retires, even so does primordial matter unfold itself before the spirit and then retire. She [matter], the helpful lady, endowed with all the dispositions, selflessly carries out, by manifold means, the purpose of the spirit which, in reality, plays no helpful part in this activity, not being made of the three dispositions.[17] Methinks, there is nothing more tender than primordial matter, that poor thing which, once it has come within the sight of the spirit, never again appears before him.

Therefore, surely, no spirit is bound, none is released, none transmigrates; primordial matter, taking different forms, transmigrates, binds herself and releases herself. By her own seven forms [virtue and vice, ignorance, detachment and attachment, mastery and the lack of it], matter binds herself; and for the purpose of the spirit, she herself, with one of her forms, namely knowledge, causes release.

"I am not like this," "This is not mine," "This is not myself"—by repeated cognizance of this truth, pure knowledge, free from all error and of the form of the discrimination of the spirit from matter, arises. Whereby the spirit, remaining unaffected like a spectator, merely looks on at primordial matter, who has, on the cessation of her purpose,[18] ceased to evolve and has turned away from her sevenfold modification.[19] The one [spirit] is indifferent, because he has seen through matter; the other [primordial matter] has ceased to be active, because she has been seen through; even though their union continues for a time, there is no evolution. When virtue, etc., have ceased to be operative as cause, as a result of the rise of perfect knowledge, the spirit continues to be in an embodied state as a result of the impressions [caused by previous karma], even as a potter's wheel.[20] When the body falls [dies], and primordial

[17] The verse is couched in a poetic vein with *double entendre* depicting the activity of primordial matter (prakriti, a feminine noun) as that of a helpful housewife and the part of the spirit (purusha, a masculine noun) as that of the idle, sit-at-home husband.

[18] The experience of the spirit and his eventual release.

[19] The eighth, knowledge, being really not her form, but a reflection of the spirit and being the cause and itself the form of that discrimination which constitutes release; the other seven, virtue, vice, etc., which constitute bondage, good and bad, are mentioned as the forms from which matter now desists.

[20] Even though the pot has been produced and the potter has ceased to rotate the wheel, the wheel yet continues its revolutions owing to the prior momentum; similarly, when perfect knowledge has been produced, no more fresh evolution of matter or its modification

matter having fulfilled her role has retired, the spirit attains release which is both certain and complete.

This secret doctrine intended for the release of the spirit was declared by the Supreme Sage [Kapila]; here are analyzed the existence, origin, and merger of beings.

SHANKARA

Commentary on the Vedānta Sūtras

If Vedānta is the dominant philosophy of India today, the credit is due almost entirely to the genius of Shankara. Shankara's expressed aim was to promote the Truth revealed in the Upanishads, which he regarded as the highest message of the Veda. He wrote commentaries to several Upanishads and to the *Gītā,* besides the present one on the *Vedānta Sūtras,* and he tried to show that all these works expressed one and the same system, i.e., the system of pure monism (Advaita).

The basic principles of Shankara's philosophy derive from this concept of absolute nonduality. All plurality is seen as unreal and as superimposed upon the absolute unqualified Brahman which is one without a second. The false notions of plurality and causality arise from delusion or māyā which though without beginning may be eliminated through knowledge. Similarly, the individual soul, which appears different from other souls and also from Brahman is in fact nothing but the one unitary Brahman. Since ignorance lies at the root of the seeming duality, knowledge alone is regarded as the means to liberation. Religious actions have only a secondary function in that they may direct the mind to knowledge, but in themselves can never bring about liberation. Devotion, too, plays a role, though subordinate. For while Brahman is absolute existence, intelligence, and bliss, it may be regarded as possessing auspicious attributes characteristic of a personalized god (*īśvara*). Contemplation of this more limited conception of Brahman purifies the mind and prepares it for the higher knowledge of the unqualified Brahman. Much of Shankara's dialectic is based on this dual standard of absolute and relative—or higher and lower—knowledge. That knowledge which leads to liberation is not mere reasoning, but involves the introspective realization of the absolute unity of the individual soul and Brahman.

The *Aphorisms on the Brahman* or *on the Upaniṣads* (*Brahma* or *Vedānta*

take place, but those modifications that had already begun must run their course and they do so as long as that body lasts; on the fall of that body, the spirit is completely released. This applies to the Vedāntic theory of knowledge and release also. The state in which one is enlightened and yet embodied, the Vedānta calls *Jīvanmukti.*

Sūtras) of Bādarāyana is an ancient codification into a single unified system of the thought of the Upanishads, whose kernel may go back several centuries before Christ. In Shankara's time it was already considered an authoritative interpretation of the Upanishads. The manner in which Shankara expounds his philosophy, in the form of a commentary on this text, is highly illustrative of his general method, which is based on the rational interpretation of revealed truth. In the introduction to his commentary, Shankara demonstrates the essential duality between the subject (Self or soul) and the object (matter). The portion extracted here forms Shankara's commentary (bhāshya) on the first four aphorisms (sūtras) which are generally taken as a concise introduction to and epitome of his extensive commentary on the whole of the *Vedānta Sūtras.*

[From Shankara, *Brahmasūtra Bhāṣya,* 1.1.1–4]

INTRODUCTION ON "SUPERIMPOSITION"

When it is well understood that "object" and "subject," comprehended as "you" and "I" and opposed in nature like darkness and light, cannot be of each other's nature, much less could the properties of the two be of each other's nature; therefore when one superimposes on the "subject" comprehended as "I" and consisting of intelligence, the "object" comprehended as "You" and its properties, and superimposes the "subject" which is the reverse thereof and its properties on the "object," this superimposition, it stands to reason to believe, is a thing to be denied.

Still, superimposing the nature and attributes of one thing on those of another and without discriminating from each other the two totally distinct things, namely, the "object" and the "subject," there is this natural usage in the world, *"I am this"* and *"This is mine,"* which is due to a sublative notion and represents a confusion of the true and the false.

One may ask, what is this thing called "superimposition"? We say, it is the "appearance" in something of some other thing previously experienced and consists of a recollection.[1] Some call it the superimposition of the attributes of one thing on another; some say that where a thing is superimposed on another, it is the illusion due to the nonperception of their difference; still others hold that where there is a superimposition, it is the fancying in a thing of a property contrary to its nature. In any case, it does not cease to have the character of one thing appearing to

[1] For example, you have met John in London; when you come upon X in New York and accost him as John, you have really met someone in whom you recollect the likeness of John whom you have previously seen; the flash of John's likeness in X is later sublated when you come closer and say, "I am sorry . . ."; here John-ness is superimposed on X.

possess another's property. And so is our experience in the world: nacre shines like silver, and one moon, as if it had a second.

But how does the superimposition of "object" and its properties on the inner Self, which is not the "object," come about? On a thing before oneself one superimposes another thing, but you say, the inner Self, which falls outside the scope of what is comprehended as "you," is never an "object." The reply is: This inner Self is not a nonobject at all times, for it is the object of the notion "I" and there is the knowledge of the inner Self by immediate intuition.[2] There is no such rule that a superimposition has to be made only in an object that exists in front of one; for even in an imperceivable thing like the ether, boys superimpose a surface, dirt, etc. Thus it is not contradictory to speak of superimposition on the inner Self of things which are non-Self.

The superimposition so characterized, the learned consider to be nescience, and the determination of the real nature of a thing by discriminating that which is superimposed on it, they say is knowledge. When this is so, that on which a thing is superimposed is not affected in the slightest degree by either the defect or the merit of the superimposed thing. And it is due to this superimposition over one thing of another in respect of the Self and the non-Self—which is termed nescience—that all worldly transactions, of the means of knowledge and the objects thereof, take place, and [under the same circumstance] again, do all the scriptures, with their injunctions, prohibitions, and means of liberation operate.

But how do you say that sources of valid knowledge like perception and the scriptures fall within the purview of that which is conditioned by nescience? I shall reply: One devoid of the sense of "I" and "Mine" in the body, senses, etc., cannot be a cognizer and cannot resort to a means of cognition; for without resorting to the senses, there can be no activity of perception, etc.; and without a basis [the body] the activity of the senses is not possible; and none ever acts without a body on which the sense of the Self has not been superimposed. Nor could the Self, the unattached, be a cognizer, when none of these [body, senses, etc.] exist; and without a cognizer, the means of cognition do not operate. Hence it is under what

[2] As a conditioned Self it is presented as object in cognitions of "I" and as the unconditioned Self, it is known by immediate intuitive knowledge; in the latter case, as the Self itself consists of knowledge and does not depend on anything outside for its knowledge, it is by courtesy that a subject-object relation is stated.

is conditioned by nescience that all means of knowledge, perception, etc., as also the scriptures, come. . . .

In respect of activities relating to scriptural teachings, although an intelligent person does not become eligible to enter upon them unless he knows the Self as having a relation to the other world, still that truth called Self, which is to be known from the Upanishads, which transcends the physical needs like hunger and the distinctions like brāhman, kshatriya, etc., and which is not subject to transmigration, is not to be included in the eligibility [for scriptural activities], because that Self is of no use and is opposed to this kind of eligibility.[3] Operating as it does before the rise of the knowledge of that kind of Self, the scripture does come under things conditioned by nescience. Thus scriptural injunctions like "A brāhman shall perform the sacrifice" operate, consequent on the superimposition on the Self of particularities like class, stage, age, and condition.

We said that superimposition is the seeing of a thing in something which is not that; thus, when son, wife, etc., are all right or not, one considers one's own Self as all right or not, one superimposes external attributes on the Self; even so does one superimpose on the Self the attributes of the *body* when one considers that "I am corpulent, I am lean, I am fair, I stand, I go, I jump"; similarly attributes of the *senses* when one says, "I am dumb, one-eyed, impotent, deaf, blind"; and in the same manner the properties of the *internal organs,* e.g., desire, volition, cogitation, and resolution. Even so, man superimposes the [conditioned] Self presented in the cognition of "I" on the inner Self which is the witness of all the activities of the internal organ; and that inner Self, the very opposite and the witness of all, on the inner organ.

Thus without beginning or end, existing in the very nature of things, this superimposition which is of the form of a knowledge that is subject to sublation and is responsible for the agency and experience of man, is something which the whole world knows. It is for casting away this superimposition which is the cause of [all] evil and for gaining the knowledge of the oneness of the Self that all the Upanishads are begun. And how this is the purport of all the Upanishads, we shall show in this system of thought called the investigation into the Self that presides over the body [*Śārīraḳa Mīmāṃsā*].

[3] That real Self which neither acts nor enjoys is beyond the realm of a desire for such result as may accrue from a meritorious act or an activity intended for attaining such a desire.

Of this system of thought [also] called the *Vedānta Mīmāṃsā* [the enquiry into the purport of the Vedānta, i.e., the Upanishads], which it is my desire to explain, this is the first aphorism:

THEN THEREFORE THE DESIRE TO KNOW THE BRAHMAN

In the commentary to this aphorism Shankara defends his position against the related system called Pūrva Mīmāmsā ("First Inquiry") in which the nature of ordained duty (dharma) and ordained action or ritual (karma) are investigated. Shankara devotes much of his attention to the refutation of other systems of thought, both orthodox and heterodox. In the passages quoted he tries to refute the claims of the Pūrva Mīmāmsakas that theirs was the only valid interpretation of the Vedas. Both schools of Mīmāmsakas ("scriptural exegetes") grew in response to the challenge of other systems of thought, chiefly Buddhism. Since the Veda was infallible it *a fortiori* had to be consistent, and to produce such a consistent system based on the Vedic scriptures was the aim of both schools. According to the Pūrva Mīmāmsā the sole purpose of scripture was to set forth ordained duty, which was otherwise unknowable; this was done in scriptural passages stating injunctions or prohibitions. Since no Vedic passage could be lacking in purpose, all other passages were viewed as *arthavāda,* helpful explanations, praises, or condemnation in connection with some injunction or prohibition. Shankara criticizes the Pūrva Mīmāmsā for holding that the meaning of the Veda consists only of prescriptions for action, whereas the Upanishads deal not with action but with knowledge (of the Brahman).

When it is accepted that the "then" [in the aphorism] has the meaning of "after" [something], just as the inquiry into dharma [duty] presupposes invariably the study of the Vedas which has just gone before that inquiry, so also, in the case of this inquiry into the Brahman, we must state what it is that has necessarily preceded it. That it is after the study of the Vedas is something common to both the inquiries, i.e., that into dharma and that into the Brahman, but is there not a difference here that the inquiry into the Brahman follows the knowledge of dharma? No; it is possible that one may have a desire to know the Brahman if one had read the Upanishads, even though one had not inquired into what dharma is. In scriptural texts like the one on the sundering of the heart [in sacrificing an animal], there is a fixed sequence of things, sequence being intended there [by the word "then"]; sequence that way is not meant here; for between the inquiry into dharma and the Brahman, there is no authority to show that one is complementary to the other or that a person qualified in the former [dharma] becomes eligible for the latter [Brahman].

Further between the two there is difference in respect of fruit as well as the object of the inquiry; the knowledge of dharma has the fruit of prosperity and it is dependent on observance of the respective duties; on the other hand, the knowledge of the Brahman has the fruit of everlasting bliss and is not dependent on any other activity. Also dharma which is desired to be known is a thing yet to come into being, as it is dependent on the person doing it; but the Brahman desired to be known here is a thing which exists already, because it is eternal and not dependent on the activity of a person. There is also difference between the two in regard to the operation of their respective sacred injunction: The sacred injunction[4] which defines dharma enlightens a person even as it engages him in the activity intended by it; on the other hand, the text relating to the Brahman[5] only enlightens a person; as knowledge is the direct result of the text, the person is not enjoined to an activity of knowing; just as an object is known when there is the contact of the sense organ and the object, even so is it here.

Therefore something must be set forth [as the preceding consideration] in close succession to which the inquiry into the Brahman is taught. I shall set it forth; the sense of discrimination as to things permanent and evanescent, nonattachment to objects of enjoyment here or in the hereafter, the accumulation of accessories like quietude and self-control,[6] and a desire to be liberated. When these are present, whether before an inquiry into dharma or after it, it is possible for one to inquire into the Brahman and know it, not when they are absent. Therefore, by the word "then," it is taught that this desire to know the Brahman follows immediately after the full acquisition of the spiritual accessories set forth above. . . .

Now that Brahman may be well known or unknown; if it is well known, there is no need to desire to know it; if on the other hand, it is unknown, it could never be desired to be known. The answer to this objection is as follows: The Brahman exists, eternal, pure, enlightened, free by nature, omniscient, and attended by all power. When the word "Brahman" is explained etymologically, it being eternal, pure and so on, are all understood, for these are in conformity with the meaning of the root *bṛh* [from which Brahman is derived]. The Brahman's existence is

[4] For example, "He who desires heaven shall perform the sacrifice" and so on.
[5] For example, "The Brahman is to be known" and so on.
[6] Others are retirement from activities, forbearance, mental concentration, and faith.

well known, because it is the Self of all; everyone realizes the existence of the Self, for none says, "I am not"; if the existence of the Self is not well known, the whole world of beings would have the notion "*I* do not exist." And the Self is the Brahman.

It may be contended that if the Brahman is well known in the world as the Self, it has already been known, and again it becomes something which need not be inquired into. It is not like that, for [while its existence in general is accepted], there are differences of opinion about its particular nature. Ordinary people and the materialists are of the view that the Self is just the body qualified by intelligence; others think that it is the intelligent sense-organs themselves that are the Self; still others, that it is the mind; some hold it as just the fleeting consciousness of the moment; some others as the void;[7] certain others say that there is some entity, which is different from the body, etc., and which transmigrates, does and enjoys;[8] some consider him as the enjoyer and not as the doer;[9] some that there is, as different from the above entity, the Lord who is omniscient and omnipotent.[10] According to still others, it is the inner Self of the enjoyer.[11] Thus, resorting to reasonings and texts and the semblances thereof, there are many who hold divergent views. Hence one who accepts some view without examining it might be prevented from attaining the ultimate good, and might also come to grief. Therefore, by way of setting forth the inquiry into the Brahman, here is begun the discussion of the meaning of the texts of the Upanishads, aided by such ratiocination as is in conformity to Scripture and having for its fruit the Supreme Beatitude.

It has been said that the Brahman is to be inquired into; on the question as to the characteristics of that Brahman, the blessed author of the aphorisms says:

WHENCE IS THE ORIGIN . . . OF THIS

. . . Of this universe made distinct through names and forms, having many agents and enjoyers, serving as the ground of the fruits of activities attended by specific places, times, and causes, and whose nature and design cannot be conceived even in one's mind—that omniscient, omnipotent cause wherefrom the origin, maintenance, and destruction of such a uni-

[7] The Buddhists. [8] The Nyāya school. [9] The Sānkhya school.

[10] This is according to the Yoga school where, besides the individual souls, there is a God.

[11] According to the Vedāntins, to whom the present text and its expounder belong.

verse proceed is the Brahman; such is the full meaning that is to be understood. . . .

It is not possible to discard the Lord, characterized as above, and suppose anything else, primordial matter devoid of intelligence,[12] atoms,[13] nonexistence, or a person subject to the transmigratory cycle as the cause of the origin, etc., of the universe characterized above.[14] Nor can it proceed from the very nature of things, for we require here [for production of a thing] a specific place, time, and cause.

This itself is taken by those philosophers who speak of the Lord as the cause of the universe, as an inference capable of demonstrating the existence, etc., of a Lord, different from the transmigrating individuals. And here, too, in the present aphorism, "whence, etc.," [15] is it not the same idea that is propounded? It is not so, for the aphorisms string together the flowers of the statements in the Vedānta [Upanishads]; [16] it is the Upanishadic statements that are cited in the form of aphorisms and examined. It is by the examination of the meaning of the scriptural texts and determining it exactly that Brahman-realization is achieved, not by inference and other sources of knowledge. The Vedāntic texts which speak of the cause of the origin, etc., of the world being there, inference, which would strengthen the understanding of their meaning and would be in conformity with the Vedāntic text, is not precluded from being one of the sources of knowledge; for ratiocination is accepted by scripture itself as an aid. Thus the Scripture says: "That Self is to be listened and thought over" [17] and shows in the text "Just as an intelligent man who has been well informed would reach the Gandhāra country," even so here, he who has a teacher knows" [18] that the Scripture takes the aid of human intellect. As

[12] This is the Sānkhya theory, refuted more fully later.

[13] This is the view of the Vaisheshika school, refuted more fully later.

[14] From aphorism four onward, these opposing views are tackled and refuted.

[15] Texts, aphorisms, verses, etc., were usually identified by citing the beginning word or words.

[16] What is meant by Shankara is that the second aphorism is not to be taken as supplying the inference to prove God, or as implying that inference is the main source of our knowledge of God; that may be so for logicians (followers of the Nyāya school), but certainly not for students of Vedānta for whom the scriptural statement about God forms the primary source of knowledge. The aphorisms are primarily a collection of statements from the scripture; when saying this Shankara presses into service also the meaning "thread," which the word *sūtra* has.

[17] *Bṛhad Āraṇyaka Upaniṣad*, 2.4.5.

[18] *Chāndogya Upaniṣad*, 6.14.2. In this text the usefulness of a personal teacher for pointing the way on the spiritual path is mentioned, and the illustration is given of an intelligent

far as the inquiry into the Brahman is concerned, scripture, etc., are not the sole source of knowledge as in the case of the inquiry into dharma; scripture, etc., and direct experience, etc., according to the occasion, are sources of knowledge; for the knowledge of the Brahman has for its object something which already exists and completes itself in its direct experience. In a thing which is to be *done,* there is no need for experience, and scripture, etc., may alone be the source of knowledge, for the thing to be done depends, for its very coming into being, on the person [who proposes to do it]. An act, whether mundane or ordained by scripture, may be done, may not be done at all, or may be done in a different manner; likewise, with reference to the scripture-ordained acts, the texts say: "One takes the *ṣoḍaśin* cup in the *Atirātra* ritual" and also [elsewhere]: "One does not take the *ṣoḍaśin* cup in the *Atirātra";* also: "One offers oblations after sunrise" and [elsewhere] "One offers oblations before sunrise." Injunctions and prohibitions too have meaning in this sphere, as also optional rules and exceptions. But a thing as such does not admit of alternative propositions like "It is thus" and "It is not thus," "It is" and "It is not"; alternative suppositions depend on the human mind, but knowledge of the truth of a thing is not dependent on the human mind; on what then does that depend? It is solely dependent on the thing itself. In respect of a pillar the knowledge of its true nature cannot take the form, "This is either the pillar or a man or something else"; "This is a man or something else" is suppositious knowledge; "This is really a pillar" is correct knowledge, because the question depends on the nature of the thing. In this manner, the validity of knowledge in respect of objects which are already in existence depends on the things themselves.

Thus the knowledge of the Brahman too is dependent on the thing, because the knowledge refers to a thing already in existence. The objection may be raised that, in so far as the Brahman is an object already in existence, it can be surely comprehended by other means of knowledge and the discussion on the Vedāntic texts becomes futile; this objection cannot hold because the Brahman is not within the provenance of the senses, the invariable relation between it and its effect is not apprehensible in its case; by nature, senses have for their object things of the world, not the Brahman. It is only when the Brahman can be the object of sense-per-

man who wants to reach the Gandhāra country, but not knowing the way, asks men and with the help of their information and direction, reaches his destination.

ception that one can apprehend that there is an effect which is related to the Brahman [its cause]; when the effect alone is apprehended [by the senses], it is not possible to decide if it is related to the Brahman or to something else; therefore the present aphorism mentioning origin, etc., is not for setting forth a theistic syllogism. But then what is it for? It is to draw attention to a Vedāntic text. What is the Vedāntic text that is intended to be indicated in this aphorism? It is the text [19] which begins with the words "Bhrigu, son of Varuna, approached his father Varuna with the request, 'O Blessed one, teach me the Brahman,'" and states: "That from which all these beings are born, that by which those born subsist and that into which those dying enter, that do you try to know; that is the Brahman." Of this Brahman [so characterized] the text which clinches its nature is the following: "From bliss it is that these beings are born; by bliss are those born sustained and into bliss do those dead enter." [20] Other texts of this kind, which speak of its being by nature eternal, pure, enlightened, and free, and of its being omniscient, and of the form of the Self and the cause, are also to be cited.

By showing the Brahman as the cause of the universe it has been suggested that the Brahman is omniscient; now to reinforce that omniscience the author of the aphorisms says:

AS IT IS THE SOURCE OF THE SCRIPTURE

Of the extensive scripture [Shāstra] comprising the *Rig Veda,* etc., reinforced and elaborated by many branches of learning, illumining everything even as a lamp, and like unto one omniscient, the source [lit. womb] is the Brahman. Of a scripture of this type, of the nature of the *Rig Veda* and the like, endowed with the quality of omniscience, the origin cannot be from anything other than the omniscient one. Whatever teaching has, for purposes of elaborate exposition, come forth from an eminent personage, as the science of grammar from Pānini, etc., though it is comprehensive of that branch of knowledge, it is well understood in the world that its exponent [e.g., Pānini] possesses knowledge far more than what is in his work; it therefore goes without saying that unsurpassed omniscience and omnipotence is to be found in that Supreme Being from whom, as the source, issued forth, as if in sport and without any effort, like the breathing of a person, this scripture in diverse recensions,

[19] *Taittirīya Upaniṣad,* 3.1.

[20] *Ibid.,* 3.6.

called *Rig Veda,* etc., which is the repository of all knowledge and is responsible for the distinctions into gods, animals, humans, classes, stages of life, etc.; this is borne out by scriptural texts like: "This that is called *Rig Veda* [and so on] is the breathings out of this Great Being." [21]

Or the scripture consisting of *Rig Veda,* etc., is the source, i.e., the authoritative means of knowing this Brahman in its real form; what is meant is that it is from the authoritative source of scripture that the Brahman, the cause of the origin, etc. of the universe is known.[22] The scriptural text concerned was cited under the previous aphorism: "That from which these things have their birth, etc." Wherefore then the present aphorism, when the Brahman being knowable from the scriptural source has already been shown by the previous aphorism which cites scriptural texts of this class? The reply is: In the previous aphorism the scripture has not been expressly stated and one might doubt that by that aphorism, "whence, etc.," a syllogistic proof of the Brahman has been set forth; to remove such a doubt, this aphorism came in, saying, "As it has the scripture as its source."

But how is it said [a Pūrva Mīmāmsaka might contend] that the Brahman is known from scripture? It has been shown by the statement: "As the scripture has action as its purpose such texts as do not have that purport are useless," [23] that the scripture refers to ritual action; therefore the Upanishads are useless as they do not have action as their purport; or as revealing the agent, the deity, etc., they are subservient to the texts which enjoin ritual action; or they are for enjoining some other activity like meditation. It is not possible that the Veda sets forth the nature of a thing already well established,[24] for a thing well established becomes the object of direct perception and other sources of knowledge; and even if such a thing is set forth, there is no human objective served by it, as there is nothing there to be avoided or desired. For this very reason, texts like "He wept," lest they should become meaningless, have been said to have meaning as recommendatory eulogies,[25] according to the statement "By

[21] *Bṛhad Āraṇyaka Upaniṣad,* 2.4.10.

[22] This is an additional interpretation of the same aphorism which reinforces what Shankara said last under the previous aphorism that the scripture is the primary source of knowledge about the Brahman, and inference or reasoning is only secondary.

[23] This is from the aphorisms of the Pūrva Mīmāmsā.

[24] The purpose of a Vedic text is to reveal what has not been known through well-known sources of knowledge.

[25] This is from a Vedic text of the class called *arthavāda,* which extols an injunction or

reason of syntactic unity with the injunctive texts, they might be for praising the injunctions."[26] Of the Vedic texts called mantras, e.g., "Thee for nourishment,"[27] the intimate association with the ritual has been shown, as they speak of an act and its accessories; no Vedic text is seen anywhere nor can it be justified without some relation to the enjoining of an act. Such enjoining of an act is not possible in respect of the nature of a thing which is well established, for injunction has for its object an action. Therefore, by reason of revealing the nature of the agent, the deity, etc., required for the ritual, the Upanishads are complementary to the texts enjoining ritual acts. If, however, this standpoint is not accepted, out of the fear that the Upanishads represent a different context altogether, still, the Upanishads may be held to have their purport in an activity like the meditation set forth in their own texts. Therefore the Brahman is not to be known from the scriptural source. In the face of that objection it is said:

THAT, HOWEVER, IS SO BECAUSE OF TEXTUAL HARMONY

The word "however" is for warding off the *prima facie* view. That Brahman, omniscient, omnipotent, and cause of the birth, existence, and dissolution of the universe *is* known from the scripture as represented by the Upanishads. How? "Because of textual harmony." In all the Upanishads the texts are in agreement in propounding, as their main purport, this idea. For example, "Dear one! this thing Existence alone was at the beginning";[28] "The one without a second";[29] "The Self, this one only, existed at first";[30] "This Brahman, devoid of anything before or after, inside or outside";[31] "This Self, the Brahman, the all-experiencing one";[32] "At first there was only this Brahman, the immortal one."[33] When it is decisively known that the purport of the words in these texts is the nature of the Brahman, and when unity is seen, to imagine a different purport is improper, as thereby one will have to give up what is expressly stated and imagine something not stated. Nor could it be concluded that their purport is to set forth the nature of the agent, deity, etc.;

condemns its opposite by various means, etymological significance, a legendary illustration, and so on. The Brāhmana part of the Veda has such texts. The present example "He wept" is from the explanation of the name Rudra.

[26] This is another aphorism from the Pūrva Mīmāmsā.

[27] Used in a particular act in one of the sacrifices.

[28] *Chāndogya Upaniṣad*, 6.2.1.

[29] *Ibid.*

[30] *Aitareya Upaniṣad*, 1.1.1.

[31] *Bṛhad Āraṇyaka Upaniṣad*, 2.5.19.

[32] *Ibid.*

[33] *Muṇḍaka Upaniṣad*, 2.2.11.

for there are texts like "Then whom should It see and with what?,"[34] which refute action, agent, and fruit.

Because the Brahman is a thing already well established, it cannot be held to be the object of perception by senses, etc.; for the truth that the Brahman is the Self, as set forth in the text "That thou art,"[35] cannot be known without the scripture. As regards the objection that since there is nothing here to be avoided or desired, there is no use in teaching it, it is no drawback; it is from the realization that the Self is the Brahman, devoid of things to be avoided or desired, that all miseries are ended and the aspiration of man is achieved. If the mention of deity, etc., means the meditations expressed in the texts themselves, there is really no contradiction; thereby, the Brahman cannot become complementary to a text enjoining a meditation; for, because the Brahman is one and devoid of things to be avoided or desired, it stands to reason that It overcomes the notion of all duality of action, agent, etc. Once thrown out by the knowledge of oneness in the Brahman, the dualistic notion cannot have that resurgence whereby one could hold that the Brahman is subservient to the meditative injunction. Although, in other parts of the scripture, texts may not be authoritative without some relation to the injunction enjoining actions, yet it is not possible to repudiate the authoritativeness of that part of the scripture concerning the knowledge of the Self, for this knowledge is seen to lead to its fruit[36] [Self-realization]. The authoritativeness of scripture is not to be deduced by inference[37] for which there is a need to look for an analogical instance experienced elsewhere. Therefore it is established that the Brahman is authoritatively known from scripture.

THE WAY OF DEVOTION

The characteristic feature of medieval Hinduism is the great upsurge and spread of devotional movements. However intense was activity in the domain of metaphysics, the worship of a personal God, in one form or another, became the dominant trend and influenced even the schools of

[34] *Bṛhad Āraṇyaka Upaniṣad,* 2.4.13. [35] *Chāndogya Upaniṣad,* 6.8.7.

[36] This is in reply to the objection of futility.

[37] That is, a syllogism based on the argument of fruitfulness as applicable to injunctive texts which prescribe action. The Nyāya school employs the analogy of the medical science in a syllogism to prove the authoritativeness of scripture.

philosophy in the direction of theism. Unquestionably the most important literary sources of this movement were the two epics, the *Rāmāyaṇa* and the *Mahābhārata,* which enshrined in the hearts of the people a divine personality adored as the fountainhead of all beauty and goodness and as the repository of infinite excellences. Following the epics, the Purānas, which dealt with the missions that the Lord fulfilled in the world by taking upon Himself many incarnations, had a wide appeal among the masses. Like the epic, the Purāna, by presenting to us the origin and cosmography of the world, the process of time, the rise and fall of kingdoms, and the conflicts of good and evil forces, reminds us that mundane possessions are ephemeral, that the Almighty alone is worth aspiring for. The Purānas, in fact, became the bibles of popular Hinduism. They expatiated on the glories and exploits of different forms of divinity, set forth in extenso the types of worship, and described the sacred shrines in different holy places to which pilgrimages were made by the devout. These Purānas were recounted to large popular audiences, who also thronged to temples which kings had dedicated to the various gods and where the same stories could be seen depicted in attractive sculpture and painting. When music, dance, and drama were added to the regular daily service of these deities, the temples not only proved great centers of attraction for the people, but also came to play a role second only to the kings as patrons of all the arts. As practices accessory to devotion, the observance of vows (*vratas*) and austerities and pilgrimages to holy waters (*tīrthas*) for baths were also approved and encouraged in the Purānas. The development of dispassion and detachment (*vairāgya*), sacrifice of possessions (*tyāga*), abstinence and moderation, and the cultivation of tranquillity and retirement were likewise recommended.

The eighteen main Purānas, the eighteen minor Purānas, and the many Samhitās and other Purāna-like compilations all dealt with the subjects set forth above. Among them, the *Purāna of the Lord* (*Bhāgavata Purāṇa,* c. eighth or ninth century A.D.) gained, by its extraordinary popularity, a place rivaled only by that of the epic *Rāmāyaṇa.* This Purāna deals with the incarnations that the Lord repeatedly takes to restore the balance of values in the world, by putting down evil and reviving virtue. The book is noteworthy for its own unique way of dealing with the story of the Lord in His incarnation as Krishna and the ecstatic type of devotion exemplified by the cowherd lasses (*gopīs*) for the Lord. There is the Supreme

Being, the Brahman, of which the Personal God is a form assumed freely for blessing the universe. That one omniscient, omnipotent God, transcendent as well as immanent, takes for the further benefit of humanity manifold forms and incarnations through His mystic potency (māyā). In these forms, He engages Himself in action in the world without being contaminated by the stain of action and its fruit, which would otherwise produce bondage and transmigration. In this role the Lord—living in the world and yet out of it, acting at His own instance, selflessly and regardless of fruit—is the exemplar of the path of true and noble action, karma-yoga, and to all who want to serve the world (*lokasaṅgraha*), He, the Yogin and expert doer (*karma-kuśala*) is the model. Emulating Him, walking in His footsteps, taking refuge under Him, abandoning the sense of oneself as the agent, having faith in His grace and compassion rather than in one's own capacity, confessing one's shortcomings and praying to Him, adoring Him, repeating His name, wearing emblems to identify oneself as belonging to Him, singing or writing of Him, worshiping Him in an image at one's home or in a temple, communing with fellow worshipers, seeing His immanence in all beings and therefore venerating all humanity—all these are ways of practicing devotion to Him and thereby realizing Him.

Each of these fundamental ideas of the cult of devotion tended to be developed into a systematic doctrine and school of its own. Thus "surrendering oneself to God" was the theme of schools which advocated one kind of surrender or another. So, too, with the doctrine of the Lord's grace. Among the Shrīvaishnavas [1] of the South, there are two well-known doctrines, one of which insists that the Lord's grace must be met with an effort on one's own part as well, while the other contends that man need do no more than place himself meekly and completely in the hands of God, who will protect the supplicant. The reciting of the Lord's name, like surrender to Him, became of great importance; throughout the nation men and women ceased to adopt fanciful proper names and everyone was named after a god or goddess, so that whatever name was uttered, one might indirectly be calling upon God. One counted God's name on a rosary or sang a hymn containing a string of the Lord's names and epithets. A body of ideas and writings grew up on the efficacy of reciting God's name and on how to do it.

[1] *Śrīvaiṣṇavas,* devotees of Vishnu with the Goddess Shrī (*Śrī*) as Mediator.

Each school of devotion had its own sacred formula or mantra, embodying the most significant of the names of the deity. For example, the celebrated five-syllabled mantra of the worshipers of Shiva runs: *Oṃ Namaḥ Śivāya,* meaning "*Oṃ,* Obeisance to Shiva." Similarly the eight-syllabled mantra of the worshipers of Vishnu-Nārāyana is: *Oṃ Namo Nārāyaṇāya,* "*Oṃ,* Obeisance to Nārāyana." The initiation into this mantra and its recitation was had at the hands of one's spiritual teacher (guru), who in all schools was esteemed as next or equal to God.

These various ways in which God was worshiped came to be codified into the school of devotion, the Bhakti Mīmāmsā (Inquiry into Bhakti), which apart from the major theistic systems of philosophy, had its own sūtras (aphoristic texts), expositions, and subsidiary literature. There are two sets of aphorisms on devotion (*Bhakti Sūtras*) ascribed to Sages Shāndilya and Nārada, which define what devotion is, emphasize its importance and superiority, and classify its forms. To illustrate the nature of man's approach to God and the degree or intensity of his devotion, various analogies were made with the relationship between friends, servant and master, son and father, etc. The most ecstatic form of devotion was considered to be that which resembled the yearning of separated lovers for each other, just as the cowherd lasses yearned for Krishna.

The three deities upon which the principal devotional movements centered were Vishnu, Shiva, and Shakti or Devī the Goddess. Each of these was worshiped under various aspects, the two most popular incarnations of Vishnu being Rāma and Krishna. The concept of the Mother Goddess Shakti carried with it a host of minor goddesses and female deities, worshiped according to esoteric practices set forth in texts called *Tantras*. Among the more prominent subsidiary sects were the worship of the Sun; Ganesha, the elephant-headed god; and Kumāra-Kārttikeya, the war-god. Even such powers as the planets (*graha*) were propitiated. Among minor devotional movements there were also some which centered around celebrated teachers and saints.

Among theistic schools of philosophy there were monistic and dualistic schools of Shaivism, chiefly in Kashmir and South India. The Nyāya system was, on its religious side, affiliated with different sects of Shaivites. The Vedānta offered a variety of interpretations of the relation between the Supreme Soul and the individual soul as developed by Bhāskara,[2]

[2] He came immediately after Shankara and held an identity-*cum*-difference in respect of the relation between the Supreme Soul and the individual soul.

Rāmānuja (d. 1137), Shrīkantha, Madhva (1199–1278), Vallabha (1479–1531), Nimbārka, and the followers of Chaitanya (b. 1485). The followers of Rāmānuja looked upon the souls as constituting the body (*śeṣa*) of the Lord (*Śeṣin*) who was the Supreme Soul. Madhva conceived of God and man as totally distinct and as Master and servant. The conception of deliverance (mukti, moksha) or salvation also differed. In most of these religious schools, emancipation was to be enjoyed in a sublime and unique world or heaven, in which case the substance of deliverance was defined as gaining a place in the Lord's world (*sālokya*) and precious proximity to Him (*sāmīpya*). According to two other views, devotees who had achieved the realization of God attained the same form as their God (*sārūpya*) or became in some way absorbed in Him (*sāyujya*).

Even the monistic philosophy of Shankara and his followers had a place for devotion to the personal God, whose grace was considered necessary to that spiritual awakening or knowledge of the Self which led to emancipation. Some of the most appealing devotional hymns are attributed to Shankara and his followers. Tradition also informs us of the reorganization of temple worship at many centers by Shankara. The distinctive feature of Shankara's teaching concerning devotion is that the various forms and names are seen as representing but one principle of divinity, whereas in the other schools one particular form and name, Shiva or Vishnu, alone is the God to be worshiped. A devotee of Shankara's school may find that a particular form of divinity appeals to him most, but he will be quite catholic in his veneration or worship of other deities; in the latter case, however, the approach is definitely sectarian.

There was thus no school of thought which failed to attach a very high value to devotion. Advocates of devotion insisted that without it all austerities, rituals, virtues, learning, or any other aspect of spiritual endeavor would be meaningless and ineffective. It was devotion that gave one real status, not birth. Among devotees there was no caste, no distinction of high or low, except that those who lacked devotion were considered the lowliest. Such a view naturally gave God's grace, called forth by true and intense devotion, an overriding power over the fate that beset one as a result of one's own actions.

The literature and school of thought styled *Āgama* and *Tantra* may best be appreciated when taken together with the literature and school of devotion. The word *Āgama,* originally applied to the Veda, means strictly a tradition of knowledge or practice handed down from teachers to pupils;

later *Āgama* came to mean a school of texts and practices of devotion to different deities, which was outside the strict scope of the Vedic teachings. A large body of texts, which their adherents believed as much revealed scriptures as the Veda, grew up under Āgama, relating to the worship of different deities, chiefly Shiva, Vishnu, and Devī or Shakti. All schools of Shaivism and Vaishnavism freely draw upon the authority of the Āgamas to reinforce their interpretation of Vedānta. The Āgama expatiates on the philosophical position, the greatness of the particular divinity upheld, and the modes and specifications of the worship of that deity. Accordingly they comprise the sections jnāna, yoga, kriyā, and charyā (philosophy, the esoteric teachings, the worship of images in temples, and religious conduct and practices).

The Tantras are of a like nature, but revel more in esoteric teachings. Apart from the teaching of mystic formulas, mantras, which are common to the Āgamas and other theistic schools, they have developed a complex mystic symbolism of letters, and employ, along with images, mystic diagrams or charts called *yantras* or *cakras.*

THE TEACHERS

NĀRADA

Aphorisms on Devotion

[From *Bhakti Sūtra,* 1–22, 25–70, 72–84]

Now then, we shall expound devotion. Devotion consists of supreme love for God. It also consists of immortality.[1] On obtaining that, man has achieved everything, he becomes immortal, he is completely satisfied. Having got it, he desires nothing else, he grieves not, he hates nothing, he delights not in anything else, he strives for nothing; having realized which, man becomes as if intoxicated, and benumbed; he delights in his own intrinsic bliss.

Devotion is not like ordinary passion, as it is the suppression of all other preoccupations. This suppression of preoccupations is the giving up of the activities of the world as well as those [namely, the rituals] ordained by the Vedas.

Devotion is complete and exclusive absorption in God and indifference

[1] Or, is supremely delectable like ambrosia. This is the double meaning of *amṛta.*

to things opposed to Him. Completeness or exclusiveness of devotion to Him means the abandoning of anything else or anybody else as one's prop and support. And indifference to things opposed to Him means the doing and observance of only those things in the world or the Vedas which are conducive to devotion towards Him.

One may observe the scriptural ordinances after one's faith in God has been firmly established, for otherwise the devotee may be deemed to have fallen off from the standard of ordained conduct. Similarly, worldly activities, like taking food, should be kept up by the devotee only to the extent needed for keeping his body.

I shall set forth the characteristics of devotion according to different views: Sage Vyāsa says that devotion is the continuous desire one has to perform the worship, etc., of God. Sage Garga opines that such a desire to listen to the stories, etc., of God is devotion. Sage Shāndilya holds that all such desires [for worship, listening to the Lord's story, etc.] should be without detriment to one's delight in the Self. But Nārada [i.e., the present author] describes devotion as dedication of all acts to God and the intense anguish when one slips from his absorption in God: there have been examples of such devotion, as in the case of the cowherd lasses of the Brindāvan.[2] . . .

Devotion is superior to action, knowledge, or yogic contemplation; for devotion is itself its fruit, and God loves the meek and dislikes those who are proud [of their attainments].

Some say that knowledge alone is the means of acquiring devotion to God, but others opine that knowledge and devotion are interdependent. According to Nārada [the writer], devotional love is itself its end. We can see this in cases like one's knowledge of a palace or a feast; certainly by one's knowledge of a palace one does not gain the satisfaction that he is a king or by one's knowledge of a feast one's hunger is not appeased. Therefore those desiring salvation should take to devotion alone.

Now, the means of acquiring devotion are set forth by teachers: 1) renunciation of sense pleasures and mundane associations; 2) ceaseless adoration of the Lord; 3) even when one is with others, engaging oneself in the listening to and the singing of the glory of the Lord; 4) chiefly the grace of the great souls or a particle of divine grace itself.

[2] The cowherd village on the banks of the Yamunā where Lord Krishna spent his childhood.

The association of the great souls [mahātman] is hard to acquire, hard to be had completely, but is always fruitful. For gaining even that association, one requires God's blessing; for between God and His men there is no difference. So try to acquire the company of the holy souls; strive for that.

And, by all means, shun evil company; for that is responsible for passion, wrath, delusion, loss of the thought of the Lord, the loss of knowledge, in fact all kinds of loss; these evil traits swell up like an ocean by reason of bad company.

Who crosses over the illusion of phenomenal existence? He who gives up evil association, who waits upon the high-souled ones, who becomes freed of the ego; he who resorts to a secluded spot, uproots worldly bondage, transcends the three dispositions and stops worrying himself about acquiring something or safeguarding something acquired; he who abandons the fruit of actions, renounces all action, and thereby transcends the pairs of joy and sorrow, gain and loss, and so on; he who lays aside even scriptures and cultivates solely uninterrupted love for God. He saves himself and becomes also the savior of the world.

Devotion is something indescribable; it is like the taste that a dumb man enjoys. But it is occasionally revealed when there is somebody deserving of it. It is absolute, not vitiated by desire for anything, multiplying every minute of its existence, and is uninterrupted; it is a highly sublime form of experience. One who has it looks at it only, listens to it alone, and thinks of nothing else.

Devotion may also be qualified in these ways, by reason of the three dispositions, as of purity, of passion, and of darkness, or by reason of the condition of the devotee, namely, one in distress, one who is curious to know, and one who has an object in view. Of these three varieties, the preceding ones are superior to the succeeding ones.

Compared to other paths, devotion is easiest. It stands in need of no external proof and it is its own proof; for it is of the very form of tranquillity and supreme bliss.

The devotee should have no anxiety if the world slips away from him; for has he not surrendered himself, the world, and the scriptures to the Lord? However, even when one is established in devotion, one should not voluntarily give up normal activities, but he should certainly give up the fruits of his actions and learn how to give them up.

The devotee should not listen to accounts of women's beauty, riches, and what unbelievers say; should cast away pride and vanity. Offering up all his activities to God, he should show his desire or anger or pride only in activities on His behalf.

Transcending the tripartite distinction of love, lover, and object of love, one should develop that love which consists of continuous service and is like the yearning of a beloved for her lover. Those who are exclusive lovers are the chief devotees; with choked voices and streaming eyes, they commune among themselves; they are the souls who sanctify our homes and the world; they make holy spots holy, sanctify acts, and render scriptures sacred. For they are full of God. . . .

Among such devotees there is no distinction of birth, learning, appearance, pedigree, wealth, or profession; for they belong to God.

A devotee should not get involved in discussion about God; for reasoning cuts in anyway and there is no finality about it. Texts which speak of devotion should be honored and the acts taught therein followed. Anxious to gain a time free from the preoccupation of pleasure or pain, desire or gain, one should not waste even a split second. One should observe nonviolence, truth, purity, compassion, faith, and other virtues.

Ever and with all heart, devotees should, without any other thought, worship only the Lord. When He is sung of, He hastens to present Himself and bestow on devotees His experience. Devotion to God is true for all times and is superior to everything else; it is superior.

Devotion, which is really one, yet takes eleven forms: attachment to the greatness of the Lord's qualities, to His form; being engrossed in His worship, and His thought; attachment to Him as a servant, as a friend, as a child or as toward a child, and as a beloved; surrendering oneself unto Him; seeing Him everywhere; and inability to bear the separation from Him.

So do they declare in one voice, without fear of what people say, the teachers of the path of devotion, Kumāra, Vyāsa, Shuka, Shāndilya Garga, Vishnu, Kaundinya, Shesha, Uddhava, Āruni, Bali, Hanumān Vibhīshana, and others. He who has faith in this wholesome teaching tha Nārada has given gains devotion and gains that most beloved objec [God]; indeed he gains that Dearest Thing.

KAPILA

The Purāna of the Lord

The *Purāna of the Lord,* dedicated to the different incarnations of the Lord including that of Krishna, has probably served to inspire and unify the devotional movements more than any other single text. Here, in one of the earlier books, Sage Kapila teaches the path of devotion to his mother Devahūti. Sage Kapila is identified as one of the manifestations of the Lord and as the promulgator of the Sānkhya philosophy. The account of the Sānkhya in Purānic literature is always theistic and the *Purāna of the Lord* completely integrates it with the path of devotion. The treatment of the doctrine also is remarkable for the way in which the same Purāna criticizes the aberrations and empty forms and rites which may unfortunately parade as devotion instead of being the true realization of the presence of the Lord everywhere.

[From *Bhāgavata Purāṇa,* 3.29.7–34; 6.1.11–18; 6.2.14; 7.5.24; 11.3.18–32; 11.27.7–51]

THE PATH OF DEVOTION (Bhakti-yoga)

[The Lord, Sage Kapila, tells His mother Devahūti:]

Blessed lady! The path of devotion is conceived in various ways according to different approaches; for by reason of nature, qualities, and approach, the minds of men differ.

That devotee, who, in a harmful manner, with vanity and intolerance, goes about ostentatiously, making distinctions between one being and another, and practices devotion, is of the lowest type, impelled by ignorance.[1]

Contemplating material enjoyment, fame, or riches, he who, still making distinctions, worships Me in images, etc., is of the middling type, impelled by desire.[2]

He who adores Me with a view to put an end to all actions [good or bad] or offering up all his actions to Me, the Supreme Being, or worships Me because I must be worshiped,[3] he is of the superior type, though he has yet the sense of difference. . . .

The characteristic of pure devotion to the Supreme Being is that it has no motive and is incessant. . . .

That devotion is described as absolute by which one transcends the

[1] The manifestation of the disposition of "darkness."
[2] The manifestation of "passion."
[3] The manifestation of "purity."

three dispositions [purity, passion, and darkness] and renders himself fit to become one with Me. . . .

I am always present in all beings as their soul and yet, ignoring Me, mortal man conducts the mockery of image-worship. He who ignores Me resident in all beings as the Soul and Master, and, in his ignorance, takes to images, verily pours oblations on ash [i.e., worships in vain]. The mind of that man who hates Me abiding in another's body, who, in his pride, sees invidious distinctions and is inimically disposed to all beings, never attains tranquillity. Blessed lady! when the worshiper is one who insults living beings, I am not satisfied with his worship in My image, however elaborate the rites and manifold the materials of his worship. Doing one's appointed duty, one should adore Me, the Master, in images and the like, only so long as one is not able to realize in one's own heart Me who am established in every being. That man of invidious perception who draws the line between himself and another, him Death pursues with his dangerous fear.

Therefore, with charity and honor and with friendship toward all and a nondifferentiating outlook, one should worship Me, the Soul of all beings, as enshrined in all beings. . . .

Honoring them, one should mentally bow to all the beings, realizing that the Lord the Master has entered them with an aspect of His own being. [3.29.7–34]

DEVOTION TO GOD THE GREATEST EXPIATION

The removal of sinful acts by expiatory rites which are also acts is not final; [4] expiatory acts are for the unintelligent; knowledge is expiation. When one keeps eating only wholesome food, diseases do not assail him; therefore one who observes the disciplines gradually qualifies himself for the supreme welfare. . . . But some, dependent solely on God, cast away all sin completely, even as the sun sweeps away the fog, solely through devotion to God. If one is averse to the Lord, no amount of expiation will purify him. [6.1.11–18]

[4] An act also carries with it the possibility of lapses; if expiation for a lapse is sought by another act, that expiatory act is liable to further lapses and so on ad infinitum; therefore an expiation of another order or plane alone can be final and that is taught here as devotion to the Lord and the recital of His name with devotion.

THE LORD'S NAME

The Teachers consider the utterance of the Lord's name as destructive of sin completely, even when the utterance is due to the name being associated with something else, or is done jocularly, or as a result of involuntary sound, or in derision.[5] [6.2.14]

NINE KINDS OF DEVOTION

Listening to the Lord's glory, singing of Him, thinking of Him, serving His feet, performing His worship, saluting Him, serving Him, friendship with Him, declaring oneself as His [surrendering oneself to Him][6] —if man could offer unto the Lord devotion of these *nine* kinds, that indeed I would consider as the greatest lesson one has learned. [7.5.24]

THE DOINGS OF THE DEVOTEE[7]

One should therefore resort to a teacher, desiring to know what constitutes the supreme welfare. . . . Taking the teacher as the deity, one should learn from him the practices characteristic of the Lord's devotees. . . . First detachment from all undesirable associations, then association with the good souls, compassion, friendliness, and due humility toward all beings, purity, penance, forbearance, silence, study of sacred writings, straightforwardness, continence, nonviolence, equanimity, seeing one's own Self and the Lord everywhere, seeking solitude, freedom from home, wearing clean recluse robes, satisfying oneself with whatever comes to one, faith in the scriptures of devotion and refraining from censure of those of other schools, subjugation of mind, speech, and action, truthful-

[5] This is the doctrine generally subscribed to on the popular level; but at the higher levels it is insisted that the true recital of God's name is that in which the devotee understands the full significance of the Lord's glory and realizes the omnipresence of the Lord.

[6] Complete surrender to the Lord, called *prapatti* or *śaraṇāgati* is the cardinal doctrine of the theology of South Indian Shrīvaishnavism; accordingly this school considers *Bhagavad Gītā*, 18.66, in which the Lord tells Arjuna: "Giving up all duties, take refuge under Me alone; I shall deliver you from all sins," as the final teaching (*carama-śloka*); and the chief sacred formula of the school, which has two parts, runs: 1) I seek as refuge the feet of Nārāyana, Lord of the Goddess of Fortune; 2) Obeisance to Nārāyana, Lord of the Goddess of Fortune (*Śrīman-nārāyaṇa-caraṇau śaraṇam prapadye; Śrīmate nārāyaṇāya namaḥ*). The Goddess from whom the Lord cannot be separated acts as the mediator between the devotee and the Lord.

[7] The following selections are taken from the eleventh book of the *Purāna of the Lord;* the second and the third selections form the part of the teachings of Lord Krishna to His best friend, devotee and kinsman, Uddhava. The range of the topics in the selections given here corresponds to that of the contents of Vaishnava Āgamas and Tantras.

ness, quietude, restraint, listening to accounts of the Lord's advents, exploits, and qualities, singing of the Lord, contemplation of the Lord of wonderful exploits, engaging in acts only for His sake, dedicating unto the Lord everything—the rites one does, gifts, penance, sacred recital, righteous conduct and whatever is dear to one like one's wife, son, house, and one's own life—cultivating friendship with those who consider the Lord as their soul and master, service to the Lord and to the world and especially to the great and good souls, sharing in the company of fellow devotees the sanctifying glory of the Lord, sharing with them one's delight, satisfaction and virtues of restraint, remembering oneself and reminding fellow-worshipers of the Lord who sweeps away all sin; bearing a body thrilled with devotion and ecstatic experience of the Lord, now in tears with some thought of the Lord, now laughing, now rejoicing, now speaking out, now dancing, now singing, now imitating the Lord's acts, and now becoming quiet with the blissful experience of the Supreme—such are the Lord's devotees, who behave like persons not of this world. [11.3.18–32]

THE METHOD OF WORSHIPING GOD IN HIS SYMBOL

[The Lord says;] My worship is of three kinds, Vedic, Tantric, and mixed. . . . In an image, on ground, in fire, in the sun, in the waters, in one's own heart, or in a brāhman, one should with suitable materials, with love, and without deception, worship Me, the Master.

First at dawn, one should have his bath, after washing his teeth, etc. . . . then do the worship of the *sandhyā* [8] and other duties ordained by the Veda; and with the rites and mantras prescribed in the Veda, one should conduct My worship, taking the resolve [9] properly; it is indeed My worship that sanctifies the observance of other duties.[10]

God's images are of eight kinds: of stone, wood, metal, plaster, painting,

[8] The *sandhyās* are the three junctions of the day, sunrise, noon, and sunset, when a twice-born is to worship *Gāyatrī,* the deity presiding over solar energy and the stimulator of intellect.

[9] This is what is called *saṅkalpa* or the utterance of the resolution of the mind that I, so and so, will perform such and such a rite or religious act for such and such a deity or other object of propitiation for such and such a purpose or according to such and such a scriptural injunction.

[10] After the first establishment of the complete theistic conviction, Vedic rites acquired a theistic orientation; the performance of *sandhyā,* of *śrāddha* in honor of manes, feasting of brāhmans, everything was for the propitiation of, and as dedication to, the Supreme Lord; and to this effect a statement was expressly made at the beginning or end of the act.

sand, *mind,* and precious gem. The image in which My spirit dwells is of two kinds, the fixed and the moving; in worship with a fixed image, there is to be no periodic calling forth of the divine presence in it and the bringing to an end of such divine presence; with a moving image, these may be done; and in a symbolic image on the ground such invocation and calling off of the divine presence have to be done. . . .

Without any deceit, the devotee should conduct My worship with well-known materials that are available and with love in his heart.

When I am worshiped in an icon, bathing Me and decorating Me are welcome; when I am worshiped on ground, the method of worship is to invoke there with the appropriate mantras the divine presence of the respective deities; when worshiped in fire, worship takes the form of the oblations with ghee. When I am to be worshiped in the sun, adoration by prostration, offering of water with mantras, muttering of prayer, etc., are best; when worshiped in the waters, the offering of water with mantras is to be done; for even some water offered to Me with love by a devotee pleases Me most; even elaborate offerings, sandal, incense, flowers, light, food, etc., made by one who is devoid of devotion, do not satisfy Me.

WORSHIP IN AN IMAGE

Having purified oneself and having gathered the materials of worship, the devotee should sit on his seat of sacred *darbha* grass, facing east or north and conduct the worship with the image in front of him. He should then utter the incantations with appropriate gestures [mudrās] which render his different limbs and hands duly charged with spiritual power; he should then invoke with mantras and proper gestures My presence in the image.

He should keep in front a vessel of sanctified water and with that water sprinkle thrice the image, the materials of worship, himself, and the vessels.

Then the devotee should, in his own body purified by the control of breath and the awakening of fire [slumbering at the basic plexus, *mūlādhāra*], contemplate in the lotus of his heart My subtle form, the form which the men of realization meditate upon as abiding on the fringes of *Oṃ*.[11] When the devotee's whole being has become pervaded

[11] *Oṃ* or *praṇava* is the greatest of all the mystic spells (mantras) of Hinduism; it is composed of five parts, A, U, M, the stop (*bindu*), and the resonance (*nāda*); beyond the

by My form, which is the inner Soul of all beings, the devotee shall, having become completely immersed in Myself, make My presence overflow into the image, etc., established in front of him, and then, with all the paraphernalia, conduct My worship.

He must first offer Me seat; My seat is made of nine elements, virtue, knowledge, dispassion, and mastery as the four feet and the opposites of these as the enclosed plank on which I sit; the other parts of My seat are the three sheets spread over the sitting plank, these three representing the three dispositions [purity, etc.] of which My own mystic potency [māyā] is composed; there are also to be established on the seat My nine powers [shakti];[12] and at the center of the seat an eight-petalled lotus, shining with its pericarp and filaments; and having prepared My seat thus, the devotee should, by the Vedic and Tantric methods and for the attainment of the two fruits of welfare here and in the hereafter, make to Me the different offerings of worship. . . .

When offering Me the bath with fragrant water, the Vedic mantras beginning with *Suvarṇagharma,*[13] the *Puruṣa Sūkta,*[14] and the *Sāma Veda* chants like *Rājana*[15] should be recited.

With clothes, sacred thread, jewels, garlands, and fragrant paste, My devotee should decorate My form suitably and with love. With faith, My worshiper should then offer Me water to wash, sandal, flower, unbroken rice,[16] incense, light, and food of different kinds; also attentions like anointing, massage, showing of mirror, etc., and entertainments like song and dance; these special attentions and entertainments may be done on festive days and even daily.

EMOTIONAL ADORATION

One should engage himself in singing of Me, praising Me, dancing with My themes, imitating My exploits and acts, narrating My stories or listening to them.

---

realm of the fifth dwells the Lord. No worship in a material image is good without such mental contemplation of the Lord.

[12] All these details which give the inner significance to the gross rituals and materials of worship are briefly referred to in the text and explained fully in the commentary. The nine powers or shaktis of the Lord are purity, exaltation, knowledge, action, mystic union, inclination, truth, mastery, and grace.

[13] *Taittirīya Āraṇyaka,* 3.11.

[14] *Rig Veda,* 10.90.

[15] Beginning with the words, *"Indram naro."* These give an indication of how the Vedic hymns were adapted to the later devotional development.

[16] Unbroken rice grain is scattered on a person or image as an auspicious act during festivities, marriage, worship, blessing, etc.

With manifold hymns of praise of Me, taken from the *Purānas* or from the local languages (Prakrits),[17] the devotee should praise and pray to Me that I bless him and prostrate himself completely before Me. With his head and hands at My feet, he should pray, "My lord, from the clutches of death [i.e., the cycle of birth and death], save me who have taken refuge under You." . . .

Whenever and wherever one feels like worshiping Me in images, etc., one should do so; I am, however, present in oneself and in all beings; for I am the Soul of everything.

Thus worshiping me with Vedic and Tantric methods, one attains through Me the desired welfare here and in the hereafter.

PUBLIC WORSHIP

Having consecrated an image of Me one should build a firm temple for Me, and beautiful flower gardens around for conducting daily worship and festivals. For the maintenance of My worship, etc., in special seasons as well as every day, one should bestow fields, bazaars, townships, and villages,[18] and thereby attain to My own lordship. [11.27.7–51]

LOKĀCHĀRYA

The Triad of Categories

The *Triad of Categories* (*Tattvatraya*) of Lokāchārya (thirteenth century) belongs to the literature of South Indian Shrīvaishnavism or Vishishtādvaita (i.e. the nondualism of the qualified Supreme), founded by Rāmānuja. Shrīvaishnavism is the most typical theistic system of thought, whose ideology inspired new devotional movements all over north India. The text followed here is a Sanskrit version of the original work written in a mixed Sanskrit-Tamil style, frequently employed by the South Indian Shrīvaishnava teachers.

[From Lokāchārya, *Tattvatraya,* pp. 85 f., 121 f.]

THE LORD

The Lord is exclusively endowed with a nature that is opposed to all evil, unlimited, and of the form of knowledge-bliss; is adorned with

[17] Cf. the section entitled, "Songs of the Saints," below. This illustrates the integration of the learned and the popular trends and traditions.

[18] The bulk of the inscriptions and grants unearthed and published by the Indian Archaeological Department relate to the foundation of these temples and the endowments made to them for divine service.

auspicious qualities, knowledge, power, etc.; He is the author of the creation, maintenance, and annihilation of the entire universe; is resorted to by the four kinds of persons [specified in the text of the *Gītā*]: namely, one in difficulty, one making a scholarly inquiry, one desirous of material gain, and one desirous of wisdom; is the bestower of the four kinds of fruits consisting of virtue, material gain, pleasure, and spiritual liberation; is possessed of a unique personality and is the consort of the three goddesses called Lakshmī, Bhūmī, and Nīlā. . . .

"His auspicious qualities, knowledge, power, etc."—these are eternal, unbounded, numberless, natural, unvitiated; there is nothing to compare them with nor to excel them; of these the objects of His qualities like affection [such as accessibility, softness, etc.] are His devotees; everybody forms the object of His qualities of knowledge, power, etc. which are at the basis of His other qualities; of the Lord's knowledge, the object is those in ignorance; of power, the weak; of forgiveness, those who have sinned; of compassion, those in misery; of affection, those who have shortcomings; of superior conduct, the inferior ones; of straightforwardness, the crooked ones; of friendliness, those who are of bad heart; of softness, those who are afraid of separation from Him; of accessibility, those who yearn to see Him. And so on.

Thus, because He is endowed with all auspicious qualities, the Lord, when He sees the sufferings of others exclaims, "Alas!" and shows His compassion; thinks always, without an exception, of their good; without either pure selfishness or a selfishness mingled with altruism, He exists exclusively for others' sake even as moonlight, southern breeze, sandal, and cool water; sees not in those who resort to Him their inferiority to Himself in respect of birth, knowledge and conduct; becomes Himself the savior when people find themselves as well as others as of no avail; performs impossible miracles like the bringing back of Sage Sāndīpini's son [drowned in the sea] [2] and the like; fulfills their desires; even creates for them [for His devotees] previously nonexistent positions like that of the Pole-star; [3] extends to them also Himself and all that is His, on the principle that what is one's own is enjoyed by oneself; [4] on the fulfillment of His devotees' purposes, He feels as if He Himself had accom-

[2] This is a story from the Purānas; the text adds one more instance also which is left out in the translation.

[3] This the Lord created and gave to the little boy-devotee, Dhruva.

[4] That is, as the beings are part of the Lord's own body, what is His is theirs also.

plished a purpose of His own; without a thought of even a single good He has done, He thinks only of the particle of a good act that the devotee might do; He Himself becomes the object of such constant delectation to the devotee that one is made to forget immemorially ingrained tastes; like a father seeing with his eyes the mistakes of his wife and sons, He goes on without minding at heart the mistakes of His devotees; even when the goddess Lakshmī [his consort] points out flaws in a devotee, He opposes Her and firmly stands by the devotee and protects him; like a lover courting even the untidy things of his beloved, He indeed accepts even the flaws of His devotees as something pleasing to Him; He is absolutely straight toward them in thought, word, and action; when they are separated, He troubles Himself so that their misery might end; places Himself freely at their service, even rendering Himself so easy as to be bound and beaten by them; and just as the mother cow, in her affection for her just-delivered calf, scares with its horns and hoofs even those who come to give feed to the calf, so the Lord wards off even Mother Lakshmī and the eternally enlightened teachers and Himself goes on displaying His own affection toward His devotees. . . .

His "personality" is, in form and qualities, something which He has taken according to His own desire; it is eternal and uniform; it is supramundane; just as a jewel cup will show transparently the gold placed in it, even so, it does not, unlike the human body which shrouds the inner Self, hide the divine nature which is of the form of knowledge, but reveals it; it is of the form of limitless effulgence; it is a reservoir of a multitude of auspicious qualities, gracefulness and the like; it is to be contemplated by yogins, so enrapturing the entire universe that one develops distaste for every other kind of mundane enjoyment; it is enjoyed by the ever-liberated souls; like a pool of lotuses blooming forth as the rays of the rising Sun strike them, it removes every kind of heat in one; it is the root of endless incarnations; it is the protector of all and resort of all; it shines adorned with arms and ornaments.

THE LORD'S FORM

The Lord's form is five-fold: the transcendent one [*para*], the manifestations [*vyūha*], the incarnations [*vibhava*], the immanent spirit [*antaryāmin*], and the images [*arcā*].

By "transcendent" is meant that it is beyond time and is in the further heaven of unbounded bliss where the eternally free souls revel in His presence. By "manifestation" is meant His taking the forms *Saṅkarṣaṇa, Pradyumna,* and *Aniruddha* for purposes of creation, maintenance, and destruction, for protecting the souls in transmigration and to bless the devotees. In the transcendent form, all the six qualities, knowledge, strength, lordship, heroism, power, and effulgence, are full; in each of the three manifestations, two of the six qualities become manifest. . . .

The "incarnations" are manifold, but chiefly of two distinct kinds, the main and subsidiary. . . . Of the incarnations, the cause is His desire; the purpose, the protection of the good, the destruction of the bad and the restoration of righteousness. "Immanence" is to enter into and control; it is also the remaining of the Lord with all sentient selves during all their states like their sojourns through heaven and hell, even as a companion who is unable to leave them; it is also the residence of the Lord in the lotus of one's heart, so that one might meditate upon Him in an auspicious form and He too, like one's kith and kin, safeguard one. The incarnation in "images" is the abiding of the Lord in temples and homes in materials of men's choice [metal, stone, etc.]; it is different from the several manifestations, Rāma, Krishna, etc., as these images are not circumscribed by the place, time, and associates connected originally with those manifestations; and all their activities are under the control of their priests whose shortcomings the Lord overlooks. Inducing the religious attitude [which any amount of mere spiritual reading does not produce], attracting the auspicious feelings of the devotee's heart, being the resort of the whole world, enjoyability—all these qualities are found to the maximum in the incarnation in images. Reversing the relationship of subordinate and Master and appearing to be innocent of knowledge, power and worship because of the overpowering influence of His unbounded compassion, He bestows on His devotee whatever the latter expects.

HYMNS IN SANSKRIT

The vast hymnal literature in Sanskrit not only gives expression to a wide range of devotional ideas and varied phases of the devotional life, but also embodies tenets of the followers of the path of devotion, the Lord's forms, incarnations, qualities, compassion, and efficacy of devotion, the potency of the Lord's name, surrender and dedication to the Lord, etc.

Devotion Alone Essential

[From Kulashekhara, *Mukundamālā*]

The Lord Nārāyana [Vishnu] is all-glorious in the absence of devotion to whose lotus feet the recital of the Vedas becomes a cry in the wilderness, the daily austerities only a means to reduce one's corpulence, all public benefactions but oblations on ash, and baths in holy waters like the bath of the elephant.[1]

[From *Bhāgavata Purāṇa,* 7.9.10]

Even a low-caste man is superior to a brāhman who is endowed with the twelve excellences but who is averse to the lotus feet of the Lord; if the former has dedicated his mind, speech, desire, and objects, and his life itself to the Lord, he sanctifies his whole race, not so the latter who is stuck up in his own enormous pride.

[From *Brahma Purāṇa,* ch. 49]

What is the use of pedigree, conduct, learning, nay even the life of those who have no devotion toward the Lord, the creator of the Universe?

[From *Bhāgavata Purāṇa,* 6.11.25]

O Lord who are the most proper object of desire! Leaving You, I desire not heaven or the status of the creator, lordship over this or the nether world, not even miraculous yogic attainments or release from rebirth!

[From Chaitanya, *Śikṣāṣṭaka* [2]]

Wealth, men, women, poesy—none of these, O Lord of the universe, do I desire; in every birth of mine, may there be unmotivated devotion to You, the Lord.

The Lord's Incarnations

[From *Bhāgavata Purāṇa,* 11.4.33]

May that Supreme Lord who, devoid of name, form, or end, yet took, for blessing those who adored His feet, names and forms through incarnations and exploits, be gracious unto me.

[1] An elephant's bath is proverbial as a futile act, for the elephant, as soon as it gets out of water, takes and throws the dirt of the street all over its body.

[2] Chaitanya (b. 1485), the founder of the Bengal school of fervent devotion to Krishna, did not write extensively. The *Octad of Instruction* (*Śikṣāṣṭaka*) extracted here is one of his two Sanskrit hymns.

The Lord's Name

[From *Vāmana Purāṇa,* ch. 83.96–99]

The sin that has accrued to me through the desire for others' women and possessions and treachery to others, through reviling others to their great agony and traducing the great ones, the sin committed by me in childhood, boyhood, youth, and old age, and in another birth—may all that sin disappear as a result of the recital of the Lord's [Vishnu's] names, Nārāyana, Govinda, Hari, and Krishna, even as a cup of salt in water.

[From Shrīdhara Venkatesha,[3] *Hymn of Sixty Verses on the Lord's Name* (*Ākhyāṣaṣṭi*)]

O Name of the Lord! Let there be the Vedas by hundreds, and by hundreds the piles of Purānas and Āgamas; are these capable of giving the thought of the Lord without You? On the other hand, You who remove all weariness completely without any effort, can bestow that thought of the Lord without the aid of any of those.

The Lord's Compassion

[From Nīlakantha Dīkshita,[4] *Ānandasāgarastava*]

If you have the compassion towards me that I should be saved, save me; why weigh my good and bad acts? You who are powerful enough to make and unmake the universe, to abide by the laws of one's karma! [5] Who will be taken in by this deception?

[From *Ādyādimahālakṣmīhṛdaya Sūtra*]

If I had not been created, there would be no question, O Lord, of Your being compassionate; if diseases had not been created, the discovery of medicine would be futile.

[3] A saint of c.1700 who lived in Tanjore District, South India, and was one of those responsible for the spread of the cult of reciting the Lord's name and the singing of congregational prayers and praises (*bhajans*).

[4] Poet and devotee of the Mother Goddess at Mathurai, South India, seventeenth century.

[5] There is always the conflict between the sphere of the Lord's mercy and the law of karma; according to the karma doctrine, one has to undergo the suffering consequent on the acts done by him, for what has been done will have its effect. But is the Lord to abide by the course of karma, which is after all subject to His sway, or will He bring His compassion into operation to save a devotee? It depends on the intensity of one's devotion to bring forth this grace of the Lord.

[From *Narasiṃha Purāṇa,* ch. 11]
That [alone] is a tongue which praises the Lord, that [alone] is a mind which is given up to You, O Lord! those alone are praiseworthy arms which do Your worship.

[From Shankara, *Subrahmaṇyabhujaṅga,* 26]
The Lord's form before the eyes, His glory in the ears, His sanctifying story always in my mouth, His work on my hand, and His service on my body—may all the aspects of my being be absorbed in God *Subrahmaṇya!* [6]

[From Shankara, *Saundaryalaharī,* 27]
Whatever I speak is the muttering of Your prayer; all art is the symbol of Your worship; all my movement is going round You in veneration; eating, etc., is offering oblations to You; if I lie down it is prostration to You; all my enjoyments are in a spirit of dedication to You; O Goddess! whatever I do may it be a synonym of Your worship.

[From Shankara, *Kāśīpañcaka,* 5]
The body is Banaras; knowledge is the expansive Ganges, the mother of the three worlds, flowing here; this devotion, this faith is the Gayā; [7] the meditation on the feet of one's spiritual teacher is Prayāga; [8] Lord *Viśveśvara* [9] is the inner Self, the witness of the minds of all and transcending the three states [of wakefulness, dream, and sleep]; if everything abides in my own body, what other shrine is there besides that?

[Verse uttered at the end of every ritual and religious act.]
Whatever I do with my body, word, mind, senses, intellect, soul, or by the course of nature, all that I dedicate to the Supreme Lord Nārāyana.

[From Utpaladeva of Kashmir,[10] *Śivastotrāvali*]
Enjoying within myself the delectation of devotion and closing my

[6] Kumāra or Kārttikeya, son of Shiva.

[7] The famous sacred spot in Bihar; associated also with the Buddha.

[8] Allahabad, place of pilgrimage at the confluence of the Ganges and Yamuna Rivers with the celestial river Sarasvati.

[9] The name of Shiva in the temple at Banaras.

[10] The school of Kashmir Shaivism is a theistic-*cum*-monistic school which incorporated the Tantric ideologies and methods of worship. One of its chief exponents is Utpaladeva (c. 900–950). The present extracts are from his beautiful hymns expressing his mystic love of Shiva.

eyes in that bliss, may I remain saying, "Obeisance to Myself, the Lord Shiva" and adoring even blades of grass!

This in brief is the definition of happiness and misery as far as I am concerned; listen to it, O Lord! Union with you is all happiness, the separation from my Lord is all misery.

To me, filled with your devotion, let there be adversity; may I not have even a succession of happy events, if they are to turn me away from your devotion.

In that seeking of Lord Shiva, all miseries become happiness, poison becomes nectar, and this life itself becomes liberation.

Laying All Burdens on the Lord and Surrendering to His Grace

[From *Pāñcarātra, "Jitaṃ te"* hymn] [11]

What is beneficial to me, that You Yourself order for me, O Lord! I am Yours, O God of gods! I have no capacity to do Your worship or praise; I am solely looking forward to Your compassion; [12] bless me please.

[From Shankara, *Śivabhujaṅga,* 16]

I am poor, wretched, broken, stricken with anguish and sorrow, exhausted, and rent into pieces; O Lord, You are the inner soul of all beings and You do not know my distress! O Lord, protect me.

[From Vedānta Deshika,[13] *Aṣṭabhujāṣṭaka*]

O Lord of the Goddess of prosperity! [14] You, by Yourself, must protect me who am solely dependent on You; if You take the initiative [to save], wherefore my exertions? And if You do not take the initiative, of what use even then are my efforts?

[From Vādirāja,[15] *Kṛṣṇastuti*]

I know not my good, I know not what is not to my good; I am powerless

[11] There are two traditions of Vishnu worship, the *Vaikhānasa* and the *Pāñcarātra,* the former older, but the latter more widespread.

[12] This attitude accords with the "southern" or more popular school of South Indian Shrīvaishnavism which says that all that man can do is, without pretending to put forth any effort of his own, realize his own meekness and keep himself ready and fit to receive the Lord's grace. The other school, called the "northern," holds that God helps those who help themselves.

[13] A brilliant, versatile, and prolific writer of the Vishishtādvaita (qualified nondualism) school (1268–1369), he wrote in Sanskrit and Tamil.

[14] The mediator between God and the devotee, according to Shrīvaishṇava theology.

[15] Vādirāja (sixteenth century) is a teacher of the dualistic and pluralistic school of theism started by Madhva in South India. In the interpretation of the Vedānta according to this school, God is only the efficient cause, not the material cause also as the schools of Shankara and Rāmānuja hold.

either to do or to refrain from doing; just as a puppet dances, even so, I exist purely at the direction of Lord Hari.

[From Vādirāja, *Haryaṣṭaka*]
O Lord Hari! Does an animal fallen into the well know how to lift itself by its own effort? Throwing about its feet and bellowing frequently, it can only excite pity, O Lord!

[From Yāmuna, *Stotraratna*] [16]
I am not one firmly established in the observance of duties; I have not known what the Self is; nor have I any devotion to Your lotus feet; destitute of everything, with no other way open, O you protector of refugees! I have taken refuge at Your feet.

There is not one despised act in the world which I have not done a thousand times; O Lord! at this hour when my sin is bearing its consequences, I am crying before you, without any other way.

O Lord! Whatever I have, whatever I am—all that is only Yours; rather, knowing full well that all this, of course, belongs to You, what shall I offer You?

[From Rāmānuja,[17] *Śaraṇāgatigadya*]
Giving up all other ordained observances, abandoning all my desires inclusive of salvation, O Lord! I took refuge under Your feet that measured the whole universe.

You alone are my mother, my father, my kinsman, my teacher, my learning, my wealth; O God of gods! You are my everything.

THE SONGS OF THE SAINTS OF MEDIEVAL HINDUISM

Just as Buddhism had gone about consolidating itself in the frontier regions and countries neighboring India—Ceylon in the south, Burma in the east, Tibet and Central Asia in the north and northwest—even so within

[16] Yāmuna Āchārya (Tamil name, Ālavandār, eleventh century), South India; one of the founders of Shrīvaishnavism in the South. Noteworthy among his three Sanskrit treatises is the *Authoritativeness of the Āgamas* (*Āgama-prāmāṇya*) which tries to establish the authority of the Āgama texts alongside of the Vedas.

[17] This great Shrīvaishnava teacher of South India and founder of the Vishishtādvaita (qualified non-dualism) school died in 1137. According to his interpretation of the Vedānta, the Lord is the efficient and material cause of the universe, but He is different from the sentient and nonsentient creation; souls are many, not one, and they are not identical with Him, but constitute His body and are dependent on Him.

India, it had gained a stronghold in areas where Brahmanical traditions were weakest. Thus the missionaries of Buddhism and Jainism established themselves in South India. Later, the leaders of the Brahmanical way found that the masses in these areas could be won over only by going to them and speaking to them in their own language. Accordingly, the truths of the Upanishads, the conclusions of the philosophical systems, the basic beliefs and practices of Hinduism—all these were brought to the people in their own language, often in a homely style, enlivened with poetry, wit, and satire, through songs by men of spiritual realization, the saints. Thus arose all over the country popular religious poetry and song.

In each region a school or succession of teachers appeared who went about making the whole countryside resound with their songs. These saints from different parts of the country subscribed to different schools of philosophy, but there was a common approach and method in their work among the people. Most of them were followers of the path of devotion (bhakti) to a personal God, and therefore their lives were marked either by continued pilgrimages to famous temples and sacred places, (which helped also their work of propagation), or by intense worship at a particular place or of a specific form of God (*iṣṭa-devatā*) to which they were most attached.

A circumstance which contributed greatly to their popularity and the success of their movement among the masses is that these saints did not come only from the highest-born and best-educated classes of society, but from every stratum of society down to the untouchables. Thus emphasis was laid on character and sincerity, not on high birth or learning.

This popular religious movement began in South India in the Tamil-speaking area where saints arose from the time of the Pallava rulers of Kāñchī (c. fourth to ninth centuries A.D.). In reclaiming the kings and the people for Hinduism, they went about singing their psalms to deities enshrined at different temples. From the Tamil country this movement of saint-singers of philosophical and religious songs in regional languages spread to the Kannada-speaking area, whence the spark was ignited in Maharashtra; then the Hindi-speaking areas took it up and the whole of North India was aflame with this resurgent and fervent faith. This popular presentation of the teaching of the Upanishads, the philosophical schools, and the Purānic lore, coincided with the linguistic phenomenon of the growth of the neo-Indo-Aryan languages of the North and the flowering forth of the literatures in the Dravidian family of languages in the South.

These songs comprised not merely stray philosophical, religious, ethical, and didactic pieces, but often musical versions of whole texts from the Sanskrit epics and Purānas. Now, under the inspiration of Vālmīki and his *Rāmāyaṇa* in the original Sanskrit, the *Rāmāyaṇa* came to be retold or sung in the local language, e.g. that of Kamban in Tamil and of Tulasīdās in Hindi. In recent times, there has been no greater votary of Rāma than Mahātmā Gāndhi, who imbibed this fervor for Rāma and his kingdom from the *Rāmāyaṇa* of Tulasīdās, as well as from the soul-stirring songs written in Gujarati and Hindi. Yet not only the *Rāmāyaṇa,* but the Upanishads, the *Gītā,* and the Purānas also had their effect. Indeed the literary renaissance of the neo–Indo-Aryan and Dravidian languages came about through the impregnation of the ideas and themes of classical Sanskrit literature, original production in which now was weakened as a result of the upsurge of creative effort in the vernacular. At the same time, popular songs, which became a dual heritage of the religiously devout and the musically minded, served as forerunners also of a musical renaissance. In them a new form of musical composition took shape, and a repertoire was provided not only for concerts but also for congregational worship or service in temples. It is these songs that one might have heard in Gāndhi's prayer meetings; it is these, too, that one hears again and again on the All-India Radio. In various localities where people met, sang, and went into devotional ecstasies, halls were erected called *bhajan maṭhs* or *nām ghars*. From the dim past when sages (rishis) in the forest hermitages (āshramas) put forth their Upanishads, to these apostles of popular spiritual culture, the saint-musicians and their *bhajan* halls, which still continue in force all over the country even in modern cities like New Delhi, Bombay, Calcutta, and Madras—the basic unity and rich flow of this spiritual heritage is clearly seen.

The readings which follow are selections from the psalms and songs of these saint-musicians of India, representing not only the geographical and linguistic regions of India, but also the chronological movement from the seventh century to the beginnings of the nineteenth.[1]

[1] Where there are no specific printed sources given for the texts of the songs which follow, they are to be understood as taken from popular printed collections of such songs available in each of the languages.

TAMIL-NĀD[2]

The Tamil saints appeared in the great days of the Pallavas when art and literature blossomed forth and Hindu culture spread from the South across the seas into the East Indies. The saints sang of Shiva and Vishnu in the temples which were then coming into prominence; the hymns on Shiva are called *Devāram* and those on Vishnu, *Divya Prabandham,* both names underlining their sacred character. Revered by the Tamils as the *Tamil Veda,* they embody the teachings of the Upanishads, and are sung to different melodic modes. The inscriptions in temples provide for endowments to maintain their recitals as part of the temple-service. The saints who adored Shiva are called *Nāyanārs,* and those who sang of Vishnu, *Ālvārs;* the contributions of these two groups of saints form the bedrock of Tamil culture and still form the most appealing part of Tamil literature. The period from the seventh century to the ninth century covers the ages of the more important ones among these; others followed and kept the tradition in full vogue throughout the subsequent centuries.

TIRUNĀVUKKARASHU

Tirunāvukkarashu (Vāgīsha, seventh century A.D.), "Master of Speech" or Appar, was reconverted to Shaivism from Jainism by his sister Tilakavatī, and in turn reconverted the Pallava King, Mahendra Varman.

We are not subject to any; we are not afraid of death; we will not suffer in hell; we live in no illusion; we feel elated; we know no ills; we bend to none; it is all one happiness for us; there is no sorrow, for we have become servants, once for all, of the independent Lord, and have become one at the beautiful flower-strewn feet of that Lord.

JNĀNASAMBANDHA

Jnānasambandha (seventh century) vanquished the Jains at Mathurai[3] and reconverted the Pāndyan king to Shaivism.

[2] *Nāḍ, nāḍu* in Tamil means country.

[3] Mathurai, the second largest city of the Tamil country, the ancient Pāndyan capital and fabled seat of Tamil learning.

The Lord's Names

The Lord's names are medicines; they are sacred mantras; they are the way to salvation in the other world, they are all the other good things, too; through them all acute miseries are destroyed; meditate only upon those names of the Lord.

The Lord Is Everything

Thou art flaw, Thou art merit, O Lord of Kūḍal Ālavāi! [4] Thou art kith and kin, Thou art Master. Thou art the light that shines without a break. Thou art the inner meaning of all the sacred texts learned. Material gain, emotional gratification [kāma], all these that man seeks art Thyself. What can I utter in praise before Thee?

MĀNIKKAVĀCHAKAR

Mānikkavāchakar ("the Ruby-worded Saint," eighth century), a minister of the Pāndyan court at Mathurai fought Buddhism and revived Shaivism. His songs are surcharged with much feeling. The collection of his devotional poems is called compendiously the *Sacred Utterances.*

[From *Tiruccataḳam,* 90]

I am false, my heart is false, my love is false; but I, this sinner, can win Thee if I weep before Thee, O Lord, Thou who art sweet like honey, nectar, and the juice of sugar-cane! Please bless me so that I might reach Thee.

From his poem on union with the Lord, called the *Puṇarcci-p-pattu,* which is typical of devotional ecstasy and the symbolism of "divine nuptials."

Melting in the mind, now standing, now sitting, now lying and now getting up, now laughing and now weeping, now bowing and now praising, now dancing in all sorts of ways, gaining the vision of the Form [of the Lord] shining like the rosy sky, with my hairs standing on end—when will I stand united with, and entered into, that exquisite Gem of mine [the Lord]!

SUNDARAMŪRTI

Sundaramūrti (ninth century) was the most humanistic of the Shaiva Nāyanārs.

[4] Meaning Mathurai.

[O Lord!] Without any other attachment, I cherished within my mind only Thine holy feet; I have been born with Thy grace and I have attained the state whereby I will have no rebirth. O Benevolent Lord at Kodumudi,[5] worshiped and lauded by the learned! Even if I forget you, let my tongue go on muttering your mantra *Namaḥ Śivāya.*[6]

POIHAI, BHŪTAM, AND PEY

Poihai of Kānchīpuram, Bhūtam of Mahābalipuram, and Pey of Mylapore, Madras, were the first three Ālvārs. On a rainy night, at Tirukkōvilūr, all three were taking shelter together in a small room which was all dark; the Lord also pressed into that small space, and to find out who the newcomer was, each of the three saints lit a lamp. What the lamp was that each lit is told by them in their verses.

Poihai: With earth as the lamp, with the swelling sea as the ghee, with the burning sun as the flame, I have seen the Lord. . . .

Bhūtam: With love as the lamp, ardent yearning as the ghee, and the mind melting in joy as the wick, I lit the light of knowledge. . . .

Pey: Lighting in my heart the bright lamp of knowledge, I sought and captured Him; softly the Lord of Miracles too entered my heart and stayed there without leaving it. . . .

NAMMĀLVĀR

Nammālvār was the most important and prolific of the Ālvār psalmists.

The Lord as Lover

This is a mood of devotion in which the devotee places himself in the position of the beloved and yearns for the Lord as the Lover. The mood is found already in the Vedic hymns; it is quite common in devotional literature and the outpourings of the mystics; in music, there is a whole body of songs, chiefly in dance, which adore the Lord in this manner.

[From *Tiruvāymoli,* 2.4.1]

[5] A Shiva shrine in Tamil country.

[6] This is typical of the devotee's complete preoccupation with the Lord and the cult of adoring the Lord by the incessant recital of His name. "*Namaḥ Śivāya*" means "Obeisance to Shiva" and forms the great "five-syllabled" mantra of Shiva; it is extracted from the Veda and is held so sacred by Shaivites that they take the expression *Namaḥ Śivāya* as a personal name.

Tossing about restlessly, with a mind that has melted, singing again and again and shedding tears, calling upon You as Narasimha[7] and seeking You everywhere, this beautiful maid[8] is languishing.

The God with Form and Beyond Form

[From *Tiruvāymoli,* 2.5.10]

He is not a male, He is not a female, He is not a neuter; He is not to be seen; He neither is nor is not; when He is sought, He will take the form in which He is sought, and again He will not come in such a form. It is indeed difficult to describe the nature of the Lord.

PERIYĀLVĀR OR VISHNUCHITTA

[From *Tiruvāymoli,* 5.2.6]

O ye ills tormenting me for long! listen, I tell you now, this body of mine has become the holy shrine of the great Lord, the Cowherd Krishna; know that, o ye ills that oppress me! I tell you one more word, you have no longer any hold here; know that and go away! This is not the old town, it has now been taken over as a protected place.

TIRUMANGAIMANNAR

Tirumangaimannar, an Ālvār and chief of a division of the Chola country, was opposed to Buddhism, of which there was a famous center in his neighborhood, at Nāgapattina on the seacoast of Tanjore.

The Lord's Name Nārāyaṇa

Nārāyaṇa is the most venerated of all the names of Vishnu as the Supreme God; the sacred formula (mantra) in which the devotees of Vishnu are initiated and which they go on repeating is *"Namo Nārāyaṇāya"*—"Obeisance to Lord Nārāyana."

The following is a widely recited verse and puts concisely all that the Lord's name and faith in it mean to the Hindu devotee.

[From *Periatirumoli,* 1.1.9]

The name *Nārāyaṇa* will bless one with high birth and affluence; it will obliterate all the sufferings of the devotees; it will endow one with the

[7] *Narasiṃha,* foremost man; means also that incarnation of Vishnu in which the Lord appeared as half-man, half-lion.

[8] That is, the heart of the devotee.

heavenly state and the service of the Lord; it will bring success and all good things; it will perform for one more beneficial acts than one's own mother; that word I have found, the name *Nārāyana.*

KARNATAKA

In this region, corresponding roughly to the state of Mysore, Kannada, a Dravidian language, is spoken.

BASAVARĀJA

Basavarāja (twelfth century), a high state official, founded the Vīrashaiva movement, a sect of worshipers of Shiva. His sententious sayings are for the most part addressed to his deity *Kūḍala Sangameśvara* (a form of Shiva).

The lamb brought to the slaughterhouse eats the leaf garland with which it is decorated. . . . The frog caught in the mouth of the snake desires to swallow the fly flying near its mouth. So is our life. The man condemned to die drinks milk and ghee. . . .

He who knows only the *Gītā* is not wise; nor is he who knows only the sacred books. He only is wise who trusts in God.

When they see a serpent carved in stone, they pour milk on it; if a real serpent comes, they say, "Kill, kill." To the servant of God, who could eat if served, they say, "Go away, go away"; but to the image of God which cannot eat, they offer dishes of food.

To speak truth is to be in heaven, to speak untruth is to continue in the world of mortals. Cleanliness is heaven, uncleanliness is hell.

Sweet words are equal to all prayers. Sweet words are equal to all penances. Good behavior is what pleases God. . . . Kindness is the root of all righteousness.

Those who have riches build temples for Thee; what shall I build? I am poor. My legs are the pillars; this body of mine is the temple.

PURANDARADĀSA

Purandaradāsa (1480–1564), the foremost and the most prolific of the Haridāsas ("Servants of Vishnu"),[9] a sect of saint-composers in Karnataka, is

[9] The Haridāsas were drawn from all classes, Kanakadāsa, one of them, being a shepherd.

deemed to have laid the foundations of the modern phase of the South Indian music system known as Karnatak music. His songs are remarkable for their literary merit, devotional fervor, and moral and philosophical teachings.

(Song: *Stomach-austerity* (*Udaravairāgya*); Melody: [10] *Nādanāmakriyā*)

This austerity is really for the sake of the stomach, this austerity devoid of devotion to the Lord—this rising in early dawn, and telling people, with a shivering frame, of having bathed in the river,[11] all the time having a mind filled with jealousy and anger; this display of a large number of images, like a shop of bronzeware and conducting worship with bright lights, to impose on others. . . .

All acts done without the abandonment of the sense of "I," without communion with the holy souls, without belief that everything goes on only at the instance of the Lord, and without the vision in silence of the Lord, are merely austerities practiced for livelihood.

MAHĀRĀSHTRA

JNĀNADEVA OR JNĀNESHVARA

Jnānadeva (1275–1296) was the foremost Mahārāshtrian saint and founder of the Marathi language and literature. His most famous work is a Marathi metrical paraphrase of the *Bhagavad Gītā* called the *Jñāneśvarī*.

[From *Jñāneśvarī*, 17.1794–1802]

Let the Lord of the Universe be pleased with this sacred literary activity of mine, and being pleased, let Him bestow on me this grace: May the wicked leave their crookedness and cultivate increasing love for the good. Let universal friendship reign among all beings. Let the darkness of evil disappear. Let the sun of true religion rise in the world. Let all beings obtain their desire. . . . May all beings be endowed with all happiness and offer ceaseless devotion to the Primeval Being. . . .

TUKĀRĀM

Tukārām (1598–1649) was the most popular shūdra saint of Mahārāshtra.

[10] Indian music belongs to the melodic or modal system, not to the harmonic system. Numberless melodic modes (rāga), based on a progression of notes, have been evolved, each with its distinct aesthetic ethos.

[11] A purification rite.

I saw my death with my own eyes. Incomparably glorious was the occasion. The whole universe was filled with joy. I became everything and enjoyed everything. I had hitherto clung to only one place, being pent up in egoism [in this body]. By my deliverance from it, I am enjoying a harvest of bliss. Death and birth are now no more. I am free from the littleness of "me" and "mine." God has given me a place to live and I am proclaiming Him to the [whole] world.

GUJARAT

MĪRĀBĀĪ

Mīrābāī (b. 1550) was an unfortunate Rājput princess who, widowed in mundane life, became, in spiritual life, the bride of the Lord whom she adored in the form of Krishna. Her songs, rhapsodies of Krishna-love, have always been popular, even today.

My only consort is Giridhar Gopāl,[12] none else—none else indeed in the whole world which I have seen through and through. I have forsaken my brothers, friends, and relations, one and all, and sitting among saintly souls, have lost regard for worldly fame or honor. My heart swells at the sight of godly persons and shrinks at the sight of the worldly. I have indeed reared the creeper of Godly Love with the water of my tears. Churning the curds, I have extracted the essence, ghee, and have thrown away the whey. The king sent me a cup of poison, even that I have drunk with pleasure! The news is now public, everyone now knows that Mīrā is deeply attached by love to God; it does not matter now; what was fated has happened!

KASHMIR

LALLĀ

Lallā (fourteenth century) was a Shaivite mystic. Her verses (*Lallāvākyāni*) are even today immensely popular in Kashmir.

[12] Names of Krishna, the former referring to his exploit in lifting a mountain, the latter to his role as cowherd.

I, Lallā, went out far in search of Shiva, the omnipresent Lord; after wandering, I, Lallā, found Him at last within my own self, abiding in His own home.

Temple and image, the two that you have fashioned, are no better than stone; the Lord is immeasurable and consists of intelligence; what is needed to realize Him is unified concentration of breath and mind.

Let them blame me or praise me or adore me with flowers; I become neither joyous nor depressed, resting in myself and drunk in the nectar of the knowledge of the pure Lord.

With the help of the gardeners called Mind and Love, plucking the flower called Steady Contemplation, offering the water of the flood of the Self's own bliss, worship the Lord with the sacred formula of silence!

BANARAS (HINDI)

KABĪR

Kabīr (1440–1518), a low caste weaver in Banares, was in many respects the pioneer of Hindi devotional verse, using the vernacular to popularize religious themes drawn from both Hindu and Muslim traditions. Though his fundamental concepts are chiefly Hindu, Muslim influence is reflected in his holding to a strict theism, opposition to all forms of idolatry and rejection of caste. God for Kabīr is usually called Rām (Skt. Rāma), and is frequently regarded as the divine Guru or Teacher. The mystical conceptions and the phraseology itself of Kabīr's verses reflect strong Sūfī influences juxtaposed to traditional Hindu doctrines. His poetry is often ungrammatical and borrows freely from both Sanskrit and Persian vocabularies, yet it is direct and forceful. Numerous couplets and didactic sayings are attributed to Kabīr and constitute much of the folk-wisdom of the average Hindu. During his lifetime Kabīr organized a religious order of monks and nuns, who furnished teachers and leaders of the community and otherwise propagated his teachings. The selections which follow were translated by the modern poet Rabīndranāth Tagore, for whom Kabīr stood as one of the most appealing and inspiring symbols of India's religious heritage.

[From Tagore, *Songs of Kabīr,* pp. 45–46, 55–57, 108–9, 112]

O servant, where dost thou seek Me?
Lo! I am beside thee.
I am neither in temple nor in mosque: I am neither in Kaaba nor in Kailash:[13]

[13] Abode of Shiva.

Neither am I in rites and ceremonies, nor in Yoga and renunciation.
If thou art a true seeker, thou shalt at once see Me: thou shalt meet Me in a moment of time.
Kabīr says, "O Sādhu! God is the breath of all breath." [p. 45]

It is needless to ask of a saint the caste to which he belongs;
For the priest, the warrior, the tradesman, and all the thirty-six castes, alike are seeking for God.
It is but folly to ask what the caste of a saint may be;
The barber has sought God, the washerwoman, and the carpenter—
Even Raidās was a seeker after God.
The Rishi Swapacha was a tanner by caste.
Hindus and Moslems alike have achieved that End, where remains no mark of distinction. [pp. 45–46]

Tell Me, O Swan, your ancient tale.
From what land do you come, O Swan? to what shore will you fly?
Where would you take your rest, O Swan, and what do you seek?
Even this morning, O Swan, awake, arise, follow me!
There is a land where no doubt nor sorrow have rule: where the terror of Death is no more.
There the woods of spring are a-bloom, and the fragrant scent "He is I" is borne on the wind:
There the bee of the heart is deeply immersed, and desires no other joy. [pp. 55–56]

O Lord Increate, who will serve Thee?
Every votary offers his worship to the God of his own creation: each day he receives service—
None seek Him, the Perfect: Brahma, the Indivisible Lord.
They believe in ten Avatārs; but no Avatār can be the Infinite Spirit, for he suffers the results of his deeds:
The Supreme One must be other than this.
The Yogī, the Sannyāsī, the Ascetics, are disputing one with another:
Kabīr says, "O brother! he who has seen the radiance of love, he is saved." [pp. 56–57]

O brother! when I was forgetful, my true Guru showed me the Way.
Then I left off all rites and ceremonies, I bathed no more in the holy water:

Then I learned that it was I alone who was mad, and the whole world beside me was sane; and I had disturbed these wise people.
From that time forth I knew no more how to roll in the dust in obeisance:
I do not ring the temple bell:
I do not set the idol on its throne:
I do not worship the image with flowers.
It is not the austerities that mortify the flesh which are pleasing to the Lord,
When you leave off your clothes and kill your senses, you do not please the Lord:
The man who is kind and who practises righteousness, who remains passive amidst the affairs of the world, who considers all creatures on earth as his own self,
He attains the Immortal Being, the true God is ever with him.
Kabīr says: "He attains the true Name whose words are pure, and who is free from pride and conceit." [pp. 108–9]

If God be within the mosque, then to whom does this world belong?
If Rām be within the image which you find upon your pilgrimage, then who is there to know what happens without?
Hari is in the East: Allāh is in the West. Look within your heart, for there you will find both Karīm and Rām;
All the men and women of the world are His living forms.
Kabīr is the child of Allāh and of Rām: He is my Guru, He is my Pīr.[14]
[p. 112]

SŪRDĀS

Sūrdās (sixteenth century) was the blind poet-singer of Agra.

I have danced my full now, O Gopāl! With passion and fury as my petticoat,[15] with lust for physical pleasure as my necklace, with delusion jingling as my anklets, with words of abuse as poetry, with mind full of false ideas as the big drum, with my movement in the company of the unholy as the steppings, with avarice as the earthen pitcher making sound inside, beating time in various ways, I have danced enough. I have worn illusion as my girdle, I have put on material craving as the mark on my

[14] Sūfī saint or teacher.

[15] The imagery employed is that of the danseuse.

forehead; I have demonstrated endless movements of my wants, without regard to time or place; O do remove all this nonsense of mine, O Son of Nanda! [16]

TULASĪDĀS

Tulasīdās (1532–1623) was the author of the great bible of the Hindi-speaking peoples, the Hindi *Rāmāyaṇa* called *Sacred Lake of the Deeds of Rāma.*

Where the Lord Dwells

[From *Rāmacaritamānasa,* 2.*Caupāī* 130]

O Rāma! Thou dwellest in the hearts of those who have no lust, anger, infatuation, pride, delusion, avarice, excitement, affection or hatred, hypocrisy, vanity, deceitfulness; those who are dear to all, benevolent to all, equable in joy and sorrow, praise and blame, who speak the truthful and the pleasant and are endowed with discrimination, who, while awake or asleep, have taken shelter under Thee and indeed have no other resort but Thyself; in their minds, O Rāma, dost Thou dwell. Those who consider other men's women as mothers and others' wealth as more poisonous than poison, those who rejoice to see others flourish and are acutely pained to see them afflicted, those to whom Thou art dearer than life, in their minds is Thy blessed abode.

[From *Vinayapattrikā,* No. 116]

O Mādhava! Such is your mystic power of illusion [māyā]; however much one may strive, one does not overcome it unless and until You bless with Your grace. . . . Knowledge, devotion, manifold spiritual means—all these are of course true; none of these is false; but Tulasī says in full confidence that the grace of the Lord alone can dispel that illusion.

[From *Vinayapattrikā,* No. 120]

Many are the means of crossing over the ocean of transmigration which the pure words of the Vedas speak of. But Tulasī says: "Real happiness of heart cannot be attained without giving up the ideas of 'I' and 'mine.'

[16] Nanda is the cowherd foster father of Krishna.

SHANKARADEVA

The spread of the Vaishnava devotional movement in Assam was primarily due to this saint. Shankaradeva (1449–1568) composed devotional narrative poems, dramas, and songs for prayers and congregational singing; founded *nām ghars,* halls for congregational prayer, and *sattras,* monastic establishments where devotional music, dance, and drama were maintained. He was a forerunner of Chaitanya of Bengal. The selection quoted below is a *ḳīrtanaghoṣa,* a song with refrain to be taken up by the congregation.

Save me O Rāma! O formless and faultless Hari! have compassion on Thy devotee and fulfill this his heart's desire. I bow to Thee, O Mādhava.[17] Thou art the giver of Law to the Law-maker.[18] Thou art the Way, the Mind; Thou art the Author of the World. Thou art the Oversoul and the sole Lord of the world, and nothing else exists besides Thee.

Thou art the cause and effect [of the world of being], the universe of the static and the moving, even as an ear ornament is inseparable from the gold of which it is made. Thou art the animals and the birds, the gods and the demons, the trees and the shrubs. Only the ignorant taketh Thee as different [from the Universe].

Being under the spell of Thy māyā, none knows that Thou art the Soul. Thou art at the heart of all beings. Blind to this truth, they go to seek Thee outside. Thou art the sole Truth; all else is illusory. The wise know this and meditate on Thee within their hearts.

I crave not for happiness, nor am I in need of salvation. Let there be naught but devotion at Thy feet. Let my mouth recite Thy name, let my ears listen to Thy tale; let Thy lotus feet shine in my heart. Let not the company of Thy devotees ever forsake me; this is the kindness I beg at Thy feet.

RĀMAPRASĀD

Rāmaprasād (1718–1775) was from Bengal.

O my mind! I tell you, worship Kālī[19] in whatever fashion you desire, repeating day and night the mantra given to you by the teacher.[20]

[17] Rāma, Hari, and Mādhava are names of Vishnu in his different forms.

[18] Brahmā, one of the Hindu trinity, the Creator.

[19] The Divine Mother.

[20] All schools of thought, devotion, and esoteric practice attach the greatest importance to

When you lie down, think you are doing obeisance to Her; in sleep meditate on the Mother; when you eat, think you are offering oblations to the Mother; whatever you hear with your ear is all the mantras of the Mother; each one of the fifty letters of the alphabet represent Her alone; Rāmaprasād declares in joy that the Mother pervades everything; when you move about in the city, consider that you are circumambulating the Mother.

An Anonymous Bhajan Song

[*Saṃsāra māyā chādiye Kṛṣṇa nāma bhaja mana*]

O Mind! Giving up attachment to the world, adore the name of Krishna. Repeat the name of Krishna and you will discover an invaluable treasure. Craving for worldly objects and all the deception caused by māyā will vanish. If you thirst for beauty, your thirst will be satisfied in an instant, for you will see with your eyes that unblemished gem, the Unbounded Supreme Being; your vision of beauty will be merged in that All-Beautiful in which all nature around is immersed. If the lotus feet of that Lord but touch you, your heart will be filled with wonderful riches.

ANDHRA (TELUGU)

TYĀGARĀJA

Tyāgarāja (1767–1847), the greatest South Indian composer, was a member of a Telugu family living in Tamil country. The major part of the songs heard in South Indian concerts are his compositions. He adored God in the form of Rāma, the incarnation of Vishnu and the hero of Vālmīki's Sanskrit epic. He believed in the full efficacy of repeating the Lord's name. His songs are noteworthy not only for his devotional fervor and ethical and spiritual preachings, but also for proclaiming the role of music an easier spiritual path than even yogic practices. On the other hand, the cultivation of mere music without devotion to the Lord would not lead one to the proper goal.

(Song: *Svara-rāga-sudhārasa*)

O Mind! devotion associated with the ambrosia of the notes and melodies of music is verily paradise and salvation. . . .

---

the guru or teacher who is to be venerated as the embodiment of divinity and from whom initiation should be taken.

To know and realize the nature of "sound" originating from the basic plexus [*mūlādhāra*] [21] is itself bliss and salvation. Likewise the knowledge of the various resonant centers of the body from which emanate the seven glorious notes of music.

Through philosophical knowledge one attains salvation only gradually after several births; but he who has knowledge of melodies along with natural devotion to God becomes a liberated soul here and now.

[21] According to esoteric physiology, there are in the body of man six centers, from the basic pelvic region to the head; the physico-spiritual energy, as well as sound, pass from the lowest where they are present in their subtlest form, to the higher ones where they become more and more manifest.

ISLAM IN MEDIEVAL INDIA

After the Ghōrid Turkish conquest at the end of the twelfth century A.D. India was, ideologically, the home of a plural society. It is disputable whether the Ghōrids and their successors revolutionized the forms of either the political or the economic life of the country; it can be argued convincingly that they only substituted one set of rulers for another without fundamentally changing the traditional functions of government or the traditional relations of rulers and ruled—that in administration, while introducing a new structure at the center, Delhi, they were conservative at the periphery, in the village; and that in economic life they merely introduced a new group of revenue receivers without changing the ways in which the people of India earned a living. What is indisputable is that, under the protection of their military power, they introduced into the heart of India a new, and in the event, unassimilable interpretation of the meaning and end of life—the Muslim.

With the memory of the partition of India along the religious frontier between Muslim and non-Muslim still fresh, it is difficult to contemplate the place of Muslim civilization in India in calm historical perspective. In the atmosphere generated by the events of 1947, it is easy either to regard Pakistan as a necessary good—as being somehow "in the womb of time" as soon as Muslim political control over Hindustan had been established in the twelfth century—and therefore to magnify the differences between Muslim and non-Muslim cultures in India; or to regard her as an unnecessary evil made possible only by the political maneuvering of modern times—and therefore to minimize the differences between these cultures.

The standpoint taken here is that the treatment of Muslims by Hindus as merely another caste; the interpenetration of Hindu customary law among Muslims in the villages; the creation of a Hindu-Muslim ruling class by the Mughal emperors with a system of rank in the imperial service and common interest in polo, elephant fighting, and common modes of dress; the development of a lingua franca, Urdu, combining Hindi grammar with a largely Arabic and Persian vocabulary; the study of Hindu thought by Muslims like al-Birūnī or Abū'l Fazl; the composition of histories in Persian by Hindus; the syncretist religions of Kabīr and Guru Nānak—all of these notwithstanding—neither educated Muslims nor educated Hindus accepted cultural coexistence as a natural prelude to cultural assimilation. Thus long before British rule and long before modern political notions of Muslim nationhood, the consensus of the Muslim community in India had rejected the eclecticism of Akbar and Dārā Shikōh for the purified Islamic teachings of Shaikh Ahmad of Sirhind and Shah Walī-Ullāh. Cultural apartheid was the dominant ideal in medieval Muslim India, in default of cultural victory.

We are not called upon here to analyze the political consequences of this fact in the modern history of India, still less to suggest what those consequences ought to have been. We may better understand, however, why Islam as an "ideology" remained unassimilated in medieval India, while yet enjoying peaceful coexistence for long periods with non-Muslim, principally Hindu, culture, if we examine briefly its religious and historical background.

CHAPTER XIV

THE FOUNDATIONS OF MEDIEVAL ISLAM

Islam in India, as elsewhere, was a civilization founded upon religion, that is, upon "the recognition on the part of man of some higher unseen power as having control of his destiny, and as being entitled to obedience, reverence, and worship" (in the words of the Oxford Dictionary). The reason for man's existence on earth, the purpose of his daily life, was submission (*islām*) to and worship of the One God, the Omnipotent. Human society was without value savc that with which Allāh had endowed it as man's proving ground for eternal salvation. The life on earth was significant—but only because Allāh had given it significance. The world was not an illusion, it was for man a dread reality, portending everlasting bliss or everlasting damnation. Man's existence on earth was not an evil to be avoided but an opportunity for service to God.

Thus the values of this world are for Muslims not of its own creation. Man does not exist merely to serve his own satisfactions according to his own manner of conceiving them. The end of man is not therefore his own perfection, his own self-realization on earth. His beliefs, his way of life, are ordained for him by Allāh who is his sovereign. A Muslim is always on active service for his Lord. No Muslim of whose thinking we have any record in medieval India forgets that he inhabits a world governed by Allāh; as a good subject he never forgets to write in the name of Allāh, nor, however distant from religion his subject may appear in our eyes, to begin with praises to his Lord. He knows that the proper study of mankind is not man but God.

ISLAM AS REVEALED IN THE QUR'ĀN AND THE SUNNA

As the means of that study Allāh has provided, in so far as He has deemed it fitting, a revealed Book, the Qur'ān, sent down in Arabic through the Angel Gabriel to His messenger the Prophet Muhammad over a period of more than twenty years from about A.D. 610, the original being in heaven as a "well-guarded tablet" (Qur'ān 85.22). But even the Prophet did not receive the whole of this tablet. The records of Muhammad's inspired utterances, found not merely in the memories of men, but according to later tradition written on shoulder blades, palm leaves, and stones, were collected after his death and under the third caliph, 'Uthmān (644–655), formed into an "authorized version" of one hundred and fourteen suras or chapters. Whatever paths Muslim thought might take in the centuries after the recension of the Qur'ān, Muslims found in the Qur'ān the very word of God, authority for those paths. The Qur'ān has remained for all ages the inspiration of the religious life of Islam.

But because the Qur'ān was the Word of God and the Prophet Muhammad the last of the prophets, at his death Divine Guidance for the community of believers came to an end. Where were the faithful to find authoritative directions amid all the vicissitudes of life? As the Arabs conquered vast territories and strange populations with highly developed religions of their own, so the need for guidance increased. The Qur'ān was indeed the final authority, but without interpretation its meaning might elude the believer. It was perhaps natural that, with so many men alive with personal memories of the words and actions of Muhammad, Muslims should seek for a model of what they should believe and do in the discourse and in the deeds of him whom God had chosen to be the bearer of His Message. By the time of the Muslim conquest of North India the principal source of Muslim belief and practice, other than the Qur'ān, had become the Sunna, or usage of the Prophet as reported in the Hadīth, the corpus of canonical tradition about Muhammad. The impression made by the personality of the Prophet upon his contemporaries and the respect paid by the Arabs to the customs (Sunna) of their forefathers provided the impetus to turn tradition into the second source of authority.

The earliest collections of Hadīth were made probably in early Ummayad times by the pious for their own edification and by lawyers and judges who had to administer the Arab conquests. At that time they did not have an overriding authority, second only to that of the Qur'ān. But there was a strong feeling among the faithful that, after the Qur'ān, belief should rest upon the authority of the Prophet and of his Companions and followers, so that any individual or sect wishing to justify its interpretation of Islam naturally appealed to a Hadīth. Hence it was not long before men began to manufacture traditions and put them into circulation. Hadīth became a report of what the Prophet, his Companions and followers would have said or done if they had been obliged to do so. The pious did not at first feel any great uneasiness at these forgeries. They doubtless thought that since their content was good and true, the Prophet would certainly have acted or spoken thus. The Hadīth became a microcosm of the religious history of the Muslim community during its formative years.

The elevation of the Prophet's Sunna as embodied in the Hadīth to a position of authority equal to that of the Qur'ān, and the reexamination of the actual practice of the Muslim community in the light of a thorough reconsideration of the original religious meaning of the Prophet's mission was, in the realm of jurisprudence, the work of al-Shāfi'ī (767–820). Unlike his predecessors who were prepared to accept the "living tradition" of the community as a basis of law, irrespective of whether that tradition could be attributed to the Prophet himself, al-Shāfi'ī persuaded his fellow Muslims to accept that only traditions from the Prophet himself should have the force of law and that the model of behavior of the Muslim community should be the model behavior of Muhammad. Undoubtedly this at first increased the tendency to invent Apostolic tradition, but in the longer run it had the effect of subjecting the actual practice of the community to scrutiny in the light of the religious insights of al-Shāfi'ī's day, and of systematizing the Law and the methods of discovering the Law. The raising of Apostolic tradition to a religious status almost equal to that of the Qur'ān was in effect a reconversion of the Muslim community to Islam at the end of the second and the beginning of the third century Hijra.

This sanctification of Hadīth and the Sunna in the province of jurisprudence hastened the appearance of collections of Hadīth which satisfied the new principles of criticism. The narrators of Hadīth were required to cite their authorities going back to the original narrator—usually a Companion of the Prophet, and then the biographies of the narrators were compiled in order to ascertain whether the narrators of the Hadīth were *prima facie* in a position to transmit the Hadīth; whether, for example, one had died before the next had been born, or whether they had ever met.

In the third century after Hijra appeared the first critical collections of Hadīth, the *Genuine Collections* (*Sahīh*) compiled by al-Bukhārī (d. 870), principally for legal purposes, and Muslim (d. 889), principally for theological purposes. These have a canonical authority in Islam second only to that of the Qur'ān. Thus, three centuries before the Turkish conquest of North India "standard" compendia of Muslim tradition had been collected, which, with the Qur'ān, provided the authoritative sources of Muslim belief.

For the orthodox (Sunni) Muslim these authoritative sources of belief and practice were not the spiritual monopoly of a divinely appointed priesthood. Anyone in the community could devote himself to the study and development of the religious sciences which came to be based upon the study of the Qur'ān and the Sunna of the Prophet as embodied in the canonical collections of Hadīth. The Caliph or head of the Muslim community had no spiritual powers; each believer was equal in his right to study how God must be obeyed (although as will be seen in the section on the Sharī'a he must be bound by the consensus of the community before him). This was not so for unorthodox Islam.

UNORTHODOX ISLAM

The most important schism in Muslim civilization is that caused by the Shī'a—the party of 'Alī.

After the death of Muhammad, a section of the faithful insisted that 'Alī, cousin and son-in-law of the Prophet, was the rightful heir to the headship of the Muslim community. The majority did not agree, and when 'Alī became caliph, the Umayyads resisted him by force of arms. 'Alī lost Syria and Egypt, and in 661 when he was murdered, Mu'awīya, an Umayyad, was proclaimed caliph in Jerusalem. 'Alī's son, Hasan, sold his rights to Mu'āwiya and died a few years later, the Shī'a asserting that he had been poisoned by Mu'āwiya. His younger brother, Husain, who had lived quietly at Medina during Mu'āwiya's reign, rebelled against Yazīd, Mu'āwiya's son. At Karbala Husain's band of two hundred was surrounded by superior forces and, as it refused to surrender, was annihilated. The tenth of Muharram, the day of Husain's death, is the culmination of ten days' lamentations among the Shī'a. 'Alī's party appeared to be finished, but it became a focus for all the discontents of the time. Although Arab in origin, the Shī'a gained support among the clients (*mawālī*), the non-Arabs who had accepted Islam and yet were not exempt from taxes and social disabilities imposed on non-Muslims.

Defeat in politics spurred elaboration of specific Shī'a doctrines. First, the "martyr's" death of Husain led to the introduction of a passion motive; the tragedy of the death of Husain paves the way to Paradise for the Shī'a. Second, the Shī'a developed the doctrine of the *Imām,* an infallible being partaking of the divine attributes sent by God to guide the faithful in every age. Some Shī'a regard the Imām as an incarnation of the Godhead itself, but they are not typical. The Imām is sinless (unlike Muhammad) and infallible, possessing a secret knowledge—the Divine Light—handed down from God to Muhammad and thence to 'Alī and his descendants. He is the final interpreter of the word of God in the Qur'ān. He is appointed by and responsible to God, not by and to the community of the faithful. His powers are much nearer those of a pope than are those of the Sunni caliphs.

The Shī'a split into many sects, the largest was that of the "Twelvers" who recognized twelve Imāms in the line from Fātima and 'Alī, ending with Muhammad al-Mahdī who disappeared from the world in 880 and is believed to be preserved against the day of his second coming to restore justice and righteousness. For the Twelvers the Imām remains mortal, but a divine light is inherent in him.

One of the most important sects of the Shī'a is that of the "Seveners" (or Ismā'īlī), so-called because they recognized as Imām the son of Ismā'īl ibn Ja'far, the sixth Imām, and not his brother Mūsā al-Kāzim. Closely connected with the Ismā'īlī were the Qarmatians who believed that Muhammad ibn Ismā'īl was the last Imām who would reappear on the last day.

In Ismā'īlī beliefs the number seven had magic importance. In their gnostic Neo-Platonic philosophy, there were seven emanations of the world intellect—God, the universal mind, the universal soul, primeval matter, space, time, and the world of earth and man. They forged a chain of manifestations of the world intellect beginning with Adam and passing through Muhammad to the Imāms. Muhammad was not, as in orthodoxy, the seal of the Prophets. They taught that the laws of the Sharī'a were not intended for those with esoteric knowledge and its prohibitions were but mere allegories. The Qur'ān itself had an inner meaning, known only to initiates.

The Ismā'īlī and the Qarmatians appealed primarily to the poor and lowly, to peasants and artisans. The Qarmatians practiced community of property, and according to their enemies, of wives also. They organized workers and artisans into guilds. They considered it legitimate to shed the blood of the orthodox. In 899 they founded an independent state at al-Ahsa on the western shores of the Persian Gulf and launched raids on neighboring Syria and Iraq. In 930 they captured Mecca and carried off the Black Stone. The Qarmatians passed on their doctrines to the Fātimids of Egypt and to the Assassins of Alamut and Syria, who terrorized the Muslim world by raids and assassinations from their mountain fortresses until stamped out by the Mongol Hūlāgū in 1256.

The Ismā'īlī and the Qarmatians owed their strength to the social discontent of later 'Abbāsid times. The disparity between rich and poor, and the decline in prosperity of the empire at the end of the ninth century, made many humble people enemies of Sunni Islam. The latter appeared to condone the social ills of the time. On the eve of the Muslim conquest of India it was customary to stigmatize enemies as Qarmatians or Bātinīs, so great was the abhorrence they aroused among those who supported the existing order.

It must be emphasized, however, that the majority of the Shī'a viewed the Ismā'īlī and the Qarmatians with an alarm equal to that of the Sunnis or orthodox Muslims, for they compromised the unity of God and disregarded the finality of Muhammad's prophethood. The majority of the Shī'a, the Twelvers, accept the Five Pillars of Islam (ritual purification, prayer, alms, fasting, and pilgrimage) and though they do not accept the principle of consensus, their law is based on the Sunna of the Prophet. Their principles occasionally diverge from those of the four Sunni schools —e.g., temporary marriage is allowed; marriage with a Christian or Jewish woman is not. Dogmatically the authority of the Imām tends to overshadow that of the Qur'ān and the Sunna.

Although the Shī'a were influential at the Mughal court in the sixteenth and seventeenth centuries and enjoyed adherents among the rulers of the Deccan Muslim kingdoms which appeared in the fourteenth and fifteenth centuries, their contribution to medieval Muslim thought in India has not been considered sufficiently distinctive in its social and political overtones to be included in the readings. Furthermore, although the Ismā'īlī and the Qarmatians infiltrated into India, they were suppressed by Muslim governments under Sunni influence and have not, so far as has been ascertained, left to posterity any direct evidence of their thought in India.

THE HISTORICAL BACKGROUND

Islam came to South Asia first as a religion, and then as a political force. The peripheral Arab conquest of Sind (beginning A.D. 711) was preceded by Muslim settlements on the western seaboard as were the Ghaznavid invasions (beginning A.D. 1000) preceded by small colonies of Muslims in the southern Punjab.

The timing and nature of Muslim conquests in North India was of decisive significance in defining the character of Muslim thought in India. The early Arab invasions of Sind under Muhammad ibn Qāsim occurred less than a hundred years after the death of the Prophet Muhammad. Islam, in 711, was still a religion composed of a few basic assertions about the oneness of God, the mission of the Prophet, the terrors of the Last Judgment, the need to perform the five daily ritual prayers, to go on the pilgrimage (*hajj*) to Mecca and to give alms (*zakāt*) to the poor. The Arabs were still sitting as pupils at the feet of the peoples they had subdued, learning the arts of civilization. The study of Arab grammar, it is true, had begun under al-Du'alī, al-Khalīl, and the Persian Sībawaih. Traditionists [1] such as al-Hasan al-Basrī, Ibn Zuhrī, and Ibn Sharāhīl al-Sha'bī were putting into circulation the religiously authoritative reports of the sayings and doings of the Prophet or his Companions. Thinkers like Wāsil ibn 'Atā were raising theological issues of divine and human ordination, while sects like the Khārijī and the Shī'a were quarreling over the government of the faithful. Even so, Islam was still forging those

[1] That is, specialists in the compilation and interpretation of the "authentic" traditions handed down from the Prophet.

intellectual weapons—the science of tradition, theology, jurisprudence, and history—which would enable it to meet argument with something more than conviction. Islam was still receptive to the impress of those civilizations of Byzantium and Persia which the Arabs had conquered. Within wide limits, Muslims were free to seek after and do God's will in their own ways. There was no established orthodoxy; there was no authority seeking to enforce one.

The century following the Arab conquest of Sind was therefore one in which Hindu culture could encounter the Arabs in the hope of giving more than it was forced to receive. For example, the scientific study of astronomy in Islam commenced under the influence of an Indian work, the *Siddhanta,* which had been brought to Baghdad about 771 and translated. The Hindu numerical system entered the Muslim world about the same time. Later, in the ninth century, India contributed the decimal system to Arab mathematics.

The background to the Ghōrid Turkish conquest of India which commenced in 1175 and blossomed into the Sultanate of Delhi under Iltutmish (1211–1236) was vastly different. The Ghōrid invasions were begun to finance the imperial ambitions of a small mountain principality in Afghanistan, were continued as a profitable outdoor occupation for Turkish adventurers, and ended in providing a home for Muslim refugees from the Mongol catastrophe of the third decade of the thirteenth century.

By the second half of the ninth century, the 'Abbāsid Caliphate had surrendered effective authority first to Persian and then to Turkish military adventurers, who recruited their chief military support from converted, purchased, and immigrant Turkish nomads from the steppes and mountains beyond the Oxus and the Jaxartes. The political headquarters of the Eastern world moved to Nishapur, Samarqand, Bukhara, and Ghaznin. The 'Abbāsid Caliph at Baghdad survived only to legitimize with robes of honor and mandates of appointment whoever had the power to compel him to do so.

Now it was unlikely that the Ghōrids and the motley host of hardy horsemen who followed them—Afghans, Turks, rough mountaineers, newly converted nomads—would themselves be the bearers of a Muslim culture remarkable for depth, variety, or subtlety. They came to Hindustan as raiders, to remain as rulers. They came as soldiers of fortune; they found fortune and stayed to organize it. It would not, therefore, have been surprising if Muslim thought in India had been stillborn of such parents. But although the Ghōrid Turks and Afghans themselves were rude and uncouth, they became nevertheless the guardians of a proud and rich emigré civilization.

For in 1220, the Mongol deluge burst upon the Muslim world; Bukhara, Samarqand, Gurganj, Balkh, Marv, and Ghaznin were in turn destroyed. Many scholars of the eastern Muslim world were killed and libraries burned. In 1258, Hūlāgū, a grandson of Chingis Khān, sacked Baghdad and slew the 'Abbāsid Caliph, Al-Musta'sim. Although by the end of the century the grandson of Hūlāgū, Ghazan Khān, had become a devout Muslim and Hūlāgū's successors (called the Īl-Khāns) had surrounded themselves with Muslim savants such as al-Juwainī and Rashīd ud-dīn, Islam was in eclipse for over half a century in Transoxania, Persia, and Iraq. But apart from a campaign on the left bank of the Indus by Chingis Khān, and forays against Lahore and Multan, India escaped Mongol visitation. The former servants of the Ghōrid sultans were left quietly, and (incidentally) by no military merit of their own, to establish a sultanate at Delhi.

From the work of the contemporary Indo-Muslim historian, Minhāj us-Sirāj Jūzjānī, himself an immigrant, and of the later historian Ziā ud-dīn Barnī, it is evident that the sultanate of Delhi offered a refuge for scholarly fugitives from the Mongols. In the thirteenth century India became a cultural colony of the Muslim world at a time when the center of that world was in enemy hands. It is not surprising, therefore, that the strong conservative trends in Islam at the beginning of the thirteenth century were, in India, strengthened. To re-establish ties with the old, rather than to embrace the new, was a reasonable desire in men who had barely escaped with their lives and who now found themselves precariously situated in an armed camp in North India, open to attack from the Mongols in the northwest and from Hindus all around them.

These immigrant Muslim scholars were now the bearers of a civilization as well as of a faith. Under the early 'Abbāsids, Muslims had not only assimilated the traditions of pre-Islamic Persia and the heritage of classical Greece, but also, in response to their religious needs, had transmuted those contributions into a unique cultural whole greater than any of its individual parts.

In religion the science of Hadīth provided Muslims with a means of formulating and defending true belief and pious practice. Muslim jurisprudence (*fiqh*) had appeared as an imposing corpus of legal principles regulating the personal, commercial, property, and sexual relations of Muslim to Muslim and of Muslim to non-Muslim. The four orthodox schools of jurisprudence, the Hanafite founded by Abū Hanīfa (d. 767), the Mālikite founded by Mālik ibn Anas (c.715–795), the Shāfi'ite founded by Muhammad ibn Idrīs al-Shāfi'ī (767–820), and the Hanbalite founded by Ahmad ibn Hanbal (d. 855), represent one of the greatest achievements of Islam and one which gave Muslim civilization in India great corporate strength. Migrant or immigrant Muslims from outside India were often appointed *qādīs* (religious judges) by the sultans in India, thus promoting Islamic knowledge there.

In theology (*kalām,* or the science of the unity of God) and philosophy, Islam had either come to terms with (or had imposed terms upon) Greek philosophy and now at the end of the twelfth century, in the theology of al-Ash'arī (873–935) and in the philosophy of al-Ghazālī (d. 1111), could rest awhile in an intellectual caravansary sufficiently fortified against assault. The challenge of the Mu'tazilites, who had attempted to interpret Islam in terms of Greek metaphysics—making God and the Qur'ān conform to human ideas of justice and reason in effect—had been met by al-Ash'arī of Baghdad and al-Māturīdī of Samarqand (d. 944), who had turned the weapons of Greek dialectic to the defeat of the Mu'tazilites in the assertion of God's unlimited sovereignty and the defense of the Qur'ān and the Hadīth.

By the end of the twelfth century, mysticism too had been domesticated in the Islamic world. Potentially a disruptive force emphasizing a direct personal relationship between the individual and his God and tending to ignore, if not to denigrate, the rules of conduct and the credal formulations of the orthodox, Sufism (Muslim mysticism) had been made respectable by al-Ghazālī. Seeking not academic knowledge but immediate experience of God, he managed to buttress the structure of theological ideas with vivid personal religious experience. It was important for Islam in India that Sufism had found accommodation in orthodox Islam by the time of the Muslim conquest—for not only did the community thereby present a united front against the infidel, but also Sufi modes of thought and worship made an appeal to Hindus so strong that many were converted to Islam. It was only after three centuries, in Mughal times, that orthodox lawyers and theologians grew fearful lest the Sufis should stray outside the Muslim fold, and, by going too far to meet kindred Hindu spirits, prepare the internal subversion of Islam in India.

Muslim historiography (*tārīkh*) had also developed as a distinctive cultural form by the time the Ghōrid Turks invaded India. Pre-Islamic Arab oral traditions, tribal genealogy, the traditions of the old Persian *Khudāy-Nāma,* the religious demand for authentic biographies of the Prophet and the early caliphs, the Persian taste for edifying anecdotes and the Turkish rulers' desire for fame, had all contributed to the rise of historical writing eminently fitted to remind Muslims in India of their great heritage. The Ghōrid invasion followed the victory of Persian as the literary language of the eastern Muslim world and, with that victory, the revival of Persian modes of thought in politics and poetry, ethics, and belles-lettres. This was encouraged by the Turkish sultans and their principal officers who found Persian easier to learn than Arabic. Persian poetry and prose with its content of epic royal deeds, its fables and moral anecdotes, its education in polite manners and in the arts of politic government, gave the society of Turkish soldiers of fortune its title deeds to civilization.

Thus the Muslim conquest of India occurred at a period when Islamic civilization had crystallized in a form which, on looking back, one can see it was to retain until the nineteenth and twentieth centuries. The scope for change in response to the challenges of the Indian environment was less than it had been at the time of the Arab invasion of Sind—indeed the Arabs had already made the major Muslim concession to India, the admission *de facto* of the Hindus to the status of *zimmīs* (tolerated and protected unbelievers).

It is remarkable that once Islam was ensconced in India, no important effort was made forcibly to evict it. For this, the political and social character of the Muslim conquest was largely responsible. The Ghōrids, and in the sixteenth century the Mughals, invaded India with organized professional armies; they did not invade India as a folk in search of a home, or as nomads in search of pasture. Neither Turk nor Mughal deprived the Hindu cultivator of his holding or settled in closed colonies on the lands of the dispossessed. Both substituted one group of revenue receivers and military chiefs for another, changing the men at the top of the social pyramid without dislodging the pyramid itself.

The Turks and the Mughals sought paramountcy rather than empire in India, suzerainty rather than government, superintendence rather than control. Neither the Delhi sultanate nor the Mughal empire interfered greatly with the daily life or the religion of the generality of their subjects. Except for acts in the heat of battle, violence did not normally characterize the relations of Muslim and Hindu. For the most part the mass of Hindus remained indifferent to their new rulers, rather than bitterly antagonistic toward them and their foreign faith.

THE COMING OF ISLAM TO INDIA

Despite the Muslim conquest of the Hindus, even at the height of the Delhi sultanate and the Mughal empire the Muslims remained a minority. Hindu chiefs enjoyed local power under Muslim suzerainty and Hindu clerks staffed all but the directing and executive posts in the administration. In the last resort, it is true, military and political power over the greater part of Hindustan rested with Muslims, yet, as with all political power, its continued exercise depended on the tacit observance of certain conditions, none the less real for being unspecified and unspoken. For the Muslims in India these were first, refraining from trespassing beyond the traditional frontiers of political activity in India, i.e., revenue collection and troop raising, to interfere actively in the beliefs and customs and laws of subject communities; and second, to preserve the cultural and religious identity of the ruling group so that it would instinctively cohere to defend its privileged political position against non-Muslims. It is this second condition with which the present section is concerned.

Before the Ghōrid conquests in India, al-Ghazālī, as will be seen, had largely stilled the theological warfare of the schools and obliged the mystics first to go on the pilgrimage to Mecca. In depriving Greek philosophy of its hold over the educated and by confining scholastic theology to a role strictly defensive of tradition, he had turned Muslims again toward the study of the Qur'ān and the Sunna as the "quickening word" for personal and social religious life. Islam entered India at a time when its learned men (*'ulamā*), mainly traditionists and canon lawyers rather than theologians, were engaged in just that practical elaboration of the daily witness of a Muslim to his beliefs which favors the solidarity of the community.

Politics, too, enhanced the influence of the ulamā. The Turks who conquered North India at the end of the twelfth century A.D. were military adventurers glad of support from the religious classes. The Ghōrid sultans recognized the legal sovereignty of the Caliph of Baghdad but in practice acted as caliphs in their own dominions, appointing religious judges (*qādīs*) and canon jurists (muftīs) to the principal towns and enforcing their decisions. The *qādīs,* muftīs, and the ulamā who taught in mosque schools and colleges, advocated obedience to the sultan and the powers that be. Although the sultans might disregard the Sharī'a when their own political position and personal habits were in question, the prestige and authority of the state stood behind the ulamā in their education of the Muslim population at large. If the state did not actively impose an orthodoxy itself, it permitted others to do so. It appears that the sultans of Delhi generally appointed orthodox Sunni ulamā of the Hanafite school of jurisprudence to office and to teaching posts.

There were occasions too when the government actively suppressed unorthodoxy. Extreme Shī'a sects—the Ismā'īlī and Qarmatians—had first appeared in Hindustan in upper Sind and established a principality with a capital at Multan. Mahmūd of Ghaznin had defeated and dispersed them in 1005 and from 1009 to 1010, but they continued underground activity in India thereafter. In the reigns of Iltutmish, Raziya, 'Alā ud-dīn Khaljī, and Fīrūz Shāh Tughluq in the thirteenth and fourteenth centuries, their adherents were slaughtered and imprisoned by the government. The Ismā'īlī and Qarmatian denial of the legitimacy of the sultanate, their egalitarian urges and their secret guild organizations caused the Delhi government as much alarm as their rejection of the orthodox caliphate, schools of law, and theology scandalized the Sunni ulamā. The relations between the Delhi sultanate and the ulamā were generally, therefore, close and harmonious, with important consequences for the outward unity and the stability of the Muslim community.

The chief ideological threat to the religious integrity of Islam in India was more subtle and insidious than that offered by the Shī'a and the Qarmatians, because it came from within the orthodox fold, from those whose lives of devotion and gentleness were often compelling arguments for their teachings—namely the mystics. The real religious tension in Indian Islam was between the Sunni ulamā and the Sufis. It was a tension between twin heirs of al-Ghazālī's heritage. The twelfth century A.D. saw the organization of the great mystic orders (*silsila*) outside India and even before the Ghōrid conquest was complete in 1195, Khwāja Mu'īn ud-dīn Chishtī of Sistan had settled in Ajmir introducing the Chishtī order to India. Within the next two centuries the great Sufi orders had spread their network of "retreats" over most of North India. These retreats were a powerful force both within and beyond the Indian Muslim community. The Sufis appealed to all classes of Muslims, particularly those less educated in the traditional sciences. Moreover, they exhibited a way of life and thought attractive to Hindus in its devotion, piety, asceticism, tolerance, and, during the sultanate period at least, in its independence of the ruling power. They were the true missionaries of Islam as a faith in India.

Nevertheless, the Sufis were under constant critical surveillance by the ulama lest they surrender Islam in the name of Islam. The fears and suspicions of the orthodox were strongest after the Mughal conquest, when Akbar and later Dārā Shikōh seemed to be encouraging or at least tolerating un-Islamic ideas and practices. The orthodox feared in Sufism its pantheistic predilections, its toleration of saint worship, and its tacit encouragement of the neglect of the study and practice of the Sharī'a. They feared too the substitution of "retreat" for mosque as the center of the life and worship of the community. Such tendencies did not need or imply Hindu influence—they existed in Islam before the conquest of India—but unless resisted they could have meant cultural absorption for Islam in India. As it was, the ulamā in their educational work among "New Muslims" needed to run fast to stand still. (Thus, for example, within living memory Muslims in Kashmir have worshiped at Buddhist shrines, Muslim cultivators in western India have offered vows to Hindu gods at harvest time, and Muslim women in the eastern Punjab have sacrificed to Shitāla, the goddess of smallpox). The orthodox ulamā did not want unnecessary hostages held out to "Hindu superstition."

But at the ideological level, the tension between the ulamā and the mystics must not be exaggerated into a parting of the bond between them. They were not enemies but rivals; partners in the mutual enjoyment of al-Ghazālī's legacy, no bitter litigants quarreling over its division. Both were traveling toward God, one by the orthodox path (Sharī'a) and the other by the mystic Way (tarīqa), from a common starting point. The mystics remained Muslim mystics and the orthodox who combated their more dangerous ideas were often mystics themselves (e.g., Shaikh

Ahmad of Sirhind). And even if it sometimes appeared, as in Akbar's and Dārā Shikōh's day, that orthodoxy and mysticism had reached the limits of mutual tolerance, the instinct of the Muslim community for unison, if not unity, in the face of unbelievers asserted itself in the person of Shah Walī-Ullāh (1702–1762) to prevent open schism and heresy hunting.

The readings that follow illustrate the different articulations of one fundamentally religious and "otherworldly" system of thought and system of law. First, we present the exposition of Islam in India by the 'ulamā, which took two main forms. One was the repetition of the mandates of the Sharī'a and of the principles of Muslim jurisprudence as set down in textbooks which were accepted as authoritative by the consensus of the Muslim community. The other was the exposition and defense of Muslim beliefs and outward observances, for the benefit of converts on the one hand and to the discredit of the mystics' extravagances on the other. The latter motive, however, did not become prominent until the fifteenth and sixteenth centuries.

Of these two forms of exposition, legal and theological, it was the former which, as we have seen, increasingly engaged the attention of the ulamā at the time of Islam's introduction to India, and which probably contributed most to the establishment of the Muslim community there. Nevertheless, implicit in this whole structure were certain basic Muslim teachings about the nature of God and Divine worship. Muslim thought in India cannot be understood without a brief appreciation of the features, methods and course of Muslim theology.

FUNDAMENTALS OF MUSLIM FAITH

The Prophet himself was no theologian and the Qur'ān was no theological treatise. Thus the followers of the Prophet were left to reduce the conceptions of the Qur'ān to a system. They were forced to do so partly by political quarrels in which opponents characterized each other as heretics and infidels, and partly by the impact of other creeds or systems of thought, notably Christianity and Greek philosophy, which challenged the convictions of pious Muslims and provoked them to defend their faith by argument.

The Qur'anic concept of Allāh is stated most simply in the formula, "There is no God save Allāh." He is the One, the Living, the Exalted, the Comprehensive, the Powerful, the Self-Sufficing, the Absolute Originator, the Eternal, the Mighty, the Dominant, the Haughty, the Great, the Laudable, the Glorious, the Generous, the Strong, the Firm, the Knower, the Subtle, the Aware, the Wise, the Hearer, the Seer. He is also the Creator, the Shaper, the Giver of Life, and the Giver of Death, the Assembler of All at the Last, the Strengthener, the Guardian, the King, the Governor, the Lord of Kingship, the Prevailer, and the Tyrant. He is the Exalter, the Abaser, the Honorer, and the Advancer. In relation to mankind Allāh is the Compassionate Compassionator, the Forgiver, the Pardoner, the Clement, the Kind, and the Loving. He is the Giver, the Provider, and the Answerer of Prayer. God's power is infinite; so is His knowledge. Although transcendent and without a peer, He is nearer to man than his jugular vein. Although not bound by human ideas of justice, He hates injustice and oppression. Man's relation to Allāh is one of utter submission and dependence. The Qur'ān deals in antinomies, as if to emphasize the temerity of human efforts to comprehend the nature and purposes of Allāh. Thus in the one text God is kind, loving, and patient; in another, He says: "I created not the jinn and mankind save that they should worship me." Again, "Whom Allāh guideth aright, he allows himself to be guided aright; whom He leads astray, they are the losers," in confrontation with "The truth is from your Lord. Let him then who will, believe; and let him be, who will be, an unbeliever," illustrates that the Qur'ān is on the issue of divine or human ordination a mine of texts for later theologians, rather than a text itself. The precise relation of Allāh to His Creation, of His Word to Himself, of His Attributes to His Essence, of Divine Command and human responsibility became questions to trouble succeeding generations of Muslims. With the aid of quotations from the Qur'ān it was possible to assert, with equal force, either the absolute transcendence over, or the complete immanence of Allāh in, His Creation. The first doctrine in general was developed by scholastic theologians, the second by some extreme Ṣufis.

Immediately after the death of Muhammad, however, the Muslim community in Mecca and Medina subscribed to an expression of faith in the one God, His Prophet, His Book, His Angels, and the Last Day, and to fulfill the duties of pilgrimage to Mecca, alms-giving, and fasting. But disputes among the followers of the Prophet together with the Arab conquest of Syria, Persia, and Egypt wrought a change. When 'Alī submitted his claim to the caliphate to arbitration after the battle of Siffin (657), some of his adherents came out against him claiming his action was unlawful. They (the Khārijites) went on to assert that they alone were true Muslims and that any other so-called Muslims must be killed on sight. This raised the question of what made a Muslim. The propaganda on behalf of the descendants of 'Alī also forced clearer and more elaborate definitions of Islam. Some said the Angel Gabriel had made a mistake and brought to Muhammad the revelation intended for 'Alī; others argued that there were two Gods; one the Imām (leader, ruler) in heaven, the other the Imām ('Alī or his descendants) on earth. The Murji'is arose who would postpone all such questions to the Last Day.

The contact between Christians and Muslims in Syria led to an efflorescence of new concepts about God, his relation to man and to the Qur'ān. Most Muslims believed at first that God was the absolute governor of the world. Christian ideas tended to emphasize human responsibility and under their influence some Muslims, the Qadarīs, affirmed the freedom of man's will. Christian doctrines of the *Logos* probably provoked the Muslim doctrine that the Qur'ān was eternal and uncreated. It was the word of God; God without a Word was unthinkable, therefore the Qur'ān was coeval with God, i.e., eternal and uncreated. His other attributes, being His, were equally eternal and uncreated. These ideas, with parallels in Christian concepts of the Trinity, could destroy his Oneness and Unity, the fundamental dogma of Islam. Another danger was Greek philosophy with its exaltation of human reason and its notions of substance and attributes. Using reason, Muslim thinkers treated the problem of the nature of Allāh in such a way as to make Him devoid of positive attributes. For example, in the Qur'ān, Allāh was the knower; therefore, He must have the quality, "knowledge." But of what was His knowledge, of something within Himself or without? If the first, there was a duality in Himself; if the latter, then His knowledge depended on something outside Himself and was not absolute, therefore He Himself, the possessor of this quality, was not absolute.

In this potentially dangerous situation, three main schools of theological thought appeared in Islam. The first, the "people of tradition," followed theological proofs which they had heard were derived from the Qur'ān, the Sunna of the Prophet, and the consensus of the Muslim community. For them reason must not be employed either to criticize or to develop doctrine; statements of belief must be accepted literally, "without enquiring how." If, for example, in the Qur'ān, it is stated that God is settled on His throne (Qur'ān 20.5), that statement must be believed as it stands without asking how He sits, or whether He sits like a man.

The second school of thought was rational in method, and its chief members were the Mu'tazilites, whose intention was to formulate Islam in philosophical terms acceptable to educated non-Arabs. They founded Muslim scholasticism. Frankly using reason to arrive at their theological position, they nevertheless reasoned from the text of the Qur'ān. Thus it is wrong to describe them as rationalists in an eighteenth-century sense.

The Mu'tazilites were concerned to vindicate Allāh's unity, His justice, and His spirituality. They denied that Allāh could be said to have any essential or eternal qualities. He could be described as Lord, Possessor, the Merciful, and so forth, but not in the sense that lordship, ownership, and mercy were attributes added to the Divine Being; rather they were attributes identical with His essence. The Mu'tazilite doctrine of the Qur'ān was also intended to preserve the unity of Allāh. If the Qur'ān was eternal and uncreated it must be another God, they argued, for it was not God, yet was other than God. Therefore it was created. The Mu'tazilites also upheld the essential justice of Allāh, conceiving Him, under the influence of Greek ideas, as Infinite Justice. All that God does is aimed at what is best for His creation. He does not desire evil and does not ordain it. All man's actions, both good and evil, result from man's free will. Man will be rewarded for his good deeds and punished for his bad. Then, the Mu'tazilites denied all anthropomorphic notions of God, explaining away those texts in the Qur'ān which speak of God's hands, eyes, face, and throne, and of His being upheld in Paradise by believers. They held that since He was infinite, He could not be in one place for that would entail His being finite. God was spirit. Their opponents said that the Mu'tazilites reduced Allāh to a vague unity of negatives. This contrasted with the vivid, personal Allāh of the Qur'ān and was completely unsatisfying to the vast majority of simple believers. The mildness of the Mu'tazilites in rejecting doctrines of absolute predestination contrasted with the hardness of their doctrines of punishment in hell for the choice of evil-doing. Moreover, when their doctrines were made the official orthodoxy under the Caliph al-Ma'mūn (813–833), they treated their opponents with great intolerance and even brutality.

The third school of thought was that which eventually, by the end of the twelfth century, became the orthodox, i.e., the Ash'arite, so-called after its founder, al-Ash'arī (873–935). In it the use of reason in Muslim theology was accepted, only now in defense, not in defiance, of the simple formulations of the Qur'ān. Applying the methods of Greek dialectic, the Ash'arites defeated the Mu'tazilites on their own ground. Briefly, their theology was as follows. God is eternal, without beginning and without end and without a likeness. He knows by knowledge, lives by life, wills by will, sees by sight, and speaks by His word. These attributes are eternal, inhere in His essence, are not He and not other than He, yet they do not detract from the unity of His essence. The Qur'ān is the speech of Allāh written in books, preserved in memories, recited by tongues, revealed to Muhammad. The speech of God is increate but the speech of Moses or other Prophets which God quotes in the Qur'ān is created. Man's pronouncing, writing, or reciting the Qur'ān is created, whereas the Qur'ān itself is uncreated.

Allāh created creatures free from unbelief and from belief. Then he gave them commandments and some disbelieved. Their denial was caused by Allāh's abandoning them. Allāh did not compel any of His creatures to be infidels or faithful. Fault and unbelief are acts of men. All the acts of man are truly his own acquisition, but Allāh creates them and they are caused by His will and His knowledge, His decision and His decree. As for anthropomorphism, God has face, hands, and soul; these belong to His qualities but it is not legitimate to inquire how.

In so far as any theology was written in medieval Muslim India—and only commentaries appear to be extant—it was largely Ash'arite in tone and content.

This is an appropriate place to add something briefly on philosophy in Islam, although there appears to have been no philosophical speculation in medieval Indian Islam. (Indeed, as will be evident from the extracts from Barnī there was sometimes active hostility to philosophy among Indian Muslims.) Translation of some of the works of Plato and Aristotle into Arabic stimulated speculation. Under the influence of Neo-Platonism and Aristotle and against the literal word of the Qur'ān, philosophers like Ibn Sīnā taught that the world was eternal, that God knew only universals (cf. the Platonic forms) and not particulars, and that there was no resurrection of the body. They asserted that it is impossible for the accustomed order of things, i.e., natural law, to be violated.

Hence philosophy was anathema to the orthodox and philosophers were often persecuted. Al-Ghazālī expressed the distaste of the orthodox in his *Incoherence of Philosophers* (*Tahāfut al-Falāsifa*), in which he showed that reason could be used to destroy reason and that the philosophers could not prove the ideas which Islam condemned. This book provoked the retort which marked the climax of philosophy in the Muslim world, *The Incoherence of Incoherence* (*Tahāfut al-Tahāfut*) by Ibn Rushd (Averroes), in which he disputes al-Ghazālī's arguments seriatim.

Interesting, from a modern standpoint, is Ibn Rushd's doctrine of nature. For Ibn Rushd the world is eternal, for everything comes into being out of something else. Becoming is the realization of potentiality, there is a causal connection between phenomena, and it is possible to formulate universal concepts which will express that nature of things, e.g. that fire burns wood because that is its nature. It is impossible here to develop Ibn Rushd's points in detail, but his practical defeat by al-Ghazālī may be important in explaining the failure of natural science in Islam to progress beyond a certain point. For the orthodox, fire burns wood because God creates inflammability in the wood when it comes into contact with the fire. Nature is not an order, it is a succession of individual Divine decrees. Space is a series of untouching atoms and time a succession of untouching moments. All change and action in the world is produced by God deciding to maintain or destroy these atoms. For example, God creates in man's mind the will to write; at the same moment He gives him the power to write and brings about the apparent motion of the hand, of the pen, and the appearance of the writing on the paper. No one of these is the cause of the other. God has brought about, by creation and annihilation of atoms, the requisite combinations to produce these appearances. Hence there is no idea of natural law. The universe is sustained by perpetual Divine intervention—in a sense, by a perpetual miracle.

THE LEGACY OF AL-GHAZĀLĪ

It was al-Ghazālī, however, who truncated philosophizing in Islam and who won an ascendancy in the Muslim world which ranks him as perhaps the greatest single force in Islam after the Prophet himself. Al-Ghazālī (1059–1111) had been brought up in an atmosphere of Sufi mysticism, but turned, before the age of twenty, to the study of theology and jurisprudence. Joining the service of the Seljuq wazir Nizām ul-Mulk, he was appointed to the Nizāmiya Madrasa[1] in Baghdad and was soon recognized as the greatest contemporary authority on theology and law. But he found no spiritual satisfaction in either. Reason merely destroyed reason; it proved nothing. Al-Ghazālī lost his faith and in his despair he could no longer teach. Finally he turned to Sufism and in mystical communion with God found peace and certainty. He abandoned his agnosticism in terror of the Divine Wrath and returned to belief in prophecy and the last judgment. After two years in Syria (1095–1097) in complete seclusion, followed by nine years in retreat, during which he wrote his great work, the *Revival of Religious Sciences* (*Ihyā' 'Ulūm al-Dīn*), in 1106 he returned under pressure from the Seljuq sultan to teaching at Nishapur. But he did not stay long in public life, returning to Tus where before his death in 1111 he had charge of a madrasa (mosque school) and a Sufi hospice.

Al-Ghazālī's *Revival of the Religious Sciences* is "a comprehensive statement of dogmatic moral ascetic and illuminative theology." He deposed jurisprudence and theology from the position they had held within Islam, teaching that the intellect should only be used to destroy trust in itself. Philosophy could not reach to the ultimate reality. Al-Ghazālī did not, however, reject dialectic; rather was he prepared, like al-Ash'arī, to use it in defense of traditional dogmas. For him the ultimate source of all knowledge was revelation from God, which reason may elucidate but cannot challenge. Hence he devoted himself to the study of tradition. After al-Ghazālī, the chief function of scholastic theology was defensive—to support and explain the doctrines of the Qur'ān and the Sunna—hence in India particularly the absence of any original theological works and the concentration on Qur'anic commentary and the study of the hadīth.

Al-Ghazālī recalled Muslims to obedience and devotion to God in their daily lives. A *faqīh,* or canon lawyer, second only to the founders of the four orthodox schools of jurisprudence and a moralist without peer in Islam, he presents in his *Revival of the Religious Sciences* the whole duty of man towards God and his fellows with the thoroughness of the ortho-

[1] A famous Muslim school in the Middle Ages.

dox schools of jurisprudence, and with the devotion of the mystic for whom the practice of duty is the cleansing of the spectacles through which the disciple catches a glimpse of God. Al-Ghazālī restored holiness to the Holy Law and law to holiness.

The creed which al-Ghazālī set forth in his *Revival of the Religious Sciences* was fundamentally that accepted by the Sunni ulamā in India and established as orthodox teaching. It is not possible to present that creed fully here, or to discuss its implications against the background of theological controversy which had raged up to his time. Nevertheless, the following represent perhaps the most essential doctrines as they were presented to the mass of the faithful and the newly converted in India:

1. God is One, without partners.
2. He is utterly transcendent, possessing no form and escaping all definition.
3. He is the Almighty Creator.
4. He knows and ordains everything that is.
5. God is all-powerful and in whatever he ordains, he cannot be unjust (that is, human concepts of justice and injustice cannot be applied to him).
6. The Qur'ān is eternal.
7. Obedience to God is binding upon man because He so decreed it through his prophets.
8. Belief in the Prophet's Divine mission is obligatory upon all.
9. Belief in the Day of Judgment is obligatory as revealed by the Prophet.
10. Belief in the excellence of the Prophet's Companions and the first four Caliphs is required by authentic tradition.

MUSLIM ORTHODOXY IN INDIA

It does not seem that any theological originality was shown by Indian Muslims in the medieval period; they sought merely to provide education in the principles of Islam. Dialectic, the study of the Qur'ān and of the Sunna, and the reiteration of the ways of witnessing outwardly to Islam, were three of the chief ways in which the ulamā in India performed this, their most important and most engrossing task. Commentaries upon commentaries upon commentaries were the typical religious literature of the time other than the mystical. The readings given are not intended to illustrate the entire range of even a single work of this class—an impossible task within the present compass—but rather to suggest the flavor of the whole. For each work quoted a number of others of its kind exists.

Piety: The Key to Paradise

This work on the goodly Muslim life was compiled not long after 1356 from various commentaries on the Qur'ān as well as from al-Ghazālī's *Revival of the Religious Sciences*. The author, Muhammad Mujīr Wajīb Adīb (dates unknown) was a disciple of the Sufi shaikh Nāsir ud-dīn Chirāgh of Delhi. The absence of tension between Sunni orthodoxy and Sufism in the fourteenth century is shown by the fact that the author quotes from the *Fawā'id ul-Fuwād* and the *Khair ul-Majālis*—records of the conversations of Sufi saints.

The *Key to Paradise* treats of the merit of repeating the formula, "There is no god but God," reading the Qur'ān, legal prayer, ablutions, fasting, almsgiving, honesty, slander, good manners, and supererogatory prayers. In reading the apparently simple teachings of *The Key to Paradise,* we should keep in mind the type of audience—Indian-born Muslims, perhaps not long converted—to which they are addressed.

[From Adīb, *Miftāh al-Jinān,* folios 4b, 9b–10, 13b, 14b, 20b–21a]

ON PRAISING GOD

It is related that the Prophet said that whoever says every day at daybreak in the name of God the Merciful and the Compassionate, "There is no god but God and Muhammad is His Prophet," him God Most High will honor with seven favors. First, He will open his spirit to Islam; second, He will soften the bitterness of death; third, He will illuminate his grave; fourth, He will show Munkar and Nakīr [1] his best aspects; fifth, He will give the list of his deeds with His right hand; sixth, He will tilt the balance of his account in his favor; and seventh, He will pass him over the eternal bridge which spans the fire of hell into Paradise like a flash of lightning. [folio 4b]

ON REMEMBERING GOD

It is reported that a man came to the Prophet and said, "O Prophet of God, the obligations of Islam are many. Advise me a little of what I

[1] The angels Munkar and Nakīr examined the dead and, if necessary, punished them in their tombs.

should do, in the letter and in the spirit." The Prophet said, "Keep your lips moist by repeating God's name." [folios 9b–10]

ON THE EXCELLENCE OF READING THE QUR'ĀN

In the illuminating commentary [of Fakhr ud-dīn al-Rāzī?] it is set down that the servant of God should make the Qur'ān his guide and his protection. On the Day of Judgment the Qur'ān will precede him and lead him toward Paradise. Whoever does not diligently stay close to the Qur'ān but lags behind, the angel will come forth and striking him on his side will carry him off to hell. . . .

It is reported in tradition that one's rank in Paradise depends upon the extent of one's recitation of the Qur'ān. They say that everyone who knows how to read a small amount of the Qur'ān will enjoy a high position in Paradise and they say that the more one knows how to read it, the higher one's status in Paradise. Utbā ibn 'Amr says that he heard the Prophet say, "Whoever reads the Qur'ān in secret is the same kind of person who gives alms in secret, and whoever reads the Qur'ān openly is like him who gives alms openly." The Prophet said that on the night of his ascent to heaven he was shown the sins of his people. He did not see any greater sin than that of him who did not know and did not read the Qur'ān. [folio 13b]

ON THE EXCELLENCE OF SAYING, "IN THE NAME OF GOD THE MERCIFUL, THE COMPASSIONATE"

It is reported in the *Salāt-i-Mas'ūdī* that Khwāja Imām Muhammad Taiyyar reported that on the morning of the Day of Resurrection, the people awaiting judgment will be deserving punishment. The angels will be hauling them up for punishment. They will say to young and old: "Come forth, you who were our followers in the world." Again they will say to the old weak ones: "You are the weak. It may be that God will have mercy on your weakness." Then they will go to the very edge of hell. When they say: "In the name of the merciful and compassionate God," the five-hundred-year-long fire of hell will avoid them. The Lord of Hell will address the fire: "Why do you not take them?" The fire will reply: "How can I take those who repeat the name of the Creator and remember Him as the Merciful and Compassionate?" God's voice will reach them, saying: "They are My servants and the fire is also My servant. He who honors My name, his name too I have held in higher esteem." On the blessings of saying: "In the name of the merciful and compassionate God," God said: "I have freed everyone in the name of God, the Merciful and the Compassionate." Therein are nineteen letters and the flames of hell are nineteen also. Every believer who repeats that rubric, to him God will give refuge from the nineteen flames of hell. [folio 14b]

ON THE MERIT OF SAYING ONE'S PRAYERS

The Prophet was sitting down with his Companions around him with Abū Bakr Siddīq [Caliph after Muhammad's death] sitting at his right hand. A young man came in; the Prophet gave instructions that he should sit nearer to him than Abū Bakr. The Companions began to think this young man was a man of the highest distinction. After the young man had left they questioned the Prophet about it; Muhammad looked toward Abū Bakr and said: "O, chief of the Companions, do not be uneasy that I bade that young man to sit higher up than you." Abū Bakr said: "O Prophet of God, what was there to say? I obeyed your command quite willingly." The Prophet said, "O, Abū Bakr, be in known unto you that this young man has sent me a harvest of such quantity as no one else has done." Abū Bakr said, "But, O Prophet of God, this young man's only occupation is that of being your disciple." The Prophet said, "He is busy with his own affairs, but every day he says his prayers once during the day and once at night. I give him a high place in our assembly because he says his prayers." [folios 20b–21a]

Theology: The Perfection of Faith

The next readings exemplify the use of reason and tradition in medieval Indian Islam to justify orthodox doctrines of God's transcendence and of His power over creation. They are taken from an exposition of Sunni doctrine called *The Perfection of Faith* by 'Abd ul-Haqq al-Dihlawī al-Bukhārī, who was born in Delhi in 1551 and died there in 1642. He was one of the most famous Sunni writers in Mughal India, winning the favor of the Emperor Jahāngīr. After performing the pilgrimage to Mecca about 1587 and studying in the Hijāz, he returned to teach for half a century in Delhi.

'Abd ul-Haqq was a prolific writer, composing biographies of the Prophet, of Indian Muslim saints, commentaries on the traditions of the Prophet, as well as a short history of India. His main contribution to Islam in India was the popularization of the study of Hadīth at a time when Sunni Islam was under the cloud raised by Akbar and the extreme mystical doctrines of Ibn 'Arabī.

The *Perfection of Faith* shows the dialectic used in orthodox theology in support of doctrines whose ultimate basis is divine revelation.

[From 'Abd ul-Haqq al-Dihlawī, *Takmīl ul-Īmān,* folios 2a–3b, 13–15]

THE ATTRIBUTES OF GOD

In truth, the creation and the proper ordering of the world will not come right except with one creator and one governor. . . . The Nourisher of the World is alive, is wise and powerful, and a free agent. Whatever He does is by His own intent and choice and not under compulsion and necessity. Without these attributes such a strange and wonderful world quite certainly would not appear or be conceivable. Such a world is not possible from a dead, ignorant, powerless, or unfree agent. These attributes [of life, wisdom, power and freedom] appear in created things. If they are not in God, from whence do they appear? He is a speaker of speech, a hearer of hearing, and a seer of seeing, because to be dumb, deaf, and blind is to be deficient and deficiencies are not proper to God. The Holy Qur'ān is eloquent as to that. It is impossible to comprehend the reality of these attributes, indeed of the totality of divine attributes by analogy and reason. But God has created a likeness of those in the essence of humankind, which he has interpenetrated in some way or other with His own attributes. But in truth, the attributes of man do not survive as God's attributes survive. "God's eternal attributes remain."

The attributes of God are eternal and are of equal duration with His essence.

Whatever He possesses—perfection and reality—is constant in eternity; because the location of accidents was created it does not become eternal. Except in a body there is neither limitation, cause, nor time; the creator of the world is not body and substance. That is to say, He is not a body and an attribute, that is to say, with the bodily qualities which the body has, like blackness and whiteness. He is not formed so that He has bodily shape and He is not compounded so that He is joined together repeatedly. He is not numbered so that it is possible to count Him. He is not limited so that He has a limit and He is not in a direction, that is to say, He is not above or below, before or after, left or right. He is not in a place and not in a moment, because all these are attributes of the world and the Nourisher of the World is not subject to worldly attributes and His purposes are not subject to time. Time does not include or circumscribe Him. His existence is not dependent upon time. For in that condition when there was not time, there was He. Now also there is time and He exists. Therefore, He is not in time. [folios 2b–3b]

THE TRANSCENDENCE OF GOD

Whatever exists, except God's essence and attributes, is created, that is to say, it comes into existence from nonexistence and is not eternal. As proof, the tradition of the Prophet, "There was God and there was nothing besides Him." As proof too, the world changes and is a place of many vicissitudes. Whatever is of this description is not eternal, and whatever is eternal does not change. We know that there is one real mode of existence—that of God's essence and attributes and there is no way for change in that mode. . . . And Almighty God is capable of extinguishing the world. After existence it passes away. As the Word of God says: "Everything perishes except the mode [Him]." Thus the angels, paradise, hell, and such like things to whose lastingness a tradition has testified, also are perishable. . . . Although God can annihilate in the twinkling of an eye, those who do not die will know that God is the creator of the world who has brought it into existence from nonexistence because, since the world is not eternal, the meaning of creation is that it was not and then it was. Whatever was of that order must have had a creator to bring it from nonexistence into existence because if it was created from itself it must always have been. Since it did not always exist, it was not created by itself but by another. The Nourisher of the World must be eternal. If He were not eternal He would be created. He would be of the world, not the self-existent Nourisher of the World. That is to say that the world's existence is by reason of its own essence and not by reason of something other than itself. But the world needs something other than itself and whatever needs something other than itself is not fit for lordship. The meaning of God's own words is future, that is, He Himself is coming into existence Himself. Certainly it must be that the end of the chain of existences is in one essence which is from itself. Otherwise it will continue in the same way endlessly and this is not reasonable. [folios 2a–2b]

FREE WILL

The next reading attempts to resolve the ethical problem posed by the doctrine of divine omnipotence. It should be noted that 'Abd ul-Haqq al-Dihlawī appeals to the Sharī'a for final illumination. This is typical of his approach to theological issues and evidence of the strong hold of the Holy Law upon the religious imagination of Muslims.

First it is necessary to understand the meaning of compulsion and choice so that the essence of this problem may become clear. Man's actions are of two kinds. One, when he conceives something, and, if that thing is desired by and is agreeable to his nature, a great desire and passion for it wells up from within him, and he follows that passion and moves after it. Or if the thing is contrary and repugnant to him, dislike and abhorrence for it wells up within him and he shuns it. His relation to the action and to stopping the action before the appearance of the desire and the loathing were on a par. It was possible that he might act or not act, whether at the stage of conception when the power to act was near, or before conceiving the idea when he was farther from acting. This motion of man is called an optional motion and the action which results from that motion is called an optional action. The other kind of action is when there is no conception, arousing of desire and wish, but motion occurs and then desire, like the trembling of a leaf. This motion is called compulsory and obligatory. If the meaning of desire and intention (as distinct from choice) is as stated, it may be objected: "Who says that man is not discerning and is not perspicacious? The creation of man occurred by choice, and such is the composition of his nature. Who says that all human motions and actions are compulsory? To say this is to deny virtue. No intelligent person will agree to this."

But there are difficulties in this conclusion. For, if, after comprehension and conversance with the eternal knowledge, intentions, decree, and ordination of God, it is conceived that it is not (really) man who brings actions into existence, that conclusion will be reached because it is realized that if God knew from all eternity that a particular action must be performed by a particular individual, that action must therefore be so performed, whether without that individual's choice, as in compulsory motion, or with his choice. If the action was optional (in form), the individual did not (really) have choice either in his decision or in his action. Furthermore, although the individual may have had choice in his action, yet he did not have any choice in its first beginnings.

For example, when an eye opens and does not see, there is no image before it. If after seeing and observing visible objects, they are desired, a rousing of passion and desire is compulsory and the existence of motion toward them is also obligatory. Thereafter, although this action occurs through the human being's choice, yet in fact this choice is obligatory and compulsory upon him. Obligation and necessity are contrary to the reality of choice. Man has choice but he has not choice in his choice; or to put it another way, he has choice in appearance, but in fact he is acting under compulsion. . . . Imām Ja'far Sādiq, who is a master of the people of the Sufi way and a chief of the people of Truth, says that there is no compulsion or freedom. But he lays down that the truth is to be found between compulsion and freedom. The Jabarites are those who say that fundamentally man has no choice and his motions are like those of inanimate nature. The Qadariya are those who say that man has choice and that man is independent in his transactions. His actions are his own creations. Imām Ja'far says that both these two schools of thought are false and go to extremes. The true school of thought is to be found between them but reason is at a loss and confounded in the comprehension of this middle way; in truth this confusion is found among people of a disputatious and contending sort who wish to found articles of faith upon reason, and who will not acknowledge anything as true and believe in it unless it pleases their reason and falls within their understanding. But for believers, the short proof of this is what is put forward in the Holy Law and the Qur'ān, in which it is written on this problem that God has both power and will and, notwithstanding that, He charges obedience and disobedience to His servants. And He says, God never commits injustice but men have inflicted injustice upon themselves. "God was not one to wrong them but they did wrong themselves."

In this verse He establishes two things. He has imputed creation to Himself and action to men. Therefore we must of necessity believe that both are true and must be believed—that creation is from God and action from man. Although we do not reach to the end of this problem and as the proof of the Holy Law and what is commanded and forbidden is itself a consequence of choice, then it is necessary to believe that. The problem of divine power and ordination and the problem of man's choice become known to us by the traditions of the right path [Sharī'a]. Since both are known from the Sharī'a, what is the controversy and the disputing about? One must believe in both. In this matter faith in the middle way is necessary. In truth, deep thought into this problem is among the indications of idleness and ignorance because no action and no truth is affected by controversy about it. One has to act. The real truth of the matter is that which is with God. [folios 13–15]

Propaganda: The Indian Proof

The *Indian Proof,* written during the reign of Jahāngīr by one Ibn 'Umar Mihrābī, avowedly aims at combating "creeping Hinduism" among Muslims living in villages far from the strongholds of Muslim culture, the towns and fortresses of the Ganges-Jumna River area. It is written in the form of a dialogue between a *sharāk* or species of talking bird who asks questions on cosmology and religion and a parrot who gives the Muslim answers. The dialogue is preceded by a mythical account of its origin. A young and accomplished Muslim falls in love with the daughter of a Mahratta raja and gives her the two talking birds whom he has made word perfect in theological discussion. The raja's daughter becomes a Muslim through listening to the two birds and has their conversation recorded in letters of gold. The golden text passes into the treasury of the Rai (prince) of Gujrat, Rai Karan, who has it interpreted to him by a young brahman secretly converted to Islam. On hearing the dialogue Rai Karan also becomes a Muslim. It is possible that the mythological form of the work is a response to the Hindu environment.

The *Indian Proof* shows clearly that the orthodox and the mystics in India were of the same faith, collaborators if not partners in the work of Muslim education. The parrot frequently quotes a Sufi work, the *Way of Eternity* (*Marsād ul-Abad*), written about 1223 by Najm ud-dīn Dāyah of Qaisariyah. Moreover, in the reading given below on the creation of the world, the *Indian Proof* expresses the doctrine of the Light of Muhammad, or the existence prior to creation of the soul of Muhammad in the form of light, from which God makes all things emanate when He decides that the universe shall be. This doctrine idealizing Muhammad is found among Sunnis, Shī'as, and mystics after the ninth century A.D. and does not necessarily impair the orthodox assertion of God's unity and transcendence. Its presence in the *Indian Proof,* however, underlines the unwisdom of forcing a cleavage between ulamā and mystics upon medieval Indian Islam.

[From Ibn 'Umar Mihrābī, *Hujjat ul-Hind,* folios 11b–13a]

The *sharāk* said: Please be kind enough to explain the manner of the coming into being of all creation and of everything which exists—mankind, the angels, jinns, devils, animals like wild beasts, birds, vegetation like trees and plants, the soul and the lower self of man and animals, the earth, mountains, seas, dry land and water, fire, wind, the skies, the world and the constellations, the signs of the zodiac, the mansions and the empyrean, the throne of God, the tablet, the pen, heaven, hell, the dwelling place in time and space of all these. Through your generous instruction it should become clear and known to everyone without doubt or obscurity what is the reality of each, in a way which explains its creation and reassures the heart and mind. And also, when you explain, do it so that all doubts disappear, reality is distinguishable from error and truth from falsehood.

The parrot answered: Know that the *Way of Eternity* (*Marsād ul-Abad*) gives an explanation of the beginning of created existences in this world and in heaven which has become the mode of existent things. If God wills, this explanation will be repeated. Now listen with your mind and from your heart to this other explanation. There is a difference between human souls and the pure soul of Muhammad the Prophet. As the prophets have said, he was the first thing God created. They called him a light and a spirit and he himself was the existence of existences, the fruit and the tree of created beings. As the tradition said, "But for you the heavens would not have been created"; for this, and no other, was the way in which creation began, like as a tree from whose seed spring the chief fruits of the tree. Then God Most High, when He wished to create created beings, first brought forth the light of Muhammad's soul from the ray of the light of His Unity as is reported in the Prophetic traditions. "I am from God and the believers are from me." In some traditions it is reported that God looked with a loving eye upon that light of Muhammad. Modesty overcame Him and the tears dropped from Him. From those drops He created the souls of the prophets. From those lights He created the souls of the saints, from their souls, the souls of believers, and from the souls of the believers He created the souls of the disobedient. From the souls of the disobedient He created the souls of hypocrites and infidels. From human souls He created the souls of the angels and from the rays of the souls of the angels He created the souls of jinns, and from their souls, devils. He created the different souls of animals according to their different kinds of ranks and states, all their descriptions of beings and souls—vegetation and minerals and compounds and elements He also brought forth.

To explain the remainder of creation; from the pearl [tear drop] which had remained, God created a jewel and looked upon that jewel with a majestic glance. With that awesome glance God melted that jewel and it became half water and half fire. Then He caused warm smoke to rise from the fire and the water and to be suspended in the air. From that came the seven heavens and from the sparks which were in the air with the smoke came forth the twinkling constellations. When He had brought forth the sun and the moon, the stars, the signs of the zodiac and the mansions of the moon from the leaping tongues of flame, He threw the wind and the water into confusion; foam appeared upon the surface and forth came the seven surfaces of the earth. Waves rose up and mountains emerged therefrom. From the remainder of the water God created the seas. He created the world in six days.

THE SHARĪ'A OR HOLY LAW OF ISLAM

Medieval Muslim society in word and deed aspired to discern and obey the pleasure of God. God was the only real object of knowledge; the understanding, however partial, of His purposes and the effort to fulfill them on earth, however feeble, was the whole duty of man. Man was thus created for worship and subjecthood, not for dominion over the world. In every thought, word, and action man was accountable to God on the Day of Judgment. Hence Muslim social ideals were not humanist ideals—the balanced and harmonious development of the human faculties or the creation of a man-conceived utopia on earth, for example. A New World for Muslims could only mean one in which they had discovered God's Will and were obeying it more fully than before.

Society was thought of, moreover, as a situation which human beings were forced to accept, rather than a relationship which might be transformed into a willing partnership for mutual companionship and welfare. It was an arithmetical total of human atoms each in geographical contiguity with the other, but significant only in relation to God.

The Muslim's individual relationship to God, however, was not stressed at the expense of social order. Belief in God and His Prophet implied acceptance of the Holy Law revealed through the Qur'ān and the Sunna of Muhammad. This Holy Law governed both doctrine and practice. It defined not merely right belief about God's Unity, His Power, and His Knowledge, but also those external acts of devotion—personal, e.g., prayer or pilgrimage, or social, e.g., almsgiving, avoidance of usury, maintenance of certain discriminations against the unbeliever—compliance with which attested one's membership in God's community before the eyes of the world. Muslim society was an organized society, though not, ideally, a humanly organized society. Its ethic was revealed to it by God, and its public life was to be informed by that revelation. Human institutions as the Muslims encountered them in their career of conquest fell into two types: they either did, or did not, conform to the will of God. If they did not, they had to be either transformed or destroyed. They could not be ignored. Nothing in life was irrelevant to the good life. Muslims were never at leisure in the sight of God. The Sharī'a or the Holy Law set the perfect standard for earthly society; it was the practical embodiment of the unity and the distinctive ideology of Islam.

As has been explained above, the Qur'ān and the Sunna of the Prophet were, after his death the two chief sources of guidance to the believer and hence of the Sharī'a. By the time of the Muslim conquest of North India, however, individuals were not permitted to investigate those sources for themselves. To later generations the knowledge of the Sharī'a is authoritatively communicated through the systems of jurisprudence worked out by the four orthodox schools of law. Jurisprudence is the science of deducing the mandates of the Sharī'a from its bases in the Qur'ān and Sunna, and in addition to the laws regulating ritual and religious observance, it embraces family law, the law of inheritance, property and contract, criminal law, constitutional law, and the conduct of war. From the Muslim viewpoint the ultimate obligation to obey regulations in any section of the Sharī'a is a religious one. They are all equally commands of Allāh. Moreover, according to the jurists, every human action falls into and may be evaluated in one or another of these five categories: commanded, recommended, legally indifferent, reprobated, or forbidden by God Himself.

According to orthodox theory, unambiguous commands or prohibitions in the Qur'ān or in the authenticated Sunna excluded the use of human reason and determination, except in so far as the resources of philology or lexicography were necessary to establish the literal sense of the text. However, when points of law or conduct not covered by a clear statement in the Qur'ān or the Sunna arose, recourse was had to argument from analogy (*qiyās*) or even to opinion (*ra'y*). Opinion, however, was rejected by the stricter sort, as introducing a fallible human element in a divine decision. It was in an academic fashion that the theologians and lawyers of the second and third centuries after Hijra developed the all-embracing regulations of the Sharī'a and created a body of jurisprudence unique in that it was the work of theorists rather than of practical men. In this they were encouraged by the 'Abbāsids, the self-proclaimed godly rulers who were determined, so they said, to abandon the ungodly ways of their Umayyad predecessors.

The whole structure was given rigidity and strength by the acceptance, in the second century Hijra, of what became the fourth basis of jurisprudence, the consensus (*ijmā'*) of the Muslim community. This was the real guarantee of the authenticity of the text of the Qur'ān, of the text of the Sunna, and of the acceptability of analogy; it was the real curb on heresy and innovation. Consensus became indeed a third channel of revelation. What the Muslim community was prepared to accept became Divine Law. When the community had attained a consensus, it was regarded as irrevocable; the formation and circulation of new doctrines and practices was in theory impossible, and, in practice, dangerous. Consensus fixed the limit between orthodoxy and heresy; to question an interpretation of Islam so arrived at was tantamount to heresy. However, consensus is not promulgated by any formal body and its existence is perceived only on looking back and seeing that agreement has tacitly been reached and then consciously accepting that tacit agreement. The spiritual mantle of Muhammad fell not upon a church and a priesthood but upon the whole community.

The chief prescriptions of the Sharī'a, founded on the four bases of the Qur'ān, Hadīth, analogy, and consensus as the "knowledge of the rights and duties whereby man may fitly conduct his life in this world and prepare himself for the future life," had been formulated by A.D. 1200. Muslims backed into their future facing the past. God's will for mankind had been revealed for men through His Prophet six hundred years ago, and since men had now worked out their understanding of that will, any impulse for change in the new environment of India would meet with tough resistance.

The good days were the good old days. The history of the world after the death of the Prophet, therefore, was a history of decadence and of retrogression, not of betterment and progresss. Change was *ipso facto* for the worse, and, therefore, to be avoided. If change did occur nevertheless, it would be disguised wherever possible as a return to the purer

Islam of seventh-century Arabia or, if not, it might be sanctified by consensus. It was certain, however, that it would not be sought or welcomed.

Through the Sharī'a Muslim society displayed and displays a deep sense of solidarity and a remarkable resilence under attack. Acceptance of the Sharī'a code of practical obligations distinguishes friend from foe. The Sharī'a itself lessens the risk of apostasy and indifference through ignorance of the practical demands made by religion upon the individual. By impressing upon Muslims that every action and social activity should be an act of worship and of humility before God, the Sharī'a nurtures the interior spiritual life while tilting the balance against the vagaries of individual religious intuition or individual speculation about the nature of God. Yet as al-Ghazālī's achievement suggests, there is room for wide variation of belief and practice within the ambit of the Holy Law. The principle of the consensus of the community has in practice permitted the tacit and peaceful acceptance of change. Muslims have usually been reluctant to extrude anyone from their society who subscribes at least to the simple basic testimony (*shahādat,* namely, "There is no god but God. Muhammad is the Prophet of God.") There has always been a hope of further education in the true Faith. This wide tolerance was to prove a major asset in the survival and the expansion of the Muslim community in India.

The Bases of Jurisprudence

A clear exposition of the bases of Muslim jurisprudence is given in the *Encyclopedia of the Sciences* by Fakhr ud-dīn al-Rāzī (1149–1209), a theologian and canon lawyer who lived for a time (c. 1185) in Ghaznīn and the Punjab under the patronage of the Ghōrid sultans, Ghiyath ud-dīn and Muhammad ibn Sām, who started the conquest of North India.

[From al-Razi, *Jāmi' ul-'Ulūm,* pp. 8–9]

The first basis is the knowledge of the evidences of the mandates of the Holy Law. These are four—God's book, the Sunna [custom and sayings] of the Prophet of God, the consensus of the community, and analogy. The explanation of the Qur'ān and the Sunna of the Prophet has been adduced. It is evident that when the Prophethood of Muhammad became acknowledged and the truth of what he said established, whatever he indicated by his practice and gave witness to as truth is right and true. Further the consensus of the community is established by the fact that God Most High said, "He who resists the Prophet after the right way has been made clear to him, we will cause him to suffer the fate he has earned. We shall cause him to burn in Hell. What an evil fate!" Since in the light of this verse it is forbidden and unlawful to follow other than the way of the believers, it follows that it is right and true to follow the way of the believers. Likewise, the Prophet said, "My community will not agree upon an error." [If a mistake had been possible in the consensus of the community, it would have been a deviation from the right path], for then the falseness of this tradition would necessarily follow and this is untrue. But what analogy proves is that the events and vicissitudes of life are infinite and the evidences are finite. To affirm the infinite by means of the finite is absurd; therefore it is evident that there is no avoiding analogy and the employment of one's own opinion [*ijtihād*].[1] Therefore it is evident that all the four sources are right and true. . . .

There are ten conditions of legal interpretation. The first is knowledge of God's Holy Book because it is a foundation of the knowledge of the mandates of the Sharīʿa. But it is not a necessary condition that there should be knowledge of the whole Book but only of those verses which are relevant to the mandates of the Holy Law—to wit, to the number of five hundred verses, and no more. It is necessary that these verses should be in the mujtahid's memory in such a way that when need of them arises it is possible to attain his object in the knowledge of one of the mandates of the Holy Law. The second condition is knowledge of the traditions of the Prophet. In the same way as in the knowledge of the word of God, where there was no need to know all, but only to remember some points, so it is with the traditions of the Prophet. Thirdly, it is a condition of legal interpretation that one should know the abrogating and the abrogated portions of the Qur'ān and of the Sunna, so that no error should occur in legal interpretation. Fourth, one should discriminate between the reason why a tradition is valid or invalid and discern the true from the false. Fifth, the interpreter of the law should be aware of the problems which have been resolved among the umma[2] because if he is

[1] A Muslim legist's interpretation of the Sharīʿa, an undertaking requiring deep scholarship and considerable ingenuity on the part of the interpreter (mujtahid), particularly if, as often, he wished to find justification in the Qur'ān and Sunna for some later custom.

[2] The Muslim community.

not aware of them he may deliver a formal legal opinion which is against the consensus of the community and this is not permissible. Sixth, knowledge of the manner of arranging Sharī'a evidence in a way which will bring forth a conclusion and distinguish truth from error in that conclusion. The interpreter of the law should know what are the occasions of error and how many there are, so that he may avoid them. The seventh is awareness of the fundamentals of the faith—knowledge of creation, of the unity of God, and of His freedom from sin and vice. The interpreter of the law should know that the Creator is eternal, knowing, and powerful. The eighth and ninth are that he should know lexicography and grammar to such an extent that by their means he can know the intentions of God and of the Prophet in the Qur'ān and the Traditions. The tenth condition is knowledge of the sciences of the bases of jurisprudence and comprehension of what is commanded and what is prohibited, the universal and the particular, the general and the special, abrogation of Qur'anic verses and the circumstances thereof, Qur'anic commentaries, and preferences and rulings and analogy.

Guidance in the Holy Law

The standard work expounding the principles of jurisprudence according to the predominant school of law in medieval Muslim India, the Hanafī, is the *Guidance* by Maulana Burhān ud-dīn Marghīnānī (d. 1197) of Transoxania. It is a digest or abstract of earlier Hanafī works and was itself the subject of several later commentaries in India. The *Guidance* commences with the compulsory religious duties (*'ibādat*) of ritual purification, prayer, alms, fasting, and pilgrimage. This exposition of religious duty precedes that of the principles of Muslim law relating among other things to marriage, adultery, fosterage, divorce, manumission of slaves, vows, punishments, larceny, holy war and the treatment of infidels, foundlings, treasure trove, loans, gifts, rules of evidence, prohibited liquors, offenses against the person, and wills. The readings given below from the *Guidance* are intended to show only the essentially religious grammar and idiom of Muslim law.

THE ALMS TAX

[From *Hidāya,* 1.1.1.2]

Alms-giving is an ordinance of God, incumbent upon every person who is free, sane, adult, and a Muslim, provided he be possessed, in full property, of such estate or effects as are termed in the language of the law a minimum, and that he has been in possession of the same for the space of one complete year. . . . The reason of this obligation is found in the word of God, who has ordained it in the Qur'ān, saying, "Bestow alms." The same injunction occurs in the traditions, and it is moreover universally admitted. The reason for freedom being a requisite condition is that this is essential to the complete possession of property. The reason why sanity of intellect and maturity of age are requisite conditions shall be hereafter demonstrated. The reason why the Muslim faith is made a condition is that the rendering of alms is an act of piety, and such cannot proceed from an infidel.

OF THE DISBURSEMENT OF ALMS, AND OF THE PERSONS TO WHOSE USE IT IS TO BE APPLIED

[From *Hidāya,* 1.1.7.53–54]

The objects of the disbursement of alms are of eight different descriptions: first, the needy; secondly, the destitute; thirdly, the collector of alms; . . . fourthly, slaves [upon whom alms are bestowed in order to enable them, by fulfilling their contract (i.e., by procuring their purchase price) to procure their freedom]; fifthly, debtors not possessed of property amounting to a legal minimum; sixthly, in the service of God; seventhly, travelers; and eighthly, the winning over of hearts. And those eight descriptions are the original objects of the expenditure of alms, being particularly specified as such in the Qur'ān; and there are, therefore, no other proper or legal objects of its application. With respect to the last, however, the law has ceased to operate, since the time of the Prophet, because he used to bestow alms upon them as a bribe or gratuity to prevent them from molesting the Muslims, and also to secure their occasional assistance; but when God gave strength to the faith, and to its followers, and rendered the Muslims independent of such assistance, the occasion of bestowing this gratuity upon them no longer remained; and all the doctors unite in this opinion. . . .

POLYGAMY

The Qur'anic influence on Muslim jurisprudence is illustrated in the following.

[From *Hidāya,* 1.2.1.88]

It is lawful for a freeman to marry four wives, whether free or slaves; but it is not lawful for him to marry more than four, because God has commanded in the Qur'ān, saying: "Ye may marry whatsoever women are agreeable to you, two, three, or four," and the numbers being thus expressly mentioned, any beyond what is there specified would be unlawful. Shāfi'ī alleges a man cannot lawfully marry more than one woman of the description of slaves, from his tenet as above recited, that "the marriage of freemen with slaves is allowable only from necessity"; the text already quoted is, however, in proof against him, since the term "women" applies equally to free women and to slaves.

TESTIMONY

The law relating to the inadmissibility of the testimony of nonbelievers and others is significant as it measures a man's "credit-worthiness" by his adherence to Muslim faith and rules of conduct.

[From *Hidāya,* 2.21.1.670–71; 2.21.2.690–91]

In all rights, whether of property or otherwise, the probity of the witness, and the use of the word *shahādat* [evidence] is requisite; even in the case of the evidence of women with respect to birth, and the like; and this is approved; because *shahādat* is testimony, since it possesses the property of being binding; whence it is that it is restricted to the place of jurisdiction; and also, that the witness is required to be free; and a Muslim. If, therefore, a witness should say: "I know," or "I know with certainty," without making use of the word *shahādat,* in that case his evidence cannot be admitted. With respect to the probity of the witness, it is indispensable, because of what is said in the Qur'ān: "Take the evidence of two just men." [2.21.1.670–71]

. . . .

The testimony of *zimmīs* [protected unbelievers] with respect to each other is admissible, notwithstanding they be of different religions. Mālik and Shāfi'ī have said that their evidence is absolutely inadmissible, because, as infidels are unjust, it is requisite to be slow in believing anything they may advance, God having said [in the Qur'ān]: "When an unjust person tells you anything, be slow in believing him"; whence it is that the evidence of an infidel is not admitted concerning a Muslim; and consequently, that an infidel stands [in this particular] in the same predicament with an apostate. The arguments of our doctors upon this point are twofold. First, it is related of the Prophet, that he permitted and held lawful the testimony of some Christians concerning others of their sect. Secondly, an infidel having power over himself, and his minor children, is on that account qualified to be a witness with regard to his own sect; and the depravity which proceeds from his faith is not destructive of this qualification, because he is supposed to abstain from everything prohibited in his own religion, and falsehood is prohibited in every religion. It is otherwise with respect to an apostate, as he possesses no power, either over his own person, or over that of another; and it is also otherwise with respect to a *zimmī* in relation to a Muslim, because a *zimmī* has no power over the person of a Muslim. Besides, a *zimmī* may be suspected of inventing falsehoods against a Muslim from the hatred he bears to him on account of the superiority of the Muslims over him. [2.21.2.690–91]

CHAPTER XV

THE MYSTICS

The majority of Muslims neither knew nor understood the theological formulations of their faith. For them life was bounded by the Sharī'a and by the round of mosque, pilgrimage, fasting, alms-giving, and ritual prayer. But many outside the comparatively small circle of scholars found this unsatisfying, particularly if, as often but not always, they were non-Arab converts with different religious traditions. They craved for a more emotional, indeed emotive religion, one in which God appeared as a loving, succoring Friend rather than as an abstract definition of undifferentiated unity incomprehensible in His Essence, inscrutable and arbitrary in His decrees. Moreover, as Islam grew to world power, the pious were scandalized at the compromises of political life and at the readiness of lawyers and theologians to accept service under "ungodly" rulers. Many withdrew into an ascetic seclusion, seeking to avoid the Divine Wrath on the Day of Judgment.

Many Muslims, therefore, found their thirst for God and for piety quenched in mysticism rather than in theology. The religious history of Islam after the twelfth century, particularly in those lands of the Eastern Caliphate which later came under the political dominance of the Turks and the Mongols, was largely that of the Sufi mystic movements and of the struggle of the ulamā to keep those movements within the Muslim fold. Although Islamic mysticism may have been stimulated by Christian, Gnostic, or Hindu mysticism, it already had a firm basis in the inspiration of the Qur'ān and in the early experience of the Prophet. His earlier revelations betray an intense consciousness of God as a living, everpresent reality. "We are nearer to him [man] than his jugular vein" (Qur'ān 50.15), and "Whenever ye turn there is the faith of God. Adore, and draw thou nigh" (96.19), or "He loveth them and they love Him" (5.59). It was this text which was particularly used by later Sufis to justify their attempts to lose themselves in the Divine Love.

Sufism was at the confluence of two streams of thought in Islam—the ascetic and the devotional. But by the second century after Hijra, the second had gained the upper hand. In many, the mystical element of love and adoration overcame the fear of the Day of Judgment. This victory is summed up in the sentence from al-Hasan al-Basrī (643–728): "I have not served God from fear of hell for I should be a wretched hireling if I served Him from fear; nor from love of heaven for I should be a bad servant if I served for what is given; I have served Him only for love of Him and desire for Him," or by the saying of the woman saint, Rabī'a al-Adawīya (d. 801): "Love of God hath so absorbed me that neither love nor hate of any other thing remain in my heart."

Before the second-century Hijra (A.D. 722–822) had ended, the Sufis had already worked out methods of attaining gnosis (*ma'rifat*) or mystic knowledge of God along a path (tarīqa) to ecstatic union with God or with one of His attributes, either by the indwelling of God in the man, or by the man's ascent to God. The true mystic was he who had cast off self and lost himself in God. The language of the Muslim Sufis during or after the moment of supreme mystical experience was often borrowed from that of inebriation or sexual love. A famous mystic, al-Hallāj, eventually, in 922, executed for heresy in Baghdad, "was so carried away by his ecstatic experience that he did not feel the dual nature of man, that is to say, his existence here as a single creature, and his rapture in mystical communion with the Divine. He taught that man was God incarnate and he looked to Jesus rather than to Muhammad as the supreme example of glorified humanity. God is love, and in His love, He created man after his own image so that man might find that image within himself and attain to union with the Divine Nature." Al-Hallāj expressed the intensity of the feeling of complete harmony with God in the following terms. "I am He whom I love and He whom I love is I. We are two spirits dwelling in one body. If thou seest me, thou seest Him, and if thou seest Him, thou seest us both."

The spiritual life which rises to this climax of insight was usually described as a journey passing through a number of stages. A typical mystic "road map" showed the following as milestones along the journey: repentance, abstinence, renunciation, poverty, patience, trust in God, satisfaction. Only when the Sufi has passed all these stages is he raised to the higher plane of consciousness (gnosis) and realizes that knowledge, knower, and known are one. Repentance is described as the awakening of the soul from the slumber of sin and heedlessness; abstinence and renunciation mean not merely the relinquishing of material pleasures but also the abandonment of all desire—even of the desire to abandon everything itself. Poverty meant the stripping away of every wish which could distract men's thoughts from God. Patience meant both patience in misfortune and patience to refrain from those things which God has forbidden to mankind. Trust in God betokened confidence in His grace toward the sinful pilgrim and satisfaction means for the pilgrim, eager acceptance of Divine decree. All these stages or stations (*maqāmāt*) were arrived at through the efforts of the pilgrim. The later part of the journey toward God was only made possible by the gift of God Himself. Indeed the light of intuitive certainty by which the heart sees God was a beam of God's Own Light cast therein by Himself. The two supreme states (*hāl*) were annihilation and subsistence. Annihilation (fanā) means a transformation of the soul through the utter extinction of all passion and desires, the contemplation of the Divine attributes, and the cessation of all conscious thought. Most Sufis were insistent that the individual human personality was not annihilated in this state. Some said that in this state the Sufi becomes like a drop of water in the ocean. Upon this follows subsistence (*baqā*) or abiding in God. This can mean either, or all, of three things—union with one of the activities symbolized by the names of God, union with one of the attributes of God, or union with the Divine Essence. When the Sufi has attained annihilation and subsistence, the veils of the flesh, of the will, and of the world have been torn aside, Truth is beheld and man is united to God. The wisest mystics, e.g., al-Ghazālī, recognized that this supreme experience could not be expressed in words; others ignored the limitation of language and scandalized the orthodox while often failing to communicate their own experience.

It is perhaps not surprising that Sufis should soon have come under suspicion from the orthodox theologians. Although early Sufis of the ascetic sort lived retired meditative lives, their claim to judge men and themselves by an inner light and to enjoy a direct personal relation to God could not but antagonize the ulamā, the doctors of a Sharī'a which claimed to regulate only outward conduct and who had no sure means of detecting hypocrisy. Although some early mystics were scrupulous in the observance of the Sharī'a, others were not recognizably within the Muslim fold at all. A friend of the philosopher Ibn Sīna, Abū Sa'īd ibn Abī'l Khair, a Persian mystic, wrote:

Not until every mosque beneath the sun,
Is ruined will our holy work be done,
And never will true Muslim appear,
Till faith and infidelity are one.

There was always the danger that, in the intensity of his personal religious experience, the Sufi would deny the value of the mandates of the Sharī'a. "The mystics learned from God, the ulamā from books." As al-Ghazālī was to ask: "In what do discussions on divorce and on buying and selling prepare the believer for the beyond?" Al-Wāsitī (d. 932) said: "Ritual acts are only impurities."

These dangerous antinomian tendencies were matched by dangerous pantheistic tendencies. It was difficult for orthodox scholars to stomach some of the expressions used by mystics in the moment of supreme insight and experience. Abū Yazīd al-Bistāmī (d. 875) cried: "Praise be to Me!"; al-Hallāj (d. 922): "I am the Truth. Is it Thou or is it I?"; Ibn Sahl Tustarī (d. 896): "I am the Proof of God, in face of the saints of my time"; Ibn Abī'l Khair: "Beneath my robe there is only God"; Ibn Sab'īn (d. 1269): "There is nothing but God." The famous Sufi teacher Muhyi' ud-dīn ibn al-'Arabī was a thorough monist. The one reality is God; the universe is His expression of Himself. The universe does not proceed from God by emanations but by manifestations; He makes himself known to Himself in everything. The mystic does not become one with God; he becomes conscious of his oneness with God. Clearly, in such a doctrine, Islam and other faiths are put on an equality. Everything (including infidels and infidelity) is for the best in the best of all possible worlds. The execution of al-Hallāj in 922 in Baghdad was a measure of the antagonism aroused among the lawyers and the dialecticians by such ideas as the above. Moreover under the 'Abbāsid Caliphs, Sufism was not popular with political authority. In the course of the third century after Hijra Sufism became popular among the artisan and minor trading classes of the cities of Iraq and Persia, uneducated in the traditional religious disciplines and sometimes the victims of the 'Abbāsid tax machine. Although Sufism was never a revolutionary movement politically, its call for a personal spiritual revival threw into sharp relief the worldliness of the ruling powers.

That orthodoxy was reconciled to mysticism within Islam was largely the achievement of the great theologian and mystic al-Ghazālī, who probably forestalled a schism in Islam. He was an Erasmus who was enough of a Luther to make a Luther unnecessary. In India, the measure of his success may be gauged by the absence of tension between the ulama and the mystics during the sultanate period. In Mughal times, however, partly because some of the Mughal rulers appeared positively to encourage unorthodoxy, antagonism broke out again.

Al-Ghazālī made the personal, emotional relation of the individual to God the core of popular Islam. Man's perfection and happiness consist in trying to imitate the qualities of God, in trying to do His Will. This Will he may discover from theology—but few are equipped to follow that severe discipline. Rather is he likely to discover the real attributes and purposes of God by mystical experience. In winning over Islam to this view, al-Ghazālī won for Sufism an abiding home in Muslim orthodoxy. In doing so, however, he pared away some of the more extreme forms of mystic expression. He refused to try to express what he himself had experienced. "To divulge the secrets of Lordship is unbelief." Al-Ghazālī held Sufism back from pantheism; at the moment of supreme illumination there is still a distinction between God and the mystic.

Al-Ghazālī's monumental exposition of Islam was accepted by consensus within a century of his death. The consequences for the Muslim world were second only perhaps to the deaths of Hasan and Husain at Karbala in 680. Many of the peoples in western Asia, particularly in the lands dominated by the Turks, were finally won over to orthodox Islam. Sufism henceforth became the most vital spiritual force in Islam with its exponents courted by princes as much as by the ordinary man. However, the victory of al-Ghazālī's synthesis altered the whole course of Muslim civilization. It opened the floodgates (and nowhere more so than in India later) to forms of religious belief and practice from which Muhammad himself would have recoiled. Principally these innovations meant the worship of saints in the teeth of the Qur'ān, tradition, and orthodox theology. Many Sufis cared little whether their practices and their teachings were in harmony with received Islamic doctrine. "Know that the principle and foundation of Sufism and knowledge of God rests on saintship," wrote al-Hujwīrī.

The victory of al-Ghazālī was followed by the invasion of Neo-Platonic and gnostic ideas into Sufism. The extreme expression of these ideas is found in Ibn 'Arabī, the Spaniard (1165–1240), in the doctrine of the Light of Muhammad. He taught that things emanate from divine prescience as ideas, and that the idea of Muhammad is the creative and rational principle of the universe. He is the Perfect Man in whom the Divine Light shines, the visible aspect of God. The aim of the Sufi should be to unite with, and in, the Perfect Man who unifies all phenomena into the manifestation of the real. The Perfect Man is "a copy of God." He is a cosmic power on which the universe depends for existence. Later, popular Islam was to attach this idea to the persons of famous mystics. At the head of the community stood prophets, and below them, saints who were the elect of the mystics. The saints formed an invisible hierarchy on which the order of the world depended. It was not surprising therefore that popular sentiment attributed miracles to the Sufi shaikhs or that after death their tombs became places of pilgrimage.

These ideas, and those of an earlier stage of Sufi belief and practice, became institutionalized in the century after al-Ghazālī's death in the great Sufi orders. Already al-Ghazālī had stated that the Sufi disciple must have recourse to a spiritual director for guidance. The novice was received into the fraternity by a ceremony of initiation. The head of the fraternity (shaikh or pīr, lit. elder) claimed the spiritual succession from the founder of the order and through him from the Prophet or 'Alī. The shaikh and his followers lived in a community endowed by supporters (who often included sultans) giving themselves up to spiritual exercises, meditation, and the attainment of mystical experience. In the twelfth century the Muslim world was covered by such retreats as a result of initiates going out from the parent retreat and founding satellite retreats linked to the parent by ties of reverence and common rituals. Membership in the orders was often very broad; it was of two kinds—a class of initiates (murīd) engaged in continual meditation or devotional exercises, and a larger number of "lay members" meeting to partake in "remembrance of God," but otherwise following their normal occupations. The total number of Sufi orders is (and was in the twelfth century) very great. The Muslim conquest of North India was contemporary with the introduction of some of these orders into India. There they were to dominate Muslim thought and social life, reaching out at times toward Hinduism.

SUFISM IN INDIA DURING THE SULTANATE PERIOD (c.1200–1500)

Muslim mysticism in India, like Muslim scholastic theology in India, entered the country in a well-developed form and did not greatly change its ideas (as opposed to its practices) in its new environment. The increasing influence of Ibn 'Arabī's pantheistic doctrines in Mughal times was due to a fresh immigration of Sufi orders new to India, rather than to changes in existing Indo-Muslim mystical schools of thought.

Between the end of the twelfth century and the end of the fifteenth, three great Sufi orders had migrated from Iraq and Persia into northern India, the Chishtī, the Suhrawardī, and the Firdausī. The first was the largest and most popular. Its "sphere of operations" was the area of the present Uttar Pradesh, where its great saints Nizām ud-dīn Auliyā (1238–1325) and Nasīr ud-dīn Muhammad Chirāgh of Delhi (d. 1356) lived and taught. Among its adherents were numbered some of the greatest luminaries of Indo-Muslim culture in the sultanate period—including Amīr Khusrau, the poet, and Ziā ud-dīn Barnī, the historian. The tombs of the mystic-saints of the order are still honored by both Hindus and Muslims. The Suhrawardī order was primarily confined to Sind. The Firdausī order could not establish itself in the Delhi area in face of the Chishtī order, and moved eastward to Bihar.

All these mystic orders were indebted for the theoretical expression of their ideas to a small number of "mystic textbooks" written in the eleventh and twelfth centuries, notably *The Unveiling of the Veiled* (*Kashf ul-Mahjūb*) by Shaikh 'Alī Hujwīrī, written partly at Lahore, the capital of the Punjab when annexed by Mahmūd of Ghaznin. In India no such systematic theoretical treatises were written, but to popularize Sufi teaching, disciples of great Sufi teachers recorded the sayings and discourses of their masters or wrote their biographies. Notable among the former is *The Morals of the Heart* (*Fawā'id ul-Fuwād*) by the poet Amīr Hasan Sijzī, a record of the conversations of Shaikh Nizām ud-dīn Auliyā in his retreat at Ghiyāspūr between A.D. 1307 and 1322. Another "Indian Sufi teachers' handbook" is the collection of letters (*Maktūbāt*) of Shaikh Sharaf ud-dīn Yahyā of Manīr, a mystic of the Firdausī order who flourished in Bihar toward the end of the fourteenth or the beginning of the fifteenth century. The letters were addressed to a disciple.

The readings will illustrate the following themes: the Sufi emphasis on the love for God as the principle of human existence on earth and their consequent unworldly attitude; the urge toward union with Him; the stages of the mystic path toward that union; the avoidance of pantheism and monism and the acceptance of the Sharī'a by the mystics of the sultanate period; and the role of the saints.

The Love of God

[From Shaikh 'Alī Hujwīrī, *Kashf ul-Mahjūb,* pp. 307–8]

Man's love toward God is a quality which manifests itself in the heart of the pious believer, in the form of veneration and magnification, so that he seeks to satisfy his Beloved and becomes impatient and restless in his desire for vision of Him, and cannot rest with anyone except Him, and grows familiar with the remembrance of Him, and abjures the remembrance of everything besides. Repose becomes unlawful to him and rest flees from him. He is cut off from all habits and associations, and renounces sensual passion and turns toward the court of love and submits to the law of love and knows God by His attributes of perfection. It is impossible that man's love of God should be similar in kind to the love of His creatures toward one another, for the former is desire to comprehend and attain the beloved object, while the latter is a property of bodies. The lovers of God are those who devote themselves to death in nearness to Him, not those who seek His nature because the seeker stands by himself, but he who devotes himself to death stands by his Beloved; and the truest lovers are they who would fain die thus, and are overpowered, because a phenomenal being has no means of approaching the Eternal save through the omnipotence of the Eternal. He who knows what is real love feels no more difficulties, and all his doubts depart.

Contemplation

[From Shaikh 'Alī Hujwīrī, *Kashf ul-Mahjūb,* pp. 329–31]

The Apostle said: "Make your bellies hungry and your livers thirsty and leave the world alone, that perchance you may see God with your hearts";

and he also said: "Worship God as though thou sawest Him, for if thou dost not see Him, yet He sees thee." God said to David: "Dost thou know what is knowledge of Me? It is the life of the heart in contemplation of Me." By "contemplation" the Sufis mean spiritual vision of God in public and private, without asking how or in what manner. . . .

There are really two kinds of contemplation. The former is the result of perfect faith, the latter of rapturous love, for in the rapture of love a man attains to such a degree that his whole being is absorbed in the thought of his Beloved and he sees nothing else. Muhammad b. Wasi' says: "I never saw anything without seeing God therein," i.e., through perfect faith. This vision is from God to His creatures. Shiblī says: "I never saw anything except God," i.e., in the rapture of love and the fervor of contemplation. One sees the act with his bodily eye and, as he looks, beholds the Agent from all things else, so that he sees only the Agent. The one method is demonstrative, the other is ecstatic. In the former case, a manifest proof is derived from the evidences of God; and in the latter case, the seer is enraptured and transported by desire; evidences and verities are a veil to him, because he who knows a thing does not reverence aught besides, and he who loves a thing does not regard aught besides, but renounces contention with God and interference with Him in His decrees and His acts. God hath said of the Apostle at the time of his Ascension: "His eyes did not swerve or transgress" (Qur'ān 53.17), on account of the intensity of his longing for God. When the lover turns his eye away from created things, he will inevitably see the Creator with his heart. God hath said: "Tell the believers to close their eyes" (Qur'ān 24.30), i.e., to close their bodily eyes to lusts and their spiritual eyes to created things. He who is most sincere in self-mortification is most firmly grounded in contemplation for inward contemplation is connected with outward mortification. Sahl b. 'Abdallāh of Tustar says: "If anyone shuts his eye to God for a single moment, he will never be rightly guided all his life long," because to regard other than God is to be handed over to other than God, and one who is left at the mercy of other than God is lost. Therefore the life of contemplatives is the time during which they enjoy contemplation: time spent in seeing ocularly they do not reckon as life, for that to them is really death. Thus, when Abū Yazīd was asked how old he was, he replied: "Four years." They said: "How can that be?" He answered: "I have been veiled [from God] by this world for seventy years, but I have seen Him during the last four years: the period in which one is veiled does not belong to one's life."

Seeking the Path

[From Shaikh Sharaf ud-dīn Maneri, *Maktūbāt-i-Sadi,* pp. 37–38]

The aspiration of the Seeker should be such that, if offered this world with its pleasures, the next with its heaven, and the Universe with its sufferings, he should leave the world and its pleasures for the profane, the next world and its heaven for the faithful, and choose the sufferings for himself. He turns from the lawful in order to avoid heaven, in the same way that common people turn from the unlawful to avoid hell. He seeks the Master and His Vision in the same way that worldly men seek ease and wealth. The latter seek increase in all their works; he seeks the One alone in all. If given anything, he gives it away; if not given, he is content.

The marks of the Seeker are as follows. He is happy if he does not get the desired object, so that he may be liberated from all bonds; he opposes the desire-nature so much that he would not gratify its craving, even if it cried therefor for seventy years; he is so harmonized with God that ease and uneasiness, a boon and a curse, admission and rejection, are the same to him; he is too resigned to beg for anything either from God or from the world; his asceticism keeps him as fully satisfied with his little all—a garment or a blanket—as others might be with the whole world. . . . He vigilantly melts his desire-nature in the furnace of asceticism and does not think of anything save the True One. He sees Him on the right and on the left, sitting and standing. Such a Seeker is called the Divine Seer. He attaches no importance to the sovereignty of earth or of heaven. His body becomes emaciated by devotional aspirations, while his heart is cheered with Divine Blessedness. Thoughts of wife and children, of this world and the next, do not occupy his heart. Though his body be on earth, his soul is with God. Though here, he has already been there, reached the Goal, and seen the Beloved with his inner eye.

This stage can be reached only under the protection of a perfect teacher, the Path safely trodden under his supervision only. . . . It is indispensable for a disciple to put off his desires and protests, and place himself before the teacher as a dead body before the washer of the dead, so that He may deal with him as He likes.

Renunciation

[From Shaikh Sharaf ud-dīn Maneri, *Maktūbāt-i-Sadi,* pp. 49–51, 78]

The first duty incumbent upon a Seeker is the practice of *Tajrīd* and *Tafrīd*. The one is to quit present possessions; the other, to cease to care for the morrow. The second duty is seclusion, outer and inner. Outer seclusion consists in flying from the world and turning thy face to the wall in order that thou mayest give up thy life on the Divine threshold; inner seclusion consists in cleansing the heart of all thoughts connected with the non-God, whether the non-God be earth or heaven. [p. 78]

. . . .

Intellect is a bondage; faith, the liberator. The disciple should be stripped naked of everything in the universe in order to gaze at the beauty of faith. But thou lovest thy personality, and canst not afford to put off the hat of self-esteem and exchange reputation for disgrace. . . .

All attachments have dropped from the masters. Their garment is pure of all material stain. Their hands are too short to seize anything tainted with impermanence. Light has shone in their hearts enabling them to see God. Absorbed in His vision are they, so that they look not to their individualities, exist not for their individualities, have forgotten their individualities in the ecstasy of His existence, and have become completely His. They speak, yet do not speak; hear, yet do not hear; move, yet do not move; sit, yet do not sit. There is no individual being in their being, no speech in their speech, no hearing in their hearing. Speakers, they are dumb; hearers, they are deaf. They care little for material conditions, and think of the True One alone. Worldly men are not aware of their whereabouts. Physically with men, they are internally with God. They are a boon to the universe—not to themselves, for they are not themselves. . . .

The knowledge that accentuates personality is verily a hindrance. The knowledge that leads to God is alone true knowledge. The learned are confined in the prison of the senses, since they but gather their knowledge through sensuous objects. He that is bound by sense-limitations is barred from supersensuous knowledge. Real knowledge wells up from the Fountain of Life, and the student thereof need not resort to senses and gropings. The iron of human nature must be put into the melting-pot of discipline, hammered on the anvil of asceticism, and then handed over to the polishing agency of the Divine Love, so that the latter may cleanse it of all material impurities. It then becomes a mirror capable of reflecting the spiritual world, and may fitly be used by the King for the beholding of His Own Image. [pp. 49–51]

THE QUEST FOR GOD THE BELOVED AND FOR KNOWLEDGE OF GOD

The quest for knowledge of God is usually described in terms of a journey or a road (tarīqa); the geography and the stages of the journey are given differently by different mystics but the mode of impulsion is the same. The Sufi must kill desire for the world, trust in God, submit to His will, and await patiently the inflowing of His Divine Grace before being able to proceed to final illumination—annihilation of the self and subsistence in God.

Repentance

[Adapted from Shaikh 'Alī Hujwīrī *Kashf ul-Mahjūb,* p. 294]

You must know that repentance is the first station of pilgrims on the way to the Truth, just as purification is the first step of those who desire to serve God. Hence God hath said: "O believers, repent unto God with a sincere repentence" (Qur'ān 66.8). And the Apostle said: "There is nothing that God loves more than a youth who repents"; and he also said: "He who repents of sin is even as one who has no sin"; then he added: "When God loves a man, sin shall not hurt him," i.e., he will not become an infidel on account of sin, and his faith will not be impaired. Etymologically *tawbat* [repentance] means "return," and repentance really involves the turning back from what God has forbidden through fear of what He has commanded. The Apostle said: "Penitence is the act of returning." This saying comprises three things which are involved in repentance, namely, 1) remorse for disobedience, 2) immediate abandonment of sin, and 3) determination not to sin again.

The Steps of a Disciple

[From Shaikh Sharaf ud-dīn Maneri, *Maktūbāt-i-Sadi,* pp. 60–61, 67–69]

The first step is holy law (Sharī'a). When the disciple has fully paid the demand of religion, and aspires to go beyond, the Path appears before him. It is the way to the heart. When he has fully observed the conditions of the Path, and aspires to soar higher, the veils of the heart are rent, and Truth shines therein. It is the way to the soul, and the goal of the seeker.

Broadly speaking, there are four stages: *Nāsūt, Malakūt, Jabarūt,* and *Lāhūt,* each leading to the next. *Nāsūt* is the animal nature, and functions through the five senses—e.g., eating, contacting, seeing, hearing, and the like. When the disciple controls the senses to the limit of bare necessity, and transcends the animal nature by purification and asceticism, he reaches *Malakūt,* the region of the angels. The duties of this stage are prayers to God. When he is not proud of these, he transcends this stage and reaches *Jabarūt,* the region of the soul. No one knows the soul but with the divine help; and truth, which is its mansion, baffles description and allusion. The duties of this stage are love, earnestness, joy, seeking, ecstasy, and insensibility. When the pilgrim transcends these by forgetting self altogether, he reaches *Lāhūt,* the unconditioned state. Here words fail.

Religion is for the desire-nature; the Path, for the heart; truth for the soul. Religion leads the desire-nature from *Nāsūt* to *Malakūt,* and transmutes it into heart. The Path leads the heart from *Malakūt* to *Jabarūt,* and transmutes it into soul. Truth leads the soul from *Jabarūt* to the divine sanctuary. The real work is to transmute the desire-nature into heart, the heart into soul, and to unify the three into one. "The lover, the Beloved and love are essentially *one.*" This is absolute monotheism. . . .

"The motive of the faithful is superior to their acts." Acts by themselves are of no value: the importance lies in the heart.

It is said that the traveler on the divine Path has three states: 1) action, 2) knowledge, 3) love. These three states are not experienced unless God wills it so. But one should work and wait. He will do verily what He has willed. He looks neither to the destruction nor to the salvation of anyone.

One who wishes to arrive at the truth must serve a teacher. No one can transcend the bondage and darkness of desires unless he, with the help of the Divine Grace, comes under the protection of a perfect and experienced teacher. As the teacher knows, he will teach the disciple according to his capacity, and will prescribe remedies suited to his ailments, so that "There is no God except Allāh" be firmly established in his nature, and the ingress of the evil spirits be cut off from his heart. All the world seeks to tread the divine Path. But each knows according to his inner purity, each seeks and aspires according to his knowledge, and each treads the Path according to his seeking and aspiration. [pp. 67–69]

. . . .

Khwāja Bāyazīd was asked: "What is the way of God?" He replied: "When thou hast vanished on the Way, then hast thou come to God." Mark this: If one attached to the Way cannot see God, how can one attached to self see God? [pp. 60–61]

The Final Stage

[From Shaikh Sharaf ud-dīn Maneri, *Maktūbāt-i-Sadi,* pp. 2–4]

The fourth stage consists in the pouring forth of the Divine Light so profusely that it absorbs all individual existences in the eyes of the pilgrim. As in the case of the absorption of particles floating in the atmosphere in the light of the sun, the particles become invisible—they do not cease to exist, nor do they become the sun, but they are inevitably lost to sight in the overpowering glare of the sun—so, here, a creature does not become God, nor does it cease to exist. Ceasing to exist is one thing, invisibility is another. . . . When thou lookest through a mirror, thou dost not see the mirror, for thou mergest into the reflection of thy face, and yet thou canst not say that the mirror has ceased to exist, or that it has become that reflection, or that the reflection has become the mirror. Such is the vision of the Divine Energy in all beings without distinction. This state is called by the Sufis absorption in monotheism. Many have lost their balance here: no one can pass through this forest without the help of the Divine Grace and the guidance of a teacher, perfect, open-eyed, experienced in the elevations and depressions of the Path and inured to its blessings and sufferings. . . . Some pilgrims attain to this lofty state only for an hour a week, some for an hour a day, some for two hours a day, some remain absorbed for the greater portion of their time. . . .

THE PRESERVATION OF GOD'S TRANSCENDENCE AT THE SUPREME STAGE OF MYSTIC EXPERIENCE

The avoidance of pantheistic doctrines by most Sufis of the Chishtī, Suhrawardī, and Firdausī orders is a significant feature of the religious history of Islam in India. The urge toward pantheism was very powerful. The Sufi might describe the moment of supreme insight in terms of complete annihilation of the self in God's being or he might develop the Muslim doctrine that God has no partners into the proposition that only God exists. Either way, the transcendence of God over the world disappears. The following readings illustrate how this heresy was avoided.

Subsistence and Annihilation

[From Shaikh 'Alī Hujwīrī, *Kashf ul-Mahjūb,* pp. 242–45, 246, 278–80]

You must know that annihilation (fanā) and subsistence (*baqā*) have one meaning in science and another meaning in mysticism, and that formalists are more puzzled by these words than by any other technical terms of the Sufis. Subsistence in its scientific and etymological acceptation is of three kinds: 1) a subsistence that begins and ends in annihilation, e.g., this world, which had a beginning and will have an end, and is now subsistent; 2) a subsistence that came into being and will never be annihilated, namely, Paradise and hell and the next world and its inhabitants; 3) a subsistence that always was and always will be, namely, the subsistence of God and His eternal attributes. Accordingly, knowledge of annihilation lies in your knowing that this world is perishable, and knowledge of subsistence lies in your knowledge that the next world is everlasting.

But the subsistence and annihilation of a state (*hāl*) denotes, for example, that when ignorance is annihilated knowledge is necessarily subsistent, and that when sin is annihilated piety is subsistent, and that when a man acquires knowledge of his piety his forgetfulness is annihilated by remembrance of God, i.e., when anyone gains knowledge of God and becomes subsistent in knowledge of Him he is annihilated from [entirely loses] ignorance of Him, and when he is annihilated from forgetfulness he becomes subsistent in remembrance of Him, and this involves the discarding of blameworthy attributes and the substitution of praiseworthy attributes. A different signification, however, is attached to the terms in question by the elect among the Sufis. They do not refer these expressions to knowledge or to state but apply them solely to the degree of perfection attained by the saints who have become free from the pains of mortification and have escaped from the prison of stations and the vicissitude of states, and whose search has ended in discovery, so that they have seen all things visible, and have heard all things audible, and have discovered all the secrets of the heart; and who, recognizing the imperfection of their own discovery, have turned away from all things and have purposely become annihilated in the object of desire, and in the very essence of desire have lost all desires of their own, for when a man becomes annihilated from his attributes he attains to perfect subsistence, he is neither near nor far, neither stranger nor intimate, neither sober nor intoxicated, neither separated nor united; he has no name, or sign, or brand, or mark.

In short, real annihilation from anything involves consciousness of its imperfection and absence of desire for it, not merely that a man should say, when he likes a thing: "I am subsistent therein," or when he dislikes it, that he should say: "I am annihilated therefrom"; for these qualities are characteristic of one who is still seeking. In annihilation there is no love or hate, and in subsistence there is no consciousness of union or separation. Some wrongly imagine that annihilation signifies loss of essence and destruction of personality, and that subsistence indicates the subsistence of God in man; both these notions are absurd. In India I had a dispute on this subject with a man who claimed to be versed in Qur'anic exegesis and theology. When I examined his pretensions I found that he knew nothing of annihilation and subsistence, and that he could not distinguish the eternal from the phenomenal. Many ignorant Sufis consider that total annilihation is possible, but this is a manifest error, for annihilation of the different parts of a material substance can never take place. I ask these ignorant and mistaken men: "What do you mean by this kind of annihilation?" If they answer: "Annihilation of substance," that is impossible; and if they answer; "Annihilation of attributes," that is only possible in so far as one attribute may be annihilated through the subsistence of another attribute, both attributes belonging to man; but it is absurd to suppose that anyone can subsist through the attributes of another individual. The Nestorians of Rūm [the Byzantine empire] and the Christians hold that Mary annihilated by self-mortification all the attributes of humanity and that the Divine subsistence became attached to her, so that she was made subsistent through the subsistence of God, and that Jesus was the result thereof, and that He was not originally composed of the stuff of humanity, because His subsistence is produced by realization of the subsistence of God; and that, in consequence of this, He and His Mother and God are all subsistent through one subsistence, which is eternal and an attribute of God. All this agrees with the doctrine of the anthropomorphistic sects of the Hashwiyya, who maintain that the Divine essence is a locus of phenomena and that the eternal may have phenomenal attributes. I ask all who proclaim such tenets: "What difference is there between the view that the eternal is the locus of the phenomenal and the view that the phenomenal is the locus of the eternal, or between the assertion that the eternal has phenomenal attributes and the assertion that the phenomenal has eternal attributes?" Such doctrines involve materialism and destroy the proof of the phenomenal nature of the universe, and compel us to say that both the Creator and His creation are eternal or that both are phenomenal, or that what is created may be commingled with what is uncreated, and that what is uncreated may descend into what is created. If, as they cannot help admitting, the creation is phenomenal, then their Creator also must be phenomenal, because the locus of a thing is like its substance; if the locus is phenomenal, it follows that the contents of the locus are phenomenal too. In fine, when one thing is linked and united and commingled with another, both things are in principle as one.

Accordingly, our subsistence and annihilation are attributes of ourselves, and resemble each other in respect of their being our attributes. Annihilation is the annihilation of one attribute through the subsistence of another attribute. One may speak, however, of an annihilation that is independent of subsistence, and also of a subsistence that is independent of annihilation: in that case annihilation means annihilation of all remembrance of other, and subsistence means subsistence of the remembrance of God. Whoever is annihilated from his own will subsists in the Will of God, because thy will is perishable and the Will of God is everlasting: when thou standest by thine own will thou standest by annihilation, but when thou art absolutely controlled by the Will of God thou standest by subsistence. Similarly, the power of fire transmutes to its own quality anything that falls into it, and surely the power of God's Will is greater than that of fire; but fire affects only the quality of iron without changing its substance, for iron can never become fire. [pp. 242–45]

Now I, 'Alī b. 'Uthmān al-Jullābī, declare that all these sayings are near to each other in meaning, although they differ in expression; and their real gist is this, that annihilation comes to a man through vision of the majesty of God and through the revelation of Divine omnipotence to his heart, so that in the overwhelming sense of His Majesty this world and the next world are obliterated from his mind, and "states" and "station" appear contemptible in the sight of his aspiring thought, and what is shown to him of miraculous grace vanishes into nothing: he becomes dead to reason and passion alike, dead even to annihilation itself; and in that annihilation of annihilation his tongue proclaims God, and his mind and body are humble and abased, as in the beginning when Adam's posterity were drawn forth from his loins without admixture of evil and took the pledge of servantship to God (Qur'ān 7.171). [p. 246]

. . . .

Unification is of three kinds: 1) God's unification of God, i.e., His knowledge of His unity; 2) God's unification of His creatures, i.e., His decree that a man shall pronounce Him to be one, and the creation of unification in his heart; 3) men's unification of God, i.e., their knowledge of the unity of God. Therefore, when a man knows God he can declare His unity and pronounce that He is one, incapable of union and separation, not admitting duality; that His unity is not a number so as to be made two by the predication of another number; that He is not finite so as to have six directions; that He has no space, and that He is not in space, so as to require the predication of space; that He is not an accident, so as to need a substance, nor a substance, which cannot exist without another like itself, nor a natural constitution (*tab'i*), in which motion and rest originate, nor a spirit so as to need a frame, nor a body so as to be composed of limbs; and that He does not become immanent (*hāl*) in things, for then He must be homogeneous with them; and that He is not joined to anything, for then that thing must be a part of Him; and that He is free from all imperfections and exalted above all defects; and that He has no like, so that He and His creature should make two; and that He has no child whose begetting would necessarily cause Him to be a stock (*asl*); and that His essence and attributes are unchangeable; and that He is endowed with those attributes of perfection which believers and Unitarians affirm, and which He has described Himself as possessing; and that He is exempt from those attributes which heretics arbitrarily impute to Him; and that He is living, knowing, forgiving, merciful, willing, powerful, hearing, seeing, speaking, and subsistent; and that His knowledge is not a state (*hāl*) in Him, nor His power solidly planted (*salābat*) in Him, nor His speech divided in Him; and that He together with His attributes exists from eternity; and that objects of cognition are not outside of His knowledge, and that entities are entirely dependent on His Will; and that He does that which He has willed, and wills that which He has known, and no creature has cognizance thereof; and that His decree is an absolute fact, and that His friends have no resource except resignation; and that He is the sole predestinator of good and evil, and the only being that is worthy of hope or fear; and that He creates all benefit and injury; and that He alone gives judgment, and His judgment is all wisdom; and that no one has any possibility of attaining unto Him; and that the inhabitants of Paradise shall behold Him; and that assimilation (*tashnīh*) is inadmissible; and that such terms as "confronting" and "seeing face to face" (*muqābalat u muwājahat*) cannot be applied to His being; and that His saints may enjoy the contemplation (*mushāhadat*) of Him in this world.

Those who do not acknowledge Him to be such are guilty of impiety. [pp. 278–80]

True Contemplation Is Ineffable

[From Shaikh 'Alī Hujwīrī, *Kashf ul-Mahjūb,* pp. 332–33]

Some Sufis have fallen into the mistake of supposing that spiritual vision and contemplation represent such an idea of God as is formed in the mind by the imagination either from memory or reflection. This is utter anthropomorphism and manifest error. God is not finite that the imagination should be able to define Him or that the intellect should comprehend His nature. Whatever can be imagined is homogeneous with the intellect, but God is not homogeneous with any genus, although in relation to the Eternal all phenomenal objects—subtle and gross alike—are homogeneous with each other notwithstanding their mutual contrariety. Therefore contemplation in this world resembles vision of God in the next world, and since the Companions of the Apostle are unanimously agreed that vision is possible hereafter, contemplation is possible here. Those who tell of contemplation either in this or the other world only say that it is possible, not that they have enjoyed or now enjoy it, because contemplation is an attribute of the heart and cannot be expressed by the tongue except metaphorically. Hence silence ranks higher than speech, for silence is a sign of contemplation, whereas speech is a sign of ocular testimony. Accordingly the Apostle, when he attained proximity to God, said: "I cannot tell Thy praise," because he was in contemplation, and contemplation in the degree of love is perfect unity and any outward expression in unity is otherness. Then he said: "Thou hast praised Thyself," i.e., Thy words are mine, and

Thy praise is mine, and I do not deem my tongue capable of expressing what I feel. As the poet says:

> I desired my beloved, but when I saw him
> I was dumbfounded and possessed neither tongue nor eye.

[From Shaikh Sharaf ud-dīn Maneri, *Maktūbāt-i-sadi,* p. 4]

Beyond the four is the stage of complete absorption, i.e., losing the very consciousness of being absorbed and of seeking after God—for such a consciousness still implies separation. Here, the soul merges itself and the universe into the Divine Light, and loses the consciousness of merging as well. "Merge into Him, this is monotheism: lose the sense of merging, this is unity." Here there are neither formulae nor ceremonies, neither being nor nonbeing, neither description nor allusion, neither heaven nor earth. It is this stage alone that unveils the mystery: "All are nonexistent save Him"; "All things are perishable save His Face"; "I am the True and the Holy One." Absolute unity without duality is realized here. "Do not be deluded; but know: everyone who merges in God is not God."

SUFI ACCEPTANCE OF ORTHODOX FORMALIST ISLAM

The Sufi orders whose adherents migrated to India before the end of the fifteenth century accepted the Islam of the Sharī'a as an essential precondition of true religion. They joined with the ulamā in teaching the simple observances of the faith to new Muslims, often in country areas outside the influence of the mosque or mosque school. The ulamā and Sufis were at peace in the house which al-Ghazālī had built—in different rooms perhaps but under the same roof.

Orthodox Practice and Spiritual Experience Both Necessary

[From Shaikh 'Alī Hujwīrī, *Kashf ul-Mahjūb,* pp. 13–15, 16]

The object of human knowledge should be to know God and His Commandments. Knowledge of "time" and of all outward and inward circumstances of which the due effect depends on "time" is incumbent upon everyone. This is of two sorts: primary and secondary. The external division of the primary class consists in making the Muslim's profession of faith; the internal division consists in the attainment of true cognition. The external division of the secondary class consists in the practice of devotion; the internal division consists in rendering one's intention sincere.

The outward and inward aspects cannot be divorced. The exoteric aspect of truth without the esoteric is hypocrisy, and the esoteric without the exoteric is heresy. So, with regard to the Law, mere formality is defective, while mere spirituality is vain.

The knowledge of the truth has three pillars: 1) Knowledge of the essence and unity of God; 2) Knowledge of the attributes of God; 3) Knowledge of the actions and wisdom of God.

The knowledge of the law also has three pillars: 1) The Qur'ān; 2) The Sunna; 3) The consensus of the Muslim community.

Knowledge of the divine essence involves recognition, on the part of one who is reasonable and has reached puberty, that God exists externally by His essence, that He is infinite and not bounded by space, that His essence is not the cause of evil, that none of His creatures is like unto Him, that He has neither wife nor child, and that He is the Creator and Sustainer of all that your imagination and intellect can conceive.

Knowledge of the divine attributes requires you to know that God has attributes existing in Himself, which are not He nor a part of Him, but exist in Him and subsist by Him, e.g., knowledge, power, life, will, hearing, sight, speech, etc.

Knowledge of the divine actions is your knowledge that God is the creator of mankind and of all their actions, that He brought the nonexistent universe into being, that He predestines good and evil and creates all that is beneficial and injurious.

Knowledge of the law involves your knowing that God has sent us Apostles with miracles of an extraordinary nature; that our Apostle, Muhammad (on whom be peace!), is a true messenger, who performed many miracles, and that whatever he has told us concerning the unseen and the visible is entirely true. [pp. 13–15]

Muhammad b. Fazl al-Balkhī says: "Knowledge is of three kinds—from God, with God, and of God." Knowledge of God is the science of gnosis whereby He is known to all His prophets and saints. It cannot be acquired by ordinary means, but is the result of divine guidance and information. Knowledge from God is the science of the Sacred Law, which He has commanded and made obligatory upon us. Knowledge with God is the science of the "stations" and the "Path" and the degrees of the saints. Gnosis is unsound without acceptance of the law, and the law is not practiced rightly unless the "stations" are manifested. [p. 16]

The Superiority of the Prophets Over the Saints

[From Shaikh 'Alī Hujwīrī, *Kashf ul-Mahjūb,* pp. 235–37]

You must know that, by universal consent of the Sufi shaikhs, the saints are at all times and in all circumstances subordinate to the prophets, whose missions they confirm. The prophets are superior to the saints, because the end of saintship is only the beginning of prophecy. Every prophet is a saint, but some saints are not prophets. The prophets are constantly exempt from the attributes of humanity, while the saints are so only temporarily; the fleeting state of the saint is the permanent station of the prophet; and that which to the saints is a station is to the prophets a veil. This view is held unanimously by the Sunni divines and the Sufi mystics, but it is opposed by a sect of the Hashwiyya—the Anthropomorphists of Khurasan—who discourse in a self-contradictory manner concerning the principles of unification, and who, although they do not know the fundamental doctrine of Sufism, call themselves saints. Saints they are indeed, but saints of the Devil. They maintain that the saints are superior to the prophets, and it is a sufficient proof of their error that they declare an ignoramus to be more excellent than Muhammad, the Chosen of God. The same vicious opinion is held by another sect of anthropomorphists, who pretend to be Sufis, and admit the doctrines of the incarnation of God and His descent [into the human body] by transmigration, and the division of His essence. I will treat fully of these matters when I give my promised account of the two reprobated sects [of Sufis]. The sects to which I am referring claim to be Muslims, but they agree with the Brahmans in denying special privileges to the prophets; and whoever believes in this doctrine becomes an infidel. Moreover, the prophets are propagandists and Imāms, and the saints are their followers, and it is absurd to suppose that the follower of an Imām is superior to the Imām himself. In short, the lives, experiences, and spiritual powers of all the saints together appear as nothing compared with one act of a true prophet, because the saints are seekers and pilgrims, whereas the prophets have arrived and have found and have returned with the command to preach and to convert the people. If anyone of the above-mentioned heretics should urge that an ambassador sent by a king is usually inferior to the person to whom he is sent, as, e.g., Gabriel is inferior to the apostles, and that this is against my argument, I reply that an ambassador sent to a single person should be inferior to him, but when an ambassador is sent to a large number of persons or to a people, he is superior to them, as the apostles are superior to the nations. Therefore one moment of the prophets is better than the whole life of the saints, because when the saints reach their goal they tell of contemplation and obtain release from the veil of humanity, although they are essentially men. On the other hand, contemplation is the first step of the apostle; and since the apostle's starting place is the saint's goal, they cannot be judged by the same standard.

The Morals of the Heart

The *Morals of the Heart* (*Fawā'id ul-Fuwād*), the "table-talk" of Shaikh Nizām ud-din Auliyā, is typical of the instruction in simple piety to which all Muslims could willingly assent.

[From Amīr Hasan Sijzī, *Fawā'id ul-Fuwād*]

ON REMEMBERING GOD

Then he [Shaikh Nizām ud-dīn] said: Once upon a time there was a great man who was called Mīra Kirāmī. A dervish wished to visit him. This dervish had the miraculous power whereby whatever he saw in a dream was correct, except for that dream which he had when the desire to see Mīra Kirāmī seized hold of him. He set out to the place where Mīra Kirāmī lived but along the way he halted for the night and fell asleep. In his dreams he heard that Mīra Kirāmī had died. When daybreak came he awoke and cried: "Alas! I have come so far to see him and he is dead. What shall I do? I will go on to the place where he was and lament at his burial place." When he reached the locality where Mīra Kirāmī lived, he began to ask everyone where Mīra Kirāmī's burial place was. They replied: "He is alive, why do you ask for his grave?" The dervish was astonished that his dream was untrue. Finally he went to see Mīra Kirāmī and greeted him. Mīra Kirāmī returned his greeting and said: "Your dream was correct as to its meaning; I am usually engaged in constant recollection of God. But on the night of your dream I was occupied otherwise; therefore the cry went forth to the world that Mīra Kirāmī had died." [conversation of the 19th Jamādī ul-Awwal, 708 after Hijra]

ON TRUST IN GOD

Talk turned to trust in God. Nizām ud-dīn said that trust has three degrees. The first is when a man obtains a pleader for his lawsuits and this pleader is both a learned person and a friend. Then the client believes: "I have a pleader who is both wise in presenting a suit and who is also my friend." In this instance there is both trust and a making of requests. The client says to his lawyer: "Answer this suit thus and bring this or that matter to such and such a conclusion." The first stage of trust is when there is both confidence in another and the giving of instructions to another.

The second degree of trust is that of a suckling whose mother is giving milk. Here there is confidence without question. The infant does not say: "Feed me at such and such times." It cries but does not demand its feed [in so many words]. It does not say, "Feed me." It does not say, "Give me milk." It has confidence in its heart in its mother's compassion.

But the third degree of trust is that of a corpse in the hands of a corpse washer. It does not make requests or change or make any motion or stay quiescent [of its own volition]. As the corpse washer decides, so he turns the corpse about—and so it goes. This is the third and highest degree of trust. [conversation of the 10th Rabī' ul-Ākhir, 710 after Hijra]

ON OBEDIENCE TO GOD

On Sunday, third Muharram 708 after Hijra, after paying respect to the shaikh, talk turned to obedience to God. Obedience to God is of two kinds, "intransitive" and "transitive." "Intransitive" obedience is that obedience whose benefits affect only the one person—for example, prayer, fasting, pilgrimage, and praising God. "Transitive" obedience is that whose benefits and comfort reaches another. Whatever kindness in companionship and compassion is shown toward others, they call "transitive" obedience. The rewards of this obedience are very great. There must be sincerity in "intransitive" obedience for it to be acceptable to God. But with "transitive" obedience, whatever one does is rewarded and acceptable to God. [conversation of the 3rd Muharram, 708 after Hijra]

ON GOING TO FRIDAY PRAYERS

A story was told that nonattendance at Friday prayers was being interpreted away [as not obligatory for a Muslim]. Shaikh Nizām ud-din said there is no such interpretation. Unless someone is a captive, on a journey, or ill, he who can go to Friday prayers and does not go has a very stubborn heart. Then he said, if a man does not go to one Friday congregational prayer, one black spot appears on his heart; if he misses two weeks' congregational prayer, then two black spots appear; and if he does not go three times in succession, his whole heart becomes black—which God forbid! [conversation of the 6th Zu'l Hijja, 719 after Hijra]

ON THE PLACE OF THE SUFI IN DAILY LIFE

Shaikh Nizām ud-dīn Auliyā said this on the real position to be adopted about abandoning the world. Abandoning the world is not stripping oneself naked, or sitting wearing only a langūta. Abandoning the world means wearing clothes and eating but not retaining what comes one's way, not acquiring anything or savoring anything, and not being attached to [worldly] things. [conversation of the 5th Shawwāl, 707 after Hijra]

CHAPTER XVI

RELIGIOUS TENSION UNDER THE MUGHALS

The religious unity of Islam in India suffered its greatest stresses during the century from A.D. c.1550 to 1650, the period of the establishment of Mughal rule and of its apogee. Many forces, some political and more religious, were conspiring to weaken the hold over Indian Muslims of Sunni orthodoxy and of "moderate" mysticism.

The Mughals were by ancestry, taste, and conviction seekers and eclectics in religion, characteristics which their political necessities and ambitions tended to confirm. The family of Chingis Khān are reported to have joined in Nestorian, Christian, Muslim, and Buddhist religious observances. Tīmūr showed greater respect to Sufi shaikhs than to the Sunni ulamā. Bābur and his son Humāyūn had been constrained to accept Shī'ism outwardly while negotiating for the support of the Persian Shī'ite Safavids. Moreover, during the sixteenth and seventeenth centuries, Shī'ism in India enjoyed political patronage. In the Deccan, Yūsuf 'Ādil Shāh of Bijapur (1489–1510) pronounced himself a Shī'a as did Burhān ud-dīn of Ahmadnagar and Qūlī Qutb Shāh of Golkonda. In North India, Bairam Khān, the guardian and minister of the young Akbar, was a Shī'a with a large Persian Shī'a following who settled down in India.

Furthermore, significant religious developments within the penumbra dividing Muslim from Hindu had softened religious acerbities in India. If from within Islam the mystic had appeared to reach out toward Hinduism, from within Hinduism, Kabīr (b. 1398), Nānak (b. 1469), and Chaitanya (b. 1485), with their condemnation of caste, Hindu rituals, and idolatry appeared to be reaching out toward Islam.

Important changes also occurred in the character of Muslim mysticism in India. New orders were introduced from Persia—the Shattārī, whose shaikh Muhammad Ghawth was Humāyūn's spiritual preceptor; the Qādirī, whose shaikh Mir Muhammad was tutor to the Mughal prince

Dārā Shikōh; and the Naqshbandī order, whose greatest luminary was Shaikh Ahmad of Sirhind. Members of the first two orders in particular were deeply influenced by the frankly pantheistic doctrines of the Spanish Muslim mystic Ibn 'Arabī (1164–1240); they observed few of the restraints in expression characteristic of the earlier Chishtī and Suhrawardī orders. What is more, their adherents were often intimately acquainted with Hindu mysticism.

None of these challenges to Sunni orthodoxy was exactly new; what was new was the political climate in India in which they had to be met. Under the Mughals, until Aurangzīb's time, the Sunni ulamā could not be confident of the exclusive support and patronage of the ruling power. Akbar came to an understanding with the Hindu Rajputs, who served to underpin his empire, and with policy reinforcing his own personal religious inclinations, set his face against Muslim militancy. The orthodox were scandalized not so much by the presence of un-Islamic ideas and practices in the Indian Muslim community as by the absence of political support in resisting them.

But resist they did, and, in the end successfully, though not without the help of a Sunni Mughal emperor, Aurangzīb (1658–1707). Readings have already been given from the works of a great traditionist of the Mughal period, 'Abd ul-Haqq al-Dihlawī. However, the greatest figure in the reaction against Akbar's and the mystics' religious syncretism was Shaikh Ahmad of Sirhind (1564–1624) who, arguing from within mystic experience itself against the pantheism of Ibn 'Arabī, recalled Muslims to a fresh realization of the religious value of traditional observance.

AKBAR'S RELIGIOUS OUTLOOK

Akbar, apparently by deliberate, mature choice, could neither read nor write; it is possible, therefore, only dimly to perceive his religious attitudes through the testimony of witnesses violently prejudiced either in his favor, as was Abū'l Fazl, his friend and confidant; or against him, as was the historian 'Abd ul-Qādir Badā'ūnī, his secret orthodox Sunni opponent, or partly through the testimony of the Jesuit fathers and of a Parsi student of religion, Muhsin-i-Fānī, who wrote half a century after Akbar's death.

As a boy in Kabul, Akbar had been open to Shī'a teachings and to the mysticism of the Persian poets. Although at the outset of his reign, however, his religious officials—the *sadr* ("minister for religious endowments") and the *qādīs* (religious judges)—were Sunni, Akbar himself visited Sufi retreats at Ajmir and Sikri. He seems to have been offended by the persecution of the Shī'a by his Sunni *sadr* and chief muftī (canon jurist) which grew violent about 1570. Meanwhile, in 1562, he had married a Hindu Rajput princess, Bihārī Mal of Amber, and had admitted Rajput princes, e.g., Rājā Mān Singh and Todar Mal, to high political and administrative office. After 1574 he was influenced by Abū'l Fazl and his brother Faizī, sons of Shaikh Mubārak Nāgōrī, and all students of Hinduism, indeed of "comparative religion." From this time, they led the discussions in the Hall of Worship which Akbar had built at Fathpur Sikri. These discussions, over which Akbar presided, were attended by Sunni ulamā, Sufi shaikhs, Hindu pundits, Parsees, Zoroastrians, Jains, and Catholic priests from Portuguese Goa. The mere fact of such discussions—in which apparently the Sunni ulamā did not shine—is the measure of the bias against orthodoxy at court. Akbar's personal religious searchings were followed by the Declaration (*Mahzar*) of 1579 that Akbar was accepted by the ulamā as the arbiter in religious disputes, by the enunciation of the "Divine Faith" (*Dīn-i-Ilāhī*), Akbar's own eclectic faith of 1582, and by a series of conciliatory gestures toward the Hindus. The Divine Faith, however, was accepted by only a small number of courtiers and was not enforced throughout the empire by political and administrative pressure.

Akbar ordered the translation of the *Atharva Veda,* the *Rāmāyaṇa,* and the *Mahābhārata.* According to Badā'ūnī he prohibited the killing of cows, refrained from eating meat on certain days and celebrated non-Islamic festivals. However, Akbar emphatically did not wish to destroy Islam in India, as Badā'ūnī implies. His quest for religious truth was that of an eclectic, not of a fanatic. Looking back, the consensus of the community appears to have pronounced against his activities, but this does not mean that they necessarily flouted the consensus at the time.

The following readings will illustrate Akbar's religious quest and the Divine Faith. The Declaration will be given in the next chapter on Muslim political thought.

The Discussion in the Hall of Worship

Readers must recall that the author of these passages is hostile to Akbar.

[Badā'ūnī, *Muntakhab ut-Tawārīkh,* II, 200–201, 255–61 *passim,* 324]

In the year nine hundred and eighty-three the buildings of the 'Ibādat-khāna were completed. The cause was this. For many years previously the emperor had gained in succession remarkable and decisive victories. The empire had grown in extent from day to day; everything turned out well, and no opponent was left in the whole world. His Majesty had thus leisure to come into nearer contact with ascetics and the disciples of his reverence [the late] Mu'īn, and passed much of his time in discussing the Word of God and the word of the Prophet. Questions of Sufism, scientific discussions, inquiries into philosophy and law, were the order of the day. [II, 200–201]

. . . .

And later that day the emperor came to Fathpūr. There he used to spend much time in the Hall of Worship in the company of learned men and shaikhs and especially on Friday nights, when he would sit up there the whole night continually occupied in discussing questions of religion, whether fundamental or collateral. The learned men used to draw the sword of the tongue on the battlefield of mutual contradiction and opposition, and the antagonism of the sects reached such a pitch that they would call one another fools and heretics. The controversies used to pass beyond the differences of Sunni, and Shī'a, of Hanafī and Shāfi'ī, of lawyer and divine, and they would attack the very bases of belief. And Makhdūm-ul-Mulk wrote a treatise to the effect that Shaikh 'Abd-al-Nabī had unjustly killed Khizr Khān Sarwānī, who had been suspected of blaspheming the Prophet [peace be upon him!], and Mīr Habsh, who had been suspected of being a Shī'a, and saying that it was not right to repeat the prayers after him, because he was undutiful toward his father, and was himself afflicted with hemorrhoids. Shaikh 'Abd-al-Nabī replied to him that he was a fool and a heretic. Then the mullās [Muslim theologians] became divided into two parties, and one party took one side and one the other, and became very Jews and Egyptians for hatred of each other. And persons of novel and whimsical opinions, in accordance with their pernicious ideas and vain doubts, coming out of ambush, decked the false in the garb of the true, and wrong in the dress of right, and cast the emperor, who was possessed of an excellent disposition, and was an earnest searcher after truth, but very ignorant and a mere tyro, and used to the company of infidels and base persons, into perplexity, till doubt was heaped upon doubt, and he lost all definite aim, and the straight wall of the clear law and of firm religion was broken down, so that after five or six years not a trace of Islam was left in him: and everything was turned topsy-turvy. . . .

And Samanas [Hindu or Buddhist ascetics] and Brahmans (who as far as the matter of private interviews is concerned gained the advantage over every one in attaining the honor of interviews with His Majesty, and in associating with him, and were in every way superior in reputation to all learned and trained men for their treatises on morals, and on physical and religious sciences, and in religious ecstasies, and stages of spiritual progress and human perfections) brought forward proofs, based on reason and traditional testimony, for the truth of their own, and the fallacy of our religion, and inculcated their doctrine with such firmness and assurance, that they affirmed mere imaginations as though they were self-evident facts, the truth of which the doubts of the sceptic could no more shake "Than the mountains crumble, and the heavens be cleft!" And the Resurrection, and Judgment, and other details and traditions, of which the Prophet was the repository, he laid all aside. And he made his courtiers continually listen to those revilings and attacks against our pure and easy, bright and holy faith. . . .

Some time before this a Brahman, named Puruk'hotam, who had written a commentary on the Book, *Increase of Wisdom* (*Khirad-afzā*), had had private interviews with him, and he had asked him to invent particular Sanskrit names for all things in existence. And at one time a Brahman, named Debi, who was one of the interpreters of the *Mahābhārata,* was pulled up the wall of the castle sitting on a bedstead till he arrived near a balcony, which the emperor had made his bed-chamber. Whilst thus suspended he instructed His Majesty in the secrets and legends of Hinduism, in the manner of worshiping idols, the fire, the sun and stars, and of revering the chief gods of these unbelievers, such as Brahma, Mahadev [Shiva], Bishn [Vishnu], Kishn [Krishna], Ram, and Mahama (whose existence as sons of the human race is a supposition, but whose nonexistence is a certainty, though in their idle belief they look on some of them as gods, and some as angels). His Majesty, on hearing further how much the people of the country prized their institutions, began to look upon them with affection. . . .

Sometimes again it was Shaikh Tāj ud-dīn whom he sent for. This shaikh was son of Shaikh Zakarīya of Ajodhan. . . . He had been a pupil of Rashīd Shaikh Zamān of Panipat, author of a commentary on the *Paths* (*Lawā'ih*), and of other excellent works, was most excellent in Sufism, and in the knowledge of theology second only to Shaikh Ibn 'Arabī and had written a comprehensive commentary on the *Joy of the Souls* (*Nuzhat ul-Arwāh*). Like the preceding he was drawn up the wall of the castle in a blanket, and His Majesty listened the whole night to his Sufic obscenities and follies. The shaikh, since he did not in any great degree feel himself bound by the injunctions of the law, introduced arguments concerning the unity of existence, such as idle Sufis discuss, and which eventually lead to license and open heresy. . . .

Learned monks also from Europe, who are called *Padre,* and have an infallible head, called *Papa,* who is able to change religious ordinances as he may deem advisable for the moment, and to whose authority kings must submit, brought the Gospel, and advanced proofs for the Trinity. His Majesty firmly believed in the truth of the Christian religion, and wishing to spread the doctrines of Jesus, ordered Prince Murād to take a few lessons in Christianity under good auspices, and charged Abū'l Fazl to translate the Gospel. . . .

Fire worshipers also came from Nousarī in Gujarat, proclaimed the religion of Zardusht [Zarathustra] as the true one, and declared reverence to fire to be superior to every other kind of worship. They also attracted the emperor's regard, and taught him the peculiar terms, the ordinances, the rites and ceremonies of the Kaianians [a pre-Muslim Persian dynasty]. At last he ordered that the sacred fire should be made over to the charge of Abū'l Fazl, and that after the manner of the kings of Persia, in whose temples blazed perpetual fires, he should take care it was never extinguished night or day, for that it is one of the signs of God, and one light from His lights. . . .

His Majesty also called some of the yogis, and gave them at night private interviews, inquiring into abstract truths; their articles of faith; their occupation; the influence of pensiveness; their several practices and usages; the power of being absent from the body; or into alchemy, physiognomy, and the power of omnipresence of the soul. [II, 255–261 *passim,* 324]

Note in the next readings the condemnation of prophethood by a philosopher at Akbar's court, which is said to have gone uncensured.

[From Muhsin-i-Fānī, *Dabistān-i-Mazāhib,* III, 78–81]

But the greatest injury comprehended in a prophetic mission is the obligation to submit to one like ourselves of the human species, who is subject to the incidental distempers and imperfections of mankind; and who nevertheless controls others with severity, in eating, drinking, and in all their other possessions, and drives them about like brutes, in every direction which he pleases; who declares every follower's wife he desires legal for himself and forbidden to the husband; who takes to himself nine wives, whilst he allows no more than four to his followers, and even of these wives he takes whichever he pleases for himself; and who grants impunity for shedding blood to whomsoever he chooses. On account of what excellency, on account of what science, is it necessary to follow that man's command; and what proof is there by his simple word? His word, because it is only a word, has no claim of superiority over the words of others. Nor is it possible to know which of the sayings be correctly his own, on account of the multiplicity of contradictions in the professions of faith. If he be a prophet on the strength of miracles, then the deference to it is very dependent; because a miracle is not firmly established, and rests only upon tradition or a demon's romances. . . .

But if it be said that every intellect has not the power of comprehending the sublime precepts, but that the bounty of the Almighty God created degrees of reason and a particular order of spirits, so that he blessed a few of the number with superior sagacity; and that the merciful light of lights, by diffusion and guidance, exalted the prophets even above these intellects —If it be so, then a prophet is of little service to men; for he gives instruction which they do not understand, or which their reason does not approve. Then the prophet will propagate his doctrine by the sword; he says to the inferiors: "My words are above your understanding, and your study will not comprehend them." To the intelligent he says: "My faith is above the mode of reason." Thus, his religion suits neither the ignorant nor the wise.

The Divine Faith

The Divine Faith was Sufi in conception, with ceremonial expressions borrowed from Zoroastrianism. It was strictly monotheistic and incorporated Shī'ite ideas of the role of the mujtahid or interpreter of the faith. In brief, it appears to owe more to Islam than to Hinduism. Unfortunately the beliefs and practices of the Divine Faith are nowhere comprehensively stated. They have to be pieced together from Abū'l Fazl's *Institutes of Akbar* (*Ā'īn-i-Akbarī*), Badā'-ūnī's *Selected Histories* (*Muntakhab ut-Tawārīkh*) and Muhsin-i-Fānī's *School of Religions* (*Dabistān-i-Mazāhib*).

THE DIVINE FAITH'S MONOTHEISM

[From Muhsin-i-Fānī, *Dabistān-i-Mazāhib,* III, 74–75]

Know for certain that the perfect prophet and learned apostle, the possessor of fame, Akbar, that is, the lord of wisdom, directs us to acknowledge that the self-existent being is the wisest teacher, and ordains the creatures with absolute power, so that the intelligent among them may be able to understand his precepts; and as reason renders it evident that the world has a Creator, all-mighty and all-wise, who has diffused upon the field of events among the servants, subject to vicissitudes, numerous and various benefits which are worthy of praise and thanksgiving; therefore, according to the lights of our reason, let us investigate the mysteries of his creation, and, according to our knowledge, pour out the praises of his benefits.

THE DIVINE FAITH'S SUFI PIETY

[From Muhsin-i-Fānī, *Dabistān-i-Mazāhib,* III, 82–84]

In the sequel it became evident to wise men that emancipation is to be obtained only by the knowledge of truth conformably with the precepts of the perfect prophet, the perfect lord of fame, Akbar, "the Wise"; the practices enjoined by him are: renouncing and abandoning the world; refraining from lust, sensuality, entertainment, slaughter of what possesses life; and from appropriating to one's self the riches of other men; abstaining from women, deceit, false accusation, oppression, intimidation, foolishness, and giving [to others] opprobrious titles. The endeavors for the recompense of the other world, and the forms of the true religion may be comprised in ten virtues, namely, 1) liberality and beneficence; 2) forbearance from bad actions and repulsion of anger with mildness; 3) abstinence from worldly desires; 4) care of freedom from the bonds of the worldly existence and violence, as well as accumulating previous stores for the future real and perpetual world; 5) piety, wisdom, and devotion, with frequent meditations on the consequences of actions; 6) strength of dexterous prudence in the desire of sublime actions; 7) soft voice, gentle words, and pleasing speeches for everybody; 8) good society with brothers, so that their will may have the precedence to our own; 9) a perfect alienation from the creatures, and a perfect attachment to the supreme Being; 10) purification of the soul by the yearning after God the all-just, and the union with the merciful Lord, in such a manner that, as long as the soul dwells in the body, it may think itself one with him and long to join him, until the hour of separation from the body arrives.

THE INFLUENCE OF ZOROASTRIANISM

[From Badā'ūnī, *Muntakhab ut-Tawārīkh,* II, 322]

A second order was given that the sun should be worshiped four times a day, in the morning and evening, and at noon and midnight. His Majesty had also one thousand and one Sanskrit names for the sun collected, and read them daily at noon, devoutly turning toward the sun; he then used to get hold of both ears, and turning himself quickly round about, used to strike the lower ends of his ears with his fists. He also adopted several other practices connected with sun-worship.

DĀRĀ SHIKŌH AND PANTHEISM

Akbar's mantle as a religious seeker fell not on his son Jahāngīr or his grandson Shāh Jahān, but on his great-grandson Dārā Shikōh (1615–1659). Dārā Shikōh addressed himself, with perhaps more enthusiasm than insight, to the study of Hindu philosophy and mystical practices. This was the more congenial because he himself was a follower of the Qādirī order of Sufis in the persons of Miān Mīrzā (d. 1635) and Mullā Shāh Badakhshānī (d. 1661).

Dārā Shikōh is important from the present standpoint because he symbolizes the major danger threatening the religious integrity of Islam in India, a mingling of the two seas of Muslim mystical pantheism and Hindu pantheism to batter down the defenses of orthodoxy. He symbolized but did not intend that threat; he himself would have rejected a charge of heresy or unbelief. The widespread Sufi acceptance of Ibn 'Arabī's mystical philosophy and their interest in Hindu mysticism should be condemned as infidelity if Dārā Shikōh is to be condemned for infidelity. However, the subsequent consensus of the Muslim community was that Dārā Shikōh's activities were dangerous to it and there is a strong presumption that Aurangzīb's political instincts were finely tuned to strong waves of Muslim sentiment when, after the war of succession, for his own ambitious purposes he had Dārā Shikōh condemned as a heretic and executed.

The readings which follow are intended to illustrate first the pantheistic tendency in Dārā Shikōh's thought—tendency, not fulfillment, for he appears to stop short of asserting the complete absorption of the mystic in God's essence—and second his efforts to find common ground between Hindu and Muslim.

The Mystic Path

[From Dārā Shikōh, *Risāla-yi-Haqq-Numā,* pp. 24, 26]

Here is the secret of unity (tawhīd), O friend, understand it;
Nowhere exists anything but God.
All that you see or know other than Him,
Verily is separate in name, but in essence one with God.

. . . .

Like an ocean is the essence of the Supreme Self,
Like forms in water are all souls and objects;
The ocean heaving and stirring within,
Transforms itself into drops, waves and bubbles. [p. 24]

So long as it does not realize its separation from the ocean,
The drop remains a drop:
So long he does not know himself to be the Creator,
The created remains a created.

. . . .

O you, in quest of God, you seek Him everywhere,
You verily are the God, not apart from Him!
Already in the midst of the boundless ocean,
Your quest resembles the search of a drop for the ocean! [p. 26]

[From Dārā Shikōh, *Hasanat ul-'Ārifīn,* p. 16]

Dost thou wish to enter the circle of men of illumination?
Then cease talking and be in the "state";

By professing the unity of God, thou canst not become a monotheist,
As the tongue cannot taste sugar by only uttering its name.

[From JRASB, Vol. V, No. 1, p. 168]

Paradise is there where no mullā exists—
Where the noise of his discussions and debate is not heard.

May the world become free from the noise of mullā,
And none should pay any heed to his decrees!

In the city where a mullā resides,
No wise man ever stays.

The Upanishads: God's Most Perfect Revelation

The following is taken from Dārā Shikōh's translation of fifty-two Upanishads, completed in 1657. He uses the third person in referring to himself.

[From Hasrat, *Dārā Shikōh,* pp. 260–68]

Praised be the Being, that one among whose eternal secrets is the dot in the [letter] ب of the bismallāh in all the heavenly books, and glorified be the mother of books. In the holy Qur'ān is the token of His glorious name; and the angels and the heavenly books and the prophets and the saints are all comprehended in this name. And be the blessings of the Almighty upon the best of His creatures, Muhammad, and upon all his children and upon his companions universally!

To proceed; whereas this unsolicitous faqīr [a religious mendicant], Muhammad Dārā Shikōh in the year 1050 after Hijra [A.D. 1640] went to Kashmir, the resemblance of paradise, and by the grace of God and the favor of the Infinite, he there obtained the auspicious opportunity of meeting the most perfect of the perfects, the flower of the gnostics, the tutor of the tutors, the sage of the sages, the guide of the guides, the unitarian accomplished in the Truth, Mullā Shāh, on whom be the peace of God.

And whereas, he was impressed with a longing to behold the gnostics of every sect, and to hear the lofty expressions of monotheism, and had cast his eyes upon many books of mysticism and had written a number of treatises thereon, and as the thirst of investigation for unity, which is a boundless ocean, became every moment increased, subtle doubts came into his mind for which he had no possibility of solution, except by the word of the Lord and the direction of the Infinite. And whereas the holy Qur'ān is mostly allegorical, and at the present day, persons thoroughly conversant with the subtleties thereof are very rare, he became desirous of bringing in view all the heavenly books, for the very words of God themselves are their own commentary; and what might be in one book compendious, in another might be found diffusive, and from the detail of one, the conciseness of the other might become comprehensible. He had, therefore, cast his eyes on the Book of Moses, the Gospels, the Psalms, and other scriptures, but the explanation of monotheism in them also was compendious and enigmatical, and from the slovenly translations which selfish persons had made, their purport was not intelligible.

Thereafter he considered, as to why the discussion about monotheism is so conspicuous in India, and why the Indian theologians and mystics of the ancient school do not disavow the Unity of God nor do they find any fault with the unitarians, but their belief is perfect in this respect; on the other hand, the ignoramuses of the present age—the highwaymen in the path of God—who have established themselves for erudites and who, falling into the traces of polemics and molestation, and apostatizing through disavowal of the true proficients in God and monotheism, display resistance against all the words of unitarianism, which are most evident from the glorious Qur'ān and the authentic traditions of indubitable prophecy.

And after verifications of these circumstances, it appeared that among this most ancient people, of all their heavenly books, which are the *Ṛig Veda,* the *Yajur Veda,* the *Sama Veda,* and the *Atharva Veda,* together with a number of ordinances, descended upon the prophets of those times, the most ancient of whom was Brahman or Adam, on whom be the peace of God, this purport is manifest from these books. And it can also be ascertained from the holy Qur'ān, that there is no nation without a prophet and without a revealed scripture, for it hath been said: "Nor do We chastise until We raise an apostle" (Qur'ān 17.15). And in another verse: "And there is not a people but a warner has gone among them" (Qur'ān 35.24). And at another place: "Certainly We sent Our apostles with clear arguments, and sent down with them the Book and the measure" (Qur'ān 57.25).

And the *summum bonum* of these four books, which contain all the secrets of the Path and the contemplative exercises of pure monotheism, are called the *Upaneḳhats* [*Upanishads*], and the people of that time have written commentaries with complete and diffusive interpretations thereon; and being still understood as the best part of their religious worship, they are always studied. And whereas this unsolicitous seeker after the Truth had in view the principle of the fundamental unity of the personality and not Arabic, Syriac, Hebrew, and Sanskrit languages, he wanted to make without any worldly motive, in a clear style, an exact and literal translation of the *Upanekhat* into Persian. For it is a treasure of monotheism and there are few thoroughly conversant with it even among the Indians. Thereby he also wanted to solve the mystery which underlies their efforts to conceal it from the Muslims.

And as at this period the city of Banares, which is the center of the sciences of this community, was in certain relations with this seeker of the Truth, he assembled together the pandits [Hindu scholars] and the sannyasis [Hindu ascetics or monks], who were the most learned of their time and proficient in the *Upanekhat* . . . in the year 1067 after Hijra; and thus every difficulty and every sublime topic which he had desired or thought and had looked for and not found, he obtained from these essences of the most ancient books, and without doubt or suspicion, these books are first of all heavenly books in point of time, and the source and the fountainhead of the ocean of unity, in conformity with the holy Qur'ān.

Happy is he, who having abandoned the prejudices of vile selfishness, sincerely and with the grace of God, renouncing all partiality, shall study and comprehend this translation entitled *The Great Secret* (*Sirr-i-Akbar*), knowing it to be a translation of the words of God. He shall become imperishable, fearless, unsolicitous, and eternally liberated.

THE REACTION AGAINST PANTHEISTIC MYSTICISM

The leader of the religious opposition to pantheistic mysticism and to neglect of the Sharī'a was Shaikh Ahmad Sirhindī al-Mujaddid-i-Alf-i-Thānī (the Renewer of Islam at the Beginning of the Second Muslim Millennium). Born at Sirhind in the East Punjab in 1564, he frequented the society of Abū'l Fazl and his brother Faizī at Agra. In 1599 he was initiated into the Naqshbandī order of mystics. He incurred the displeasure of Jahāngīr for his unbending opposition to the Shī'a who were powerful at court, but was restored to favor before his death in 1624.

Shaikh Ahmad Sirhindī's great achievement was paradoxically to win Indian Islam away from Sufi extremism by means of mysticism itself. Perhaps his success was due to deep personal understanding of the meaning and value of what he rejected. To explain briefly: the mystical school of Ibn 'Arabī holds that Being is one; is Allāh, and that everything is His manifestation or emanation. God is neither transcendent nor immanent. He is All. Creation is only God's yearning to know Himself by expressing Himself. At the end of the mystic path (fanā) the mystic knows himself to be Himself. God's essence and His attributes (e.g., individual Sufi seekers) are One.

Shaikh Ahmad of Sirhind replied that Ibn 'Arabī and his school were merely talking of the mystic stage of annihilation (fanā) and that this is not the final stage of reality. At the stage of annihilation the mystic is *ipso facto* absorbed in the being of God and utterly oblivious to anything other than God. Ibn 'Arabī is confusing the subjective with the objective. In fact, says Shaikh Ahmad, Ibn 'Arabī must still be aware of the world in order to identify it with God, otherwise he would have talked only of God. Shaikh Ahmad argues that beyond annihilation is a state which, he says, Ibn 'Arabī did not reach, in which the mystic experiences the truth that God is beyond comprehension through intuition. Hence man must revert to revelation and to the religious sciences based on revelation, in other words to the Sharī'a of the ulamā. Shaikh Ahmad insists that the only relation between God and the world is that of Creator and created and all talk of union or identity is heresy born of subjective mystic misconceptions.

These views Shaikh Ahmad propagated in his *Letters* (*Maktūbāt*), written to his disciples and others. About five hundred and thirty in all, they form a great classic of Indo-Muslim religious literature.

Mystic Union With God Is Only Subjective

[From Shaikh Ahmad Sirhindi, *Maktubat,* folios 52–53b]

The divine unity which Sufis encounter on their way is of two kinds, "unity of experience" (*tauhīd-i-shuhūdī*) and "unity of existence" (*tauhīd-i-wujūdī*). "Unity of experience" is seeing only one thing, that is to say, the traveler on the mystic path witnesses only oneness. "Unity of existence" is considering that only one thing exists and conceiving all else as nonexistent, believing that nonexistence is a mere reverse and antithesis [logically] of that one existence. "Unity of existence" is of the order of positive knowledge and "unity of experience" is of the order of absolutely certain knowledge. "Unity of experience" is among the necessary stages of the mystic path because annihilation of the self is not established without this oneness and without that real insight is not possible.

The overwhelming power of the vision of the unity of God is such that it is impossible to see what is beyond the state of annihilation of the self (fanā). Contrary to that is the "unity of existence"; . . . There is nothing in the heart which shall cause the denial of knowledge of what is beyond at the time of attaining knowledge of the unity of God. For example, when someone obtains a certain knowledge of the existence of the sun, the attainment of that knowledge does not cause him to think that the stars do not also exist at the same time. But at the time when he saw the sun he will certainly not see the stars, what he has witnessed will only be the sun. At the time when he does not see the stars, he knows that the stars are not nonexistent; indeed he knows they exist, but are hidden and overcome by the brilliance of the sun. This person is in a position to contradict those who deny the existence of the stars for he knows it was only that the knowledge of their existence had not yet been attained by him. Then the doctrine of unity of existence, which is the denial of everything except the Self of the Divine, is at war with both reason and the Sharī'a in contradistinction to unity of experience in which in its visualizing of unity no opposition to them occurs. For example, at the time of sunrise to deny the existence of the stars is to deny fact. At the same time when the stars are not seen, there is no opposition; rather their invisibility is due to the superiority of the light of the sun; if one's vision becomes so powerful as not to be affected by the light of the sun, the stars will be seen separately from the sun. This power of vision is possible in the "station" of absolute truth.

Thus the statements of some shaikhs who are apparently opposed to the True Way, and lead some men toward the doctrine of unity of existence as, for example, Abū Mansūr al-Hallāj in his statement, "I am God," and Abū Yazīd Bistāmī, "Praise be to Me!" and such like. It is proper that people must be led toward "unity of experience" and that opposition to that doctrine be repelled. Whenever what is other than God Most High was hidden to them, they uttered those phrases in the grip of ecstasy and they did not affirm anything but God. The meaning of "I am the Truth" is that He is the Truth, not "I" [al-Hallāj]; since he does not see himself he [al-Hallāj] does not establish that it is he who sees himself and he calls what he sees God. This is unbelief. Here no one may speak because not to affirm a thing is not [necessarily] to deny its existence and this is exactly what "unity of existence" does. For I say that to affirm nothing is not to deny anything. Indeed at this stage on the mystic path there is utter amazement [at the Glory of God] and all commands become ineffective.

And in "Praise be to Me!" the holiness of God is meant, not the holiness of the mystic, because God has become completely raised beyond the mystic's sight. . . . Some mystics do not give vent to such expressions in the state of real certainty, which is a state of amazement. When they pass beyond this stage and arrive at absolute certainty, they avoid such expressions altogether and do not transgress proper bounds.

In these times, many of those who claim to live as Sufis have propagated "unity of existence" and do not know anything beyond that; they have remained behind in real knowledge and have reduced the statements of the shaikhs to meanings of their own imagining and have held them up as guides for their own generation making current their own wicked secrets by means of these conceptions. If there are expressions in the statements of some of these shaikhs which lead to unity of existence, they must be attacked. . . .

The Sharī'a Is the True Religious Way

[From Shaikh Ahmad Sirhindī, *Maktūbāt,* folios 46a–b]

The Prophet says that there are three parts to the Sharī'a, knowledge, action, and sincere belief. Until these three parts are verified the Sharī'a is not verified. When the Sharī'a is verified God's satisfaction is obtained and this is superior to all else, "May God Most High be satisfied with all of them!" Therefore the Sharī'a is a guarantee of all these blessings and there is no purpose in seeking anything beyond the Sharī'a. The Way and the Truth, which for the Sufis have become distinct, both are servants of the Sharī'a. On the perfection of the third part of the Sharī'a which is sincere belief—the aim in acquiring the first two parts of the Sharī'a is the perfection of the Sharī'a and not anything else. The states and stations and gnosis which happen to the Sufi along his way are not among the purposes of the Sharī'a. The imaginings, the ideas, and the dark thoughts of the novice of the Way, having passed beyond all these must reach the stage of acquiescence in God, the end of the stages of the pilgrims of the mystic path and the object of the greatest desire. Unfortunately, the aim of passing beyond the stages of the Way to the reality beyond is not just to obtain that sincere belief which is the real cause of acquiescence in God. . . . Short-sighted people count the attainment of the various states and stages of the mystic path among their aims and consider the appearance of God and His manifestations among the things to be most desired. In the end, they remain imprisoned in their thoughts and in their imaginings and deprive themselves of the perfections of the Sharī'a.

Revelation and Inspiration Reconciled

[From Shaikh Ahmad Sirhindī, *Maktūbāt,* folios 50–51b]

The Prophet of God is the beloved of God; everything which is good and desired is for the sake of the beloved of God. As God has said in the holy Qur'ān, "No doubt your conduct and character is the best," and, "You are without doubt among the prophets and on the right path," and, "This is the only right path that you follow, and you do not follow the wrong path." His people have called him the straight road and what is outside his way of life is forbidden. As the Prophet has said, "Thanks should be given that the Prophet has shown a right path for the people." He also said that inner belief perfects outward observance and that there is not a hair-breadth of contradiction between the two. For example, not to tell lies is Sharī'a and to condemn lying thoughts in the heart is the Way (tarīqa) and inner reality (*haqīqat*). If this condemnation is possible but with hesitation and great effort, it is the Way and if it comes about without great hesitation it is inner reality. Then in truth, interior belief, which is both the Way and the Truth, is shown forth; this is the Sharī'a. When the travelers who follow the way of reproach encounter anything which is openly at war with the Sharī'a and adopt it, they fall victim to intoxication and are overcome by the mystic state (*hāl*). If they pass beyond that stage and return to sobriety, opposition to the Sharī'a is completely removed and destroyed.

For example, a group of the intoxicated limit their imagination to themselves and consider the Person of God to be encompassed by the world. This view is opposed to the opinion of the orthodox ulamā. They assert the way of (traditional) knowledge. Whenever, despite the fact that the Person of God is unlimited by any categorical mandates, and despite the fact that to inject something into the Person of God is to oppose the clear statement that He is ineffable and inscrutable, the Sufis assert that His Person is limitrophe with the world, then indeed they dwell in confusion, folly, and mere ignorance. What has God to do with the injection of human ideas and limitations into His Person? The Sufis must give the excuse that their intention is to understand the first manifestation of God and that when they see that manifestation they do not know it for what it is, and they interpret it as God Himself. . . .

The Person of God Most High is most nearly understood by the orthodox ulamā when they say that He is ineffable and incomparable and that whatever is beyond Him is something additional to that manifestation. If that manifestation of Him is proved it will be known that it is beyond the bounds of His essence and it will not be said that the limits of that manifestation are the limits of God's essence. Thus the viewpoint of the ulamā is more lofty than the viewpoint of the Sufis. The Person of God according to the Sufis is in fact implied in the essence of God according to the orthodox ulamā. Nearness and association with the Person of God and the agreement of interior knowledge with the sciences of the Sharī'a is perfect and complete. . . .

The station of truth is higher than the station of saintship; higher than that still is the station of prophethood and the knowledge which came by inspiration and by revelation to the holy Prophet. Between knowledge by revelation and knowledge by inspiration there is only a difference of process. . . . Revelation is clear cut and inspiration, opinion. For revelation is through the medium of angels and angels are innocent; there is no imputation of error to them.

Although inspiration has a high religious status and is of the heart, and the heart is of the Divine Order, nevertheless, it is connected with the reason and the lower self and however much one is on guard against the lower self, it never rises beyond its own qualities. The ability to err finds a home in it. But one must know that the survival of the qualities of the lower self and its contentment is a benefit and an advantage. If the lower self is completely forbidden from manifesting its qualities, the way of moral and spiritual development is obstructed. The soul would attain the rank of an angel and it would be imprisoned. Its progress is by means of opposition between it and the lower self. If no opposition remains how shall development occur?

Against Rulers Misled by Wicked Ulamā

[From Shaikh Ahmad Sirhindī, *Maktūbāt,* folios 58b–59b]

The sultan in relation to the world is like the soul in relation to the body. If the soul is healthy, the body is healthy, and if the soul is sick, the body is sick. The integrity of the ruler means the integrity of the world; his corruption, the corruption of the world. It is known what has befallen the people of Islam. Notwithstanding the presence of Islam in a foreign land, the infirmity of the Muslim community in previous generations did not go beyond the point where the Muslims followed their religion and the unbelievers followed theirs. As the Qur'ān says, "For you, your way, for me, my way." . . .

In the previous generation, in the very sight of men, unbelievers turned to the way of domination, the rites of unbelief prevailed in the abode of Islam, and Muslims were too weak to show forth the mandates of the faith. If they did, they were killed. Crying aloud their troubles to Muhammad, the beloved of God, those who believed in him lived in ignominy and disgrace; those who denied him enjoyed the prestige and respect due to Muslims, and with their feather brains condoled with Islam. The disobedient and those who denied Muhammad used to rub the salt of derision and scorn into the wounds of the faithful. The sun of guidance was hidden behind the veil of error and the light of truth was shut out and obscured behind the curtain of absurdity.

Today, when the good tidings of the downfall of what was prohibiting Islam [i.e., the death of Akbar] and the accession of the king of Islam [i.e., Jahāngīr] is reaching every corner, the community of the faithful have made it their duty to be the helpers and assistants of the ruler and to take as their guide the spreading of the Holy Law and the strengthening of the community. This assistance and support is becoming effective both by word and deed. In the very early days of Islam the most successful pens were those which clarified problems of Holy Law and which propagated theological opinions in accordance with the Qur'ān, the Sunna, and the consensus of the community, so that such errors and innovations as did appear did not lead people astray and end in their corruption. This role is peculiar to the orthodox ulamā who should always look to the invisible world.

Worldly ulamā whose worldly aspirations are their religion—indeed their conversation is a fatal poison and their corruption is contagious. . . . In the generation before this, every calamity which appeared arose from the evil desires of these people. They misled rulers. The seventy-two sects who went on the road of error were lost because the ruler enforced his errors on others and the majority of the so-called ignorant Sufis of this time upheld the decisions of the wicked ulamā—their corruption was also contagious. Obviously, if someone, notwithstanding assistance of every kind, commits an error, and a schism occurs in Islam, that error should be reprehended. But these hateful people of little capital always wish to enroll themselves among the helpers of Islam and to beg importunately. . . . These disobedient people worm their way into the confidence of the generous and consider themselves to be like heroes. . . . It is hoped that in these times, if God wills, the worthy will be honored with royal company.

SHAH WALĪ-ULLĀH

The instinct of Indian Islam for tolerance and flexibility as a condition of its survival is symbolized in the life and thought of Shah Walī-Ullāh of Delhi (1703–1762), who wrote during the decline of the Mughal empire and before Indian Islam felt the impact of Western thought. He translated the Qur'ān into Persian, wrote Qur'anic commentaries, was a student of tradition, scholastic theology, and jurisprudence, and practiced Sufism. His significance as a religious thinker is still being estimated but his writings indicate that Indian Islam had survived the intellectual and religious trials of the sixteenth and seventeenth centuries without loss of vitality and catholicity. Shah Walī-Ullāh helped to insure that at least among Muslims there was no bitter religious strife to complement the political strife in India after Aurangzīb's death. Shah Walī-Ullāh, in the readings which follow, is to be observed teaching the old lessons of devotion to the Sunna of the Prophet and the need for breadth and tolerance in interpreting the mandates of the Sharī'a.

Legal Interpretation

Ijtihād or legal interpretation is the process whereby the student of the Sharīʿa arrives at determinations of the Holy Law in circumstances not already covered by previous decisions. Legal interpretation is the sole means of adapting the Sharīʿa to changing social circumstances while yet preserving the ideal of orthodoxy, i.e., of following in the footsteps of the Prophet in obedience to a God-revealed law. The problem of legal interpretation has come to the fore in every period of crisis for the Indo-Muslim community, whether in the newly founded state of Pakistan or in Shah Walī-Ullāh's eighteenth century, when Muslim power was rapidly disintegrating. Shah Walī-Ullāh advises interpreters of the law to avoid arbitrariness and destructive controversy, and rather to apply the Golden Mean.

[From *The Muslim World,* Vol. XLV, No. 4, pp. 347–54 *passim;* 357–58]

The true nature of legal interpretation (*ijtihād*), as understood from the discourse of scholars, is exhaustive endeavor in understanding the derivative principles of the Holy Canon Law by means of detailed arguments, their genera being based on four departments: 1) The Holy Book [the Qur'ān]; 2) The example and precept of the Prophet [the Sunna]; 3) The consensus of opinion of the Muslim community; 4) The application of analogy.

Let it be understood from this that legal interpretation is wider than [i.e., not confined to] the exhaustive endeavor to perceive the principle worked out by earlier scholars, no matter whether such an endeavor leads to disagreement or agreement with these earlier scholars. It is not limited by the consideration whether this endeavor is made with or without aid received from some of the earlier scholars in their notification of the aspects of questions involved in a given issue and their notification over the sources of the principles through detailed arguments. . . .

[Al-Baghawī said] "An interpreter of the Law is one who combines in himself five types of knowledge: 1) the knowledge of the Book of God the Glorious; 2) the knowledge of the example and precept of the Prophet (peace be on him and his descendants); 3) the knowledge of the speeches of the scholars of yore recording their consensus of opinion and their difference of opinion; 4) the knowledge of the Arabic language; and 5) the knowledge of analogy, which is the method of eliciting the principle from the Qur'ān or the Hadīth when the principle is not found unequivocally in the statutes of the Qur'ān, the Hadīth, and the consensus of opinion.

"It is incumbent that of the knowledge of the Holy Book he should possess the knowledge of the abrogating and the abrogated passages, the summary expressions and the full expressions, the general ordinances and the particular ones, the sound verses and the ambiguous verses, the disapprovals, prohibitions, permissions and approvals, and obligations.

"And of the Hadīth he must recognize the perfectly sound Hadīth, the weak ones, the ones supported by complete chains of narrators going back to the Prophet, the ones in which the chains of narrators omit the names of the Companions who transmitted the Hadīth. And he must know the application of the Hadīth upon the Qur'ān and of the Qur'ān upon the Hadīth, so that if he finds a Hadīth, the outward meanings of which do not conform to the meanings of the Book, he should get guided rightly to bring out its bearing, for the Hadīth is an exposition of the Book, and does not contradict it. Of the Hadīth it is obligatory upon him to know only those which relate to the principles of the Holy Law, and not the rest which contain stories, accounts of events, and admonitions.

"And likewise, it is incumbent that he should possess the lexical knowledge necessary to understand the passages in the Qur'ān and the Hadīth. But it is not required that he should encompass the entire vocabulary of Arabic. He should so polish up his linguistic knowledge that he may be in a position to understand the real import of Arabic phrases to an extent which may guide him to the intended meanings in different contexts and circumstances. This requirement is there because the Holy Canon Law is addressed in Arabic. He who does not know Arabic will not recognize the meaning intended by the Law-giver [i.e., the Prophet], nor will he understand what the companions and the successors of the companions said of principles, nor will he understand the most important judgments given by the jurisconsults of the community. He should know Arabic well so that his judgment does not stand opposed to theirs, in which case his judgment will involve violation of the consensus. And when he knows the major portion of each of these departments of knowledge, he is an interpreter of the Law, and the exhaustive knowledge of all these is not a condition. And if he is ignorant of one of these five departments then his path is to follow [i.e., not to indulge in legal interpretation], even if he is profoundly learned in the school of one of the bygone Imāms [the founders of one of the four schools of Muslim law]. It is not allowable for such a man to be invested with the status of a judge, or to be a candidate for a position in which he might give judgments. And if these sciences are combined in him, and he shuns evil passions and innovations, clothes himself with robes of piety, and abstains from major sins, not persisting in minor sins, then it is allowable that he may take up the responsibility of the office of a judge and may exercise his personal discretion in the Holy Law using legal interpretation and may pronounce his judgment. And he who does not combine in himself these conditions must, in matters that might concern him, follow him who does combine them." [The quotation from al-Baghawī ends here.] . . .

Scholars have differed in the matter of ratification of interpreters of the law, pronouncing differently on the derivative issues where no conclusive judgment is to be found. Is each of these interpreters of the law correct or is only one of them correct? . . . . [The author reviews the opinions of various authorities, and finally quotes al-Baidāwī.]

Al-Baidawī said in *The Stages* (*Al-Minhāj*): "The most preferable view is that which comes soundly from al-Shāfi'i: 'In every occurrence there is a fixed verdict upon which there is an indication.' Whichever interpreter of the law finds out that indication, hits the target, and whichever fails to find it out, misses the target, although he is not sinful on that account, for legal interpretation, which is the sum total of the search of arguments, is preceded by arguments; and the indication upon the error made comes after the verdict. If two different legal interpretations were to be regarded true, this would be a concurrence of two contradictions. And the interpreter of the law, missing the target of truth is not sinful either because the Prophet (peace be on him!) said: 'Whoso hits the target, shall have two rewards, and whoso misses it, shall have only one reward.'

"It is said that if the verdict is fixed, then he whose position is contrary to it does not judge according to what Allāh had revealed, and so is a transgressor, for Allāh the Exalted says: 'Whoso judges not in accordance with what Allāh has revealed, they are the transgressors.' We say answering this objection that he [i.e., the error-maker] pronounced judgments in accordance with what he thought was right, even though his judgment mistook the meaning of what God has revealed." . . .

And in reality the opinion attributed to the four Imams [the opinion that only one legal interpreter out of many, pronouncing on the same issue, is correct] is drawn out from some of their statements and there is no final unequivocal ruling (*nass*) given by them on this matter.

And in fact the community of Islam has not differed from the position that you can ratify legal interpreters pronouncing judgment in a matter wherein the community is given choice by an unequivocal holy text or by consensus (ijmā'), e.g., the Seven Variant Readings of the Qur'ān, the formulae of invocations, and the number of prostrations in Witr Prayers, which may be seven, nine, or eleven. And likewise the ulamā [i.e., scholars] should not differ [from the position that both the legal interpreters could be ratified] in matters wherein choice is given by some indication [if not by an unequivocal text or by consensus].

And the truth is that there are four types of difference: 1) That in which the truth is decisively determined, and it is necessary in such a case that its opposite be contradicted for it is false; 2) That in which the truth is determined by the dominant opinion. The opposite of it is false by dominant opinion; 3) That in which definite choice has been given to adopt any of the two alternative sides of difference; and 4) That in which the above choice is given by the dominant opinion.

And the detailed explanation of the above is that if the issue at hand is such that the verdict of the verdict giver is violated by both the alternative ways of settling it, i.e., if there is found an unequivocal, sound, and well-known Hadīth of the Prophet, and both legal interpretations stand opposed to it, then both will be false. But yes. The legal interpreter in such a matter will sometimes be excused upon grounds of his ignorance of the unequivocal Hadīth of the Prophet (peace be upon him) until that Hadīth reaches him, and the argument gets established. And if the legal interpretation is exercised in the ascertainment of an event which happened but the state whereof becomes dubious, like in the question whether Mr. A is dead or alive, unquestionably the truth in such a case will be one of the two alternatives. But the interpreter making a mistake in such a case will sometimes be excused in his legal interpretation. . . . The important cases of difference are of many types:

1. One interpreter of the law receives a Hadīth and the other one does not. Now in this case the right interpreter is already known.

2. Every interpreter engaged in the same issue has some conflicting Hadīth and he exercises legal interpretation in bringing about congruence

between some of them and preference of some over others, and his legal interpretation leads to a certain judgment of his own and so difference of this nature appears.

3. They may differ in the explanation of the words used and their logical definitions, or regarding the supply of what might be considered omitted in speech [and left to be understood], or in eliciting the *manat* [i.e., the common factor which justifies the application of a primary principle from the Qur'ān or the Hadīth to a derivative situation, or in application of general to particulars, etc.].

4. They may differ in primary principles leading to difference in derivative principles.

In all these cases each of any two interpreters of the law will be right provided the sources from which they get support are easily acceptable to intellects. . . .

Now whoever recognizes the true nature of this problem will realize: 1) that in the majority of cases of legal interpretation the truth lies somewhere between the two extremes of difference; 2) that in the matter of religion there is breadth and not narrowness; 3) that being unreasonably stubborn and determined to deny what the opponent says is ridiculous; 4) that the construing of definitions if it aims at bringing concepts closer to the understanding of every literate person, assists knowledge. But if these definitions are far-fetched and try to discriminate between involved matters by means of innovated premises, it will soon lead to an unworthy and innovated system of Sharī'a; 5) the true opinion is that pronounced by Izz al-Dīn 'Abd al-Salām who says: "He attains the goal who stands firm on what is agreed upon by scholars and abstains from what they have unanimously disallowed, and regards allowable that which is unanimously thus regarded by scholars, and does that which is unanimously approved by scholars, and keeps away from that which they have unanimously regarded as hateful."

Shah Walī-Ullāh and Mysticism

In his attitude toward mysticism, Shah Walī-Ullāh was conciliatory. For him, Ibn 'Arabī's doctrine of the unity of existence and Shaikh Ahmad of Sirhind's doctrine of the unity of experience, *i.e.,* the apparent but illusory unity of existence are both true statements about the same thing. In a letter to one Afandī Ismā'īl he writes:

[Adapted from *Visva-Bharati Annals,* IV, 35–36 (tr. by Asiri), 1951]

Unity of existence and unity of experience are two relative terms used at two different places in an argument about God. Unity of existence here implies scrutiny of the encompassing truth which has filled the universe by unfolding itself with various commands on which is based knowledge about good and evil. Both revelation and reason support it. One should know that created things are one in one respect and different in another. This can only be perceived by the saints who are really perfect. The stage of unity of experience is higher than unity of existence. . . . Now some Sufis saw the contingent and created as connected with the eternal; also they perceived the modes of God's existence combined with His essence. This can be explained by the example of wax forms of man, horse and ass, which have wax in common, but different shapes. This is the belief of the real pantheists. But the others maintain that the Universe is a reflection of the names and attributes of the necessary being [God] reflected in their opposite, nonexistence. These attributes and names are reflected in the mirror of nonexistence which is powerless.

In the same manner one can imagine the appearance of each name and attribute of God in the mirror of non-being. The former is unity of existence, and the latter unity of experience. To me both are based on true revelations. Unity of experience of Shaikh Ahmad does not contradict but confirms Ibn 'Arabī's unity of existence. In short, if real facts are taken into account and studied without their garb of simile and metaphor, both doctrines will appear almost the same.

CHAPTER XVII

THE MUSLIM RULER IN INDIA

For Muslims, God is the all-mighty and ever active sovereign of His Universe who has made His Will and Pleasure for mankind known in His Holy Law (Sharī'a). The government of His community on earth is therefore one of the innumerable and, strictly speaking, indeterminate expressions of this total Divine sovereignty, and "political theory" is merely one specification or aspect of the Holy Law.

The problems to which Muslim thought on temporal government stands as the succession of answers have not been, for example, those of the origin and nature of political power or of the relation of "church" and "state," but of how the pious Muslim might recognize that the government of the community is in the right hands and be assured that it is being exercised for the right purposes. After early attempts to define the conditions of the appointment of legitimate authority over the community however, the majority of the ulamā—the students of Islamic revelation—preferred to concentrate on persuading the *de facto* ruler to do his duty toward Islam no matter how he had gained his position, thereby enabling pious Muslims to obey the "powers that be" with a good conscience. In this they were doubtless impelled by the desire to avoid a political chaos in which the practice of the good Muslim life might become impossible, and by a human reluctance to believe that, in accepting a particular ruler, they had sinned against God.

As long as the Prophet lived, Muslims did not have to "theorize politically." Muhammad was the divinely appointed Messenger of God, communicating to mankind what God had wished them to know. Muhammad united in himself, legislative, executive, and judicial functions. But with him died the Revelation of Divine Command and the exercise of Divine government organically united in one person. However, the period of the *ridda* wars (632–634) against seceding Arab tribes determined that rebellion was the same as apostasy and that ideally, at least, the community was neither a political nor a religious one, but both.

After the Prophet's death, Muslims could not agree upon one interpretation of God's will for the government of the community. Some, the party of 'Alī, the Prophet's cousin and son-in-law, thought he should have been accepted as head of the community at the Prophet's death, in place of those who were actually accepted successively, namely, Abū Bakr, 'Umar, and 'Uthmān. Faced with opposition, the supporters of the actual succession of caliphs idealized their rule, and what later generations believed was their practice, was held to embody true Islamic government on earth. This, the Sunni doctors of the Holy Law stated, involved the necessity of a Khalīfa as the divinely ordained ruler of the community, symbolizing the supremacy of the Holy Law. He was selected by the community (or by the senior members of it) to enforce the Holy Law, but not to define it himself. The Khalīfa, the Sunnis held, was a magistrate, not a pope; the guardian, not the chief of the ulamā.

The pious charged the Ummayads (661–750) with introducing a worldly hereditary monarchy. The 'Abbāsid caliphs (750–1258) advertised their religiousness and patronized the ulamā, but hardly fulfilled the ideal of the early caliphate—they were not elected and their authority was certainly not exercised solely to enforce the Holy Law.

Moreover from the middle of the ninth century, the 'Abbāsid caliphs were proposed and deposed by their Turkish guards, while between 945 and 1055, they were the puppets of the Buyid princes, Shī'a's who only recognized the 'Abbāsid caliph as nominal head of the community for political reasons.

Confronted with this chasm between the ideal and the actual, and unwilling to convict the community of living in sin by reason of its acquiescence, Sunni jurists attempted to sanctify, or at least to condone, the actual course of history by appeal to texts from the Qur'ān and the Sunna, and to ijmā'—in this context, passive acceptance of the political *fait accompli*. Faced with the "amirate by seizure"—the forceful imposition of his rule by a military chief over a part of the Muslim world—a jurist like al-Māwardī (d. 1058) argued in his *al-Ahkām us-Sultāniyya* that such a ruler was to be accepted as legitimate providing that he paid deference to the nominal headship of the caliph and entered into a kind of "concordat" whereby the caliph invested him with authority in return for an undertaking to rule according to Holy Law and defend Muslim territory.

As for India, the Ghōrid conquerors, the sultans of Delhi, and, *a fortiori,* the Mughals were clearly not agents of the caliph. Although Iltutmish in 1229 received investiture as the lieutenant of the then 'Abbāsid caliph, the Mongol Hūlāgū's slaying of the 'Abbāsid Caliph al-Musta'sim in 1258 denied his successors even that title to legitimacy. Indo-Muslim theory met the situation by stressing the divine ordination of the function of temporal government, the duty of obedience, and the desirability of the sultanate in India acting as caliph *de facto* for its own dominions—that is by ascribing to it those functions, including the defense and maintenance of true religion and the Holy Law, of dispensing justice and of appointing the god-fearing to office, which Sunni jurists had earlier ascribed to the caliphate. The test of the Muslim ruler was not how he came to be where he was, but what he did when he arrived there.

In essence, the bulk of Indo-Muslim writing on government embodies a conception of partnership between the doctors of the holy law and the sultan in the higher interests of the faith—a partnership between pious professors and pious policemen. In the sixteenth century, members of Akbar's circle, under the influence of Shī'ī doctrines and ideas mediated from Greek philosophy, were inclined to allow the "just Imām" discretion to decide points of Holy Law where there was disagreement among the doctors and no clear guidance was offered by the Sharī'a. Still, it is doubtful whether in this they were going beyond the ambit of the administrative discretion (*siyāsa*) already allowed the ruler by some jurists and writers so that he might act in the best interest, though not according to the formal terms, of the Holy Law. Abū'l Fazl, however, appears to associate some of the sanctity which had always attached to the office of the just Imām with the person of the just ruler. The orthodox, for their part, reacted strongly against this, fearing that the supremacy of the Holy Law over a Muslim's realm (and the authority of the ulamā as its interpreters) was about to be abandoned even in principle, as it had long since been ignored for the most part in practice. Certainly Abū-l Fazl's ideas threatened to wipe out the distinction made in later Sunni thought between the religious and the ruling institution.

The readings in this section illustrate the political thinking of writers who accept the sultanate as a necessary fact and who wish to consecrate it to Islamic purposes. They have been taken from the following works of the sultanate period—The *Genealogies* (*Shajara-yi-Ansāb*) written about 1206 by Fakhr ud-dīn Mubārak Shāh, a learned man at the court of Qutb ud-dīn Aibak; Ziā ud-dīn Barnī's *Rulings on Temporal Government* (*Fatāwa-yi-Jahāndārī*); and *The Treasuries of Kings* (*Zakhīrat ul-Mulūk*), written in the second half of the fourteenth century by one said to be largely responsible for the conversion of Kashmir to Islam, Shaikh Hamadānī. Along with these are presented under each topic pertinent selections from writing of the Mughal period, including Muhammad Bāqir Khān's *Advice on Government* (*Mau'iza-yi-Jahāngīrī*); the *Ethics of Government* (*Akhlāq-i-Jahāngīrī*), written in 1620–1622 by Nūr ud-dīn Muhammad Khagānī; Abū Tālib al-Husaini's *Institutes of Tīmūr* (c. 1637); and Abū'l Fazl's *Ā'īn-i-Akbarī.*

The Final End of Human Society Is the Worship of God

Ziā ud-dīn Barnī was the most important writer on politics during the era of the Delhi sultanate (c.1210–1556). Born about 1285, he belonged to the Muslim aristocracy, with his father, paternal uncle, and grandfather all holding important administrative positions under the sultan of Delhi. He himself held no government post but was a *nadīm* or boon companion of Sultan Muhammad ibn Tughluq (1325–1351) for over seventeen years. At the death of Muhammad ibn Tughluq he fell out of favor and was banished from court, suffering imprisonment for a few months. It was during this period of poverty and exile from court that he wrote his works on government and religion, hoping thereby both to prepare himself for the hereafter and also to win back the favor of Sultan Fīrūz Shāh Tughluq. In the latter hope he was disappointed, dying in poverty not long after 1357.

Barnī wrote to set forth for the sultans of Delhi their duty toward Islam. His two most important works, the *Rulings on Temporal Government* (*Fatāwa-yi-Jahāndārī*) and *Fīrūz Shāh's History* (*Tārīkh-i-Fīrūz Shāhī*) form the reverse and obverse of the same doctrinal coin. Barnī was a Sunni Muslim, hostile to the Shī'a and to the influence of Greek philosophy, while convinced of the virtues of Sufi mysticism. In the *Fatāwa-yi-Jahāndārī* he sets forth his conception of the duties of the sultan toward orthodox Sunni Islam, a conception which, it should be emphasized, is not original in the wider context of Islamic political or legal thought. In the *Tārīkh-i-Fīrūz Shāhī,* he interprets the history of the Delhi sultans from Balban (1266–87) to Fīrūz Shāh Tughluq (1351–88) in such a manner as to convey that sultans who followed his precepts prospered, and those who sinned against them, met Nemesis.

[From Barnī, *Fatāwa-yi-Jahāndārī,* folios 44b, 143, 199a–199b]

The king of all kings and rulers is God. God maintains the world by His wrath and His grace and the indications of His grace and His wrath are manifest in His mercy and His bounty toward the good and the wicked.

He has created Paradise for the good and the obedient and has promised it for them. He has created hell for the wicked and the disobedient and has frightened the stubborn and the infidels with it. He has created Rizwān [the porter at the gate of Paradise] out of his mercy and Malāk [the guardian of hell] out of his wrath. So, earthly "rulers" must [metaphorically speaking] follow the practices of the Real Ruler and treat the inhabitants of their kingdoms in accordance with the contrasting qualities which are essential for temporal government. [folio 199a–b]

. . . .

God is the real king and earthly "kings" are the playthings of His decree and Divine Power. In His government, God forgives some sinners and does not accept the repentance of others and treats them sternly. Some He will punish in the next world and does not punish in this world; others he punishes in this world and will not punish in the next. Some He keeps safe and some He keeps under the umbrella of His protection, compassion, and favor. Some He raises to the pinnacle of esteem, greatness, glory, and good fortune. Others He rolls in the dust of dishonor and disgrace. Upon some He bestows wealth and prosperity, others He causes to live in a middling state, others He keeps in poverty, indigence, and wretchedness. Some He brings to life and some He causes to die. Toward people of every sort, condition and kind He exercises His Lordship by different treatment, in accordance with His Ripe Judgment. He maintains the order of the world and keeps it coherent. He is the real King and to him alone is Kingship proper. [folio 143]

. . . .

Mankind was created for submission to God. As God Most High has said, "We have not created men or jinns except that they may worship Us." [folio 44b]

Prophets and Kings

All power is ultimately God's but is exercised over human society through prophets, the learned, and kings. The substitution of sultans for caliphs is an adjustment of Muslim thinking to the historical situation in the Muslim world after the destruction of the 'Abbāsid caliphate. God ordains the sultanate as a necessary corrective for human weakness and as a necessary means of salvation.

[From Barnī, *Fatāwa-yi-Jahāndārī,* folios 247b–248a]

Religion and temporal government are twins; that is, the head of religion and the head of government are twin brothers. As the world will not come right or stay right through kingship alone there must be both prophets and kings in the world so that mankind's business in both the worlds may be carried through in accordance with God's wishes. If there be a king and no prophet, then the affairs of this world may come aright, but no one created of God will be saved in the next. If there is a prophet but no king, then without the power and majesty of kingship, the world will seek the right in vain and religious commands will not prevail and affairs will fall into confusion and disorder. Almighty God has adorned prophets and kings with inborn virtues and praiseworthy qualities. These two high attributes—prophethood and kingship—do not mix well with base morals and vile qualities. Almighty God (may His name be glorified) has only created prophets that they may bestow the gift of humble submission to God out of their own nature. He has created them innocent of major and minor sin so that everyone in the world may draw nigh to Him who lacks nothing and become His nearest and dearest. They hear the word of God and bring it to men; they show men the way to those laws which are pleasing to God. They show them the right path and keep them away from the wrong path. Everyone of those so pleased to hearken unto those words and follow their authority draws nearer to God and is worthy of the bounty of Paradise. But he who counts their words as nothing, rejects their prophethood and the commands from God which out of their God-fearing characters the prophets give, is deserving of Hell and remains estranged from God.

[From Shaikh Hamadānī, *Zakhīrat ul-Mulūk,* folio 75a]

Know ye that among the great ones of the learned, those possessed of intelligence and wisdom, it is established and proved that, at the very first moment of creation, by reason of the different qualities and admixture of ability which are bestowed by the bounty of God like a lustrous and bejeweled costume, the souls and natures of men have fallen out differently. Hence, the inclinations, motives and purposes of men have become different and the difference is manifested in all their words, deeds, and fundamental articles of faith.

The qualities of beastliness and of base morals—tyranny and injustice, hatred, and rancor, and avarice are implanted in the dispositions of men. Then, in the perfection of His great Wisdom, God has decreed that there be a just and competent ruler of mankind so that, by the power of judicial process, the affairs of the progeny of Adam and the rules for managing the affairs of mankind may be kept and preserved on the right path; also a ruler has been ordained by God so that he may endeavor, as far as possible, to put into operation the mandates of the Sharī'a and to be on guard to preserve the prescriptions and rules of Islam among people of all classes and, with the prohibitions of punishment and the curb of command, to prevent tyranny over and oppression of the weak by the strong. Thus the physical world may be assured of stability, the bounds of the Sharī'a not invaded by the disorder of oppression and innovation, and the characteristics of brute beasts and camels may not be manifested among people of all classes.

[From Muhammad Bāqir Khān, *Mau'iza-yi-Jahāngīrī,* folios 5–7]
Moreover, in order to order and arrange the affairs of the world and the concerns of mankind there must be rules whereby, each living with the other, no one may suffer injustice and oppression. Therefore God has raised up from among mankind itself prophets and messengers, each one of whom is a pearl in the sea of purity and a lodestar in the constellations possessing the qualities of attachment to the world and of separation from it, of care for the world and of detachment from it. Thus, having obtained holiness through separation and detachment from the world, they may, by their connection and their strong ties with it, guide the rebellious and those wallowing in black error and eager to be deceived, to the abode of true guidance and the fountain of divine protection. And they keep those laws which are called the Sharī'a so that everyone may be put on the straight road of its mandates and, enjoying security through the majesty and wrath of God, attain to eternal bliss and felicity. Everyone who strays from the straight path shall be afflicted by the lash of divine displeasure and be placed in the next world in "durance vile." . . .

After the time of Muhammad who is the seal and the last of the prophets, in order that the principles of religion may be established and properly ordered, the actions of God's servants directed aright and their welfare secured, and the boon of peace and tranquillity obtained by the existence of one governor and ruler who should be worthy of imitation and possessed of exalted power, and whose praiseworthy person should be adorned with the jewel of justice and equity; in order too, that through the full exercise of the power or by the nonexercise of the power of a warrior's wrath, the shadow of man's base and animal passions may be shunned and avoided in order that all this may be achieved and the people not forget their sincere friends [the prophets], not follow after their own desires, not let their lusts overwhelm them, not indulge in wanton pastimes and arrogant contention for superiority, one against another—and if the different generations of God's creatures are to live quietly on a bed of peace and tranquillity, then there is no escaping, indeed it is necessary and unavoidable, that there shall exist that chosen being of creation whom they call a king.

He, the king, being created with the morals of a doctor of holy law and basing his conduct of affairs upon the mandates of the Holy Law shall therefore make his authority distinguished for some of the qualities which can be the embroidery of the garments of the sultanate. Furthermore, directing all his high aspirations toward understanding what wise men say and opening the secrets of the ulamā, he shall make their advice, counsel and decisions his model, so that both the head of his kingdom shall be adorned with the crown of success and the garment of the kingdom be ornamented by respect for religion. Both the kingdom and the subjects of every prudent king who is distinguished for these worthy qualities and who is adorned with the jewel of these laudable dispositions, shall become prosperous, happy, contented, obedient, and loyal, and with the garden of his authority containing such trees and seeds, year by year for numberless generations, his reputation for goodness shall remain inscribed on the pages of time.

Obedience to the Sultan Is Commanded by God

[From Fakhr-i-Mudir, *Shajara,* pp. 12–13]

And the Prophet, Peace be upon him! saith: "Whoever obeys me, verily and truly will have obeyed God and whoever obeys the Imām [leader], that is to say, the sultan, will have obeyed me, and whoever rebels against me will have rebelled against God, and whoever rebels against the sultan, verily and truly he will have rebelled against me." The Prophet also said: "Obey your kings and governors though they be Abyssinian slaves."

Kingship Is Incompatible with Religious Ideals

Some thinkers, on the other hand, hold that the sultanate is un-Islamic; that it is an unholy heir of Persian traditions of monarchy. Ziā ud-dīn Barnī, for example, insists that monarchy is essentially antithetical to religion and that rulers must consecrate themselves to God's service if they are to have any hope of escaping God's wrath. Only the four Rightly-Guided Caliphs were true Muslim rulers.

[From Barnī, *Fatāwa-yi-Jahāndārī,* folios 87b–100a, 224a–b *passim*]

The governance of men is not feasible and has not been feasible without the ways of rulers and the majesty and pomp of governors. And that one generation when the Rightly-Guided Caliphs exercised the authority of the successors of the Prophet with a life of abstinence and poverty, and the world became subject to them, was only possible because the time of the Prophet Muhammad was so near and the effects of his miracles were still being felt. From Adam's day until the extinction of the world their generation has been and will always be considered the wonder of time and the rarity of the ages. The behavior of these caliphs in all things followed the Sunna of the Prophet. But if succeeding caliphs and kings wished to follow their example they would not be able to maintain their caliphate or royal authority for a single day. Moreover, those four [the Rightly-Guided Caliphs] who did not adopt the habits and customs of sultans for fear of opposing the practice of the Prophet, with all the power of the Prophet's practices, lost their lives. 'Umar, 'Uthmān, and 'Alī were martyred by fearless fanatics. No other Muslim caliph or ruler has found the opportunity—or will ever find it—to rule and to proclaim the practice of the Prophet, by embracing their way of life and livelihood; for the world is full of those who have the character of devils, the habits of carnivorous beasts, of wild animals, and beasts of prey; without the terror and dominion of powerful and successful sultans, command and control over them is never achieved. . . .

The helpers and supporters of the orthodox caliphs were the noble Companions of the Prophet who eagerly sacrificed their lives and property, wives, sons, and belongings in the way of Truth. Because they had been associates, friends, and companions of the Chosen One of the Lord Most High and had witnessed Divine Revelation, they were such lovers of God and the Prophet that the whole world was not worth a farthing in their sight. . . . Because they had such helpers and companions, the path of poverty and self-denial was practicable in the government of the Rightly-Guided Caliphs. . . .

But now . . . real belief in God and certainty and firmness in the true faith remain conspicuous in only a small number of individuals. The outward appearance of Islam has assumed many guises; the world has returned to the ways of mere mimics [i.e., men only follow Islam as a matter of custom] and of seekers after this world. Just as before the advent of the Prophet, the aspirations and desires of mankind were centered on this world, so the same is appearing again. Never will the power and authority of the caliphate be asserted and become well constituted without the terror and majesty and pomp of temporal rulership which are the ways by which rulers secure submission of the unruly, reduce the forward and the rebellious to impotence. Rule, dominion, and conquest are not possible with a life of poverty. Without the majesty and pomp of the sultanate, man will swallow man, the obedient will become disobedient, the prestige of authority will melt away, and obedience to command will completely disappear. No one will fear the governors and *muqta's* whom the Commander of the Faithful has appointed, and they will become without respect or authority; every day revolt and tumult will break out and tyranny and oppression will appear. . . .

After them [the first four caliphs] the caliphs and kings of Islam were faced by two opposed alternatives, both necessary for religion and the realm. If they followed the traditions of the Prophet and his mode of life, government and kingship would be impracticable for them; claiming to be kings and yet living the life of a mendicant they would not remain alive; authority, which is the essence of government, would not be enforced among the people at all.

If they follow the practices of the Khusraus [the Persian emperors] and adopt their mode of sitting and rising, eating and dressing, and their general manner of life—the destruction of the headstrong, the subduing of the forward, and the taking of any steps necessary for the enforcement of authority among the people, it is necessary to transgress the Sunna of the Prophet, the sum and essence of true religion. In the persons and in the environment of kings no traditions are admissible because prophethood is the perfection of religiousness, and kingship that of earthly bliss; these two perfections are opposed and contradictory to each other and their combination is not within the bounds of possibility.

For servitude to God is the necessary condition of religion, and the necessary conditions of this servitude are submission, supplication, poverty, self-abasement, abjectness, need, and humility. On the other hand, the requisites of kingship, which is the perfection of worldly good fortune, are haughtiness, pride, aloofness from others, luxurious and soft living, lack of civility, grandeur, and might. The qualities enumerated here are among the attributes of God. And since kingship is the deputyship and the vice-regency of God, kingship is not compatible with the characteristics of servitude.

Consequently, it became necessary for the rulers of Islam to adopt the customs of the kings of Persia to ensure the greatness of the True Word, the supremacy of the Muslim religion, the superiority of Truth, the rooting out of the enemies of the Faith, the carrying on of the affairs of religion, and the maintenance of their own authority. . . . Nevertheless, the religion of Islam totally prohibits the iniquities committed by the Persian kings.

But just as the eating of carrion, though prohibited, is yet permitted in time of dire need, similarly the customs and traditions of the sultans of 'Ajam [1]—the crown and the throne, aloofness from others, pride, rules about sitting down and getting up in the king's court, high palaces, court ceremonials, asking people to prostrate themselves before the king, collecting treasures, misappropriating properties, wearing gold garments and jewels and silk cloth and making other people wear them, putting people to death on grounds of policy, keeping large harems, spending recklessly without any right and seizing countries without any claims of inheritance, and whatever else is a necessity of his aloof status, his pride and haughtiness without which a king is not deemed or called a king—should, from the viewpoint of truth and the correct faith, be considered like the eating of carrion in time of dire need. It is the duty of religious kings to fear and regret the commission of such actions as a danger to religion, to ask for divine forgiveness during the night with weeping and lamentations, to be certain themselves that all the customs and traditions of kingship are opposed to the traditions of the Prophet and in that they and their followers and their servants are involved.

Piety consists in following the practices of the Prophet. During the period of his mission as Prophet, the Prophet never ate meat by cutting it with a knife. The Companions asked: "O Prophet of God, is it forbidden to cut meat with a knife and to eat it?" "It is not forbidden," he replied, "but it is one of the practices of the sultans of 'Ajam and I who

[1] 'Ajam, lit. "dumb," refers to the non-Arabs, especially to the inhabitants of Persia.

have been sent to overthrow their customs and practices completely, and forbid them absolutely in my faith, have not eaten in the way that they have eaten."

So, O sons of Mahmūd, know and know well that kingship is not feasible without adopting the customs and practices of kings of 'Ajam. It is known to all the ulamā that the customs and practices of the sultans of 'Ajam are opposed to the Sunna of the Prophet and to his way of life and livelihood. [folios 87b–89b, 99b–100a]

. . . .

It has been said that in former times in 'Ajam, Rūm,[2] Yaman, India, Syria, and Egypt kingship was confined to the royal dynasty of every country and the desire of usurpation did not enter the hearts of the members of any other class of people. Thus, if in 'Ajam the ruler did not belong to the dynasty of the Khusraus, the people did not obey him. Similarly, in Rūm, if the ruler did not belong to the family of the Qaisars, the Romans did not bow their heads to him. Whenever such a principle had become customary among the people for generations and ages, usurpation was not tried. . . . Further, among the ancients, kingship was hereditary, and if a king died, one of his sons, in accordance with his nomination, ascended the throne. He kept the old officers at their posts and did not injure any leader, tribal chief, or noble family. This way and custom was very admirable.

After the rule of these monarchs in whose dynasties kingship had been enduring came to an end, kingship was established in many countries by usurpation and force and no attention was paid to the origin and descent of kings. Anyone who could obtain power, prestige, and a following by any means whatsoever, established himself over a territory, overthrew its previous ruler, took possession of the royal authority and caused himself to be called "king." . . .

Among the Muslims this untoward event came about through the Umayyad sultans who have been called Yazīdīs and Marwānids. During the generation of the Companions of the Prophet the government of the Muslim countries belonged by right to the Rightly-Guided Caliphs through the consensus of the community and appointment by their predecessors. The caliphate passed down to the Commander of the Faithful,

[2] The Eastern Roman or Byzantine Empire.

Hasan, son of 'Alī, both of whom were of the Hāshim clan. Not until Mu'āwiya, Yazīd, and the Marwānids had overthrown the Hāshim clan, their helpers, supporters, friends, and well-wishers, and blackened their own faces in this world and the next, was their eighty years of rule possible. Not until Abū Muslim Marūzī had sought vengeance for the family of the Prophet from the Umayyad sultans and disinterred Mu'āwiya, Yazīd, and the Marwānids from their graves and burnt them and extirpated their helpers, supporters, sympathizers, and sincere friends, did the caliphate of the 'Abbāsids in Baghdad become possible. . . .

Now reflect with a clear mind on how this bad practice and wicked custom has become habitual among the kings of Islam. First, without any rightful claim, external or domestic, they seize a territory; then out of religious or worldly expediency they obtain permission from the caliph of Baghdad for their usurpation. In addition to this, for the preservation of their own lives, which are certainly worthy of ultimate destruction and death, they overthrow and reduce to poverty and distress, by every means that comes to hands, many tribes, families, and illustrious families of the preceding regime. Some they spare, others they kill; some they imprison, others they exile; and some they deprive of their properties. Owing to the weakness of their faith, they do not care for Islam or the rights of Muslims, and they never consider the answer they will have to give on the Day of Judgment. To this sort of "overthrowing" they give the name of "political expediency." [folios 224a–224b *passim*]

[From Shaikh Hamadānī, *Zakhīrat ul-Mulūk*, folios 76a–b]
There were two offices united in Adam's illustrious person—the office of prophet and the office of sultan and ruler. In the office of prophet there is no place for the domination of lust and self-will. Undoubtedly the reality of this office was never manifested except in the pure bodies and open vessels of the prophets (may God bless them all and give them peace). But the conduct of the office of sultan and ruler are as if susceptible to the assaults of passionate and lustful behavior. There is a great measure of the two reprehensible qualities of lust and self-will attaching to the dangerous office of sultan. For that reason, in most ages and seasons it appears as an offensive manifestation and as a vessel of contamination, with its holders drawn from among tyrants, felons, oppressors, and the rich. From the time of Adam there has only been a limited number of

people among the great Prophets—Joseph, Moses, David, Solomon, and Muhammad (Peace be upon him)—and after the prophets, the Rightly-Guided Caliphs—Abū Bakr, 'Umar, 'Uthmān, and 'Alī (may God be satisfied with all of them)—in whose noble persons the good qualities of rulership have been manifested. They attended to the performance of the duties of their office in the way they should and made their own good qualities an argument against the oppressor and the unjust, the unheeding and the contumacious.

A few stories from the annals of the sultanate and governorship of prophets, a few traditions of the government and caliphate of the God-fearing and Rightly-Guided Caliphs have been set down for remembrance in this chapter for the admonition of those evil tyrants and wicked oppressors who have made the office of sultan and ruler over the people of Islam a source of pride and arrogance, and authority and governorship over the Muslim community a base thing of lust and self-will, and who consider wickedness and injustice the normal practice of kingship and corrupt and filthy behavior the normal practice of the great.

The War Between Good and Evil

The world has been created a battlefield between good and evil in which evil cannot be annihilated but only temporarily kept in check. The integral relation between "political theory" and theology should be noted.

[From Barnī, *Fatāwa-yi-Jahāndārī,* folios 117b–118a]

The meaning of "truth being established at the center" is not that falsehood totally vanishes while truth alone remains in this world. For Almighty God has said: "We have created two spirits"—that is, God has created things in pairs and has brought into existence one thing in opposition to another. Opposite to truth he has created falsehood, for example. Opposite to moral soundness he has created corruption. In the disorder of good, he created evil. Opposite obedience to God there is rebellion against him and opposed to obedience there is disobedience. Similarly, day and night, light and darkness, sky and earth, belief and unbelief, the unity of God and polytheism have been created in pairs and as contraries of each other.

The object of the above preamble is this. "Truth being established at the center" does not mean that falsehood is totally overthrown. For if all the prophets and kings of Islam gather together and try to remove and eliminate falsehood (which includes infidelity, sin, disobedience, and wickedness) from this world so that only truth (which includes Islam, moral soundness, obedience, and virtue) may prevail, they most certainly will not be able to succeed. It is not within the realm of possibility that there should be only goodness on this earth and no evil, only morality and no corruption, only Islam and theism and no infidelity and polytheism. For truth becomes luminous through the existence of falsehood, good through the existence of evil, Islam through the existence of infidelity, and theism through the existence of polytheism. In this way it becomes clear that this is truth and this is falsehood, that this is good and this is evil, that this is Islam and this is polytheism. . . .

Man's Opposing Qualities and Their "Political" Implications

Men have been created with contrasting qualities of good and evil dispositions; so with rulers—only rulers must control and employ their different dispositions so as to ensure the superiority of true religion and the maintenance of peace and order.

[From Barnī, *Fatāwa-yi-Jahāndārī,* folios 193a–195a *passim*]

God Most High has formed man with contrasting qualities. In every creature whom He has created as a human being and taken out of the animal circle, the contradictory qualities of contraction of the heart [against the entry of divine revelation] and its expansion [to receive divine revelation], wrath and grace, generosity and meanness, humility and pride are to be observed. But he in whom contrasting qualities are to be seen to perfection yet whose human nature is very much present is one of the wonders of the world. . . .

All the subjects of the ruler at the time of having dealings with him, or of his exercising temporal authority over them, are dependent upon him, and he is lord and judge over all. Consequently, wrath and grace, power and compassion, severity and sympathy, pride and humility, harshness and softness, anger and forbearance, mercy and hardness of heart, which are opposing qualities, should adorn the king in the most perfect manner and should be employed at proper times and on appropriate occasions. With these perfect dispositions, a king can deal with thousands of men who are different in their qualities and dispositions, temperaments and natures. If all is wrathfulness in the ruler and no kindness, what will become of the submissive, the weak, and the yielding? How will they endure violent usage or conquest? And if there is mildness and no wrathfulness, how will the ruler restrain the rebellious, the contumacious, the refractory and the disobedient from rebellion, contumacy, and disobedience and make them instead obedient, submissive, resourceless, and impotent? The same underlying truth as holds good for the attributes of men and beasts holds good also for the contrasting attributes of the ruler.

It is one of the wonders of the world when the contrasting qualities of the king are perfect and when he shows them forth in all their splendor at the appropriate and fitting occasions, and when he does not show wrath at the time for mildness or mildness at the time for wrath. One so endowed is complete with a portion of Godlike attributes. A person whose contrasting qualities are innate and display themselves to perfection and which are employed on occasions of good and evil, probity and dishonesty, obedience and disobedience, is worthy of and has a claim to kingship—which is the deputyship and vice-regency of God. . . . Such are the kings who have the position of Axes of the World on earth and who find a place in the shadow of the Divine Throne. Recounting their praises and their great deeds becomes a means of salvation and not of perdition.

The Duties and Responsibilities of the True King

The extent to which Muslim thinkers in India transfer the obligations of the caliph to the sultan will be observed in these readings.

The first excerpt indicates the proper relationship between those learned in the Holy Law and political authority. Sultans should be police chiefs to enforce the Sharī'a, not legislators.

[From Fakhr-i-Mudir, *Shajara,* pp. 9–14]

It is evident to mankind that after the prophets and the messengers (on whom be peace!) comes the rank and station of the true friends of God, the martyrs and the learned. The learned are also the true friends of God and enjoy superiority over the martyrs; as the Prophet says: "The learned are the heirs of the prophets." He also says: "When the Day of Judgment cometh, they will weigh the ink of the scholar and the blood of the martyr and the ink of the scholar will prevail over the blood of the martyr."

The world is maintained through legal opinions of the learned and by their piety; the world is kept prosperous through the blessings of their knowledge, their adherence to religion, and their fear of God. The mandates of the Sharī'a and the ordinances of divine worship are entrusted to their station. Prohibitions and sins are concealed and hidden through their superintendance and the commands to do what is right are known to them. The religion of God Most High is firm through their persons and the fixing of the limits of punishment and of royal justice is dependent upon their faith in God. The Prophet says: "One wise doctor of jurisprudence is more troublesome to the Devil than a thousand worshipers."

The Prophet also, in giving the reason for the standing and excellence of the learned says: "The best amīrs [rulers] and kings are those who visit men learned in the Sharī'a, and the worst learned men are those who wait on amīrs and kings." This tradition is recorded so that amīrs and kings may seek out learned men and hear wisdom from them, and so that they may take their advice and do what they say, leaving alone what they prohibit. Thus they may be the best of amīrs and kings. It is forbidden for learned men to wait on amīrs and sultans lest they become the worst of learned men. And this is a merciful prohibition against going to visit kings, although it may be necessary, lest someone should despise them and condemn them, for God Most High has made learned men dear to him [pp. 9–11]

. . . .

Some of the mandates of the Sharī'a are dependent upon the person and the orders of kings—as the Friday *Khutba* [sermon], and the two festivals of the breaking of the fast of Ramazān and of sacrifices at Mecca, the fixing of the limits of the land tax and alms, the making of war; the giving of judgment between litigants; the hearing of lawsuits; in addition, the protection of the country from foreign armies, the organization of armies, the provision of rations for the soldiery, the awarding of capital punishment in the interests of the subjects, the doing of justice among the people and the avenging of the oppressed. [pp. 13–14]

[From Barnī, *Fatāwa-yi-Jahāndārī,* folios 7a–9a]

The essence of protection and promotion of the Faith by the ruler is the enforcement in his kingdom of the commands to do what is lawful and the prohibition of what is unlawful, and the making current of the mandates of the Holy Law among the seventy-two creeds. [folio 8a]

. . . .

The greatness of a king who protects religion is beyond description, for it is through his protection and promotion of the faith that Muslims give themselves to obedience to God and the performance of their religious duties in peace of mind, that the mandates of the Holy Law of the Prophet may become operative over different realms, that the pure faith may predominate over others, and that the honor and lives of both Muslims and the protected people are protected and secured and the banners of Islam may reach unto the highest heavens. [folio 7a]

. . . .

The religious scholars of the past have written clearly and in detail concerning the tests of the firm and sincere faith of kings. One of these tests is that they appoint harsh-tempered censors of morals and honest judicial officers in their capitals, cities, and towns, and strengthen their authority in every way, so that these officers can make manifest the splendor of "ordering the good and prohibiting the evil" among the Muslims, and may embitter the lives of all open, persistent, and public sinners through their severe punishments. . . . By the purity of their surveillance of the above sinful acts, they may check wine-sellers, flute-players, and dice-players. If prohibitions, stern orders, and insults cannot restrain them, if in spite of their claim to be Muslims, they do not openly give up their shameless acts of disobedience, and if respect for the Faith and fear of the ruler's orders is unable to dissuade them, then the rich among them should be punished with deprivation of property and the poor with imprisonment and fines. Wine-sellers should be sent out of the towns to live in distant corners; if they happen to be Muslims, they should be treated heartlessly, and it should be so arranged that no Muslim acts as a wine-seller. All male prostitutes should be prevented with severe blows from adorning themselves like women, wailing like women, and indulging in their other sins; they should also be treated with harshness and severity so that they may leave the capital, go to the countryside, and obtain their livelihood there by agriculture and other lawful occupations. . . . These people who have made filthy sin and disobedience their profession, and whose open parade of their behavior in the capital of Islam brings disgrace on the banners of Islam, should be prohibited in all cities and be ordered to leave them and conceal themselves in hovels and out-of-the-way places in the countryside. The construction and public use of pleasure houses should not be permitted; if they have been constructed already, they should be pulled down, "brick by brick." In short, the public practice of anything prohibited by the Law should not be allowed. But if in secret and privately habitual sinners indulge in their practices, severe investigations about their activities should not usually be made. If anything prohibited by the Holy Law is seen by the censors of morals, judicial officers, and the general public, it should be totally suppressed. But what is secret and hidden should not be so revealed and published.

The innovations which are injurious to the traditions should be overthrown as far as possible; at no places where they are seen should innovations, under any pretext, be allowed to become established.

The Muslim should be insistently asked, city quarter by city quarter, street by street, and house by house, to observe the five basic Muslim duties, i.e., reciting the Muslim profession of faith, the five obligatory prayers, the giving of alms, fasting during the month of Ramazan, and the pilgrimage to Mecca. It should be the duty of the censors to warn people who are slack about their obligatory prayers by various means; people who ignore their prayers altogether should be compelled by severe measures to pray. The rich should be asked to give alms (*zakāt*) to the poor and no excuse from them should be heard. And as to those reckless people, who either eat openly or practice their disgusting acts of disobedience in public during the fasting month [Ramazān] regardless of the respect due to the Faith and with no fear of the king, they should be arrested and brought before the ruler, so that as a general warning he may in his discretion and with his firm judgment punish them with long imprisonment, exile to distant places, death, or the shedding of blood. [folios 8a–9a]

In the next reading Barnī is advocating what he suggests was the actual practice of Sultan Mahmūd of Ghaznīn as the ideal for succeeding rulers in the Islamic world—that is, the suppression of the *falāsifa* (philosophers).

[From Barnī, *Fatāwa-yi-Jahāndārī,* folios 10b, 121a]

No other "sciences" were allowed to be publicly taught in the kingdom of Sultan Mahmūd except Qur'anic commentary, the traditions of the Prophet, and law divested of all false interpretation—in short, apart from the "sciences" which were based on the affirmation, "God has said," and "The Prophet has said," all other "sciences" were banned.

When Sultan Mahmūd conquered Khwārazm, he heard that Mu'tazilite doctrines were current there and that many men of learning were Mu'tazilites. He ordered these Mu'tazilite scholars to be exiled from Khwārazm; if anyone after the promulgation of this order followed the Mu'tazilite creed or even took its name, he was to be sent bound to Ghaznin. By the God who has succored Sultan Mahmūd in every difficulty, if Ibn Sīnā, who is the reviver of the philosophy of Greece and the leader of philosophers in Muslim countries, had fallen into the hands of Sultan Mahmūd, he would have ordered Ibn Sīnā to be cut to pieces and his flesh given to kites. [folio 10b]

Further, if kings like and approve that philosophers and all other people of false doctrine who are opponents of the true religion and enemies of the Prophet should teach their books openly; that these people should give to the sciences of the Greeks, which are the enemies of the traditional commands of the early and later prophets, the name of rational knowledge and to the sciences of the Sharī'a they give the name of traditional knowledge; that they should proclaim the world to be eternal and consider God not to have a cognition of details; that they should be disbelievers in the Day of Judgment, in the rising up of men from their graves, in the account-taking [on Judgment Day], and in Heaven and Hell (though belief in these things is the basis of the Faith and has been asserted in three hundred and sixty revealed books of the prophets); that they should both speak and write their rationalistic books in denial of these things—now if such people are allowed to live with honor and dignity in the capital of the king, to propagate their doctrines and to affirm their preference for the rationalistic over the traditional—how is the true Faith to prevail over the false creeds, or the banners of Islam raised, or "Truth established at the Center," or the honor of "ordering the good or prohibiting the unlawful," appear? [folio 121a]

[From Abū Tālib Husainī, *Tūzuk-i-Tīmūrī,* pp. 338, 340, 342]

It is your duty to act in obedience to the commands of God and of the Prophet of God and to give help to his posterity. Those rulers who feed on the bounty of God, and yet rebel against Him and against His Prophet, you must expel from God's kingdom. Act with justice in the land of your Creator; for it is said that the kingdom of the unbelievers may remain, but that of the unjust, never.

You must root out from God's kingdom all pollution and abomination; for evil practices have that effect on the world which bad food has upon the body.

Do not ascribe the continuance of the tyrant in the world to his own merits; the cause of the long duration of the oppressive and the wicked is this, that they may realize their power for evil in action and then be overtaken by the wrath and fury of Almighty God.

It shall happen that the omnipotence of the Creator shall chastise the cruel, the wicked, and the impious, by chains and imprisonment, by famine and hunger and plague, and by sudden death, all at one time.

And it shall sometimes happen that the just, the devout and the virtuous, and the innocent shall be overtaken and be caught in the disasters which afflict the evil-doers. For the fire which occurs in the reed bed burns both the moist green reeds and the dry reeds.

The general attitude of benevolence toward his Muslim subjects which was expected of the godly Muslim ruler is expressed in the following reading from Shaikh Hamadānī's *Treasuries of Kings.*

[From Shaikh Hamadānī *Zakhīrat ul-Mulūk,* folios 88a–93b]

Subjects are of two kinds, believers and unbelievers, and the mandates for and duties toward them are different according to whether they are believers or unbelievers.

There are twenty duties toward their Muslim subjects which are laid upon governors and kings and which they are obliged to perform.

The first is to show respect toward all Muslims; not to behave haughtily toward any Muslim, in full realization that God considers any haughty tyrant his enemy. . . . Second, not to listen to vulgar tittle-tattle one about another for that only leads in the end to strife and regret; in particular to consider vicious the words of scoundrels, intriguers, the jealous and the greedy, because covetousness will cause harm to a people through greed for a morsel, and envy will destroy all talents. . . . The third duty is that when a ruler becomes angry with a Muslim for some fault or weakness, he should as far as possible not delay forgiveness beyond three days, unless his anger has been caused by some action harmful to religion, wherefore it is permissible for him to shun him for the rest of his life. However, in a worldly matter forgiveness is more fitting. The Prophet [on whom be peace] has said: "Whoever forgives the sin of a brother

Muslim will have his sins forgiven by God on the Day of Judgment." . . .

The fourth duty upon rulers is to make the bounty of justice and righteousness general over all the people and in spreading the fruits of benevolence not to discriminate between the worthy and the unworthy; for the king is the shadow of God's justice and as the mercy of God embraces both infidel and believer alike, so the justice of the ruler should embrace both the good and the wicked. . . .

The fifth duty is not, in the arrogance of power, to pry into the private households of Muslims and not to enter the houses and storehouses of subjects without permission, because when the Prophet, in all his glory as a ruler and prophet, approached the door of a Muslim's house, he asked three times for permission to enter; if permission was not given, he went away and was not vexed. . . .

The sixth duty is, in speaking and dealing with all kinds of people, to treat each man according to his own proper rank and degree, neither looking for gentle speech from the mean and the ruffianly, nor elegance from the ignorant, and not demanding the manners of polite society from mountain and desert folk. Show courtesy to each according to his station and excuse every man according to his rank and do not disdain to meet anyone face to face. . . . The seventh duty upon rulers is to hold old men in great respect at meetings and discussion and especially to look upon the godly and the young with a kindly eye. As the Prophet said: "He who does not treat the old men of my people with respect and who is not merciful toward the young of the Muslim community is not one of us." . . .

The eighth obligation upon a ruler is that when he makes a promise in conversation with any Muslim, he keep it and allow nothing contrary to it. As the Prophet said: "Religion is the making of a promise [by the believer]." The Prophet said: "There are three indications of a hypocrite—when he speaks he lies, when he makes a promise he does precisely the opposite, and when he is trusted he acts treacherously." . . .

The ninth duty is not to speak severely when giving judgment and to show an open face to men of all classes and to show benevolence to those in distress. As the Prophet said: "In Paradise there are mansions whose interiors appear from outside to be of wondrous precious stones." They asked: "O Prophet of God, and whose are these mansions?" and he said: "They belong to those who speak pleasantly to the servants of God, to those who feed the hungry, and to those who say their prayers at night when the rest of mankind are asleep."

The tenth duty is to show fairness in the exercise of the royal office and jurisdiction. As the ruler asks fair dealing from his people, so they ask fair dealing from him. Moreover, he should deal with the affairs of Muslims in the same way that he would conclude the bargain with them if they were dealing with him. The Prophet said: "He who wishes to escape hell-fire and enter into the blessings of Paradise should do toward men as he would have them do toward him."

The eleventh duty is to consider the establishment of peace and concord a first duty, so that no delay is permitted in deciding an issue between Muslims and there is no delay in the decision between two opposing sides which might end in the matter becoming a cause of hatred, enmity, and eventual violence. The Prophet said: "I will inform you of a deed better than fasting, almsgiving, and prayer." They said: "Yes, yes, O Prophet of God?" He said: "It is peacemaking between Muslims."

The twelfth duty is not to attempt to investigate Muslims' sins and not to distress unfortunate subjects for their errors; the ruler should wink at his people's faults as far as possible and keep their mistakes hidden. The Prophet said: "Whoever conceals the sins and faults of Muslims will have his sins concealed by God on earth and on the Day of Judgment."

The thirteenth duty is not to arraign the people for acts of disobedience when they follow their own desires; to prevent suspicion and avoid arousing suspicion; if from time to time the ruler succumbs to sin, he should keep the fact concealed because the generality follow their ruler and judge in virtue and in vice, and if they see their ruler on the high road of virtue, they will follow the same path and the reward for that will be credited to his account. If the subjects observe corruption in their ruler they will also stray into iniquity, debauchery, and vice, and the sin of that will be debited to his account. The Prophet said: "Whoever follows good practices will reap the reward for that, and the reward of whoever follows him in those good practices will also be put to his account; whoever follows evil practices will receive the punishment for that, and the punishment of him who acts wickedly as a consequence will also be put down to him who was responsible originally for those evil practices."

The fourteenth duty upon the ruler is, that when a decision on the requirements of a Muslim is held up for words of intercession, to see that he puts in the requisite word of intercession and allows no negligence in carrying the decision out. One of the special features of the work of a judge is that many important matters may be brought to a successful conclusion by one word from him. The ruler should seize the opportunity to obtain the blessings of this reward. The Prophet said: "There is no more excellent act of almsgiving than speech." They asked him: "How so?" He replied: "It is intercession which preserves lives, brings benefit to another, and prevents harm to another."

The fifteenth duty is to keep the position of those who are poor and weak preponderant over that of those who are rich and powerful. Most of the time the ruler should sit with the poor and the people of God and once a day he should brighten the mirror of his heart with the advice and counsel of the pious because the personal superintendence of the business of government and the mixing with all and sundry darkens the heart, as does also association with the worldly and the rich. When these two darknesses embitter the heart, one must fear danger to religion; this is a cause for eternal bondage and everlasting mortification. . . . The Prophet said: "You are sitting with the dead." "O Prophet of God, who are the dead?" "The rich," he replied. . . .

The sixteenth duty is not to neglect the position of the poor and humble and not to allow any omission of almsgiving to the weak and those in distress. The ruler should consider diligent inquiry into the position of orphans an obligation upon himself and should consider the account to be rendered on the Day of Judgment; on that day possessions and a kingdom are no help and all the rightful claimants will demand their dues from the ruler. Today, when he is able, he should strive to redeem his time. Abū Harīra said that the Prophet said: "On the Day of Judgment God will summon his servant. God the Avenger will address him by name. 'O servant of Mine, on earth I asked you for bread and apparel and you did not give me any.' His servant will ask: 'O God, how is that?' and God will say: 'So-and-so was hungry in your company and so and so was naked and you did not look after them and treat them kindly. As you deprived them by your power and might of the means of subsistence so we now deprive you.' "

The seventeenth obligation on rulers is to keep, by punishment, the highways used by Muslims free from the fear of highwaymen and thieves, by exemplary and public punishment to make an example, as a warning to others, of him who causes injury to Muslims on the highroads by molestation and extortion. At every place in the country where there is a dangerous spot infested by robbers, erect buildings there if it is at all possible and, if not, station watchmen there. . . .

The eighteenth duty upon the ruler is, as far as possible, and where there is need, to exert himself in the good work of building bridges and resting places for travelers; not to permit any negligence in this respect. . . . The nineteenth duty is to build a mosque in any place where Muslims congregate and to appoint an Imām and a muezzin and to furnish the means of livelihood for them, so that, in freedom from anxiety they can perform prayer assiduously at the proper times without offering the excuse that seeking the means of carrying out that commandment prevents them in fact from doing so. . . .

The twentieth duty is not to abandon the command of God to do what is lawful and His injunction against doing what is unlawful, and not to deny people of all classes religious exhortation. Also, to command the subjects to perform their religious duties, to prevent them from disobedience to God and by means of punishment restrain them from sin.

One of the most important duties imposed by Muslim writers on the sultanate was the subjection of unbelievers. This was a duty of peculiar importance in India with its large Hindu population.

In practice both the sultans of Delhi and the Mughal emperors extended toleration to their Hindu subjects. It is doubtful whether they levied *jizya* or a poll tax as such upon non-Muslims. There is no evidence that a separate branch of the revenue department existed for this purpose, and those historians who allege that some sultans did levy *jizya* can be shown to be extolling a sultan in stock Islamic idiom. There is no doubt that for orthodox writers, it was a merit to abase the infidel and levy *jizya*. The view of the Muslim legists of the Hanafī school was that payment of *jizya* implying political submission entitled a non-Muslim to toleration, subject to certain discriminations—detailed in the reading later from Shaikh Hamadānī's *Treasuries of Kings*. Strictly, only a "people of a [revealed] book," i.e., Jews, Christians, and Sabaeans (which has been interpreted to cover Zoroastrians), may be accepted as *zimmīs* or "people of the covenant or obligation." Thus, Hindus should be excluded from toleration. Ziā ud-dīn Barnī was dismayed that the sultan of Delhi did tolerate them, as he implies in the first passage below. Barnī's ideals are expressed in the second and third readings. To support his contention he quotes an (uncanonical?) tradition to the effect that unbelievers have only the choice of Islam or the sword.

[From Barnī, *Fatāwa-yi-Jahāndārī,* folios 12a, 119a–20b]

If the desire for the overthrow of infidels and the abasing of idolators and polytheists does not fill the hearts of the Muslim kings; if, on the other hand, out of the thought that infidels and polytheists are payers of tribute and protected persons, they make the infidels eminent, distinguished, honored, and favored; if they bestow drums, banners, ornaments, cloaks of brocade, and caparisoned horses upon them; if they appoint them to governorships, high posts, and offices; and if in their capital [Delhi?] where the raising of the banners of Islam raises those banners in all Muslim cities, they allow idol-worshipers to build houses like palaces, to wear clothes of brocade, and to ride Arab horses caparisoned with gold and silver ornaments, to be equipped with a hundred thousand sources of strength, to live amid delights and comforts, to take Muslims into their service and to make them run before their horses, with poor Muslims begging of them and at their doors in the capital of Islam, through which the palace of Islam raises itself, so that Muslims call them kings, princes, warriors, bankers, clerks, and pandits [Brahman scholars]—how then may the banners of Islam be raised? [folios 120–120b]

. . . .

If the kings of Islam, with all their majesty and power, take for granted infidelity and infidels, polytheism and polytheists throughout their dominions in return for the land revenue (*kharāj*) and *jizya,* how will the tradition, "If I fight people until they say, 'There is no god but God,' and if they say, 'There is no god but God,' they are immune from me and their persons and property exist only by virtue of Islam," be observed? And how will infidelity and infidels, polytheism and polytheists be overthrown—the purpose of the mission of 124,000 prophets and the domination of sultans of Islam since Islam appeared? If the kings of Islam do not strive with all their might for this overthrow, if they do not devote all their courage and energies to this end for the satisfaction of God and of the prophet, for the assistance of the Faith and the exalting of the True Word; if they become content with extracting the *jizya* and the land tax from the Hindus who worship idols and cow-dung, taking for granted the Hindu way of life with all its stipulations of infidelity, how shall infidelity be brought to an end, now that Muhammad's Prophethood has come to an end—and it was by the prayers of the prophets that infidelity was being ended? How will "Truth be established at the Center" and how will the

Word of God obtain the opportunity for supremacy? How will the True Faith prevail over other religions, if the kings of Islam, with the power and prestige of Islam which has appeared in the world, with three hundred years of hereditary faith in Islam, permit the banners of infidelity to be openly displayed in their capital and in the cities of the Muslims, idols to be openly worshiped and the conditions of infidelity to be observed as far as possible, the mandates of their false creed to operate without fear? How will the True Faith prevail if rulers allow the infidels to keep their temples, adorn their idols, and to make merry during their festivals with beating of drums and *dhols* [a kind of drum], singing and dancing? [folios 119a–b]

. . . .

If Mahmūd . . . had gone to India once more, he would have brought under his sword all the Brahmans of Hind who, in that vast land, are the cause of the continuance of the laws of infidelity and of the strength of idolators, he would have cut off the heads of two hundred or three hundred thousand Hindu chiefs. He would not have returned his "Hindu-slaughtering" sword to its scabbard until the whole of Hind had accepted Islam. For Mahmūd was a Shāfi'ite, and according to Imām Shāfi'i the decree for Hindus is "either death or Islam"—that is to say, they should either be put to death or embrace Islam. It is not lawful to accept *jizya* from Hindus as they have neither a prophet nor a revealed book. [folio 12a]

Shaikh Hamadānī was, however, prepared to admit idol worshipers to the status of *zimmīs,* as the first of his conditions below implies.

[From Shaikh Hamadānī, *Zakhīrat ul-Mulūk,* folios 94a–95a]

There is another mandate relating to those subjects who are unbelievers and protected people (*zimmīs*). For their governance, the observance of those conditions which the Caliph 'Umar laid down in his agreement for establishing the status of the fire worshipers and the People of the Book [Jews and Christians] and which gave them safety is obligatory on rulers and governors. Rulers should impose these conditions on the *zimmīs* of their dominions and make their lives and their property dependent on their fulfillment. The twenty conditions are as follows:

1. In a country under the authority of a Muslim ruler, they are to build no new homes for images or idol temples.
2. They are not to rebuild any old buildings which have been destroyed.
3. Muslim travelers are not to be prevented from staying in idol temples.
4. No Muslim who stays in their houses will commit a sin if he is a guest for three days, if he should have occasion for the delay.
5. Infidels may not act as spies or give aid and comfort to them.
6. If any of their people show any inclinations toward Islam, they are not to be prevented from doing so.
7. Muslims are to be respected.
8. If *zimmīs* are gathered together in a meeting and Muslims appear, they are to be allowed at the meeting.
9. They are not to dress like Muslims.
10. They are not to give each other Muslim names.
11. They are not to ride on horses with saddle and bridle.
12. They are not to possess swords and arrows.
13. They are not to wear signet rings and seals on their fingers.
14. They are not to sell and drink intoxicating liquor openly.
15. They must not abandon the clothing which they have had as a sign of their state of ignorance so that they may be distinguished from Muslims.
16. They are not to propagate the customs and usages of polytheists among Muslims.
17. They are not to build their homes in the neighborhood of those of Muslims.
18. They are not to bring their dead near the graveyards of Muslims.
19. They are not to mourn their dead with loud voices.
20. They are not to buy Muslim slaves.

At the end of the treaty it is written that if *zimmīs* infringe any of these conditions, they shall not enjoy security and it shall be lawful for Muslims to take their lives and possessions as though they were the lives and possessions of unbelievers in a state of war with the faithful.

A passage from a Mughal writer on the same theme.

[From Abū Tālib Husainī, *Tūzuk-i-Tīmūrī,* p. 330]

If tyranny and oppression and iniquity exists in any kingdom, it is the duty of sultans, out of a regard for justice, to resolve on the removal and extirpation of the tyranny and oppression and to conduct a rapid excursion against it. For God Most High will take that kingdom from the oppressor and entrust it to the just ruler. . . . And in every country where the Sharī'a is feeble, where they do not respect those whom God Most High has made great and distress His chosen servants, it is the duty of a conquering sultan, who intends to make current the religion and the law of Muhammad, to invade that country, for the Prophet will strengthen him in that undertaking. Thus I seized the capital of Hindustan from Sultan Mahmūd, the grandson of Fīrūz Shāh, from Mallū Khān, and from Sarang, reestablishing the True Faith and the Sharī'a and destroying the idol temples of that country.

Justice Is Indispensable to Temporal Rulership

Muslim writers in Persia who, after the practical breakdown of the Sunni jurists' theory of the caliphate, discussed the duties of the sultanate (e.g. Nizām ul-Mulk, author of the *Siyāsat-Nāma,* al-Ghazālī in his *Nasīhat ul-Mulūk* and Wassāf in his *Akhlāq us-Sultānat*) were prepared to choose justice in preference to legality, if they could not have both. Although a sultan was often obliged, out of political expediency, to contravene, or to go beyond the ideal prescriptions of the Sharī'a, they argued that he could still serve God if he dispensed justice and equity, thus preventing social disorder provoked by oppression. Indo-Muslim thought was (as usual) very similar.

[From Fakhr-i-Mudir, *Shajara,* p. 13]

And the Prophet also says, "The sultan is the shadow of God. The shadow consists of care and tranquillity because justice and security are found there, and in the shelter and protection of kings there is a resting place for the oppressed and a refuge from the oppressors."

[From Barnī *Fatāwa-yi-Jahāndārī,* folios 43b–44b]

From the time of Adam to our own days the people of all communities throughout history are united in the opinion that justice is a requisite of religion and that religion is a requisite of justice. For it is not possible for men to live without having dealings with each other; and in these mutual dealings a man may be strong or weak, good or bad, Muslim or non-Muslim, wise or foolish, learned or ignorant, townsman or villager, resident or traveler, deceptive or straightforward, ruler or subject, an adult or a minor. Now justice is the balance in which the actions of people, right or wrong, are weighed. The distinction between one's desserts and the opposite is clarified by justice. Justice exposes cruelty, oppression, usurpation, and plunder. Consequently, there can be no stability in the affairs of men without justice. No religion which is founded on divine commandments can do without justice. Both ancient and succeeding authorities have said: "Religion and justice are twins." For justice breaks the strong arm of the tyrannical, the oppressive, and the mighty—of misappropriators, plunderers, rebels, the froward, the "people of license," and disbelievers in the Day of Judgment and accounts—to protect the money, property, women, and children of the weak, the obedient, the helpless, the orphans, the submissive, and the friendless. Justice prevents tyranny and oppression through the mandates of religion. If there is no justice or equity on the earth, there will be complete community of women and property; the distinction between one man's property and another's will vanish; no time or place will be free from disorder, and no man will be able to drink his cup of water in his corner in peace or to stretch his legs and sleep on his bed in security for a single night; and, finally, the world will cease to be prosperous owing to immense tumults and disorders. Nevertheless if all the wise men of the earth tried to govern a village, or even a household, through mere policy or precepts of wisdom without judges endowed with power, they would not succeed. The origin of peace and stability is justice and equity which prevails among the people [only] through strong command.

The real justification for the authority of kings and of their power and dignity is the manifestation of justice, so that through their royal power and dignity they may remove all recourse to oppression and cruelty in the dealings of the servants of God, the seventy-two creeds may attain to contentment of heart, and everyone may devote himself to his craft, profession, trade and work, and the world may become populous and prosperous. If there is no justice, there will be no trade and no one will be able to obtain any fruit from his work. Finally, if the affairs of men are not "organized at the center," there will be no permanency in the works of Muslim faith or the commandments, and recompense and punishment will not bear their fruits.

[From Muhammad Bāqir Khān, *Mau'iza-yi-Jahāngīrī,* folios 10a–11a]

Kings must consider their sitting on a throne to be for the sake of dispensing justice and not for the sake of living a life of enjoyment, and should consider justice and equity the cause of the continuance of their rule, of the persistence of their fame, and of obtaining reward in the next world. . . .

If there is no control by government and administration, great enterprises would not stay in [good] order and if there was no correction and punishment, man's affairs would be ruined. Administration is the ornament of the king and of the state, and it is expedient for both religion and government. Without the kings' rules of administration the mandates of the Sharī'a would not be put into effect, nor would the foundations of the sultanate be firm. If the sword of administrative punishment is not drawn from the scabbard of retribution, the foundations of sedition and the basis of oppression will not be subverted and undermined. If the vile dross of injustice is not destroyed by the flame of royal power, the young plant of security will not be nurtured in the garden of hope. When the seditious see that the flame of such punishment is sharp, they will slink away. If they observe little to be alarmed at in the work of administration, there will be rebellion on every side and all kinds of disturbances will ensue.

Moreover, kings must show the mercy which God does toward the good and the peaceable and the wrath of God toward the wicked and the evildoers. They must tip the point of their authority with the honey of kindness and sweeten the bitterness of their harshness with the sugar of kindness. There must be a conjunction of justice and punishment, so that the meadow of the hopes of the good may be kept verdant by the moisture of kindness and the bases of the existence of the wicked may be uprooted by the gale of punishment.

Rulership Is a Sacred Trust

Indo-Muslim writers emphasize the responsibility of rulers before God for the welfare of His creatures. Power is a sacred trust, for which rulers will answer on the Day of Judgment.

[From Nūr ud-dīn Muhammad Khaqānī, *Akhlāq-i-Jahāngīrī,* folio 279b]

It is said that when the father of 'Umar ibn 'Abd al-'Azīz lay dying, his son asked him when he would see him again. 'Abd al-'Azīz replied that it would be in the next world. His son said he hoped it would be sooner than that. 'Abd al-'Azīz then said: "You may see me in a dream during the first, second, or third nights [after my death]." Twelve years passed without his son seeing him in a dream. At last he did so. Replying to his son's question why he had not seen him as promised, 'Abd al-'Azīz said: "O son I have been very occupied; near Baghdad there was a broken bridge with no one appointed to keep it in repair. Once when a flock of sheep were passing over it, the forefeet of one of them went through a hole in the bridge. I have been answering [to God] for that until this very moment.

[From Shaikh Hamadānī, *Zakhīrat ul-Mulūk,* folios 72b–73a]
Sulaimān Fāris (may God be satisfied with him) reported that the Prophet of God (on whom be peace) said that every governor who has anything to do with the affairs of Muslims in the exercise of his authority will on the Day of Judgment be brought forward with both hands tied around his neck. Nobody and nothing will release his hands except justice. . . . If he has been a benefactor of mankind, his benevolence frees him; if he has been a wicked man, an oppressor, and a sinner and a rebel against God . . . he falls into the pit; it must be seventy years before he reaches the bottom of that pit.

[From Nūr ud-dīn Muhammad Khaqānī, *Akhlāq-i-Jahāngīrī,* folios 264a–269]
It is reported from Abū Sa'īd that the Prophet said that every sultan and ruler who does not show compassion toward his subjects will be forbidden to enter Paradise and enjoy its delights. And 'Abdullāh 'Umar al-Khattāb reported that the Prophet said that God will, on the day of need, when the ruler is surrounded by enemies, close the door of His mercy in the face of that ruler who, placed in a position of authority over Muslims, shuts the door of his house against the weak and the needy. And Abū Mūsā Ash'arī said that the Prophet said that the basest fellow in creation is he who as a ruler puts himself in pledge for Muslims and does not discharge that pledge, while the most noble is he who dispenses justice and equity among Muslims. [folios 264a, b]

. . . .

It is related that in the time of Sultan Abū Sayyid Khudābanda, his amīrs [nobles] were treating his subjects harshly and forcibly confiscating their goods. One day the sultan said to his amīrs: "Until now I have had regard for my subjects, but after today I shall cease doing so. If it is expedient, then we must plunder everybody and not allow them anything from our treasuries; but on the condition, furthermore, that you do not ask for any salary or stipend from me; if henceforth any one of you makes this sort of request to me, I shall punish him." The amīrs said: "How can we do without salaries or stipends, what kind of service can we then perform?" Abū Sayyid replied: "The successful conduct of all our affairs depends on the efforts made by the subjects in building, agriculture, in crafts, and in commerce. When we plunder them, from whom can we expect to receive anything? You should consider that if the mass of the people have their livestock and its products taken away, and their grain eaten, they must of necessity abandon cultivation and engage in it no more; thus there will be no revenue and what will you do?" When the amirs heard these words, they began to treat the people kindly. [folios 268b–269]

The Selection of Officials

If he is to escape divine punishment, the sultan must employ and consult god-fearing aides and officials of true Muslim belief and avoid employing low and impious persons. The aim of the royal officials, as of the sultan himself, must be the furtherance of true religion.

[From Barnī, *Fatāwa-yi-Jahāndārī,* folios 59a, b, 205b–10a]

How can the ruler . . . act according to the Sharī'a in his government without good helpers, praiseworthy supporters, pious friends, and trusty well-wishers who are adorned with lineage, descent, and praiseworthy morals? How can he discharge the duties of such a high and delicate office with the help of the worthless and the shameless, with the assistance and concurrence of the godless and the idle? [folio 205b]

. . . .

In the choice of helpers and companions, religious kings have laid down a few things as obligatory. First, the person selected should be one on whom the search for true religion predominates over the quest for worldly good, even though it be only by a needle's point, for if all his efforts are devoted to religion he will not become one of the helpers and companions of the king and will not dabble in the world's business. . . . From a man whose loyalty and well-wishing toward them springs out of love of the world and desire for place and who is a captive and slave of this world, no deed, which is in the ultimate praiseworthy and commendable, can be expected. . . . A man who is not fit to be trusted in affairs of religion, is not fit to be trusted in affairs of state. [folio 210a]

. . . .

My advice to you, my dear son, is do justice to the qualities of the people of God and make clear the balance and scales for measuring the virtue of the people. Create a rank for every excellence and accordingly confer honor, position, dignity, and grandeur upon every description of people. In the bestowal of robes and gifts, employment in office, the right of sitting and rising, of speaking and listening in your presence, deal with your servants in a manner in keeping with their capacity as wazirs, wise men, learned in the Holy Law, and ascetics. Do not blindly undertake with the servants of God some project affecting your kingdom in an incongruous way and do not start any project which the wise men of your kingdom will attribute to your lack of reason or to self-will. Let it be known to you, my son, that God has made the ruler greater than all human creation, and, with all that greatness, has entrusted the world to him. Thus it is necessary that the great should receive the gift of greatness from the ruler and that he be the cause of their position in the world and their dignity. He should be the means of the prestige which appears among men. Royal actions are indeed very important. The consequences of royal actions quickly appear among the people and remain a long time. It is a long time before a person honored by him becomes base, or a person made contemptible by him becomes excellent. But the honor in which those who forsake the world and retire to an ascetic way of life are held among the generality is due to their renunciation of the world (which is the beloved of mankind) and their withdrawal from human society. The king has no part in conferring this honor and has no hand in its attainment. Thus, my son, it is incumbent upon you not to lower the offices and dignities of your state by conferring them upon the foolish, the ignorant, the sinful, the low-born, and those in the grip of vice. The royal dynasty itself is disgraced and becomes infamous through baseness and infamy among the officers of state. [folios 59a–59b]

[From Muhammad Bāqir Khān, *Mau'iza-yi-Jahāngīrī,* folios 27b–28b]

The ruler is he who, having nurtured those who are distinguished among their equals for the perfection of their sagacity, probity, ability, chastity, sincerity, devotion to religion, piety, faithfulness, and loyalty, acquired prestige from the fact of each one being employed in the capacity for which he is fitted. He gives them appointments one by one as occasion arises in accordance with their judgment, courage, intelligence, and capacity. He does not give one person two employments lest an intended task is not completed; one person, one task; one task, one person. The ruler himself should look into the circumstances and the nature of the employments entrusted to his officers and trusted servants so that when they are performed he should know which among his agents cherish his subjects and are upright in religion, and which are treacherous and seditious knaves. So, he who ministers to the people's welfare and sincerely performs the duty assigned to him may be favored by the ruler and enjoy security in his office. He who does not sympathize with the subjects, who neglects the essentials of his duty, does not let slip an opportunity for treachery, and makes baseness his upper and his nether garments—his name is to be struck from the roll of office.

In the following reading, Barnī states that among usurpers are those who do not employ subordinates in those ranks for which God has fitted them; usurpers, thinking of the preservation of their own power and not of God's glory, employ those whom they believe meet for their own worldly purposes, irrespective of merit. The basis of Barnī's moral and religious distinctions, which should be mirrored in social distinctions, is more fully illustrated in the chapter on the Muslim social ideal.

[From Barnī, *Fatāwa-yi-Jahāndārī,* folios 56a, b]

But one who collects a large number of people on his side, caring for no desert or merit in them except their loyalty to himself, he is to be called "conqueror" and not "king." He rules the country through the power of his followers; he strikes, takes, seizes, and bestows, and thus every day he is able to show more favors to his supporters. He increases their power and dignity, thinking that the permanence of his kingdom is due to them, and he strives for their prosperity without paying any regard to their defects and their merits. The eyes of such a man are turned away from God Almighty; he is all the time exclusively busy with his helpers and supporters till matters come to such a pass that he turns all low, mean, base, defective, and worthless men, who are of bad and low origin, into the pillars of his state, provided he sees in them great loyalty toward himself combined with substantial power and dignity. No doubt thousands and thousands of such usurpers have risen on this earth from every stock that can be imagined; they have ruled for a while with the support of a body of partisans and have left the world having made themselves and their followers fit for Hell. Thus neither their names nor any traces of them have remained in the conversations or the hearts of the people. But all rulers, whose eyes have been wholly fixed on God Almighty, have made clear scales and measures of merit, real worth, piety, nobility, free-birth, wisdom, skill, and morality, who have discharged their obligations to every merit through the resources of their government and to the full extent of their power, and who in that discharge have looked at everyone with that one vision—their memory will remain till the Day of Judgment among the people of God and this fact will have been a sufficient proof of their salvation and of their status in the next world.

The Importance of Consultation

[From Barnī, *Fatāwa-yi-Jahāndārī,* folios 17a, 23a–24a]

You should know that the supreme object of that part of a man's soul which commands to evil, higher than which it is impossible to conceive, is self-will and self-indulgence. This is specially the case with kings, whose souls owing to their great power become equal in strength to a thousand elephants in heat. If the king subdues this power and madness of his soul, refrains from being self-willed, and decides the affairs of his kingdom in consultation with his counsellors, will not the kindness of God shine on his forehead and all his undertakings end in success and virtue? [folio 17a]

. . . .

Great kings have observed many conditions and have been very cautious in the matter of consultation; consequently, the opinion of their counsellors has seldom erred. The first condition of consultation is the frank expression of the opinion of the counsellors—that is, the very condition of holding a council is that all counsellors should be able to say whatever comes to their minds without fear, to give reasons and arguments for their opinions about the execution of state enterprises, and to consult frankly with each other. Ultimately, when all their minds are in agreement and no objection remains, they should apply themselves to the accomplishment of their purpose. This, in the terminology of consultation, is known as "agreement of opinion." If there is no unanimous agreement about the matter among the counsellors, no reliance can be placed upon any course of action. Secondly, the counsellors ought to be [properly] appointed; they should be nearly equal to each other in their experience, in their loyalty, and in their status before the king. If one counsellor is perfect in intelligence and the other defective, one high in status and the other "on the way down," there will be a danger of incongruity in the decision. Thirdly, all counsellors should be admitted to the secrets of the realm and none of them should be unworthy of being taken into confidence. If a counsellor is not cognizant of the secrets of the realm, he will not be able to arrive at a correct decision, just as a physician cannot prescribe effective remedies unless he knows the real symptoms and diseases of a patient. Fourthly, the counsellors, besides being chosen by the ruler and being near to him, ought to have perfect security of life and position so that they may not for any reason resort to flattery in the council chamber. They should be able to express their real opinion, with lips unsealed, and they should be convinced that this will lead to increased recognition of their loyalty. They should not be afraid of the ill-temper of the ruler, for so long as the fear of the king tortures their breasts, sincere advice will not come from their hearts to their tongues. Fifthly, the king should keep his opinions a secret from his counsellors. He should, first, acquaint himself with the opinion of his counsellors, hear the views they have to express and wait for the decision they arrive at. If the ruler expresses his opinion in the council at the very beginning, the counsellors will find it necessary, willingly or unwillingly, to praise his decision and to suppress their own views. No one will have the courage to oppose the decision of the king or to give reasons against it. This fact has been proved by experience. [folios 23a–24a]

Organizing the Government

Rulers must appoint pious, efficient, and trustworthy army commanders, wazirs or finance officers, judges, and intelligence officers. The task of the latter particularly is to report on the welfare of the people and to bring oppressive acts by officials to the ruler's notice.

[From Muhammad Bāqir Khān, *Mau'iza-yi-Jahāngīrī,* folios 26b–27b]

You should know that "pillars of the state," ministers, and other servants, are essential for sultans and kings. It is an unquestioned need of rulers to have capable counsellors and trusty officers who have the privilege of intimacy with the king's secrets, and have ability and authority for important undertakings. It is said that a realm has four legs. If one is missing the foundations of important transactions will not be firm. The first leg of the kingdom is the existence of great amīrs, who are the people of the sword and guard the frontiers of the kingdom and prevent the wickedness of enemies from affecting the king and the people. They are the pillars of the dynasty and the foundation of the sultanate. Second are the capable finance officers and religious revenue officers who are the ornament of the kingdoms, the cause of the stable foundations of the sultanate, and the regulators of the affairs of the realm. The undertakings of the ruler of the kingdom do not reach a successful conclusion without the people of the pen, and indeed in some ways, the people of the pen aspire to superiority over the people of the sword, arguing first that the sword is only used for enemies and not for friends, whereas the pen is used both to benefit friends and to ward off enemies, something which the sword cannot do. The second argument is that the people of the sword in secret betray ambitions to be kings themselves. This is something which never happens with the people of the pen. Thirdly, the people of the sword empty the treasury, and the people of the pen fill it, and occasions of income are better than occasions of expenditure. In any event, failure will never overtake nor calamity stalk the kingdom of him who places in charge of his affairs a wise, sensible wazir, with excellent moral qualities, without greed and with high aspirations. For, if the opposite occurs and an unholy wazir with a lewd nature meddles with the business of the realm, however much the ruler may be humane and beneficient himself, the benefits of his own justice and compassion will be prevented from reaching his subjects and fear of him will not cause reports of oppressors to be made to him—just as it is impossible for a thirsty man to touch the pure sweet water which is to be seen on the skin of a crocodile, however thirsty he may be. The third leg of the realm is the judge who, on behalf of the sultan, inquires into the state of the people, obtains justice for the weak from the strong, and abaṣes and subdues the seditious and the forward. The fourth leg is the trusty intelligence officers who report continually the actions of the royal officials and the condition of the subjects. They bring to the royal notice any signs of harshness and negligence. For when information about the country and realm is hidden from the ruler, he is careless of friend or foe, good or evil, and everyone does as he likes. When the ruler is without information, the foundations of his sultanate become shaky from all the rebellions which spring up in all parts of the country.

[From Barnī, *Fatāwa-yi-Jahāndārī,* folios 82a–84a *passim*]

In the appointment of intelligence officers, auditors, and spies, religious rulers have had good intentions and objects. First, when it becomes clear to the officers, judges, governors, and revenue collectors both far and near, that their good and bad actions will be brought to light, they do not demand bribes or accept presents or show favor or partiality. They do not depart from the path of righteousness or take to sinfulness and wrong-doing, and they are always fearful and trembling concerning their own private affairs. Owing to this caution on their part they may be safe from their real superior [God] and from their figurative superior [the sultan].

Secondly, when the people are convinced that the good and bad deeds of all classes are being reported to the king and that officeholders have been appointed for this particular purpose, they will behave like good subjects; they will neither conspire nor rebel nor attempt to overpower each other nor oppress the weak. Thirdly, if revenue collectors and accountants know that their actions will be brought to the notice of the king, they will refrain from stealing and misappropriating and thus remain secure from the ruler and escape dishonor and disgrace. Lastly, it will be an advantage even to the king's sons, brothers, and high officers if they are aware that the king will be informed of all their actions, for they will not then, presuming on their close relationship with the king, step beyond the bounds of justice in their dealings with their own people and strangers, or their slaves and servants. . . .

The intelligence officer should be truthful in speech, truthful in writing, reliable, well-born, worthy of confidence, sober and careful where he lives, and not much given to social and convivial intercourse so that his object, which is obtaining correct information for the king's business, may be attained. But if the intelligence officer is a thief, a man without rectitude, low-born, mean, a frequenter of every place and a caller at every door, corrupt, greedy, covetous, and reckless, then what should be the predicate of the ruler's intentions, his designs and his search for the welfare of his subjects, will become the opposite. For the dishonest and low-born intelligence officer, who is a master of intrigue and "wire-pulling," spins many lies that look like truth, and through his testifying to false information, affairs are thrown into disorder. Where benefits should be rendered, injuries are inflicted; men worthy of punishment are favored while men deserving of favor are punished.

The Army

Following the Persian pre-and post-Muslim tradition Muslim writers on government in India always stress the importance of the maintenance of a large and efficient army. It is doubtful whether this stress is specifically related to the military problems facing the Muslim rulers in India.

[From Barnī, *Fatāwa-yi-Jahāndārī,* folios 64a–b]

O sons of Mahmūd, you and every one whom God raises to be a ruler and a refuge of religion, ought to know that without a large, powerful, and magnificent army, maintained in good order, it has not been possible to exercise government and maintain rule, or plan conquest, to direct administration, to awe the hearts of the people by conquests, to bring the world under rule and government, to overcome the rebellious and the refractory, to bring the stubborn and the disobedient under control, to suppress the contentions of rivals and the opposition of equals and the enmity of the powerful, to overthrow those who injure the religion and realm of Muhammad, to extirpate those who molest the Sharī'a of Muhammad and to make manifest the glory of the true faith over false doctrines and to enforce the mandates of the Sharī'a over the seventy-two creeds, to seize by force countries, regions, provinces, and territories from the irreligious, to obtain booty for the warriors of the faith and those entitled to it among the Muslims, to close all breaches open to the enemies of the kingdom and those troublesome to the dynasty and, in short, to seek relief from the heavy responsibility of rulership.

[From Muhammad Bāqir Khān, *Mau'iza-yi-Jahāngīrī,* folios 35a–b]

Similarly since the world is a place of unforeseen vicissitudes and no one knows what time will have in store, or from what direction rebellion will appear, rulers must consider the raising of a large army their principal concern and must always keep it equipped and ready for war and, having appointed and confirmed amīrs, aides, and pillars of the kingdom, confer upon each, according to merit, his command (*mansab*) and a *jāgīr*,[1] so that he may maintain his appropriate contingent. From year to year rulers should take care that their armies and amīrs are ready for muster, that all their weapons, equipment, and warlike apparatus is ready and prepared; if sultans and amīrs become so engrossed in collecting money that they do not recruit an army, in an emergency they will be at a loss; there will be no benefit to be derived from their chests of gold and however much "they may bite the finger of regret with the teeth of blame," it will not profit them.

The Perfect Rule

The religious consequences which Muslim writers hoped and believed would flow from sultans taking upon themselves the responsibilities and duties previously borne by the caliphs are perhaps best expressed in the reading below from Barnī's *Rulings on Temporal Government.*

[From Barnī, *Fatāwa-yi-Jahāndārī,* folios 122a–122b; 231b–232a]

Whenever the ruler, with truly pious intent, high aspirations, and all solicitude, strives with the help of his supporters and followers, and with all the might and power of his office in the conviction that the glory of Muhammad's religion is the most important task of his own faith and dynasty [then the following consequences follow]: obedience to the command to do what is lawful and the prohibition of what is unlawful manifests itself in his capital and in the provinces; the banners of Islam are always exalted; virtue and merit grow and good works and obedience to God arise, and arise with the beat of drums; sin and iniquity, wickedness and wrongdoing, sink low and remain concealed and in hiding; justice and beneficence become diffused while oppression and tyranny are doomed and cast out; the sciences of tradition become agreeable to men's minds, and they avoid concealed innovations and the knowledge and the literature of concealed innovations; the religious and the protectors of religion attain to dignity and high positions while members of false sects, men of evil faith and heretics, enemies of true religion, become base and contemptible, powerless, and of no account. Those mandates of true religion are enforced and those forbidden by the Holy Law (Sharī'a)

[1] Lands (or land revenues) assigned in return for service to the ruler, originally only for the lifetime of the grantee but often becoming hereditary.

sink low and become as if they had never been; love of God and of the Prophets is strengthened in the Muslim community and love of the world (which is a temptation in the path of truth and a longing and an evil in men's hearts) lessens, and desire for the next world increases and desire for this world becomes wearisome and vexatious. The virtues of the people prevail over their vices; truth and the truthful obtain glory and honor, lying and liars, dishonor. Descendants of Muhammad [Saiyyids], doctors of Sharī'a, mystics, ascetics, devotees, recluses appear great, honored, distinguished, and illustrious in the sight and in the minds of men, while the ignorant, the corrupt, the irreligious, the negligent [in performing their prayers], and the shameless appear contemptible, powerless, and unworthy in men's sight. In Holy War sincere zeal is manifested, and the desire for martyrdom graces the warriors and strivers for the faith. Truth and honesty become such; perfidy and dishonesty are reduced to a sorry plight; the good and the just take up occupations in religion and government; the tyrannical and the wicked are left to roam at large "unwept, unhonored, and unsung," or by a change in their dispositions, to behave justly and well; the rich and propertied discharge their obligations to God, and give alms, and perform charitable good works; the poor and the needy are not left in want and are freed from hunger and nakedness. [folios 122a, b]

However, if rulers do not fulfill their religious duty and act as tyrants, no "constitutional" remedy is provided. Tyranny is a visitation from God.

If God Most High views the people of a country and clime with eyes of wrath, and wishes them to remain in toil, trouble, suffering, distress, and disorder, he appoints over them a ruler who is a slave to innate depravity, so that they may be at a loss to know what to do through his evil character and filthy habits, and be utterly confounded through his vicious qualities. [folios 231b–232a]

Abū'l Fazl's Theory of Rulership

The next reading is taken from the preface to the famous *Institutes of Akbar* and "imperial gazeteer" of Akbar's empire. Abū'l Fazl 'Allāmī, friend and companion of the Mughal emperor Akbar, was born in 1551 at Agra. His father, Shaikh Mubārak, was a prominent scholar and mystic, and Abū'l Fazl, though given an orthodox education, stood at the confluence of the many religious currents of his age. He was presented at court by his brother, the poet Faizī, in 1574, and soon gained the emperor's favor by his wit, learning, and moral earnestness. He joined in influencing Akbar against Sunni orthodoxy and in obtaining the assent of Muslim doctors of law to a declaration giving Akbar the deciding voice on religious questions in narrowly defined circumstances. Abū'l Fazl attracted the enmity of Prince Salīm (Jahāngīr) for his influence over Akbar and was murdered at the former's instance in 1602.

Abū'l Fazl's thinking on government was influenced by Shī'ī teachings and by ideas mediated from classical Greece by Muslim philosophers (*falāsifa*). The Shī'a believed that from the creation of Adam a divine light had passed into the substance of a chosen one in each generation and that this Imam possessed esoteric knowledge of God and enjoyed immunity from sin. By Mughal times, this conception of an immaculate and infallible guide for mankind had been transferred to the person of the temporal ruler (*pādshāh*). Furthermore, the Platonic idea of "philosopher kings" had been received into the Muslim world and transmitted with Islamic overtones by such writers, for example, as al-Fārābī (d. 950), Ibn Rushd (d. 1198), and al-Rāzī (d. 1209), reaching Indian Mughal circles through Jalāl ud-dīn Dawwānī's *Akhlāq-i-Jalālī* (*Jalālī's Ethics*), written in Persia about 1470. In his writing, Abū'l Fazl treated Akbar as an incarnation of these conceptions. Akbar himself, of a deeply religious and inquiring mind, was not loath to exercise that initiative in religious questions which Abu'l Fazl was willing to allow him in theory.

[From Abū'l Fazl, *Ā'īn-i-Akbarī,* pp. ii–iv]

No dignity is higher in the eyes of God than royalty, and those who are wise drink from its auspicious fountain. A sufficient proof of this, for those who require one, is the fact that royalty is a remedy for the spirit of rebellion, and the reason why subjects obey. Even the meaning of the word *Pādshāh* [emperor] shows this; for *pād* signifies stability and possession. If royalty did not exist, the storm of strife would never subside, nor selfish ambition disappear. Mankind, being under the burden of lawlessness and lust, would sink into the pit of destruction; this world, this great market place, would lose its prosperity, and the whole world become a barren waste. But by the light of imperial justice, some follow with cheerfulness the road of obedience, while others abstain from violence through fear of punishment; and out of necessity make choice of the path of rectitude. *Shāh* is also a name given to one who surpasses his fellows, as you may see from words like *shāh-suwār* [royal horseman], *shāh-rāh* [royal road]; it is also a term applied to a bridegroom—the world, as the bride, betroths herself to the king, and becomes his worshiper.

Silly and shortsighted men cannot distinguish a true king from a selfish ruler. Nor is this remarkable, as both have in common a large treasury, a numerous army, clever servants, obedient subjects, an abundance of wise men, a multitude of skillful workmen, and a superfluity of means of enjoyment. But men of deeper insight remark a difference. In the case of the former, these things just now enumerated are lasting, but in that of the latter, of short duration. The former does not attach himself to these things, as his object is to remove oppression and provide for everything which is good. Security, health, chastity, justice, polite manners, faithfulness, truth, and increase of sincerity, and so forth, are the result. The latter is kept in bonds by the external forms of royal power, by vanity, the slavishness of men, and the desire of enjoyment; hence everywhere there is insecurity, unsettledness, strife, oppression, faithlessness, robbery.

Royalty is a light emanating from God, and a ray from the sun, the illuminator of the universe, the argument of the book of perfection, the receptacle of all virtues. Modern language calls this light the divine light, and the tongue of antiquity called it the sublime halo. It is communicated by God to kings without the intermediate assistance of anyone, and men, in the presence of it, bend the forehead of praise toward the ground of submission.

Again, many excellent qualities flow from the possession of this light:

1. A paternal love toward the subjects. Thousands find rest in the love of the king, and sectarian differences do not raise the dust of strife. In his wisdom, the king will understand the spirit of the age, and shape his plans accordingly.

2. A large heart. The sight of anything disagreeable does not unsettle him, nor is want of discrimination for him a source of disappointment. His courage steps in. His divine firmness gives him the power of requittal, nor does the high position of an offender interfere with it. The wishes of great and small are attended to, and their claims meet with no delay at his hands.

3. A daily increasing trust in God. When he performs an action, he considers God as the real doer of it [and himself as the medium] so that a conflict of motives can produce no disturbance.

4. Prayer and devotion. The success of his plans will not lead him to neglect, nor will adversity cause him to forget God and madly trust in man. He puts the reins of desire into the hands of reason; in the wide field of his desires he does not permit himself to be trodden down by restless-

ness; nor will he waste his precious time in seeking after that which is improper. He makes wrath, the tyrant, pay homage to wisdom, so that blind rage may not get the upper hand, and inconsiderateness overstep the proper limits. He sits on the eminence of propriety, so that those who have gone astray have a way left to return, without exposing their bad deeds to the public gaze. When he sits in judgment, the petitioner seems to be the judge, and he himself, on account of his mildness, the suitor for justice. He does not permit petitioners to be delayed on the path of hope; he endeavors to promote the happiness of the creatures in obedience to the will of the Creator, and never seeks to please the people in contradiction to reason. He is forever searching after those who speak the truth and is not displeased with words that seem bitter, but are in reality sweet. He considers the nature of the words and the rank of the speaker. He is not content with committing violence, but he must see that no injustice is done within his realm.

The Declaration of Akbar's Status as a Mujtahid

The next reading is the Declaration (*mahzar*) by certain of the ulamā at Akbar's court allowing limited powers of religious interpretation to the Mughal emperor. It should be emphasized that these powers were allowed only when there was no clear prescription already in the Holy Law and only where there was disagreement among the ulamā. It is quite wrong to conceive Akbar as being granted "papal" powers by those who subscribed to the *mahzar*.

[From 'Abd ul-Qādir Badā'ūnī, *Muntakhab ut-Tawārīkh,* II, 271–72]

The intention in laying this foundation and accepting this statement is that, since Hindustan has become a center of security and peace and a land of justice and beneficence through the blessings of the ruler's justice and policy, groups of people of all classes, especially learned scholars and men accomplished in minute study, have migrated to Hindustan and have chosen this country for their home, having left the lands of "'Arab and 'Ajam." All the distinguished scholars who embrace the study of the roots and derivations of the Sharī'a and the sciences based on reason and tradition, and who are characterized by religious faith, piety, and honesty, have very carefully and deeply considered the abstruse meanings of the Qur'anic verse: "Obey God and obey the Prophet and those who have authority among you," and the sound traditions: "Surely the man who is dearest to God on the Day of Judgment is the just Imām [leader, king]. Whoever obeys the amīr [commander], obeys you and whoever rebels against him rebels against you." Also other proofs established by reason and report. The learned have given a decision that the status of a just king is greater before God than the status of an interpreter of the Law (mujtahid) and that the Sultan of Islam, the asylum of the people, the Commander of the Faithful, the shadow of God over mankind, Abū'l Fath Jalāl ud-dīn Muhammad Akbar Pādshāh Ghāzī (whose kingdom God perpetuate!) is a most just, most wise king and one most informed of God.

Accordingly if a religious problem arises regarding which there are differences among the interpreters of the Law, and if His Majesty with his penetrating understanding and clear wisdom chooses one side with a view to facilitating the livelihood of mankind and the good order of the world's affairs and gives the decision to that side, that shall be agreed upon and it shall be necessary and obligatory for everyone of all sorts and conditions to follow it. Furthermore, if, in accordance with his own just opinion, he should promulgate a decision which is not opposed to the [clear] text of the Qur'ān and the Traditions and would be for the convenience of mankind, it is necessary and obligatory for everyone to act upon it and opposition to it shall be a cause of hardship in the next world and of detriment in both religious and worldly affairs.

This sincere written statement, for the sake of God and the promulgation of the duties of Islam, is signed as a declaration of the scholars of religion and of the holy lawyers. (Done in the month of Rajab 987 after Hijra [August–September, 1579])

CHAPTER XVIII

THE IDEAL SOCIAL ORDER

Writing in medieval India on the ideal Muslim social order, as on other aspects of the Islamic revelation, was confined to those educated in Muslim religious sciences. Therefore its approach is academic and doctrinaire. This is no crisis-literature; it does not offer practical answers to contemporary social problems, but rather repeats ideas which entered Hindustan from the ouside Muslim world. Any correspondence between the ideal categories of Muslim "social" thought and the actualities of the Indian scene is attributable more to the general similarity of the economic order and class structure of Asian society in the pre-industrial age, whether in Hindustan, Persia, or Iraq, than to actual observation of society in India.

The ideal Muslim social order is essentially a religious order. Society is not a venue for individual self-realization, a contrivance for the satisfaction of human wants; the only kind of human happiness which it should make possible is the happiness which comes from obedience to God. Since obedience to God meant obedience to a revealed Holy Law, the Sharīʿa, Muslim social ideals envisage a conservative order in which repetition and submission are reckoned more worthy than innovation and enterprise. The good society was the old society—that which existed during the lifetime of the Prophet. The modern American hopes and intends change to be for the better; the medieval Muslim believed it to be for the worse.

As has been seen, for the Muslim, earthly society should be so ordered as to make possible the godly life and the welfare of the students of the godly life, the ulamā and the mystics. Harmony is the keyword; man should be in harmony with God, nature, and his fellows. If he is not in harmony with his fellows, his attention will be diverted from God, for then he will be intent upon self-preservation. But harmony depends upon being in his proper place and a man's proper place is that for which his nature fits him. The ultimate whole within which each individual finds his place is not economic, although economic activity is essential to the welfare of that whole. The ultimate whole is Islamic—the Muslim community defending itself successfully against attack from outside, devoting itself to the practice of the True Faith, and providing itself with a livelihood sufficient both to bear the cost of its own defense and to keep its members alive and active in the service of God.

In India (following pre-Muslim Iranian tradition) society is seen as four main classes—men of the pen, men of the sword, men of business, and men of the soil. The first are guardians of religion and learning, the second are the guardians of those guardians, and the third and fourth are the sustainers of the first two classes. Attempts by any member of any class to change from his class can only, it is believed, result in chaos and disorder. Muslim social ideas are essentially hierarchical and organic. But how was each to be sure of his proper class and function? Indo-Muslim thinkers, adapting Greek and Persian ideas, answered that God had decided the problem at the creation. Social harmony between classes of men endowed with different aptitudes is willed by God.

The ideal social classification advocated by Indo-Muslim theorists of the ulamā class did correspond in large measure to the social stratification, viewed from a Muslim point of observation, in that area of Hindustan under Muslim rule—except that the people of the sword took precedence in practice over the people of the pen and often ignored them. But it was nevertheless very much the theory of a pen-man's utopia which ignored actual social differences in Muslim India—the distinction between Turk and non-Turk in the first century of Muslim rule, between immigrant Muslim and Indian-born Muslim, between hereditary Muslim and converted Muslim, Delhi Muslim and Bengali Muslim, between descendants of Afghan tribes and non-Afghans, between those with light skins and those with dark, between slaves and free men. However, in its picture of a static society in which men performed those duties for which heredity and inherited education had designated them—of soldiers who would not conceive of becoming agriculturists or traders, and of traders who would not think of becoming ulamā or soldiers—the idea was not very far from the actual: a society of small cultivators and traders supporting, with its labor and taxes, a military and learned aristocracy.

The institution of slavery was important in politics, administration, and in household economy in medieval India under Muslim rule; it does not figure as an important theme in Indo-Muslim writing on the ideal social order. Turkish rulers like Qutb ud-dīn Aibak (1206–1210), Iltutmish (1211–1236), and Balban (1266–1287), began their careers as slaves, and slaves from within the sultans' households were often appointed to high administrative and military offices, but no organized system of slave training, promotion and rule, similar to the Janissary system under the Ottoman Turks, existed in medieval India.[1]

Similarly, the status of women in Muslim law and thought did not change with the conquest of Hindustan by Muslims, although, in practice, Hindu customary law was influential among certain groups of Muslim converts from Hinduism.[2]

For statements on the social and political discrimination which, ideally, should be enforced against non-Muslims, reference should be made to Chapter XVII.

The Four-Class Division of Society

The first reading has been taken from a Persian work on ethics written outside India in the second half of the fifteenth century. The work is *Jalālī's Ethics* (*Akhlāq-i-Jalālī*), by Muhammad ibn Asad Jalāl ud-dīn al-Dawwānī (1427–1501). It was popular in Mughal India.

[From Thompson, *Practical Philosophy of the Muhammadan People,* pp. 388–90]

In order to preserve this political equipoise, there is a correspondence to be maintained between the various classes. Like as the equipoise of bodily temperament is effected by intermixture and correspondence of four elements, the equipoise of the political temperament is to be sought for in the correspondence of four classes.

1. *Men of the pen,* such as lawyers, divines, judges, bookmen, statisticians, geometricians, astronomers, physicians, poets. In these and their exertions in the use of their delightful pens, the subsistence of the faith and of the world itself is vested and bound up. They occupy the place in politics that water does among the elements. Indeed, to persons of ready understanding, the similarity of knowledge and water is as clear as water itself, and as evident as the sun that makes it so.

[1] For an extensive discussion of the status of slaves under Muslim law, see the article, " 'Abd" in the *Encyclopaedia of Islam* (new edition, 1954). No changes in legal doctrine on slavery appear to have occurred in medieval Muslim India; readings from lawbooks used in India have not been given.

[2] See the article, " 'Āda" in the *Encyclopaedia of Islam* (1954).

2. *Men of the sword,* such as soldiers, fighting zealots, guards of forts and passes, etc.; without whose exercise of the impetuous and vindictive sword, no arrangement of the age's interests could be effected; without the havoc of whose tempest-like energies, the materials of corruption, in the shape of rebellious and disaffected persons, could never be dissolved and dissipated. These then occupy the place of fire, their resemblance to it is too plain to require demonstration; no rational person need call in the aid of fire to discover it.

3. *Men of business,* such as merchants, capitalists, artisans, and craftsmen, by whom the means of emolument and all other interests are adjusted; and through whom the remotest extremes enjoy the advantage and safeguard of each other's most peculiar commodities. The resemblance of these to air—the auxiliary of growth and increase in vegetables—the reviver of spirit in animal life—the medium by the undulation and movement of which all sorts of rare and precious things traverse the hearing to arrive at the headquarters of human nature—is exceedingly manifest.

4. *Husbandmen,* such as seedsmen, bailiffs, and agriculturists—the superintendents of vegetation and preparers of provender; without whose exertions the continuance of the human kind must be cut short. These are, in fact, the only producers of what had no previous existence; the other classes adding nothing whatever to subsisting products, but only transferring what subsists already from person to person, from place to place, and from form to form. How close these come to the soil and surface of the earth—the point to which all the heavenly circles refer—the scope to which all the luminaries of the purer world direct their rays—the stage on which wonders are displayed—the limit to which mysteries are confined—must be universally apparent.

In like manner then as in the composite organizations the passing of any element beyond its proper measure occasions the loss of equipoise, and is followed by dissolution and ruin, in political coalition, no less, the prevalence of any one class over the other three overturns the adjustment and dissolves the junction. Next attention is to be directed to the condition of the individuals composing them, and the place of every one determined according to his right.

The four-class classification is found in India in Abū'l Fazl, by whom the learned are relegated to the third position.

[From Abū'l Fazl, *Ā'īn-i-Akbarī,* iv–v]

The people of the world may be divided into four classes:

1. *Warriors,* who in the political body have the nature of fire. Their flames, directed by understanding, consume the straw and rubbish of rebellion and strife, but kindle also the lamp of rest in this world of disturbances.

2. *Artificers and merchants,* who hold the place of air. From their labors and travels, God's gifts become universal, and the breeze of contentment nourishes the rose-tree of life.

3. *The learned,* such as the philosopher, the physician, the arithmetician, the geometrician, the astronomer, who resemble water. From their pen and their wisdom, a river rises in the drought of the world, and the garden of the creation receives from their irrigating powers, a peculiar freshness.

4. *Husbandmen and laborers,* who may be compared to earth. By their exertions, the staple of life is brought to perfection, and strength and happiness flow from their work.

It is therefore obligatory for a king to put each of these in its proper place, and by uniting personal ability with due respect for others, to cause the world to flourish.

Social Precedence

The essentially religious color of the medieval Muslim ideal social order is brought out in the following passage, which purports to be an order by the Caliph Ma'mūn establishing social precedence. The passage is from the *Rulings on Temporal Governments,* by Ziā ud-dīn Barnī.

[From Barnī, *Fatāwa-yi-Jahāndārī,* folios 128a–129b *passim*]

It is commanded that the inhabitants of the capital, Baghdad, and the entire population of the Muslim world should hold in the greatest honor and respect all men of the Hāshimite family who are related to the Prophet by ties of blood, especially the 'Abbāsids to whose line the caliphate of the Muslim community has been confirmed, and, in particular the saiyids whose descent from and relationship to the Prophet is certain. In all circumstances they should strive to reverence and honor them and not allow them to be insulted and humiliated. They should consider the rendering of honor and respect to them to be among their religious duties and a way of doing homage to the Prophet himself. People should consider the causing of any harm or injury to them as equal to infidelity and unbelief.

In accordance with God's commands, a share of the fifth of the spoils of war which accrues to the public treasury, after having been converted to cash, should be delivered to them at their homes for their maintenance. They are to have precedence in seating over all my [the Caliph Ma'mūn's] helpers, supporters, courtiers, and high officers and dignitaries of the realm. In other assemblies and meetings, religious scholars, shaikhs, wazirs, maliks [princes], and the well-known and distinguished people of Baghdad are to sit below them. All classes of the Baghdad population are to pay them due regard and to deem the salvation of Muslims of all classes attainable through paying the relations of the Prophet honor and respect.

As regards the Sunni religious scholars and the Sufis of Baghdad, it is commanded that they should be respected in the capital; to do them honor is to be considered a part of piety. It should be thought that the mandates of the True Faith are adorned by their words and deeds and the elevation of the banners of Islam is a result of honor paid to them.

[And Ma'mūn ordered that] in accordance with the instructions of the Chief Qādī and with the records kept by the Shaikh ul-Islām, they should cause religious scholars and Sufis to be given what would be sufficient and salutary for them, and enable them to live in the best of circumstances and to avoid that neediness which makes both knowledge and the learned contemptible.

For the warriors and champions of the Faith, he commanded sufficient salaries, allowances, and assistance to be given them in cash from the public treasury of the Muslims, in accordance with the instructions of the muster master at Baghdad and the ranks and grades named and fixed by the muster master's department. Respect and honor are to be paid to holy warriors both in the caliph's palace and in all Baghdad, for they are the protectors of the territory of Islam and of its inhabitants. They fight in the way of God and overthrow the enemies of God and of His Prophet.

Divine Origin of the "Division of Labor"

Ideally a man's status in the godly society is related to his innate virtues or vices for which God as Creator is responsible. A man's occupation denotes his moral degree in God's sight. The superior social rank of the learned and the literary, implied in the first reading, should be noted.

[From Barnī, *Fatāwa-yi-Jahāndārī,* folios 216b–217b]

All men in creation are equal and in outward form and appearance are also equal. Every distinction of goodness and wickedness which has appeared among mankind has so appeared as a result of their qualities and of their commission of acts. Virtue and vice have been shared out from all eternity and were made the associate of their spirits. The manifestation of human deeds and acts is a created thing. Whenever God obliges good actions and wicked actions, and good and evil, He gives warning of it so that those good and bad deeds, that good and that evil, may be openly manifested, and when, in the very first generation of Adam, the sons of Adam appeared and multiplied, and the world began to be populated, and in their social intercourse the need for everything befell mankind, the Eternal Craftsman imparted to mens' minds the crafts essential to their social intercourse. So in one he implanted writing and penmanship, to another horsemanship, to one the craft of weaving, to another farriery, and to yet another carpentry. All these crafts, honorable and base, from penmanship and horsemanship to cupping and tanning, were implanted in their minds and breasts by virtue of those virtues and vices which, in the very depths of their natures, have become the companions of their spirits. To the hearts of the possessors of the virtues, by reason of their innate virtue, have fallen the noble crafts, and in those under the dominion of vice, by reason of their innate vice, have been implanted the ignoble occupations. Those thus inspired have chosen those very crafts which have been grafted upon their minds and have practiced them, and from them have come those crafts and skills and occupations with which they were inspired; for them the bringing of those crafts into existence was made feasible.

These crafts, noble and ignoble, have become the hidden companions of the sons of the first sons of Adam. In accordance with their quickness of intelligence and perspicacity, their descendants have added to the crafts of their ancestors some fine and desirable features, so that every art, craft, and profession, of whose products mankind has need, has reached perfection.

As virtues were implanted in those who have chosen the nobler occupations, from them alone come forth goodness, kindness, generosity, valor, good deeds, good works, truthfulness, keeping of promises, avoidance of slander, loyalty, purity of vision, justice, equity, recognition of one's duty, gratitude for favors received, and fear of God. These people are said to be noble, freeborn, virtuous, religious, of high lineage, and of pure birth. They alone are worthy of offices and posts in the realm and under the government of the ruler who, in his high position as the supreme governor, is singled out as the leader and the chief of mankind. Thus the government of the ruler and his activities are given strength and put in an orderly condition.

But whenever vices have been inserted into the minds of those who chose the baser arts and the mean occupations, only immodesty, falsehood, miserliness, perfidy, sins, wrongs, lies, evil-speaking, ingratitude, stupidity, injustice, oppression, blindness to one's duty, cant, impudence, bloodthirstiness, rascality, conceit and godlessness appear. They are called lowborn, bazaar people, base, mean, worthless, "plebeian," shameless, and of impure birth. Every act which is mingled with meanness and founded on ignominy comes very well from them. The promotion of the low and the lowborn brings no advantage in this world, for it is impudent to act against the wisdom of creation.

Rulers to Preserve the Social Order Willed by God

[From Barnī, *Fatāwa-yi-Jahāndārī,* folios 58a–58b, 130a]

It is a [religious] duty and necessary for kings whose principal aims are the protection of religion and stability in affairs of government to follow the practices of God Most High in their bestowal of place. Whomsoever God has chosen and honored with excellence, greatness, and ability, in proportion to his merit so should he be singled out and honored by kings. . . . He whom God has created with vile qualities and made contemptible in his sin, rascality, and ignorance, who as a sport of the Devil has been brought into existence as a slave of this world and a helpless victim of his lower self, should be treated and lived with according to the way he was created, so that the wisdom of the creation of the Creator may illumine the hearts of all. But if the ruler, out of a natural inclination or base desire, self-will, or lack of wisdom honors such a scoundrel, then the ruler holds God in contempt and treats Him with scorn. For the ruler has honored, in opposition to the wisdom of creation, one whom God has dishonored and treats him as one distinguished and honorable, making him happy out of the bounty of his power and greatness. Such a ruler is not worthy of the caliphate and deputyship of God. To use the name of king for him becomes a crime for he has made the incomparable bounty of God into an instrument of sin. Opposition to the wisdom of creation hurts him in this world and finally he will be punished in the next world.

. . . .

Teachers of every kind are to be strictly enjoined not to thrust precious stones down the throats of dogs or to put collars of gold round the necks of pigs and bears—that is, to the mean, the ignoble, the worthless; to shopkeepers and the lowborn they are to teach nothing more than the mandates about prayer, fasting, alms-giving, and the pilgrimage to Mecca, along with some chapters of the Qur'ān and some doctrines of the Faith, without which their religion cannot be correct and valid prayers are not possible. They are to be instructed in nothing more lest it bring honor to their mean souls. They are not to be taught reading and writing, for plenty of disorders arise owing to the skill of the lowborn in knowledge. The disorders into which all the affairs of religion and government are thrown is due to the acts and words of the lowborn, whom they have made skillful. For by means of their skill they become governors, revenue-collectors, accountants, officers, and rulers. If the teachers are disobedient and it is discovered at the time of investigation that they have imparted knowledge or taught letters or writing to the lowborn, inevitably punishment for their disobedience will be meted out to them. [folio 130a]

The next two readings from the Mughal period express a similar point of view to Barnī's. The first work, Muhammad Bāqir Khān's *Admonitions on Government,* was written in 1612–13; the second, though entitled *Institutes of Tīmūr,* was written about 1637 by Abū Tālib al-Husainī.

[From Muhammad Bāqir Khān, *Mau'iza-yi-Jahāngīrī,* folios 29–31 *passim*]

Rulers should not permit unworthy people with evil natures to be put on an equality with people with a pure lineage and wisdom and they should consider the maintenance of rank among the fundamental customs and usages of rulership. For, if the differences between classes disappear and the lowest class boast of living on an equality with the "median" class, and the "median" boast of living on an equality with the upper, rulers will lose prestige and complete undermining of the bases of the kingdom will appear. For this reason rulers of former days used not to allow base people of rascally origin and who had been taught writing to understand problems of fulfilling promises and rules of order because, when this habit is perpetuated and they emerge from their professions to take their place among the servants of the government, verily, injury will spread and the life of all classes become disordered. . . . Consider worthy of education him who has an intrinsically fine nature and avoid educating rascals with an intrinsically bad nature, for every stone does not become a jewel nor all blood fragrant musk. In him who has a vile person, a base nature, and an inner nastiness, there will not be seen either sincerity, capacity for government, or regard for religion—and when the quality of sincerity and of piety, which is the root of intellect, has been removed, every fault which it is possible to have can be expected from him.

[From Abū Tālib al-Husainī, *Tūzuk-i-Tīmūrī,* pp. 158–60]
Fourthly, by advice and institute, I regulated the affairs of my household and by advice and institute I firmly established my authority so that the amirs [nobles] and ministers, soldiers and subjects, could not transgress the just bounds of their ranks and degrees, and each one was the keeper of his own station. [p. 160]

. . . .

Be it known to Abū Mansūr Tīmūr (on whom be the blessing of Almighty God!) that the organization of the business of this world is patterned on the organization of the business of the next, in which there are public functionaries and officials, deputies and chamberlains, each in his own station performing his own work. They do not overstep their bounds and they await the commands of God. Therefore you must take precautions that your wazirs, soldiers, officials, servants, and officials, each being within the confines of their own stations, await your commands. Keep every class and group within their proper limits so that your dominion may be properly established and ordered. But if you do not keep everything and everybody in their proper place, then chaos and sedition will make their way into your state. Therefore you should watch that everything and everybody remain in their rank and degree. [p. 158]

CHAPTER XIX

THE IMPORTANCE OF THE STUDY OF HISTORY

Medieval Indo-Muslims, no less than medieval Arab or Persian Muslims, were historically minded people. The Muslim conquest of Hindustan ushered in a succession of historical works, chiefly written in Persian, without precedent (except for the Kashmir Chronicle, 1148–49) and certainly without parallel in Hindu India. Such well-known works as Ziā ud-dīn Barnī's *Tārīkh-i-Fīrūz Shāhī* (c.1357), Abū'l Fazl's *Akbar-Nāma* (1590s), and 'Abd ul-Qādir Badā'ūnī's *Muntakhab ut-Tawārīkh* (c.1596) are but the most imposing peaks of a Himalayan range of histories.

Islam as a religion had intensified and redirected the pre-Muslim Arab interest in the past, which had found expression in the oral battle-day traditions (*ayyām*) and tribal genealogies (*ansāb*). The Qur'ān was the confirmation of a progressive revelation in history of God's will for man (6.92; 35.31), recalling mankind to an awareness of a Truth previously communicated by an historical succession of prophets (4.163), but neglected. Man should study the history of the world before Muhammad for the good of his soul. Furthermore, the Qur'ān emphasizes man's accountability to God for his deeds—that is to say, for his history—on the Day of Judgment (17.13, 14). Hence the facts about what men do are instinct with a truly awful significance.

Then too, the study of the life of the Prophet, his actions, and his sayings, and those of his Companions, was essentially an historical study. For most Muslims this had added significance inasmuch as they viewed the good life as one modeled upon the life of the Prophet and upon those of his Companions. Again, the dogma of the infallibility of consensus, and for Sunnis, the belief that the religious role of Muhammad had descended upon the community as a whole, invested a record of the past with a new seriousness. Such a record was essential for true servanthood of God and a reasonable hope of salvation.

Before the Muslim conquests in India, interest in history in the Muslim world had also been excited by such nonreligious considerations as pride in the story of Muslim conquests and in the part played therein by family and tribe, and by the emergence of independent military rulers who encouraged the production of histories retailing their power, piety, and patronage of learning. Such rulers were as interested in enjoying stories and traditions from pre-Muslim Iran and Turkestan as in knowing the biography of the Prophet and the story of the infant Muslim community after his death. Tabarī's (d. 923) monumental *History of Prophets and Kings* (*Tārīkh ul-Rusūl wa'l Mulūk*) stood at the confluence of both the Islamic and the non-Islamic streams in Muslim historiography.

Indo-Muslim historiography (as indeed that elsewhere in the Muslim world), reflected, and sometimes consciously propagated, the religio-politico-social ideas illustrated in the previous chapters. Written chiefly by courtiers, royal confidants, and officials, the purpose of Indo-Muslim histories was utilitarian in the sense that they aimed some to teach true religion by historical example, some to preserve a record of great deeds for the edification of succeeding generations of Muslims, some to glorify the history of Islam in Hindustan, some to praise a particular ruler or a line of rulers, and some to do all these. Many such histories were written either at the behest of the ruler or in hope of his patronage.

Medieval Muslim historiography in India, as in medieval Muslim Persia, implicitly accepted therefore (where it did not seek actively to underpin) notions of a religious and social order founded upon a tacit partnership between the ulamā and their patron and protector, the godly ruler, in the furtherance of the good life. Furthermore, by concentrating upon the deeds of the ruling power, Indo-Muslim historians helped to confirm autocracy as the typical Indo-Muslim political institution. Such tendencies will be illustrated from the preface to Abū'l Fazl's *Akbar-Nāma,* where he indeed destroys even the theory of a balance between separate religious and ruling institutions.

Almost all Indo-Muslim historians assume that only the history of Muslims is deserving of attention. Many, particularly after the establishment of Mughal rule, give a conspectus of the political history of Muslims in Hindustan from the time of the Ghōrid conquest, or sometimes perhaps, of the raids of Mahmūd of Ghaznin. The stimulation among the literate and the powerful of an Indo-Muslim awareness of themselves as a separate community, divided from the Hindus by history as well as by ideology, must be accounted an important by-product of Indo-Muslim historical writing.

Relevance and space do not permit the discussion and illustration of Indo-Muslim historical technique. The aim of the readings is merely to illustrate three themes related to those of earlier chapters. It is not suggested that they are even an index to the scope of Indo-Muslim historical writing.[1]

The Study of History As an Integral Support of the Orthodox Muslim Conception of World Order

[From Barnī, *Tārīkh-i-Fīrūz Shāhī,* pp. 9–17]

After the science of Qur'anic commentary, of tradition, of jurisprudence, and the mystic path of the Sufi shaikhs, I have not observed such advantages from any branch of learning as I have from history. History is the knowledge of the annals and traditions of prophets, caliphs, sultans, and of the great men of religion and of government. Pursuit of the study of history is particular to the great ones of religion and of government who are famous for the excellence of their qualities or who have become famous among mankind for their great deeds. Low fellows, rascals, unfit and unworthy persons, inferior people, and those with base aspirations, people of unknown stock and mean natures, of no lineage and low lineage, loiterers and bazaar loafers—all these have no connection with history. It is not their trade and skill. A knowledge of history does not advantage such people and profits them in no circumstance. For history is the annals of the good qualities of greatness and the story of the virtues, excellences, and the fine deeds of great men of religion and government, and not a record of the vices of rascals, low fellows, people of inferior birth and bazaar stock, who love base qualities by reason of their rascally nature and who have no desire for history. Rather it is harmful to base and mean fellows for them to read and know history, not an advantage at all. What higher honor for history is it possible to conceive than that mean and low people have no desire or inclination for this rare form of knowledge, that it is of no profit to them in their low dealings and filthy

[1] For this see C. A. Storey, "Persian Literature," Section II, 2, *History of India* (London, 1939).

morals, and that history is the only science of learning in any quarter from which they desire no benefit whatever?

But those who have been born of excellent lineage and good stock, in whose seed the honor of greatness and of great birth has been inscribed—they cannot escape knowing history and employing it. They cannot live without using history. Among great people, those born great, those of high lineage and those born of high lineage, the historian is dearer than life and they wish to follow\the footsteps of historians whose writings are a means whereby the great people of religion and of government find eternal life.

Leaders of religion and of government have spoken at length on the value of history. The first value is that the heavenly books which are the word of God are filled with reports of most of the deeds of prophets—the best of created beings—and of the annals of sultans—the rulers of men—their violence and oppression. History is the form of knowledge which provides a stock of warnings to be heeded by those with eyes to see. Second, the science of Hadīth—all the words and deeds of the Prophet and the most precious form of knowledge after Qur'anic commentary, the discovery and confirmation of narrators, and of events recorded in tradition, the warlike activities of the Holy Prophet, the establishment of a chronology, the abrogation of traditions—all these are connected with history and it is on this account that the science of history is entirely bound up with the science of tradition. The great Imāms of tradition have said that history and tradition are twins and if the traditionist is not an historian he will not be informed of the activities of the Holy Prophet, and of the Companions who are the original reporters of Hadīth. Without history, the true circumstances of the real Companions and the followers of the Companions as distinct from spurious companions and followers will become evident. Whenever the traditionist is not an historian, their activities will not be authenticated and the traditionist will not be able to give a true account of tradition or explain it correctly. Furthermore, the circumstances and events which occurred in the time of the Prophet and his companions and their explanation and analysis—which is a cause of encouragement and confidence for the hearts of all generations of the Muslim community—these too became known through history.

The third boon to be derived from history is that it is a means of increasing the intelligence and understanding and also a means of correct decision and planning [a course of action]. From the study of the experience of others a person becomes experienced himself and through knowing, by a knowledge of history, what has previously happened, a firm resolve emerges. Aristotle and Buzurjmihr [wazir to the Sassanian ruler Noshirwan] have stated that a knowledge of history strengthens and confirms right judgment in that the knowledge of previous circumstances is a testimony to the justice and soundness of subsequent opinion.

The fourth advantage to be gained from history is that through its knowledge, and through awareness of events both recent and remote in time, the hearts of sultans, maliks, wazirs, and other great men remain firm and if some terrible calamity from heaven happens to rulers, they do not lose their serenity and the remedy for healing the ills of the kingdom becomes clear to them from the remedies applied by their predecessors. In their hearts they may avoid schemes and projects which they would otherwise have planned and they observe signs of untoward happenings before they occur. This advantage is one of the greatest possible.

The fifth advantage from history is that the knowledge of the annals of the prophets and their vicissitudes, and the way in which they accepted whatever came to them, patiently and with resignation, may become a cause of patience and resignation for those who know history. The eventual finding by the prophets of salvation from calamity becomes a means of hope for those who know history. Since it became evident from history that calamities of all kinds have rained upon prophets (who are the best of men), the hearts of Muslims will not despair when unforeseen calamity descends upon them.

The sixth advantage from a knowledge of history is that the natural qualities of the elect, of the just, and of the benevolent, their salvation and their high status, find a seat in the heart and the evil deeds of the contumacious, the tyrannical, and the oppressive, their ultimate destruction and the plague affecting them become evident to the sultans, wazirs, and rulers of Islam. The rewards of virtue and the results of evil deeds are proved in the affairs of worldly government, and fortunate caliphs, sultans, and rulers incline toward virtue and excellence, and kings of Islam do not fall into the clutches of tyranny and oppression, avoid haughty behavior in exercising their dominion, and do not abandon what their character as servants of God requires. The benefits of the right dealing of caliphs and sultans, wazirs and rulers, spread among all the people and stretch near and far.

The seventh benefit from history is that it is inseparable from truth.

Great men of religion and government in all ages have said that the foundation of the science of history has been placed on truth. Thus Abraham made this request from God and offered this prayer: "May I have a good report among later generations." In rebuking those who write lies, God has said: "They corrupt the Word from its proper meaning." God has made lying and slandering perilous matters.

The composition of history is special to great men and the sons of great men who are connected with the administration of justice, freedom, truth, and right, because history is the narration of good and evil, justice and injustice, merit and unmerit, praiseworthy qualities and offensive qualities, acts of obedience and acts of disobedience, virtues and vices, in times gone by so that succeeding readers may take warning from them and comprehend the advantages and the dangers of worldly government and the benevolence and the wickedness of empire and follow that benevolence and avoid that wickedness. And if, which God forfend! a liar and rogue uses falsehoods, and, with his low and filthy nature grafts a story of unfitting actions upon the lives of previous great men, incorporates it in his writing and gives currency to lying and slander with many colored accounts, makes lies seem like truth, and writes them down, and does not, out of criminality, fear either this world or the next, and does not fear having to answer on the Day of Judgment so that the good are called and described as wicked for hidden crimes of which they speak—all this is terrible and worse. To speak and write of the wicked as if they were good, that is the worst form of evil conduct.

Since the annals of history are without [written] warrant and proclaim the dealings of sultans and great men, therefore, it is necessary that the historian be one of the kind worthy of respect and known and famous for his truth and just dealing, so that students may have firm confidence in what he writes without written authority and so that he may obtain credit among the honorable. For there is no assurance for the honorable unless in the writing of one worthy of respect and unless there is not the slightest doubt as to his true faith and piety. . . .

It must be known that whatever people worthy of respect have written in their histories has been relied upon by others, and whatever the self-willed people of unknown stock have written, the wise have not trusted. History written by rascals has grown old in booksellers' shops and has been returned to the papermakers for repulping.

As the historian must be among the notables and the respected, so the soundness of his religion and sect is a condition of his writing history. Otherwise, what happens is as in the case of some people of wrong religion and of evil faith from hereditary prejudice and hereditary hatred—such as the Shi'a and the Khārijites who have woven lying tales about the Companions of the Prophet. Previous writers of wrong faith and evil religion have mixed truth and error in their histories. They have set down well-known and rejected traditions in their works. Whenever the religion, sect, and evil belief of an historian is not evident to readers and they reckon the writers of history among their predecessors, they think that perhaps they are writing the truth. Whoever does not recognize the deceits of people of false religion—that the way of such people is to keep their erroneous beliefs and filthy faith hidden among the Sunnis and mix the lies and tissue of inventions which have found a place among their horrid doctrines with the kinship of well-known true traditions; that they set them down in their own rejected writings so that the student who has not had warning of previous circumstances may come to know of their false beliefs and their crooked ways and understand the religion of lying historians—trouble will indeed come upon his own true faith by studying those writers who have mingled with error, and he will consider correct what irreligious authors have composed.

One great benefit from the understanding of history is that through it the Sunnis of time gone by become known from the unorthodox, those of true from those of untrue belief, and faithful supporters of Islam from unfaithful. Trustworthy accounts of events are distinguished from rejected doctrines and the Imāms of the Sunna and the community turn with renewed strength to the orthodox faith.

One of the indispensable conditions of history writing, and one which is absolutely obligatory in the interests of piety, is that when the historian writes of the excellences, the good deeds, the justice and equity of the ruler or of a great man, he must also not conceal his vices and evil deeds and not employ the ways of conviviality in writing history. If he considers it expedient he should speak openly, but if not, he should speak by insinuations, in hints, and in covert and learned allusions. If out of fear and terror he cannot write about the crimes of contemporaries he is excused, but he must write the truth about the past. If the historian has received blows from the ruler, wazir, or great men of his time, or has received much favor and patronage, he should write in such a way that it is impossible to perceive that he has received kindness or ill treatment, patronage or payment from the great, lest as a consequence he should write against truth of excellences and of vices that were not, and of deeds and events that did not happen. But the attention of the truthful, pious, and sincere historian should be directed toward writing the truth. He should be in fear of answering on the Day of Judgment. . . .

In sum, history is a rare and useful form of knowledge and its writing is a very great obligation. Its advantages spread far and wide, both as regards spreading the knowledge of deeds and praiseworthy qualities and perpetuating them on the scrolls of time and as regards the many boons it confers upon readers when they study it. The historian has many duties and responsibilities toward those of whose annals and deeds he writes and spreads on the pages of time. If they are alive, the publication of their deeds becomes a means whereby they are loved, spoken well of, and wished well. Friendship for them becomes engraved on the hearts both of those who know them and of strangers. If they are dead, the recollection of their deeds ensures them a second life, and they become greatly deserving of God's mercy. The historian also has duties toward the readers and hearers of history because by means of his writing they may obtain considerable rewards.

[From Badā'ūnī, *Muntakhab ut-Tawārīkh*, II (tr. by Lowe), 272]

I have made bold to chronicle these events, a course very far removed from that of prudence and circumspection. But God (He is glorious and honored!) is my witness, and sufficient is God as a witness, that my inducement to write this has been nothing but sorrow for the faith, and heartburning for the deceased religion of Islam. . . .

[From Badā'ūnī, *Muntakhab ut-Tawārīkh*, III (tr. by Haig), 529, 530 *passim*]

I shall now explain what it was that originally led me to collect these fragments. Since a complete revolution, both in legislation and in manners, greater than any of which there is any record for the past thousand years, has taken place in these days, and every writer who has had the ability to record events and to write two connected sentences has, for the sake of flattering the people of this age, or for fear of them, or by reason of his ignorance of matters of faith, or of his distance from court, or for his own selfish ends, concealed the truth, and, having bartered his faith for worldly profit, and right guidance for error, has adorned falsehood with the semblance of truth, and distorted and embellished infidelity and pernicious trash until they have appeared to be laudable . . . it is incumbent on me, who am acquainted with some, at least, of the affairs narrated, and have even been intimately connected with these transactions, to place on record what I have seen and what I have heard, for my evidence regarding these things is that of an eyewitness who is certain of what he relates, and does not spring from mere supposition and guesswork ("and when can that which is heard resemble that which is seen?") in order that, on the one hand, my record may be an expiation of the writings, past and present, which I have been compelled and directed to undertake, and, on the other, right may be proved to be on the side of the Muslims and mercy may be shown to me.

Historical Literature in the Service of Autocracy

Indo-Muslim historiography tended to focus on the deeds of the ruler, who was sometimes glorified in the extreme, as is shown by this excerpt from Nizām ud-dīn Ahmad's *Tabaqāt-i-Akbarī,* written in 1592–93.

[From Nizām ud-dīn Ahmad, *Tabaqāt-i-Akbarī,* I (tr. by De), iii–v *passim*]

But, after that, this insignificant particle—Nizām ud-dīn Ahmad, the son of Muhammad Muqīm the Harāwī, who is a humble dependent and a faithful adherent of the sublime Court of the Great Emperor, the Sultan of the Sultans of the world, the beneficent shadow of God, the viceregent of the Omnipotent, the strengthener of the pillars of world-conquest, the founder of the rules for governing the world, the ruler of the world and of all who inhabit it, the lord of all time and of all that exists in it, the embodiment of Divine secrets, the personification of spiritual essences, the most potent conqueror and the most successful ruler, the lion in the wilderness of political and religious warfare Abū'l Fath Jalāl ud-dīn Muhammad Akbar Pādshāh Ghāzī; may God perpetuate his dominion and empire, and fill the table of his justice and benefaction!—represents that from his childhood, according to the instructions of his worthy father, he occupied himself with the study of historical works, which brightens the intellect of the studious, and inspires the intelligent with awe. . . . Now that all the provinces and divisions of Hindustan have been conquered by the world-opening sword of His Majesty, the viceregent of God, and the many have been unified into the one, and even many of the countries outside of India, which had never been acquired by any of the former great sultans have become part and parcel of his dominions, and it is hoped, that the seven climes would become the abode of peace and quiet under the shadow of His Majesty's auspicious standard, it came to the dull understanding of the author, that he should, with the pen of truth and candor, write a comprehensive history which should present in a clear style, in its different sections, an account of the Empire of Hindustan from the time of Sabuktigīn which began with the year 367 after Hijra when Islam first appeared in the country of Hindustan, to the year 1001 after Hijra, corresponding with the thirty-seventh year of the Divine era, which was inaugurated at the epoch-making accession of His Majesty, the vice-regent of God; and should embellish the glorious army, which is as it were an introduction to the sublime chronicle of renown. . . .

The next reading, from Abū'l Fazl's *Akbar-Nāma,* betrays his efforts to have Akbar regarded as heir both to the prophets and to caliphs and kings.

[From Abū'l Fazl, *Akbar-Nāma,* I (tr. by Beveridge), 16–17]

So long as the spiritual supremacy over the recluse, which is called Holiness, and the sway over laymen, which is called Sovereignty, were distinct, there was strife and confusion among the children of Noah [mankind]. Now that in virtue of his exaltation, foresight, comprehensive wisdom, universal benevolence, pervading discernment, and perfect knowledge of God, these two great offices (mansab) which are the guiding thread of the spiritual and temporal worlds, have been conferred on the opener of the hoards of wisdom and claviger of Divine treasuries, a small portion at least—if his holy nature grant the necessary faculty—may be brought from the ambush of concealment to the asylum of publicity. Knowest thou at all who is this world-girdling luminary and radiant spirit? Or whose august advent has bestowed this grace? 'Tis he who by virtue of his enlightenment and truth is the world-protecting sovereign of our age, to wit, that Lord (Shāhanshāh) of the hosts of sciences—theater of God's power —station of infinite bounties—unique of the eternal temple—confidant of the dais of unity—jewel of the imperial mine—bezel of God's signet-ring —glory of the Gurgān family—lamp of the tribe of Tīmūr—lord of incomparable mystery—heir of Humāyūn's throne—origin of the canons of world-government—author of universal conquest—shining forehead of the morning of guidance—focus of the sun of holiness—[etc., etc.] . . . Akbar.

INDIC WORD LIST

The following is a list of Sanskrit (S) and Pali (P) terms and proper names printed in roman type in the text together with the corresponding transliteration in accordance with L. Renou's *Grammaire Sanscrite* (Paris, 1930). There is no listing for those terms whose orthodox spellings do not differ from popular ones as used in the text. Some Hindi (H), Bengali (B), and Dravidian (D), i.e., Tamil, Telegu, etc., words are also included in cases where a significant word is borrowed from the Sanskrit or where the orthography may be misleading.

āchārya	ācārya
Agneya	Āgneya
ahimsā	ahiṃsā
Amar Dās (H)	Amar Dās
Ambashtha	Ambaṣṭha
Amritachandra	Amṛtacandra
Anāthapindaka	Anāthapiṇḍaka
Angiras	Aṅgiras
Apabhramsha	Apabhraṃśa
Āranyaka	Āraṇyaka
Ardha-magadhi	Ardha-māgadhī
Āruni	Āruṇi
Aryan	Āryan
Asanga	Asaṅga
Āshmarathya	Āśmarathya
Ashoka	Aśoka (Pali, Asoka)
āshrama	āśrama
Ashvaghosha	Aśvaghoṣa
Āshvalāyana	Āśvalāyana
ashvamedha	aśvamedha
Ashvin	Aśvin
Asur (H)	Asura (S)
Audulomi	Auḍulomi
Avalokiteshvara	Avalokiteśvara
avatār (H)	avatāra (S)
Ayodhya	Ayodhyā
Bādarāyana	Bādarāyaṇa
bhajan (H)	bhajana
Bhartrihari	Bhartṛhari
bhāshya	bhāṣya
Bhatta Lollata	Bhaṭṭa Lollaṭa
Bhatta Nāyaka	Bhaṭṭa Nāyaka
Bhavananda	Bhavānanda
bhikshu	bhikṣu
Bhīshma	Bhīṣma
Bhoodan (H)	Bhūdāna (S)
Bhrigu	Bhṛgu
brahmachārī	brahmacārī
brahmacharya	brahmacarya
brāhman	brāhmaṇa
Brāhmana	Brāhmaṇa
Brahmanaspati	Brahmaṇaspati
Brihaspati	Bṛhaspati
Brindavan (H)	Vṛndāvana (S)
Chaitanya	Caitanya
Chāndāla	Cāṇḍāla
Chandragupta	Candragupta
Charkha (H)	Carkha
Chaulukya	Caulukya
Chetaka	Ceṭaka
chit	cit
Chola (D)	Cōḷa
Dadu	Dādū
Dadu-panthi	Dādū-panthī
Daksha	Dakṣa
Damayanti	Damayantī
Dandin	Daṇḍin

darshana	darśana
Devanagri (H)	Devanāgarī
Dhananjaya	Dhanañjaya
Dhritarāshtra	Dhṛtarāṣṭra
dhyana	dhyāna
Dinnāga	Diṅnāga
Drona	Droṇa
Duhshanta	Duḥṣanta (Duṣyanta)
Ganesha	Gaṇeśa
Ganges	Gaṅgā (S)
Garuda	Garuḍa
Gaudapāda	Gauḍapāda
Gauri	Gaurī
Gaya	Gayā
ghee	ghī (H)
Giridhar	Giridhara (S)
Gokul (H)	Gokula (S)
Gopāl (H)	Gopāla (S)
Gudākesha	Guḍākeśa
guna	guṇa
gyana (B)	jñāna (S)
Harsha	Harṣa
Hemachandra	Hemacandra
Himalaya	Himālaya
Īshvara	Īśvara
Īshvarakrishna	Īśvarakṛṣṇa
Jagannath	Jagannātha (S)
Jain	Jaina
Jan(a) Sangh (H)	Jana Saṅgha (S)
Jayasimha	Jayasiṃha
jnāna	jñāna
Jnānadeva	Jñānadeva
Jnāneshvara	Jñāneśvara
Jnātrika	Jñātṛka
Kailash(a)	Kailāsa
Kalinga	Kaliṅga
Kanāda	Kaṇāda
Kanchi	Kāñcī
Kānchīpuram	Kāñcīpura
Karana	Karaṇa
Karna	Karṇa
Kāshakritsna	Kāśakṛtsna
Kashi	Kāśī
Kaundinya	Kauṇḍinya
Kautilya	Kauṭilya
Kayastha	Kāyastha
Krishna	Kṛṣṇa
Krita	Kṛta
kshatra	kṣatra
Kshatriya	Kṣatriya
Kshemendra	Kṣemendra
Kurukshetra	Kurukṣetra
Kushāna	Kuṣāṇa
Kusinara (P)	Kusināra
Lakshmī	Lakṣmī
Lila	Līlā
Lingayat	Liṅgāyat
Lokāchārya	Lokācārya
Mahadev (H)	Mahādeva (S)
Maha Muni	Mahāmuni (S)
maharaja(h)	mahārāja
Maharashtra	Mahārāṣṭra
maharshi	maharṣi
Mahāsānghika	Mahāsāṅghika
Mahendra Sinha	Mahendra Siṅha
Māhishya	Māhiṣya
Maladhārī Hemachandra	Maladhārī Hemacandra
Mammata	Mammaṭa
Marīchi	Marīci
Mathura	Mathurā
Mīmāmsā	Mīmāṃsā
Mīmāmsaka	Mīmāṃsaka
moksha	mokṣa
Mrigaputra	Mṛgaputra
Narasimha	Narasiṃha
Nārāyana	Nārāyaṇa
Nigantha Nātaputta	Nirgrantha Jñātṛputra (S); Nigaṇṭha Nātaputta (P)
Nīlakantha Dīkshita	Nīlakaṇṭha Dīkṣita
Nirvāna	Nirvāṇa
Nishāda	Niṣāda
Om	Oṃ
Pakudha Kacchāyana (P)	Pakudha Kaccāyana
Pali	Pāli
Pāndava	Pāṇḍava
pandit (H)	paṇḍita (S)
Pāndu	Pāṇḍu
Pāndya	Pāṇḍya
Pānini	Pāṇini
Parameshvara	Parameśvara
Parashurāma	Paraśurāma

Pārshva	Pārśva
Parthiva Puja	Pārthiva Pūjā
Pataliputra	Pāṭaliputra
Patanjali	Patañjali
Pava	Pāvā
Pindaree	Piṇḍarī
prajna	prajñā
Prakrit (Prākrit)	Prākṛta (S)
prakriti	prakṛti
prāna	prāṇa
Pranayama	Prāṇāyāma
Prithā	Pṛthā
purāna	purāṇa
Purāna Kassapa (P)	Purāṇa Kassapa
Purandaradāsa	Puraṅdaradāsa
purusha	puruṣa
purushārtha	puruṣārtha
Pūrva Mīmāmsā	Pūrva Mīmāṃsā
Pūrva Mīmāmsaka	Pūrva Mīmāṃsaka
Pūshan	Pūṣan
Pushyamitra Shunga	Puṣyamitra Śuṅga
raj (H)	rājya (S)
raja (H)	rājā
rakshasa (Rakkhshas)	rākṣasa (Rakṣas)
Ramakrishna	Rāmakṛṣṇa
Rāmana Maharshi	Rāmaṇa Maharṣi
Ramananda	Rāmānanda
Rām Rājya Pārishad (H)	Rām Rājya Pariṣad
Rashtriya Svayam Sevak Sangh (H)	Rāṣṭriya Svayam Sevak Saṅgh
Rāvana	Rāvaṇa
Rig Veda	*Ṛg Veda*
Rishabhadeva	Ṛṣabhadeva
rishi	ṛṣi
rita	ṛta
Sabha	Sabhā
Sādhāran (Brahmo Samaj) (B)	Sādhāraṇa Brahma Samāja (S)
Sakar ki Churi	Sakar kī chūrī (H)
Sāl (H)	Śāla
Samāj (H)	Samāja
samhitā	saṃhitā
samsāra	saṃsāra
samskāra	saṃskāra
Sanatan Dharma (H)	Sanātana Dharma (S)
Sandhya	Sandhyā
Sanjaya Belatthiputta (P)	Sañjaya Belaṭṭhiputta
Sānkhya	Sāṅkhya
Sanskrit	Saṃskṛta (S)
Saraswatī	Sarasvatī
sati, suttee	satī (S)
satyagrahi	satyāgrahī
Saurashtra	Saurāṣṭra
Savitar	Savitṛ
Shaiva	Śaiva
Shakra	Śakra
shakti	śakti
Shakuntalā	Śakuntalā
Shākya	Śākya
Shālīki	Śālīki
Shāndilya	Śāṇḍilya
Shankara	Śaṅkara
Shankaradeva	Śaṅkaradeva
Shāntideva	Śāntideva
Shantiniketan	Śāntiniketana
Shāriputra	Śāriputra
Shārngadeva	Śārṅgadeva
shāstra	śāstra
Shauraseni	Śaurasenī
Shesha	Śeṣa
Shitala	Śītalā
Shiva	Śiva
Shivajī	Śivaji
Shrāvastī	Śrāvastī
Shrī	Śrī
Shrīdhara Venkatesha	Śrīdhara Veṅkateśa
Shrīkantha	Śrīkaṇṭha
Shrīvaishnava	Śrīvaiṣṇava
shruti	śruti
Shuddhi	Śuddhi
shūdra	śūdra
Shuka	Śuka
Shukra	Śukra
Shunga	Śuṅga
Shvetaketu	Śvetaketu
Shvetāmbara	Śvetāmbara
Singāla (P)	Siṅgāla

smriti	smṛti
Sri	Śrī
Swadeshī (H)	Svadeśī (S)
Swami	Svāmi
Swamiji	Svāmiji
swaraj (H)	svarājya (S)
Tīrthankara	Tīrthaṅkara
Trishalā	Triśalā
Tukārām	Tukārāma
Tvashtar	Tvaṣṭṛ
Uddālaka Āruni	Uddālaka Āruṇi
Ujjain	Ujjayinī (S)
Upanishad	Upaniṣad
Uttara Mīmāmsā	Uttara Mīmāṃsā
Uttar Pradesh	Uttara Pradeśa (S)
Vāch	Vāc
Vāgīsha (Tirunāvukkarashu, D)	Vāgīśa
Vaishali	Vaiśālī
Vaisheshika	Vaiśeṣika
Vaishnava	Vaiṣṇava
Vaishravana	Vaiśravaṇa
Vaishya	Vaiśya
varna	varṇa
Varuna	Varuṇa
Vedānta Deshika	Vedānta Deśika
Vibhīshana	Vibhīṣaṇa
Vijnānavāda	Vijñānavāda
Vijnānavādin	Vijñānavādin
Vīrashaiva	Vīraśaiva
Virochana	Virocana
Virūdhaka	Virūḍhaka
Virūpāksha	Virūpākṣa
Vishishtādvaita	Viśiṣṭādvaita
Vishnu	Viṣṇu
Vishnuchitta (Periyālvār, D)	Viṣṇucitta
Vishva-Bhārati	Viśva-Bhārati
Vrishni	Vṛṣṇi
Vritra	Vṛtra
Vyakaran (H)	Vyākaraṇa (S)
Yādavaprakāsha	Yādavaprakāśa
Yajna	Yajña
yaksha	yakṣa
Yamuna	Yamunā (Jumna)
Yāmuna Āchārya (Ālavandār, D)	Yāmunācārya (S)
Yogāchāra	Yogācāra
yogi	yogī
Yudhishthira	Yudhiṣṭhira

INDEX

'Uthmān, 456
Utpaladeva, 343*n*
Uttara Mīmāmsā, 296; *see also* Mīmāmsā

Vādirāja, 344-45
Vaipulya Sūtras, 158
Vaisheshika school (Skt., *Vaiśeṣika*), 272, 297, 317*n*
Vaishnavism, 188, 327; *see also* Shrīvaishnava
Vaishyas (third social order), 14, 132, 133, 218, 236
Vajra ("thunderbolt"), 11
Vajradhvaja Sūtra (Shāntideva), 160
Vajrayāna Buddhism (Vehicle of the Thunderbolt), 180, 189, 190
Vakroktijīvita: Life of Striking Expression (Kuntaka), 260*n*
Vallabha Āchārya, 302, 326
Vālmīki, 210, 347
Vāmana Purāṇa, 342
Vardhamāna, *see* Mahāvīra
Varna-āshrama-dharma, 213, 216, 219-20
Varuna, 3, 5, 9-10
Vātsyāyana, 254-56
Vedānt (Uttara Mīmāmsā), 306-22
Vedānta, 24; defined, 295; influence of Shankara in, 310
Vedānta Deshika, 344
Vedānta Sūtras, 295-98, 301, 302, 310-22
Vedāntic school, 272-73, 295-302
Vedas, 1, 2, 5-18, 200, 201, 202, 203, 216-18, 239, 257; *see also* specific Veda, e.g., Atharva Veda
Vedic ritual, 19; see also *Śrauta* fires
Vegetarianism, 169-70
Vehicle of the Thunderbolt, *see* Thunderbolt Vehicle
Vessa (Skt., *vaiśya*), 132; *see also* Vaishyas
Vijñānavāda, 155, 156-57, 177, 179
Viññāna (consciousness or conscious thought), 93
Virochana, 28-30
Vishnu, 5, 13; cult of, 188*n,* 201, 202; doctrine of the incarnations of, 193, 204, 210, 277; salvation and, 302
Vishnu-Nārāyana, worshipers of, 325
Visuddhimagga: The Way of Purification, 98
Vritra, 3, 7, 11

Walī-Ullāh, Shah, 363, 378, 448-54
War and peace: Jain attitude toward, 86-87; Buddhism on, 118-19, 125-27, 138, 181-82; Hinduism on, 231, 246-49
West, the, 151
Women: rights as wives, 119, 123; in Tantric Buddhism, 194; in Hinduism, 215, 227-28, 234; Muslim thought on, 503
World of Radiance (*Ābhassara*), 127-28
World Soul, in Mahāyāna Buddhism, 154, 179
Worship, types of, in Hinduism, 322-61

Yājñavalkya Smṛti: Lawbook of Yājnavalkya, 207, 212, 216, 221-23
Yajur Veda, 2, 239
Yoga (self discipline), 41, 217, 239, 273, 276-77; school of, 297, 298, 300, 316*n; see also* Bhakti-yoga; Karma-yoga
Yudhishthira, 207, 275
Yusuf Adil Shah of Bijapur, 429

Zakhīrat ul Mulūk: The Treasuries of Kings (Shaikh Hamadānī), 458
Zīa ud-dīn Barnī, 372, 382, 410, 511; readings from, 458-60, 463-67, 469-70, 471-74, 479-81, 483-84, 487-88, 489-91, 493-94, 495-96, 504-9, 513-18
Zimmīs, 402-3, 479, 481-82
Zoroastrianism, 153, 436, 479